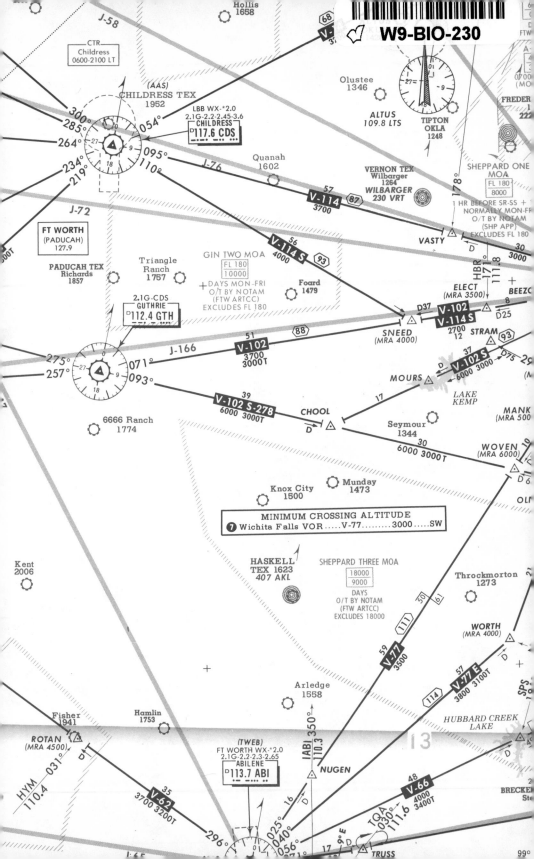

Advanced Pilot Manual

© 1981 Jeppesen Sanderson, Inc.
All Rights Reserved — Published Simultaneously in Germany
International Standard Book Number 0-88487-068-5

JS314298A

INTRODUCTION

The new *Jeppesen Sanderson Advanced Pilot Manual* is designed for pilot applicants who are training under FAR Part 141 in FAA approved schools. The manual and supplementary materials also meet the requirements of a home study course for pilot applicants who are seeking certification under FAR Part 61 and are not affiliated with an approved school.

The Advanced Manual is an authoritative textbook reference which is flexible, comprehensive, and well illustrated for easy study and understanding. It can be used for the combined instrument/commercial course or for either of the courses separately. Part I of the manual contains the commercial knowledge areas and Part II presents the instrument knowledge areas. In addition, the appendix provides an analysis of flight maneuvers and procedures required for instrument/commercial pilot certification.

Jeppesen Sanderson Advanced Courses contain several other complementary components for study and review of essential material.

1. Instrument/Commercial Pilot Audiovisual presentations review and reinforce the concepts presented in the Advanced Manual. These motivating visual aids present essential subject areas in brilliant color and synchonized sound.
2. The *Advanced Pilot Workbook* contains comprehensive exercises which cover the material presented in the audiovisual course and in the manual. The workbook is designed for individual study and self-checking. These exercises are integrated into the ground training lessons in the Training Syllabus.
3. The Advanced Pilot Stage Examination Set includes five exam booklets containing questions over specific chapters of the manual. The exams are designed to evaluate the applicant's progress at various intervals throughout the advanced courses.
4. The Instrument Pilot and Commercial Pilot Final Exams evaluate the applicant's comprehension of subject areas emphasized in the actual FAA written tests. The exam booklet consists of 140 self-contained, multiple-choice questions and two question selection sheets. Thus, two separate exams are provided; both cover the two main subject areas. Answer keys and comprehensive critiques are also available.
5. The *Advanced Pilot Training Syllabus* provides a lesson-by-lesson guide for completion of the ground and flight training required under FAR Part 141. The Training Syllabus is required for all applicants who are enrolled in approved schools and also is beneficial for applicants seeking certification outside of approved schools.

The information presented in these Jeppesen Sanderson Courses provides the necessary framework for a successful advanced training program. Applicants who complete this course of study under the guidance of a qualified instructor will be well prepared for the FAA written examinations and flight tests.

TABLE OF CONTENTS

PART I—COMMERCIAL

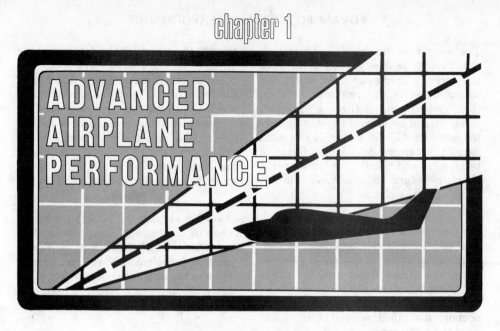

chapter 1

ADVANCED
AIRPLANE
PERFORMANCE

INTRODUCTION

The instrument/commercial pilot must have a thorough understanding of the factors which affect airplane performance. These include accurate computation of weight and balance information, use of performance information provided by the airplane manufacturer, and aerodynamics. This chapter provides a review of these areas as they relate to performance under various flight conditions.

SECTION A — WEIGHT AND BALANCE CONTROL

AIRPLANE WEIGHT

The maximum allowable weight of an aircraft is determined by the manufacturer after conducting stress analysis, static tests, and flight tests. This procedure insures that the aircraft structure exceeds the strength requirements for safe operation. All civil aircraft in the United States are licensed by the FAA to be operated at weights up to a maximum allowable weight. Manufacturers may designate maximum allowable weights for various phases of flight operations, such as maximum ramp weight, maximum takeoff weight, and maximum landing weight.

Aircraft manufacturers use a large safety factor in these tests, and modern aircraft are actually capable of carrying loads that are well above those expected during normal operations. The engineers provide at least a 50 *percent safety factor* in the design of their aircraft. This means that an aircraft licensed in the utility category, which is designed for a maximum load factor of 4.4 Gs, is built to withstand a load factor of 6.6 Gs before structural failure of a component occurs. However, the pilot must be cautioned against operating an aircraft at a greater load factor than that for which it is licensed. Although structural failure will generally not occur until *at least 150 percent* of the licensed load factor is exceeded, some structural damage (bending of parts) can occur. In addition, repeated overstressing of the aircraft structure can weaken certain parts with a resultant failure during a later period of operation.

The weight of an aircraft at rest is considered to be one G, which is the force that gravity exerts upon an object. As shown in figure 1-1, an aircraft at rest on the ground, in either a uniform climb/descent or in level flight, will have the same one-G load factor. If the same aircraft is subjected to a load factor of two Gs, the additional force increases the effective weight to *two times* the airplane's actual weight.

For example, an aircraft that is turning in a 60° bank and maintaining a constant altitude is subjected to a load factor of two Gs. This means the wings are lifting two times the actual weight of the aircraft. If the aircraft weighs 2,300 pounds, the effective weight in a 60° bank is 4,600 pounds.

Normally, the G-force or load factor exerted on an aircraft is dependent upon the aircraft's speed and the amount of control pressure a pilot uses. However, there is another important factor to be considered. Gusty air can subject the

aircraft to sudden jolts and, therefore, an increase in load factor. The loads imposed on the aircraft are dependent upon the force of the gust and the speed at which the aircraft penetrates them. It is similar to driving a car over a bumpy street. If a person drives over a bump slowly, the car will bounce mildly; but if the same bump is crossed at a higher speed, the car will bounce more violently.

Gusts are actually turbulent columns or layers of air that are rising, descending, or moving at different velocities. Flying through turbulent air at high speeds causes the wings to be subjected to severe bumps, which result in high load factors.

When flying in gusty conditions, the pilot should slow the aircraft to *maneuvering speed*, which is the speed at which abrupt control travel will not exceed the design load factor. At or below this speed, gusty conditions will not cause the designed load factor to be exceeded.

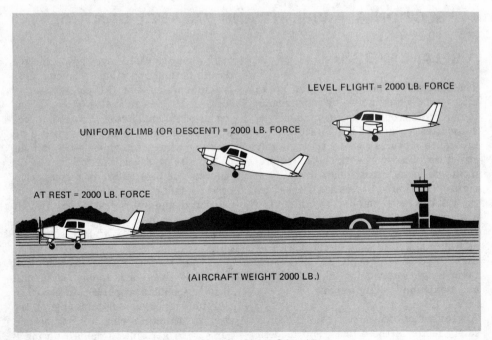

LEVEL FLIGHT = 2000 LB. FORCE

UNIFORM CLIMB (OR DESCENT) = 2000 LB. FORCE

AT REST = 2000 LB. FORCE

(AIRCRAFT WEIGHT 2000 LB.)

Fig. 1-1. Aircraft with a 1-G Load Factor

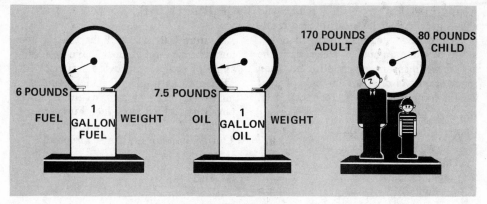

Fig. 1-2. Standard Weights

MAXIMUM LANDING WEIGHT

To gain a greater load carrying capacity and, therefore, greater utilization of the aircraft, some manufacturers designate a maximum landing weight in addition to the maximum takeoff weight. This is done to increase the useful load of an aircraft without costly redesign of the landing gear and associated aircraft structure, since it is assumed that a portion of the fuel load will be expended during the flight.

EMPTY WEIGHT

The empty weight of the aircraft is the *standard empty weight*. This weight is found on the weight and balance papers supplied by the manufacturer. It includes the weight of the aircraft, the *unusable* fuel, full oil, and full operating fluids.

The standard empty weight of the airplane plus optional equipment is called the *basic empty weight*. This weight is also found in the weight and balance papers. Aircraft of the same basic type and model often have basic empty weights that vary from one another because of the various combinations of optional equipment.

CHECKING WEIGHT

The *actual* weight of the aircraft can be checked by adding together the following weights:

1. Basic empty weight
2. Usable fuel on board
3. Pilot and passengers
4. Baggage or cargo

The basic empty weight of the aircraft should be listed first. In newer aircraft this weight is shown on the aircraft *Weight & Balance Record*, located in the aircraft data file, or in the pilot's operating handbook. On earlier model airplanes, this weight was called the *licensed empty weight*. When this term is used, engine oil must be included in weight and balance computations. Oil weighs 7.5 pounds per gallon; thus, the weight of oil can be determined by multiplying 7.5 times the number of gallons of drainable oil in the engine.

The pilot and passengers of average stature are considered to weigh 170 pounds. This average figure was chosen by the FAA to simplify weight and balance calculations. Children whose ages range from 2 to 12 years are considered to have an average weight of 80 pounds. These standard weights are illustrated in figure 1-2.

Actual weights of the pilot and passengers should be used if the aircraft is being loaded near the forward or aft limits of the moment envelope, or if the actual weights are much different than the average weights. An example of total weight computations is as follows:

Basic empty weight .... 1,422 lbs.
Pilot and front passenger ...... 340 lbs.
Rear passengers .... 295 lbs.
Fuel (38 gals.) .... 228 lbs.
Baggage .... 15 lbs.
Total weight .... 2,300 lbs.

EFFECTS OF OVERLOAD

When total weight exceeds the maximum allowable figure, the aircraft is overloaded and performance will be degraded. The performance degradation is in proportion to the amount of the overload.

TAKEOFF

The pilot attempting a takeoff with an aircraft over maximum weight will find that the aircraft needs a much longer takeoff roll, and the effect of the overload will have a compound effect on the takeoff. First, it will take longer to accelerate to normal takeoff speed; and second, the aircraft must be accelerated to a greater speed to provide additional lift to support the added weight.

CLIMBOUT

The rate-of-climb and angle-of-climb speeds are based on the maximum takeoff weight of the aircraft. Therefore, an overloaded aircraft will not climb as fast as it would under normal loading conditions. The pilot will find that the *time to climb* is extended considerably. The fuel consumption also will increase due to the longer time period during which climb power is used. In an extreme case, the pilot may be able to take off but unable to climb out of ground effect, since ground effect gives additional lift to the aircraft when it is within one wingspan distance of the ground.

CRUISE FLIGHT

An aircraft in cruise flight that is over maximum weight must have a higher angle of attack to provide sufficient lift. This greater angle of attack results in increased drag which requires more power and, thus, more fuel. Furthermore, the aircraft will have a shorter range and a lower than normal cruise airspeed.

STALL

Since an overloaded aircraft must have additional lift to support its weight, the stall speed also will increase and the airplane will have a much greater tendency to stall on takeoff and climbout due to the slow airspeed and the higher angle of attack. The possibility of an unintentional stall at an *excessive* weight is one of the most dangerous flight characteristics of an overloaded aircraft.

As long as a pilot observes weight and balance limitations, the aircraft characteristics and performance will be within the normal range; on the other hand, an aircraft loaded in excess of the maximum weight will have dangerous characteristics. Loading within acceptable limits is a prerequisite for successful and efficient flight operations; however, weight is only one of the major loading considerations.

IMPORTANCE OF BALANCE

The distribution of weight in an aircraft can be as significant as the weight. Thus, pilots must also check weight distribution or balance. The longitudinal stability of the aircraft is dependent upon the location of the center of gravity. An aircraft that has the center of gravity (CG) within the proper range is said to be balanced.

The forward CG limits are based upon the effective use of elevator control in the aircraft. To be safe and stable in all phases of flight, the aircraft must have sufficient elevator control to lift the nose of the aircraft to a pitch attitude which will sustain normal flight at that speed.

With the load too far forward, the elevator control will be insufficient to hold the nose at the required pitch attitude. The aft limits of the CG range are based on the relationship between the center of gravity and the *center of lift* (CL). The aircraft with a CG that is too far aft in relationship to the CL becomes unstable and hard to control.

EFFECTS OF LOADING FORWARD OF THE CG LIMIT

Longitudinal stability is the resistance of an aircraft to nose-up or nose-down pitching motions. The static longitudinal stability of an aircraft increases as the CG moves ahead of the forward limit; in this condition, it is possible for the aircraft to become *too stable.* If it is too stable, the aircraft will be resistant to control by the elevators.

TAKEOFF

A nose-heavy aircraft will require a longer ground run and faster speed before the nose can be raised for takeoff. This is because additional speed is required to provide the downward pressure on the tail necessary to "rotate" the aircraft. (See Fig. 1-3.) If the runway is short, an aircraft loaded extremely forward of the CG limit could fail to become airborne in time to clear obstacles at the end of the runway.

CRUISE

The additional downward pressure on the tail, which is needed to hold the

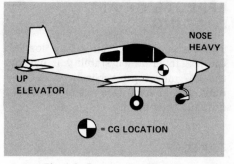

Fig. 1-3. Extreme Forward CG

nose up, places an *extra load* on the aircraft wings. Therefore, more lift is needed to sustain level flight. As shown in figure 1-4, the weight that must be supported by the wings equals the total weight of the aircraft *plus* the weight that must be exerted downward on the tail.

The drag created by the up elevator and the additional lift that must be generated "team up" to reduce aircraft performance. The aircraft loaded forward of the limit will have a slower cruise speed and greater fuel consumption.

LANDING

An aircraft which is loaded with the center of gravity ahead of the forward limit may experience a loss of elevator effectiveness during the landing flare. This loss will cause the airplane to land in a nose-low attitude which may result in structural damage to the nosewheel assembly.

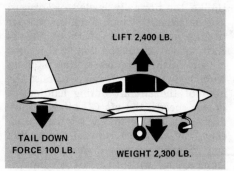

Fig. 1-4. Total Lift Required

EFFECTS OF AFT LOADING

The further aft the aircraft is loaded, the less longitudinal stability it has. As the CG moves progressively aft of the limit, the aircraft becomes unstable and difficult to control.

TAKEOFF

The aircraft loaded aft of limits will easily become airborne. This is because the tail-down force necessary to hold the nose up will be reduced or eliminated. Also, this reduction in tail-down force reduces the weight the wings must support and thereby reduces the amount of lift necessary for flight. As the aircraft loaded aft of the limits "breaks ground," it may pitch up and stall. Also, gusty air and crosswinds will have a greater tendency to flip or ground loop the airplane.

CRUISE

Under cruise conditions, the aircraft loaded aft of the envelope is *unstable* and hard to control. The use of elevator trim has little effect on the aircraft, and the pilot finds that he is constantly making pitch attitude adjustments to maintain level flight.

LANDING

Unlike the normally loaded or forward loaded aircraft (which tends to recover from a nose-up pitch attitude), the aircraft loaded aft of the limit will remain in, or further aggravate, the pitch-up tendency. The aft CG tends to raise the nose of the aircraft during landing; at slower speeds, the aft CG tends to produce a stall. Due to the pitch-up tendency, the aircraft is more prone to stall and possibly enter a spin. Recovery from a spin with a CG aft of limits is difficult, and sometimes impossible.

ADVANTAGES OF PROPER LOADING

When the CG is within limits, the pilot will find that the aircraft flight characteristics and performance will be at the optimum. The aircraft will rotate easily on takeoff (with little pitch change), and it will tend to be stable during the transition from ground control to flight control. During cruise, the aircraft loaded within CG limits will achieve the best cruise speed and will be stable and easy to trim in level flight. The aircraft's landing performance is characterized by a smooth, easy flare with a rate of descent that is gentle and easy to control. Furthermore, throughout the full speed range of the aircraft, the controls will have the proper effectiveness. It should be mentioned that an aircraft loaded near, but within, the aft limits will have the fastest cruise speed. This is due to the reduced *tail-down force* needed to balance the aircraft in level flight; therefore, the total load the wings must carry is less. (See Fig. 1-4.)

WEIGHT AND BALANCE COMPUTATIONS

DEFINITIONS AND THEORY

The balanced condition of an aircraft can be determined by locating the center of gravity, which is the *imaginary point* where all the aircraft weight is considered to be concentrated. To provide the proper balance between longitudinal stability and elevator control, the center of gravity normally is located slightly forward of the center of lift.

This is of great value if the aircraft is slowed near the stall speed. As the aircraft decelerates, the elevator becomes less effective and the CG, being located forward of the center of lift, lowers the nose and consequently, the angle of attack. Thus, the aircraft will tend to resist stalling.

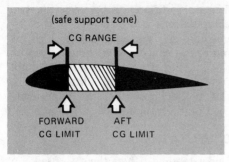

Fig. 1-5. Center of Gravity Range

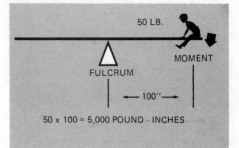

Fig. 1-6. Moment = 5,000 Pound-Inches

The safe support zone, as shown in figure 1-5, is called the center of gravity range, or CG range. The extremities of the CG range are called the forward CG limit and aft CG limit.

The center of gravity limits usually are specified in inches from a *datum reference*. The datum is an arbitrarily fixed position somewhere along the longitudinal axis of the aircraft.

There is no fixed rule to establish the location of the datum for all aircraft. The design engineers determine the datum reference location for each aircraft. It is often located on the nose or at some other point on the aircraft, such as the firewall or the wing's leading edge. It may also be located at a point on the projected longitudinal axis ahead of the nose of the aircraft.

The distance from the datum to a component of the aircraft or any object in the aircraft is called the *arm*. When the object or component is located aft of the datum, the arm is measured in positive inches. However, when the component or object is located forward of the datum reference, the arm is measured and indicated as negative or minus inches.

If the *weight of an object is multiplied by the arm*, the resultant value is known as the *moment*. The moment is the twisting force applied about the fulcrum by the weight. To understand balance computations, the datum line of

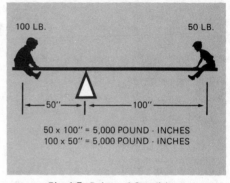

Fig. 1-7. Balanced Conditions

an aircraft and the fulcrum of the teeter totter, as shown in figure 1-6. are collocated at the same point. The boy sitting on the teeter totter weighs 50 pounds and is 100 inches from the datum line. By multiplying 50 pounds by 100 inches, the moment of 5,000 pound-inches is determined.

To balance the teeter totter, 5,000 pound-inches must be applied on the other end. As shown in figure 1-7, this moment can be added to the teeter totter by placing a 100-pound boy 50 inches from the datum. In this condition, the 5,000 pound-inches on the left of the fulcrum and the 5,000 pound-inches on the right cancel each other and the teeter totter load is balanced at the fulcrum.

Figure 1-8 illustrates the method used in aircraft weight and balance computations. The fulcrum, which is the balance point, remains in the same loca-

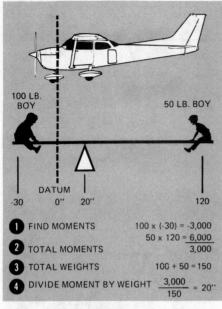

100 LB. BOY

50 LB. BOY

DATUM

-30   0″   20″   120

1 FIND MOMENTS   100 x (-30) = -3,000
                       50 x 120 = 6,000
2 TOTAL MOMENTS   3,000
3 TOTAL WEIGHTS   100 + 50 = 150
4 DIVIDE MOMENT BY WEIGHT $\frac{3,000}{150} = 20″$

Fig. 1-8. Comparison: Airplane and Teeter Totter

tion. The only difference is the datum reference is now moved to a convenient place (any convenient place) to the left. The 100-pound boy on the left can be compared to the engine of the aircraft. The 50-pound boy on the far right can be visualized as the long, but light-weight, empennage of the aircraft. The datum reference is the aircraft's firewall.

To make this computation, proceed as follows:

1. Find the moments by multiplying the weight of each boy by his distance from the datum (100 x -30 = -3,000; 50 x 120 = 6,000).

2. Add the moments (-3,000 + 6,000 = +3,000).

3. Add the weights (50 + 100 = 150).

4. Divide total moment by total weight (3,000 ÷ 150 = 20).

5. Therefore, the balance point is 20 inches aft of the datum reference.

The only difference between the two computations is the location of the datum lines and the methods by which the moments cancel each other. Because the fulcrum (CG) of the aircraft is not fixed, but varies with different loads, this method is the one that is normally used on most aircraft.

COMPUTATIONS

Understanding the theory used in weight and balance calculations provides a basis for understanding the three most common methods of weight and balance computations. These three methods are known as the computation method, the graph method, and the table method.

COMPUTATION METHOD

The weight and balance worksheet, illustrated in figure 1-9, shows the aircraft weight, moment, and CG, as calculated using the computation method. The steps involved in these computations are as follows:

1. List the aircraft basic empty weight, the weight of pilot, passengers, baggage, and fuel.

2. Add the weights to get the loaded weight of the aircraft. If the total weight exceeds the allowable weight, adjust the amount of weight before determining the moments. This can possibly save steps later if the weight is over the maximum value.

3. Multiply the weights and arms to obtain the moments of each item.

4. Add the moments to get the total moment of the aircraft.

5. Divide the total moment by the total weight to obtain the CG arm of the loaded aircraft.

6. Compare the CG arm to the approved limits shown in figure 1-10.

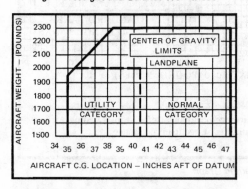

ITEM	WEIGHT (pounds)	ARM (inches)	MOMENT (pound-inches)
BASIC EMPTY WT.	1,437	38.75	55,684
FUEL (38 GAL.)	228	48.0	10,944
PILOT & PASSENGER	340	37.0	12,580
REAR PASSENGERS	280	73.0	20,440
BAGGAGE	15	95.0	1,425
TOTAL	2,300		101,073
CG =	43.9	INCHES	

WEIGHT and BALANCE FORM

Fig. 1-9. Weight and Balance Worksheet

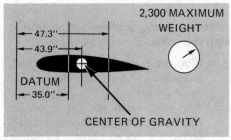

Fig. 1-10. Weight and Balance Limits

While some aircraft use the computation method, many aircraft use either the graph or table methods for figuring weight and balance. However, a thorough knowledge of the computation method provides the pilot with an understanding of the other two methods.

GRAPH METHOD

In this method, the multiplication and division steps are already completed and presented on a graph. The graph method contains separate graphs for de-

termining aircraft moments and center of gravity limits.

The loading graph contains a separate load line for each item. For example, the graph shown in figure 1-11 has loading lines for pilot and front passenger, fuel, rear passengers, and baggage or passenger on child seat.

SAMPLE PROBLEM USING LOADING GRAPH METHOD

To better acquaint the pilot with the graph method, a sample problem will be worked. In this problem, the aircraft will be loaded as follows:

Fuel . . . . 38 gals.
Pilot. . . . . 170 lbs.
Front seat passenger . . . . 170 lbs.
Rear seat passengers . . . . 280 lbs.
Baggage . . . . 15 lbs.
Basic empty weight . . . . 1,437 lbs.
Moment/1000 . . . . 55.7 lb.-in.

Using the graph method, the problem is worked as follows:

1. Enter the aircraft load items on a worksheet. (See Fig. 1-12.)
2. Find the moment for the pilot and front passenger, as shown on the graph in figure 1-11, as follows:
   a. First, locate the load line labeled "pilot and front passenger" on the load graph (item 1).
   b. On the left side of the graph, locate 340 pounds, which is the total weight of the pilot and front seat passenger (item 2).
   c. Proceed horizontally to the right to the "pilot and front seat passenger" load line intersection, which is marked as item 3.
   d. From the intersection point on the load line, proceed vertically downward to the hori-

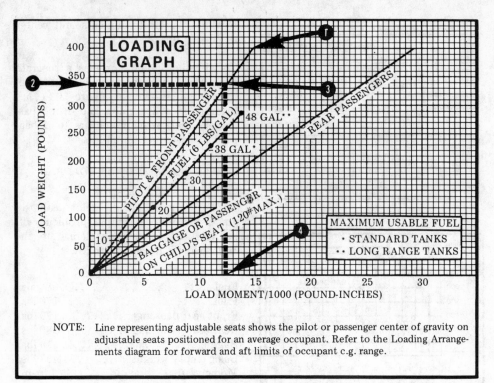

Fig. 1-11. Loading Graph

zontal scale at the bottom of the graph represented by item 4. This shows a *moment/1000* to be 12.6.

e. Enter 340 pounds in the weight column and 12.6 in the moment column on the worksheet.

At this point, it is appropriate to note that the graph method provides the moments in abbreviated numerical form. By referring to the load moment reference at the bottom of figure 1-11, the load moment *divided by 1,000 pound-inches* can be observed. The graph method presents numbers that are small and easy to compute; however, because of chart interpretation and rounding off, slight inaccuracies may exist. In this case, the moment is actually 12,600 pound-inches and the number that represents this value is 12.6. The

solution to the problem is completed with these remaining steps.

3. Find the moment/1000 for the fuel, baggage, and rear passengers in the same manner.

4. Add the weight column to obtain the loaded weight of the aircraft and the moment column to obtain the total moment.

5. Using figure 1-13, find the loaded aircraft weight by proceeding horizontally to the right until the loaded aircraft weight line intersects the loaded aircraft moment line. Since this point falls within the moment envelope, the aircraft is loaded safely within the weight and center of gravity limits; therefore, no further calculations are required.

SHIFTING THE LOAD

In another aircraft weight and balance problem illustrated in figure 1-14, the

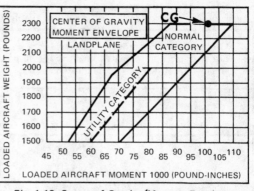

Fig. 1-12. Weight and Balance Worksheet

Fig. 1-13. Center of Gravity/Moment Envelope

pilot finds that the CG location is too far aft. Since the loaded weight of the aircraft is within the maximum allowable weight, the pilot needs only to shift part of the load forward to move the CG within the approved limits. This can be done by moving some of the cargo from area C to cargo area B.

In order to decide how much load to move from cargo area C, the procedure listed below should be followed.

1. Determine how far the CG is out of the envelope. To do this, scan horizontally to the left *from the CG position* and count the number of squares between the CG location and the first vertical line within the CG moment envelope. In the example illustrated in figure 1-14, the CG moment is 3.3 squares aft of the first vertical line within the envelope. Since each square is equal to a moment of 1,000 pound-inches, the CG is 3,300 pound-inches too far aft.

2. Determine the distance between cargo area C and cargo area B. From the loading data illustrated in figure 1-15, cargo area C is located 99 inches aft of the datum and cargo area B is 70 inches aft. Subtracting 70 from 99 inches, it is found that area B is 29 inches forward of C.

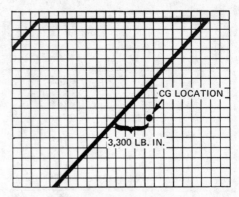

Fig. 1-14. CG Aft of Limits

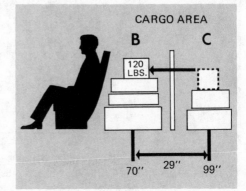

Fig. 1-15. Load Shifted to Place CG Within Limits

3. Divide the moment of 3,300 pound-inches (the moment the CG is aft of the envelope) by 29 inches (the distance from cargo area C to cargo area B) to determine the load to be moved (3,300

Useful Load Weights and Moments					
*Note: The moments listed in this table are actual values divided by 100, or moment/100. For example, the tabulated moment for 30 pounds of fuel is the weight (30), times the arm (117), divided by 100, and listed as 35.					
		FUEL ARM 117			
Gallons	Weight	Moment*	Gallons	Weight	Moment*
5	30	35	35	210	246
10	60	70	40	240	281
15	90	105	45	270	316
20	120	140	50	300	351
25	150	176	55	330	386
30	180	211	59	354	414

Occupants Front Seat ARM 110 0		Rear Seat or Baggage ARM 142	
Weight	Moment*	Weight	Moment*
120	132	120	170
130	143	130	185
140	154	140	199
150	165	150	213
160	176	160	227
170	187	170	241
180	198	180	256
190	209	190	270
200	220	200	284

Sample Loading Problem	Sample Airplane		Actual Airplane	
	Weight (lbs.)	Moment (/100)	Weight (lbs.)	Moment (/100)
Basic empty weight	1340	1442		
Fuel	240	281		
Front seat occupants	340	374		
Rear seat baggage or occupant	270	383		
Total airplane (loaded)	2190	2480		

The total airplane loaded figures, weight 2190 pounds and the moment/100 of 2480 pounds-inches, are the values used to enter the Center of Gravity Envelope Chart.

Fig. 1-16. Weights and Moments

÷ 29 = 114). To balance the load, at least 114 pounds must be moved from cargo area C to B.

4. Analyzing the load, the pilot finds that one of the boxes in cargo area C weighs 120 pounds. If this box is moved to area B, as illustrated in figure 1-15, the aircraft will be safely loaded.

TABLE METHOD

The table method eliminates both the multiplication and division calculations. Instead of graphs, tables which list the

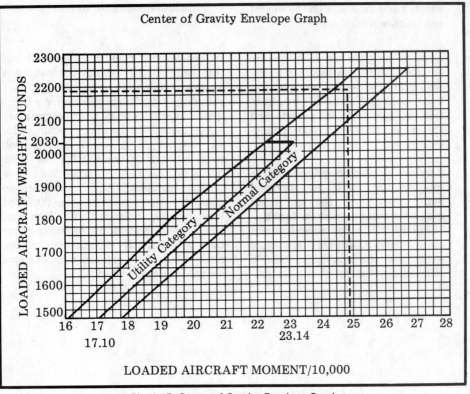

Fig. 1-17. Center of Gravity Envelope Graph

weights and moments for each type of useful load are provided; however, interpolation may be necessary to compute some moments. For example, to determine the moment for a 165-pound passenger, the pilot should refer to the table in figure 1-16 and locate the moment/100 for 160 pounds, which is 176; then for 170 pounds, which is 187. By interpolation, the moment/100 for the 165-pound passenger is determined to be 182. The moment/100 for other passengers, baggage, and fuel should be computed in this same manner.

The table method may also provide a *center of gravity envelope graph* to insure that the total aircraft weight and moment are within acceptable limits. This graph, shown in figure 1-17, will be used with the following sample problem.

Sample Problem Using Table Method

Assume the aircraft is loaded with 40 gallons of fuel, pilot and front seat passenger, and baggage weighing a total of 270 pounds. The aircraft empty weight is 1,340 pounds and it has a moment/100 of 1,442. What are the weight and balance conditions of the aircraft?

This problem is calculated as follows:

1. Refer to the *occupants front seat* portion of the load table. The moment for each of the 170-pound occupants is 187 for a total moment/100 of 374.

2. Add these values to the aircraft weight and balance worksheet.

3. In like manner, find the moments for the fuel and then enter the

weights and moments on the weight and balance worksheet.

4. After all weights and moments are obtained, add them together to get the aircraft's loaded weight and total moment. The loaded weight in this problem is 2,190 pounds and the moment is 248,000 pound-inches.

5. Compare the loaded weight and the total moment with the approved limits shown on the center of gravity envelope graph in figure 1-17. Since the loaded weight is less than the maximum allowable weight and the moment of 248,000 falls within the envelope, the air-craft is determined to be within CG limits.

In conclusion, it must be pointed out that weight and balance computations are an important part of preflight planning. All pilots preparing for a flight must determine that their aircraft are safely loaded. If the pilot regularly flies an aircraft in a consistent loading condition (for instance, with the same business associate and/or the same product samples), it is redundant to compute the complete weight and balance data for each flight. However, any time an aircraft is loaded in other than a previously computed condition, new weight and balance computations should be accomplished.

SECTION B—ADVANCED PERFORMANCE CONTROL

AIRCRAFT PERFORMANCE

Performance figures are based on how the aircraft performs under standard atmospheric conditions. These are:

1. A sea level pressure of 29.92 inches of mercury
2. A sea level temperature of 15° Celsius
3. A *standard* temperature and pressure lapse rate with an increase in altitude

Together, these values provide a "common denominator" with which to evaluate aircraft performance when actual atmospheric conditions are nonstandard.

DENSITY ALTITUDE

The standard conditions stated above seldom exist. Thus, the atmosphere is constantly in a state of flux. The factor which contributes greatest to changing conditions is the density of the air. It has a direct bearing on engine power output, propeller efficiency, and lift generated by the wings. As air temperature or altitude *increases*, the density of the air *decreases*. Since it is possible to describe the density of the air by referring to a corresponding altitude in the standard atmosphere, the term "density altitude" is employed.

PRESSURE ALTITUDE

Density altitude changes directly with pressure altitude. When pressure altitude is corrected for nonstandard temperature variations, density altitude can then be determined.

When all conditions are standard, as shown in figure 1-18, an aircraft flying at an indicated altitude of 5,000 feet MSL will have a *true altitude* of 5,000

feet, assuming no altimeter error is present and the altimeter is properly set. The *pressure altitude* (the measurement from the point at which an atmospheric pressure of 29.92 inches of mercury is found) is also 5,000 feet, because the pressure level (29.92 in. Hg) occurs at sea level.

In this example, pressure and temperature have no effect on air density from standard; therefore, the density altitude is *identical* to the true altitude of 5,000 feet. Under these conditions, the aircraft will perform as predicted by the manufacturer. In figure 1-18, the *absolute altitude* above the terrain is also 5,000 feet as the aircraft is flying over the ocean.

Conversely, when the pressure at sea level drops below 29.92 in. Hg, as shown in figure 1-19, the point where 29.92 in. Hg is found will theoretically be below sea level. In this case, the pressure at sea level is 29.72 inches of mercury. Based on a conversion factor of one inch of mercury equals 1,000 feet of altitude, the point where the standard pressure datum occurs will be 200 feet below sea level. That is:

$$\begin{array}{r} 29.92 \text{ in. Hg} \\ -29.72 \hphantom{\text{ in. Hg}} \\ \hline .20 \text{ in. Hg (or 200 feet)} \end{array}$$

Thus, the pressure altitude has increased 200 feet to an altitude of 5,200 feet, even though the true altitude has not changed. To further illustrate this concept, assume the airplane is flying over terrain which has an altitude of 2,000 feet AGL. (See Fig. 1-19.)

When sea level pressure is *higher* than 29.92 in. Hg, the standard datum plane will be above sea level. In this case, the pressure altitude measured from the

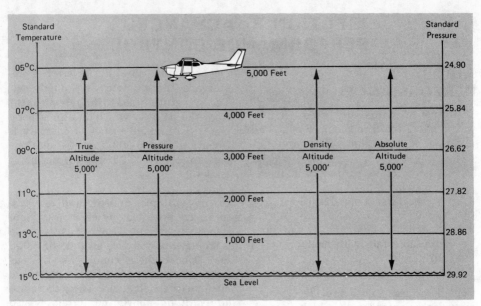

Fig. 1-18. Standard Atmospheric Conditions

standard datum is less than the MSL altitude. As stated previously, the true altitude and the absolute altitude each remain constant, assuming a standard pressure and temperature lapse rate, no altimeter error, and a properly set altimeter.

COMPUTING PRESSURE ALTITUDE

Pressure altitude may be calculated in one of two ways. The conversion factor of one inch of mercury equals approximately 1,000 feet of altitude can be employed (as shown in a previous example), and the barometric scale of the altimeter can be adjusted to 29.92 inches of mercury. After this is done, the altimeter compares the pressure sensed through the static air source to the standard datum plane and displays the differential pressure on the instrument face as pressure altitude.

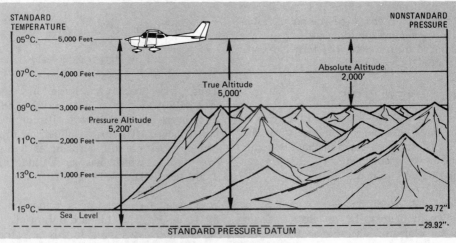

Fig. 1-19. Standard Pressure Datum

TEMPERATURE

As temperature increases, the density of the air decreases. The aircraft will then fly as if it were at a higher altitude. Conversely, as the temperature decreases, air density increases and the aircraft responds as if flying at a lower altitude. As shown in figure 1-20, item 1, an increase in temperature above the standard temperature of plus five degrees Celsius at 5,000 feet will raise the apparent altitude at which the aircraft is flying. In other words, because of the 10° Celsius increase above standard temperature, the airplane now will *perform* as if flying at an approximate altitude increase of 1,100 feet. When taking off on a hot day, the density altitude may be 2,000 or 3,000 feet higher than the *airport elevation.* Even when other conditions (such as pressure and humidity) remain the same, an aircraft will need more runway for takeoff on a hot day than on a cold day.

When deviations from standard occur in both pressure and temperature, both factors must be considered when computing density altitude. As shown in figure 1-20, the pressure below standard increases the pressure altitude (item 2) and the density altitude as measured from the standard pressure datum (item 3).

HUMIDITY

Air contains moisture in three forms: solid, liquid, and gaseous (water vapor). As a result of evaporation, the air always contains some moisture in the form of water vapor. Water vapor weighs less than dry air; therefore, a given volume of moist air will weigh less (be less dense) than an equal volume of dry air.

The primary result of high humidity is a loss of engine power. This is due to:

1 a loss in the *weight per unit volume* of combustible air,

2 an excessive *enrichment* of the mixture, and

3 a *"drowning"* effect on the burning process.

The "drowning" effect results in retarding the flame propagation in the combustion chamber. On a very humid day, this effect will decrease takeoff and

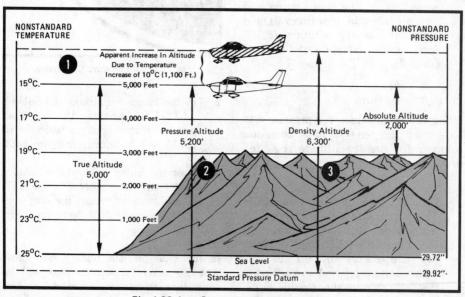

Fig. 1-20. Low Pressure — High Temperature

climb performance by approximately seven percent.

It was formerly thought that humid air would support less weight and, therefore, provide less lift. However, it is now known that the effect of humid air on lift is minimal.

COMPUTING DENSITY ALTITUDE

There are two basic methods for computing density altitude. One utilizes a density altitude chart, and the other utilizes a flight computer.

CHART METHOD

If an aircraft is departing an airport with a pressure altitude of 5,000 feet and a temperature of 95° Fahrenheit, density altitude may be computed by using the chart in figure 1-21 and proceeding as follows:

1. Draw a line straight up from 95° (item 1) to the point it intersects 5,000 feet pressure altitude (item 2).

2. Proceed horizontally from the intersection of the temperature and pressure altitude lines (item 2), and read the density altitude (8,500 feet) on the left side of the chart (item 3).

COMPUTER METHOD

Using the same values for pressure altitude and temperature, the computer solution for density altitude is as follows:

1. Convert the temperature from Fahrenheit to Celsius using the temperature conversion scale on the computer. Looking opposite the temperature of 95° on the Fahrenheit scale, find the temperature of 35° on the Celsius scale. (See Fig. 1-22.)

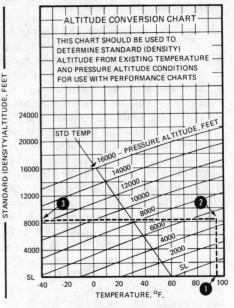

Fig. 1-21. Density Altitude Chart

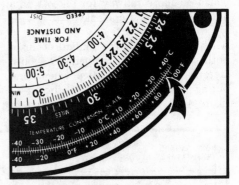

Fig. 1-22. Temperature Conversion

2. In the window marked PRESSURE ALTITUDE, position the +35° Celsius over the pressure altitude of 5,000 feet, as shown in figure 1-23.

3. Over the index mark at the bottom center of the DENSITY ALTITUDE window, read the approximate answer 8,500 feet. (See Fig. 1-23.)

In this example, the pilot would know that his aircraft performance will be equivalent to operations at 8,500 feet under standard conditions.

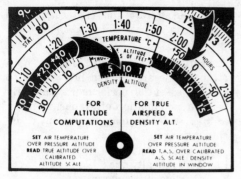

*Fig. 1-23. Setting Temperature
and Pressure Altitude*

GROUND OPERATIONS

Although the airplane is primarily designed for air operations, it also must function as a ground machine during transition to and from flight. Therefore, aircraft performance computations also must take into consideration the ground factors affecting the aircraft during these transitions.

WEIGHT

Weight is defined as the gravitational force pulling a body toward the center of earth. Thus, a direct relationship exists between weight and power; less power is required to overcome a force as weight decreases. Performance information is based on maximum takeoff weight. Under given atmospheric conditions and a fixed power value, the following characteristics will be evident in an aircraft with a decreased load.

1. Takeoff and landing rolls will be shorter.
2. Climb will be greater.
3. Cruise will be faster.

Conversely, more power is required to overcome a weight increase. Thus, increased load requires a longer ground run since more speed is needed to meet the additional lift requirement. Further, excess weight affects three additional

phases of the flight performance profile. This weight causes a reduction in the rate of climb, a slower cruise speed, and a longer landing roll.

SURFACE WINDS

During takeoff, a headwind will shorten the takeoff run and a tailwind will increase the takeoff run. A headwind on takeoff, if of sufficient velocity, can help compensate for lost performance due to a high density altitude. On the other hand, a tailwind takeoff under the same atmospheric conditions can produce disastrous results.

Theoretically, takeoff ground run can be reduced by about 19 percent with a direct headwind equal to 10 percent of liftoff speed. A tailwind of the same velocity in relation to liftoff speed can increase ground run by 21 percent. For flight planning, however, pilots should use figures provided by the aircraft manufacturer in the pilot's operating handbook.

RUNWAY GRADIENT

The effect of runway gradient must be considered when computing the accelerate-stop distance for multi-engine aircraft. This is very important when runway length and takeoff distance are critical. The FAA has established two percent as the maximum upslope for general aviation VFR airports. Normally, a one percent upslope will increase takeoff ground run by two to four percent. Pilots should also expect an increase in landing run distances on a downslope runway.

RUNWAY CONDITIONS AFFECTING TAKEOFF ROLL

The condition of the runway surface usually has a greater effect on takeoff than does gradient. The rougher the surface of the runway, the higher the coefficient of friction between the wheels and the runway surface. As a result, the rolling resistance increases, making greater thrust necessary for takeoff. The same is true for soft, muddy, or snow-covered runways.

RUNWAY CONDITIONS AFFECTING LANDING ROLL

The braking effectiveness of the aircraft is directly affected by the runway surface conditions. The ideal situation to attain the shortest landing roll is a dry, hard-surfaced runway with an upslope. Since these conditions are not always present, the pilot should be aware that on grassy, wet, or hardpacked snow-covered runways stopping distance is significantly increased, and uneven braking action may cause a dangerous ground control situation.

PERFORMANCE CHARTS

Airplane performance refers to how well the airplane will react under a given set of circumstances. Generally, the pilot can accurately predict this performance by use of graphs and charts. Pilot's operating handbooks contain those charts and graphs that enable the pilot to determine what may be expected during takeoff and in flight under known conditions. Before any presentation is given on the use of specific performance data, it is necessary to understand what a graph is and how it is used.

Graphs and charts conveniently display the relationship between two or more variables. In aviation, graphs and charts are used for computing range, fuel consumption, takeoff distance, available power, and rate of climb. For example, a power setting selected from the range charts is more efficient than a random setting. These charts provide accurate fuel flow settings from which close estimates of fuel consumption can be made. The data in the charts and graphs have been compiled from actual flight tests (using average pilotage techniques)

with the aircraft and engines in good condition.

Aircraft flight manuals can use both straight line and curved line graphs to present essential performance data. By using a combination of graphs, as many as five variables may be presented, including:

1. Pressure altitude
2. Outside air temperature
3. Airplane weight
4. Headwind
5. Distance

By compensating for these five variables, the pilot can determine normal takeoff distance, accelerate-stop distance, single-engine takeoff distance, and additional performance items.

The preceding paragraphs presented background information on aircraft and engine performance factors. In the following paragraphs, these factors will be applied to various calculations. The charts will be presented and discussed in the general order of their occurrence in the flight profile — takeoff, accelerate-stop, climb, cruise, and landing. These charts and graphs are typical of those found in the flight manuals for multi-engine aircraft; however, similar types of charts and graphs are used for light, single-engine aircraft as well.

TAKEOFF PERFORMANCE

Takeoff performance is frequently a critical consideration in flight planning. Takeoff limits the load since every airplane can handle a considerably heavier load in flight than it can handle during takeoff. Because of variations in atmospheric conditions, available power, and pilot technique, it is not a simple matter to accurately predict takeoff performance.

Normal takeoff procedures and considerations are standard in that computations are predicated on the basis of:

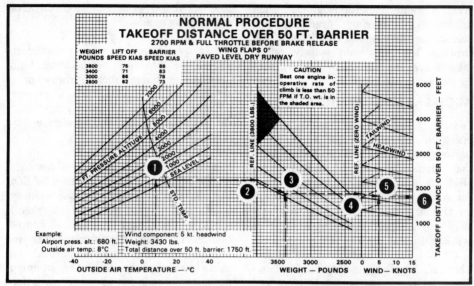

Fig. 1-24. Takeoff Distance Chart

1. A level, hard-surfaced, dry runway
2. Full power
3. The takeoff weight of the aircraft

Although weight is the primary factor determining takeoff speed, there are several factors that determine the length of the takeoff run. These factors are:

1. Type of runway
2. Atmospheric pressure
3. Air temperature
4. Wind direction and velocity

The accompanying takeoff distance chart (See Fig. 1-24) is used for calculating takeoff distance for a multi-engine airplane. For example, referring to the chart shown, the pilot can determine the ground roll and distance to clear a 50-foot obstacle under the following conditions:

Temperature .... 8°C
Pressure altitude............ 680 ft.
Takeoff weight............ 3,430 lbs.
Headwind .... 5 kts.

The solution to the example is as follows:

1. Locate the temperature of 8° Celsius at the bottom of the chart.
2. Move vertically to the diagonal line representing 680 feet of pressure altitude (item 1).

3. Move horizontally (right) to the weight reference line (item 2).
4. Move parallel to the weight lines and proceed to the area that represents 3,430 pounds (item 3).
5. Proceed horizontally to the zero wind reference line (item 4).
6. Proceed parallel to the headwind lines until reaching the headwind component of 5 knots (item 5), then move horizontally (right) to find the takeoff distance over the 50-foot barrier (item 6).

Pilots are often tempted to compute takeoff distance on only the amount of ground roll needed. Since most runways are not located in the middle of an unobstructed flat plain or desert, the competent pilot will compute the takeoff distance over a 50-foot barrier to assure clearance of any obstacle at the end of the runway or climbout area.

By consulting the takeoff distance charts and computing the distance based on known or estimated atmospheric conditions, it is possible, under extreme circumstances, to find that a takeoff is impossible within the confines of the available runway. Therefore, minor factors not allowed for in the performance charts should be considered.

When marginal conditions appear, such as humidity, runway gradient, turbulence, or the age and condition of the airplane, the pilot may wisely refuse takeoff even though *basic* performance figures are favorable.

ACCELERATE-STOP DISTANCE

Federal Aviation Regulations require pilots to determine (prior to flight) if runway lengths are sufficient at airports they intend to use. Additionally, the pilot of a multi-engine airplane must determine if the runway is long enough for the airplane to accelerate to a safe single-engine speed then stop while there is still sufficient runway remaining.

The safe single-engine speed is determined by the aircraft manufacturer and is used in accelerate-stop distance charts. Engine failure at any critical airspeed, however, necessitates an instantaneous decision to stop or to continue the takeoff. This decision must be based on

the calculated accelerate-stop distance and runway available.

In many instances where maximum takeoff weights, high temperature, high pressure altitudes, short runway, or a combination of these factors are involved, the available runway length may fall short of the required accelerate-stop distance.

When such is the case, a speed-distance relationship must be determined to find the maximum weight for the runway length and a speed above which takeoff must be continued in case of engine failure. The pilot should remember accelerate-stop distances are based on using maximum braking. The stopping distance is subject to some variation according to the procedure used and runway condition.

The accelerate-stop distance can be calculated by use of a table, as shown in

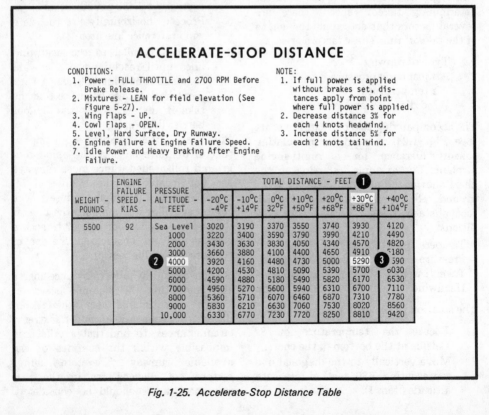

ACCELERATE-STOP DISTANCE

CONDITIONS:
1. Power - FULL THROTTLE and 2700 RPM Before Brake Release.
2. Mixtures - LEAN for field elevation (See Figure 5-27).
3. Wing Flaps - UP.
4. Cowl Flaps - OPEN.
5. Level, Hard Surface, Dry Runway.
6. Engine Failure at Engine Failure Speed.
7. Idle Power and Heavy Braking After Engine Failure.

NOTE:
1. If full power is applied without brakes set, distances apply from point where full power is applied.
2. Decrease distance 3% for each 4 knots headwind.
3. Increase distance 5% for each 2 knots tailwind.

WEIGHT - POUNDS	ENGINE FAILURE SPEED - KIAS	PRESSURE ALTITUDE - FEET	TOTAL DISTANCE - FEET						
			-20°C -4°F	-10°C +14°F	0°C 32°F	+10°C +50°F	+20°C +68°F	+30°C +86°F	+40°C +104°F
5500	92	Sea Level	3020	3190	3370	3550	3740	3930	4120
		1000	3220	3400	3590	3790	3990	4210	4490
		2000	3430	3630	3830	4050	4340	4570	4820
		3000	3660	3880	4100	4400	4650	4910	5180
		4000	3920	4160	4480	4730	5000	5290	5590
		5000	4200	4530	4810	5090	5390	5700	6030
		6000	4590	4880	5180	5490	5820	6170	6530
		7000	4950	5270	5600	5940	6310	6700	7110
		8000	5360	5710	6070	6460	6870	7310	7780
		9000	5830	6210	6630	7060	7530	8020	8560
		10,000	6330	6770	7230	7720	8250	8810	9420

Fig. 1-25. Accelerate-Stop Distance Table

figure 1-25. Certain criteria must be adopted in computing accelerate-stop distance in order to obtain maximum safety without optimum pilot technique. This is accomplished by considering the same variables that were present when computing normal takeoff distance. Those variables are temperature, pressure altitude, takeoff weight, and wind.

In the following example, determination of accelerate-stop distance is predicated on a takeoff from a hard-surfaced runway with the pilot applying full power before releasing the brakes, wing flaps up, and mixture set at the recommended setting. Engine failure occurs at takeoff speed, and the pilot exerts heavy braking. Use the table in figure 1-25 to find the accelerate-stop distance under the following conditions:

Temperature .... 30 °C
Pressure altitude .... 4,000 ft.
Takeoff weight. .... 5,500 lbs.
Headwind .... 12 kts.

The steps to take in solving the accelerate-stop distance are as follows:

1. Locate the temperature of 30° Celsius (item 1) on the referenced illustration.

2. Under the data for 5,500 pounds, find the pressure altitude of 4,000 feet (item 2).

3. Move right horizontally to the +30° Celsius column to find the no-wind distance (item 3).

4. Find the headwind correction factor under Note 2 on the top of the table.

5. For 12 knots of headwind, reduce the accelerate-stop distance 9% (12 ÷ 4 = 3; 3 × 3% = 9%). The ac-

celerate-stop distance for the stated conditions is 4,814 feet (5,290 × .09 =476.1; 5,290 − 476 = 4,814).

Caution should always be exercised in computing accelerate-stop distances, since wind velocity readings are usually obtained at some height above the ground; hence, the actual wind on the runway may be less. It is generally advantageous to be conservative when calculating the effects of headwind. If the other existing conditions indicate that the operation can be conducted safely with regard to accelerate-stop distance, any headwind component will tend to provide an increased margin of safety.

TAKEOFF

Performance data for takeoff also is presented in some handbooks in tabular form, as illustrated in figure 1-26. In this example, the information pertains to a single-engine aircraft; however, the format is representative of many commonly used takeoff tables.

CLIMB

The climb segment of the flight profile is complex; that is, there is usually a broad variety of speeds associated with the ascent to altitude. The different types of climbs can be broadly classified as multi-engine climbs and single-engine climbs.

MULTI-ENGINE CLIMBS

The first classification of climbs concerns the aircraft performance with both engines functioning normally. In this realm of performance, there are three essential climb speeds for the pilot to keep in mind — best angle-of-climb, best rate-of-climb, and the recommended cruising climb speeds.

TAKEOFF DISTANCE
MAXIMUM WEIGHT 2300 LBS

SHORT FIELD

CONDITIONS:
Flaps Up
Full Throttle Prior to Brake Release
Paved, Level, Dry Runway
Zero Wind

NOTES:
1. Short field technique as specified in Section 4.
2. Prior to takeoff from fields above 3000 feet elevation, the mixture should be leaned to give maximum RPM in a full throttle, static runup.
3. Decrease distances 10% for each 9 knots headwind. For operation with tailwinds up to 10 knots, increase distances by 10% for each 2 knots.
4. For operation on a dry, grass runway, increase distances by 15% of the "ground roll" figure.

WEIGHT LBS	TAKEOFF SPEED KIAS LIFT OFF	TAKEOFF SPEED KIAS AT 50 FT	PRESS ALT FT	0°C GRND ROLL	0°C TOTAL TO CLEAR 50 FT OBS	10°C GRND ROLL	10°C TOTAL TO CLEAR 50 FT OBS	20°C GRND ROLL	20°C TOTAL TO CLEAR 50 FT OBS	30°C GRND ROLL	30°C TOTAL TO CLEAR 50 FT OBS	40°C GRND ROLL	40°C TOTAL TO CLEAR 50 FT OBS
2300	52	59	S.L.	720	1300	775	1390	835	1490	895	1590	960	1700
			1000	790	1420	850	1525	915	1630	980	1745	1050	1865
			2000	865	1555	930	1670	1000	1790	1075	1915	1155	2055
			3000	950	1710	1025	1835	1100	1970	1185	2115	1270	2265
			4000	1045	1880	1125	2025	1210	2175	1300	2335	1400	2510
			5000	1150	2075	1240	2240	1335	2410	1435	2595	1540	2795
			6000	1265	2305	1365	2485	1475	2680	1585	2895	1705	3125
			7000	1400	2565	1510	2770	1630	3000	1755	3245	1890	3515
			8000	1550	2870	1675	3110	1805	3375	1945	3670	2095	3990

Fig. 1-26. Takeoff Performance Data

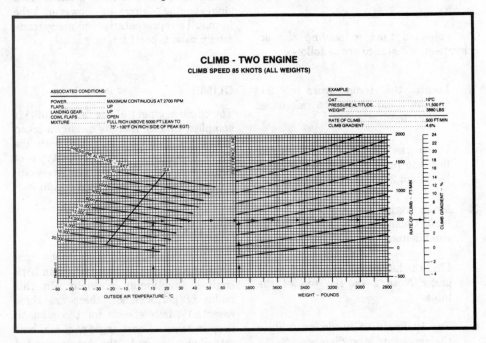

CLIMB - TWO ENGINE
CLIMB SPEED 85 KNOTS (ALL WEIGHTS)

ASSOCIATED CONDITIONS:

POWER . . . . MAXIMUM CONTINUOUS AT 2700 RPM
FLAPS . . . . UP
LANDING GEAR . . . . UP
COWL FLAPS . . . . OPEN
MIXTURE . . . . FULL RICH (ABOVE 5000 FT LEAN TO
75° - 100°F ON RICH SIDE OF PEAK EGT)

EXAMPLE:

OAT . . . . 10°C
PRESSURE ALTITUDE . . . . 11,500 FT
WEIGHT . . . . 3880 LBS

RATE OF CLIMB . . . . 500 FT/MIN
CLIMB GRADIENT 4.6%

Fig. 1-27. Climb Performance Chart

BEST ANGLE OF CLIMB

The best angle-of-climb speed provides the greatest gain in altitude for any given distance traveled over the ground. This speed is used for obstacle clearance immediately after takeoff. Due to excess drag, the best angle-of-climb speed is not as efficient as a faster climb speed. It is for this reason that the aircraft should be accelerated to at least the best rate-of-climb speed as soon as obstructions have been cleared.

BEST RATE OF CLIMB

As the nose of the aircraft is lowered from the best angle-of-climb position, the speed increases. Even though the climb angle is less, this reduced climb angle provides the best rate of climb because the airplane flies faster and climbs higher per *unit of time*. As the climb angle is further reduced, the speed increases, but the rate of climb decreases.

The best rate of climb is often used to reach an assigned altitude in the least amount of time. This climb might be used because of terrain, wind, and altitude factors. If used, the best rate-of-climb speed tends to decrease as the altitude increases.

The climb performance chart shown in figure 1-27 illustrates that at 11,500 feet, and a weight of 3,880 pounds, a pilot can expect a rate of climb of approximately 500 feet per minute. This chart also demonstrates that the rate of climb decreases with an increase in altitude or temperature. Under these conditions, the airplane will climb 46 feet per 1,000 feet of ground distance traversed.

CRUISE CLIMB

The airspeed used in a climb is often a compromise between the best rate of climb and an airspeed that produces adequate engine cooling along with some degree of fuel economy. The airspeed at which the climb is most economically accomplished is near the airspeed for maximum range. Such a speed usually will be specified in the pilot's operating handbook. Cruise climb normally is performed at 75 percent power.

SINGLE-ENGINE CLIMBS

An astute pilot will plan in sufficient detail to know what action to take in the event of a single-engine emergency. During the takeoff and climb segments of the flight profile, there are two speeds relevent to the safe continuation of the flight should an engine failure occur after liftoff. These two speeds are the single-engine best angle-of-climb speed (V_{XSE}) and the single-engine best rate-of-climb speed (V_{YSE}).

Most twin-engine aircraft can be controlled satisfactorily on the ground should an engine failure occur prior to reaching the air minimum control speed (V_{MCA}) on the takeoff roll. If the airplane is airborne below V_{MCA} and suddenly loses all power on one engine, it cannot be satisfactorily controlled.

An efficient climbing path (with both engines operating) is one which leaves the ground at V_{MCA} plus 5 knots, accelerates quickly to the recommended safe single-engine speed, and then continues to the best single-engine angle-of-climb speed. By this point in the flight profile, the gear should be retracted with the aircraft accelerating rapidly to the single-engine best rate-of-climb speed (V_{YSE}). The primary purpose of the initial climb is to gain a safe, single-engine maneuvering altitude. For normal multi-engine takeoffs, airspeed in excess of V_Y during initial climbout is not as valuable as the altitude that would have been gained. This is true because the drag of a failed engine prevents efficient conversion of excess airspeed to altitude. If an engine failure occurs during climb after the airplane is in the clean configuration at an airspeed of V_{YSE} or V_Y, the possibility of a sustained single-engine climb is greatly improved.

1-25

CRUISE

When planning the cruise segment of the flight profile, the pilot should be economy conscious; however, the attainment of economy depends largely on an ability to read and interpret cruise performance charts. The cruise charts provided in the pilot's operating handbook (POH) indicate the true airspeed, range, endurance, and fuel consumption that can be expected for a given power setting at various altitudes.

To accurately project flight endurance, compensation must be made for time, fuel consumed, and distance covered during taxi, warmup, takeoff, climb, and descent. If the pilot consults the appropriate charts in the POH, an adequate and accurate fuel reserve can be planned.

The cruise performance charts for the aircraft illustrated in figure 1-28 are based on aircraft weights up to 5,500 pounds. One can see that, at a standard temperature of 0° Celsius and 2,400 r.p.m., 21 inches of manifold pressure (item 1) are required to achieve 62.4

percent brake horsepower at 7,500 feet (item 2). This should deliver a true airspeed of 178 knots with a total fuel consumption rate of 158 pounds of fuel per hour. Any desired flight condition can be determined by referring to the chart appropriate to the altitude.

If the planned flight altitude falls between the altitudes covered by the charts, the value sought can be found by a process known as "interpolation." When the desired reading falls between two values given on the charts, the difference between these two values should be divided into 10 equal parts. Then the point at which the reading is desired can be said to be so many tenths from either value and added or subtracted to obtain the desired figure.

LANDING

Performance information for the landing phase also is included in the pilot's operating handbook. The landing operation begins at the end of the flight profile and in the traffic pattern. Landing and stopping distances are plotted on

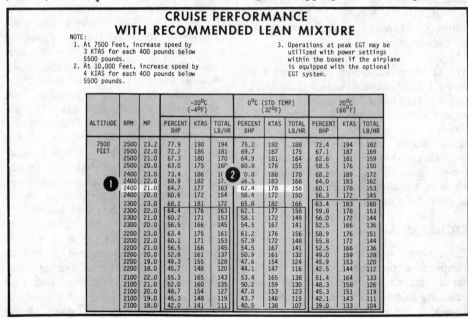

CRUISE PERFORMANCE
WITH RECOMMENDED LEAN MIXTURE

NOTE:
1. At 7500 Feet, increase speed by 3 KTAS for each 400 pounds below 5500 pounds.
2. At 10,000 Feet, increase speed by 4 KIAS for each 400 pounds below 5500 pounds.

3. Operations at peak EGT may be utilized with power settings within the boxes if the airplane is equipped with the optional EGT system.

ALTITUDE	RPM	MP	-20°C (-4°F)			0°C (STD TEMP) (32°F)			20°C (68°F)		
			PERCENT BHP	KTAS	TOTAL LB/HR	PERCENT BHP	KTAS	TOTAL LB/HR	PERCENT BHP	KTAS	TOTAL LB/HR
7500 FEET	2500	23.2	77.9	190	194	75.2	192	188	72.4	194	182
	2500	22.0	72.2	185	181	69.7	187	175	67.1	187	169
	2500	21.0	67.3	180	170	64.9	181	164	62.6	181	159
	2500	20.0	63.0	175	160	60.8	176	155	58.5	176	150
	2400	23.0	73.4	186	18	70.8	188	178	68.2	189	172
	2400	22.0	68.9	182	17	66.5	183	168	64.0	183	162
	2400	21.0	64.7	177	163	62.4	178	158	60.1	178	153
	2400	20.0	60.6	172	154	58.4	172	150	56.3	172	145
	2300	23.0	68.2	181	172	65.8	182	166	63.4	183	160
	2300	22.0	64.4	176	163	62.1	177	158	59.8	178	153
	2300	21.0	60.2	171	153	58.1	172	149	56.0	172	144
	2300	20.0	56.5	166	145	54.5	167	141	52.5	166	136
	2200	23.0	63.4	175	161	61.2	176	156	58.9	176	151
	2200	22.0	60.1	171	153	57.9	172	148	55.8	172	144
	2200	21.0	56.5	166	145	54.5	167	141	52.5	166	136
	2200	20.0	52.8	161	137	50.9	161	132	49.0	159	128
	2200	19.0	49.3	155	128	47.6	154	124	45.9	153	120
	2200	18.0	45.7	148	120	44.1	147	116	42.5	144	112
	2100	22.0	55.3	165	143	53.4	165	138	51.4	164	133
	2100	21.0	52.0	160	135	50.2	159	130	48.3	158	126
	2100	20.0	48.7	154	127	47.0	153	123	45.3	151	119
	2100	19.0	45.3	148	119	43.7	146	115	42.1	143	111
	2100	18.0	42.0	141	111	40.5	138	107	39.0	133	104

Fig. 1-28. Cruise Performance Chart (Excerpt)

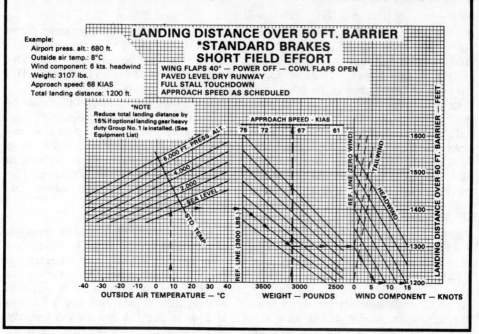

Fig. 1-29. Landing Performance Chart

the landing performance chart shown in figure 1-29. Wing flaps have little direct effect on aircraft stopping distances but, *indirectly, they have an appreciable effect* since the use of full flaps will materially reduce landing speed and, in turn, reduce ground roll.

The information presented in the landing chart (See Fig. 1-29) is based on maximum braking, 40° flap extension, and a hard-surfaced runway. Theoretically, maximum braking is realized just before the point at which skidding occurs. The chart directly makes allowances for temperature, pressure altitude, wind, and aircraft weight.

The following steps are used in determining landing distance over a 50-foot barrier:

1. Determination of temperature and pressure altitude
2. Determination of effect of aircraft weight
3. Determination of effect of headwind

SECTION C—ADVANCED AERODYNAMICS

An aircraft in flight is acted upon by four forces—lift, weight, thrust, and drag. *Lift* is the upward acting force; *weight* is the downward acting force; *thrust* acts in a forward direction; and *drag* is the backward, or retarding force.

Lift opposes weight and thrust opposes drag. When an aircraft is in straight-and-level flight, the opposing forces balance each other; lift equals weight and thrust equals drag. Any inequality between thrust and drag, while maintaining straight-and-level flight, results in acceleration or deceleration until the two forces become balanced. (See Fig. 1-30.)

LIFT

Efficient airplane operation depends on the pilot's knowledge of lift—how it is created and how it is sustained. To aid in understanding the aerodynamic forces involved in the production of lift, a review of the terminology associated with airfoils is presented in figure 1-31.

There is only one condition that must be present for an airfoil to produce lift—the air pressure above the wing must be less than the air pressure below the wing. The lower air pressure above the wing of an aircraft in flight results from a differential in airflow velocity above and below the wing.

Bernoulli's Principle can be used to explain how this occurs. As the airflow increases in velocity, it decreases in pressure. To illustrate this, examine the subsonic airflow as it passes through the venturi tube shown in figure 1-32. The airflow at point A has a given velocity, static pressure, and density. As it ap-

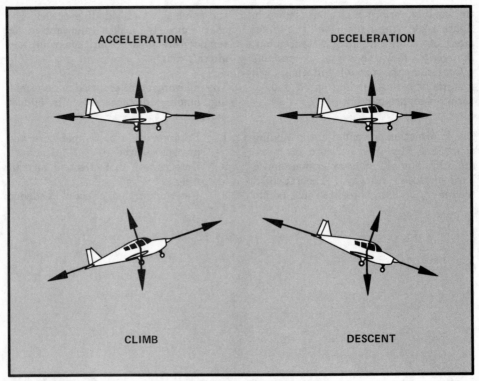

Fig. 1-30. Forces Acting on an Airplane

proaches the constriction at point B, a change in the velocity, pressure, or density must occur to maintain the original mass flow of air. In subsonic airflows, there is very little change in density; therefore, a change in the velocity and static pressure occurs. As the airflow reaches point B, the velocity increases, resulting in a decrease of the static pressure. The upper wing surface corresponds with the lower half of the tube and the decrease in static pressure above the wing results in the lifting action.

LIFT FORMULA

From Bernoulli's Principle, it is known that an airfoil must create a circulation in the airstream to produce a decrease in static pressure above the airfoil. As the angle of attack is increased, the decrease in pressure above the airfoil becomes greater. At the same time, additional pressure is created on the bottom of the airfoil due to the airflow striking the lower surface. This factor contributes approximately 25 to 30 percent of the total lift at angles of attack near that for maximum lift. This additional pressure, called the *dynamic pressure*, varies considerably as the angle of attack and airfoil velocity change, resulting in a variation of its contribution to the total lift. As illustrated in the following lift formula, total lift is a combination of many factors, including the dynamic pressure.

$$L = C_L S \frac{\rho_0}{2} V_I^2$$

L = Lift (in pounds)

C_L = Coefficient of lift (changes with airfoil design and angle of attack)

S = Wing area (in square feet)

$\frac{\rho_0}{2}$ = Air density at sea level and standard temperature, divided by 2

V_I^2 Indicated airspeed in feet per second; the technical notation for IAS is $V\sqrt{\sigma}$, where V is true airspeed

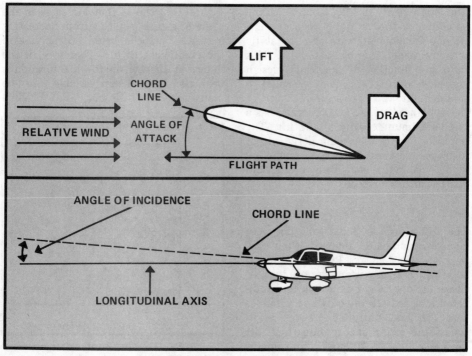

Fig. 1-31. Airfoil Terminology

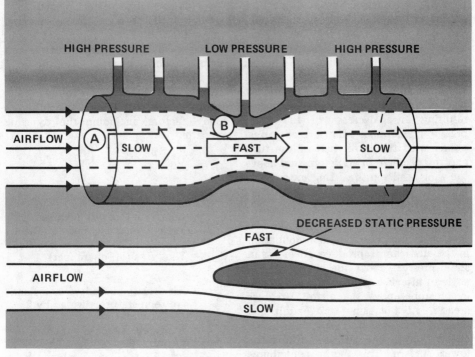

Fig. 1-32. Bernoulli's Principle

The coefficient of lift, as used in the equation, is the ratio between the airstream dynamic pressure and the static pressure generated by the wing. This ratio is a function of the wing's design and angle of attack. A wing designed to produce lift at slow airspeeds, such as the type used on a STOL aircraft, has a high maximum coefficient of lift. The opposite is true of a wing designed for high speed aircraft. This type of wing has a low maximum coefficient of lift and stalls at higher airspeeds.

The lift formula indicates that any change in indicated airspeed, wing size, or angle of attack results in a change of total lift. It is important to note that, of these factors, angle of attack and indicated airspeed are the only two variables that can be controlled by the pilot, unless the airfoil incorporates high lift devices which are discussed later in this section.

Figure 1-33 shows that increases in the angle of attack resulting from decreasing indicated airspeed cause an increase in the coefficient of lift. Therefore, if the indicated airspeed in the lift formula is decreased, some other variable must be increased to maintain the original

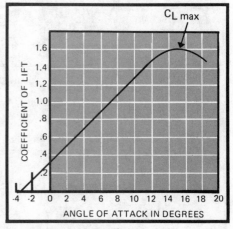

Fig. 1-33. Coefficient of Lift vs. Angle of Attack

amount of lift. Because the angle of attack is the only other variable which can be controlled readily, it must be increased to maintain constant lift.

Flight at minimum controllable airspeed provides an application of the lift formula. As the indicated airspeed *decreases*, the angle of attack must increase to maintain the same amount of lift necessary to sustain level flight. However, as each pilot knows, the angle of attack cannot be increased indefinitely. The angle of attack can be increased only until $C_{L_{max}}$ is reached. (See Fig. 1-33.) At this point, the pilot can no longer increase lift by increasing the angle of attack.

Because the ability to change airspeed and/or angle of attack is limited, a given amount of lift cannot be maintained during all conditions of flight. The pilot must know the performance capabilities of his aircraft and fly within those capabilities.

HIGH LIFT DEVICES

High lift devices can be incorporated in an airfoil to enable the pilot to have a greater degree of control over the production of lift. In general, high lift devices serve to increase the coefficient of lift.

TRAILING EDGE FLAPS

One of the most common high lift devices is the trailing edge flap. The deflection of this flap produces a large increase in airfoil camber and moves the effective lift force toward the trailing edge of the wing. The four basic types of flaps found on general aviation airplanes are illustrated in figure 1-34.

Plain Flap

The plain flap is the simplest of the four types. It increases the airfoil camber, resulting in a significant increase in the coefficient of lift ($C_{L_{max}}$). At the same time, it greatly increases drag and moves the center of lift aft on the airfoil, resulting in a nose-down pitching moment.

Split Flap

The split flap is deflected from the lower surface of the airfoil and produces a slightly greater increase in lift than does the plain flap. However, more drag is created because of the turbulent air pattern produced behind the airfoil.

Slotted Flap

The slotted flap provides an even greater increase in lift. This flap configuration allows the airflow from below the airfoil to flow over the upper flap surface,

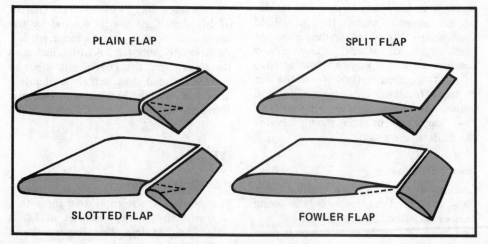

PLAIN FLAP

SPLIT FLAP

SLOTTED FLAP

FOWLER FLAP

Fig. 1-34. Trailing Edge Flaps

delaying airflow separation at high lift coefficients. This flap also provides an increase in wing camber to aid in increasing lift.

Fowler Flap

Of the four common flap types, the fowler flap is the most efficient. This flap not only moves down to increase wing camber, but also moves aft to increase the wing area. These two factors combine to provide large increases in lift with comparatively small increases in drag.

LEADING EDGE HIGH LIFT DEVICES

High lift devices also can be applied to the leading edge of the airfoil. The most common types are fixed slots, movable slats, and leading edge flaps. These devices are shown in figure 1-35.

Fixed Slots

Fixed slots direct airflow to the upper wing surface and delay airflow separation at higher angles of attack. The slot does not increase the wing camber, but allows a higher maximum coefficient of lift because the stall is delayed until the wing reaches a higher angle of attack.

Movable Slats

Movable slats consist of a leading edge segment which is free to move on tracks. At low angles of attack, the slat is held flush against the wing's leading edge. At high angles of attack, either a low pressure area at the wing's leading edge or pilot operated controls force the slat to move forward. This opens a slot and allows the air below the wing to flow over the wing's upper surface, delaying the airflow separation.

Leading Edge Flaps

Leading edge flaps, like trailing edge flaps, are used to increase the wing camber to effect an increase in $C_{L_{max}}$. This type of leading edge device is used frequently in conjunction with trailing

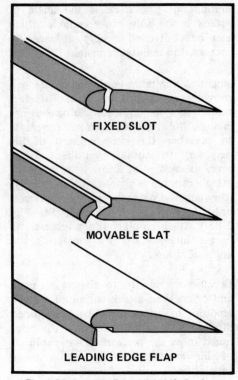

FIXED SLOT

MOVABLE SLAT

LEADING EDGE FLAP

Fig. 1-35. Leading Edge High Lift Devices

edge flaps and can reduce the nose-down pitching moment produced by the trailing edge flap.

The use of high lift devices gives the pilot greater control over the coefficient of lift, but their use is limited by the airplane's performance characteristics. Additionally, any device which increases the maximum lift coefficient also increases induced drag, which is of prime importance to the airplane's overall performance.

DRAG

INDUCED DRAG

The portion of the total drag force that is created by the production of lift is called *induced drag*. This drag is induced as the wing creates lift.

EFFECTS OF AIRSPEED AND ANGLE OF ATTACK

Because induced drag is a byproduct of lift, it is greatly affected by changes in airspeed. As indicated airspeed is decreased, induced drag increases, but at a much faster rate. If all other factors remain constant, induced drag varies inversely with the square of the airspeed. For example, if the indicated airspeed decreases by one-half, the induced drag increases four times, as illustrated in figure 1-36, points 1 and 2.

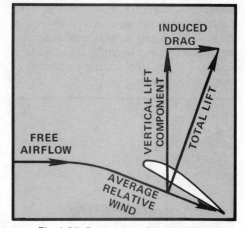

Fig. 1-37. Production of Induced Drag

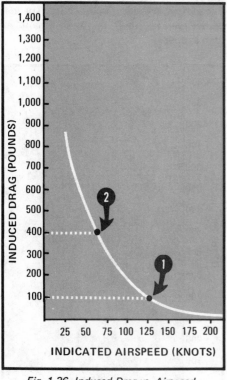

Fig. 1-36. Induced Drag vs. Airspeed

Induced drag is greatest at high angles of attack. Figure 1-37 illustrates how lift results in the creation of induced drag. The pilot should remember that induced drag is an unavoidable byproduct of the development of lift and varies inversely with changes in the indicated airspeed.

As the airflow approaches the wing, a portion of it is deflected downward,

resulting in a slight change in the actual relative wind. The lift produced by the wing acts perpendicular to the new relative wind, while the vertical lift component directly opposes the aircraft's weight. The rearward component of the total lift results in the retarding force of induced drag.

PARASITE DRAG

Parasite drag includes any drag which is *not* associated with the production of lift. Parasite drag is created by the airplane's surface as it displaces the airmass, generates turbulence, and retards smooth airflow.

EFFECT OF AIRPLANE SHAPE

The parasite drag created because of the shape of the airplane is called *form drag*. Form drag can be minimized by streamlining. This explains why airplane manufacturers attempt to streamline any airplane surface which is exposed to the passing airstream. It has been found that one of the most effective shapes for reducing form drag is the "teardrop."

An additional consideration in airplane shape is *interference drag*. This is the parasite drag created when various airflows over the airplane meet and form turbulent currents. In figure 1-38, the air flowing over the fuselage and wing of airplane A abruptly meets at the wing root, forming an area of turbulent airflow. On airplane B, this area has been streamlined, or "faired," to provide a smooth joining of the airflow and reduction of turbulence.

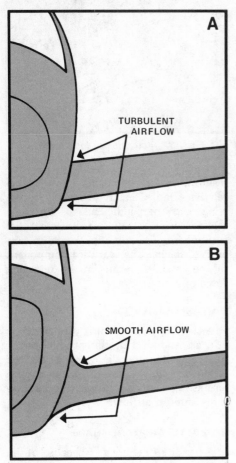

Fig. 1-38. Prevention of Interference Drag

Changes in airplane configuration can create substantial increases in total parasite drag. The primary cause of this increase is increases in the parasite drag area. For example, lowering the landing gear and flaps can increase the parasite drag area up to 80 percent.

EFFECT OF AIRSPEED

The actual parasite drag created by a given airplane varies with airspeed. For example, the same airplane at a constant

altitude has four times as much parasite drag at 200 knots as it has at 100 knots. This factor necessitates "clean" aerodynamic designs for high speed airplanes.

TOTAL DRAG

The total drag of an airplane in flight is the sum of the induced and parasite drag. Figure 1-39 illustrates the variation of total drag with *indicated airspeed* for a given airplane at a constant weight and configuration. For example, the parasite drag *increases* with velocity, while induced drag *decreases* with velocity. Induced drag is predominant at low speeds, while parasite drag is predominant at high speeds.

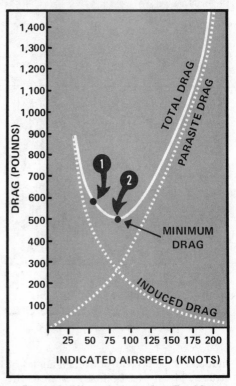

Fig. 1-39. Effect of Airspeed on Total Drag

Figure 1-39 also illustrates that minimum total drag occurs at the airspeed where induced and parasite drag meet. This is the point where the airplane is operating with the best *lift-to-drag ratio;* the airplane is producing the least drag for a given amount of lift. A practical application of the lift-to-drag ratio is the power-off glide. During a power-off glide, the maximum horizontal distance can be obtained when the airspeed which produces the maximum lift-to-drag ratio is used. This airspeed normally is given in the pilot's operating handbook for the specific airplane.

The minimum drag speed varies slightly with changes in airplane weight but, in light aircraft, the change in weight is not great enough to appreciably affect this speed. This same airspeed produces the maximum range. Because the airplane is operating at the peak ratio between lift and drag, the most efficient use of fuel for each mile traveled is obtained.

THRUST

Thrust is the force that must be produced to overcome the total drag. In a steady flight condition, thrust must equal total drag. If thrust exceeds drag, the airplane accelerates until the thrust and drag forces reach equilibrium.

The jet engine produces thrust by increasing the velocity of the air from the inlet to the exhaust of the engine. The thrust leaving the engine results in forward motion of the aircraft through an equal and opposite reaction. The propeller produces thrust by changing the velocity of the air passing the propeller blades. For the purpose of this discussion, only the thrust produced by a propeller and the factors that affect propeller efficiency are considered.

PROPELLER EFFICIENCY

The propeller converts the shaft horsepower of the engine into thrust horsepower. How efficiently this power is converted to thrust is important to airplane performance. Because the propeller is an airfoil, its efficiency is subject to all the factors which affect airfoil efficiency. The maximum efficiency is greatly affected by the angle of attack and rotational speed.

The fixed pitch propeller obtains maximum efficiency at either low airspeeds and high r.p.m. (climb propeller) or at high airspeeds and low r.p.m. (cruise propeller). The climb propeller provides greater efficiency during takeoff and climb, while the cruise propeller is most efficient at cruise airspeeds.

Variable pitch or constant speed propellers normally are used with high performance engines. With the constant speed propeller, the pilot can select the optimum propeller r.p.m. to use engine power efficiently. For takeoff and climb, a low pitch, high r.p.m. setting is used, but for cruise, a high pitch, low r.p.m. setting is selected. Although the constant speed propeller generally is considered to have optimum aerodynamic efficiency, the fixed pitch propeller also has some significant benefits. These include lower initial cost, less maintenance, and simplicity of operation. A detailed discussion of propeller efficiency is contained in Chapter 3.

FLIGHT IN THE AREA OF REVERSE COMMAND

Thrust and power are not synonymous terms. Thrust is the force created by the propeller to overcome drag, while power is the measure of work performed by the engine to turn the propeller. Although thrust and power are not the same, the curve representing power in figure 1-40 closely resembles that of the drag or thrust curve. This power curve is used throughout the following discussion to explain flight in the area of reverse command or flight "behind the power curve."

The line dividing the area of normal command from that of reverse command is the speed for maximum endurance. At point 1, the power required for level flight is at a minimum; therefore, the lowest *rate* of fuel consumption is obtained while maintaining a constant, level flight airspeed. Point 2 represents the airspeed for maximum range, or the

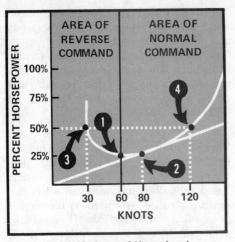

Fig. 1-40. Areas of Normal and Reverse Command

best fuel consumption *per mile* traveled. Points 1 and 2 correspond to points 1 and 2 on the total drag curve in figure 1-39. The point representing maximum range is determined by drawing a line tangent to the power curve. The point of tangency indicates the power for maximum range.

As figure 1-40 illustrates, a decrease in airspeed to the left of point 1 or an increase in airspeed to the right of point 1, require progressively higher power settings. It is important to note that in the area of reverse command, each airspeed reduction requires an increase in angle of attack to maintain altitude. Because of the drag increase accompanying the change in angle of attack, the power must be increased to balance the drag forces.

The graph also illustrates that one power setting can provide level flight at two different airspeeds, one in the area of reverse command (point 3) and one in the area of normal command (point 4). The important concept to remember is that when operating in the area of reverse command, slower airspeeds require the use of higher power settings to maintain level flight. If this area of flight could be avoided, problems would not

arise, but airplanes frequently operate in this speed range during maneuvers such as short-field landings. Therefore, the pilot should have an understanding of the airplane's flight characteristics in the area of reverse command.

An airplane trimmed for level flight at 40 knots requires a specific power setting. If the pitch attitude is temporarily reduced until an airspeed of 50 knots is reached, excess power is available, causing the airplane to climb. Conversely, if the pitch attitude is increased, a descent results because insufficient power is being used to maintain altitude. A further increase in angle of attack increases induced drag, increasing the need for power to maintain altitude. The pilot must remember that when flying in the area of reverse command, raising the nose while maintaining a fixed power setting results in a descent because insufficient power is available to maintain altitude at the lower airspeed.

WEIGHT

Weight, or gravity, is the simplest of the four forces. This is the actual weight of the airplane, termed one-G, and it always acts downward, toward the center of the earth. The effective weight, or load factor, can be increased above the normal one-G by flight maneuvers or turbulence. For this reason, airplane structures are designed to withstand load factors greater than the one-G weight of the airplane.

AIRCRAFT STABILITY

STATIC STABILITY

Static stability is the tendency of an airplane to return to a state of equilibrium following a displacement from that condition. If *positive* static stability is present, the airplane has a tendency to return to the original point of equilibrium. As shown in figure 1-41, part 1, when the ball is moved from point A, it has a tendency to return to the original position.

Part 2 illustrates *negative* static stability. When the ball is displaced from point A, it has a tendency to move farther from the point of equilibrium.

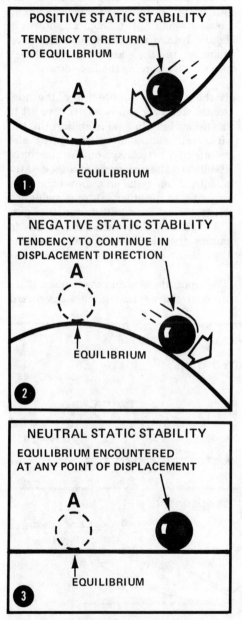

Fig. 1-41. Static Stability

Neutral static stability is illustrated by part 3. When the ball is displaced from equilibrium at point A, it does not have a tendency to return to, or move farther from, its original point of equilibrium.

DYNAMIC STABILITY

Dynamic stability refers to the time required for an airplane's response to its static stability. The static and dynamic stability must be considered in combination to understand the effects on an airplane.

Airplanes are designed with positive static and positive dynamic stability. This results in the airplane's tendency to return to equilibrium through a series of decreasing oscillations, as shown in figure 1-42, airplane A. If airplane B displays positive static, but neutral dynamic stability, it attempts to return to equilibrium but the oscillations do not decrease in magnitude with time; therefore, equilibrium is not regained. Positive static and negative dynamic stability are indicated by airplane C. After the displacement from equilibrium occurs, the oscillations increase in magnitude as time progresses.

LONGITUDINAL STABILITY

If the aircraft is statically stable along its longitudinal axis, it will resist any force which might cause it to pitch, and it will return to level flight when the force is removed. This is the most important of the three types of stability of an aircraft in flight.

To obtain longitudinal stability, an airplane may be designed to be either slightly tail-heavy or nose-heavy while trimmed in straight-and-level flight. Additionally, the CG location can affect the nose-heavy or tail-heavy condition. If the airplane is loaded near the forward CG limit, a nose-heavy condition can occur. Conversely, if it is loaded near the aft CG limit, a tail-heavy condition may result. Consequently, the horizontal stabilizer is designed with the capability of producing either the positive or negative lift necessary to longitudinally stabilize the airplane.

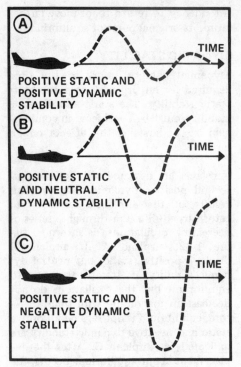

Fig. 1-42. Oscillatory Stability

If an airplane is tail-heavy during straight-and-level flight, the horizontal stabilizer produces positive lift to maintain longitudinal stability. If turbulence or control input pitches the nose up, the horizontal stabilizer experiences an increased angle of attack, as shown in figure 1-43, part A. This results in an increase in the horizontal stabilizer's positive lift, forcing the nose down.

If the airplane is nose-heavy, the horizontal stabilizer produces negative lift to maintain longitudinal stability. In this situation, a nose-up displacement also results in a lift change on the horizontal stabilizer. The new angle of attack of the stabilizer can result in a conversion from negative to positive lift or a reduction in negative lift, as illustrated in figure 1-43, part B. Either situation results in raising the airplane's tail and lowering the nose.

The opposite reaction takes place if the nose of the airplane pitches downward.

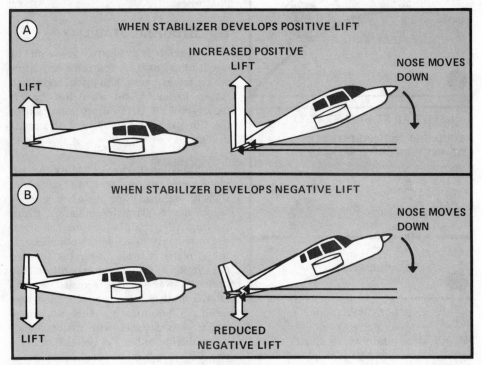

Fig. 1-43. Longitudinal Stability

A horizontal stabilizer producing positive lift experiences a decrease in angle of attack; therefore, less tail lift is developed and the tail lowers as the nose raises. If the stabilizer is producing negative lift to maintain stability, the pitch change results in an increase in the angle of attack, causing the stabilizer to produce greater negative lift. This situation also forces the tail down, returning the airplane to the trimmed condition.

LATERAL STABILITY

Lateral stability refers to an airplane's tendency to return to wings-level flight following a displacement. It is considered generally undesirable to design an airplane with *strong* lateral stability. *Strong* lateral stability has a detrimental effect on rolling performance and handling characteristics during crosswind takeoffs and landings.

The tendency of an airplane to right itself after being displaced from wings-level flight actually is the result of a side slip which is induced by corrective control movements. If a wing is displaced, another force, such as a control input, must be introduced before the airplane's lateral stability becomes evident. As illustrated in figure 1-44, position 1, a wing develops stable rolling moments when a side slip is introduced. When the relative wind strikes the airplane from the side, the upwind wing experiences an increased angle of attack and increased lift. The downwind wing has a reduced angle of attack and decreased lift. The differential in lift results in a rolling moment, which tends to raise the low wing.

Dihedral, as illustrated in figure 1-44, position 2, is a wing design consideration used to obtain lateral stability. Dihedral increases the stabilizing effect of side slips by increasing the lift differential between the high and low wing during the slip.

Sweepback, which frequently is used on corporate jet airplanes, also has a lateral stabilizing effect. When an aircraft with sweepback wings begins to slip, the leading edge of the low wing meets the relative wind more nearly perpendicular than the higher wing. This results in more lift on the low wing and causes a restoring force to return the wing to a level position. (See Fig. 1-45.)

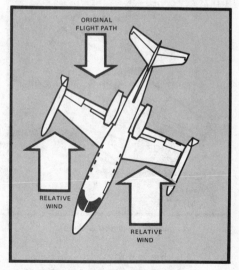

Fig. 1-45. Effect of Sweepback

DIRECTIONAL STABILITY

Directional stability is the tendency of the airplane to remain stationary about

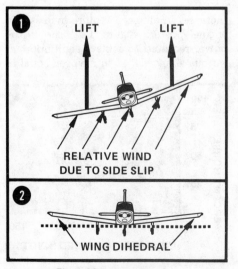

Fig. 1-44. Lateral Stability

the vertical or yaw axis. Figure 1-46, aircraft A, illustrates that when the relative wind is parallel to the longitudinal axis, the airplane is in equilibrium. If some force yaws the airplane, producing a side slip, a positive yawing moment also is developed, which returns the airplane to equilibrium.

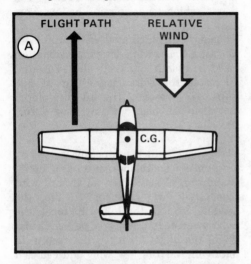

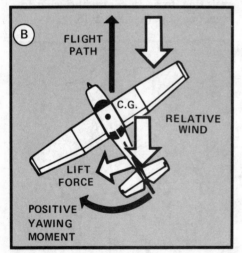

Fig. 1-46. Yaw and Side Slip

To obtain this stability, the side area of fuselage ahead of the center of gravity must be less than that behind the center of gravity. This difference in fuselage area is usually insufficient for a high degree of stability, so a vertical stabilizer is added.

The vertical stabilizer is a symmetrical airfoil, capable of producing lift in either direction. As shown by aircraft B, a positive side slip angle changes the relative wind on the vertical stabilizer, creating a higher coefficient of lift in one direction. In the illustration, the airplane is in a side slip to the right, resulting in positive lift to the left of the stabilizer. Additional lift moves the tail to the left, causing the longitudinal axis to align with the relative wind.

AERODYNAMICS AND FLIGHT PERFORMANCE

STRAIGHT-AND-LEVEL FLIGHT

When an airplane is in straight-and-level, unaccelerated flight, a condition of equilibrium exists. Lift equals weight, and thrust equals total drag. To accelerate or decelerate in level flight, the power must be changed to produce an unbalanced condition. But as the power is changed and the airspeed changes, an adjustment of the angle of attack must be simultaneously accomplished, or level flight will not be maintained. This relates back to the basic lift equation; a change in velocity results in a change in total lift, unless one of the other variable factors is changed.

Increases in airspeed require increases in engine power. Figure 1-47 shows the power required to achieve equilibrium at various airspeeds. If an airspeed equal to

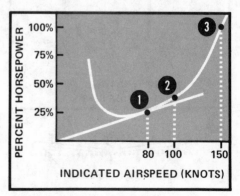

Fig. 1-47. Power Required vs. Airspeed

point 1 is desired, the power required curve shows the engine power that must be available to maintain equilibrium. If a speed equal to point 2 is desired, the power required for equilibrium is considerably greater. The maximum level flight speed, shown in point 3, is obtained when the power required equals the power available from the powerplant.

The airplane will continue to be accelerated in straight-and-level flight until the power required equals the power available. At this point, the increase in drag associated with the increased airspeed has reached equilibrium with the power required and the power available, and the airplane no longer accelerates.

Maximum endurance and maximum range in level flight are two other important performance considerations. The power settings necessary to achieve maximum endurance or maximum range normally can be determined from the performance data in the pilot's operating handbook. Maximum endurance occurs at the point where the least power is required to maintain level flight, but the maximum range occurs where the ratio of airspeed to power required is the greatest.

The value of maximum range is obvious, but the speed for maximum endurance is equally valuable. During flight in IFR conditions, a pilot may be requested to hold at a given point due to other air traffic. The pilot's objective is to expend time with a minimum consumption of fuel. In this situation, maximum endurance airspeed is the most economical, because it requires the lowest power setting and, therefore, the lowest fuel flow.

CLIMBS

Maximum climb performance is *not* a result of excess lift, but a result of excess thrust horsepower and/or thrust. The angle of climb is a function of thrust, while rate of climb is a function of thrust horsepower. During most phases

of flight, the maximum rate of climb is used. As illustrated in figure 1-48, the maximum rate of climb occurs at the airspeed with the greatest difference between thrust horsepower available (product of shaft horsepower and propeller efficiency) and thrust horsepower required.

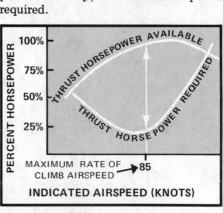

Fig. 1-48. Maximum Rate of Climb

If excess thrust horsepower is not available, the airplane is in steady, level flight. If excess thrust horsepower is available, the rate of climb produced is proportional to the amount of excess power.

For any given airplane weight, the maximum angle of climb (greatest altitude gain in least horizontal or forward distance) is dependent upon the amount of excess *thrust* available. This occurs where there is the greatest differential between thrust and drag. Figure 1-49 shows the thrust available and required curves in relation to airspeed. It should be noted that thrust available decreases as the airspeed increases, but the thrust required curve increases with airspeed. Therefore, the maximum angle-of-climb airspeed occurs at the point with the greatest differential between thrust available and thrust required.

The thrust available curve shows that propeller thrust is the highest at low airspeeds and decreases as airspeed increases. Therefore, the maximum excess thrust is available at an airspeed very close to the stall speed.

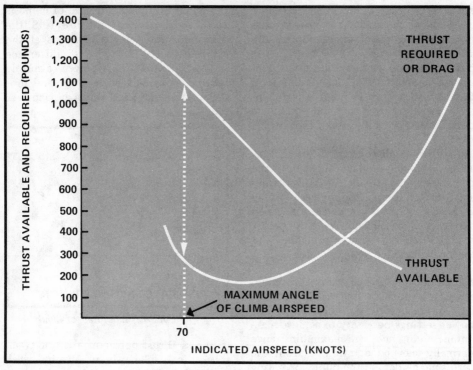

Fig. 1-49. Maximum Angle of Climb

FACTORS AFFECTING CLIMB PERFORMANCE

Airspeed affects both the angle and rate of climb. At a given airplane weight, a specific airspeed is required for maximum performance. Generally, the larger the speed variation from that required, the larger the performance variation.

Weight also affects climb performance. A change in weight changes the drag and power required. Increases in weight reduce the maximum rate and angle of climb.

Increases in altitude generally have the greatest effect on climb performance. This occurs because an increased altitude increases the power and thrust required, but decreases the power and thrust available. Therefore, both the angle-of-climb and rate-of-climb performance decrease with altitude. At the same time, the airspeed necessary to obtain the

maximum angle of climb increases with altitude, but the airspeed for best rate of climb decreases, as shown in figure 1-50. The point where these two speeds converge is the airplane's *absolute* ceiling;

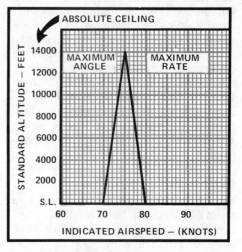

Fig. 1-50. Change in Climb Speed with Altitude

neither excess power nor thrust is available to produce a climb. At the absolute ceiling, the rate of climb becomes zero, and only the airspeed where the angle and rate of climb converge results in steady, level flight.

GLIDES

In the event of an engine failure, the pilot of a single-engine airplane usually is interested in flying the airplane at the minimum glide angle to obtain the maximum distance for the altitude lost. This minimum glide angle is obtained under the aerodynamic conditions which produce the least drag. Since the lift is basically equal to the weight, the minimum drag is obtained at the maximum lift-to-drag ratio (L/D_{max}). This occurs at a specific value of the lift coefficient and, therefore, at a specific angle of attack.

Power-off glide performance also can be correlated to airspeed. Figure 1-51 illustrates that the rate of descent varies with changes in airspeed. An attempt to stretch a glide by flying at speeds above or below the best glide speed is futile, and results in increased rates of descent. This figure also illustrates that increases in drag, such as lowering the landing gear or flaps, decrease the maximum glide distance. Additionally, as the drag increases, the airspeed for the maximum glide distance decreases for that configuration.

TURNS

Turns are made by canting the vertical component of lift to one side to produce a force which turns the aircraft. The lift force can be subdivided and represented as two forces: one acting vertically and one acting horizontally. (See Fig. 1-52.) The horizontal component of lift accel-

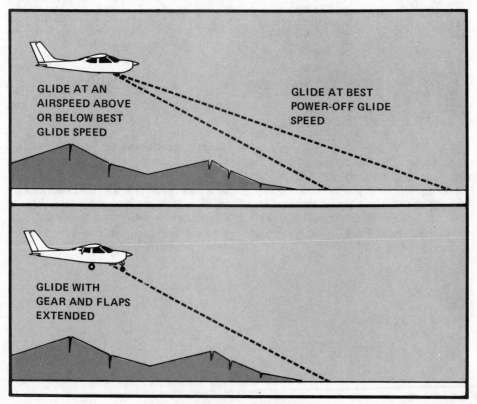

Fig. 1-51. Maximum Power-Off Glide

erates the aircraft toward the center of the turn, while the vertical component overcomes weight.

In a level turn, there are pairs of opposing forces in balance. The centrifugal force acting on the aircraft is equal and opposite to the turning force. The vertical component of lift is opposite and equal to the aircraft's weight. The combined centrifugal force and weight is called the resultant force and is opposite and equal to the total lift.

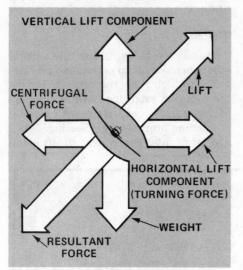

Fig. 1-52. Balanced Forces in a Coordinated Turn

The steeper the bank, the greater the total lift needed and the greater the force required to make the airplane turn. This also means that the centrifugal and gravitational forces combine to make a greater resultant force and higher load factor. (See Fig. 1-53.)

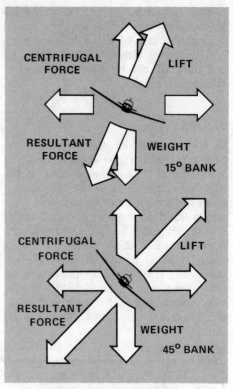

Fig. 1-53. Increases in Bank and Load Factor

In level flight, the total lift force is equal to weight. When the aircraft is banked, the total lift is diverted from vertical. Since the total lift is still equal to weight, insufficient lift is acting vertically to counteract weight and the aircraft descends. In order to maintain altitude in a turn, the total lift must be increased until sufficient lift acts vertically to counteract weight. This is done by increasing the angle of attack and, therefore, the coefficient of lift.

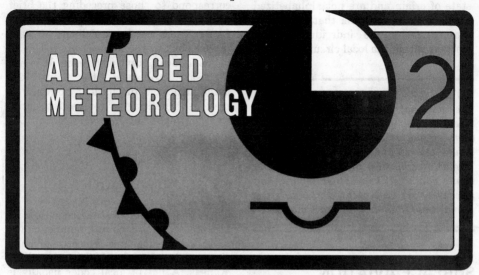

chapter 2

ADVANCED
METEOROLOGY

INTRODUCTION

This manual covers those subjects of meteorology that are applicable to the instrument/commercial pilot's training program. Since all pilots use basically the same weather facilities and operate in varying degrees of the same weather conditions, the weather knowledge required of the private pilot is also applicable to the instrument/commercial pilot.

Advanced meteorology is presented to provide the pilot with a better understanding of various weather phenomena and a detailed knowledge of how to utilize existing weather services. To determine the safety and practicality of a proposed flight, it is essential for the instrument/commercial pilot to analyze the weather conditions which may be encountered on a flight and realize personal limitations, as well as those of the aircraft.

SECTION A—ADVANCED WEATHER TELETYPE REPORTS AND FORECASTS

Weather observations are taken and transmitted at periodic intervals along Federal airways, and at important points off airways. Teletype circuits are used to provide various weather stations throughout the country with up-to-date weather information. Each station is part of a circuit that consists of all stations in a geographical region. A request/reply system is available for non-local data.

Each station in a local circuit sends its own report in assigned order. The monitoring station on the circuit then relays selected reports to other stations,

beginning with nearby circuits and followed by circuits at a greater distance. The result is that stations on the local circuit receive reports from all stations on their own circuit and selected reports from other circuits. Fewer reports are received from more distant stations.

To enable pilots and briefers to locate weather reports with ease, relays are subdivided according to the state of origin. Reporting stations within the state are alphabetized when part of a relay. However, reporting stations on a local circuit do not appear according to state of origin and are not alphabetized. They appear in the order that the reports were sent by the individual issuing stations within the local circuit.

NOTE:

The National Weather Service is considering the use of metric values in weather reports and forecasts. If metric values are adopted in the future, cloud heights, visibilities, and other measurements contained in weather reports and forecasts may be presented in a different format than that shown in this manual.

SURFACE AVIATION WEATHER REPORTS

The surface aviation weather report, sometimes referred to as an "hourly" report, is used to compile information concerning existing surface weather at the various observation stations. This report is given every hour.

Figure 2-1 shows a sample hourly report. It is read as follows: The tenth day of the month, 1106 GMT . . . Wichita . . . special report at 1102 GMT . . . 300 scattered . . . measured ceiling 800 broken . . . 2,000 overcast . . . 1-1/2 miles visibility with thunderstorms and moderate rain showers . . . barometer reading, in millibars converted to sea level, 1013.2 . . . temperature 72° Fahrenheit . . . dewpoint 64° Fahrenheit . . .wind from 020° at 14 knots with gusts to 18 knots . . . altimeter setting 29.92, converted to sea level . . . along runway 01, visual range variable 3,000 to 5,000 feet . . . thunderstorm southwest of the station, moving east, frequent lightning from cloud to cloud . . . rain began at 15 minutes after the hour.

The numbered callouts on the hourly aviation weather report in figure 2-1

correspond to those preceding the brief descriptions in the second portion of the figure. These numbered callouts also are placed next to the appropriate headings in the following text discussion. It is not necessary to refer to figure 2-1 throughout the discussion; however, it may be beneficial to review the entire weather report at intervals during the discussion.

① STATION IDENTIFICATION

The station identification code follows the state or local circuit number, date, and transmission time. The code given in the sample report is "ICT" for Wichita, Kansas. A list of local codes usually is placed along the edge of clipboards or bulletin boards where the reports are displayed. All location identifiers are listed in a booklet of the same name available at all Weather Service offices.

② SPECIAL REPORT

The letters "SP" are the code for a special report. Sometimes special reports are transmitted on the teletype separately; however, they usually are imbedded in a series of weather reports.

③ SKY CONDITION

This segment of the report covers the sky condition, layer by layer. The illustrated report indicates 300 feet scattered, measured 800 feet broken, and 2,000 feet overcast.

To determine the cloud heights, two zeros are added to the number given in the report; for example, "8" means "800 feet." The amount of cloud coverage is coded according to the listing shown in figure 2-1. If the ceiling is variable, the letter "V" will follow the ceiling height.

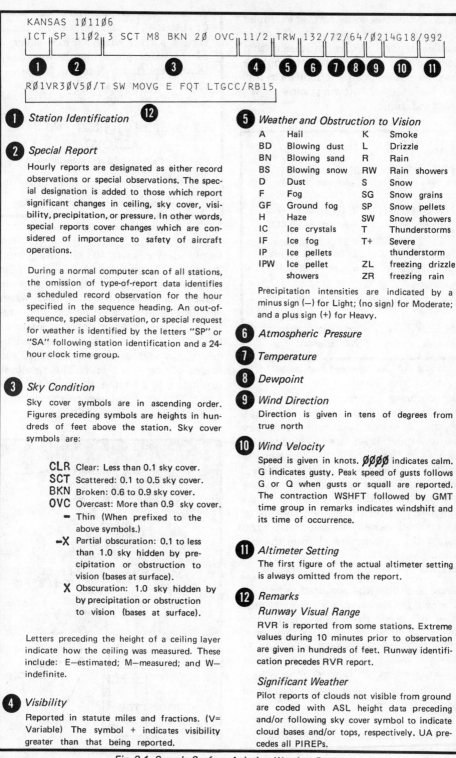

KANSAS 1Ø11Ø6
ICT SP 11Ø2 3 SCT M8 BKN 2Ø OVC 11/2 TRW 132/72/64/Ø214G18/992
① ② ③ ④ ⑤ ⑥ ⑦ ⑧ ⑨ ⑩ ⑪

RØ1VR3ØV5Ø/T SW MOVG E FQT LTGCC/RB15

① Station Identification ⑫

② Special Report

Hourly reports are designated as either record observations or special observations. The special designation is added to those which report significant changes in ceiling, sky cover, visibility, precipitation, or pressure. In other words, special reports cover changes which are considered of importance to safety of aircraft operations.

During a normal computer scan of all stations, the omission of type-of-report data identifies a scheduled record observation for the hour specified in the sequence heading. An out-of-sequence, special observation, or special request for weather is identified by the letters "SP" or "SA" following station identification and a 24-hour clock time group.

③ Sky Condition

Sky cover symbols are in ascending order. Figures preceding symbols are heights in hundreds of feet above the station. Sky cover symbols are:

CLR Clear: Less than 0.1 sky cover.
SCT Scattered: 0.1 to 0.5 sky cover.
BKN Broken: 0.6 to 0.9 sky cover.
OVC Overcast: More than 0.9 sky cover.
 − Thin (When prefixed to the above symbols.)
 −X Partial obscuration: 0.1 to less than 1.0 sky hidden by precipitation or obstruction to vision (bases at surface).
 X Obscuration: 1.0 sky hidden by by precipitation or obstruction to vision (bases at surface).

Letters preceding the height of a ceiling layer indicate how the ceiling was measured. These include: E—estimated; M—measured; and W—indefinite.

④ Visibility

Reported in statute miles and fractions. (V= Variable) The symbol + indicates visibility greater than that being reported.

⑤ Weather and Obstruction to Vision

A	Hail	K	Smoke
BD	Blowing dust	L	Drizzle
BN	Blowing sand	R	Rain
BS	Blowing snow	RW	Rain showers
D	Dust	S	Snow
F	Fog	SG	Snow grains
GF	Ground fog	SP	Snow pellets
H	Haze	SW	Snow showers
IC	Ice crystals	T	Thunderstorms
IF	Ice fog	T+	Severe
IP	Ice pellets		thunderstorm
IPW	Ice pellet	ZL	freezing drizzle
	showers	ZR	freezing rain

Precipitation intensities are indicated by a minus sign (−) for Light; (no sign) for Moderate; and a plus sign (+) for Heavy.

⑥ Atmospheric Pressure

⑦ Temperature

⑧ Dewpoint

⑨ Wind Direction

Direction is given in tens of degrees from true north

⑩ Wind Velocity

Speed is given in knots. ØØØØ indicates calm. G indicates gusty. Peak speed of gusts follows G or Q when gusts or squall are reported. The contraction WSHFT followed by GMT time group in remarks indicates windshift and its time of occurrence.

⑪ Altimeter Setting

The first figure of the actual altimeter setting is always omitted from the report.

⑫ Remarks

Runway Visual Range

RVR is reported from some stations. Extreme values during 10 minutes prior to observation are given in hundreds of feet. Runway identification precedes RVR report.

Significant Weather

Pilot reports of clouds not visible from ground are coded with ASL height data preceding and/or following sky cover symbol to indicate cloud bases and/or tops, respectively. UA precedes all PIREPs.

Fig. 2-1. Sample Surface Aviation Weather Report

Figure 2-2 shows some further examples of the sky coverage segments of hourly weather reports. *Obscured* means that the overlying sky condition cannot be observed due to such phenomena as fog, dust, smoke, or blowing snow. "W" means *indefinite*.

I CT CLR	Clear
I CT 3 SCT	300' scattered (add two zeros)
I CT 2Ø BKN 2ØØ OVC	2,000' broken with overcast at 20,000'
I CT 2Ø BKN 2ØØ BKN	2,000' broken with broken at 20,000'
I CT – X	Partial Obscuration
I CT W2 OVC	Indefinite ceiling 200' overcast

Fig. 2-2. Sky Coverage Examples

Sky coverage information accumulates from the ground up. In other words, if a lower layer covers two-tenths of the sky and an upper layer covers four-tenths, the lower layer will be reported as "SCT" and the upper layer as "BKN," even though the upper layer covers less than one-half of the sky. This means that a greater portion of the sky appears to be covered when viewed from the ground than when viewed from the air.

CEILING

Figure 2-3 gives the accepted definition of a *ceiling*. However, for practical purposes, pilots can think of a ceiling as the lowest height at which more than one-half of the sky is covered by clouds. If the sky coverage in the example had indicated "8-BKN" (800 feet, thin broken), this cloud layer would not have constituted a ceiling.

A measured ceiling (M) means that the ceiling was determined through the use of a rotating beam *ceilometer*, an elec-

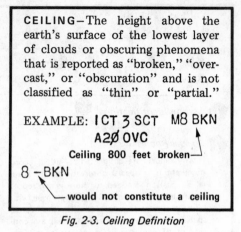

CEILING—The height above the earth's surface of the lowest layer of clouds or obscuring phenomena that is reported as "broken," "overcast," or "obscuration" and is not classified as "thin" or "partial."

EXAMPLE: I CT 3 SCT M8 BKN
A2Ø OVC
Ceiling 800 feet broken—

8 – BKN

would not constitute a ceiling

Fig. 2-3. Ceiling Definition

tronic device used to measure cloud bases, as illustrated in figure 2-4. The projector rotates in a vertical plane while radiating a brilliant beam of light. When clouds are illuminated, some light reflects to the detector and the angle of projected light is converted automatically to a vertical measurement of the height of the cloud base. The resultant readings may be remotely indicated in a control tower, flight service station, or a National Weather Service Office.

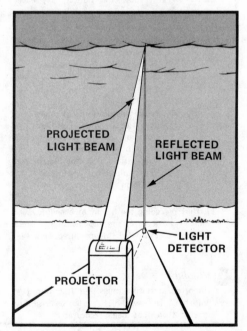

PROJECTED LIGHT BEAM

REFLECTED LIGHT BEAM

LIGHT DETECTOR

PROJECTOR

Fig. 2-4. Electronic Ceiling Measurement

Balloon, aircraft and observer-determined ceilings are collectively formed *estimated ceilings* (E). The balloon-estimated ceiling is determined by releasing a weather balloon and noting how long it takes to reach the cloud base. It is observed through a *theodolite* (an instrument for measuring angles) or by a directional radio antenna and the cloud height is determined by triangulation. The accuracy of this method is rather limited, however, because vertical air currents often cause the balloon to rise at speeds other than the normal ascent rate.

An aircraft-estimated ceiling is received by the local ATC facility or flight service station as a pilot report, then forwarded to the weather observer as a reliable source of information on cloud bases and tops. In the absence of the above methods of determining cloud height, a weather observer can estimate the ceiling height by relying on his experience and knowledge of cloud forms.

If a ceiling is *variable*, the letter "V" will follow the ceiling height. For example, the hourly weather report " ICT E15VOVC " indicates that there is an estimated ceiling of 1,500 feet overcast with varying ceilings in the area.

An indefinite ceiling exists whenever the base of an existing ceiling cannot be determined due to vision-limiting precipitation, haze, or fog. This ceiling represents vertical visibility into the obscuring elements, rather than the height of an actual cloud base.

When an observer reports an obscuration, he is, in effect, saying that the sky is obscured from his vision by surface-based phenomena. He cannot see any clouds above it or determine actual cloud cover. If he reports a partial obscuration, the sky is partially obscured by surface-based phenomena; however, enough of the sky can be seen to report the sky conditions that exist above it.

Due to the communication delay between an observation and its dissemination, hourly weather reports are actually recent history. Because of this, flight planning should be based on *trends*. Several consecutive reports should be studied to get an idea of the sequence of events which may occur.

4 VISIBILITY

This segment in the sample hourly weather report contains the visibility (1-1/2 statute miles). In a situation where the visibility is not the same in each direction, the reported visibility is whatever can be observed over at least one-half of the horizon. This is *prevailing visibility*. If a patch of dense ground fog lies over the approach end of the runway, but prevailing visibility is five miles in haze, visibility will be reported as five miles. For this reason, a pilot should check for *sector* visibilities in the remarks section.

Prevailing visibilities are determined by viewing prominent objects against the horizon. At night, lighted objects are used. This is significant because, at night, a pilot may be able to see lighted obstructions five miles away, but he would have to be much closer to an unlighted obstruction to see it. If the surrounding countryside has few or no lights, a pilot may be flying IFR at night and not realize it, since the visibility using unlighted objects could easily be less than one mile.

5 WEATHER AND OBSTRUCTION TO VISION

The fifth segment of the hourly report can be one letter or a combination of letters that indicate the present weather or obstruction to visibility at the observation station. The "TRW" shown in the sample report stands for thunderstorms and moderate rain showers.

If rain or snow is falling steadily, VFR conditions probably will not last and marginal situations are likely to worsen.

Moderate rain can easily obstruct the view through the windshield and reduce five miles visibility to a single, blurry mile or less. Snow showers *severely* reduce forward visibility and, in addition, cover the ground so that visual cues are virtually eliminated as the runway is approached. For this reason, descending to improve visibility is not effective in snow.

Besides indicating the major causes of visibility restrictions, the present weather section contents also can provide insight into the vertical cross-section of the atmosphere. By knowing the form of precipitation reaching the ground and applying basic knowledge of what must happen aloft to produce it, some idea of conditions aloft may be obtained.

6 ATMOSPHERIC PRESSURE

This segment of the sample hourly report provides the atmospheric pressure in millibars. The numbers given in the hourly report are the last three digits of the pressure reading, 132 (1013.2 millibars, corrected to sea level). This item may not seem as useful as the altimeter setting, but it may assist in establishing a mental relationship between teletype reports and chart presentations of isobars.

The following steps can be used to read the barometric pressure from an hourly report.

1. If the first two numbers are less than 56, prefix the number with 10. For example, 132 becomes 1013.2.
2. If the first two numbers are 56 or greater, prefix the number with 9. For example, 584 becomes 958.4. Note that the last digit of the barometric pressure reading is always in tenths.

7 TEMPERATURE

Item 7 of the hourly report is the surface temperature in degrees Fahrenheit. The example shows that the temperature at the station is 72° Fahrenheit. A sudden rapid rise or fall in the temperature may indicate a frontal passage.

8 DEWPOINT

In this section of the sample report, 64° is the dewpoint in degrees Fahrenheit. The dewpoint is that temperature to which air must be cooled to become saturated. For example, if the air temperature is 60° Fahrenheit and the dewpoint is 50° Fahrenheit, the air would be saturated if cooled to 50° Fahrenheit. If the air were further cooled to 49° Fahrenheit, it could no longer hold all the water vapor and the water vapor would condense to liquid. If this type of cooling takes place only in the fraction of an inch or so of the air above the ground, dew will form. However, it is more likely that the cooling will affect a deeper layer of the lower atmosphere and fog will form.

The dewpoint is important to the pilot because it indicates the temperature at which fog normally starts to form. When the air is saturated, the relative humidity is 100 percent; if the air is not saturated, the temperature is higher than the dewpoint and the relative humidity is less than 100 percent.

A high relative humidity is of prime importance in the formation of fog, since condensation will not occur unless the relative humidity is near 100 percent. The natural conditions which bring about a high relative humidity are also fog-producing processes. Relative humidity can be estimated from hourly weather reports by determining the spread (difference in degrees) between the temperature and dewpoint. Fog is rare when the spread is more than four degrees Fahrenheit. It is most frequent when the temperature/dewpoint spread is less than two degrees Fahrenheit.

A light wind is generally favorable for fog formation. It causes a gentle mixing action which spreads surface cooling through a deeper layer of air and increases the thickness of the fog. If calm winds exist when other factors are favorable for fog formation, only dew, frost, or a shallow layer of fog will form.

❾ WIND DIRECTION

The wind direction is reported to the nearest 10° by means of a two-digit number. In the example, the wind is blowing from 020°. A zero must be added to the two-digit number to obtain the correct wind direction. Figure 2-5 shows how various wind directions are given in an hourly report.

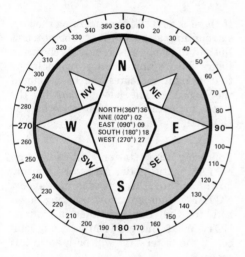

NORTH(360°) 36
NNE (020°) 02
EAST (090°) 09
SOUTH (180°) 18
WEST (270°) 27

Fig. 2-5. Wind Direction

Pilots should observe the terrain surrounding frequently visited airports and the wind direction which produces an upslope flow. This information, noted in the margin of the appropriate approach chart, is a valuable tool for forecasting fog when the temperature/dewpoint spread is small.

❿ WIND VELOCITY

This segment of the report gives the wind velocity in knots. At this station, the wind velocity is 14 knots, with gusts (indicated by the G) to 18 knots. A gust is a variation in wind speed of at least 10 knots between lulls and peaks.

A *squall* is a sudden increase in speed of at least 15 knots to a sustained speed of 20 knots, or more, lasting for at least one minute. The squall is indicated by the letter "Q" immediately after the average wind velocity, followed by the speed of the squall wind; for example, 0214Q25. Squalls indicate turbulence near the surface and differ from gusts due to their longer duration.

A *calm* wind is shown by four zeros. A steady wind without gusts or squalls is shown without a letter following the wind velocity, such as the 16 knots shown in figure 2-6. An "E" preceding the wind segment denotes the speed is estimated.

∅∅∅∅	– Calm
3416	– From 340° at 16 knots
E 2727	– From 270° estimated at 27 knots
E 3414G28	– From 340° estimated 14 knots with gusts to 28 knots

Fig. 2-6. Hourly Wind Reports

Analysis of wind direction and velocity can be used as a forecasting aid. If winds created by a nearby front slow down, very low ceilings and visibilities are a distinct possibility. If they begin to gain speed noticeably, it may indicate the front is growing in intensity.

⓫ ALTIMETER SETTING

The next item in the surface aviation report is the altimeter setting. This example indicates the altimeter setting is 29.92.

If the first number is 8 or 9, it should be prefixed with 2. For example, if 896 is prefixed with the number 2, the number becomes 28.96. If the first number is 0 or 1, it should be prefixed with 3. For example, if 102 appears on the hourly report, it is prefixed with 3. The value then becomes 31.02. All altimeter settings are already converted to sea level. This means that if a weather station at

5 ,000 feet above sea level has a baro-metric reading of 24.92 inches, the reading is reduced to sea level by allow-ing one inch of mercury for every 1,000 feet that the station is located above sea level. Therefore, five inches are added to the altimeter setting and this setting, reduced to sea level, becomes 29.92 inches of mercury. All altimeters set in relation to sea level pressure indicate altitude above sea level, not above the terrain, as illustrated in figure 2-7.

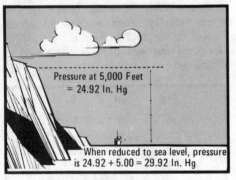

Fig. 2-7. Altimeter Setting
Converted to Sea Level

12 REMARKS

In the remarks section of hourly weather reports, there may be information con-cerning runway visual range. At the approach end of runway 01, as indicated by "R01" in the example, the visual range is 3,000 feet variable to 5,000 feet. These values are averages recorded dur-ing a 10-minute period.

In the remarks is the notation: "Thun-derstorm southwest, moving east, fre-quent lightning cloud to cloud." Al-though hourly reports consist of symbols and abbreviations, this example shows their simplicity and the ease of reading them. The final remark on the hourly report shows that rain began 15 minutes past the hour.

The following list contains other com-mon remarks that may be found on hourly reports.

BINOVC	—Breaks in overcast
CB	—Cumulonimbus clouds
CU FRMG	—Cumulus forming
OCNL SPKL	—Occasional sprinkle
RB48	—Rain began 48 minutes past the hour
RE10	—Rain ended 10 minutes past the hour
CIG RGD	—Ceilings ragged

There are many more abbreviations used in the remarks column. However, this list should give an idea of how to read some of them.

NOTAMs

If there is a *NOTAM* concerning the area surrounding a station, it will be noted at the end of the hourly report, as shown in figure 2-8. A horizontal arrow pointing to the right indicates the beginning of the NOTAM. The letters following the arrow indicate the station reporting the NOTAM.

Following the station letters is the NOTAM status code. An arrow pointing down and to the left denotes a new NOTAM, while an arrow pointing down and to the right denotes a current NOTAM. If the NOTAM is being can-celed, the letter "C" will be used in this space.

The NOTAM serial number follows the status code. It consists of one or two numerals to indicate month of issuance, a slant mark, and one or more numerals to identify the chronological sequence of each NOTAM. Numbers are assigned consecutively, beginning with the num-ber "1" for the first NOTAM issued during the month. The example shown in figure 2-8 indicates that this is the fourth NOTAM issued at this station during September.

Figure 2-9 shows examples of NOTAMs found in the "Remarks" sections of hourly reports. The NOTAMs listed in this illustration are read as follows.

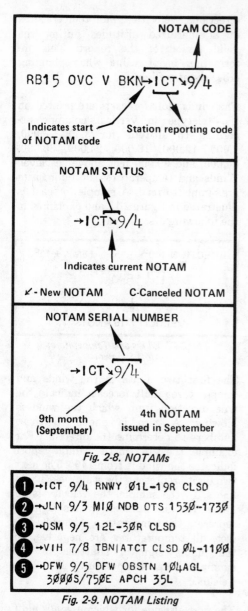

Fig. 2-8. NOTAMs

① →ICT 9/4 RNWY Ø1L-19R CLSD

② →JLN 9/3 MIØ NDB OTS 153Ø-173Ø

③ →DSM 9/5 12L-3ØR CLSD

④ →VIH 7/8 TBN|ATCT CLSD Ø4-11ØØ

⑤ →DFW 9/5 DFW OBSTN 1Ø4AGL
3ØØØS/75ØE APCH 35L

Fig. 2-9. NOTAM Listing

① Wichita NOTAM No. 9/4, runways 01L and 19R closed

② Joplin NOTAM No. 9/3, Miami, Oklahoma, nondirectional beacon out of service from 1530Z until 1730Z

③ Des Moines NOTAM No. 9/5, runways 12L and 30R closed

④ Vichy NOTAM No. 7/8, Tribune Air Traffic Control Tower closed from 0400Z until 1100Z

⑤ Dallas-Ft. Worth NOTAM No. 9/5, at the Dallas-Ft. Worth Regional Airport, there is an obstruction 104 feet AGL, 3,000 feet south and 750 feet east of the approach end of runway 35L

It can be seen that the NOTAMs cover such things as runway closures, hours of operation of navigational aids and control towers, and obstructions in the approach and departure paths of an aircraft. Generally, anything that can affect the safe conduct of a flight is reported as a NOTAM. These notices may be carried in the remarks section or they may be listed directly after the station concerned in the weather report, as shown in figure 2-10.

PRACTICE SURFACE AVIATION WEATHER REPORTS

Figure 2-11 is an example of an hourly weather report series. It lists the weather reports that were transmitted by teletype from Kansas City as a cold front approached, moved overhead, and passed the city.

```
CALIFORNIA 251613
LAX M16OVC 21/2HK 132/62/56/2003/992/BASE CLDS W 15 HND BINOVC
OAK 300-SCT 20 130/66/51/0000→OAK↘5/6
→OAK 5/6 OAK GS 27R OTS THRU 7/18
SAC CLR 25 124/71/31/3212G22/990→SAC↘5/5 5/21
→SAC 5/5 SAC 12-30 CLSD
→SAC 5/21 SAC N 1900 2 CLSD
SAN M14OVC 7 139/61/52/2105/994 SML BINOVC→SAN↘5/3 5/11
→SAN 5/3 SAN 9-27 CLSD 0715-1330 WKDAY EXCP HOL
→SAN 5/11 SDM RWY LGTS OTS 06-1400 DLY EXCP PPO CTC 123.0/CRCG
SFO CLR 7 132/65/48/0705/992
```

Fig. 2-10. NOTAM Location

Cold front approaching (15ØØZ)
MKC 1ØØ SCT 15+ 132/64/58/131Ø/992

Cold front passing (17ØØZ)
MKC M5 OVC 2TRW 962/56/55/3221G25/946

After cold front passage (19ØØZ)
MKC M2Ø BKN 12RW 222/5Ø/42/3615/Ø17

Fig. 2-11. Consecutive Reports

When the cold front approaches, Kansas City reports: 10,000 scattered . . . greater than 15 miles visibility . . . barometric pressure 1013.2 . . . temperature 64°F . . . dewpoint 58°F . . . wind from 130° at 10 knots . . . altimeter setting, 29.92.

Two hours later, as the cold front passes over Kansas City, the hourly weather report is: Kansas City . . . measured ceiling 500 overcast . . . two miles visibility due to thunderstorms and rain showers . . . pressure down to 996.2 millibars . . . temperature down to 56°F . . . dewpoint 55°F . . . wind shift from 130° to 320° at 21 knots with gusts to 25 knots . . . altimeter setting down to 29.46.

After cold front passage, the report is: Kansas City . . . measured ceiling 2,000 broken . . . visibility 12 miles . . . still some rain showers . . . pressure up to 1022.2 millibars . . . the cold airmass moved in and lowered temperature to 50°F . . . dewpoint down to 42°F . . . wind shift from 320° to 360° at 15 knots . . . altimeter up to 30.17.

The weather, moving across the continent, can be observed by watching the weather reports from the various stations. These reports can be used to determine the speed of frontal movements.

WINDS AND TEMPERATURES ALOFT FORECASTS

Another teletype service is transmission of the winds and temperatures aloft forecasts. These forecasts predict wind directions, velocities, and temperatures at standardized altitudes during the valid period of the report. This information is of value when planning cross-country flights.

The winds aloft forecasts are printed on the teletype in vertical columns according to altitude for 3,000, 6,000, 9,000, 12,000, 18,000, 24,000, 30,000, 34,000, and 39,000 feet above sea level. Winds and temperatures aloft forecasts are simple to read. A sample forecast is illustrated in figure 2-12 and explained in the following discussion.

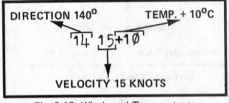

Fig. 2-12. Winds and Temperatures Aloft Segment

The first two digits in the winds and temperatures aloft forecast indicate the true direction from which the wind is blowing. A zero is added to these numbers to determine the direction. For example, the "14" in the sample report indicates the wind is from 140°. The next two digits represent the wind velocity in knots. In the sample, the velocity is 15 knots. The last numbers in this segment represent the temperature. Above 24,000 feet, all temperatures are negative, so the minus sign is omitted. In the example, the temperature is +10° Celsius.

The first altitude for which a winds aloft forecast is issued is always at least 1,500 feet above the station elevation. Temperature is forecast for all altitudes 2,500 feet or more above a station, except for the 3,000-foot level.

A sample winds and temperatures aloft forecast is illustrated in figure 2-13. Four segments of this forecast are numbered. The station is Wichita and the forecast is read as follows.

```
     FDUS2 KWBC  240545
DATA BASED ON 240000Z

VALID 241800Z  FOR USE 1500-2100Z.  TEMPS NEG ABV 24000

FT  3000   6000   9000   12000  18000  24000  30000  34000   39000

ICT 1415 1819+10 2022+08 2325+05 2930-01 3338-07 354518 015326 035032
     1      2       3       4
```

Fig. 2-13. Practice Winds Aloft Forecast

1 3,000-foot level ... wind from 140° at 15 knots ... no temperature provided.

2 6,000-foot level ... wind from 180° at 19 knots ... temperature +10° Celsius.

3 9,000-foot level ... wind from 200° at 22 knots ... temperature +8° Celsius.

4 12,000-foot level ... wind from 230° at 25 knots ... temperature +5° Celsius.

To obtain the most accurate wind forecast available, a pilot should check to see that his planned flight time occurs within the "for use" period and as close as possible to the "valid" time. Both are circled in figure 2-13. As a general rule, an updated wind forecast should be requested anytime the "data based on" time, also shown in figure 2-13, is over 12 hours old. This is when the actual wind was observed.

TERMINAL FORECASTS

Terminal forecasts (FTs) are issued three times daily and each is valid for a 24-hour period. The last six hours of the forecasts project an outlook expressed categorically as VFR, MVFR (marginal VFR), IFR, or LIFR (low IFR). The categories are defined in the table.

Ceiling	Visibility	Category
more than 3000'	more than 5 miles	VFR
1000' to 3000'	3 to 5 miles	MVFR
500' to 1000'	1 to 3 miles	IFR
less than 500'	less than 1 mile	LIFR

The symbols used for the first 18 hours of a terminal forecast are the same, both in appearance and sequence, as those used in aviation weather reports. However, the ceiling is indicated in a terminal forecast by the letter "C" preceding the altitude of the sky condition symbol.

A forecast of the visibility is included only if visibility is expected to be six statute miles or less. Additionally, the wind forecast is included only if the wind is expected to be 10 knots or greater. As in the aviation weather report, the wind direction is given in reference to true north. Figure 2-14 shows examples of terminal forecasts.

The first forecast is read as follows: Albuquerque (ABQ) terminal forecast sent on the tenth day of the month ... valid from 1100Z that day to 1100Z the next day ... ceiling 2,000 feet broken ... 3,500 feet over-

```
NEW MEXICO 101044
ABQ 101111 C20 BKN 35 OVC 3RW 2925G30. 18Z 50 SCT 90 -BKN
2310G. 05Z VFR..
SAF 101111 80 SCT C120 BKN 0112G. 18Z C60 BKN SW- OMTNS.05Z VFR..
```

Fig. 2-14. Terminal Forecasts

cast . . . three miles visibility in rain showers . . . winds 290° at 25 knots gusting to 30. At 1800Z . . . 5,000 feet scattered . . . 9,000 feet thin broken . . . seven miles visibility . . . winds from 230° at 10 knots and gusting . . . outlook, beginning 05Z . . . VFR conditions to continue to the end of the valid time.

The forecast for Sante Fe (SAF) is decoded as follows: terminal forecast . . . valid from the 10th day of the month at 1100Z to the 11th day of the month at 1100Z . . . 8,000 feet scattered . . . ceiling 12,000 feet broken . . . visibility seven miles or more . . . wind from 010° at 12 knots, gusting. At 1800Z . . . 6,000 feet broken . . . visibility seven miles or more . . . wind less than 10 knots . . . light snow showers over the mountains . . . outlook, beginning at 05Z, VFR conditions to continue to the end of the forecast period.

The practice of using hourly weather reports to confirm the validity of terminal forecasts is standard practice. When this is done, however, pilots must remember that the sky cover in forecasts *is not* a summation from the ground up as it is in hourly weather reports. An overcast layer, if *forecast*, is expected to actually be more than nine-tenths sky coverage. If an overcast subsequently occurs on an *hourly report*, it may or may not confirm the overcast level which was forecast. Its accuracy depends on the masking effect of lower cloud levels. This disparity in the relationship between forecasts and actual observations becomes especially important during marginal conditions when pilot judgment is based on this relationship.

AREA FORECASTS

Area forecasts (FAs) are issued two times daily by the Weather Service Forecast Office (WSFO). The area forecasts are issued for a specific area and are used primarily to determine enroute weather conditions. These forecasts include spec-

ific information for an *18-hour period* and a general outlook for an *additional 12-hour period*. Area forecasts give information on pressure systems, fronts, precipitation, cloud bases and tops, icing, and other weather phenomena which is of general importance for flight planning purposes.

The extent of the weather area covered and the type of weather forecast can be seen by referring to the area forecast, as shown in figure 2-15. The reading of an area forecast can be difficult due to the numerous word contractions which are used within them. With some practice, however, it becomes quite easy to read and understand area forecasts.

The following discussion refers to figure 2-15. The area forecast is divided into five categories: heading, forecast area, synopsis, significant clouds and weather, and icing. The outlook is included in each paragraph of the significant clouds and weather portion of the forecast.

Heading—The area forecast originated in Kansas City on the first day of the month at 1240Z. The valid time for this forecast is from 1300Z Wednesday until 0700Z Thursday. The outlook extends from 0700Z to 1900Z Thursday.

Forecast area—The area in this forecast includes Colorado, Wyoming, Kansas, Nebraska, South Dakota, and North Dakota.

Synopsis—The synopsis is a brief discussion of the overall weather picture. The synopsis of the illustrated forecast reads as follows: arctic front in the vicinity of the eastern slopes of the mountains of Wyoming and Colorado . . . weak upslope airflow east of the arctic front in Colorado, Wyoming, and western Nebraska . . . strong northwesterly windflow aloft.

Significant clouds and weather—This section of the forecast reads as follows:

```
MKC FA Ø1124Ø
13Z WED-Ø7Z - 19Z THU.
OTLK Ø7Z - 19Z THU

CO WY KS NE SD ND

HGTS ASL UNLESS NOTED
SYNOPSIS...ARTIC FNT VCNTY ERN SLPS MTNS WY CO. WK UPSLP
E ARTIC FNT IN CO WY AND WRN NB. STG NWLY FLOW ALF.

SIGCLDS AND WX...
CO WY E FNT...
HIR TRRN FQTLY OBSCD. 15-25 BKN V OVC 4Ø-6Ø BKN V OVC AGL
OCNL RAIN SE CO. TOPS 1ØØ-12Ø TOPS CU TO 2ØØ
OTLK...MVFR CIG.

RMNG PTNS WY AND CO.
HIR MTNS OBSCD CO AND LCLY OBSCD WY 1ØØ-12Ø SCT V BKN
15Ø-18Ø SCT V BKN TOPS 2ØØ. SCT SNW MTNS.
OTLK...VFR WIND.

KS NB SD ND...
W PTNS 2Ø-4Ø SCT V BKN AGL WITH FEW SHWRS DURG AFTN
BCMG CLR BY MIDN. E PTNS 5Ø-7Ø BKN AGL BCMG 2Ø-4Ø OVC
AGL BY MIDN. TOPS 1ØØ-12Ø. OTLK...MVFR CIG.

ICG...MDT ICGIC BLO 14Ø. FRZLVL AT OR NR SFC OVR AND NR
MTNS 4Ø-6Ø ELSW.
```

Fig. 2-15. Area Forecast

Colorado and Wyoming, east of the front . . . high terrain frequently obscured . . . 1,500 to 2,500 feet broken variable overcast . . . 4,000 to 6,000 feet broken variable to overcast AGL . . . occasional rain in southeast Colorado . . . tops of clouds 10,000 to 12,000 feet . . . tops of cumulus to 20,000 feet . . . outlook, marginal VFR due to low ceilings.

The next section reads: Remaining portions of Wyoming and Colorado . . . higher mountains obscured in Colorado and locally obscured in Wyoming . . . cloud conditions of 10,000 to 12,000 feet scattered variable to broken . . . 15,000 to 18,000 feet scattered variable to broken with tops at 20,000 . . . scattered snow showers in the mountains . . . outlook, VFR; however, winds in excess of 25 knots are expected.

The Kansas, Nebraska, South Dakota, and North Dakota section reads as follows: West portions of these states . . . 2,000 to 4,000 feet scattered variable to broken above ground level with a few showers during the afternoon, becoming clear by midnight. East portions . . . 5,000 to 7,000 feet broken above ground level, becoming 2,000 to 4,000 feet overcast above ground level by midnight . . . tops 10,000 to 12,000 . . . outlook, marginal VFR, again due to ceilings.

Icing—The icing section of the area forecast reads as follows: Moderate icing in clouds below 14,000 feet . . . freezing level at or near the surface over and near the mountains . . . 4,000 to 6,000 feet elsewhere.

SEVERE WEATHER FORECASTS

A specialized weather forecasting center in Kansas City, known as the National Severe Storms Forecast Center, issues severe weather forecasts whenever significant weather is anticipated any place in the United States. These forecasts are published in the form of severe weather watch bulletins, or in-flight advisories, such as AIRMETs, SIGMETs, and convective SIGMETs.

SEVERE WEATHER WATCH BULLETINS

A severe weather watch bulletin (WW) defines areas of possible severe thunderstorm or tornado activity. WWs are unscheduled and issued as required. Subsequent bulletins are provided, as needed, to show progress of storms and to delineate areas no longer under the threat of severe storm activity. As indicated in the heading excerpt (Fig. 2-16), each WW is assigned a number. Follow-on bulletins are assigned new watch numbers in sequence. For example, the next WW pertaining to this storm would be designated watch number 105. Effective times and void times for previous bulletins are indicated in the plain language text. Density of coverage within an area may indicate isolated, few, scattered, or numerous. These terms are defined in figure 2-17.

BULLETIN—IMMEDIATE BROADCAST REQUESTED
TORNADO WATCH NUMBER 104
NATIONAL WEATHER SERVICE KANSAS CITY MO
143 PM CDT THU APR 17 19--

A . . . THE NATIONAL SEVERE STORMS FORECAST CENTER SAYS THERE IS A POSSIBILITY OF TORNADOES AND SEVERE THUNDERSTORMS . .

Fig. 2-16. Severe Weather Watch Bulletin

Adjective	Coverage
Isolated	Extremely small number
Few	15% or less of area or line
Scattered	16% to 45% of area or line
Numerous	More than 45% of area or line.

Fig. 2-17. Area Coverage of Showers and Thunderstorms

IN-FLIGHT ADVISORIES

In-flight advisories are also unscheduled forecasts to advise enroute aircraft of potentially hazardous weather. An in-flight advisory may be one of three types, depending on the severity of the weather — AIRMETs for less hazardous weather, SIGMETs for relatively severe conditions other than thunderstorms, and *convective* SIGMETs for thunderstorm-related activity. AIRMETs and SIGMETs are distributed over teletype circuits and broadcast periodically on the voice facilities of flight service stations.

SIGMETs and AIRMETs are listed chronologically each day to identify separate weather systems within a geographic area such as low ceilings, icing, or turbulence. Each series is numbered using the phonetic alphabet; for example, Alpha 1, Alpha 2, etc., until the condition ends. Should a different weather phenomenon arise in a forecast area on a specific day, the Bravo series is started and continued until that condition ends. For example, the Alpha series may deal with turbulence, while Bravo may identify an icing condition. In this manner, each weather situation can be identified quickly by its name and number. The names and numbers from one forecast office are unrelated to those from other offices.

AIRMETs

AIRMETs concern conditions that are potentially hazardous to aircraft that have limited capability because of smaller size and lack of equipment or instrumentation. They cover moderate icing, moderate turbulence over an extensive area, extensive areas of visibilities less than three miles or ceilings less than 1,000 feet (including mountain ridges and passes), and sustained winds of 30 knots or more at or within 2,000 feet of the surface.

AIRMETs are issued when the above conditions exist or are expected within two hours. These advisories are broadcast at 30-minute intervals (15 and 45 minutes past the hour) for the first hour after issuance. This schedule continues for the flight precaution portion of the AIRMET during the valid period of the advisory. An AIRMET can be considered to be an amendment of an area forecast.

The AIRMET shown in figure 2-18 is read as follows: AIRMET foxtrot 6 . . . Flight precaution . . . in southeastern Colorado, southern and western Kansas, ceilings will generally be below 1,000 feet with the visibility below three statute miles in fog and snow . . . locally freezing precipitation in southern Kansas . . . moderate mixed icing can be expected in clouds and in precipitation . . . conditions will continue beyond 0100Z.

SIGMETs

SIGMET stands for *significant meteorology*. This category of in-flight advisory includes weather phenomena that are particularly hazardous to light aircraft and potentially hazardous to all aircraft. SIGMET advisories cover severe and extreme turbulence, severe icing, and widespread duststorms or sandstorms which lower visibility below three miles.

These advisories may be included in relevant portions of an area forecast; however, most SIGMETs are issued separately and they automatically amend the area forecast for the period of the advisory. Separate area forecast

amendments may also be issued subsequently, if a significant change occurs. The purpose of this type of advisory service is to notify pilots of the possibility of hazardous flying conditions which were probably unknown prior to takeoff. Whether or not the condition described is potentially hazardous to a particular flight is for the pilot to decide, based on individual experience and operational limits of the aircraft.

Figure 2-19 is an example of a SIGMET. It is read as follows: SIGMET Alpha 1 . . . flight precautions . . . severe icing is forecast below 16,000 feet in New Hampshire and western Maine . . . overrunning conditions resulting in severe icing in clouds and in precipitation can be expected from the surface to 16,000 feet . . . these conditions will continue beyond 0300Z.

FAA flight service stations within 150 miles of the affected area broadcast SIGMETs at 15-minute intervals for the first hour. Then, an alert notice (flight precaution) simply stating the phrase "SIGMET (name/number) is current," will be broadcast at 15 and 45 minutes past the hour during the remaining valid period of the SIGMET.

CONVECTIVE SIGMETs

Convective SIGMETs are issued, when required, on a scheduled and non-scheduled basis whenever one or more of the following conditions exist.

1. Tornadoes
2. Lines of thunderstorms

```
MKC WA Ø52Ø55
Ø52100-Ø6010ØZ

AIRMET FOXTROT 6 FLT PRCTN SE CO SRN AND WRN KS CIG GENLY
BLO 1Ø VSBY BLO 3 IN FOG AND SNW. LCL FRZG PCPN SRN KS. MDT MXD
ICGCIP CONDS CONTG BYD Ø1Z
```

Fig. 2-18. AIRMET

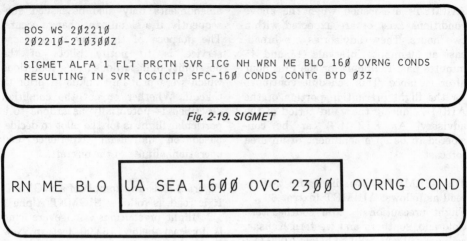

```
BOS WS 2Ø221Ø
2Ø221Ø-21Ø3ØØZ

SIGMET ALFA 1 FLT PRCTN SVR ICG NH WRN ME BLO 16Ø OVRNG CONDS
RESULTING IN SVR ICGICIP SFC-16Ø CONDS CONTG BYD Ø3Z
```

Fig. 2-19. SIGMET

```
RN ME BLO  UA SEA 16ØØ OVC 23ØØ  OVRNG COND
```

Fig. 2-20. PIREP

3. Embedded thunderstorms
4. Isolated or areas of intense thunderstorms
5. Hail of 3/4 of an inch or greater in diameter

The individual report is given in two parts. In the first part the location and description of the phenomena is listed. The second part contains the location of the activity in relation to six specified VORs which form a special grid covering the conterminous United States. Each convective SIGMET is valid for one hour; subsequent messages are numbered consecutively (01-99) each day beginning at 0000Z.

PIREPs

Pilot reports, or PIREPs, are another source of valuable weather information which the flight service stations broadcast. Pilots are urged to cooperate and volunteer reports of cloud tops, upper cloud layers, thunderstorms, ice, turbulence, strong winds, and other significant flight condition information.

No observation is more timely and authoritative than one from a pilot in flight. In fact, the only direct means of confirming or observing some weather conditions, such as cloud tops, icing, or turbulence, is through a pilot report.

Weather briefers, forecasters, and other pilots welcome PIREPs.

Normally, pilots should submit a PIREP whenever unforecast, hazardous, or potentially hazardous conditions are encountered. In addition pilots should report, in *plain language*, information of a non-meteorological nature that could affect the safety of flight operations. For example, knowledge of the location of a large flock of birds is helpful to air traffic controllers and other pilots.

Pilots usually report height values as above mean sea level, since they determine heights with an altimeter. In reports disseminated as PIREPs, height references are always given above mean sea level. In the prescribed format, the letters "UA" identify the message as a PIREP. Next in order are location, time, phenomena, altitude, and type of aircraft, if turbulence or icing is reported. An example of a PIREP is shown in figure 2-20. It is read as: Pilot reports over Seattle at 1600Z, overcast at 2,300 feet MSL.

A computerized format for PIREPs is being used at many larger stations. Figure 2-21 provides an example of this type of report and the codes used to identify its contents.

CODED PIREP

UA/OV DCA 275Ø45 1745 F33Ø/TP B727/SK 185 BKN 22Ø/28Ø THN-OVC 29Ø/TA -53/WV 29Ø12Ø/TB LGT-MDT-CAT ABV-31Ø

DECODED PIREP

Washington 275 radial 45 NM at 1745Z altitude of 33,000 feet, type aircraft Boeing 727, two layers of clouds: 1st layer base 18,500 broken top 22,000, 2nd layer base 28,000 thin overcast top 29,000, outside air temperature minus 53 degrees celsius spot wind 290 degrees true at 120 kts., light to moderate clear air turbulence above 31,000.

CODE EXPLANATIONS

UA — Message type (Pilot report as appended to surface aviation weather report)
UUA — Urgent pilot report (special transmission)
OV — Locations (navaid identification, bearing from navaid, distance from navaid, route segment, time, altitude in hundreds of feet)
TP — Type aircraft
SK — Cloud base and top (multiple layers separated by /)
TA — Temperature (°C)
WV — Airborne computer-derived wind data (three-digit direction; three-digit speed, kts.)
TB — Turbulence
IC — Icing
WX — Conditions not reported in previous sections

Fig. 2-21. Computer-Coded PIREPs

SECTION B—ADVANCED WEATHER CHARTS

In addition to the teletype reports, the National Weather Service has a variety of weather charts that provide valuable weather information. By referring to these charts, the pilot is provided with a pictorial representation of the weather across the nation and along his route of flight.

The following are some of the more common charts.

1. Surface analysis
2. Weather depiction
3. Radar summary
4. Low-level prognostic

SURFACE ANALYSIS CHART

Surface analysis charts provide a general picture of the atmospheric pressure pattern at the surface of the earth by showing the positions of highs, lows, and

fronts. They also indicate wind, temperature, dewpoint, and other weather data in a manner similar to the printed daily weather map illustrated in figure 2-22. Pilots should, however, use the more current teletype reports for specific station weather.

Surface analysis charts are reproduced in the Weather Service Office on a facsimile machine like the one shown in figure 2-23. The original weather chart is drawn by National Weather Service personnel in Washington, D.C., and transmitted to weather stations across the country every three hours.

The basic building block of the surface analysis chart is the station model. The station model presents pertinent weather data in symbolic and number form. Although the hourly aviation weather reports provide more current station

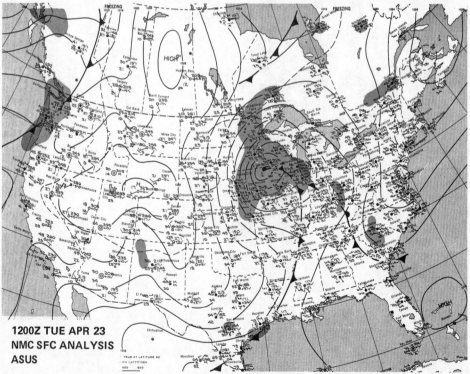

1200Z TUE APR 23
NMC SFC ANALYSIS
ASUS

Fig. 2-22. Daily Weather Map

Fig. 2-23. Facsimile Machine

weather, it is helpful to become familiar with the station model when interpreting the surface analysis chart.

Figure 2-24 shows a station model as it appears on a surface analysis chart. It is read as follows:

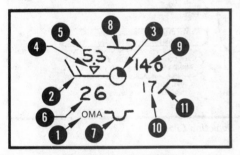

Fig. 2-24. Station Model

1. The station, Omaha (OMA), (item 1) is reporting the wind from the west at 15 knots (item 2) with a one-tenth to five-tenths sky cover (item 3), and intermittent rain showers (item 4).

2. The temperature is 53° Fahrenheit (item 5) and dewpoint is 26° (item 6) with stratocumulus low clouds (item 7).

3. There are high scattered cirrus clouds, or "mare's tails," over this station (item 8).

4. The barometric pressure is 1014.0 millibars (item 9) and the pressure has risen 1.7 millibars (item 10) in the past three hours. The barometric tendency has been rising, but is now steady (item 11).

Isobars are drawn on the surface analysis chart at four millibar intervals and are labeled with the last two digits of the pressure reading. For example, figure 2-25 shows an isobar that is labeled "08." This represents 1008 millibars.

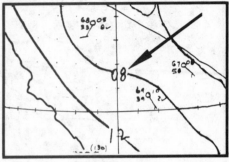

Fig. 2-25. Isobars

High-pressure and low-pressure areas are labeled as "H" or "L" on the chart. Fronts are shown with conventional symbols.

WEATHER DEPICTION CHART

Weather depiction charts, such as the one illustrated in figure 2-26, also are reproduced on the facsimile machine every three hours. A comparison should be made between this chart and the surface aviation weather reports to get an up-to-date weather picture. An abbreviated station model is used on this type of chart. The visibility, type of weather, amount of sky-cover, and height of cloud bases are the types of data portrayed. (See Fig. 2-27.)

A typical station model used on the weather depiction chart is shown in figure 2-28. The number and symbol on the left represent the visibility in statute miles (item 1) and type of weather (item 2). The example shows the visibility as 2-1/2 miles with fog. The visibility value is omitted when visibility is over six miles.

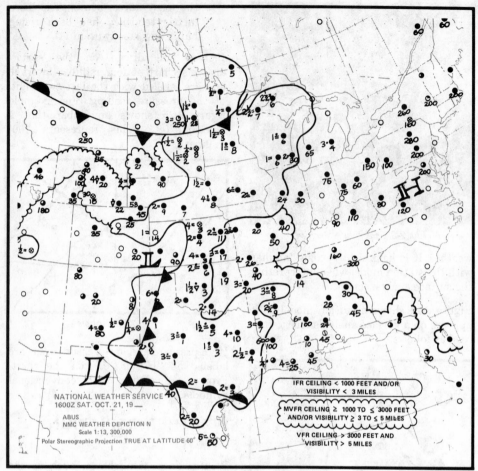

Fig. 2-26. Weather Depiction Chart

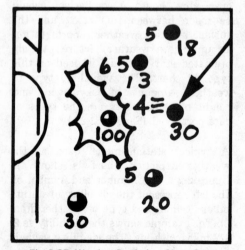

Fig. 2-27. Weather Depiction Chart Data

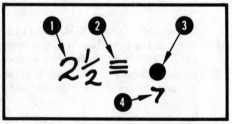

Fig. 2-28. Typical Station Model

The center of the station symbol represents the amount of sky covered by clouds. The sky coverage symbols used on weather depiction charts are the same as those used on the surface chart. The solid area denotes a complete overcast. (See Fig. 2-28, item 3.)

A number or numbers beneath the cloud coverage symbol lists the height of the ceiling in hundreds of feet above ground level. If the coverage does not constitute a ceiling, the height refers to the lowest scattered layer. Figure 2-28, item 4, shows a ceiling of 700 feet overcast.

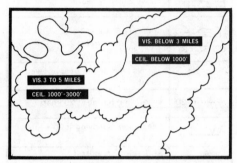

Fig. 2-29. Ceilings and Visibilities

A scalloped boundary line is drawn around areas in which the ceiling height is between 1,000 and 3,000 feet and/or the visibility is between three and five statute miles. A smooth boundary line is drawn around areas in which the visibility is below three miles and/or the ceiling is less than 1,000 feet. By observing the smooth and scalloped borders, depicted in figure 2-29, pilots can see IFR and marginal weather areas across the nation at a glance. Frontal positions also are shown on the weather depiction chart.

RADAR SUMMARY CHART

Another chart which provides weather information is the radar summary chart. (See Fig. 2-30.) Normally, it is reproduced on the facsimile machine every hour. Since radar echoes change in shape and intensity in a matter of minutes, the data shown on this map is not current. However, it does show general storm areas and movements over the nation. By learning to read this chart, the pilot can interpret current radar plottings on display in the Weather Service office.

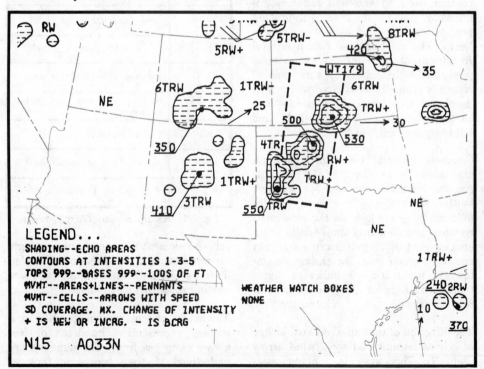

Fig. 2-30. Radar Summary Chart

ADVANCED METEOROLOGY

Weather radar is used primarily for detecting and tracking severe storms, such as thunderstorms, tornadoes, and hurricanes. This type of radar equipment is adjusted to a wave length that gives the best signal return from water droplets and other precipitation particles. A storm does not actually produce a radar signal. Instead, water droplets produce "echoes" on the radar scope. The size and number of water droplets, as well as the distance to the storm, determine the strength of the return signal.

Echoes are classified as light and moderate (level 1), heavy or very heavy (level 3), or intense and extreme (level 5). The various symbols used on the radar summary chart are shown in figure 2-31.

Figure 2-32 shows a drawing of a typical radar echo as it would appear on a radar summary chart. The basic contour outlines the area of radar return intensity one (item 1). A superimposed contour (item 2) shows a radar return intensity level of three, indicating precipitation classified as heavy or very heavy. The most intense return is level five (item 3). The intense or extreme precipitation indicated by this type of return is normally associated with a well developed thunderstorm. Hazards such as hail, turbulence, strong winds, and lightning may exist in these areas.

Complete or solid coverage within an area may be as depicted by item 4. Another method uses a number to report tenths of total sky coverage, usually followed by symbology for the associated weather. Item 5 shows three-tenths of an area covered by thunderstorms and rain showers which are increasing in intensity, while item 6 indicates eight-tenths coverage of thunderstorms and rain showers decreasing in intensity.

The direction of motion of an area or line of echoes is indicated by a wind arrow (item 7). This area is moving east-northeast at 20 knots. Individual cell or

RADAR SUMMARY CHART	
Symbol	Meaning
	Intensity 1 Light and moderate
	Intensity 3 (Second Contour) Heavy and very heavy
	Intensity 5 (Dark Area) Intense and extreme
	dashed lines define areas of severe weather
→ 20	echoes are moving at 20 knots
	line or area is moving at 20 knots (10 knot barbs)
240/80	echo top 24,000' MSL echo base 8,000' MSL
INTENSITY AND TREND OF PRECIPITATION	
+	increasing precipitation
−	decreasing precipitation
ECHO COVERAGE	
Symbol	Meaning
SLD	solid, over 9/10 coverage
BKN	broken, 6/10 to 9/10 coverage
SCT	scattered 1/10 to 5/10 coverage
NE	No echo — Equipment operating but no echoes
NA	Observation not available
OM	equipment out for maintenance
●	Strong cell identified by one station

Fig. 2-31. Radar Summary Chart Symbols

echo movement is shown by a single arrow pointing in the direction of motion (item 8). In this illustration, cells are moving southeast at 25 knots.

The height of echo tops is specified by a number representing hundreds of feet above mean sea level. The numbers are underlined if they represent tops of echoes. In figure 2-32, the top of the

2-22

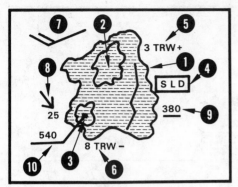

Fig. 2-32. Typical Radar Echo Plotting

echoes in the thunderstorm area are 38,000 feet (item 9) and the top of the isolated thunderstorm echo is 54,000 feet (item 10).

The echoes in the upper part of figure 2-33 depict an area with seven-tenths echo coverage which is composed of thunderstorms and rainshowers. The echoes are primarily of level one intensity and decreasing. However, a single storm cell exists with intensity level five. The top of the precipitation within this cell is at 43,000 feet MSL. The entire system is moving to the east-northeast at 25 knots.

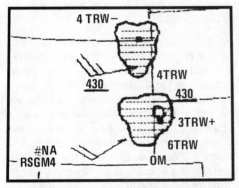

Fig. 2-33. Radar Summary Chart Excerpt

LOW-LEVEL PROGNOSTIC

The low-level prognostic chart, shown in figure 2-34, is divided into *two* forecast periods. The two panels on the left show the weather prognosis for a 12-hour period and those on the right for a 24-hour period. The valid times and titles

for each panel are shown in the lower left-hand corner.

The panels on the top indicate the forecaster's best estimate of where low or middle clouds will exist. Also depicted are freezing levels, plus areas and altitudes of turbulence. The lower panels are the forecaster's best estimate of the location of frontal and pressure systems, as well as the areas and types of precipitation. The two panels on the right (valid for 24 hours) contain the same information as the panels on the left (valid for 12 hours), but with the movement *expected between* the two time frames indicated.

Low-level prognostic charts are issued four times a day or every six hours. The valid time of each panel appears on the lower left-hand corner of that panel. For example, the weather "picture" on the left-hand panel, containing "1800Z WED APR 26," represents a prediction of the weather situation that is expected to exist at 1800 Zulu time on Wednesday, April 26.

The ceiling and visibility legend is the same as that used with the weather depiction chart. The smooth lines in figure 2-34, item 1, enclose areas where the ceiling is expected to be below 1,000 feet AGL and/or visibility less than three miles. Those areas with expected ceilings from 1,000 to 3,000 feet AGL and/or visibilities of three to five miles are enclosed in scalloped lines (item 2).

A dotted line broken only by the notation 32° F, illustrated by item 3, indicates the predicted location of the freezing isotherm at the surface. An isotherm is a line of equal temperature (an isobar is a line of equal pressure).

The broken lines represent heights in hundreds of feet of the lowest forecast freezing level. As shown by item 4, a line broken by "40" shows that the freezing level will be at 4,000 feet MSL. All temperatures will be above freezing at altitudes below 4,000 feet at all locations along the broken line.

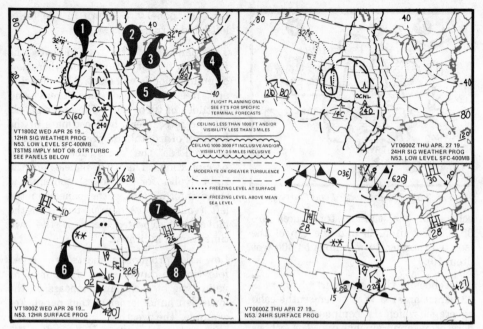

Fig. 2-34. Low-Level Significant Weather Prognostic Chart

The symbol used to mark areas with turbulence is a spike. The number "80" with a dash beneath it means that moderate turbulence is predicted below 8,000 feet MSL in that region (item 5). Areas of turbulence also are enclosed in a heavy dashed line.

On the lower panels, those areas which are expected to have showers are enclosed by a broken line of dots and dashes. If the precipitation is expected to be more *persistent* (continuous or intermittent), the area will be enclosed by a solid line (item 6). If more than half the area is expected to be covered by precipitation (showers, intermittent or continuous), the area will be shaded. If less than half the area is expected to have precipitation, the area will not be shaded. Various symbols may be used within the precipitation areas to indicate rain showers, snow showers, or thunderstorms. These symbols are found in figure 2-35.

Arrows may be used to show the predicted direction of movement of the pressure system, as shown by figure 2-34, item 7. The speed of the high pressure

area, 15 knots in this example, is often shown near the arrows. The predicted atmospheric pressure in millibars is depicted near the major pressure systems. For example, as shown in item 8, 26 stands for 1026 millibars. The rule previously discussed for prefixing a 9 or 10 still applies.

While the accuracy of these charts has improved greatly over the past decade, the pilot should remember that these charts are *still forecasts*. If the pilot compares an *actual* synoptic chart for an earlier time period with the *prognostic* chart for the same time period, these charts will probably look somewhat different. For example, if the weather system decelerates and deepens, more widespread weather will occur. Conversely, if the weather system accelerates and diminishes in size, the bad weather area will be less extensive.

CONSTANT PRESSURE CHARTS

The constant pressure charts show wind direction and velocity, temperature, dewpoint, and altitudes of the various

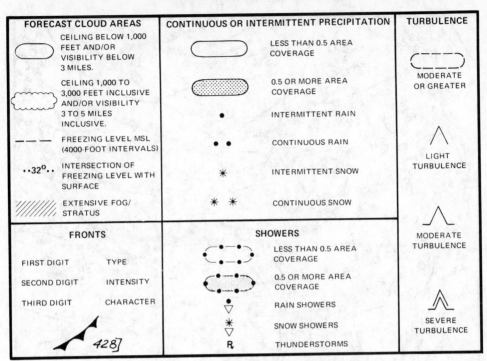

Fig. 2-35. Low-Level Prognostic Chart Symbols

pressure levels. These charts are issued every 12 hours for pressure levels of 850, 700, 500, 300, and 200 millibars.

These charts represent undulating surfaces above sea level. Where the *height* of the pressure surface is high, there is warm air over the underlying stations. Low *heights* indicate cold, dense air.

850 MILLIBAR

The 850-millibar constant pressure chart portrays conditions for low-level flight. It most often relates to weather at approximately 5,000 feet MSL, which is the general level of clouds associated with bad weather. This chart is valuable for forecasting thunderstorms, rain, snow, overcast, and heavy cloudiness. (See Fig. 2-36.)

Figure 2-37 provides a closeup of a plotting model used to portray wind, temperature, dewpoint, and altitude on the constant pressure chart. The shaft shows the approximate direction of the

wind, with the nearest 10° depicted by a small number adjacent to the pennants. For example, the "4" (item 1) with a north-northwest arrow means the wind is blowing from 340°. The wind velocity is depicted by the barbs at the end of the shaft. Each full barb represents 10 knots and each half barb equals five knots. This symbol shows that the wind has a velocity of 25 knots.

Figure 2-38 shows some examples of wind directions as they might appear on a constant pressure chart. At the top, the wind is from 30°. The center example shows a wind from 120°, and the bottom symbol from 250°.

The constant pressure height at which this data was recorded is shown as an abbreviated number of meters above mean sea level. It always consists of three digits, with the first digit of the height omitted on the 850-millibar chart. For example, the height value of 435 signifies 1,435 meters. This is shown in figure 2-37, item 2.

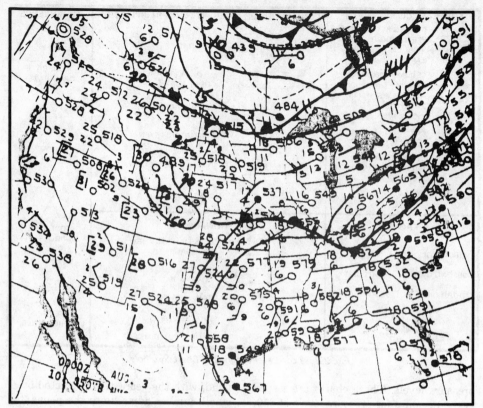

Fig. 2-36. 850 Millibar Constant Pressure Chart

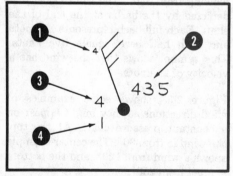

Fig. 2-37. Plotting Model

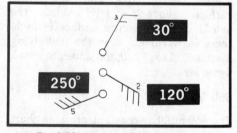

Fig. 2-38. Wind Direction Examples

Height values on 500, 300, and 200 millibar charts are plotted in dekameters, or tens of meters, and a zero must be added to obtain the correct height value in meters.

The number on the left side of the plotting model is the temperature in degrees Celsius (item 3.) The temperature is plus four degrees Celsius. If it had been minus four degrees, this number would have been preceded by a minus sign. The temperature/dewpoint spread (item 4) at this altitude, shown directly under the temperature, is one degree Celsius.

The center of the plotting model consists of either a solid dot or a circle. A solid dot is used when the temperature and dewpoint are within five degrees of each other. A circle is used when this difference is more than five degrees.

The solid continuous lines, on all constant pressure charts are contour, equal height lines. The height value of these lines is expressed in meters. These lines are usually drawn for intervals of 60 meters on the 850-millibar chart. For example, the contour line, shown in figure 2-39, is labeled 138. To read this number, one zero should be added to the end of the number to get 1,380 meters. Since there are about 3.28 feet per meter, the metric values shown on the map can be converted to feet by multiplying meters by 3.28 (1,380 meters $\times$ 3.28 = 4,526 feet).

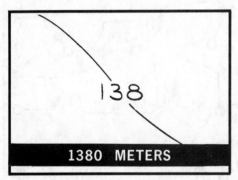

Fig. 2-39. Equal Height Lines

The winds blow parallel to the contour lines, and the speed of the wind is directly proportional to the spacing of the contour lines. The closer the contour lines, the stronger the wind. The dashed lines are isotherms. These lines connect points of equal temperature and normally are drawn at intervals of five degrees Celsius.

The positions of fronts are indicated in the same symbolic manner as on surface charts, provided the front extends up to the pressure level of the chart. Fronts are observed most frequently on the 850-millibar and 700-millibar charts. Highs and lows are also depicted on the constant pressure charts.

Upper cold lows, as shown on these charts, are producers of bad weather, as the injection of cold air from aloft creates instability. Thus, the area underneath upper cold lows will generally have poor flight conditions.

700 MILLIBAR

The 700-millibar chart shows weather data in the vicinity of the 10,000-foot level and provides weather information for pilots operating at that approximate altitude. It shows wind conditions associated with heavy clouds and rain, but only well-developed fronts appear on this type of chart. The symbols used on the 700-millibar chart are the same as those used for the 850-millibar chart.

500 MILLIBAR

The 500-millibar chart shows conditions at about the 18,000-foot level and represents average troposphere conditions. These charts are useful in determining average wind and temperature conditions for long range flights at and near flight level 180.

300 AND 200 MILLIBAR

The 300-millibar and 200-millibar constant pressure charts show conditions in the upper atmosphere and provide weather data of interest to jet pilots. The 300-millibar chart depicts weather at about the 30,000-foot level and the 200-millibar chart, at the 39,000-foot level. Wind velocities on these charts are depicted with wind arrows in the same manner as noted on the other constant pressure charts, except that the wind velocities are often higher.

WINDS AND TEMPERATURE ALOFT CHARTS

Winds and temperatures aloft patterns are computer prepared and routinely transmitted by facsimile. They are transmitted twice daily and depict the winds and temperatures for eight levels; 6,000, 9,000, 12,000, 18,000, 24,000, 30,000, 34,000 and 39,000 feet. Figure 2-

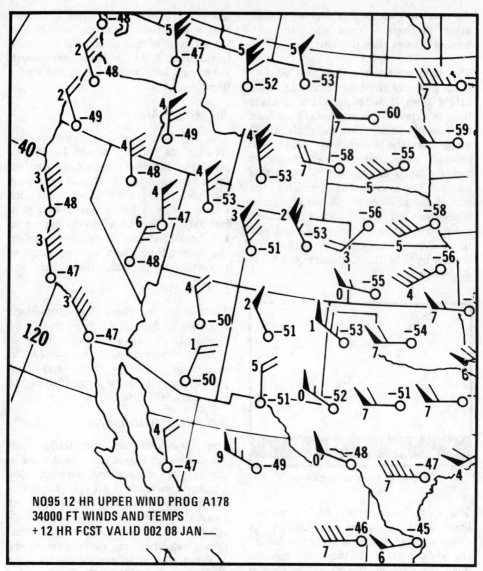

NO95 12 HR UPPER WIND PROG A178
34000 FT WINDS AND TEMPS
+12 HR FCST VALID 002 08 JAN—

Fig. 2-40. Forecast Winds and Temperatures Aloft Chart Excerpt

40 is an example of the 34,000-foot level chart. Wind direction and speed are indicated by the wind shaft with barbs or pennants in the same manner as used on the surface and constant pressure charts. Figure 2-41 shows a wind arrow depicting a wind from 200° true at 25 knots and a temperature of −43° Celsius. A pilot using these charts can observe overall wind flow patterns and choose an appropriate route and/or cruising altitude.

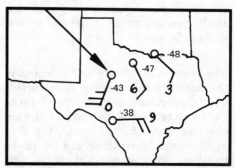

Fig. 2-41. Sample Wind Arrow and Temperature

SATELLITE CHARTS

Another observation tool is the meteorological satellite system. One of the satellites is shown in figure 2-42. Automatic picture-taking equipment aboard the orbiting satellite transmits a picture to earth every six minutes. Meteorologists with receiving equipment can receive this data directly or receive a similar chart on the facsimile circuit. Pictures of the earth's surface show cloud cover and locate severe storm areas. Very often, satellite photographs indicate overcast conditions between weather reporting stations.

The cloud cover chart, shown in figure 2-43, is made from satellite picture data superimposed on an outline map of North America and Central America and distributed via the facsimile circuit. The lighter areas show cloud coverage.

Fig. 2-42. Satellite Weather Gathering

Fig. 2-43. Cloud Cover Chart

SECTION C—WEATHER CONSIDERATIONS

The National Weather Service is well equipped with a vast communications system, measuring instruments, maps, charts, and radar information to perform many important services for the pilot. It is essential that all pilots have a knowledge of how weather is created in order to thoroughly understand all of the weather reports, and forecasts, inflight advisories, and weather broadcasts on the radio. To help the pilot gain this knowledge, the third part of this chapter is devoted to a review of theory.

First, it must be remembered that the sun, shining on the earth, heats the surface, which, in turn, heats the adjacent air in the atmosphere. This phenomenon is one of the main causes of weather. It is known as normal convection, or radiation. Air, warmed by the sun, causes columns of rising air.

Radiation takes place all over the earth's surface. The heated air columns rise into the atmosphere and, at high levels, circulate to the north and south poles of the earth. The circulation of this air causes prevailing winds, such as the trade winds.

The major portion of the warm air rises and flows to the northern or the southern parts of the earth, where it is cooled and becomes heavy. Then, it settles to the earth's surface and starts moving toward lower latitudes where it frequently forms large cold airmasses. The circulation pattern is illustrated in figure 2-44.

AIRMASSES

The large masses of air often create high-pressure areas which are labeled on weather charts with the letter "H." It should be recalled that lines on a weather chart showing the pressure patterns around a high-pressure area are known as *isobars*, and connect points of equal barometric pressure. The lines close to the center of a high-pressure area have

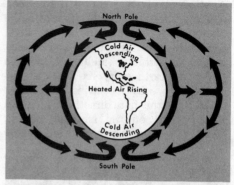

Fig. 2-44. General Air Circulation Pattern

higher pressure values, in millibars, than the lines farther away from the center of the area. All isobars on a weather chart are generally four millibars apart.

In the high-pressure area pattern, the wind flows around the high-pressure area in a clockwise direction in the Northern Hemisphere, as shown in figure 2-45. The pressure gradient of the high-pressure area is shown at the bottom of the illustration. This gradient is determined by the distance between the isobars. The closer the isobars, the steeper the mountain of air that forms the high-pressure area.

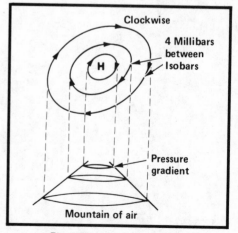

Fig. 2-45. High-Pressure Area

The valleys between the high-pressure areas, into which these huge airmasses are trying to move, are known as lows and are labeled with the letter "L." A low is nothing more than a valley between hugh mountains of air.

Circulation is counterclockwise around low pressure areas in the Northern Hemisphere, as shown in figure 2-46, and clockwise in the Southern Hemisphere. As in high pressure areas, the closer the isobars, the higher the wind velocity. The spaces between the isobars determine the pressure gradient of the valley between the high-pressure areas.

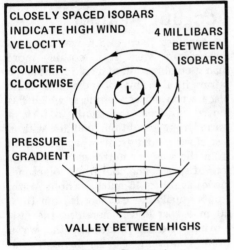

Fig. 2-46. Low-Pressure Area

High-pressure airmasses, which are trying to move into low-pressure areas or valleys, circulate in a counterclockwise direction around the lows. The cold air, from the north, will force all of the air in front of it aloft. The boundary, between the moving airmass and the airmass that is being replaced, is illustrated by the symbol shown in figure 2-47. This is known as a cold front.

COLD FRONT

Figure 2-48 shows a profile of a cold front that is moving along the surface. As it moves, the warm air in front of it is forced into the cold upper atmosphere where the moist air condenses. This condensation, along the edge of the cold

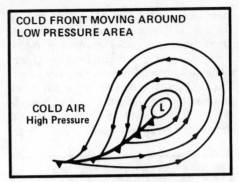

Fig. 2-47. Cold Front Moving Around Low-Pressure Area

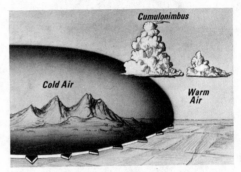

Fig. 2-48. Cold Front Profile

front boundary, creates cumulonimbus clouds.

The following weather could be expected with a cold front.

1. Cumulus clouds
2. Turbulence
3. Precipitation
4. Atmospheric pressure drop, then rise
5. After the frontal passage, a temperature drop, which means that the cold air is moving into the area
6. Wind shift with the frontal passage because of the circulation around the low and along the frontal boundary
7. Good visibility because of the cold, unstable air moving into the area

WARM FRONT

As a warm airmass moves in from the south and starts its circulation around a low-pressure area, a different weather condition, known as a *warm front*, is formed. It is represented on the weather chart by the symbol shown in figure 2-49. A warm front circulates counter-clockwise around a low-pressure area. The isobars are farther from the low-pressure center along the frontal boundary, indicating that there is a pressure drop at the boundary itself.

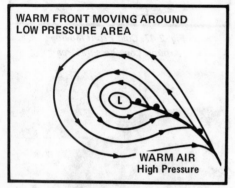

Fig. 2-49. Warm Front Moving Around Low-Pressure Area

In a warm front, the warm air overruns the cold air. As the warm air is forced aloft, up the cold air slope, it creates various types of stratus clouds, such as nimbostratus, altostratus, cirrostratus, and cirrus. The approach of cirrus clouds is sometimes an indication of an approaching warm front, as illustrated in figure 2-50.

The weather found with a warm front is as follows.

1. Stratus clouds, if enough moisture is present
2. Little turbulence, except when the warm airmass is unstable
3. Precipitation ahead of the front
4. Atmospheric pressure drop, then rise
5. After the frontal passage, a temperature rise, which means that the warm air is moving into the area
6. Wind shift with the frontal passage
7. Poor visibility due to heavy overcast, precipitation, and haze or fog associated with the front.

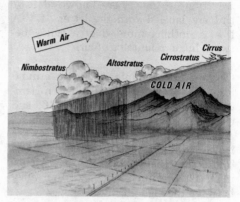

Fig. 2-50. Warm Front Profile

OCCLUDED FRONT

An *occluded front* also moves around a low-pressure area. It is nothing more than a combination of a cold front and a warm front. This phenomenon takes place when a warm airmass, which has moved up from the south to form a warm front condition, collides with a fast-moving cold front which moves in from the west, or northwest, at a faster rate of speed. The cold front sometimes moves at 40 to 45 miles per hour. Warm fronts usually move at speeds from 10 to 20 miles per hour. Therefore, the fast-moving cold air underruns the warm front condition, forcing it aloft and creating an occluded front, as shown in figure 2-51.

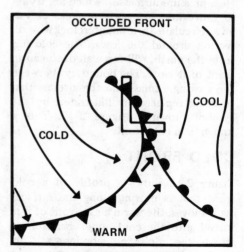

Fig. 2-51. Occluded Front

Figure 2-52 shows an occluded front profile in which the cold air has overtaken the warm front weather conditions aloft. The occluded front creates cumulonimbus clouds, associated with the cold front, plus all of the stratus clouds and weather conditions associated with the warm front. This can be a dangerous and complicated phenomenon.

STATIONARY FRONT

After these fronts dissipate, or the temperature on each side of the front becomes almost equal, and the pressure does likewise, the movement of these frontal conditions will stop, and spread out over a large area. This condition is known as a stationary front and has its own symbol, consisting of the cold front symbol pointing one direction, and the warm front symbol pointing in the other, as in figure 2-53. With this condition, there may be very low ceilings, poor visibility, and some icing conditions. The stationary front may remain in the area for days.

WEATHER IN MOUNTAINOUS AREAS

Terrain, as well as fronts, can cause air to be lifted and cooled until cloudiness results. When the wind blows against a

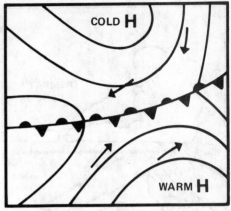

Fig. 2-53. Stationary Front

mountain barrier, the moisture content of the air and its stability determine the amount and height of clouds, their thickness, and their type. As the air descends on the leeward side of the terrain, it is warmed and clouds disappear, as shown in figure 2-54.

Fronts and low-pressure systems moving through mountainous regions create more cloudiness and precipitation, turbulence, and icing conditions on the windward slopes than they do over flat terrain. This is because the terrain lifting effect is added to the frontal lifting forces at work.

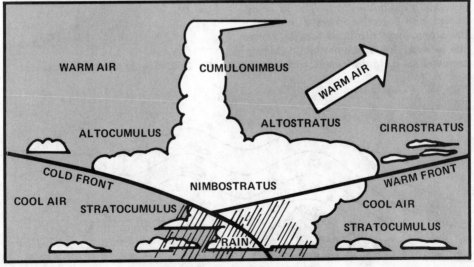

Fig. 2-52. Occluded Front Profile

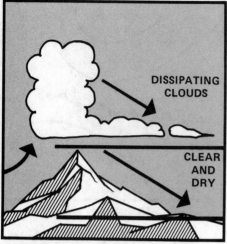

Fig. 2-54. Mountainous Area Weather

It also causes a wave or ripple in the atmosphere which can extend for miles downwind from the mountain range.

The only way a pilot has of knowing that this tremendous turbulence exists is by noticing the various clouds that form in this area, as shown in figure 2-55. A lenticular, or lens-shaped, cloud usually is located at the crest of one of the standing mountain waves. Roll, or rotor, clouds may form at about the same level as the mountain peak or the ridge of the mountain range. The pilot should watch for this type of warning in mountainous areas. The associated downdrafts and turbulence are very severe and can cause the pilot to lose control of his aircraft.

Because of the rapid changes in elevation in mountainous areas, weather conditions frequently change rapidly in short distances. Cloud heights above ground level, in particular, vary significantly from place to place even though the mean sea level elevation of clouds may be uniform. Pilots should understand the effects of terrain on weather especially in mountainous areas.

MOUNTAIN WAVE

The movement of air over the mountain ridges also causes turbulence and may generate a *mountain wave*. The air being cooled and forced up over a mountain has a tendency to roll, or tumble, down the leeward side of the mountain causing tremendous downdrafts and turbulence.

A mountain wave should be anticipated whenever winds of 20 knots or greater are blowing perpendicular to a mountain range. Aircraft should fly at a level at least 50 percent greater than the height of the range to avoid mountain turbulence. For example, a pilot should fly

Fig. 2-56. Avoiding Mountain Turbulence

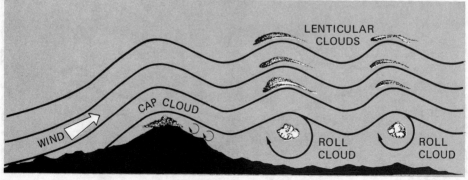

Fig. 2-55. Mountain Wave

at 15,000 feet for a 10,000-foot range of mountains, as illustrated in figure 2-56. Pilots of small aircraft with performance ceilings close to the suggested height should not attempt to cross the mountain ranges.

WEATHER NEAR LARGE BODIES OF WATER

Large bodies of water sometimes have pronounced effects on local weather conditions. For example, during the winter season, the Great Lakes are warmer than the surrounding land areas and the cold airmasses that move southward from Canada. Heat and moisture are added to these cold airmasses as they pass over the lakes. The resulting convection causes cumulus-type clouds and rain or snow showers and squalls. The areas on the downwind side of large bodies of water are usually affected by this type of weather.

WEATHER HAZARDS

POOR VISIBILITY

One of the most common aviation weather hazards is low visibility. The pilot is concerned with three types of visibility: horizontal surface visibility, air-to-air visibility, and air-to-ground or slant visibility. (See Fig. 2-57.) Usually, the only information available to the pilot is horizontal surface visibility which is reported by the weather observer. However, air-to-air and air-to-ground visibility can be quite different from that reported to him. Pilots are the only source of information for visibility aloft.

Clouds, haze, and dust aloft interfere with air-to-air visibility. While an aircraft is flying in clouds, the pilot's visibility is similar to that experienced in dense fog on the ground.

Air-to-ground visibility is restricted by clouds and haze aloft as well as by surface phenomena such as fog or blowing dust. The slant visibility may be

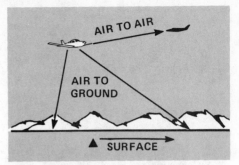

Fig. 2-57. Types of Visibility

greater or less than the surface horizontal visibility depending on the depth of the surface condition. Slant visibility is important in the approach zone to the runway and to enroute VFR operations for finding checkpoints.

Horizontal visibility at the surface is most important during landing and take-off operations. Poor visibility creates the greatest hazard when it exists together with a low cloud ceiling.

FOG

Fog is the most common restriction to visibility. It is a cloud resting on the ground and is composed of small water droplets. Conditions favorable for fog are light winds and a small difference between temperature and dewpoint.

A characteristic of fog that makes it very hazardous to aviation is the rapidity with which it can form. It is not unusual for the visibility to drop from above three miles to less than one-half mile in a few minutes.

As illustrated in figure 2-58, *radiation fog* usually occurs at night or early in the morning over a land surface. It is caused by the radiational cooling of the ground and the air in the layers immediately above the land's surface.

Advection fog is formed by the horizontal movement of air over a surface colder or warmer than the air. This fog can be formed in one place and trans-

Fig. 2-58. Radiation Fog

Fig. 2-60. Upslope Fog

ported to another by horizontal air movements. The most common type of fog found on the west coast of the United States is advection fog, as illustrated in figure 2-59.

Fig. 2-59. Advection Fog.

Another type of fog is known as *upslope fog*. In this condition, moist air is forced up over the elevations of the earth and becomes cooled and condenses into fog as it reaches higher altitudes, as shown in figure 2-60.

In the same way, clouds can also be formed in the crests of mountain peaks by warm moist air being forced up the mountain slope and reaching its dewpoint in the cold air along the crest of the mountain. This is also known as mechanical convection. (See Fig. 2-61.)

Rain-induced fog results from the addition of moisture to the air by the

OROGRAPHIC CONVECTION OR MECHANICAL LIFTING   COLD AIR

WARM AIR

Fig. 2-61. Orographic Convection

evaporation of cold rain falling from above. This type of fog usually becomes more dense as night approaches and the air near the ground cools. (See Fig. 2-62.)

Detailed forecasting of fog is difficult, but there are some general rules which should prove helpful for anticipating fog on a short range basis.

Fig. 2-62. Rain-Induced Fog

1. Fog frequently forms during night-time or early morning if the sky is clear, the wind almost calm, and the dewpoint within 15° of the temperature at dusk.
2. Expect shallow fog to clear within a few hours after sunrise if there are no clouds above the fog. Expect thick fog or fog which has heavy cloudiness above to clear slowly.
3. Be alert for fog formation when the temperature dewpoint spread is small and continuous drizzle or light rain sets in.
4. Monitor surface weather reports at the area of concern for decreasing temperature dewpoint spread. Be alert to fog formation if the spread is decreasing and getting as small as five degrees.

HAZE

Haze is caused by the concentration of dust or salt particles into a stable layer of air and occasionally may extend from the surface to 15,000 feet. Haze layers often have definite tops above which air-to-air visibility is good. Air-to-ground visibility may be poor, however, even from above the haze layers.

Visibility in haze varies greatly, depending upon whether the pilot is facing the sun or has it at his back. Visibility may be very poor when flying toward the sun and landing could be hazardous during this condition.

DUST, SAND, OR SNOW

Strong surface winds and vertical currents may carry aloft loose materials from the surface, such as dust, sand, or snow, and thereby reduce surface visibility to near zero over extensive areas. Under some conditions, dust can be carried aloft as high as 15,000 feet and restrict slant, flight, and surface visibility. Blowing sand and snow are seldom carried aloft beyond a few hundred feet.

PRECIPITATION

Precipitation may occur as rain, drizzle, snow, ice pellets, or hail. The effect of rain on the visual range of the pilot is very noticeable, because when rain flows over the windshield, the cockpit visibility is greatly reduced. Heavy snow frequently reduces horizontal flight visibility to zero. Drizzle is often accompanied by fog, haze, or smoke, resulting in lower visibility than rain.

ICING

Aircraft icing is a major hazard because it can alter the flight characteristics of an aircraft until it is unable to fly. It also can choke the engine induction system until insufficient power is available to maintain flight.

Carburetor ice is a frequent cause of engine failure. The cooling resulting from the vaporization of fuel, together with the expansion of air as it goes through the carburetor, causes temperatures to drop as much as 70° Fahrenheit almost instantly. Water vapor is condensed by the cooling and ice can result, as shown in figure 2-63.

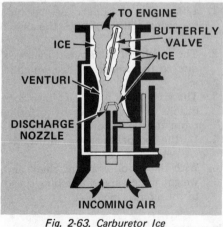

Fig. 2-63. Carburetor Ice

The application of carburetor heat as soon as carburetor ice is suspected usually will remove this ice in a few seconds. Each type of aircraft has different carburetor ice characteristics and the aircraft owner's manual should be consulted for most efficient use of the carburetor heat control.

The effects of ice buildup on aircraft are cumulative. Thus, a pilot encountering icing must quickly change his flight procedure or alter his course or altitude to maintain safe flight. In extreme cases, two to three inches of ice can form on the leading edge of an aircraft in less than five minutes.

One-half inch of ice on the leading edge of an airfoil can noticeably reduce the lifting power of an aircraft as well as increase the drag. Ice on an aircraft results in the following. (See Fig. 2-64.)

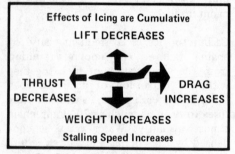

Fig. 2-64. Effects of Structural Icing

1. Lift of the wings decreases because ice accumulation changes the airfoil shape.
2. The weight of the aircraft increases due to the weight of accumulated ice.
3. The combination of the above conditions increases drag by offering more resistance to the atmosphere.
4. If the propeller ices, thrust decreases.
5. With the airfoil changing shape and weight increasing, the stalling speed of the aircraft increases.

Two conditions are necessary for a substantial accumulation of ice on an aircraft.

1. The aircraft must be flying through visible moisture such as rain or clouds.

2. The temperature of the water or of the aircraft must be 0° Celsius or lower.

When water droplets are cooled below the freezing temperature, they are in an unnatural state, and turn to ice quickly when disturbed by an aircraft passing through them. Liquid water below freezing is called supercooled.

Icing is most heavily concentrated in cumuliform clouds in the range of temperature from 0° to -10° Celsius, usually from near the freezing level to 5,000 feet above the freezing level. However, supercooled water and icing have been encountered in thunderstorms as high as 40,000 feet with a temperature of -40° Celsius.

Icing occurs in layer, or stratiform, clouds as well as in cumulus clouds. However, the rate of ice accumulation is not as fast in stratiform clouds. Continuous icing at a slower rate is normally associated with stratus clouds in the range from 0° to -15° Celsius.

Clear ice appears as a smooth glaze and is formed by the freezing of large water drops, such as are found in cumuliform clouds or freezing rain. Accumulation of this type of ice is rapid because large drops spread out and assume the shape of the surface on which they freeze. Clear ice adheres very strongly to the surface of the aircraft and is quite difficult to remove. If water runs back to aileron or elevator hinges before freezing, it may restrict control movement. (See Fig. 2-65.)

Rime ice is formed by small water drops freezing quickly on the aircraft surface. The drops retain their round shape and air is trapped in the ice. Rime ice has an opaque appearance and usually has an uneven surface. It occurs most frequently in stratiform clouds. It builds up more slowly than clear ice and is easier to dislodge. (See Fig. 2-65.)

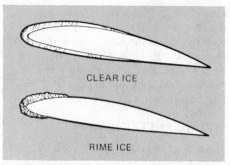

Fig. 2-65. Differences in Structural Icing

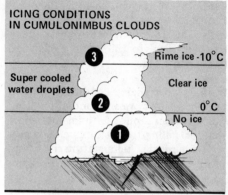

Fig. 2-66. Icing Conditions
in Cumulonimbus Clouds

In weather forecasts or pilot reports, aircraft structural icing normally is classified as trace, light, moderate or severe, depending on the accumulation rate. A *trace* means ice is perceptible, but accumulation is nearly balanced by its rate of sublimation. The use of de-icing equipment is unnecessary, unless icing is encountered for an extended period of time. *Light* ice accumulation can be a problem during prolonged exposure (over one hour) without adequate de-icing/anti-icing equipment. In *moderate* icing conditions, even short encounters become potentially hazardous unless de-icing/anti-icing equipment is used. *Severe* icing produces a rate of accumulation greater than the reduction or control capabilities of the de-icing/anti-icing equipment.

Figure 2-66 depicts various icing conditions in cumulonimbus clouds.

1. At the lower level of the storm where temperatures are above freezing (position 1), ice usually is not encountered.
2. In the middle section of the storm (position 2), clear ice and possibly rime ice will be present. Clear ice in this area will be caused by supercooled water droplets.
3. In the upper levels of the storm (position 3), the temperatures are much lower and the moisture content is much less. Rime ice will be the dominant type of ice encountered. However, clear or rime icing seldom exists without at least a trace of the other.

The supercooled water droplets found in cumulonimbus clouds are nothing more than large beads of moisture suspended in the heavy clouds. They exist at a temperature level below freezing, even though they are still in a liquid state. Whenever these water droplets come into contact with an aircraft, they spread over the aircraft's surface and freeze into clear ice.

Hail is often caused by supercooled water droplets. As shown in figure 2-67, the water droplets are picked up by the rising air currents and carried through lower temperatures in the upper level of the cloud. Then, when they are heavy enough to overcome the rising air currents, they fall out of the cloud as hail.

The hailstones sometimes make many cycles through the storm in the updrafts and downdrafts, accumulating more and

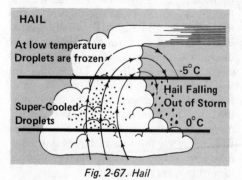

Fig. 2-67. Hail

more ice in layers, before they are thrown clear of the cloud and fall to earth. The size of the hailstone generally is proportional to the number of cycles it has completed.

Another serious icing condition exists in the vicinity of a warm front. Rime icing is likely when a pilot is flying into snow which is falling from stratus clouds at a level where the temperature is below zero degrees Celsius, as shown in figure 2-68, position A.

In the vicinity of the warm front, more than one freezing level may be present. For example, if the surface temperature is 35° Fahrenheit (or approximately 2° Celsius), the lowest freezing level will be about 700 feet above the surface. In the warm air above the front, the temperature may be above freezing, as illustrated by the seven degrees Celsius level shown in the figure. A second freezing level will always exist at some higher point, as shown by the zero degree Celsius level.

When an aircraft proceeds toward and under a warm front, it may encounter ice pellets (raindrops which have frozen while falling through colder air). When the rain is frozen, it generally does not adhere to a cold aircraft. However, when the snow changes to ice pellets, a greater icing problem should be expected, because the aircraft is approaching the warmer temperatures of the frontal zone.

If the aircraft continues to fly under the frontal zone, the pilot should anticipate freezing rain (position B), which results from rain falling through cold air with below freezing temperatures or from rain striking the cold aircraft. Depending on the slope of the frontal boundary and temperatures on each side of the front, the area of freezing rain may be quite narrow or may extend for some miles. Regardless of the width, structural icing may be severe enough to become a hazard in a very short time.

A mixture of rime and clear ice should be expected at position C. If the aircraft were flying in the upper level of clouds associated with this warm front, where the temperatures are far below freezing, rime ice would be the dominant type of icing encountered (position D).

FINDING FREEZING LEVEL

The rate at which air cools with altitude without losing or gaining in heat content is called the adiabatic lapse rate and is expressed in degrees per 1,000 feet. (See Fig. 2-69.) For dry air, the rate of cooling is constant at three degrees Celsius per 1,000 feet, but moist air is variable, depending upon original temperature, pressure, and moisture content.

The average lapse rate, obtained from measurements throughout the world, is approximately 2° Celsius or 3-1/2° Fahrenheit per 1,000 feet. This average has been adopted as the "standard lapse rate." By using the standard lapse rate and the following formula, pilots may estimate the level of freezing temperature.

1. Using Fahrenheit temperatures, subtract 32° Fahrenheit from the surface temperature and divide this by 3-1/2° Fahrenheit, the standard lapse rate. The answer will be the freezing level in thousands of feet AGL.
2. Using Celsius temperatures, divide the surface temperature by two degrees Celsius. This also will provide the freezing level in thousands of feet AGL.

SAMPLE FREEZING LEVEL PROBLEM

If the surface temperature at the airport is 60° Fahrenheit, what is the freezing level? This problem can be worked in two ways.

1. Using Fahrenheit
   a. Subtract 32°F from 60°F (60 - 32 = 28°F).
   b. Divide 28°F by 3-1/2°F (28 ÷ 3-1/2 = 8).

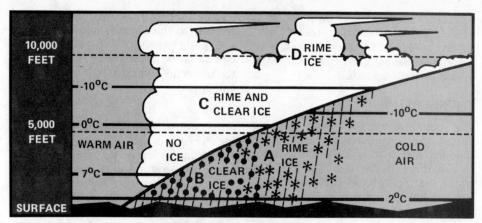

Fig. 2-68. Warm Front Icing

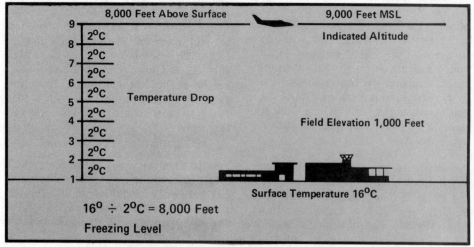

Fig. 2-69. Finding Freezing Level

c. Multiply 8 times 1,000. The answer is 8,000 feet above the surface.

2. Using Celsius
   a. First, convert 60° F to Celsius using the conversion scale on the computer. 60° F is equal to 16° C.
   b. Divide 16° C by 2° (16 ÷ 2 = 8).
   c. Multiply 8 times 1,000. The answer is 8,000 feet above the surface.

If ice is encountered, there are two things that can be done to eliminate it or decrease its accumulation.

1. Descend to a level where the temperature is above 32° Fahrenheit. This action melts, or eliminates, the ice.
2. Climb to a higher altitude where the temperature is lower and moisture content is less. This reduces the rate of ice accumulation.

Ice formed on an aircraft in the air can be dangerous, but frozen mud on the wings may be equally hazardous. An aircraft may pick this up while taxiing. It is advisable to remove this foreign matter from the wings before attempting to take off. Such accumulations disturb the airflow over the wing and drastically reduce the aircraft's performance.

Another ground icing hazard is frost, which may increase the takeoff and stalling speeds of an aircraft enough to prevent a takeoff. For safety, frost should be removed before takeoff.

THUNDERSTORMS

The thunderstorm is another weather hazard often encountered by pilots. The thunderstorm is truly a weather factory. In it, and near it, are found gusty surface winds, extreme turbulence, rain, hail, heavy icing, and variable pressure that make altimeters unreliable.

A thunderstorm may cover an area as large as 50 miles in diameter, and may be alive and active for many hours. When well developed, thunderstorms have numerous cells and vertical currents which may travel much faster than some small airplanes fly horizontally. However, every thunderstorm starts as a single convective cell, which first produces a simple cumulus cloud. (See Fig. 2-70, part A.)

Eventually, as the cloud builds further, water droplets condense, become larger and begin to fall. The falling rain drags air along with it and starts downdrafts. When the rain and downdrafts begin to reach the ground, the cell is said to be mature. The downdrafts spread out horizontally at the ground, producing strong and gusty winds. Within and near the cloud, severe downdrafts exist adjacent to powerful updrafts. (See Fig. 2-70, part B.)

Supercooled water droplets often cause hail. The water droplets are picked up by the rising air currents, carried through lower temperatures in the upper level of the cloud, and then, when they are heavy enough to overcome the rising air currents, they fall out of the cloud as hail. The supercooled droplets sometimes make many cycles through the storm, in the updrafts and downdrafts, in the form of ice before they are thrown clear of the cloud or fall to earth. The number of cycles to which the hail has been subjected contributes to the size of the hailstones. There are records in this country which show that hail has been as large as 5-1/4 inches in diameter.

At the time the rain reaches the ground and gustiness has set in, the cell usually has reached a height of 25,000 feet or more. The height growth continues until the rising currents of air reach a stable layer.

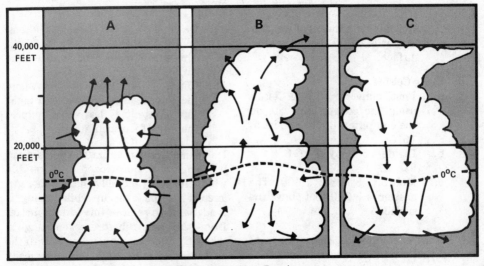

Fig. 2-70. Thunderstorm Development

As the vertical currents decrease, they turn with the prevailing winds at high levels. This results in the "anvil" top characteristic of the dissipating stage of a thunderstorm. (See Fig. 2-70, part C.) The height at which this occurs varies depending on the degree of instability of the air. The average height of thunderstorms is 35,000 feet, but they can range from 25,000 to over 60,000 feet.

By the time the anvil is well established, downdrafts are characteristic of the middle and lower portions of the cloud. This downward motion heats and dries the air causing the cloud formation to dissipate.

The chances of severe or extreme turbulence within thunderstorms are greater at higher altitudes. Most cases of severe turbulence are encountered between 8,000 and 15,000 feet above the terrain. Lightning is found throughout the thunderstorm cloud, but is most frequent and severe from the freezing level up to -10° Celsius.

To avoid these hazards, the pilot should not fly into the center of an active thunderstorm. When circumnavigating thunderstorm activity, the pilot should keep in mind that turbulence can exist in the clear air around the buildup. Light-

ning can also strike an aircraft in the clear in the vicinity of a thunderstorm. (See Fig. 2-71.)

Fig. 2-71. Avoid Thunderstorms

The horizontal spreading out of the downdrafts beneath the thunderstorm causes a rapid change in wind direction and speed immediately before the passage of the storm. The gusty shifting winds are hazardous for landing operations. Usually the first gust is an extremely turbulent condition and precedes the arrival of the roll cloud and the onset of rain as the thunderstorm approaches, as shown in figure 2-72.

A band of active thunderstorms is called a squall line. Typically, they develop a

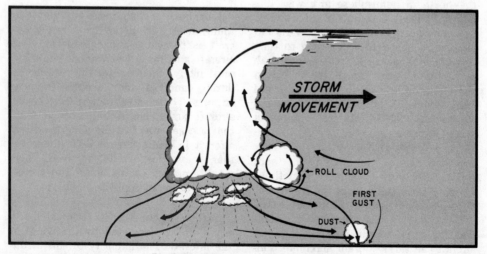

Fig. 2-72. Thunderstorm—Shifting Winds

few hundred miles ahead of a cold front in moist, unstable air. The line of thunderstorms may be several hundred miles long and vary in width from 30 to 50 miles. Squall lines usually form quickly and have rapid movement. Generally, their life cycle is completed in 24 hours with maximum intensity during late afternoon or early at night. They are very hazardous to light aircraft because severe turbulence is often associated with them. (See Fig. 2-73.)

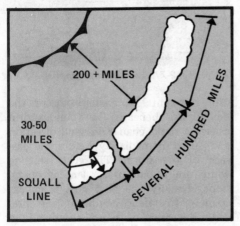

Fig. 2-73. Squall Lines

JET STREAM

The jet stream is a high-level stream of strong westerly winds that moves across the northern hemisphere in a wave-like pattern. (See Fig. 2-74.) The jet stream oscillates northward and southward and also varies in height from time to time and place to place. With each outbreak of cold air from the north, the jet stream generally intensifies, moves southward and lowers in altitude. Wind speeds approaching 200 knots are common in the jet stream.

On the edge of the jet stream, there exists turbulence which is sometimes severe. Within the core of the jet stream, however, little or no turbulence exists and the winds are uniformly strong. This core area is where jet and turbojet aircraft can safely obtain maximum tailwinds in the atmosphere. While the jet

Fig. 2-74. Jet Stream Path

stream may stretch across the country for several thousand miles, its width is only a few hundred miles, and its thickness varies from 3,000 to 7,000 feet.

Clear air turbulence, associated with the jet stream and the tropopause, can usually be avoided by changing altitude. Very often a change in altitude of a few thousand feet will take a flight into smoother air while a lateral displacement of 100 miles might be required to clear the turbulence.

WAKE TURBULENCE

All airplanes in flight cause turbulence in their wake. Turbulence from heavy aircraft is particularly dangerous to light aircraft and must be avoided. Pilots are most likely to encounter this turbulence during landings and takeoffs at busy airports. The greatest danger from heavy aircraft turbulence results from vortices that are generated at the wingtips of an aircraft in flight. Figure 2-75 illustrates that if vortices could be seen, they would resemble twin horizontal tornadoes, rotating in opposite directions.

The rotating cones of air are created as a result of lift generated by the wings of the aircraft. The intensity of this turbulence is related to the wing span, weight, and forward speed of the aircraft, and the density of the air. In general, turbulence intensity is directly proportional to the weight of the airplane and inversely proportional to its speed and wing span. Viewed from the rear, vortex cores rotate clockwise from the left wing and counterclockwise from the right wing. These cores, if generated more than a few span lengths above the ground, settle downward from the flight path of the aircraft.

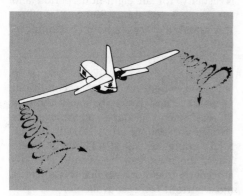

Fig. 2-75. Wingtip Vortices

When the aircraft is on the ground, the weight of the aircraft is off the wings so the vortex cores cannot be generated. Prior to liftoff or after touchdown, wingtip vortices are nonexistant. Therefore, in takeoff and landing operations, the rotation or touchdown point of the large aircraft is critical. Wake turbulence will not be created before rotation or after touchdown and will not exist above the airplane's flight path.

1. If taking off behind a large aircraft, start the takeoff roll where the large aircraft did, lift off at a point before its liftoff point and climb out above its flight path.
2. If taking off after a large aircraft lands, delay the takeoff for at least two minutes and plan the liftoff point to be beyond the touchdown point of the large aircraft.
3. Remember, a light crosswind of three to seven knots may cause the upwind vortex to remain in the touchdown zone for a longer period than with other wind conditions.
4. During intersection takeoffs, be alert to large aircraft operations and avoid any heading which will cross below a large aircraft's path.

The following procedures are recommended for landing behind a large aircraft.

1. If cleared to land close behind a large aircraft, stay above the large aircraft's final approach path and land beyond its touchdown point.
2. While in the pattern, avoid crossing the path of the large aircraft, if possible. This can be done by keeping the pattern inside or above that of the large aircraft.
3. If a large aircraft has just taken off, plan the touchdown and landing roll in advance of the large aircraft's liftoff point.
4. When landing on an intersecting runway behind a departing or landing large aircraft, note the other aircraft's position in relation to the intersection. The large aircraft must be either in the takeoff roll or the landing roll-out when the runway intersection is crossed. Otherwise, the pilot of the light aircraft must be able to complete the roll-out *prior* to reaching the intersection or he should abandon the approach.
5. When landing on a parallel runway, consider the possible drift of a vortex generated by a large aircraft on the adjacent runway. Stay at or above the aircraft's final approach path and land beyond its touchdown point.
6. Continue to apply wake turbulence precautions during taxi operations.

A thorough discussion of heavy aircraft turbulence is given in the "Safety of Flight Section" of the *Airman's Information Manual*. All pilots should read this section and be familiar with the recommended procedures.

SOURCES OF WEATHER INFORMATION

Aviation weather for preflight planning is available in all major metropolitan areas and many smaller cities. The telephone numbers or radio frequencies of these outlets can be found in the *Airport/ Facility Directory* and/or in the local telephone directory under the United States Government listing. One or more of the following should be contacted when a weather briefing for a flight is desired.

1. National Weather Service (NWS) offices
2. Flight service stations (FSS)
3. Pilots automatic telephone weather answering service (PATWAS)
4. Transcribed weather broadcasts (TWEB)
5. Automatic aviation weather services (AAWS)

IN-PERSON BRIEFINGS

Where possible, the pilot should go to the flight service station or National Weather Service Office for his weather briefing. Current and forecast weather information is available at these offices, and briefers are able to provide assistance necessary for preflight planning.

TELEPHONE BRIEFINGS

At times, when an in-person briefing is not possible, a telephone briefing is appropriate. When requesting a briefing by telephone, the pilot should have his writing materials at hand and be comfortably situated so he can copy the necessary information. The main disadvantage of a telephone briefing is that he will not have the charts and reports to view and study, but must mentally picture what the briefer describes. However, the advantage of asking questions and obtaining additional information is still available.

RECORDED BRIEFINGS

There will be times when it is not feasible to contact an FSS or NWS office. In these situations, two types of telephone recordings and one transcribed radio broadcast are available for weather information.

PATWAS

The pilots automatic telephone weather answering service (PATWAS) is a recorded forecast of flight conditions along specified, well-traveled routes diverging from the PATWAS station. This forecast is usually for an eight-hour period and for distances of about 200 to 350 miles. It is updated every six hours beginning at 0000Z.

Additionally, the PATWAS forecast is amended whenever weather conditions necessitate and the FSS places the new forecast on the tape recording. The criteria for issuing an AIRMET or SIGMET apply to the PATWAS as well. Thus, the pilot can be assured that the automatic telephone service is issuing the most current forecast available.

AAWS

The automatic aviation weather service (AAWS) is a recorded enroute forecast prepared and transcribed by the FAA flight service station personnel. These forecasts cover specified routes in certain directions out to distances of about 200 miles from the FSS which prepared the recording. AAWS forecasts are similar to PATWAS. However, their valid time is longer than eight hours, and is variable depending upon the time of issue.

TWEB

The transcribed weather broadcasts (TWEBs) are transmitted over low frequency nondirectional beacons and over some VORs, and can be received on the ground up to 90 miles or more from the broadcasting station. TWEBs and PATWAS are identical in forecast content and valid time. An advantage of TWEBs over some PATWAS recordings is that they combine the PATWAS issuances from several surrounding stations, thus

ADVANCED METEOROLOGY

enlarging the enroute coverage to 400 miles or more from the broadcast outlet.

TWEB and PATWAS transcriptions provide forecast and synoptic data in a format useful for route planning. Normal order and content consists of the following:

1. Synopsis
2. Flight precautions
3. Route forecasts
4. Outlook
5. Winds aloft forecast
6. Radar reports
7. Surface reports
8. PIREPs/NOTAMs

IN-FLIGHT WEATHER SERVICES

The FAA maintains air-to-ground two-way communications for distribution of weather information through the voice portions of VORs and selected communications frequencies. These communications facilities are used to transmit various types of weather information.

CURRENT WEATHER

Although routine *scheduled* weather broadcasts have been discontinued (except in Alaska), the FAA provides *unscheduled* weather broadcasts over VOR and NDB frequencies on an as-required basis. These broadcasts contain significant aeronautical information and are made at random times. Each unscheduled broadcast begins with the announcement, "aviation broadcast" followed by the significant data. For example, *aviation broadcast, special weather report,* (Notice to Airmen, Pilot Report, etc.) (location name twice) *three seven* (past the hour) *observation* . . .

Since these broadcasts contain information gathered within approximately 150 nautical miles of the location, the pilot can keep abreast of the important weather changes as the flight progresses. Along with this current weather information, these broadcasts include SIGMETs, AIRMETs, and other notices of a critical nature.

REQUEST AND REPLY SERVICE

If unexpected weather conditions are encountered, a pilot may request specific weather information. By communicating directly with FSSs, current information on convective SIGMETs, SIGMETs, AIRMETs, thunderstorms, radar reports, winds and temperatures aloft forecasts, pilot reports, terminal and enroute forecasts can be obtained.

ENROUTE FLIGHT ADVISORY SERVICE

The FAA has developed an *enroute flight advisory service* (Flight Watch) to provide specific enroute weather information. This service is made available to all pilots by selected flight service stations throughout the United States.

Each of the selected flight service stations provides the enroute flight advisory service in its own geographical area and the area served by its remote communication outlet. To request this service, the appropriate call sign and the words "Flight Watch" should be transmitted; i.e., *"Seattle Flight Watch."* The communications frequency used for this service is 122.00 MHz.

Flight Watch enables a pilot to obtain routine weather information, plus current reports on the location of thunderstorms and other hazardous weather, as observed and reported by pilots or noted on radar. To increase the efficiency of this service, all pilots are encouraged to report weather encountered in flight.

ADVANCED METEOROLOGY

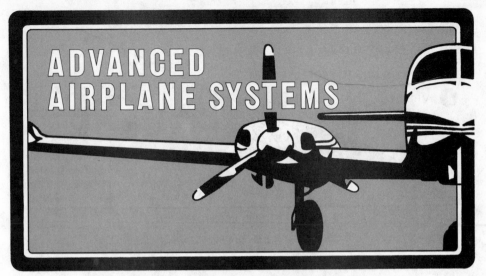

chapter 3

ADVANCED AIRPLANE SYSTEMS

INTRODUCTION

Advanced airplane systems have significantly increased the safety, economy, and utility of high performance aircraft. Operation of these complex airplanes requires a high level of knowledge and proficiency on the part of the pilot. In addition, commercial pilot certification standards specify that the applicant must gain experience in complex aircraft. This chapter introduces controllable pitch propellers, fuel injection, turbocharging, and landing gear systems.

SECTION A
CONTROLLABLE-PITCH PROPELLERS

PROPELLER EFFICIENCY

The aircraft engine has been designed to provide a large amount of power with the least possible engine weight. The development of constant-speed propellers was a major step toward gaining high performance from small powerplants.

Each blade of a propeller is essentially a rotating wing. As a result of their construction, the propeller blades produce forces that create thrust to pull or push the airplane through the air. The thrust which is created is a result of the propeller blades producing lift parallel to the airplane's longitudinal axis. The lifting action imparts a momentum change on the airstream. The highest propulsive efficiency is obtained when a large mass of air is moved with a relatively small velocity change.

If a propeller could perform with 100 percent efficiency, all of the engine's power output to the propeller would be converted to thrust. Therefore, it is important to maintain high propeller efficiency, as well as high horsepower.

Propeller efficiency is determined by numerous factors. Since the propeller is an airfoil, its *angle of attack* is the principal factor in determining efficiency. The angle of attack of a propeller is determined by the propeller pitch (called blade angle), propeller r.p.m., and the airflow along the propeller axis. These factors are illustrated in figure 3-1.

To produce the effective pitch angle that provides the angle of attack necessary for optimum thrust or peak efficiency, a

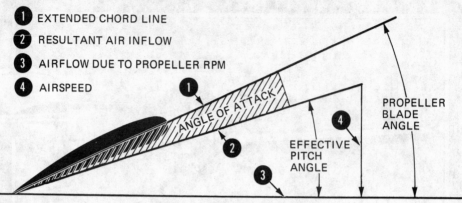

① EXTENDED CHORD LINE
② RESULTANT AIR INFLOW
③ AIRFLOW DUE TO PROPELLER RPM
④ AIRSPEED

ANGLE OF ATTACK

PROPELLER BLADE ANGLE

EFFECTIVE PITCH ANGLE

PLANE OF PROPELLER ROTATION

Fig. 3-1. Effective Pitch Angle

fixed-pitch propeller must be operated at a specific r.p.m. and airspeed. Since slow airspeeds tend to produce small effective pitch angles and, consequently, excessive angles of attack, "climb props," normally used on aircraft operating from short fields or high field elevations, have a small blade angle. Conversely, "cruise props," used on aircraft to obtain a higher airspeed, have a large blade angle. The relationship between these two kinds of fixed-pitch propellers is shown in figure 3-2.

The efficiency of a fixed-pitch propeller increases with an increase in effective pitch angle until *peak efficiency* at the optimum angle of attack is reached. Then, the efficiency of the fixed-pitch propeller decreases rapidly, as shown in figure 3-2 (item 1). The variable-pitch, constant-speed propeller can maintain the optimum angle of attack by changing the propeller blade angle with changes in the effective pitch angle. In this way, a high plateau of propeller efficiency can be maintained over a wide range of air-

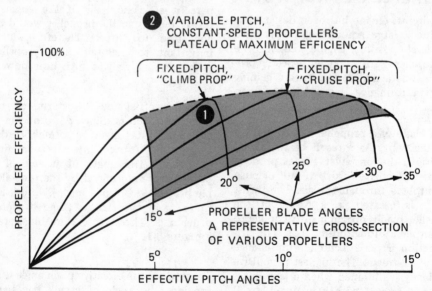

② VARIABLE-PITCH, CONSTANT-SPEED PROPELLER'S PLATEAU OF MAXIMUM EFFICIENCY

100%

FIXED-PITCH, "CLIMB PROP"

FIXED-PITCH, "CRUISE PROP"

PROPELLER EFFICIENCY

15° 20° 25° 30° 35°

PROPELLER BLADE ANGLES
A REPRESENTATIVE CROSS-SECTION OF VARIOUS PROPELLERS

5° 10° 15°

EFFECTIVE PITCH ANGLES

Fig. 3-2. Propeller Efficiency

speed and r.p.m. combinations (item 2). If a particular variable-pitch, constant-speed propeller has blade angle limits of 15° minimum and 35° maximum, the propeller efficiency that may be gained over fixed-pitch propellers having blade angles of either 15° or 35° is shown by the shaded area of figure 3-2.

RPM CONTROL

The variable-pitch propeller allows the *blade angle* to be changed, as necessary, to provide the desired angle of attack. However, since the angle of attack is also determined by the effective pitch angle, a change in either the r.p.m. or airspeed will cause a change in the angle of attack and, therefore, a change in propeller efficiency.

When an aircraft equipped with a fixed-pitch propeller accelerates, as in a dive, the propeller r.p.m. tends to increase. Additionally, if the airspeed decreases, the propeller r.p.m. tends to decrease. If the r.p.m. of a variable-pitch propeller is to be held constant, the propeller blade must be designed so that the *blade angle* may automatically be *increased* with an increase in airspeed. Conversely, it must be designed so that the blade angle may automatically be decreased as the airspeed decreases. Maintaining a constant r.p.m. by variation of the propeller blade angle also tends to maintain the desired angle of attack and optimum propeller efficiency.

The constant-speed propeller system utilizes a hydraulic governor and a pitch-change mechanism. The governor is mounted on the engine and is geared to the engine crankshaft so that it senses engine speed. The governor is adjusted by the pilot through the r.p.m. or propeller control on the control console. The pitch change mechanism is mounted in the propeller hub to control the blade angle.

When the engine's speed begins to increase above the r.p.m. for which the governor is adjusted, the governor activates the pitch-change mechanism in the propeller hub so that the blade angle increases. This increases the blade's angle of attack and, therefore, its drag loading, which slows the blade's speed. As the engine r.p.m. decreases, the governor reverses the process in the hub's pitch-change mechanism, returning the blade angle to the original pitch, and the engine to the desired speed. When the engine speed decreases below the selected r.p.m., the process is carried out in the reverse order, first decreasing the blade angle, then returning it to the selected pitch.

PITCH–CHANGE MECHANISM

Aerodynamic forces and spring tension acting on the blades of a spinning, constant-speed propeller tend to twist the blades to the angle of attack that produces the least drag and thrust in the plane of propeller rotation. The smallest amount of drag and thrust is produced at a small, or zero, angle of attack.

In the most elementary form, hydraulic pitch-change mechanisms found on single-engine airplanes utilize oil pressure to oppose the twisting forces acting on the blades. This arrangement allows the mechanism to increase the blade angle, as shown in figure 3-3 (item 1). A hydraulic piston in the hub of the propeller is connected to each blade by means of a piston rod. This rod is attached to forks that slide over the single pitch-change pin mounted in the root of each blade (item 2).

The cylinder is attached to the propeller hub. Oil under high pressure is fed into the cylinder from the governor through the center of the propeller shaft and piston rod. The oil pressure moves the piston toward the rear of the cylinder, thereby moving the piston rod and forks aft. The forks push the pitch-change pin of each blade toward the rear of the hub, thus causing each blade to twist in the hub toward the high pitch position. The

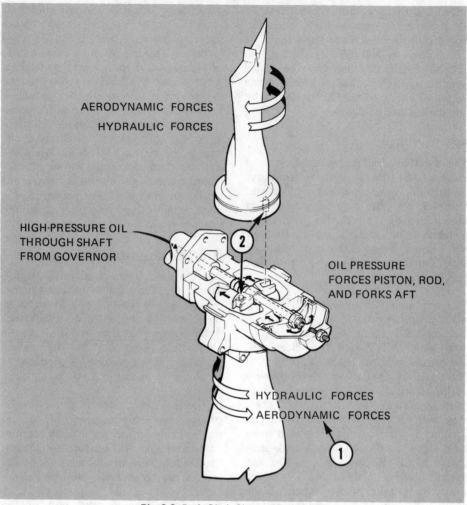

Fig. 3-3. Basic Pitch-Change Mechanism

governor regulates the oil pressure sent to the pitch-change mechanism to the amount necessary to maintain an equilibrium between aerodynamic and hydraulic pitch-changing forces at the selected r.p.m.

Multi-engine aircraft, as opposed to single-engine aircraft, provide higher performance and increased safety; however, their propeller pitch-change mechanisms are necessarily more complex. Since the *windmilling* propeller of an inoperative engine generates excessive drag, the propellers of most multi-engine aircraft can be *feathered* (twisted to an extremely

high pitch position) in order to stop propeller rotation and reduce the drag to a minimum.

The basic propeller pitch-change mechanism depends on an engine-driven oil pump for a supply of oil under high pressure. If the pitch-change mechanism of a featherable propeller depended on oil pressure to increase the blade angle to the feathered position, the loss of oil or a governor failure would prevent the propeller from being feathered. To avoid this problem, an *alternate method* of increasing the blade angle is used in featherable pitch-change mechanisms.

COUNTERWEIGHTS

*Fig. 3-4. Counterweights Attached
to a Featherable Prop*

The aerodynamic twisting forces acting on the propeller blade may be countered by altering the blade's center of mass in lieu of opposing oil hydraulic pressure. Featherable propellers have "counterweights" attached to the shank of each blade, as shown in figure 3-4. When the propeller is spinning, the counterweight's center of mass tends toward the blade's plane of rotation, thus increasing the blade angle, as shown in figure 3-5. The counterweight's centrifugal twisting force is designed to be slightly *greater* than the aerodynamic twisting force, and hydraulic pressure is used to aid the aerodynamic force in decreasing the blade angle. The various types of featherable pitch-change mechanisms use hydraulic pressure in one of several configurations. (See Fig. 3-6.)

Some types of featherable propellers utilize compressed air in the tip of the cylinder to oppose the hydraulic pressure and aid the counterweights in feathering the blades, as shown in figure 3-6. A locking device in the propeller hub prevents inadvertent feathering during operations at low r.p.m. settings, such as during ground operations.

ADVANTAGES OF CONSTANT-SPEED PROPELLERS

The principal advantage of a constant-speed propeller is that it converts a very high percentage of engine power into thrust over a wide range of r.p.m. and

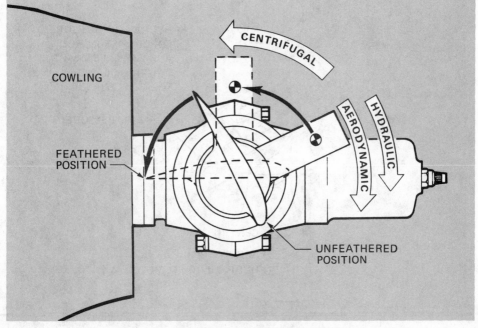

COWLING

CENTRIFUGAL

AERODYNAMIC

HYDRAULIC

FEATHERED POSITION

UNFEATHERED POSITION

Fig. 3-5. Counterweights Tend to Increase Pitch

airspeed combinations. In addition to being more efficient, constant-speed propeller operation enables the pilot to select optimum combinations of engine power and r.p.m.

Maintaining a constant r.p.m. stabilizes the fuel consumption rate. Also, at any given power setting, the pilot may select the r.p.m. that produces the least noise and vibration, further reducing the fatigue forces acting on the engine, airframe, and pilot. The term "good performance" can have various connotations. To one pilot, obtaining the "best overall performance" from an airplane may mean achieving the highest rate of climb or fastest airspeed; to another pilot, this performance may be described as the least engine wear, longest range, or lowest fuel consumption. Since individual pilot requirements vary and different aircraft sometimes have widely differing operational characteristics, it is impractical to detail the manner in which a pilot may use a constant-speed propeller to his best advantage. There are, however, general considerations that apply to all engines equipped with constant-speed propellers.

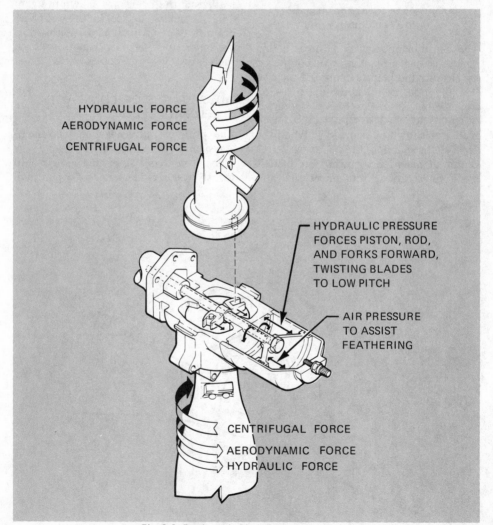

HYDRAULIC FORCE
AERODYNAMIC FORCE
CENTRIFUGAL FORCE

HYDRAULIC PRESSURE
FORCES PISTON, ROD,
AND FORKS FORWARD,
TWISTING BLADES
TO LOW PITCH

AIR PRESSURE
TO ASSIST
FEATHERING

CENTRIFUGAL FORCE
AERODYNAMIC FORCE
HYDRAULIC FORCE

Fig. 3-6. Featherable Pitch-Change Mechanism

CONSTANT-SPEED PROPELLER OPERATION

In addition to providing the optimum pitch angle for a wide range of airspeed and r.p.m. combinations, the pitch control itself directly affects engine horsepower. The horsepower developed by the engine depends on the internal engine pressures and on the engine r.p.m. Increasing the manifold absolute pressure (MAP), the r.p.m., or both, will increase the engine's horsepower output, as shown in figure 3-7.

An engine's maximum horsepower output is obtained at the *maximum* MAP and r.p.m. the engine can sustain at a given altitude, temperature, and airspeed. An engine's maximum horsepower output produces the maximum potential thrust, fastest airspeed, greatest

rate of climb, and maximum fuel consumption rate. Obtaining maximum thrust is critically important for takeoff and climb performance; therefore, the maximum permissible or obtainable MAP and r.p.m. are used during these periods. During climbs, when the climb performance is not critical, or during cruise, decreasing the horsepower output slightly may result in significant savings in fuel consumption and engine wear, without a large reduction in thrust or airspeed. The manner in which engine horsepower is best reduced varies from system to system; however, with a constant-speed propeller, decreasing the r.p.m., manifold pressure, or both may achieve the desired results.

Figure 3-8 compares the effects of a slight r.p.m. reduction on an airplane

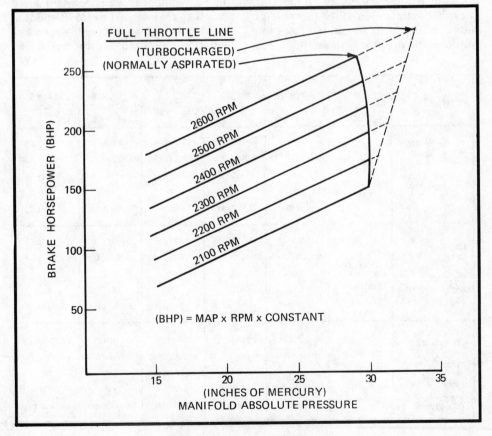

Fig. 3-7. R.P.M. Affects Horsepower

equipped with a fixed-pitch propeller, to the effects on a turbocharged, twin-engine airplane equipped with a constant-speed, three-bladed propeller.

The table applies to light, general aviation aircraft having engines in the 150 to 400 horsepower range. The data in the left-hand column indicates the amount of r.p.m. reduction. The second column shows that the manifold pressure of the engine with the fixed-pitch propeller is reduced, but not measured. The third column indicates this same propeller-engine combination has lost a significant amount of horsepower. The fourth column, under true airspeed, shows that the aircraft with a constant-speed propeller has experienced a minimal reduction in airspeed, while the airspeed of the aircraft with the fixed-pitch propeller has been reduced by nearly 10 percent. A careful examination of the fuel savings shown in the fifth column indicates the relationship of fuel consumption to

horsepower. Finally, columns six and seven indicate that the endurance and range of each aircraft has been increased significantly.

The eight percent reduction in r.p.m has caused a slight reduction in airspeed, but has greatly reduced fuel consumption, increased range, and immeasurably increased the engine's time between overhauls.

The pilot must exercise his good judgment in selecting the power and r.p.m. combination most suitable to his performance needs. Furthermore, he must observe the manufacturer's recommendations concerning engine operating procedures and limitations.

The general operating procedures for engines equipped with constant-speed propellers are intended to aid the pilot in keeping the engine within its operating limitations. For example, the engine may

PILOT REDUCES RPM	EFFECT ON MAP	EFFECT ON BHP	EFFECT ON TAS	EFFECT ON FUEL CONSUMPTION	EFFECT ON ENDURANCE	EFFECT ON RANGE
FIXED-PITCH PROPELLER 2,700 RPM REDUCED 7.5% TO 2,500 RPM	MAP IS REDUCED (AMOUNT NOT INDICATED)	123 BHP REDUCED BY 17% TO 102 BHP	134 KNOTS REDUCED BY 10% TO 121 KNOTS	9.0 GPH REDUCED BY 18% TO 7.4 GPH	5.3 HOURS INCREASED BY 21% TO 6.4 HOURS	710 MILES INCREASED BY 9.4% TO 776 MILES
CONSTANT-SPEED PROPELLER 2,500 RPM REDUCED 8.0% TO 2,300 RPM	22 IN. HG INCREASED 4.5% TO 23 IN. HG	188 BHP REDUCED BY 10.6% TO 168 BHP	167 KNOTS REDUCED BY 5% TO 159 KNOTS	15.2 GPH REDUCED BY 12% TO 13.4 GPH	5.2 HOURS INCREASED BY 12% TO 5.8 HOURS	870 MILES INCREASED BY 6% TO 922 MILES
THREE-BLADED CONSTANT-SPEED, TURBOCHARGED, TWIN ENGINE 1,950 RPM REDUCED 7.8% TO 1,800 RPM	32.IN. HG * MAINTAINED AT 32 IN. HG	276 BHP REDUCED BY 18% TO 226 BHP	220 KNOTS REDUCED BY 9% TO 200 KNOTS	47.5 GPH REDUCED BY 22% TO 38.5 GPH	6.0 HOURS INCREASED BY 23% TO 7.4 HOURS	1,320 MILES INCREASED 12% TO 1,480 MILES

*MAP maintained by turbocharger system

Fig. 3-8. Effects of Slight R.P.M. Reduction

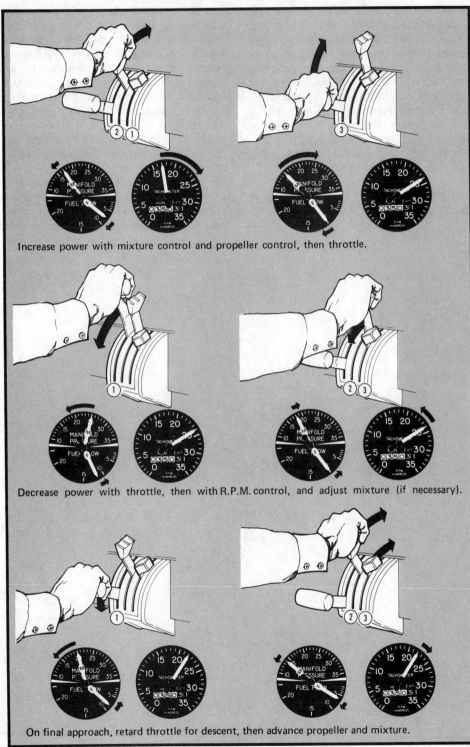

Increase power with mixture control and propeller control, then throttle.

Decrease power with throttle, then with R.P.M. control, and adjust mixture (if necessary).

On final approach, retard throttle for descent, then advance propeller and mixture.

Fig. 3-9. General Operating Procedures

be damaged by attempts to obtain a high manifold pressure at a low r.p.m. setting. Hence, when increasing the engine's horsepower output, the r.p.m. normally is increased first by using the propeller control. Then, the manifold pressure may be increased, using the throttle. When decreasing the engine power output, the manifold pressure should be reduced first, using the engine throttle. Then, the r.p.m. should be reduced, using the propeller control.

Operating procedures for certain engines may differ slightly, and the pilot must consult the appropriate flight manual. It also is possible to damage an engine by maintaining high r.p.m. at higher altitudes and airspeed when the manifold pressure is reduced to the low power setting. The internal pressures in an engine tend to absorb the shock at the end of a piston stroke, and the absence of those pressures at a high r.p.m. may be damaging. In flight, it is necessary to maintain both the manifold pressure and the r.p.m. within their respective operating ranges, as indicated by the green arc on the manifold pressure gauge and the tachometer. The procedures for operating an engine with a constant-speed propeller are summarized in figure 3-9.

SECTION B
FUEL INJECTION AND TURBOCHARGING

FUEL INJECTION SYSTEM

A high performance engine must be operated within a very narrow range of limitations. Controlling the amount of fuel and air entering the combustion chamber is one of the most critical factors in operating this type of engine. Extremes in fuel-air mixtures, pressures, and temperatures can greatly reduce an engine's performance, or even cause it to fail. Although float carburetion may be an adequate means of control in some cases, fuel injection provides a more accurate method of measuring and distributing the desired amount of fuel to each cylinder. The contribution of fuel injection to an engine's overall performance can be shown in terms of lower fuel consumption per unit of horsepower, increased horsepower per unit of weight, lower operating temperatures, longer engine life, and increased reliability.

DISADVANTAGES OF FLOAT CARBURETION

Disadvantages of the float carburetor and other similar fuel distribution systems result from the manner in which the fuel is *vaporized and distributed* to each cylinder. In an ideal engine, each cylinder should receive the same amount of fuel. Ideal fuel distribution is most difficult to achieve, however, when the fuel is mixed with the inflow of air at the carburetor. Some of the fuel sprayed from the discharge nozzle is not entirely vaporized and remains in the form of minute, liquid droplets of different sizes. Due to variations in the mass of the atomized droplets, the droplets flow *unevenly* around the bends and restrictions in the intake manifold. Subsequently, this causes an uneven distribution of droplets to the cylinders. After the atomized droplets have been unevenly divided between cylinders, they may or may not be vaporized before entering the combustion chamber; in either case,

each cylinder receives a slightly different total amount of fuel. These small differences can reduce an engine's power output at peak power settings.

Since engine power depends on gas expansion, the temperature of the vaporized fuel entering the combustion chamber is extremely important. The greatest engine power will result when the vaporized fuel temperature is low.

Vaporizing the fuel at the carburetor cools the intake air. The air is reheated as it passes through the induction system and past the valves, prior to entering the combustion chamber. Additionally, vaporizing the fuel at the carburetor increases susceptibility to carburetor ice.

An ideal solution to both detrimental aspects of vaporizing the fuel at a single, central carburetor might be to have an identical carburetor collocated with each cylinder's intake port. This solution is nearly obtained by fuel injection systems which vaporize the fuel at each discharge nozzle just prior to entering the combustion chamber.

FUEL INJECTION SYSTEM COMPONENTS

Fuel injection systems are found on most new engines. Since each aircraft may have slightly different operating procedures and characteristics, careful review of the appropriate flight manual is required prior to operating an unfamiliar system.

As shown in figure 3-10 the continuous flow fuel injection system has four basic components: an engine-driven fuel pump (item 1), fuel injector (fuel-air control) unit (item 2), fuel flow (distribution manifold) divider (item 3), and individual fuel discharge nozzles (item 4).

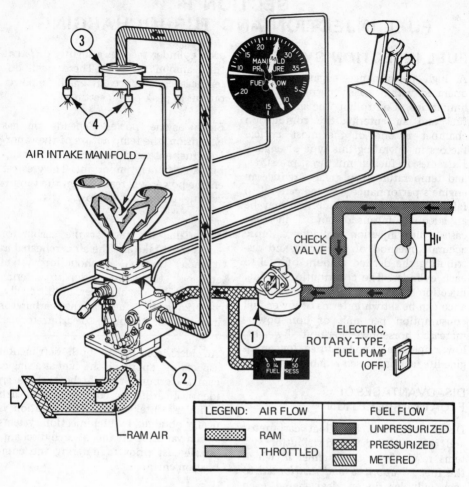

Fig. 3-10. Fuel Injection System

Fuel is delivered from the aircraft's tanks to the engine-driven fuel pump where the fuel is put under pressure.

The pressurized fuel is routed through the fuel injector unit where the fuel flow is metered by a set of valves according to the mixture setting and flow of air to the engine. Also, the intake airflow is throttled in the fuel injector unit. The metered fuel is then sent to the fuel flow divider where it is divided equally among the individual fuel lines that lead to each cylinder. The fuel lines carry the metered and divided fuel flow to the individual discharge nozzles where the fuel is readily atomized and then vaporized at the cylinder's intake port. If proper techniques are employed, operating a modern engine equipped with a fuel injection system is no more difficult for the pilot than operating an engine with a conventional float carburetor.

ENGINE-DRIVEN FUEL PUMP

The engine-driven fuel pump is the only constantly moving part in the continuous flow fuel injection system. This fuel pump is attached to the engine's accessory drive section. An electric fuel pump also is incorporated to provide fuel pressure for starting and to deal with possible failure of the engine-driven pump.

FUEL INJECTOR UNIT

The fuel injector unit is analogous to the carburetor in a conventional fuel-air induction system. The difference is that the fuel and air are not combined in the fuel injector unit. Instead, this unit regulates the air flowing through the air induction manifold and meters the correct amount of fuel required for the fuel injectors.

FUEL—FLOW DIVIDER

The fuel-flow divider, sometimes termed the fuel manifold, is designed to divide the fuel evenly between each of the cylinders. Valves are built into the flow divider which provide an automatic and positive fuel-shutoff mechanism when the mixture control is moved to idle--cutoff.

FUEL INJECTION NOZZLES

The fuel injection nozzles "inject" the metered fuel into the air induction manifold. This occurs in the cylinder head just outside the intake valves and ports leading to the combustion chambers. Thus, the fuel is mixed with the intake air just prior to entering the combustion chamber.

FUEL—FLOW INDICATOR

A fuel-flow indicator enables the pilot to monitor the operation of the system, as well as determine the extent to which the system may be "leaned." The fuel-flow indicator is actually a pressure gauge connected to the fuel manifold. The pressure gauge often is marked in both pounds per square inch and gallons or pounds of fuel flow per hour.

NORMAL STARTING PROCEDURES

Starting a fuel-injected engine is similar to starting a float-carbureted engine, except that the electric fuel pump is used to pressurize and prime the fuel injection system. The mixture control is placed in the *idle-cutoff* position. The propeller control is placed in the low pitch/high r.p.m. position, and the throttle is opened slightly. After the electric fuel pump is turned on, the mixture control is advanced until sufficient fuel flow is indicated by the fuel-flow indicator; normally, a flow *rate* of four to six gallons an hour is recommended. Then the pilot should return the mixture control to idle-cutoff. When these steps are accomplished, the engine is ready to start; once it fires, the mixture control is smoothly advanced toward the FULL RICH position.

DETONATION

Detonation is the *uncontrolled, explosive* combustion of fuel. The rate of burning is extremely rapid, producing excessive pressure and temperature within the engine. Detonation can cause the immediate failure of an engine by destroying a piston, valve, or part of the cylinder. Less severe detonation can cause overheating, loss of power, roughness, and reduced engine life.

The causes of detonation can be understood by first examining the normal combustion process, shown in figure 3-11. This figure depicts the inside of a cylinder, as seen through the top of the cylinder head during five phases of compression and combustion.

Normal combustion begins with the spark plugs igniting the fuel-air mixture as it is compressed in the cylinder (item 1). As the piston reaches the end of its compression stroke, two "flame fronts" are advancing evenly through the unburned fuel-air mixture toward the center of the cylinder (item 2). The fuel is burned in the area immediately behind the advancing flame front, as shown by the heavy black lines (item 3). The evenly burning fuel causes a smooth increase in temperature and pressure.

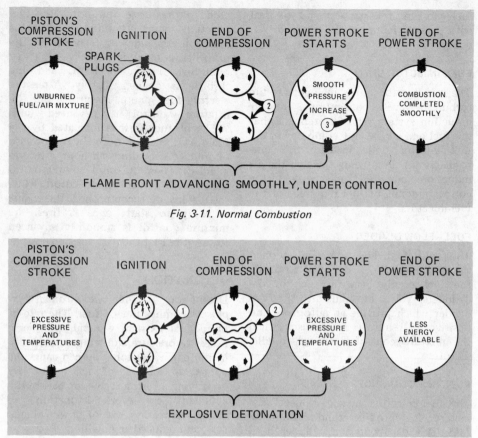

Fig. 3-11. Normal Combustion

Fig. 3-12. Detonation

This increasing pressure provides the engine with a controlled amount of energy during the piston's power stroke.

Detonation occurs when the fuel-air mixture is compressed at an abnormally high temperature and/or pressure. (See Fig. 3-12.) As this mixture is ignited by the spark plugs and the flame front begins to advance across the cylinder, the temperature and pressure within the area of the unburned fuel air mixture increases still further.

Eventually, the temperature and pressure become great enough to support explosive combustion and the fuel is ignited *spontaneously* (item 1). The resultant flame fronts advance erratically and rapidly (item 2), creating pressure increases which cause the engine to lose power. The pressure may build to such

an extreme that it is in excess of the engine's structural capacity.

Care must be taken to avoid the following common causes of detonation.

1. Takeoff with an overheated engine (this also should include other operations at more than 75 percent power)
2. Operations with an extremely high manifold pressure and extremely low r.p.m.
3. Operations over 75 percent power with extremely lean mixture

PREIGNITION

Preignition and detonation are interrelated in that preignition can cause detonation and detonation can cause preignition. Preignition is the *premature burning* of fuel, caused by a "residual hotspot." This hotspot can be a glowing piece of carbon deposit on a spark plug, as shown in figure 3-13 (item 1), or a cracked, ceramic spark plug insulator.

The rough edge of a valve, broken piston ring, cracked piston, or scored cylinder wall may become incandescent and cause preignition (item 2). By the time normal ignition occurs, a large quantity of the fuel-air mixture has already been consumed. The premature burning can easily lead to excessive pressures and temperatures; in turn, these can result in detonation (item 3).

EXHAUST GAS TEMPERATURE GAUGE

The exhaust gas temperature (EGT) gauge measures the exhaust temperature at a point just outside the combustion chamber. The EGT sensor is a thermocouple-type probe made of dissimilar metals that generate a minute electrical current when heated. This probe is sensitive to temperature changes and provides an accurate means of determining the relative combustion temperatures. Thus, by using the EGT gauge, the mixture control (fuel/air ratio) can be adjusted with great accuracy and efficiency.

MIXTURE LEANING

"Leaning" an engine to the proper fuel-air ratio for the current operating conditions can significantly increase the engine's performance. Leaning the engine too much can cause excessive

combustion temperatures, resulting in detonation and/or preignition. Operating the engine with an excessively rich mixture can cause spark plug fouling and power loss. To avoid this, it is imperative that high-performance engines be operated with a fuel-air ratio appropriate for the current operating conditions. General procedures for leaning the mixture are illustrated in figure 3-14. Since each engine type and model has slightly different characteristics, the numbers shown in this figure are representative averages for light aircraft engines.

Takeoff power requires a rich mixture to prevent detonation, as shown in figure 3-14 (item 1). Normally, the mixture control should be in the FULL RICH position prior to applying takeoff power. At density altitudes above 5,000 feet it may be necessary to lean the mixture slightly to achieve smooth engine operation.

Best fuel economy may be obtained at the peak EGT, or at slightly richer or leaner settings, depending on the engine (item 2). Most engines may *not* be safely leaned to peak EGT when the engine is developing more than 75 percent power. Hence, the power usually must be reduced to 75 percent or less *before* leaning to peak EGT.

Best cruise power usually is obtained with a mixture slightly richer than the mixture producing peak EGT and best fuel economy (item 3). It can not be emphasized too strongly that the engine

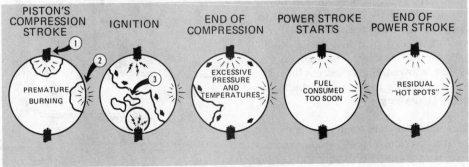

Fig. 3-13. Preignition

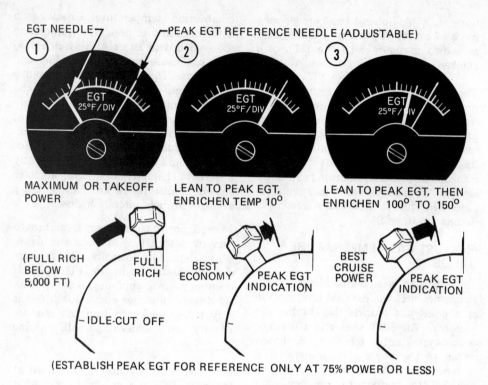

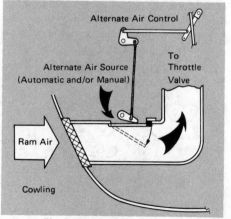

Fig. 3-14. Mixture Leaning Procedures

should be operated in accordance with the manufacturer's recommendations, and the professional pilot should make every effort to inform himself of the most current information regarding his equipment.

ALTERNATE AIR SOURCE

Fuel injection has the added advantage over float carburetion of being *less* susceptible to induction system icing. The refrigeration process in a carburetor is caused by both the cooling, due to a large pressure reduction in the throttle venturi, and by heat loss during the fuel vaporization process. The fuel injection system allows the greatest cooling effect at the cylinder head where icing is least likely to develop.

The induction air supply in a fuel injection system is filtered prior to entering the throttle and intake manifold. The familiar intake screen facing the airflow at the front of the cowling is a potential source of induction icing. To prevent engine failure due to an iced-over or unusually clogged intake filter, the induction air system of a fuel-injected engine must have an alternate air source, as shown in figure 3-15. The alternate air door may be

Fig. 3-15. Alternate Air Source

opened either manually or automatically, depending on the system's design.

TURBOCHARGING

Controlling the amount of atmospheric pressure in the induction system goes hand-in-hand with controlling fuel induction and vaporization. Unfortunately, atmospheric pressure varies from location to location and decreases with an increase in altitude. Any decrease in the intake MAP causes a decrease in engine power output. Pressurizing the air in the intake manifold as the aircraft climbs to altitude is one solution to the problem of power loss due to a decreasing MAP.

TURBOCHARGERS

The principles of turbocharger operation are surprisingly simple. The actual turbocharger is, however, a carefully designed, very sophisticated piece of machinery.

The compressor is driven by the exhaust turbine, which derives its energy from the engine's hot exhaust gases. The compressor receives ram air from the air inlet or alternate air source. This air is pressurized by centrifugal force as it is whirled around by the impeller vanes. The compressed air is then "collected" from the ring surrounding the impeller and directed into the fuel injector unit's throttle valve.

SYSTEM COMPONENTS

If the full force of the exhaust is used to drive the turbine at lower altitudes, the compressor will produce excessive pressure and a very high inlet air temperature. To avoid overboosting the manifold pressure, the compressor output is regulated by an exhaust bypass valve, as shown in figure 3-16, which controls the flow of exhaust gases acting on the drive turbine. Opening the exhaust bypass valve, often termed a "waste gate," allows the exhaust to bypass the turbine. The waste gate position is governed by a pressure-sensing control mechanism and a waste gate actuator.

OPERATING CHARACTERISTICS

The waste gate and its control mechanism are designed to maintain the

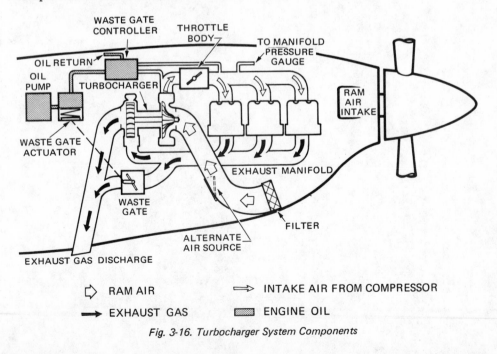

Fig. 3-16. Turbocharger System Components

compressor output at the desired constant pressure. As the airplane climbs, the waste gate closes gradually, forcing more engine exhaust gases to drive the turbine. The altitude at which the turbine is driven at its maximum rated speed is called the turbocharger's *critical altitude*. Although it may be possible on some aircraft for the compressor to maintain the maximum MAP to a higher altitude, the turbine on such aircraft would have to be driven at an excessive speed. Above the critical altitude, the throttle must be retarded and the MAP reduced to prevent the turbine from overspeeding.

SECTION C—LANDING GEAR SYSTEMS

RETRACTABLE LANDING GEAR

Retractable landing gear systems enable the pilot to achieve more efficient operations from his airplane. As the gear is retracted, the airflow around the aircraft is "cleaned up" and parasite drag is reduced. Under these conditions, the aircraft is capable of climbing at a greater rate and cruising at a higher speed without an increase in power. Additionally, the landing gear can be used as an airbrake during high rates of descent.

Gear retraction systems are classified according to the power source used for retraction and extension. Electrical and hydraulic actuating mechanisms are used most frequently.

ELECTRICAL SYSTEM

In the electrical landing gear system, a series of rods, levers, cables, and bellcranks may be utilized for extension and retraction. The source of energy required to operate this system is supplied by a reversible electric motor. Through a gear assembly, the electric motor turns a bellcrank operating the push-pull cables and tubes that extend and retract the landing gear.

For emergency operation, some systems utilize a handcrank for gear extension. When using the handcrank, the landing gear can be lowered, but should not be retracted.

HYDRAULIC SYSTEM

In the hydraulic landing gear system, the energy to extend and retract the landing gear is transmitted by hydraulic fluid through a series of valves, pipes, and actuators. When the gear lever is placed in the UP position, hydraulic fluid is channeled through the plumbing and into the actuators. The actuator cylinder retracts, pulling the gear up into the wheel wells. When the lever is placed in the DOWN position, the movement of the hydraulic fluid is reversed. Pressure is applied to the opposite end of the actuator, forcing the cylinder to extend. This, in turn, extends the landing gear.

The hydraulic systems installed in many large multi-engine aircraft utilize engine-driven pumps to supply hydraulic pressure. Hydraulic fluid is channeled through the gear selector valve to control the fluid for extension and retraction. For emergency gear operation a hand hydraulic pump, compressed carbon dioxide pressure, or a combination of both may be used.

ELECTRO-HYDRAULIC SYSTEM

The electro-hydraulic system utilizes a reversible electric motor to drive the hydraulic pump. In this system, the hydraulic plumbing is located between the pump and the actuating cylinders. The gear selector is an electrical switch that turns on the electric motor and controls its direction. A typical electro-hydraulic system used on many single-engine and light multi-engine aircraft is the basis of the following discussion. This system is illustrated in figure 3-17.

GENERAL DESCRIPTION

The main gear and nose gear operate in a similar manner, except for steering provisions of the nose gear and the pivoting action required during its retraction (item 1). The nosewheel is steerable through a linkage connected to the rudder pedals (item 2). A hydraulic damper on the nosewheel strut (item 3) compensates for any tendency of the wheel to shimmy. The main gear retracts into the wings, while the nose gear rotates 90° and retracts for storage in the lower part of the cowling. Each gear is held in the retracted position by hydraulic pressure, but the main gear has an additional hydraulically actuated uplock (item 4). Overcenter travel of the

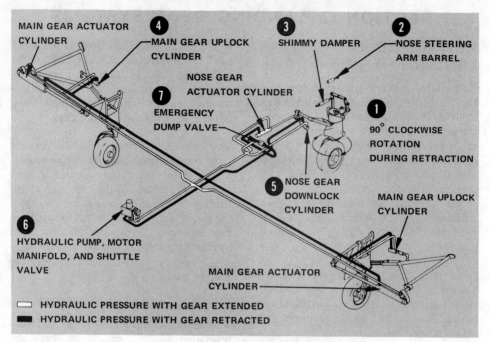

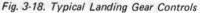

Fig. 3-17. Typical Landing Gear System

spring-held side brace, in conjunction with hydraulic pressure, locks the main gear down. The nose gear is locked down by overcenter travel of a draglink and a hydraulically actuated downlock (item 5). Pressure for the hydraulic system is supplied by a hydraulic pump (item 6), which is driven by a reversible electric motor. The pump motor is activated by the landing gear control switch. When hydraulic pressure is exerted in one direction, the gear is extended; when exerted in the other direction, the gear is retracted. A hydraulic pressure dump valve (item 7) is provided for emergency extension of the landing gear.

SYSTEM OPERATION

CONTROL SWITCH

The landing gear is controlled by a two-position switch, as illustrated in figure 3-18, item 1. The switch is operated by moving it upward to retract and downward to extend the gear. In this system, the switch handle must be lifted across a center detent when moving it from one position to the other.

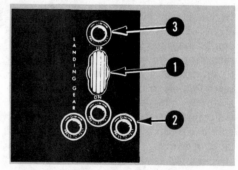

Fig. 3-18. Typical Landing Gear Controls

POSITION INDICATORS

The landing gear position indicator lights (item 2) are located just below the landing gear control switch. Three green lights, one for each gear, illuminate when the respective landing gear is down and locked. A red light above the landing gear control switch (item 3) illuminates whenever one or more of the landing gear are in transit or in any intermediate position. When all gears are up and locked, all the lights are off. Each of the lights has a press-to-test feature to verify that the bulbs are working.

SAFETY SWITCH

A mechanical switch on the landing gear strut breaks the electrical circuit to prevent inadvertent landing gear retraction while on the ground. The switch, which is actuated by strut compression, prevents activation of the hydraulic pump until the strut is fully extended.

WARNING HORN

A warning horn sounds continuously if the landing gear is in the retracted position when the throttle is retarded below 12 to 14 inches of manifold pressure. The switch which activates the warning horn is located on the throttle control linkage.

CIRCUIT BREAKERS

Circuit breakers are used to protect the landing gear circuitry. One usually protects the landing gear motor. Another protects the remainder of the circuitry, including the gear warning system.

AIRSPEED LIMITATIONS

During normal operations, the limiting airspeeds that apply to the landing gear should be observed. These speeds are listed in the pilot's operating handbook. The *maximum landing gear extended speed* is the maximum speed at which an aircraft can be flown safely with the landing gear extended. The *maximum landing gear operating speed* is the maximum speed for cycling the landing gear. In addition, many airplanes have a *maximum landing gear retraction speed*. This limitation is due to the additional operating loads placed on the retraction mechanism as it opposes gravitational and airstream forces on the landing gear.

GEAR SYSTEM MALFUNCTIONS

Landing gear position lights provide the primary means for determining whether the gear has extended or retracted properly. However, several flight characteristics may provide useful indications of a gear malfunction. When the gear extends, for example, the airspeed decreases and the pitch attitude may change slightly. Conversely, when the gear is retracted, the airspeed should accelerate to normal climb speed when using normal climb power. In cases where all of the gears do not extend, a change in flight control pressures is noticable because of induced yaw. Any one of these characteristics may indicate a gear malfunction.

If a gear light does not illuminate when the gear is selected DOWN and airspeed and pitch indicate that the gear has extended, the press-to-test feature on the position lights may reveal an inoperative lightbulb. When the gear does malfunction, all of the landing gear circuit breakers should be checked and reset. The electric gear motor may not be receiving power due to an overload, or a malfunction in the remaining circuitry may have caused a circuit breaker to trip.

EMERGENCY GEAR EXTENSION

An emergency gear extension feature also is provided. Since the landing gear is held up by hydraulic pressure, the only requirement for extension is to relieve the system pressure. A hydraulic pressure valve may be located under an access door near the pilot's seat. The access door is identified by a placard, such as the one shown in figure 3-19. An emergency gear extension checklist and a handle for opening the emergency dump valve to relieve the hydraulic pressure are provided inside the door. When the pressure is relieved, the gear free falls into the DOWN AND LOCKED position.

Prior to activating this valve, it is advisable to slow the aircraft, pull out the circuit breaker for the landing gear motor, and place the landing gear switch handle in the DOWN position. If the aircraft is not slowed, air pressure working against the weight of the gear may prevent it from freefalling into the DOWN AND LOCKED position.

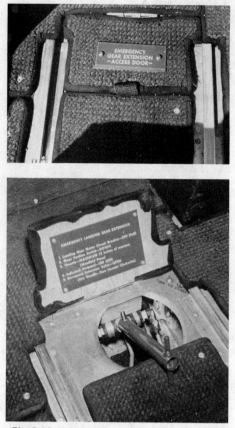

Fig. 3-19. Emergency Landing Gear Extension

If the hydraulic system fails in flight due to a hydraulic leak, electric motor failure, or other factor, emergency extension should be performed immediately. Otherwise, the gear may extend slowly as pressure is lost and fail to lock down as it does when freefalling.

OPERATIONS IN WATER AND SNOW

Cold weather operations in water, slush, or snow can be detrimental to proper operation of retractable landing gear systems. Moisture which is splashed onto gear linkages can freeze, resulting in a gear retraction malfunction. Additionally, if the temperature at ground level is above freezing and temperatures aloft are below freezing, the gear may retract normally, only to have the moisture freeze in flight and prevent gear extension.

Several preventive measures are available to the pilot to prevent gear malfunctions caused by freezing moisture.

1. If water, slush, or snow is present on the ramp area, the airplane should be taxied at a slow speed to prevent splashing the moisture onto the gear mechanism.

2. Isolated areas of water, slush, or snow should be avoided.

3. If moisture is unavoidable, the landing gear can be cycled several times after takeoff to prevent a solid bond of ice from adhering to movable gear parts.

4. If gear retraction is prevented by ice formation, the pilot should return for a landing and have the airplane heated to melt the ice and dry the landing gear mechanism.

chapter 4

RADIO NAVIGATION SYSTEMS

INTRODUCTION

In order to fully utilize national airspace, the advanced pilot must possess a thorough understanding of radio navigation systems. To develop an operational orientation in this subject, the pilot must not only learn the tracking procedures of radio navigation, but must become familiar with the respective ground and airborne components. Advanced radio navigation, principles of radar, and operation of the transponder are discussed in this chapter.

SECTION A—VOR NAVIGATION AND DME

VOR NAVIGATION

The federal airway system is based primarily upon the very high frequency omnidirectional range (VOR). This extensive system consists of several hundred ground stations that transmit navigation course guidance signals utilized by aircraft in flight.

ADVANTAGES OF VOR NAVIGATION

The VOR navigational system has many advantages for the IFR and VFR pilot.

1. *Freedom from interference* — The VOR transmits in the very high frequency range of 108.00 through 117.95 megaHertz (MHz) and is relatively free from precipitation static and annoying interferences, which are caused by storms or other weather phenomena.

2. *Extreme accuracy* — A course accuracy of plus or minus one degree is possible when flying the VOR.

3. *Automatic wind correction* — Wind drift is compensated for automatically by flying with the course deviation indicator.

VOR signals are transmitted on an approximate line-of-sight basis. Any obstacles (mountains, buildings, or terrain features, including the curvature of the earth) block VOR signals and restrict the distance from which they can be received at a given altitude. Certain terrain features may produce areas where VOR navigation signals are unusable. These abnormalities are published in the *Airport/Facility Directory* under the individual VOR listing.

CLASSES OF VOR FACILITIES
TERMINAL VOR

The lowest usable classification of the VOR is the terminal VOR (TVOR). The operational requirements of this facility are such that it normally should not be used more than 25 nautical miles from the station or over 12,000 feet mean sea level. Terminal VORs are used primarily as approach navigation aids for airports and are not used as part of the VOR enroute structure.

LOW ALTITUDE VOR

The low altitude VOR (LVOR) may be used reliably at 40 nautical miles below 18,000 feet. This altitude is the highest altitude at which stations with identical frequencies will not interfere with each other.

HIGH ALTITUDE VOR

High altitude VORs (HVORs) are frequency protected to 100 nautical miles below 18,000 feet within the conterminous United States. Above 18,000 feet, they are protected to 130 miles.

VOR COMPONENTS

Figure 4-1 displays those components that make up the aircraft VOR equipment. These components function together to present the pilot with the display information necessary for accurate navigation.

Fig. 4-1. VOR Components

VOR RECEIVER

In many modern aircraft, the *VOR receiver* is built into the same case with the VHF communications transceiver. When collocated, the radio is called a nav/com or a one and one-half radio. The radio in figure 4-1 is the nav/com type.

VOR signals are received by an antenna that normally is located on a vertical stabilizer or on top of the fuselage. This antenna appears to be a "V" that is lying in a horizontal plane. The signals from the antenna are converted by the VOR receiver into the indications that are displayed on the navigation indicator.

NAVIGATION INDICATOR

The VOR *navigation indicator* presents aircraft position information to the pilot. The indicator has three functional components to perform this job — the course selector, the TO/FROM flag, and the course deviation indicator.

The *course selector*, sometimes called *omnibearing selector* or OBS, rotates the azimuth ring which displays the VOR course selected. This ring may also show the reciprocal of the selected course.

The TO/FROM flag indicates whether the course selected will take the pilot to or from the station. If the aircraft is out of station range and cannot receive a reliable, usable signal, the TO/FROM indicator will display OFF. Also, the OFF flag will be displayed when the aircraft is directly over the station or abeam the station; that is, when crossing a radial which is plus or minus 90° of the course selector setting.

When the aircraft heading is in general agreement with the course selector, the *course deviation indicator* (CDI) shows the pilot the position relative to the course selected and indicates whether the radial is to the right or left. The CDI needle has a 10° spread from center to either side when receiving a VOR signal. Figure 4-2 shows that an aircraft five

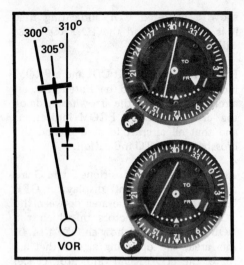

Fig. 4-2. CDI Deflections

degrees off course will have the CDI deflected one-half of the way from center to the outside edge. If the aircraft is 10° off course, the needle will be completely to one side. Each dot on the navigation indicator represents two degrees when navigating by VOR.

VOR ORIENTATION AND NAVIGATION

To effectively use the vast network of federal airways, the pilot must be thoroughly familiar with VOR navigation. Additionally, the pilot must have an understanding of VOR orientation.

COURSE ARROW

Each time a course is selected with the course selector, the area around the VOR station is divided into two halves. It is helpful to think of the dividing line between the two halves or envelopes as a course arrow. The course arrow passes through the station and points in the direction of the selected course. Figure 4-3 shows the divisions or segments around a VOR station.

Once a course is selected, the CDI shows the pilot in which of these two "envelopes" he is located. If the aircraft is located along the course line, the indicator will have a centered CDI needle, as

shown by the indicator on the course arrow in figure 4-3. If the aircraft is located at position A, the VOR indicator will display a right CDI indication. Any aircraft on the same side of the course arrow as position A will have a right CDI indication.

The CDI will not move to the other side of the indicator until the aircraft crosses the course arrow. If an aircraft moves from position A to position B, the indications on the CDI will be the same as B.

Whenever the pilot changes the course selector, he should visualize an imaginary course arrow placed over the station. In this way, the pilot can look at his CDI and tell in which envelope the aircraft is located.

CROSSBAR

Selecting a course also establishes the position of another line—the crossbar—which runs perpendicular to the course arrow at the station. The crossbar divides the VOR reception area into two additional envelopes. The area forward of the crossbar is the FROM envelope, and the area aft of the crossbar is the TO envelope. The TO/FROM indicator shows in which envelope the aircraft is located. As shown in figure 4-4 both aircraft on the arrowhead side of the

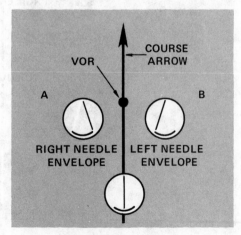

Fig. 4-3. Course Envelopes

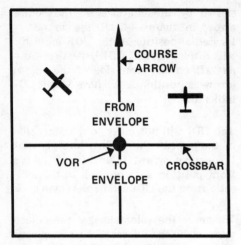

Fig. 4-4. Course Crossbar

show a centered CDI, indicating that it is on course, and the TO/FROM flag will show FROM.

Position B shows a left CDI and a FROM indication. It should be noted that all aircraft located on the arrowhead side of the crossbar have a FROM indication, and that all aircraft located behind the crossbar have a TO indication.

Aircraft located at positions C and G are over the crossbar and display an OFF indication. This is the area between the TO and FROM sectors in which the VOR indicator will show an OFF flag. In this area, the opposing signals that actuate the TO/FROM indicator cancel each other and produce an OFF indication. A movement across the transition area is indicated by the TO/FROM flag changing from a positive TO or FROM indication to OFF and then to the opposite indication. The farther the air-

course arrow will display a FROM indication on the TO/FROM indicator.

Figure 4-5 shows CDI indications in eight different locations around the VOR station. In position A, the aircraft will

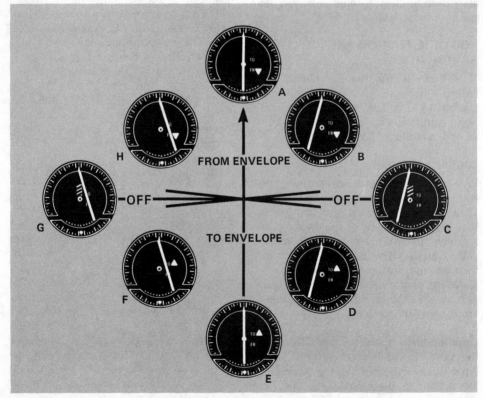

Fig. 4-5. VOR Indications

craft is from the VOR, the longer the OFF flag will be displayed during the TO/FROM transition.

BRACKETING A VOR RADIAL

The method used to intercept and maintain a predetermined radial is called *bracketing.* When no crosswind is present, bracketing consists simply of intercepting a VOR radial, turning the aircraft to a heading identical to the course set on the VOR course selector, and maintaining that heading. A crosswind component complicates the procedure, requiring the pilot to make a series of slight corrections to reintercept the selected radial. Drift information gained from this procedure is used to determine the heading required to hold the desired radial.

In figure 4-6, the pilot wishes to track inbound to the VOR station on the 165° radial. In this case, the inbound *course* is 345°, or the reciprocal of 165°. This is also the aircraft's *heading* when it is established inbound along the radial under no-wind conditions.

If the pilot tunes his VOR receiver to the station and sets 345° in the course selector, he will note a full needle deflection to the right, as shown in item 1. At this time he should take up an intercept heading 30° to the right of the inbound course.

When the course needle moves away from full deflection and begins to work its way towards the center position, as in item 2, the pilot should judge the rate of needle movement, For example, if it appears too rapid, there is a possibility of overshooting the desired radial. In this case, the pilot should consider reducing his intercept angle.

Item 3 depicts the ideal situation. At the moment of interception, the aircraft is aligned on a magnetic heading which equals the magnetic course inbound. This heading should be held while the pilot monitors the course needle for any left/right movement indicating the presence of a crosswind. If the indicator begins a progressive movement to the left, the aircraft is drifting to the right, as shown in item 4, and correction is needed in the direction of needle movement. At this time, a value judgment must be made concerning the amount of correction needed. (This is largely a matter of experience.)

In item 5, the pilot has chosen to correct 20° to the left of the inbound course. The new heading is 325°. Again, the pilot maintains this heading while monitoring course needle movement. If this new heading results in a needle movement toward center, it is maintained until centering occurs, as in item 6. At this time, the pilot should realize that returning to a heading which equals the inbound magnetic course of 345° will cause the aircraft to drift back to the right of the desired radial, and that a heading of 325° will take the aircraft left of the radial. Therefore, the magnetic heading required to hold the desired course is somewhere between these two values. By narrowing down this information, an experimental heading of 335° is established in item 7. This heading results in the aircraft deviating slightly left of course as shown in item 8. This narrowing process continues in item 9. Through use of the slight, definite heading adjustments dictated by the results of earlier corrections, a final heading eventually will be found which produces exactly the amount of wind correction necessary to track along the desired radial. Item 10 illustrates this desired end result.

Corrections made to reintercept the inbound course when wind changes occur should be made following this same procedure. Drift should be determined and the intercept heading estimated. Then, that heading should be held, its effect noted, and the drift information used for further correction, if needed.

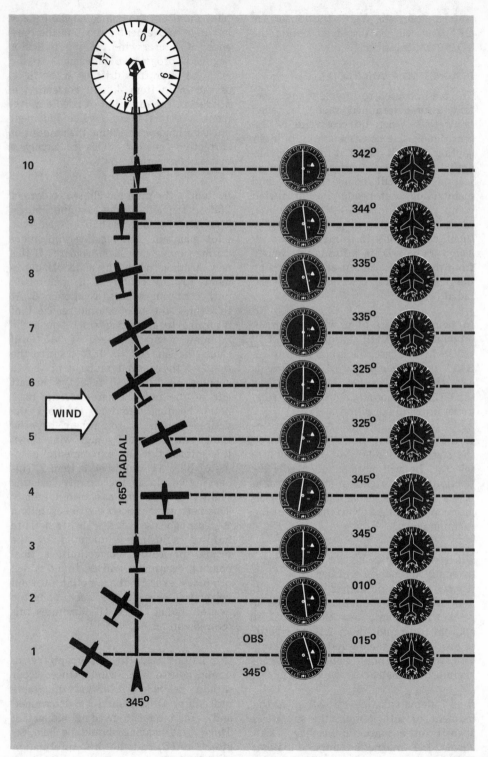

Fig. 4-6. Bracketing a VOR Radial

TRACK TO THE STATION

The most common use of VOR navigation is tracking a radial from station to station. The pilot sets the course on the course selector and tracks that course by keeping the CDI needle centered.

When the course selector is in general agreement with the heading indicator, the CDI will always point toward the selected course. For example, if the course is to the right, the indicator will point to the right and the pilot must turn in this direction to intercept the course.

It is important that the heading indicator be checked against the magnetic compass at the beginning of tracking. The VOR indicator only tells the pilot the position of his aircraft along a certain radial, which means he must rely on his heading indicator for aircraft heading information.

As the aircraft passes the VOR station, the pilot has two basic indications of station passage. The most positive indication is that the TO/FROM indicator changes to the opposite reading. The second indication, although not as positive, is the fluctuation of the CDI. If the aircraft passes directly over the station, the needle will fluctuate from side to side and return to its original position. If the aircraft is left of course, the needle will not fluctuate, but will continue to point to the right. Similarly, if the aircraft is right of course, the needle will point to the left and not fluctuate as the pilot passes abeam the station.

AIRCRAFT HEADING

Figure 4-7 shows that aircraft heading has absolutely no effect on the VOR indication. Regardless of which direction the aircraft is heading, the pilot will receive the same indication, provided he remains in the same course envelope. This is because the course arrow and crossbar divide the area surrounding the VOR into envelopes or sectors. These

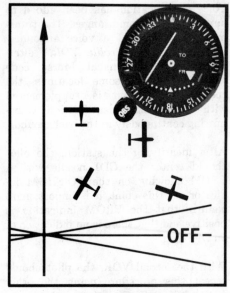

Fig. 4-7. Effect of Heading on VOR Indications

sectors are based upon the magnetic course that is indicated on the course selector and not the aircraft heading.

DETERMINING POSITION

Since the VOR gives only direction, not distance, from the VOR station, the pilot must use two stations to obtain a positive fix. By the use of a cross-check with two VOR facilities, the pilot can pinpoint his location.

The pilot desiring to make a position fix should tune his number one VOR to one of the desired stations and make positive identification. The only positive method of identifying a VOR is by its Morse code identification or by the recorded, automatic voice identification which is always indicated by use of the word "VOR" following the name. The identification of an omnirange should never be determined solely by listening to voice transmissions of the flight service station or approach control facility involved. If a VOR station is shut down for maintenance or the signal is unreliable because of a malfunction, the identification is turned off.

Voice identification has been added to numerous VHF omniranges. The transmission consists of a voice announcement, such as *"Airville VOR,"* alternating with the usual Morse code identification. At some locations, the coded identification is supplemented with VOR voice identification transmitting continuously in the background.

After identifying the station, the pilot should center the CDI needle with a FROM showing on the TO/FROM indicator. At this point, it is important to confirm that the FROM indication is positive and that there is no indication of an OFF flag.

With the second VOR, the pilot should repeat this procedure using the other VOR station. Then, using a chart, the pilot can draw a line outbound from the VORs using the radials indicated by the course selectors. The intersection of these radials will be the aircraft's position.

VOR ACCURACY

Federal Aviation Regulation 91.25 and good judgment dictate that the VOR equipment of aircraft flying under instrument flight rules be within specified tolerances. Airborne VOR equipment to be used on an IFR flight must be either maintained, checked, and inspected under an approved procedure, or it must be operationally checked within 30 days preceding the flight.

Although the regulations do not state who must make this operational check, normally it is performed by the pilot in command. An entry must then be made in the aircraft log or other reliable record. The entry must show the date, location, bearing error, and the signature of the person who completed the operational check. A pilot preparing for an IFR flight should check the aircraft records to ensure that VOR equipment meets both the accuracy and currency requirements.

The Federal Aviation Administration has approved several different methods for checking the accuracy of VOR equipment in an aircraft. These checking methods, found in FAR 91.25 and also in the AIM, are explained in this section. The methods for performing the checks are listed in their order of preference. The dual VOR check, although listed last, may be substituted for the other checks. The maximum permissible bearing error for each of the checks is shown in the table.

VOR TEST FACILITY

The first method is to use a VOR test facility signal (VOT). This is an approved test signal located on an airport which provides the pilot with a convenient and accurate means to determine the status of the VOR receivers.

The pilot should tune the VOR receiver to the VOT frequency. These frequencies are coded with a series of Morse code dots or a continuous 1,020-cycle tone. With the course selector set to zero degrees, the course deviation indicator (CDI) should center and the TO/FROM indication should be FROM. Conversely, when 180° is used, the TO/FROM indication reading will be TO and the CDI, again, should be centered. The exact error in a particular receiver can be determined by turning the course selector until the CDI is centered and then noting the degrees difference between 180° or 0°. The maximum permissible bearing error with this system check is plus or minus four degrees.

MAX. ERROR	TYPE OF CHECK
Ground ± 4°	1. VOT 2. Designated VOR System Checkpoint on Airport Surface
Flight ± 6°	3. Designated Airborne VOR Checkpoint 4. Made-up Check
Ground and Flight 4°	5. Dual VORs, both tuned to same VOR

VOT facilities are listed in a separate section in the back of the *Airport/Facility Directory*. Since the VOT signal is a special test signal only, it may be received and used regardless of the aircraft's position on the airport.

GROUND CHECKPOINT

On certain airports, the aircraft can be taxied to a point on the airport surface designated as a VOR system checkpoint. This system uses a VOR radial from a station that is located on or in close proximity to the airport. The maximum permissible bearing error is plus or minus four degrees. Designated VOR checkpoints are listed in the same section as the VOT facilities in the *Airport/Facility Directory*.

AIRBORNE CHECKPOINT

If neither a test signal nor a designated checkpoint on the surface is available, the pilot can use an airborne checkpoint designated by the FAA. These checkpoints, also listed in the Directory, are geographic locations in the immediate vicinity of the airport. The maximum permissible bearing error is plus or minus six degrees using a designated airborne check.

AIRWAY CHECKPOINT

If a designated checkpoint is not available, the pilot may use the following steps to check the VOR receiver while in flight.

1. Select a VOR radial that lies along the centerline of an established VOR airway.
2. Along this route, select a prominent ground point on the radial, preferably more than 20 miles from the VOR facility.
3. Maneuver the aircraft directly over the point at a reasonably low altitude and note the VOR bearing indicated by the receiver. The maximum permissible variation between the published radial and the indicated bearing is six degrees.

4. This check must be performed along an airway. The United States airway system is tested to plus or minus one degree and guarantees accuracy of the VOR.

DUAL VOR CHECK

If dual VOR systems, independent of each other except for the antenna, are installed in the aircraft, the person checking the equipment may check one system against the other. The pilot should tune both VORs to the same VOR facility and note the indicated bearings to that station. The maximum permissible variation between the two indicated bearings is four degrees.

DISTANCE MEASURING EQUIPMENT

Distance measuring equipment (DME) consists of ground equipment, usually installed at a VORTAC station, and the airborne equipment installed in the aircraft. The DME provides distance and groundspeed information only from a VORTAC, VOR/DME, or TACAN ground facility.

The DME in use by the general aviation pilot utilizes the UHF distance signal that is provided by TACAN. For convenience of operation, the FAA has placed most TACAN stations on VOR sites. Since there are paired frequencies in use between VORs and TACANs, the pilot using a DME need only tune the radio to the VHF frequency listed for the VORTAC station.

IDENTIFICATION FEATURE

VORTAC and VOR/DME facilities are identified by synchronized identifications which are transmitted on a time-share basis. The DME or TACAN coded identification is transmitted one time for each three or four times the VOR coded identification is transmitted. However, the DME identification is heard through the DME receiver, not the VOR receiver.

Where VOR code and voice identification are used, the DME or TACAN code identification is transmitted once for each three times the VOR identification is transmitted. At some VORTAC facilities, the VOR and DME coded identification is supplemented with VOR voice identification transmitting continuously in the background. When either the VOR or the DME is inoperative, it is important to recognize which identifier is retained for the operative facility. A single coded identification transmitting approximately every 30 seconds indicates that only the DME is operative. The absence of the single coded identification every 30 seconds indicates only the VOR is operative.

ACCURACY

The DME operates in the ultrahigh frequency (UHF) band and, therefore, is subject to the characteristic line-of-sight limitation. With adequate altitude, the DME signals may be reliably received at distances up to 199 nautical miles with an error of less than one-half mile or three percent of the distance, whichever is greater.

DME THEORY

The DME operates by transmitting to, and receiving paired pulses from, the VORTAC or VOR/DME station. The DME transmitter in the aircraft sends out very narrow pulses at a frequency of about 1,000 MHz. These signals are picked up by a receiver at the VORTAC station and trigger a reply transmission on a different frequency.

The reply pulses from the VORTAC station are then received by timing circuits in the aircraft's receiver, which measure the elapsed time between transmission and reception. Electronic circuits within the radio convert this measurement to electrical signals which operate the distance and groundspeed indicators.

DME COMPONENTS

The transceiver that sends out the interrogating signal to the VORTAC station incorporates an internal computer to measure the time interval that has passed. The antenna that the DME uses for both transmission and reception is a very small shark's fin antenna that normally is mounted on the underside of the aircraft. A typical transceiver and UHF antenna are shown in figure 4-8.

Fig. 4-8. Distance Measuring Equipment

The DME displays information in the form of distance to the station and the aircraft's groundspeed. Most DME radios have this display information on the face of the radio. It must be noted that the distance to the station is read as a slant range in nautical miles. The DME measures distance to the station as a direct line, without regard to aircraft altitude. If an aircraft is directly over the DME station at 6,076 feet AGL, the distance indicator will read one mile.

The DME gives a groundspeed readout in knots when the pilot turns the function control knob to groundspeed. The groundspeed displayed is accurate only if the aircraft is flying directly to or from the station. Since the DME measures groundspeed by comparing the time lapse between a series of pulses, flight in any direction other than directly to or away from the station will give an unreliable reading.

HORIZONTAL SITUATION INDICATOR

The advantages of a horizontal situation indicator (HSI) are resulting in greater utilization of this unique navigation instrument. The HSI combines a heading indicator and a VOR indicator in one display, resulting in a simplified navigation situation for the pilot. The HSI also presents localizer/glide slope information.

The horizontal situation indicator is illustrated in figure 4-9. The HSI features a *compass card* (item 1) which is slaved to a remotely mounted magnetic compass and a *lubber line* or *index* (item 2) that functions as the aircraft heading indicator. The *green heading select bug* (item 3) is controlled by the *heading select* knob (item 9). When the heading select bug is moved, using the autopilot HDG mode, the aircraft will turn automatically to the new heading.

The *course arrow* (item 4) is controlled by the *course select knob* (item 11) and is used to select the VOR or inbound localizer course, which in this case is 010°. The *lateral deviation needle* (item 5) functions like a CDI and senses the aircraft position with respect to the selected course. When the aircraft is on course, the needle is aligned with the course arrow. Off-course position is reflected by the *lateral deviation scale* (item 6). The scale is marked with a center circle, three dots, and a line on each of side of center; each mark signifies two degrees in the VOR mode and one-half of a degree in the localizer mode.

Travel to or from the VOR is shown on the *ambiguity indicator* (item 7). The *symbolic aircraft* (item 8) represents the position of the aircraft with respect to the navigation situation. The *reciprocal course pointer* (item 10) is attached to the course arrow and is also controlled by the course selector knob (item 11). The *glide slope pointer* (item 12) indicates the aircraft's position on the glide slope. For example, when the pointer is above the center position, the aircraft is below the glide slope, and vice versa.

The HSI incorporates three off flags to alert the pilot to unreliable signals or equipment malfunctions. Both the navigation (NAV) flag and the heading (HDG) flag are red in color; when displayed, they appear over the azimuth of the compass card on the upper portion of the instrument. The glide slope (GS OFF) flag, which is black and white, is displayed on the left side of the instrument.

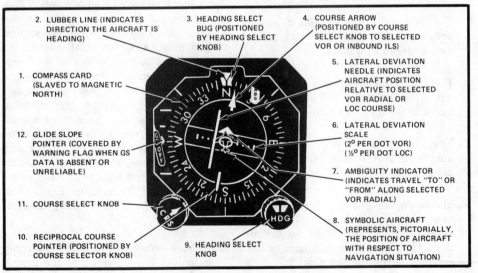

Fig. 4-9. Horizontal Situation Indicator

2. LUBBER LINE (INDICATES DIRECTION THE AIRCRAFT IS HEADING)

3. HEADING SELECT BUG (POSITIONED BY HEADING SELECT KNOB)

4. COURSE ARROW (POSITIONED BY COURSE SELECT KNOB TO SELECTED VOR OR INBOUND ILS)

1. COMPASS CARD (SLAVED TO MAGNETIC NORTH)

5. LATERAL DEVIATION NEEDLE (INDICATES AIRCRAFT POSITION RELATIVE TO SELECTED VOR RADIAL OR LOC COURSE)

12. GLIDE SLOPE POINTER (COVERED BY WARNING FLAG WHEN GS DATA IS ABSENT OR UNRELIABLE)

6. LATERAL DEVIATION SCALE (2° PER DOT VOR) (½° PER DOT LOC)

7. AMBIGUITY INDICATOR (INDICATES TRAVEL "TO" OR "FROM" ALONG SELECTED VOR RADIAL)

11. COURSE SELECT KNOB

10. RECIPROCAL COURSE POINTER (POSITIONED BY COURSE SELECTOR KNOB)

9. HEADING SELECT KNOB

8. SYMBOLIC AIRCRAFT (REPRESENTS, PICTORIALLY, THE POSITION OF AIRCRAFT WITH RESPECT TO NAVIGATION SITUATION)

SECTION B—ADF AND AREA NAVIGATION

AUTOMATIC DIRECTION FINDER

One of the older types of radio navigation is the automatic direction finder (ADF). The ADF receiver provides a "backup" navigation system for VHF equipment and can be used when line-of-sight transmission becomes unreliable. ADF is used as a means of identifying positions, receiving low and medium frequency voice communications, homing, and tracking.

NONDIRECTIONAL BEACON

The facilities used by the ADF are the low/medium frequency navigation stations. These facilities include nondirectional beacons, compass locators, and commercial broadcast stations. Since commercial broadcast stations normally are not used in navigation, this section will discuss only the nondirectional beacon and compass locator.

Nondirectional radio beacons, according to their power output and usage, include three types of radio beacons and the compass locator.

1. The MH radio beacon has a power output of less than 50 watts and a usable range of 25 miles.

2. The H classification has a power output of 50 through 1,999 watts, with a usable range up to 50 miles.

3. The HH radio beacon has a power output of 2,000 watts or more and a usable range of 75 miles.

4. The compass locator is collocated with the outer marker (LOM) or middle marker (LMM) of an instrument landing system. It normally has a power output of less than 25 watts and a usable range of 15 miles.

ADF CHARACTERISTICS

BENEFITS

NDBs are used to provide homing and navigational facilities in terminal areas. The ADF system offers two distinct benefits — economical cost of installation and relatively low maintenance. Also, the installation of NDBs has enabled smaller airports to utilize an instrument approach which otherwise would not be economically feasible.

The NDB transmits a low frequency signal, which is in the range of 200 to 415 kHz. This signal is not transmitted on a line of sight as with VHF or UHF; rather, it follows the curvature of the earth, providing reception at low altitudes over great distances. In Alaska, Canada, and certain other countries, the ADF is used for enroute navigation over long distances.

LIMITATIONS

To obtain maximum utilization from the ADF, the pilot should familiarize himself with the following L/M frequency characteristics and limitations.

1. *Twilight effect* — Radio waves reflected by the ionosphere return to the earth 30 to 60 miles from the station and may cause the ADF pointer to fluctuate. Twilight effect is *most pronounced* during the period just before and just after sunrise and sunset. Generally, the greater the distance from the station, the greater the effect. This effect can be *minimized* by averaging the fluctuation, flying at a higher altitude, or selecting a station with a lower frequency. NDB transmissions on frequencies lower than 350 kHz have very little twilight effect.

2. *Terrain effect* — Mountains or other sharply rising portions of the earth's surface have the ability to reflect

radio waves and may have magnetic deposits which can cause indefinite indications. Only strong stations that give definite directional indications should be used.

3. *Shoreline effect* — Shorelines have the ability to refract (bend) low frequency radio waves. The direction of these radio waves may change as they pass from land to water. However, radio waves passing from land to water at an angle greater than 30° will have little or no shoreline effect. Therefore, if the pilot is using a land-based NDB while over water, he should select a bearing which crosses the shoreline at an angle greater than 30°, as shown in figure 4-10.

4. *Thunderstorm effect* — In close proximity to electrical storms, the ADF needle will point to the source of lightning flashes, rather than to the station being used. Since this electrical activity sends out radio waves which are received by the ADF, the pilot should note the flashes of lightning and not use the resulting ADF indications.

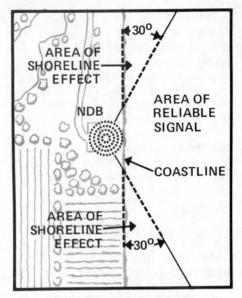

Fig. 4-10. Shoreline Effect

ADF COMPONENTS

The major ADF components are illustrated in figure 4-11. The only component not shown is the sense antenna which, on most light aircraft, is a thin wire running from an insulator on top of the cabin to the vertical stabilizer.

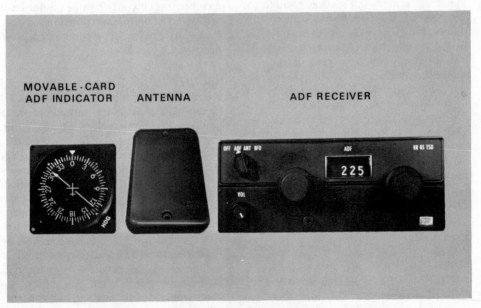

Fig. 4-11. ADF Components

RECEIVER

Controls on the ADF receiver permit the pilot to tune the desired station and select the *mode* of operation. When the pilot tunes the receiver, he must identify the station positively. This is accomplished by continuous Morse code identifiers, *except* during voice communications. All radio beacons transmit a three-letter identification in Morse code, except the compass locator which transmits a continuous two-letter identifier.

ANTENNAS

The ADF receives signals on both the loop and sense antennas. The loop antenna, which is used most often, is a small, flat antenna without moving parts. Within the antenna are several coils spaced at various angles. The loop antenna senses the direction of the station from the antenna by the strength of the signal on each coil. The sense antenna corrects for the inability of the loop to determine whether the bearing *is to or from the station*. The sense antenna also is used for voice reception.

BEARING INDICATOR

The direction of the station relative to the nose of the aircraft is displayed by the bearing indicator. If the aircraft is flown directly to the station, the bearing indicator will point to zero degrees. It should be emphasized that an ADF with a fixed-card bearing indicator will always represent the nose of the aircraft as zero degrees and the tail of the aircraft as 180°. In the following discussion, it is assumed the bearing indicator has a fixed card. Movable-card ADF indicators are discussed later in this section.

TUNING THE ADF

To tune the ADF, the following steps should be used.

1. Place the function knob at the ANT (RECEIVE) mode. This turns the set to the mode that provides the best reception. The ANT mode is used for tuning the ADF and for continuous listening when the ADF function is not required.

2. Select the desired frequency band and adjust the volume until background noise is heard.

3. Tune the desired frequency with the tuning controls, then readjust volume for the best listening level and identify the station.

4. To operate the radio as an automatic direction finder, switch the function knob to ADF.

5. Read the bearing to the station in relation to the nose of the aircraft from the pointer on the bearing indicator.

To test for reliable bearing indication the ANT function is selected. The ADF needle will then move 90° away from the original position. After the pointer reaches 90° from the original bearing, the function selector should be moved back to ADF. The needle should move rapidly to the *original homing position* and remain steady if the station is being received reliably. If the needle does not return to the homing position or continues to "hunt," inadequate reception or tuning is indicated.

The BFO mode is used for tuning and identification of continuous wave (CW) signals. CW signals are unmodulated, as compared to normal NDB signals. Within the conterminous United States, the BFO system usually is not required for station identification. However, in many countries where CW stations are used, the BFO is useful for station tuning and identification at long range. During tuning using the BFO function, maximum signal reception is determined by the strength of the audio tone; that is, a maximum signal provides the strongest audio reception. After the station has been tuned and identified, the function selector is returned to the ADF mode.

DEFINITIONS

The fixed-card bearing pointer measures, in a clockwise direction, the number of degrees between the nose of the aircraft and the station. This measurement is termed *relative bearing*, as shown in figure 4-12, item 1.

A magnetic bearing to the station is obtained by *adding the relative bearing shown on the indicator to the magnetic heading of the aircraft.* For example, if the magnetic heading of the aircraft is 40° and the relative bearing is 210°, the magnetic bearing to the station will be 250°. The magnetic bearing illustrated in figure 4-12, item 2, is the angle formed by the intersection of a line drawn from the aircraft to the radio station and a line drawn from the aircraft to magnetic north.

For position orientation, it is advantageous to know the aircraft's location from the NDB. This can be determined by computing the reciprocal of the bearing to the station. Figure 4-12, item 3, illustrates that a reciprocal bearing is obtained by adding or subtracting 180° from the magnetic bearing. If the bearing is less than 180°, a pilot will find the easiest way to do this is to add 200° and then subtract 20°. Likewise, if the bearing is more than 180°, the pilot will add 20° and then subtract 200°. Therefore, in the example shown, the reciprocal bearing would be 070°. By using the "200-20" method the pilot is able to work these problems quickly and with greater ease.

HOMING

One of the most common uses of the ADF is called "homing to a station." In this procedure, the pilot flies to a station by keeping the bearing indicator needle on zero. The procedures used to home to a station, as shown in figure 4-13, are as follows.

1. Tune the desired frequency and identify the station.

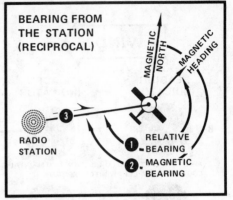

Fig. 4-12. ADF Bearings

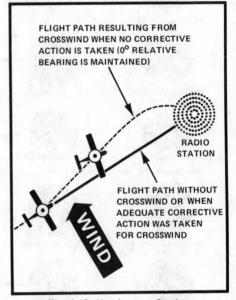

Fig. 4-13. Homing to a Station

2. Set the *function selector knob* to ADF and note the relative bearing.

3. Turn the aircraft toward the relative bearing until the bearing indicator pointer is at zero degrees.

4. Continue flight to the station by maintaining a relative bearing of zero degrees.

Figure 4-13 illustrates that, if the **mag**netic heading must be changed to hold the bearing indicator on zero degrees

RADIO NAVIGATION SYSTEMS

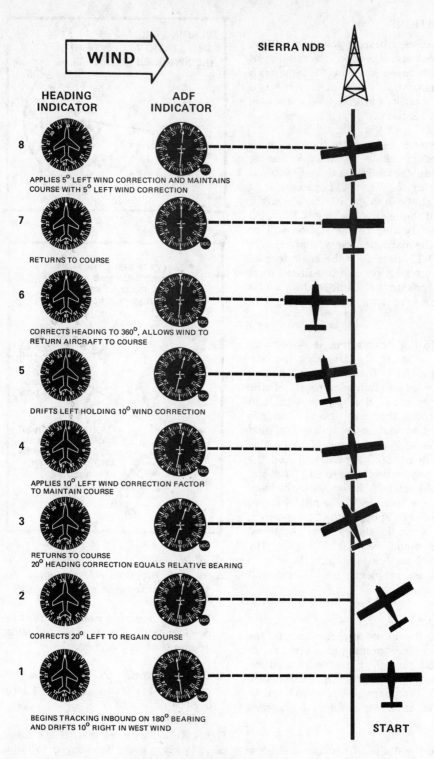

Fig. 4-14. Bracketing a Magnetic Bearing

relative bearing, the aircraft is drifting due to a crosswind. If a turn is made only to return to zero degrees relative bearing, crosswind correction is not applied, and the aircraft will fly a curved path to the station. The pilot will need to keep changing aircraft heading to maintain the zero degrees relative bearing while flying to the station.

BRACKETING A MAGNETIC BEARING

Crosswind correction using ADF is somewhat more involved, since, unlike VOR, ADF does not provide an automatic wind correction angle. In the bracketing illustration, shown in figure 4-14, the pilot has been tracking inbound to an NDB on the 360° magnetic bearing to the station with a wind from the west. In position 1, the aircraft has drifted 10° right of course. In positions 2 through 8, the aircraft reintercepts the course and wind correction is applied. When following the steps in the bracketing procedure, the five degree left heading correction in step 8 is equal to the five degree relative bearing. Regardless of the number of degrees correction left or right, when on course, the *wind correction angle* should be exactly *equal to the number of degrees a station bears to the left or right* of the nose of the aircraft (MH + RB = MB).

When crossing an NDB, the ADF indicator may show side-to-side needle deflections or steady movement toward a wingtip position. The pilot should maintain a constant aircraft heading and avoid "chasing" the needle. This will result in a straight ground track across the station, and normal navigation procedures may be resumed after station passage. Station passage using ADF equipment is indicated by 180° *reversal of the bearing indicator* from the nose to the tail position.

TRACKING FROM A STATION

The principles of bracketing a magnetic bearing are used to track *from* a station

as well as *to* a station. Figure 4-15 illustrates an aircraft tracking outbound from a station with a crosswind from the north. The reciprocal bearing is found by subtracting 180° from the magnetic bearing of 270°, equaling 090°. If a 10° wind correction angle is required, the pilot knows he is tracking the desired reciprocal bearing because the heading (080°) and relative bearing (190°) equal the magnetic bearing (270°) to the station.

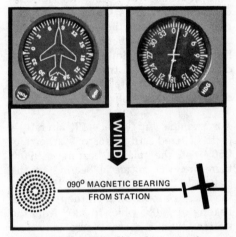

Fig. 4-15. ADF Tracking from a Station

POSITION FIX BY ADF

The ADF receiver can aid the pilot in making a definite position fix by using two or more stations and the process of triangulation. To determine the exact location of the aircraft, the following procedure should be used.

1. Locate two stations in the vicinity of the aircraft and note the frequency of each station.

2. With the function selector knob set to ANT, tune in and identify each station.

3. Set the function selector knob to ADF, then note the magnetic heading of the aircraft on the heading indicator. Continue to fly this heading and tune in the stations previously identi-

fied, recording the relative bearing for each station.

4. Plot each magnetic bearing on the chart. The aircraft is located at the intersection of the bearing lines, as shown in figure 4-16.

MOVABLE-CARD ADF INDICATORS

The movable-card ADF indicator provides an easier solution to ADF orientation problems. When using the movable-card indicator, the azimuth ring may be rotated to reflect the heading of the aircraft. Using this method, the magnetic heading to the station can be read directly from the instrument. The calculations required with the fixed-card indicator are eliminated.

For example, in figure 4-17, aircraft A (with a fixed-card indicator) is heading 050° and the relative bearing is 090°; therefore, the magnetic bearing to the station is 140° ($050^o + 090^o$). However, the aircraft's location is on the reciprocal bearing of 140°, which is 320° from the station. With a movable-card indicator, the pilot of aircraft B can set 050° (aircraft heading) below the upper azimuth index and read the magnetic bearing to the station directly as 140°, thus solving the orientation problem. The movable-card indicator also may be used as a fixed-card indicator when zero degrees is set under the index.

RMI

Originally a military development, the radio magnetic indicator is being utilized frequently in light, general aviation aircraft. The RMI has several advantages which lighten the pilot's workload, minimize errors, and provide constant orientation.

The equipment requires only one navigational display, which usually features *two bearing indicators* superimposed over a *slaved compass card*. This slaved compass card responds identically to the

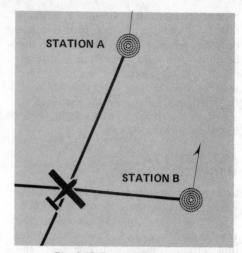

Fig. 4-16. Position Fix by ADF

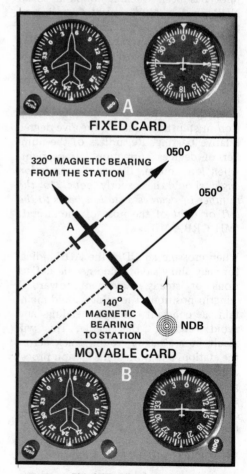

Fig. 4-17. Fixed-Card and Movable-Card Indicators

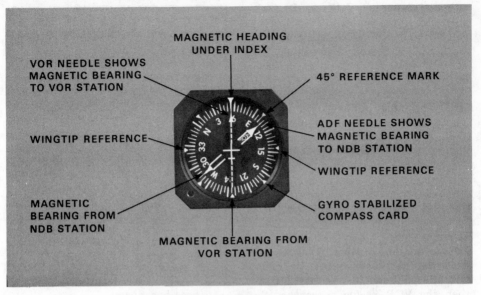

Fig. 4-18. Radio Magnetic Indicator

movements of the aircraft heading indicator. Whereas the fixed-card ADF indicator requires the use of a formula to determine magnetic bearing to the station, the RMI bearing indicator always *shows the magnetic bearing directly.* RMI equipment is shown in figure 4-18.

USING RMI

The RMI presents VOR and ADF bearing information simultaneously over one display. An RMI display using ADF and VOR simultaneously is illustrated in figure 4-19. Assume a pilot is tracking

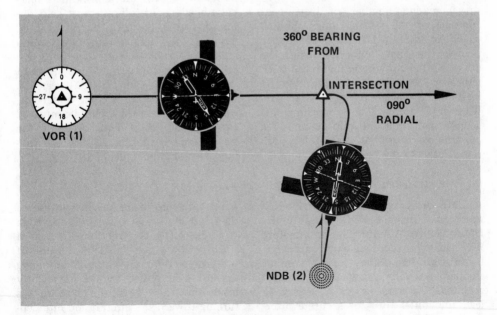

Fig. 4-19. RMI Navigation

outbound from the VOR on the 090°
radial, with the number one bearing
indicator tuned to the VOR, and number
two bearing indicator tuned to the NDB.
Since the slaved compass card reflects
the magnetic heading (090°), the pilot
will turn right and proceed direct to the
NDB when the number two bearing
indicator reflects a magnetic bearing of
180°. No equipment adjustments are
required, and the RMI provides the pilot
with *constant orientation* to his position
with respect to the selected navaids.

The RMI also may be used effectively
for airway intercepts. Regardless of the
intercept angle, the VOR needle will
point to the inbound magnetic course of
the airway upon interception. In figure
4-20, the pilot should turn left to 010°
when the VOR needle approaches the
inbound course (010°). In this case, the
intercept angle is 40°; however, if other
intercept angles are used, the pilot will
still turn inbound when the VOR needle
approaches 010°. In addition, position
orientation from the NDB is available to
the pilot throughout course interception.

DME ARCS AND RMI

An increasing number of instrument
approach procedures are being published
which incorporate DME arcs for transition to the final approach course. The
use of RMI in conjunction with the DME
indicator provides a simple, accurate
method for navigation of a DME arc.
While intercepting and flying the arc, it
is important that the pilot maintain a
continuous mental picture of his position relative to the facility.

INTERCEPTING THE ARC

A DME arc may be intercepted while
flying to or from a VORTAC or VOR/
DME facility. A turn of approximately
90° usually is required when intercepting a DME arc. Since a 90° turn at
standard rate (three degrees per second)
requires 30 seconds, it is necessary to
lead the initial turn for accurate interception. The determination of a lead-

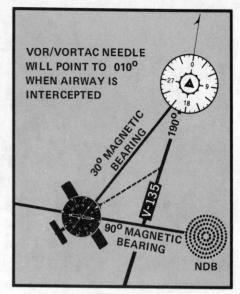

Fig. 4-20. RMI Airway Intercept

point prevents overshooting or undershooting the arc. For groundspeeds below
150 knots, a .5 nautical mile leadpoint
usually is satisfactory. The interception
procedure is illustrated in figure 4-21.

Prior to reaching the leadpoint, the
direction of turn and approximate magnetic heading for roll-out must be determined. During the turn, the pilot should
monitor the VOR bearing pointer and
attempt to roll out with the pointer on
or near the appropriate left or right
wingtip reference on the RMI (item 1).
If it appears the arc is being undershot,
roll-out from the turn should be initiated
early. If the arc is being overshot, the
turn should be continued past the roll-
out point originally planned.

MAINTAINING THE ARC

Larger arcs are easier to fly because of
their gradual rate of curvature. High
groundspeeds in conjunction with arcs of
small radii are more difficult because of
the higher rate of curvature. Maintaining
the arc is simplified by keeping slightly
inside the curve. Thus, the arc always is
turning toward the aircraft and interception may be accomplished by holding a

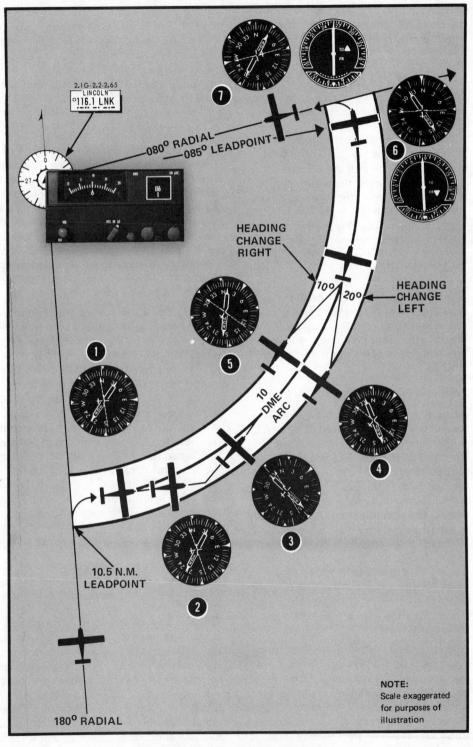

Fig. 4-21. Flying the DME Arc with RMI

straight course. If the aircraft is outside the curve, the arc is "turning away" and a greater correction is required.

Theoretically, a pilot using RMI would be able to fly an exact circle around a facility in a no-wind condition by maintaining the bearing pointer on the wingtip reference. In actual practice, a series of short legs are flown. With the bearing pointer on the appropriate left or right wingtip reference and the aircraft at the desired DME range, the heading should be maintained and the bearing pointer allowed to move 5° to 10° behind the wingtip (item 2). This will cause the DME distance to increase slightly.

Next, the aircraft should be turned toward the facility to place the bearing pointer 5° to 10° ahead of the wingtip reference (item 3) and the heading maintained until the pointer is again behind the wingtip. This procedure is repeated, as necessary, to maintain the approximate arc.

OFF-COURSE CORRECTIONS

As a guide in making course corrections, the relative bearing may be changed 10° to 20° for each one-half mile deviation from the desired arc. For example, if the aircraft is one-half mile outside the arc and the bearing pointer is on the wingtip reference, as illustrated in figure 4-21, item 4, the aircraft should be turned 20° toward the facility to return to the arc. If the off-course position is one-half mile inside the arc and the bearing pointer is on the wingtip reference (item 5), a turn of 10° away from the facility is appropriate.

WIND CORRECTION

Since the wind correction angle is changing constantly throughout the arc, wind orientation is important. A reference other than the wingtip must be used when operating in a crosswind. If a crosswind is blowing the aircraft *away* from the facility, the bearing pointer should be maintained *ahead* of the wing-

tip. If a crosswind is blowing the aircraft *toward* the facility, the bearing pointer should be established *behind* the wingtip. The selected reference point should be displaced from the wingtip by an amount equal to the required wind correction angle.

INTERCEPTING A RADIAL FROM A DME ARC

There is no essential difference between intercepting a radial from an arc and intercepting it from a straight course. The lead will vary with the arc's radius and the aircraft's groundspeed. A lead of five degrees or less is sufficient at speeds up to 150 knots when flying DME arcs like those depicted on most approach charts.

With an RMI, the rate of bearing movement should be monitored closely while flying the arc. The approximate lead radial should be determined and the bearing selector of the VOR navigation indicator should be set to the outbound course of the lead radial. When the CDI shows the aircraft crossing the appropriate radial (item 6), the turn to intercept the inbound course is initiated. During the turn, the OBS should be reset to the inbound course. Following the rollout, the CDI should be centered and the VOR bearing indicator should point directly ahead of the aircraft (item 7).

RMI ACCURACY CHECKS

Since the VOR bearing pointer of an RMI is part of the VOR equipment of an aircraft, it must meet the tolerances specified in FAR 91.25 for IFR flight. The accuracy of the VOR bearing pointer may be checked using a VOT. When the VOR receiver which operates the RMI is tuned to the VOT frequency, an accurate VOR bearing pointer will indicate 180°. The 180° indication is not affected by the magnetic heading of the aircraft or the OBS setting of a VOR navigation indicator which operates from a common receiver.

The accuracy also may be checked using VOR airborne and ground checkpoints. When these checkpoints are used, the VOR bearing pointer should indicate the magnetic bearing to the station.

AREA NAVIGATION

Area navigation (RNAV) has been developed and designed to provide more lateral freedom and, thus, more complete use of available airspace. This method of navigation does not require a track directly to or from any radio navigation aid. Area navigation capability has three principal applications.

1. It permits a direct route between any given departure and arrival point to reduce flight distances and traffic congestion.

2. It permits aircraft to be flown in terminal areas on varied prepro-grammed arrival and departure flight paths to assist and expedite traffic flow.

3. It permits instrument approaches (within certain limitations) at airports not equipped with local instrument landing aids.

There are three RNAV systems presently in common use. These are the course-line computer, Doppler radar, and inertial naviation systems. The Doppler radar and inertial navigation systems are not dependent upon ground based navigation aids, but are essentially self-contained units. Since Doppler radar and inertial navigation systems are used primarily aboard airlines and military aircraft, only the course-line computers will be discussed in this text.

COURSE-LINE COMPUTERS

Course-line computers provide a method of operating on an RNAV basis by utilizing the signals of VORTAC stations. The CLC permits the pilot to set up electronic waypoints (phantom VORTACs) at appropriate points within the reception range of the station. Because the pilot can electronically displace any usable VORTAC station to a different location, it is possible to fly the most direct route with airways, checkpoints, and airport locators tailored to individual needs. Use of course-line computers for VFR navigation affords the pilot great flexibility. Ultimately, this can reduce the total time for a given flight and provide significant savings in fuel and operating costs.

Fig. 4-22. CLC Components

CLC COMPONENTS

In addition to the VHF navigation receiver and the DME in the aircraft, the
course-line computer system has an
RNAV computer, waypoint selector, and
an RNAV indicator. (See Fig. 4-22.) The
heart of the CLC area navigation system
is an analog computer. With two simple
settings on the control panel, the analog
computer displaces a VORTAC to the
desired radial and distance from the
original location. It then relays information to the CLC display, providing the
pilot with the position of the aircraft in
relation to this new phantom station.

The CLC display looks like a standard
VOR and ILS indicator. When the CLC
display is being used in the VOR mode,
the CDI shows displacement from the
selected course in degrees. In the CLC
(RNAV) mode, each deviation dot on
the VOR indicator signifies an off-course
position based on nautical miles, rather
than the normal two degrees in the VOR
mode. Values of .5, 1, 2, or 10 nautical
miles may be used for each dot, depending on design and/or manufacturer.

While using the CLC, the DME distance
indication is given in relationship to the
waypoint (phantom VORTAC station)
and not the original VORTAC. However,
the *DME groundspeed readout* is in
relation to the original VORTAC and
not the waypoint on some general aviation CLC equipment.

SECTION C—RADAR AND TRANSPONDER

RADAR

Radar is a method of gathering information about distant objects by means of reflected radio waves. When electronically processed, the radio waves can be used to determine the distance and bearing of an object from the radar transmission site. Radar units operated by the Federal Aviation Administration are located throughout the United States and are available to both military and civilian pilots.

Radar utilizes a highly directional rotating antenna to transmit high frequency radio energy. The radio energy emitted by the radar transmitter is either a sequence of short pulses or a continuous wave. The pulses are used for obtaining range (distance) information while the continuous wave transmission is used to measure speed, as in Doppler radar. The radar units to be discussed in this section are those that will be used for obtaining range information.

When a pulse of radio waves is transmitted by a radar unit, it travels from the antenna *at the speed of light*. If an object is within the range of these transmissions, the energy pulse is reflected back from the object to its point of transmission. Generally, the antenna that transmits the pulse waves also receives the reflected signals. The radar receiver then automatically computes the time it took the pulse of energy to travel out and return. Once the time is known, the distance of the object may be electronically computed since a radio impulse travels at a constant rate; thus, the following relationship may be used:

$$distance = rate \times time$$

When a target is located, the *angle* of the antenna from true north at the time the reflected radio wave is received indicates the azimuth (horizontal direction) of the target.

PRIMARY RADAR

The radar units in operation by the FAA are divided into two categories — primary and secondary radar. Primary radar includes both surveillance and precision radar.

AIRPORT SURVEILLANCE RADAR

Airport surveillance radar (ASR) is designed to provide relatively short range coverage in the general vicinity of an airport and is used to expedite the handling of traffic. ASR is normally used by approach control, departure control, and tower personnel to provide vectors and aircraft separation within the immediate vicinity of the airport. ASR also can be utilized to perform instrument approaches.

AIR ROUTE SURVEILLANCE RADAR

Air route surveillance radar (ARSR) is a long range radar system designed primarily to provide a display of aircraft located in controlled airspace. ARSR is used for air traffic control of cross-country flights.

PRECISION RADAR

Precision radar is designed for use as a landing approach aid rather than for vectoring and spacing aircraft. Precision approach radar (PAR) equipment may be used as a *primary landing aid*, or it may be used to *monitor* other types of approaches. PAR is designed to display range, azimuth, and elevation information. Two antennas are used in the system — one scanning a vertical plane and the other scanning horizontally.

The radar display scope is divided into two parts. The upper half presents altitude and distance information, and the lower half represents azimuth and distance information. The range of PAR systems is limited to a distance of approximately 10 miles, the azimuth to 20° on each side of centerline, and the elevation to seven degrees above a horizontal plane; therefore, radar coverage is provided only for the final approach area.

SECONDARY SURVEILLANCE RADAR

Secondary surveillance radar is the international term for the air traffic control beacon system. This term refers to the form of radar used only in air traffic control. Secondary radar is a separate system and is capable of independent operation. However, in normal traffic control use, it is interconnected with either the long range air route surveillance radar or the short range airport surveillance radar. A display of both the primary and secondary radar "targets" is presented on the same radar screen.

Secondary surveillance radar is used to provide greater effectiveness in the airspace system. First, it counteracts some of the shortcomings inherent in primary radar. With secondary radar, aircraft targets will not vary in size as they do with primary radar. Second, the radar display is not degraded by weather conditions, such as precipitation and ground clutter (caused by reflections on the earth's surface), which frequently impair the primary radar display. Third, the radar beacon transponders transmit definite codes which permit the controller to make positive identification more easily. When using only primary radar, the controller must have the pilot execute a series of turns for positive identification. Fourth, it allows the controller to select aircraft within a certain altitude range or certain area of coverage.

GROUND EQUIPMENT

The ground equipment used with the radar beacon system is divided into three major components: the *interrogator*, *antenna*, and *decoder*. The major function of the interrogator is to trigger the airborne transponder and cause it to reply on the selected code. The interrogations are transmitted on

1030.0 MHz and replies from the airborne equipment are received on 1090.0 MHz. One section of the interrogator receives replies from the airborne transponder and transmits them to the decoder. The decoder accepts beacon signals from the interrogation unit and displays targets on the radar screen. Interrogations are transmitted and received by a highly directional rotating antenna, such as shown in figure 4-23.

Fig. 4-23. Radar Antenna

ARTS—III

At certain busy terminal areas around the United States, the automated radar terminal systems (ARTS-III) are installed. Computer controlled ARTS-III equipment automatically provides a continuous display of the aircraft's identification number, actual altitude, groundspeed, and other pertinent information on the radar screen. Figure 4-24 illustrates the ARTS-III display. Computer data processing equipment follows and updates each aircraft position from the time the aircraft enters the terminal approach area until final touchdown. Maximum utilization with this system requires each aircraft in the area to be equipped with a transponder and altimeter which have altitude encoding capability.

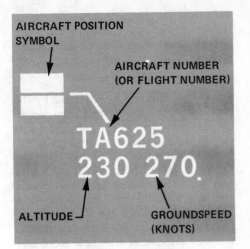

AIRCRAFT POSITION SYMBOL

AIRCRAFT NUMBER (OR FLIGHT NUMBER)

TA625
230 270.

ALTITUDE

GROUNDSPEED (KNOTS)

Fig. 4-24. ARTS-III Display

TRANSPONDER

The transponder is the airborne portion of the air traffic control beacon (secondary radar) system. The coded interrogation signal transmitted by the ground equipment causes the aircraft transponder to reply automatically and send back a coded signal. This causes the aircraft to appear as a distinctive pattern on the radar controller's scope. Figure 4-25 illustrates a radar scope with the various types of displays which are explained in the following paragraphs. The controller will see transponder-enhanced targets on the scope as blips with a coded signal. All other replies are the normal blips, commonly referred to as "skin paint."

TRANSPONDER MODES

Most general aviation transponders are equipped for Modes A and A/C operations. Mode A is used by the pilot for most general transponder replies. Mode A/C is for altitude reporting. The Federal Aviation Administration is equipping the major air terminals with ARTS-III capabilities. Altitude reporting equipment also is being installed with the air route traffic control radar equipment.

Most transponders in use today are equipped with the capability of altitude encoding. When a transponder of this type is used in conjunction with an altimeter designed for automatic pressure altitude reporting, a distinctive signal is sent to the ground radar station. This provides the controller with a visual display of the aircraft's altitude. With this type of equipment, the pilot should operate the transponder on Mode A/C, unless directed otherwise by the controller.

TRANSPONDER CODES

On the face of the transponder are controls used to select a numerical code requested by the air traffic controller. A typical transponder is shown in figure 4-26. Pilots will be informed of the code they must use. For example, the controller might tell the pilot to "squawk 1100." The term "squawk 1100" means the pilot should operate the transponder on code 1100.

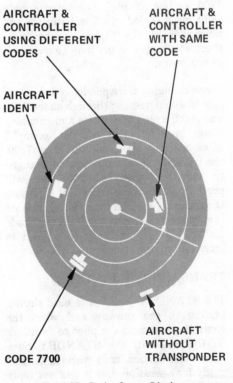

AIRCRAFT & CONTROLLER USING DIFFERENT CODES

AIRCRAFT & CONTROLLER WITH SAME CODE

AIRCRAFT IDENT

CODE 7700

AIRCRAFT WITHOUT TRANSPONDER

Fig. 4-25. Radar Scope Displays

Fig. 4-26. Typical Transponder

There are certain standard codes set aside for special use. The pilot should learn these codes and use them as needed or directed. Code 1200 has been assigned for all normal VFR operations regardless of altitude.

The pilot of an aircraft that experiences an emergency may alert air traffic control by squawking code 7700. Since there is a remote possibility that the pilot may not be within an area of radar coverage, radio communications should be established with an air traffic control facility as soon as possible. To alert ATC to a loss of two-way radio communications, the pilot should squawk 7700 for one minute, then squawk code 7600 for a period of 15 minutes, or the remainder of the flight, whichever is shortest. The procedure may be repeated, as necessary.

When changing transponder codes, pilots should avoid passing through codes 7700 and 0000, which may cause a momentary alarm in ATC facilities. For example, when changing from code 2700 to 7200, the transponder should first be changed to 2200 and then to 7200. This will preclude the possibility of passing through the emergency code. A number that must be avoided at all times is code 0000. This is a military code used in interception operations.

TRANSPONDER CONTROLS

The STANDBY position is used during taxiing to the runway and when the controller instructs the pilot to "squawk STANDBY." In the STANDBY position, the transponder is warmed up and ready for operation, but it *will not* reply to an interrogating signal. The controller will request STANDBY to eliminate clutter on the scope caused by too many aircraft on the ground or in the immediate vicinity, which appear on the screen as distorted blips.

The LO position may be requested by the controller when the aircraft transponder causes the target on the radar scope to extend into a broad arc, making it difficult for the controller to determine the aircraft's actual position. The FAA is now in the process of updating ground facilities with the addition of *side lobe suppression* to eliminate this condition. Because of the side lobe suppression features on ground facilities, some new transponders are being built *without* a LO control position.

NORMAL or ON is the transponder setting normally utilized unless the pilot is instructed otherwise by the controller. On most transponders, the term ON is used in place of NORMAL. The pilot should switch to ON just prior to takeoff. After completing the landing roll, the transponder should be turned to OFF or STANDBY unless instructed to perform this function earlier by the controller.

When asked to "IDENT," the pilot should press and immediately release the IDENT button. This causes the transponder to send strong radar target presentations, or blossoms, for a few seconds for positive identification. IDENT should not be used unless the controller specifically calls for it.

Most transponders also have a small reply or monitor light. This light blinks each time the transponder replies to a ground interrogation signal, thus informing the pilot the transponder is being interrogated. Many transponders incorporate a *test switch* to test internal circuitry; when the pilot pushes the test switch, a signal is sent through the transponder circuitry to evaluate the unit for correct operation. If the transponder is operating properly, the reply monitor light will flash.

WEATHER AVOIDANCE RADAR

Weather avoidance radar allows the pilot to avoid thunderstorms, areas of heavy precipitation, and the associated turbulence. A normal radar system of this type consists of a transmitter/receiver, an antenna, and a display scope mounted on the instrument panel. As shown in figure 4-27, the operating controls are grouped around the display scope and normally consist of the following major controls.

 An intensity control which adjusts the brightness of the radar returns

2 A tilt control which controls the tilt on the antenna

3 A combination off/range/test control, which activates the system, allows various range selections (20 and 80 miles, in this case), and provides a test function

4 A normal/contour switch to select the type of radar returns displayed

5 A dimness control which adjusts the background lighting of the radar display

When the normal/contour switch is in the normal mode, weather avoidance radar will show a brilliant image of heavy rainfall ahead. In the contour mode, all pulses above a preselected strength are blocked. This rejection of signals highlights areas of maximum cell activity as black holes, outlined by areas of lesser rainfall, as shown by the arrow in figure 4-27. Rules for avoiding these areas vary, but there is a general agreement that 20 to 30 miles is a safe, comfortable distance from strong echoes. However, all echoes should be avoided because there are no predictable turbulence-free areas.

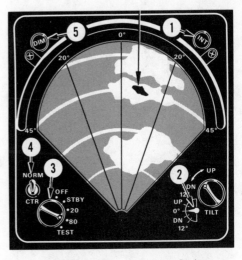

Fig. 4-27. Weather Avoidance Radar

Interpreting weather avoidance radar images is both an art and a skill and requires practice in using this equipment to gain proficiency. There is no substitute for keeping the weather avoidance radar on in all kinds of weather and learning proper interpretation of the images.

chapter 5

INSTRUMENT/COMMERCIAL PILOT FEDERAL AVIATION REGULATIONS

INTRODUCTION

This chapter contains selected regulations from Parts 61, 91, 135, and the NTSB Procedural Regulations. Parts 61 and 91 have been edited to present those regulations pertinent to the instrument and commercial pilot. In addition, a table of contents is provided at the beginning of each part for easy reference to specific regulations.

The section covering Part 135 is limited in its coverage and is intended only to *familiarize* the pilot with this part of the regulations. It should be noted that in order to fly under Part 135, a pilot is required to have formal training, which includes coverage of these FARs in their entirety. Concerned applicants also should review FAR Part 133, "Rotorcraft External-Load Operations," and FAR Part 137, "Agricultural Aircraft Operations." These regulations are briefly described at the end of the Part 135 section. The last section contains a summary of the Hazardous Materials Regulation (HMR), Part 175, and the National Transportation and Safety Board (NTSB) Regulation, Part 830.

The content of the Federal Aviation Regulations is revised periodically as new rules become effective and others become obsolete. Thus, occasional review is necessary. All pilots are responsible for knowledge of FARs pertaining to their flight operations.

SECTION A—FAR PART 61

TABLE OF CONTENTS

FEDERAL AVIATION REGULATIONS

TABLE OF CONTENTS

SUBPART A—GENERAL

61.1 APPLICABILITY.

(a) This part prescribes the requirements for issuing pilot and flight instructor certificates and ratings, the conditions under which those certificates and ratings are necessary, and the privileges and limitations of those certificates and ratings.

(b) Except as provided in 61.71 of this Part, an applicant for a certificate or rating may, until November 1, 1974, meet either the requirements of this Part, or the requirements in effect immediately before November 1, 1973. However, the applicant for a private pilot certificate with a free balloon class rating must meet the requirements of this part.

61.3 REQUIREMENT FOR CERTIFICATES, RATING, AND AUTHORIZATIONS.

(a) *Pilot certificate.* No person may act as pilot in command or in any other capacity as a required pilot flight crewmember of a civil aircraft of United States registry unless he has in his personal possession a current pilot certificate issued to him under this part. However, when the aircraft is operated within a foreign country a current pilot license issued by the country in which the aircraft is operated may be used.

(b) *Pilot certificate: foreign aircraft.* No person may, within the United States, act as pilot in command or in any other capacity as a required pilot flight crewmember of a civil aircraft of foreign registry unless he has in his personal possession a current pilot certificate issued to him under this part, or a pilot license issued to him or validated for him by the country in which the aircraft is registered.

(c) *Medical certificate.* Except for free balloon pilots piloting balloons and glider pilots piloting gliders, no person may act as pilot in command or in any other capacity as a required pilot flight crewmember of an aircraft under a certificate issued to him under this part, unless he has in his personal possession an appropriate current medical certificate issued under Part 67 of this chapter. However, when the aircraft is operated within a foreign country with a current pilot license issued by that country, evidence of current medical qualification for that license, issued by that country, may be used. In the case of a pilot certificate issued on the basis of a foreign pilot license under 61.75, evidence of current medical qualification accepted for the issue of that license is used in place of a medical certificate.

(e) *Instrument rating.* No person may act as pilot in command of a civil aircraft under instrument flight rules, or in weather conditions less than the minimums prescribed for VFR flight unless—

    (1) In the case of an airplane, he holds an instrument rating or an airline transport pilot certificate with an airplane category rating on it;

(h) *Inspection of certificate.* Each person who holds a pilot certificate, flight instructor certificate, medical certificate, authorization or license required by this part shall present it for inspection upon the request of the Administrator, an authorized representative of the National Transportation Safety Board, or any Federal, State, or local law enforcement officer.

61.5 CERTIFICATES AND RATINGS ISSUED UNDER THIS PART.

(a) The following certificates are issued under this part:

    (1) Pilot certificates:
        (i) Student pilot.
        (ii) Private pilot.
        (iii) Commercial pilot.
        (iv) Airline transport pilot.
    (2) Flight instructor certificates.

(b) The following ratings are placed on pilot certificates (other than student pilot) where applicable:

    (1) Aircraft category ratings:
        (i) Airplane.
        (ii) Rotorcraft.
        (iii) Glider.
        (iv) Lighter-than-air.
    (2) Airplane class ratings:

        (i) Single-engine land.
        (ii) Multiengine land.
        (iii) Single-engine sea.
        (iv) Multiengine sea.
    (3) Rotorcraft class ratings:
        (i) Helicopter.
        (ii) Gyroplane.
    (4) Lighter-than-air class ratings:
        (i) Airship.
        (ii) Free balloon.
    (5) Aircraft type ratings are listed in Advisory Circular 61-1 entitled "Aircraft Type Ratings." This list includes ratings for the following:
        (i) Large aircraft, other than lighter-than-air.
        (ii) Small turbojet-powered airplanes.
        (iii) Small helicopters for operations requiring an airline transport pilot certificate.
        (iv) Other aircraft type ratings specified by the Administrator through aircraft type certificate procedures.
    (6) Instrument ratings (on private and commercial pilot certificates only):
        (i) Instrument—airplanes.
        (ii) Instrument—helicopter.

61.11 EXPIRED PILOT CERTIFICATES AND REISSUANCE.

(a) No person who holds an expired pilot certificate or rating may exercise the privileges of that pilot certificate, or rating.

(c) A private or commercial pilot certificate or a special purpose pilot certificate, issued on the basis of a foreign pilot license, expires on the expiration date stated thereon. A certificate without an expiration date is issued to the holder of the expired certificate only if he meets the requirements of 61.75 for the issue of a pilot certificate based on a foreign pilot license.

61.13 APPLICATION AND QUALIFICATION

(a) Application for a certificate and rating, or for an additional rating under this part is made on a form and in a manner prescribed by the Administrator.

(b) An applicant who meets the requirements of this part is entitled to an appropriate pilot certificate with aircraft ratings. Additional aircraft category, class, type and other ratings, for which the applicant is qualified, are added to his certificate. However, the Administrator may refuse to issue certificates to persons who are not citizens of the United States and who do not reside in the United States.

(c) An applicant who cannot comply with all of the flight proficiency requirements prescribed by this part because the aircraft used by him for his flight training or flight test is characteristically incapable of performing a required pilot operation, but who meets all other requirements for the certificate or rating sought, is issued the certificate or rating with appropriate limitations.

(d) An applicant for a pilot certificate who holds a medical certificate under 67.19 of this chapter with special limitations on it, but who meets all other requirements for that pilot certificate, is issued a pilot certificate containing such operating limitations as the Administrator determines are necessary because of the applicant's medical deficiency.

(e) A Category II pilot authorization is issued as a part of the applicant's instrument rating or airline transport pilot certificate. Upon original issue the authorization contains a limitation for Category II operations of 1,600 feet RVR and a 150 foot decision height. This limitation is removed when the holder shows that since the beginning of the sixth preceding month he has made three Category II ILS approaches to a landing under actual or simulated instrument conditions with a 150 foot decision height.

61.15 OFFENSES INVOLVING NARCOTIC DRUGS, MARIHUANA, AND DEPRESSANT OR STIMULANT DRUGS OR SUBSTANCES

(a) No person who is convicted of violating any Federal or State statute relating to the growing, processing, manufacture, sale, disposition, possession, transportation, or importation of narcotic drugs, marihuana, and depressant or stimulant drugs or substances, is eligible for any certificate or rating issued under this part for a period of 1 year after the date of final conviction.

(b) No person who commits an act prohibited by 91.12(a) of this chapter is eligible for any certificate or rating issued under this part for a period of 1 year after the date of that act.

(c) Any conviction specified in paragraph (a) of this section or the commission of the act referenced in paragraph (b) of this section, is grounds for suspending or revoking any certificate or rating issued under this part.

61.17 TEMPORARY CERTIFICATE

(a) A temporary pilot or flight instructor certificate, or a rating, effective for a period of not more than 120 days, is issued to a qualified applicant pending a review of his qualifications and the issuance of a permanent certificate or rating by the Administrator. The permanent certificate or rating is issued to an applicant found qualified and a denial thereof is issued to an applicant found not qualified.

(b) A temporary certificate issued under paragraph (a) of this section expires —
(1) At the end of the expiration date stated thereon; or
(2) Upon receipt by the applicant of —
  (i) The certificate or rating sought; or
  (ii) Notice that the certificate or rating sought is denied.

61.19 DURATION OF PILOT AND FLIGHT INSTRUCTOR CERTIFICATES

(a) *General.* The holder of a certificate with an expiration date may not, after that date, exercise the privileges of that certificate.

(b) *Student pilot certificate.* A student pilot certificate expires at the end of the 24th month after the month in which it is issued.

(c) *Other pilot certificates.* Any pilot certificate (other than a student pilot certificate) issued under this part is issued without a specific expiration date. However, the holder of a pilot certificate issued on the basis of a foreign pilot license may exercise the privileges of that certificate only while the foreign pilot license on which that certificate is based is effective.

(e) *Surrender, suspension, or revocation.* Any pilot certificate or flight instructor certificate issued under this part ceases to be effective if it is surrendered, suspended, or revoked.

(f) *Return of certificate.* The holder of any certificate issued under this part that is suspended or revoked shall, upon the Administrator's request, return it.

61.23 DURATION OF MEDICAL CERTIFICATES.

(a) A first-class medical certificate expires at the end of the last day of—

(1) The sixth month after the month of the date of examination shown on the certificate, for operations requiring an airline transport pilot certificate;

(2) The 12th month after the month of the date of examination shown on the certificate, for operations requiring only a commercial pilot certificate; and

(3) The 24th month after the month of the date of examination shown on the certificate, for operations requiring only a private or student pilot certificate.

(b) A second-class medical certificate expires at the end of the last day of—

(1) The 12th month after the month of the date of examination shown on the certificate, for operations requiring a commercial pilot certificate; and

(2) The 24th month after the month of the date of examination shown on the certificate, for operations requiring only a private or student pilot certificate.

(c) A third-class medical certificate expires at the end of the last day of the 24th month after the month of the date of examination shown on the certificate, for operations requiring a private or student pilot certificate.

61.25 CHANGE OF NAME.

An application for the change of a name on a certificate issued under this part must be accompanied by the applicant's current certificate and a copy of the marriage license, court order, or other document verifying the change. The documents are returned to the applicant after inspection.

61.27 VOLUNTARY SURRENDER OR EXCHANGE OF CERTIFICATE.

The holder of a certificate issued under this part may voluntarily surrender it for cancellation, or for the issue of a certificate of lower grade, or another certificate with specific ratings deleted. If he so requests, he must include the following signed statement or its equivalent:

This request is made for my own reasons, with full knowledge that my (insert name of certificate or rating, as appropriate) may not be reissued to me unless I again pass the tests prescribed for its issue.

61.29 REPLACEMENT OF LOST OR DESTROYED CERTIFICATE.

(a) An application for the replacement of a lost or destroyed airman certificate issued under this part is made by letter to the Department of Transportation, Federal Aviation Administration, Airman Certification Branch, Post Office Box 25082, Oklahoma City, OK 73125. This letter must—

(1) State the name of the person to whom the certificate was issued, the permanent mailing address (including zip code), social security number (if any), date and place of birth of the certificate holder, and any available information regarding the grade, number, and date of issue of the certificate, and the ratings on it; and

(2) Be accompanied by a check or money order for $2, payable to the Federal Aviation Administration.

(b) An application for the replacement of a lost or destroyed medical certificate is made by letter to the Department of Transportation, Federal Aviation Administration, Aeromedical Certification Branch, Post Office Box 25082, Oklahoma City, OK 73125, accompanied by a check or money order for $2.

(c) A person who has lost a certificate issued under this part, or a medical certificate issued under Part 67 of this chapter, or both, may obtain a telegram from the FAA confirming that it was issued. The telegram may be carried as a certificate for a period not to exceed 60 days pending his receipt of a duplicate certificate under paragraph (a) or (b) of this section, unless he has been notified that the certificate has been suspended or revoked. The request for such a telegram may be made by letter or prepaid telegram, including the date upon which a duplicate certificate was previously requested, if a request had been made, and a money order for the cost of the duplicate certificate. The request for a telegraphic certificate is sent to the office listed in paragraph (a) or (b) of this section, as appropriate. However, a request for both airman and medical certificates at the same time must be sent to the office prescribed in paragraph (a) of this section.

61.31 GENERAL LIMITATIONS.

(a) *Type ratings required.* A person may not act as pilot in command of any of the following aircraft unless he holds a type rating for that aircraft:

   (1) A large aircraft (except lighter-than-air).

   (2) A helicopter, for operations requiring an airline transport pilot certificate.

   (3) A turbojet powered airplane.

   (4) Other aircraft specified by the Administrator through aircraft type certificate procedures.

(b) *Authorization in lieu of a type rating.*

   (1) In lieu of a type rating required under paragraphs (a)(1), (3), and (4) of this section, an aircraft may be operated under an authorization issued by the Administrator, for a flight or series of flights within the United States, if—

      (i) The particular operation for which the authorization is requested involves a ferry flight, a practice or training flight, a flight test for a pilot type rating, or a test flight of an aircraft, for a period that does not exceed 60 days;

      (ii) The applicant shows that compliance with paragraph (a) of this section is impracticable for the particular operations; and

      (iii) The Administrator finds that an equivalent level of safety may be achieved through operating limitations on the authorization.

   (2) Aircraft operated under an authorization issued under this paragraph—

      (i) May not be operated for compensation or hire; and

      (ii) May carry only flight crewmembers necessary for the flight.

   (3) An authorization issued under this paragraph may be reissued for an additional 60-day period for the same operation if the applicant shows that he was prevented from carrying out the purpose of the particular operation before his authorization expired.

The prohibition of paragraph (b)(2)(i) of this section does not prohibit compensation for the use of an aircraft by a pilot solely to prepare for or take a flight test for a type rating.

(c) *Category and class rating: Carrying another person or operating for compensation or hire.* Unless he holds a category and class rating for that aircraft, a person may not act as pilot in command of an aircraft that is carrying another person or is operated for compensation or hire. In addition, he may not act as pilot in command of that aircraft for compensation or hire.

(d) *Category and class rating: Other operations.* No person may act as pilot in command of an aircraft in solo flight in operations not subject to paragraph (c) of this section, unless he meets at least one of the following:

   (1) He holds a category and class rating appropriate to that aircraft.

   (2) He has received flight instruction in the pilot operations required by this part, appropriate to the category and class of aircraft for first solo, given to him by a certificated flight instructor who found him competent to solo that category and class of aircraft and has so endorsed his pilot logbook.

   (3) He has soloed and logged pilot-in-command time in that category and class of aircraft before November 1, 1973.

(e) *High performance airplanes.* A person holding a private or commercial pilot certificate may not act as pilot in command of an airplane that has more than 200 horsepower, or that has a retractable landing gear, flaps, and a controllable propeller, unless he has received flight instruction from an authorized flight instructor who has certified in his logbook that he is competent to pilot an airplane that has more than 200 horsepower, or that has a retractable landing gear, flaps, and a controllable propeller, as the case may be. However, this instruction is not required if he has logged flight time as pilot in command in high performance airplanes before November 1, 1973.

(f) *Exception.* This section does not require a class rating for gliders, or category and class ratings for aircraft that are not type certificated as airplanes, rotorcraft, or lighter-than-air aircraft. In addition, the rating limitations of this section do not apply to—

(1) The holder of a student pilot certificate;

(2) The holder of a pilot certificate when operating an aircraft under the authority of an experimental or provisional type certificate;

(3) An applicant when taking a flight test given by the Administrator; or

(4) The holder of a pilot certificate with a lighter-than-air category rating when operating a hot air balloon without an airborne heater.

61.33 TESTS: GENERAL PROCEDURE.

Tests prescribed by or under this part are given at times and places, and by persons, designated by the Administrator.

61.35 WRITTEN TEST: PREREQUISITES AND PASSING GRADES.

(a) An applicant for a written test must—

(1) Show that he has satisfactorily completed the ground instruction or home study course required by this part for the certificate or rating sought:

(2) Present as personal identification an airman certificate, driver's license, or other official document; and

(3) Present a birth certificate or other official document showing that he meets the age requirement prescribed in this part for the certificate sought not later than 2 years from the date of application for the test.

(b) The minimum passing grade is specified by the Administrator on each written test sheet or booklet furnished to the applicant.

This section does not apply to the written test for an airline transport pilot certificate or a rating associated with that certificate.

61.37 WRITTEN TESTS: CHEATING OR OTHER UNAUTHORIZED CONDUCT.

(a) Except as authorized by the Administrator, no person may—

(1) Copy, or intentionally remove, a written test under this part;

(2) Give to another, or receive from another, any part or copy of that test;

(3) Give help on that test to, or receive help on that test from, any person during the period that test is being given;

(4) Take any part of that test in behalf of another person;

(5) Use any material or aid during the period that test is being given; or

(6) Intentionally cause, assist, or participate in any act prohibited by this paragraph.

(b) No person whom the Administrator finds to have committed an act prohibited by paragraph (a) of this section is eligible for any airman or ground instructor certificate or rating, or to take any test therefor, under this chapter for a period of 1 year after the date of that act. In addition, the commission of that act is a basis for suspending or revoking any airman or ground instructor certificate or rating held by that person.

61.39 PREREQUISITES FOR FLIGHT TESTS.

(a) To be eligible for a flight test for a certificate, or an aircraft or instrument rating issued under this part, the applicant must—

(1) Have passed any required written test since the beginning of the 24th month before the month in which he takes the flight test;

(2) Have the applicable instruction and aeronautical experience prescribed in this part;

(3) Hold a current medical certificate appropriate to the certificate he seeks or, in the case of a rating to be added to his pilot certificate, at least a third-class medical certificate issued since the beginning of the 24th month before the month in which he takes the flight test;

(4) Except for a flight test for an airline transport pilot certificate, meet the age requirement for the issuance of the certificate or rating he seeks; and

(5) Have a written statement from an appropriately certificated flight instructor certifying that he has given the applicant flight instruction in preparation for the flight test within 60 days preceding the date of application, and finds him competent to pass the test and to have satisfactory knowledge of the subject areas in which he is shown to be deficient by his FAA airman written test report. However, an applicant need not have this written statement if he—

(i) Holds a foreign pilot license issued by a contracting State to the Convention on International Civil Aviation that authorizes at least the pilot privileges of the airman certificate sought by him;

(ii) Is applying for a type rating only, or a class rating with an associated type rating; or

(iii) Is applying for an airline transport pilot certificate or an additional aircraft rating on that certificate.

(b) Notwithstanding paragraph (a)(1) of this section, an applicant for an airline transport pilot certificate or an additional aircraft rating on that certificate who has been since passing the written examination, continuously employed as a pilot, or as a pilot assigned to flight engineer duties by, and is participating in an approved pilot training program of a U.S. air carrier or commercial operator, or who is rated as a pilot by, and is participating in a pilot training program of a U.S. scheduled military air transportation service, may take the flight test for that certificate or rating.

61.41 FLIGHT INSTRUCTION RECEIVED FROM FLIGHT INSTRUCTORS NOT CERTIFICATED BY FAA.

Flight instruction may be credited toward the requirements for a pilot certificate or rating issued under this part if it is received from—

(a) An Armed Force of either the United States or a foreign contracting State to the Convention on International Civil Aviation in a program for training military pilots; or

(b) A flight instructor who is authorized to give that flight instruction by the licensing authority of a foreign contracting State to the Convention on International Civil Aviation and the flight instruction is given outside the United States.

61.43 FLIGHT TESTS: GENERAL PROCEDURES.

(a) The ability of an applicant for a private or commercial pilot certificate, or for an aircraft or instrument rating on that certificate to perform the required pilot operations is based on the following:

(1) Executing procedures and maneuvers within the aircraft's performance capabilities and limitations, including use of the aircraft's systems.

(2) Executing emergency procedures and maneuvers appropriate to the aircraft.

(3) Piloting the aircraft with smoothness and accuracy.

(4) Exercising judgment.

(5) Applying his aeronautical knowledge.

(6) Showing that he is the master of the aircraft, with the successful outcome of a procedure or maneuver never seriously in doubt.

(b) If the applicant fails any of the required pilot operations in accordance with the applicable provisions of paragraph (a) of this section, the applicant fails the flight test. The applicant is not eligible for the certificate or rating sought until he passes any pilot operations he has failed.

(c) The examiner or the applicant may discontinue the test at any time when the failure of a required pilot operation makes the applicant ineligible for the certificate or rating sought. If the test is discontinued the applicant is entitled to credit for only those entire pilot operations that he has successfully performed.

61.45 FLIGHT TESTS: REQUIRED AIRCRAFT AND EQUIPMENT.

(a) *General.* An applicant for a certificate or rating under this part must furnish, for each flight test that he is required to take, an appropriate aircraft of United States registry that has a current standard or limited airworthiness certificate. However, the applicant may, at the discretion of the inspector or examiner conducting the test, furnish an aircraft of U.S. registry that has a current airworthiness certificate other than standard or limited, an aircraft of foreign registry that is properly certificated by the country of registry, or a military aircraft in an operational status if its use is allowed by an appropriate military authority.

(b) *Required equipment (other than controls).* Aircraft furnished for a flight test must have—

(1) The equipment for each pilot operation required for the flight test;

(2) No prescribed operating limitations that prohibit its use in any pilot operation required on the test;

(3) Pilot seats with adequate visibility for each pilot to operate the aircraft

safely, except as provided in paragraph (d) of this section; and

(4) Cockpit and outside visibility adequate to evaluate the performance of the applicant, where an additional jump seat is provided for the examiner.

(c) *Required controls.* An aircraft (other than lighter-than-air) furnished under paragraph (a) of this section for any pilot flight test must have engine power controls and flight controls that are easily reached and operable in a normal manner by both pilots, unless after considering all the factors, the examiner determines that the flight test can be conducted safely without them. However, an aircraft having other controls such as nose-wheel steering, brakes, switches, fuel selectors, and engine air flow controls that are not easily reached and operable in a normal manner by both pilots may be used, if more than one pilot is required under its airworthiness certificate, or if the examiner determines that the flight can be conducted safely.

(d) *Simulated instrument flight equipment.* An applicant for any flight test involving flight maneuvers solely by reference to instruments must furnish equipment satisfactory to the examiner that excludes the visual reference of the applicant outside of the aircraft.

(e) *Aircraft with single controls.* At the discretion of the examiner, an aircraft furnished under paragraph (a) of this section for a flight test may, in the cases listed herein, have a single set of controls. In such case, the examiner determines the competence of the applicant by observation from the ground or from another aircraft.

(1) A flight test for addition of a class or type rating, not involving demonstration of instrument skills, to a private or commercial pilot certificate.

61.47 FLIGHT TESTS: STATUS OF FAA INSPECTORS AND OTHER AUTHORIZED FLIGHT EXAMINERS.

An FAA inspector or other authorized flight examiner conducts the flight test of an applicant for a pilot certificate or rating for the purpose of observing the applicant's ability to perform satisfactorily the procedures and maneuvers on the flight test. The inspector or other examiner is not pilot in command of the aircraft during the flight test unless he acts in that capacity for the flight, or portion of the flight, by prior arrangement with the applicant or other person who would otherwise act as pilot in command of the flight, or portion of the flight. Notwithstanding the type of aircraft used during a flight test, the applicant and the inspector or other examiner are not, with respect to each other (or other occupants authorized by the inspector or other examiner), subject to the requirements or limitations for the carriage of passengers specified in this chapter.

61.49 RETESTING AFTER FAILURE.

An applicant for a written or flight test who fails that test may not apply for retesting until after 30 days after the date he failed the test. However, in the case of his first failure he may apply for retesting before the 30 days have expired upon presenting a written statement from an authorized instructor certifying that he has given flight or ground instruction as appropriate to the applicant and finds him competent to pass the test.

61.51 PILOT LOGBOOKS.

(a) The aeronautical training and experience used to meet the requirements for a certificate or rating, or the recent flight experience requirements of this part must be shown by a reliable record. The logging of other flight time is not required.

(b) *Logbook entries.* Each pilot shall enter the following information for each flight or lesson logged:

(1) *General.*
   (i) Date.
   (ii) Total time of flight.
   (iii) Place, or points of departure and arrival.
   (iv) Type and identification of aircraft.

(2) *Type of pilot experience or training.*
   (i) Pilot in command or solo.
   (ii) Second in command.
   (iii) Flight instruction received from an authorized flight instructor.
   (iv) Instrument flight instruction from an authorized flight instructor.
   (v) Pilot ground trainer instruction.
   (vi) Participating crew (lighter-than-air).
   (vii) Other pilot time.

(3) *Conditions of flight.*
  (i) Day or night.
  (ii) Actual instrument.
  (iii) Simulated instrument conditions.

Logging of pilot time —

(1) *Solo flight time.* A pilot may log as solo flight time only that flight time when he is the sole occupant of the aircraft. However, a student pilot may also log as solo flight time that time during which he acts as the pilot in command of an airship requiring more than one flight crewmember.

(2) *Pilot-in-command flight time.*
  (i) A private or commercial pilot may log as pilot in command time only that flight time during which he is the sole manipulator of the controls of an aircraft for which he is rated, or when he is the sole occupant of the aircraft, or when he acts as pilot in command of an aircraft on which more than one pilot is required under the type certification of the aircraft, or the regulations under which the flight is conducted.
  (ii) An airline transport pilot may log as pilot in command time all of the flight time during which he acts as pilot in command.
  (iii) A certificated flight instructor may log as pilot in command time all flight time during which he acts as a flight instructor.

(3) *Second-in-command flight time.* A pilot may log as second in command time all flight time during which he acts as second in command of an aircraft on which more than one pilot is required under the type certification of the aircraft, or the regulations under which the flight is conducted.

(4) *Instrument flight time.* A pilot may log as instrument flight time only that time during which he operates the aircraft solely by reference to instruments, under actual or simulated instrument flight conditions. Each entry must include the place and type of each instrument approach completed, and the name of the safety pilot for each simulated instrument flight. An instrument flight instructor may log as instrument time that time during which he acts as instrument flight instructor in actual instrument weather conditions.

(5) *Instruction time.* All time logged as flight instruction, instrument flight instruction, pilot ground trainer instruction, or ground instruction time must be certified by the appropriately rated and certificated instructor from whom it was received.

(d) *Presentation of logbook.*
  (1) A pilot must present his logbook (or other record required by this section) for inspection upon reasonable request by the Administrator, an authorized representative of the National Transportation Safety Board, or any State or local law enforcement officer.
  (2) A student pilot must carry his logbook (or other record required by this section) with him on all solo cross-country flights, as evidence of the required instructor clearances and endorsements.

61.53 OPERATIONS DURING MEDICAL DEFICIENCY.

No person may act as pilot in command, or in any other capacity as a required pilot flight crewmember while he has a known medical deficiency, or increase of a known medical deficiency, that would make him unable to meet the requirements for his current medical certificate.

61.57 RECENT FLIGHT EXPERIENCE: PILOT IN COMMAND.

(a) *Flight review.* After November 1, 1974, no person may act as pilot in command of an aircraft unless, within the preceding 24 months, he has—
  (1) Accomplished a flight review given to him, in an aircraft for which he is rated, by an appropriately certificated instructor or other person designated by the Administrator; and
  (2) Had his logbook endorsed by the person who gave him the review certifying that he has satisfactorily accomplished the flight review.

However, a person who has, within the preceding 24 months, satisfactorily completed a pilot proficiency check conducted by the FAA, an approved pilot check airman or a U.S. armed force for a pilot certificate, rating or operating privilege, need not accomplish the flight review required by this section.

(b) *Meaning of flight review.* As used in this section, a flight review consists of—

  (1) A review of the current general operating and flight rules of Part 91; and

  (2) A review of those maneuvers and procedures which in the discretion of the person giving the review are necessary for the pilot to demonstrate that he can safely exercise the privileges of his pilot certificate.

(c) *General experience.* No person may act as pilot in command of an aircraft carrying passengers, nor of an aircraft certificated for more than one required pilot flight crewmember, unless within the preceding 90 days, he has made three takeoffs and three landings as the sole manipulator of the flight controls in an aircraft of the same category and class and, if a type rating is required, of the same type. If the aircraft is a tailwheel airplane, the landings must have been made to a full stop in a tailwheel airplane. For the purpose of meeting the requirements of the paragraph a person may act as pilot in command of a flight under day VFR or day IFR if no persons or property other than as necessary for his compliance thereunder, are carried. This paragraph does not apply to operations requiring an airline transport pilot certificate, or to operations conducted under Part 135.

(d) *Night experience.* No person may act as pilot in command of an aircraft carrying passengers during the period beginning 1 hour after sunset and ending 1 hour before sunrise (as published in the American Air Almanac) unless, within the preceding 90 days, he has made at least three takeoffs and three landings to a full stop during that period in the category and class of aircraft to be used. This paragraph does not apply to operations requiring an airline transport pilot certificate.

(e) *Instrument* —

  (1) *Recent IFR experience.* No pilot may act as pilot in command under IFR, nor in weather conditions less than the minimums prescribed for VFR, unless he has, within the past 6 months—

    (i) In the case of an aircraft other than a glider, logged at least 6 hours of instrument time under actual or simulated IFR conditions, at least 3 of which were in flight in the category of aircraft involved, including at least six instrument approaches, or passed an instrument competency check in the category of aircraft involved.

  (2) *Instrument competency check.* A pilot who does not meet the recent instrument experience requirements of paragraph (e)(1) of this section during the prescribed time or 6 months thereafter may not serve as pilot in command under IFR, nor in weather conditions less than the minimums prescribed for VFR, until he passes an instrument competency check in the category of aircraft involved, given by an FAA inspector, a member of an armed force of the United States authorized to conduct flight tests, an FAA-approved check pilot, or a certificated instrument flight instructor. The Administrator may authorize the conduct of part or all of this check in a pilot ground trainer equipped for instruments or an aircraft simulator.

61.59 FALSIFICATION, REPRODUCTION, OR ALTERATION OF APPLICATIONS, CERTIFICATES, LOGBOOKS, REPORTS, OR RECORDS.

(a) No person may make or cause to be made—

  (1) Any fraudulent or intentionally false statement on any application for a certificate, rating, or duplicate thereof, issued under this part;

  (2) Any fraudulent or intentionally false entry in any logbook, record, or report that is required to be kept, made, or used, to show compliance with any requirement for the issuance, or exercise of the privileges, or any certificate or rating under this part;

  (3) Any reproduction, for fraudulent purpose, of any certificate or rating under this part; or

  (4) Any alteration of any certificate or rating under this part.

(b) The commission by any person of an act prohibited under paragraph (a) of this section is a basis for suspending or revoking any airman or ground instructor certificate or rating held by that person.

61.60 CHANGE OF ADDRESS.

The holder of a pilot or flight instructor certificate who has made a change in his permanent mailing address may not after 30 days from the date he moved, exercise the privileges of his certificate unless he has notified in writing the Department of Transportation, Federal Aviation Administration, Airman Certification Branch, Box 25082, Oklahoma City, OK 73125, of his new address.

SUBPART B—AIRCRAFT RATINGS AND SPECIAL CERTIFICATES

61.61 APPLICABILITY.

This subpart prescribes the requirements for the issuance of additional aircraft ratings after a pilot or instructor certificate is issued, and the requirements and limitations for special pilot certificates and ratings issued by the Administrator.

61.63 ADDITIONAL AIRCRAFT RATINGS (OTHER THAN AIRLINE TRANSPORT PILOT).

(a) *General.* To be eligible for an aircraft rating after his certificate is issued to him an applicant must meet the requirements of paragraphs (b) through (d) of this section, as appropriate to the rating sought.

(b) *Category rating.* An applicant for a category rating to be added on his pilot certificate must meet the requirements of this Part for the issue of the pilot certificate appropriate to the privileges for which the category rating is sought. However, the holder of a category rating for powered aircraft is not required to take a written test for the addition of a category rating on his pilot certificate.

(c) *Class rating.* An applicant for an aircraft class rating to be added on his pilot certificate must—

(1) Present a logbook record certified by an authorized flight instructor showing that the applicant has received flight instruction in the class of aircraft for which a rating is sought and has been found competent in the pilot operations appropriate to the pilot certificate to which his category rating applies; and

(2) Pass a flight test appropriate to his pilot certificate and applicable to the aircraft category and class rating sought.

(d) *Type rating.* An applicant for a type rating to be added on his pilot certificate must meet the following requirements:

(1) He must hold, or concurrently obtain, an instrument rating appropriate to the aircraft for which a type rating is sought.

(2) He must pass a flight test showing competence in pilot operations appropriate to the pilot certificate he holds and to the type rating sought.

(3) He must pass a flight test showing competence in pilot operations under instrument flight rules in an aircraft of the type for which the type rating is sought or, in the case of a single pilot station airplane, meet the requirements of paragraph (d)(3)(i) or (ii) of this section, whichever is applicable.

(i) The applicant must have met the requirements of this subparagraph in a multiengine airplane for which the type rating is required.

(ii) If he does not meet the requirements of paragraph (d)(3)(i) of this section and he seeks a type rating for a single-engine airplane, he must meet the requirements of this subparagraph in either a single or multiengine airplane, and have the recent instrument experience set forth in 61.57(e), when he applies for the flight test under paragraph (d)(2) of this section.

(4) An applicant who does not meet the requirements of paragraphs (d)(1) and (3) of this section may obtain a type rating limited to "VFR only." Upon meeting these instrument requirements or the requirements of 61.73(e)(2), the "VFR only" limitation may be removed for the particular type of aircraft in which competence is shown.

(5) When an instrument rating is issued to the holder of one or more type ratings, the type ratings on the amended certificate bear the limitation described in paragraph (d)(4) of this section for each airplane type rating for which he has not shown his instrument competency under this paragraph.

61.65 INSTRUMENT RATING REQUIREMENTS.

(a) *General.* To be eligible for an instrument rating (airplane) or an instrument rating (helicopter), an applicant must—

  (1) Hold a current private or commercial pilot certificate with an aircraft rating appropriate to the instrument rating sought;

  (2) Be able to read, speak, and understand the English language; and

  (3) Comply with the applicable requirements of this section.

(b) *Ground instruction.* An applicant for the written test for an instrument rating must have received ground instruction, or have logged home study in at least the following areas of aeronautical knowledge appropriate to the rating sought.

  (1) The regulations of this chapter that apply to flight under IFR conditions, the Airman's Information Manual, and the IFR air traffic system and procedures;

  (2) Dead reckoning appropriate to IFR navigation, IFR navigation by radio aids using the VOR, ADF, and ILS systems, and the use of IFR charts and instrument approach plates;

  (3) The procurement and use of aviation weather reports and forecasts, and the elements of forecasting weather trends on the basis of that information and personal observation of weather conditions; and

  (4) The safe and efficient operation of airplanes or helicopters, as appropriate, under instrument weather conditions.

(c) *Flight instruction and skill—airplanes.* An applicant for the flight test for an instrument rating (airplane) must present a logbook record certified by an authorized flight instructor showing that he has received instrument flight instruction in an airplane in the following pilot operations, and has been found competent in each of them:

  (1) Control and accurate maneuvering of an airplane solely by reference to instruments.

  (2) IFR navigation by the use of the VOR and ADF systems, including compliance with air traffic control instructions and procedures.

  (3) Instrument approaches to published minimums using the VOR, ADF, and ILS systems (instruction in the use of the ADF and ILS may be received in an instrument ground trainer and instruction in the use of the ILS glide slope may be received in an airborne ILS simulator).

  (4) Cross-country flying in simulated or actual IFR conditions, on Federal airways or as routed by ATC, including one such trip of at least 250 nautical miles, including VOR, ADF, and ILS approaches at different airports.

  (5) Simulated emergencies, including the recovery from unusual attitudes, equipment or instrument malfunctions, loss of communications, and engine-out emergencies if a multi-engine airplane is used, and missed approach procedure.

(e) *Flight experience.* An applicant for an instrument rating must have at least the following flight time as a pilot:

  (1) A total of 200 hours of pilot flight time, including 100 hours as pilot in command, of which 50 hours are cross-country in the category of aircraft for which an instrument rating is sought.

  (2) 40 hours of simulated or actual instrument time, of which not more than 20 hours may be instrument instruction by an authorized instructor in an instrument ground trainer acceptable to the Administrator.

  (3) 15 hours of instrument flight instruction by an authorized flight instructor, including at least 5 hours in an airplane or a helicopter, as appropriate.

(f) *Written test.* An applicant for an instrument rating must pass a written test appropriate to the instrument rating sought on the subjects in which ground instruction is required by paragraph (b) of this section.

(g) *Practical test.* An applicant for an instrument rating must pass a flight test in an airplane or a helicopter, as appropriate. The test must include instrument flight procedures selected by the inspector or examiner conducting the test to determine the applicant's ability to perform competently the IFR operations on which instruction is required by paragraph (c) or (d) of this section.

61.69 GLIDER TOWING: EXPERIENCE AND INSTRUCTION REQUIREMENTS

No person may act as pilot in command of an aircraft towing a glider unless he meets the following requirements:

(a) He holds a current pilot certificate (other than a student pilot certificate).

(b) He has an endorsement in his pilot logbook from a person authorized to give flight instruction in gliders, certifying that he has received ground and flight instruction in gliders and is familiar with the techniques and procedures essential to the safe towing of gliders, including airspeed limitations, emergency procedures, signals used, and maximum angles of bank.

(c) He has made and entered in his pilot logbook —
  (1) At least three flights as sole manipulator of the controls of an aircraft towing a glider while accompanied by a pilot who has met the requirements of this section and made and logged at least 10 flights as pilot-in-command of an aircraft towing a glider; or
  (2) At least three flights as sole manipulator of the controls of an aircraft simulating glider towing flight procedures (while accompanied by a pilot who meets the requirements of this section), and at least three flights as pilot or observer in a glider being towed by an aircraft.

However, any person who, before May 17, 1967, made, and entered in his pilot logbook, 10 or more flights as pilot in command of an aircraft towing a glider in accordance with a certificate of waiver need not comply with paragraphs (c)(1) and (2) of this section.

(d) If he holds only a private pilot certificate he must have had, and entered in his pilot logbook at least —
  (1) 100 hours of pilot flight time in powered aircraft; or
  (2) 200 total hours of pilot flight time in powered or other aircraft.

(e) Within the preceding 12 months he has—
  (1) Made at least three actual or simulated glider tows while accompanied by a qualified pilot who meets the requirements of this section; or
  (2) Made at least three flights as pilot in command of a glider towed by an aircraft.

61.71 GRADUATES OF CERTIFICATED FLYING SCHOOLS: SPECIAL RULES

(a) A graduate of a flying school that is certificated under Part 141 of this chapter is considered to meet the applicable aeronautical experience requirements of this part if he presents an appropriate graduation certificate within 60 days after the date he is graduated. However, if he applies for a flight test for an instrument rating he must hold a commercial pilot certificate, or hold a private pilot certificate and meet the requirements of 61.65(e)(1) and 61.123 (except paragraphs (d) and (e) thereof). In addition, if he applies for a flight instructor certificate he must hold a commercial pilot certificate.

(b) An applicant for a certificate or rating under this part is considered to meet the aeronautical knowledge and skill requirements, or both, applicable to that certificate or rating, if he applies within 90 days after graduation from an appropriate course given by a flying school that is certificated under Part 141 of this chapter and is authorized to test applicants on aeronautical knowledge or skill, or both.

However, until January 1, 1977, a graduate of a flying school certificated and operated under the provisions of 141.29 of this chapter, is considered to meet the aeronautical experience requirements of this part, and may be tested under the requirements of Part 61 that were in effect prior to November 1, 1973.

SUBPART E — COMMERCIAL PILOTS
61.121 APPLICABILITY
This subpart prescribes the requirements for the issuance of commercial pilot certificates and ratings, the conditions under which those certificates and ratings are necessary, and the limitations upon those certificates and ratings.

61.123 ELIGIBILITY REQUIREMENTS: GENERAL
To be eligible for a commercial pilot certificate, a person must —

(a) Be at least 18 years of age;

(b) Be able to speak, read, and understand the English language, or have such operating limitations placed on his pilot certificate as is necessary for safety, to be removed when he shows he can read, speak, and understand the English language;

(c) Hold at least a valid second-class medical certificate issued under Part 67 of this chapter, or, in the case of a glider or free balloon rating, certify that he has no known medical deficiency that makes him unable to pilot a glider or a free balloon, as appropriate;

(d) Pass a written examination appropriate to the aircraft rating sought on the subjects in which ground instruction is required by 61.125;

(e) Pass an oral and flight test appropriate to the rating he seeks, covering items selected by the inspector or examiner from those on which training is required by 61.127; and

(f) Comply with the provisions of this subpart which apply to the rating he seeks.

61.125 AERONAUTICAL KNOWLEDGE.

An applicant for a commercial pilot certificate must have logged ground instruction from an authorized instructor, or must present evidence showing that he has satisfactorily completed a course of instruction or home study, in at least the following areas of aeronautical knowledge appropriate to the category of aircraft for which a rating is sought.

(a) *Airplanes.*
   (1) The regulations of this chapter governing the operations, privileges, and limitations of a commercial pilot, and the accident reporting requirements of the National Transportation Safety Board;
   (2) Basic aerodynamics and the principles of flight which apply to airplanes; and
   (3) Airplane operations, including the use of flaps, retractable landing gears, controllable propellers, high altitude operation with and without pressurization, loading and balance computations, and the significance and use of airplane performance speeds.

61.127 FLIGHT PROFICIENCY.

The applicant for a commercial pilot certificate must have logged instruction from an authorized flight instructor in at least the following pilot operations. In addition, his logbook must contain an endorsement by an authorized flight instructor who has given him the instruction certifying that he has found the applicant prepared to perform each of those operations competently as a commercial pilot.

(a) *Airplanes.*
   (1) Preflight duties, including load and balance determination, line inspection, and aircraft servicing;
   (2) Flight at critically slow airspeeds, recognition of imminent stalls, and recovery from stalls with and without power;
   (3) Normal and crosswind takeoffs and landings, using precision approaches, flaps, power as appropriate, and specified approach speeds;
   (4) Maximum performance takeoffs and landings, climbs, and descents;
   (5) Operation of an airplane equipped with a retractable landing gear, flaps, and controllable propeller(s), including normal and emergency operations; and
   (6) Emergency procedures, such as coping with power loss or equipment malfunctions, fire in flight, collision avoidance precautions, and engine-out procedures if a multiengine airplane is used.

61.129 AIRPLANE RATING: AERONAUTICAL EXPERIENCE.

(a) *General.* An applicant for a commercial pilot certificate with an airplane rating must hold a private pilot certificate with an airplane rating. If he does not hold that certificate and rating he must meet the flight experience requirements for a private pilot certificate and airplane rating and pass the applicable written and practical test prescribed in Subpart D of this part. In addition, the applicant must hold an instrument rating (airplane), or the commercial pilot certificate that is issued is endorsed with a limitation prohibiting the carriage of passengers for hire in airplanes on cross-country flights of more than 50 nautical miles, or at night.

(b) *Flight time as pilot.* An applicant for a commercial pilot certificate with an airplane rating must have a total of at least 250 hours of flight time as pilot, which may include not more than 50 hours of instruction from an authorized instructor in a ground trainer acceptable to the Administrator. The total flight time as pilot must include—
   (1) 100 hours in powered aircraft, including at least—
      (i) 50 hours in airplanes, and

FEDERAL AVIATION REGULATIONS

(ii) 10 hours of flight instruction and practice given by an authorized flight instructor in an airplane having a retractable landing gear, flaps, and a controllable pitch propeller; and

(2) 50 hours of flight instruction given by an authorized flight instructor, including—

(i) 10 hours of instrument instruction, of which at least 5 hours must be in flight in airplanes, and

(ii) 10 hours of instruction in preparation for the commercial pilot flight test; and

(3) 100 hours of pilot in command time, including at least—

(i) 50 hours in airplanes;

(ii) 50 hours of cross-country flights, each flight with a landing at a point more than 50 nautical miles from the point of departure, including a flight with landings at three points each of

which is more than 200 nautical miles from the other two points, except that those flights conducted in Hawaii may be made with landings at points which are 100 nautical miles apart; and

(iii) 5 hours of night flying including at least 10 takeoffs and landings as sole manipulator of the controls.

61.139 COMMERCIAL PILOT PRIVILEGES AND LIMITATIONS: GENERAL.

The holder of a commercial pilot certificate may:

(a) Act as pilot in command of an aircraft carrying persons or property for compensation or hire;

(b) Act as pilot in command of an aircraft for compensation or hire; and

(c) Give flight instruction in an airship if he holds a lighter-than-air category and an airship class rating, or in a free balloon if he holds a free balloon class rating.

SECTION B—FAR PART 91

TABLE OF CONTENTS

FEDERAL AVIATION REGULATIONS

TABLE OF CONTENTS

SUBPART A — GENERAL

91.1 APPLICABILITY

(a) Except as provided in paragraph (b) of this section, this Part prescribes rules governing the operation of aircraft (other than moored balloons, kites, unmanned rockets and unmanned free balloons) within the United States.

(b) Each person operating a civil aircraft of U.S. registry outside of the United States shall —

   (1) When over the high seas, comply with Annex 2 (Rules of the Air) to the Convention on International Civil Aviation and with 91.70(c) and 91.90 of Subpart B;

   (2) When within a foreign country, comply with the regulations relating to the flight and maneuver of aircraft there in force.

   (3) Except for 91.15(b), 91.17, 91.38 and 91.43, comply with Subparts A, C and D of this Part so far as they are not inconsistent with applicable regulations of the foreign country where the aircraft is operated or Annex 2 to the Convention on International Civil Aviation.

91.3 RESPONSIBILITY AND AUTHORITY OF THE PILOT IN COMMAND

(a) The pilot in command of an aircraft is directly responsible for, and is the final authority as to, the operation of that aircraft.

(b) In an emergency requiring immediate action, the pilot in command may deviate from any rule of this Subpart or of Subpart B to the extent required to meet that emergency.

(c) Each pilot in command who deviates from a rule under paragraph (b) of this section shall, upon the request of the Administrator, send a written report of that deviation to the Administrator.

91.5 PREFLIGHT ACTION

Each pilot in command shall, before beginning a flight, familiarize himself with all available information concerning that flight. This information must include:

(a) For a flight under IFR or a flight not in the vicinity of an airport, weather reports and forecasts, fuel requirements, alternatives available if the planned flight cannot be completed, and any known traffic delays of which he has been advised by ATC.

(b) For any flight, runway lengths at airports of intended use, and the following takeoff and landing distance information;

   (1) For civil aircraft for which an approved airplane or rotorcraft flight manual containing takeoff and landing distance data is required, the takeoff and landing distance data contained therein; and

   (2) For civil aircraft other than those specified in subparagraph (1) of this paragraph, other reliable information appropriate to the aircraft, relating to aircraft performance under expected values of airport elevation and runway slope, aircraft gross weight, and wind and temperature.

91.7 FLIGHT CREWMEMBERS AT STATIONS

(a) During takeoff and landing, and while en route, each required flight crewmember shall —

   (1) Be at his station unless his absence is necessary in the performance of his duties in connection with the operation of the aircraft or in connection with his physiological needs; and

   (2) Keep his seat belt fastened while at his station.

(b) After July 18, 1978, each required flight crewmember of a U.S. registered civil airplane shall, during takeoff and land-

ing, keep the shoulder harness fastened while at his station. This paragraph does not apply if —
(1) The seat at the crewmember's station is not equipped with a shoulder harness; or
(2) The crewmember would be unable to perform his required duties with the shoulder harness fastened.

91.8 PROHIBITION AGAINST INTERFERENCE WITH CREWMEMBERS

No person may assault, threaten, intimidate, or interfere with a crewmember in the performance of the crewmember's duties aboard an aircraft being operated.

91.9 CARELESS OR RECKLESS OPERATION

No person may operate an aircraft in a careless or reckless manner so as to endanger the life or property of another.

91.10 CARELESS OR RECKLESS OPERATION OTHER THAN FOR THE PURPOSE OF AIR NAVIGATION

No person may operate an aircraft other than for the purpose of air navigation, on any part of the surface of an airport used by aircraft for air commerce (including areas used by those aircraft for receiving or discharging persons or cargo), in a careless or reckless manner so as to endanger the life or property of another.

91.11 LIQUOR AND DRUGS

(a) No person may act as a crewmember of a civil aircraft —
(1) Within 8 hours after the consumption of any alcoholic beverage;
(2) While under the influence of alcohol; or
(3) While using any drug that affects his faculties in any way contrary to safety.
(b) Except in an emergency, no pilot of a civil aircraft may allow a person who is obviously under the influence of intoxicating liquors or drugs (except a medical patient under proper care) to be carried in that aircraft.

91.12 CARRIAGE OF NARCOTIC DRUGS, MARIHUANA, AND DEPRESSANT OR STIMULANT DRUGS OR SUBSTANCES

(a) Except as provided in paragraph (b) of this section, no person may operate a civil aircraft within the United States with knowledge that narcotic drugs, marihuana, and depressant or stimulant drugs or substances as defined in Federal or State statutes are carried in the aircraft.
(b) Paragraph (a) of this section does not apply to any carriage of narcotic drugs, marihuana, and depressant or stimulant drugs or substances authorized by or under any Federal or State statute or by any Federal or State agency.

91.13 DROPPING OBJECTS

No pilot in command of a civil aircraft may allow any object to be dropped from that aircraft in flight that creates a hazard to persons or property. However, this section does not prohibit the dropping of any object if reasonable precautions are taken to avoid injury or damage to persons or property.

91.14 USE OF SAFETY BELTS

(a) Unless otherwise authorized by the Administrator —
(1) No pilot may take off a U.S. registered civil aircraft (except a free balloon that incorporates a basket or gondola and an airship) unless the pilot in command of that aircraft ensures that each person on board is briefed on how to fasten and unfasten that person's safety belt.
(2) No pilot may take off or land a U.S. registered civil aircraft (except free balloons that incorporate baskets or gondolas and airships) unless the pilot in command of that aircraft ensures that each person on board has been notified to fasten his safety belt.
(3) During the takeoff and landing of U.S. registered civil aircraft (except free balloons that incorporate baskets or gondolas and airships), each person on board that aircraft must occupy a seat or berth with a safety belt properly secured about him. However, a person who has not reached his second birthday may be held by an adult who is occupying a seat or berth, and a person on board for the purpose of engaging in sport parachuting may use the floor of the aircraft as a seat.
(b) This section does not apply to operations conducted under Part 121, 123, or 127 of this chapter. Paragraph (a)(3) of this section does not apply to persons subject to 91.7.

91.15 PARACHUTES AND PARACHUTING

(a) No pilot of a civil aircraft may allow a parachute that is available for emergency use to be carried in that aircraft unless it is an approved type and—
  (1) If a chair type (canopy in back), it has been packed by a certificated and appropriately rated parachute rigger within the preceding 120 days; or
  (2) If any other type, it has been packed by a certificated and appropriately rated parachute rigger —
    (i) Within the preceding 120 days, if its canopy, shrouds, and harness are composed exclusively of nylon, rayon, or other similar synthetic fiber or materials that are substantially resistant to damage from mold, mildew, or other fungi and other rotting agents propagated in a moist environment; or
    (ii) Within the preceding 60 days, if any part of the parachute is composed of silk, pongee, or other natural fiber, or materials not specified in subdivision (i) of this subparagraph.

(b) Except in an emergency, no pilot in command may allow, and no person may make, a parachute jump from an aircraft within the United States except in accordance with Part 105 (New) of this chapter.

(c) Unless each occupant of the aircraft is wearing an approved parachute, no pilot of a civil aircraft, carrying any person (other than a crewmember) may execute any intentional maneuver that exceeds —
  (1) A bank of 60 degrees relative to the horizon; or
  (2) A nose-up or nose-down attitude of 30 degrees relative to the horizon.

(d) Paragraph (c) of this section does not apply to —
  (1) Flight tests for pilot certification or rating; or
  (2) Spins and other flight maneuvers required by the regulations for any certificate or rating when given by
    (i) A certificated flight instructor; or
    (ii) An airline transport pilot instructing in accordance with 61.169 of this chapter.

(e) For the purposes of this section, "approved parachute" means —
  (1) A parachute manufactured under a type certificate or a technical standard order (C-23 series); or
  (2) A personnel-carrying military parachute identified by an NAF, AAF, or AN drawing number, an AAF order number, or any other military designation or specification number.

91.17 TOWING: GLIDERS

(a) No person may operate a civil aircraft towing a glider unless:
  (1) The pilot in command of the towing aircraft is qualified under 61.69 of this chapter.
  (2) The towing aircraft is equipped with a towhitch of a kind, and installed in a manner, approved by the Administrator.
  (3) The towline used has a breaking strength not less than 80 percent of the maximum certificated operating weight of the glider, and not more than twice this operating weight. However, the towline used may have a breaking strength more than twice the maximum certificated operating weight of the glider if—
    (i) A safety link is installed at the point of attachment of the towline to the glider, with a breaking strength not less than 80 percent of the maximum certificated operating weight of the glider, and not greater than twice this operating weight; and
    (ii) A safety link is installed at the point of attachment of the towline to the towing aircraft with a breaking strength greater, but not more than 25 percent greater, than that of the safety link at the towed glider end of the towline, and not greater than twice the maximum certificated operating weight of the glider.
  (4) Before conducting any towing operations within a control zone, or before making each towing flight within a control zone if required by ATC, the pilot in command notifies the control tower if one is in operation in that control zone. If such a control tower is not in operation, he must notify the FAA flight service station serving the control zone before conducting any towing operations in that control zone.
  (5) The pilots of the towing aircraft and the glider have agreed upon a general course of action including takeoff and release signals, air-

speeds, and emergency procedures for each pilot.

(b) No pilot of a civil aircraft may intentionally release a towline, after release of a glider, in a manner so as to endanger the life or property of another.

91.18 TOWING: OTHER THAN UNDER 91.17

(a) No pilot of a civil aircraft may tow anything with that aircraft (other than under 91.17) except in accordance with the terms of a certificate of waiver issued by the Administrator.

(b) An application for a certificate of waiver under this section is made on a form and in a manner prescribed by the Administrator and must be submitted to the nearest Flight Standards District Office.

91.19 PORTABLE ELECTRONIC DEVICES

(a) Except as provided in paragraph (b) of this section, no person may operate, nor may any operator or pilot in command of an aircraft allow the operation of, any portable electronic device on any of the following U.S. registered civil aircraft:
   (1) Aircraft operated by an air carrier or commercial operator; or
   (2) Any other aircraft while it is operated under IFR.

(b) Paragraph (a) of this section does not apply to:
   (1) Portable voice recorders;
   (2) Hearing aids;
   (3) Heart pacemakers;
   (4) Electric shavers; or
   (5) Any other portable electronic device that the operator of the aircraft has determined will not cause interference with the navigation or communication system of the aircraft on which it is to be used.

(c) In the case of an aircraft operated by an air carrier or commercial operator, the determination required by paragraph (b)(5) of this section shall be made by the air carrier or commercial operator of the aircraft on which the particular device is to be used. In the case of other aircraft, the determination may be made by the pilot in command or other operator of the aircraft.

91.21 FLIGHT INSTRUCTION; SIMULATED INSTRUMENT FLIGHT AND CERTAIN FLIGHT TESTS

(a) No person may operate a civil aircraft (except a manned free balloon) that is being used for flight instruction unless that aircraft has fully functioning, dual controls. However, instrument flight instruction may be given in a single-engine airplane equipped with a single, functioning throwover control wheel, in place of fixed, dual controls of the elevator and ailerons, when:
   (1) The instructor has determined that the flight can be conducted safely; and
   (2) The person manipulating the controls has at least a private pilot certificate with appropriate category and class ratings.

(b) No person may operate a civil aircraft in simulated instrument flight unless —
   (1) An appropriately rated pilot occupies the other control seat as safety pilot;
   (2) The safety pilot has adequate vision forward and to each side of the aircraft, or a competent observer in the aircraft adequately supplements the vision of the safety pilot; and
   (3) Except in the case of lighter-than-air aircraft, that aircraft is equipped with fully functioning dual controls. However, simulated instrument flight may be conducted in a single-engine airplane, equipped with a single, functioning, throwover control wheel, in place of fixed, dual controls of the elevator and ailerons, when —
      (i) The safety pilot has determined that the flight can be conducted safely; and
      (ii) The person manipulating the control has at least a private pilot certificate with appropriate category and class ratings.

(c) No person may operate a civil aircraft that is being used for a flight test for an airline transport pilot certificate or a class or type rating on that certificate, or for a Federal Aviation Regulation Part 121 proficiency flight test, unless the pilot seated at the controls, other than the pilot being checked, is fully qualified to act as pilot in command of the aircraft.

91.22 FUEL REQUIREMENTS FOR FLIGHT UNDER VFR

(a) No person may begin a flight in an airplane under VFR unless (considering wind and forecast weather conditions) there is enough fuel to fly to the first point of intended landing and, assuming normal cruising speed —
   (1) During the day, to fly after that for at least 30 minutes; or
   (2) At night, to fly after that for at least 45 minutes.

(b) No person may begin a flight in a rotorcraft under VFR unless (considering wind and forecast weather conditions) there is enough fuel to fly to the first point of intended landing and, assuming normal cruising speed, to fly after that for at least 20 minutes.

91.23 FUEL REQUIREMENTS FOR FLIGHT IN IFR CONDITIONS

(a) Except as provided in paragraph (b) of this section, no person may operate a civil aircraft in IFR conditions unless it carries enough fuel (considering weather reports and forecasts, and weather conditions) to —
   (1) Complete the flight to the first airport of intended landing;
   (2) Fly from that airport to the alternate airport; and
   (3) Fly after that for 45 minutes at normal cruising speed.
(b) Paragraph (a)(2) of this section does not apply if —
   (1) Part 97 of this subchapter prescribes a standard instrument approach procedure for the first airport of intended landing; and
   (2) For at least 1 hour before and 1 hour after the estimated time of arrival at the airport, the weather reports or forecasts or any combination of them, indicate —
      (i) The ceiling will be at least 2,000 feet above the airport elevation; and
      (ii) Visibility will be at least 3 miles.

91.24 ATC TRANSPONDER AND ALTITUDE REPORTING EQUIPMENT AND USE

(a) *All airspace: U.S. registered civil aircraft.* For operations not conducted under Parts 121, 123, 127, or 135 of this chapter, ATC transponder equipment installed after January 1, 1974, in U.S. registered civil aircraft not previously equipped with an ATC transponder, and all ATC transponder equipment used in U.S. registered civil aircraft after July 1, 1975, must meet the performance and environmental requirements of any class of TSO-C74b or any class of TSO-C74c as appropriate, except that the Administrator may approve the use of TSO-C74 or TSO-C74a equipment after July 1, 1975, if the applicant submits data showing that such equipment meets the minimum performance standards of the appropriate class of TSO-C74c and en-

vironmental conditions of the TSO under which it was manufactured.

(b) *Controlled airspace: all aircraft.* Except for persons operating helicopters in terminal control areas at or below 1,000 feet AGL under the terms of a letter of agreement, and except for persons operating gliders above 12,500 feet MSL but below the floor of the positive control area, no person may operate an aircraft in controlled airspace, after the applicable dates prescribed in paragraphs (b)(1) through (b)(4) of this section, unless that aircraft is equipped with an operable coded radar beacon transponder having a Mode 3/A 4096 code capability, replying to Mode 3/A interrogation with the code specified by ATC, and is equipped with automatic pressure altitude reporting equipment having a Mode C capability that automatically replies to Mode C interrogations by transmitting pressure altitude information in 100-foot increments. This requirement applies —
   (1) In Group I Terminal Control Areas governed by 91.90(a);
   (2) In Group II Terminal Control Areas governed by 91.90(b), except as provided therein;
   (3) In Group III Terminal Control Areas governed by 91.90(c), except as provided therein; and
   (4) In all controlled airspace of the 48 contiguous States and the District of Columbia, above 12,500 feet MSL, excluding the airspace at and below 2,500 feet AGL.

(c) *ATC authorized deviations.* ATC may authorize deviations from paragraph (b) of this section —
   (1) Immediately, to allow an aircraft with an inoperative transponder to continue to the airport of ultimate destination, including any intermediate stops, or to proceed to a place where suitable repairs can be made, or both;
   (2) Immediately, for operations of aircraft with an operating transponder but without operating automatic pressure altitude reporting equipment having a Mode C capability; and
   (3) On a continuing basis, or for individual flights, for operations of aircraft without a transponder, in which case the request for a deviation must be submitted to the ATC facility having jurisdiction over the airspace concerned at least four hours before the proposed operation.

91.25 VOR EQUIPMENT CHECK FOR IFR OPERATIONS

(a) No person may operate a civil aircraft under IFR using the VOR system of radio navigation unless the VOR equipment of that aircraft —
   (1) Is maintained, checked, and inspected under an approved procedure; or
   (2) Has been operationally checked within the preceding 30 days and was found to be within the limits of the permissible indicated bearing error set forth in paragraph (b) or (c) of this section.

(b) Except as provided in paragraph (c) of this section, each person conducting a VOR check under paragraph (a)(2) of this section shall—
   (1) Use, at the airport of intended departure, an FAA operated or approved test signal or a test signal radiated by a certificated and appropriately rated radio repair station or, outside the United States, a test signal operated or approved by appropriate authority, to check the VOR equipment (the maximum permissible indicated bearing error is plus or minus 4 degrees);
   (2) If a test signal is not available at the airport of intended departure, use a point on an airport surface designated as a VOR system checkpoint by the Administrator or, outside the United States, by appropriate authority (the maximum permissible bearing is plus or minus 4 degrees);
   (3) If neither a test signal nor a designated checkpoint on the surface is available, use an airborne checkpoint designated by the Administrator or, outside the United States, by appropriate authority (the maximum permissible bearing error is plus or minus 6 degrees); or
   (4) If no check signal or point is available, while in flight —
      (i) Select a VOR radial that lies along the centerline of an established VOR airway;
      (ii) Select a prominent ground point along the selected radial preferably more than 20 miles from the VOR ground facility and maneuver the aircraft directly over the point at a reasonably low altitude; and
      (iii) Note the VOR bearing indicated by the receiver when over the ground point (the maximum permissible variation between the published radial and the indicated bearing is 6 degrees).

(c) If dual system VOR (units independent of each other except for the antenna) is installed in the aircraft, the person checking the equipment may check one system against the other in place of the check procedures specified in paragraph (b) of this section. He shall tune both systems to the same VOR ground facility and note the indicated bearings to that station. The maximum permissible variation between the two indicated bearings is 4 degrees.

(d) Each person making the VOR operational check as specified in paragraph (b) or (c) of this section shall enter the date, place, bearing error, and sign the aircraft log or other record. In addition, if a test signal radiated by a repair station, as specified in paragraph (b)(1) of this section, is used, an entry must be made in the aircraft log or other record by the repair station certificate holder or the certificate holder's representative certifying to the bearing transmitted by the repair station for the check and the date of transmission.

91.27 CIVIL AIRCRAFT: CERTIFICATIONS REQUIRED

(a) Except as provided in 91.28, no person may operate a civil aircraft unless it has within it the following:
   (1) An appropriate and current airworthiness certificate. Each U.S. airworthiness certificate used to comply with this subparagraph (except a special flight permit, a copy of the applicable operations specifications issued under 21.197(c) of this chapter, appropriate sections of the air carrier manual required by Parts 121 and 127 of this chapter containing that portion of the operations specifications issued under 21.197(c), or an authorization under 91.45), must have on it the registration number assigned to the aircraft under Part 47 of this chapter. However, the airworthiness certificate need not have on it an assigned special identification number before 10 days after that number is first affixed to the aircraft. A revised airworthiness certificate having on it an assigned special identification number, that has been affixed to an aircraft, may only be obtained upon application to an FAA Flight Standards District Office.

(2) A registration certificate issued to its owner.

(b) No person may operate a civil aircraft unless the airworthiness certificate required by paragraph (a) of this section or a special flight authorization issued under 91.28 is displayed at the cabin or cockpit entrance so that it is legible to passengers or crew.

91.29 CIVIL AIRCRAFT AIRWORTHINESS

(a) No person may operate a civil aircraft unless it is in an airworthy condition.

(b) The pilot in command of a civil aircraft is responsible for determining whether that aircraft is in condition for safe flight. He shall discontinue the flight when unairworthy mechanical or structural conditions occur.

91.31 CIVIL AIRCRAFT OPERATING LIMITATIONS AND MARKING REQUIREMENTS

(a) Except as provided in paragraph (d) of this section, no person may operate a civil aircraft without compliance with the operating limitations for that aircraft prescribed by the certificating authority of the country of registry.

(b) No person may operate a U.S. registered civil aircraft —
   (1) For which an Airplane or Rotorcraft Flight Manual is required by 21.5 unless there is available in the aircraft a current approved Airplane or Rotorcraft Flight Manual or the manual provided for in 121.141(b); and
   (2) For which an Airplane or Rotorcraft Flight Manual is not required by 21.5, unless there is available in the aircraft a current approved Airplane or Rotorcraft Flight Manual, approved manual material, markings, and placards, or any combination thereof.

(c) No person may operate a U.S. registered civil aircraft unless that aircraft is identified in accordance with Part 45 of this chapter.

(d) Any person taking off or landing a helicopter certificated under Part 29 of this chapter at a heliport constructed over water may make such momentary flight as is necessary for takeoff or landing through the prohibited range of the limiting height-speed envelope established for that helicopter if that flight through the prohibited range takes place over water on which a safe ditching

can be accomplished, and if the helicopter is amphibious or is equipped with floats or other emergency flotation gear adequate to accomplish a safe emergency ditching on open water.

(e) The Airplane or Rotorcraft Flight Manual, or manual material, markings and placards required by paragraph (b) of this section must contain each operating limitation prescribed for that aircraft by the Administrator, including the following:
   (1) Powerplant (e.g., r.p.m., manifold pressure, gas temperature, etc.).
   (2) Airspeeds (e.g., normal operating speed, flaps extended speed, etc.).
   (3) Aircraft weight, center of gravity, and weight distribution, including the composition of the useful load in those combinations and ranges intended to ensure that the weight and center of gravity position will remain within approved limits (e.g., combinations and ranges of crew, oil, fuel, and baggage).
   (4) Minimum flight crew.
   (5) Kinds of operation.
   (6) Maximum operating altitude.
   (7) Maneuvering flight load factors.
   (8) Rotor speed (for rotorcraft).
   (9) Limiting height-speed envelope (for rotorcraft).

91.32 SUPPLEMENTAL OXYGEN

(a) *General.* No person may operate a civil aircraft of U.S. registry —
   (1) At cabin pressure altitudes above 12,500 feet (MSL) up to and including 14,000 feet (MSL), unless the required minimum flight crew is provided with and uses supplemental oxygen for that part of the flight at those altitudes that is of more than 30 minutes duration;
   (2) At cabin pressure altitudes above 14,000 feet (MSL), unless the required minimum flight crew is provided with and uses supplemental oxygen during the entire flight time at those altitudes; and
   (3) At cabin pressure altitudes above 15,000 feet (MSL), unless each occupant of the aircraft is provided with supplemental oxygen.

(b) *Pressurized cabin aircraft.*
   (1) No person may operate a civil aircraft of U.S. registry with a pressurized cabin —
      (i) At flight altitudes above flight level 250, unless at least a 10-minute supply of supplemental oxygen in addition to any

oxygen required to satisfy paragraph (a) of this section, is available for each occupant of the aircraft for use in the event that a descent is necessitated by loss of cabin pressurization; and

(ii) At flight altitudes above flight level 350, unless one pilot at the controls of the airplane is wearing and using an oxygen mask that is secured and sealed, and that either supplies oxygen at all times or automatically supplies oxygen whenever the cabin pressure altitude of the airplane exceeds 14,000 feet (MSL), except that the one pilot need not wear and use an oxygen mask while at or below flight level 410 if there are two pilots at the controls and each pilot has quick-donning type of oxygen mask that can be placed on the face with one hand from the ready position within five seconds, supplying oxygen and properly secured and sealed.

(2) Notwithstanding subparagraph (1)(ii) of this paragraph, if for any reason at any time it is necessary for one pilot to leave his station at the controls of the aircraft when operating at flight altitudes above flight level 350, the remaining pilot at the controls shall put on and use his oxygen mask until the other pilot has returned to his station.

91.33 POWERED CIVIL AIRCRAFT WITH STANDARD CATEGORY U.S. AIRWORTHINESS CERTIFICATES; INSTRUMENT AND EQUIPMENT REQUIREMENTS

(a) *General.* Except as provided in paragraphs (c)(3) and (e) of this section, no person may operate a powered civil aircraft with a standard category U.S. airworthiness certificate in any operation described in paragraphs (b) through (f) of this section unless that aircraft contains the instruments and equipment specified in those paragraphs (or FAA approved equivalents) for that type of operation, and those instruments and items of equipment are in operable condition.

(b) *Visual flight rules (day).* For VFR flight during the day the following instruments and equipment are required:
(1) Airspeed indicator.
(2) Altimeter.
(3) Magnetic direction indicator.
(4) Tachometer for each engine.

(5) Oil pressure gauge for each engine using pressure system.
(6) Temperature gauge for each liquid-cooled engine.
(7) Oil temperature gauge for each air-cooled engine.
(8) Manifold pressure gauge for each altitude engine.
(9) Fuel gauge indicating the quantity of fuel in each tank.
(10) Landing gear position indicator, if the aircraft has a retractable landing gear.
(11) If the aircraft is operated for hire over water and beyond power-off gliding distance from shore, approved flotation gear readily available to each occupant, and at least one pyrotechnic signaling device.
(12) Except as to airships, an approved safety belt for all occupants who have reached their second birthday. After December 4, 1980, each safety belt must be equipped with an approved metal to metal latching device. The rated strength of each safety belt shall not be less than that corresponding with the ultimate load factors specified in the current applicable aircraft airworthiness requirements considering the dimensional characteristics of the safety belt installation for the specific seat or berth arrangement. The webbing of each safety belt shall be replaced as required by the Administrator.
(13) For small civil airplanes manufactured after July 18, 1978, an approved shoulder harness for each front seat. The shoulder harness must be designed to protect the occupant from serious head injury when the occupant experiences the ultimate inertia forces specified in 23.561(b)(2) of this chapter. Each shoulder harness installed at a flight crewmember station must permit the crewmember, when seated and with his safety belt and shoulder harness fastened, to perform all functions necessary for flight operations. For purposes of this paragraph —
(i) The date of manufacture of an airplane is the date the inspection acceptance records reflect that the airplane is complete and meets the FAA Approved Type Design Data; and

(ii) A front seat is a seat located at flight crewmember station or any seat located alongside such a seat.

(c) *Visual flight rules (night).* For VFR flight at night the following instruments and equipment are required:

(1) Instruments and equipment specified in paragraph (b) of this section.

(2) Approved position lights.

(3) An approved aviation red or aviation white anti-collision light system on all U.S. registered civil aircraft. Anti-collision light systems initially installed after August 11, 1971, on aircraft for which a type certificate was issued or applied for before August 11, 1971, must at least meet the anti-collision light standards of Parts 23, 25, 27, or 29, as applicable, that were in effect on August 10, 1971, except that the color may be either aviation red or aviation white. In the event of failure of any light of the anti-collision light system, operations with the aircraft may be continued to a stop where repairs or replacement can be made.

(4) If the aircraft is operated for hire, one electric landing light.

(5) An adequate source of electrical energy for all installed electric and radio equipment.

(6) One spare set of fuses, or three spare fuses of each kind required.

(d) *Instrument flight rules.* For IFR flight the following instruments and equipment are required:

(1) Instruments and equipment specified in paragraph (b) of this section and for night flight, instruments and equipment specified in paragraph (c) of this section.

(2) Two-way radio communications system and navigation equipment appropriate to the ground facilities to be used.

(3) Gyroscopic rate-of-turn indicator, except on the following aircraft:

(i) Large airplanes with a third attitude instrument system usable through flight attitudes of 360 degrees of pitch and roll and installed in accordance with 121.305(j) of this chapter; and

(ii) Rotorcraft, type certificated under Part 29 of this chapter, with a third attitude instrument system usable through flight attitudes of ±80 degrees of pitch and ±120 degrees or roll

and installed in accordance with 29.1303(g) of this chapter.

(4) Slip-skid indicator.

(5) Sensitive altimeter adjustable for barometric pressure.

(6) A clock displaying hours, minutes, and seconds with a sweep-second pointer or digital presentation.

(7) Generator of adequate capacity.

(8) Gyroscopic bank and pitch indicator (artificial horizon).

(9) Gyroscopic direction indicator (directional gyro or equivalent.)

(e) *Flight at and above 24,000 feet MSL.* If VOR navigational equipment is required under paragraph (d)(2) of this section, no person may operate a U.S. registered civil aircraft within the 50 states, and the District of Columbia, at or above 24,000 feet MSL unless that aircraft is equipped with approved distance measuring equipment (DME). When DME required by this paragraph fails at and above 24,000 feet MSL, the pilot in command of the aircraft shall notify ATC immediately, and may then continue operations at and above 24,000 feet MSL to the next airport of intended landing at which repairs or replacement of the equipment can be made.

91.52 EMERGENCY LOCATOR TRANSMITTERS

(a) Except as provided in paragraph (e) and (f) of this section, no person may operate a U.S. registered civil airplane unless it meets the applicable requirements of paragraphs (b), (c), and (d) of this section.

(b) To comply with paragraph (a) of this section, each U.S. registered civil airplane must be equipped as follows:

(1) For operations governed by the supplemental air carrier and commercial operator rules of Part 121 of this chapter, or the air travel club rules of Part 123 of this chapter, there must be attached to the airplane an automatic type emergency locator transmitter that is in operable condition and meets the applicable requirements of 37.200 of this chapter;

(2) For charter flights governed by the domestic and flag air carrier rules of Part 121 of this chapter, there must be attached to the airplane an automatic type emergency locator transmitter that is in operable condition and meets the applicable requirements of 37.200 of this chapter;

(3) For operations governed by Part 135 of this chapter, there must be at-

tached to the airplane an automatic type emergency locator transmitter that is in operable condition and meets the applicable requirements of Part 37.200 of this chapter; and

(4) For operations other than those specified in subparagraphs (1), (2), and (3) of this paragraph, there must be attached to the airplane a personnel type or an automatic type emergency locator transmitter that is in operable condition and meets the applicable requirements of 37.200 of this chapter.

(c) Each emergency locator transmitter required by paragraphs (a) and (b) of this section must be attached to the airplane in such a manner that the probability of damage to the transmitter, in the event of crash impact, is minimized. Fixed and deployable automatic type transmitters must be attached to the airplane as far aft as practicable.

(d) Batteries used in the emergency locator transmitters required by paragraphs (a) and (b) of this section must be replaced (or recharged, if the battery is rechargeable) —

(1) When the transmitter has been in use for more than one cumulative hour; or

(2) When 50 percent of their useful life (or, for rechargeable batteries, 50 percent of their useful life of charge), as established by the transmitter manufacturer under 37.200(g)(2) of this chapter, has expired.

The new expiration date for the replacement (or recharge) of the battery must be legibly marked on the outside of the transmitter and entered in the aircraft maintenance record. Subparagraph (d)(2) of this paragraph does not apply to batteries (such as water-activated batteries) that are essentially unaffected during probable storage intervals.

(e) Notwithstanding paragraphs (a) and (b) of this section, a person may —

(1) Ferry a newly acquired airplane from the place where possession of it was taken to a place where the emergency locator transmitter is to be installed; and

(2) Ferry an airplane with an inoperative emergency locator transmitter from a place where repairs or replacement cannot be made to a place where they can be made.

No person other than required crewmembers may be carried aboard an airplane being ferried pursuant to paragraph (e) of this section.

(f) Paragraphs (a) and (b) of this section do not apply to —

(1) Turbojet-powered aircraft;

(2) Aircraft while engaged in scheduled flights by scheduled air carriers certificated by the Civil Aeronautics Board;

(3) Aircraft while engaged in training operations conducted entirely within a 50-mile radius of the airport from which such local flight operations began;

(4) Aircraft while engaged in flight operations incident to design and testing;

(5) New aircraft while engaged in flight operations incident to their manufacture, preparation, and delivery;

(6) Aircraft while engaged in flight operations incident to the aerial application of chemicals and other substances for agricultural purposes;

(7) Aircraft certificated by the Administrator for research and development purposes;

(8) Aircraft while used for showing compliance with regulations, crew training, exhibition, air racing, or market surveys;

(9) Aircraft equipped to carry not more than one person; and

(10) An aircraft during any period for which the transmitter has been temporarily removed for inspection, repair, modification or replacement, subject to the following:

(i) No person may operate the aircraft unless the aircraft records contain an entry which includes the date of initial removal, the make, model, serial number and reason for removal of the transmitter, and a placard is located in view of the pilot to show "ELT not installed."

(ii) No person may operate the aircraft more than 90 days after the ELT is initially removed from the aircraft.

SUBPART B — FLIGHT RULES: GENERAL

91.61 APPLICABILITY

This subpart prescribes flight rules governing the operation of aircraft within the United States.

91.63 WAIVERS

(a) The Administrator may issue a certificate of waiver authorizing the operation of aircraft in deviation of any rule of this subpart if he finds that the proposed operation can be safely conducted under the terms of that certificate of waiver.

91.65 OPERATING NEAR OTHER AIRCRAFT

(a) No person may operate an aircraft so close to another aircraft as to create a collision hazard.
(b) No person may operate an aircraft in formation flight except by arrangement with the pilot in command of each aircraft in the formation.
(c) No person may operate an aircraft, carrying passengers for hire, in formation flight.
(d) Unless otherwise authorized by ATC, no person operating an aircraft may operate his aircraft in accordance with any clearance or instruction that has been issued to the pilot of another aircraft for radar Air Traffic Control purposes.

91.67 RIGHT-OF-WAY RULES; EXCEPT WATER OPERATIONS

(a) *General.* When weather conditions permit, regardless of whether an operation is conducted under Instrument Flight Rules or Visual Flight Rules, vigilance shall be maintained by each person operating an aircraft so as to see and avoid other aircraft in compliance with this section. When a rule of this section gives another aircraft the right of way, he shall give way to that aircraft and may not pass over, under, or ahead of it, unless well clear.
(b) *In distress.* An aircraft in distress has the right of way over all other air traffic.
(c) *Converging.* When aircraft of the same category are converging at approximately the same altitude (except head-on, or nearly so) the aircraft to the other's right has the right of way. If the aircraft are of different categories —
   (1) A balloon has the right of way over any other category of aircraft;
   (2) A glider has the right of way over an airship, airplane or rotorcraft; and
   (3) An airship has the right of way over an airplane or rotorcraft.
However, an aircraft towing or refueling other aircraft has the right of way over all other engine-driven aircraft.
(d) *Approaching head-on.* When aircraft are approaching each other head-on, or nearly so, each pilot of each aircraft shall alter course to the right.
(e) *Overtaking.* Each aircraft that is being overtaken has the right of way and each pilot of an overtaking aircraft shall alter course to the right to pass well clear.

(f) *Landing.* Aircraft, while on final approach to land, or while landing, have the right of way over other aircraft in flight or operating on the surface. When two or more aircraft are approaching an airport for the purpose of landing, the aircraft at the lower altitude has the right of way, but it shall not take advantage of this rule to cut in front of another which is on final approach to land, or to overtake that aircraft.
(g) *Inapplicability.* This section does not apply to the operation of an aircraft on water.

91.69 RIGHT-OF-WAY RULES; WATER OPERATIONS

(a) *General.* Each person operating an aircraft on the water shall, insofar as possible, keep clear of all vessels and avoid impeding their navigation, and shall give way to any vessel or other aircraft that is given the right of way by any rule of this section.
(b) *Crossing.* When aircraft, or an aircraft and a vessel are on crossing courses, the aircraft or vessel to the other's right has the right of way.
(c) *Approaching head-on.* When aircraft, or an aircraft and a vessel, are approaching head-on or nearly so, each shall alter its course to the right to keep well clear.
(d) *Overtaking.* Each aircraft or vessel that is being overtaken has the right of way, and the one overtaking shall alter course to keep well clear.
(e) *Special circumstances.* When aircraft, or an aircraft and a vessel, approach so as to involve risk of collision, each aircraft or vessel shall proceed with careful regard to existing circumstances, including the limitations of the respective craft.

91.70 AIRCRAFT SPEED

(a) Unless otherwise authorized by the Administrator, no person may operate an aircraft below 10,000 feet MSL at an indicated airspeed of more than 250 knots (288 m.p.h.).
(b) Unless otherwise authorized or required by ATC, no person may operate an aircraft within an airport traffic area at an indicated airspeed of more than —
   (1) In the case of a reciprocating engine aircraft, 156 knots (180 m.p.h.); or
   (2) In the case of a turbine-powered aircraft, 200 knots (230 m.p.h.)
Paragraph (b) of this section does not apply to any operations within a terminal control area. Such operations shall comply with paragraph (a) of this section.

(c) No person may operate an aircraft in the airspace underlying a terminal control area, at an indicated airspeed of more than 200 knots (230 m.p.h.).

However, if the minimum safe airspeed for any particular operation is greater than the maximum speed prescribed in this section, the aircraft may be operated at that minimum speed.

91.71 ACROBATIC FLIGHT

No person may operate an aircraft in acrobatic flight —

(a) Over any congested area of a city, town, or settlement;

(b) Over an open air assembly of persons;

(c) Within a control zone or Federal airway;

(d) Below an altitude of 1,500 feet above the surface; or

(e) When flight visibility is less than three miles.

For the purposes of this section, acrobatic flight means an intentional maneuver involving an abrupt change in an aircraft's attitude, an abnormal attitude, or abnormal acceleration, not necessary for normal flight.

91.73 AIRCRAFT LIGHTS

No person may, during the period from sunset to sunrise (or, in Alaska, during the period a prominent unlighted object cannot be seen from a distance of three statute miles or the sun is more than six degrees below the horizon) —

(a) Operate an aircraft unless it has lighted position lights;

(b) Park or move an aircraft in, or in dangerous proximity to, a night flight operations area of an airport unless the aircraft —

(1) Is clearly illuminated;

(2) Has lighted position lights; or

(3) Is in an area which is marked by obstruction lights.

(c) Anchor an aircraft unless the aircraft—

(1) Has lighted anchor lights; or

(2) Is in an area, where anchor lights are not required on vessels; or

(d) Operate an aircraft, required by 91.33(c)(3) to be equipped with an anticollision light system, unless it has approved and lighted aviation red or aviation white anticollision lights. However, the anticollision lights need not be lighted when the pilot in command determines that, because of operating conditions, it would be in the interest of safety to turn the lights off.

91.75 COMPLIANCE WITH ATC CLEARANCES AND INSTRUCTIONS

(a) When an ATC clearance has been obtained, no pilot in command may deviate from that clearance, except in an emergency, unless he obtains an amended clearance. However, except in positive controlled airspace, this paragraph does not prohibit him from cancelling an IFR flight plan if he is operating in VFR weather conditions. If a pilot is uncertain of the meaning of an ATC clearance, he shall immediately request clarification from ATC.

(b) Except in an emergency, no person may, in an area in which air traffic control is exercised, operate an aircraft contrary to an ATC instruction.

(c) Each pilot in command who deviates, in an emergency, from an ATC clearance or instruction shall notify ATC of that deviation as soon as possible.

(d) Each pilot in command who (though not deviating from a rule of this subpart) is given priority by ATC in an emergency, shall, if requested by ATC, submit a detailed report of that emergency within 48 hours to the chief of that ATC facility.

91.77 ATC LIGHT SIGNALS

ATC light signals have the meaning shown in the following table.

Color and type of signal	Meaning with respect to aircraft on the surface	Meaning with respect to aircraft in flight
Steady green Flashing green	Cleared for takeoff Cleared to taxi	Cleared to land Return for landing (to be followed by steady green at proper time)
Steady red	Stop	Give way to other aircraft and continue circling
Flashing red	Taxi clear of runway in use	Airport unsafe — do not land
Flashing white	Return to starting point on airport	Not applicable
Alternating red and green	Exercise extreme caution	Exercise extreme caution

91.79 MINIMUM SAFE ALTITUDES; GENERAL

Except when necessary for takeoff or landing, no person may operate an aircraft below the following altitudes:

(a) *Anywhere.* An altitude allowing, if a power unit fails, an emergency landing without undue hazard to persons or property on the surface.

(b) *Over congested areas.* Over any congested area of a city, town, or settlement, or over an open air assembly of persons, an altitude of 1,000 feet above the highest obstacle within a horizontal radius of 2,000 feet of the aircraft.

(c) *Over other than congested areas.* An altitude of 500 feet above the surface, except over open water or sparsely

FEDERAL AVIATION REGULATIONS

populated areas. In that case, the aircraft may not be operated closer than 500 feet to any person, vessel, vehicle, or structure.

(d) *Helicopters.* Helicopters may be operated at less than the minimums prescribed in paragraph (b) or (c) of this section if the operation is conducted without hazard to persons or property on the surface. In addition, each person operating a helicopter shall comply with routes or altitudes specifically prescribed for helicopters by the Administrator.

91.81 ALTIMETER SETTINGS

(a) Each person operating an aircraft shall maintain the cruising altitude or flight level of that aircraft, as the case may be, by reference to an altimeter that is set, when operating—
  (1) Below 18,000 feet MSL, to —
    (i) The current reported altimeter setting of a station along the route and within 100 nautical miles of the aircraft;
    (ii) If there is no station within the area prescribed in subdivision (i) of this subparagraph, the current reported altimeter setting of an appropriate available station; or
    (iii) In the case of an aircraft not equipped with a radio, the elevation of the departure airport or an appropriate altimeter setting available before departure; or
  (2) At or above 18,000 feet MSL, to 29.92" Hg.

(b) The lowest usable flight level is determined by the atmospheric pressure in the area of operation, as shown in the following table:

Current altimeter setting	Lowest usable flight level
29.92 or higher	180
29.91 through 29.42	185
29.41 through 28.92	190
28.91 through 28.42	195
28.41 through 27.92	200
27.91 through 27.42	205
27.41 through 26.92	210

(c) To convert minimum altitude prescribed under 91.79 and 91.119 to the minimum flight level, the pilot shall take the flight-level equivalent of the minimum altitude in feet and add the appropriate number of feet specified below, according to the current reported altimeter setting:

Current altimeter setting	Adjustment factor
29.92 or higher	None
29.91 through 29.42	500 feet
29.41 through 28.92	1,000 feet
28.91 through 28.42	1,500 feet
28.41 through 27.92	2,000 feet
27.91 through 27.42	2,500 feet
27.41 through 26.92	3,000 feet

91.83 FLIGHT PLAN; INFORMATION REQUIRED

(a) Unless otherwise authorized by ATC each person filing an IFR or VFR flight plan shall include in it the following information:
  (1) The aircraft identification number and, if necessary, its radio call sign.
  (2) The type of the aircraft or, in the case of a formation flight, the type of each aircraft and the number of aircraft, in the formation.
  (3) The full name and address of the pilot in command or, in the case of a formation flight, the formation commander.
  (4) The point and proposed time of departure.
  (5) The proposed route, cruising altitude (or flight level), and true airspeed at that altitude.
  (6) The point of first intended landing and the estimated elapsed time until over that point.
  (7) The radio frequencies to be used.
  (8) The amount of fuel on board (in hours).
  (9) In the case of an IFR flight plan, an alternate airport, except as provided in paragraph (b) of this section.
  (10) The number of persons in the aircraft, except where that information is otherwise readily available to the FAA.
  (11) Any other information the pilot in command or ATC believes is necessary for ATC purposes.

(b) *Exceptions to applicability of paragraph (a)(9) of this section.* Paragraph (a)(9) of this section does not apply if Part 97 of this subchapter prescribes a standard instrument approach procedure for the first airport of intended landing and, for at least one hour before and one hour after the estimated time of arrival, the weather reports or forecasts or any combination of them, indicate —
  (1) The ceiling will be at least 2,000 feet above the airport elevation; and
  (2) Visibility will be at least 3 miles.

(c) *IFR alternate airport weather minimums.* Unless otherwise authorized

5-30

by the Administrator, no person may include an alternate airport in an IFR flight plan unless current weather forecasts indicate that, at the estimated time of arrival at the alternate airport, the ceiling and visibility at that airport will be at or above the following alternate airport weather minimums:

(1) If an instrument approach procedure has been published in Part 97 of this chapter for that airport, the alternate airport minimums specified in that procedure, or, if none are so specified, the following minimums:

    (i) Precision approach procedure: Ceiling 600 feet and visibility 2 statute miles.

    (ii) Nonprecision approach procedure: Ceiling 800 feet and visibility 2 statute miles.

(2) If no instrument approach procedure has been published in Part 97 of this chapter for that airport, the ceiling and visibility minimums are those allowing descent from the MEA, approach, and landing, under basic VFR.

(d) *Cancellation.* When a flight plan has been activated, the pilot in command, upon cancelling or completing the flight under the flight plan, shall notify an FAA Flight Service Station or ATC facility.

91.84 FLIGHTS BETWEEN MEXICO OR CANADA AND THE UNITED STATES

Unless otherwise authorized by ATC, no person may operate a civil aircraft between Mexico and Canada and the United States without filing an IFR or VFR flight plan, as appropriate.

91.85 OPERATING ON OR IN THE VICINITY OF AN AIRPORT; GENERAL RULES

(a) Unless otherwise required by Part 93 of this chapter, each person operating an aircraft on or in the vicinity of an airport shall comply with the requirements of this section and of 91.87 and 91.89.

(b) Unless otherwise authorized or required by ATC, no person may operate an aircraft within an airport traffic area except for the purpose of landing at, or taking off from, an airport within that area. ATC authorizations may be given as individual approval of specific operations or may be contained in written agreements between airport users and the tower concerned.

91.87 OPERATION AT AIRPORTS WITH OPERATING CONTROL TOWERS

(a) *General.* Unless otherwise authorized or required by ATC, each person operating an aircraft to, from, or on an airport with an operating control tower shall comply with the applicable provisions of this section.

(b) *Communications with control towers operated by the United States.* No person may, within an airport traffic area, operate an aircraft to, from, or on an airport having a control tower operated by the United States unless two-way radio communications are maintained between that aircraft and the control tower. However, if the aircraft radio fails in flight, he may operate that aircraft and land if weather conditions are at or above basic VFR weather minimums, he maintains visual contact with the tower, and he receives a clearance to land. If the aircraft radio fails while in flight under IFR, he must comply with 91.127.

(c) *Communications with other control towers.* No person may, within an airport traffic area, operate an aircraft to, from, or on an airport having a control tower that is operated by any person other than the United States unless —

(1) If that aircraft's radio equipment so allows, two-way radio communications are maintained between the aircraft and the tower; or

(2) If that aircraft's radio equipment allows only reception from the tower, the pilot has the tower's frequency monitored.

(d) *Minimum altitudes.* When operating to an airport with an operating control tower, each pilot of —

(1) A turbine-powered airplane or a large airplane shall, unless otherwise required by the applicable distance from cloud criteria, enter the airport traffic area at an altitude of at least 1,500 feet above the surface of the airport and maintain at least 1,500 feet within the airport traffic area, including the traffic pattern, until further descent is required for a safe landing;

(2) A turbine-powered airplane or a large airplane approaching to land on a runway being served by an ILS, shall, if the airplane is ILS equipped, fly that airplane at an altitude at or above the glide slope between the outer marker (or the point of interception with the glide slope, if compliance with the applicable distance from clouds criteria

requires interception closer in) and the middle marker; and,

(3) An airplane approaching to land on a runway served by a visual approach slope indicator, shall maintain an altitude at or above the glide slope until a lower altitude is necessary for a safe landing.

However, subparagraphs (2) and (3) of this paragraph do not prohibit normal bracketing maneuvers above or below the glide slope that are conducted for the purpose of remaining on the glide slope.

(e) *Approaches.* When approaching to land at an airport with an operating control tower, each pilot of —

(1) An airplane, shall circle the airport to the left; and

(2) A helicopter, shall avoid the flow of fixed-wing aircraft.

(f) *Departures.* No person may operate an aircraft taking off from an airport with an operating control tower except in compliance with the following:

(1) Each pilot shall comply with any departure procedures established for that airport by the FAA.

(2) Unless otherwise required by the departure procedure or the applicable distance from clouds criteria, each pilot of a turbine-powered airplane and each pilot of a large airplane shall climb to an altitude of 1,500 feet above the surface as rapidly as practicable.

(g) *Noise abatement runway system.* When landing or taking off from an airport with an operating control tower, and for which a formal runway use program has been established by the FAA, each pilot of a turbine-powered airplane and each pilot of a large airplane, assigned a noise abatement runway by ATC, shall use that runway.

However, consistent with the final authority of the pilot in command concerning the safe operation of the aircraft as prescribed in 91.3(a), ATC may assign a different runway if requested by the pilot in the interest of safety.

(h) *Clearances required.* No person may, at any airport with an operating control tower, operate an aircraft on a runway or taxiway, or takeoff or land an aircraft, unless an appropriate clearance is received from ATC. A clearance to "taxi to" the takeoff runway assigned to the aircraft is not a clearance to cross that assigned takeoff runway, or to taxi on that runway at any point, but is a clearance to cross other runways that intersect the taxi route to that assigned takeoff runway. A clearance to "taxi to"

any point other than an assigned takeoff runway is a clearance to cross all runways that intersect the taxi route to that point.

91.89 OPERATION AT AIRPORTS WITHOUT CONTROL TOWERS

Each person operating an aircraft to or from an airport without an operating control tower shall —

(a) In the case of an airplane approaching to land, make all turns of that airplane to the left unless the airport displays approved light signals or visual markings indicating that turns should be made to the right, in which case the pilot shall make all turns to the right;

(b) In the case of a helicopter approaching to land, avoid the flow of fixed-wing aircraft; and

(c) In the case of an aircraft departing the airport, comply with any FAA traffic pattern for that airport.

91.90 TERMINAL CONTROL AREAS

(a) *Group I terminal control areas.*

(1) *Operating rules.* No person may operate an aircraft within a Group I terminal control area designated in Part 71 of this chapter except in compliance with the following rules:

(i) No person may operate an aircraft within a Group I terminal control area unless he has received an appropriate authorization from ATC prior to the operation of that aircraft in that area.

(ii) Unless otherwise authorized by ATC, each person operating a large turbine engine powered airplane to or from a primary airport shall operate at or above the designated floors while within the lateral limits of the terminal control area.

(2) *Pilot requirements.* The pilot in command of a civil aircraft may not land or take off that aircraft from an airport within a Group I terminal control area unless he holds at least a private pilot certificate.

(3) *Equipment requirements.* Unless otherwise authorized by ATC in the case of in-flight VOR, TACAN or two-way radio failure; or unless otherwise authorized by ATC in the case of a transponder failure occurring at any time, no person may operate an aircraft within a Group I terminal control area unless that aircraft is equipped with —

(i) An operable VOR or TACAN receiver (except in the case of helicopters);

(ii) An operable two-way radio capable of communicating with ATC on appropriate frequencies for that terminal control area; and

(iii) The applicable equipment specified in 91.24.

(b) *Group II terminal control areas*

(1) *Operating rules.* No person may operate an aircraft within a Group II terminal control area designated in Part 71 of this chapter except in compliance with the following rules:

(i) No person may operate an aircraft within a Group II terminal control area unless he has received an appropriate authorization from ATC prior to operation of that aircraft in that area, and unless two-way radio communications are maintained, within that area, between that aircraft and the ATC facility.

(ii) Unless otherwise authorized by ATC, each person operating a large turbine engine powered airplane to or from a primary airport shall operate at or above the designated floors while within the lateral limits of the terminal control area.

(2) *Equipment requirements.* Unless otherwise authorized by ATC in the case of in-flight VOR, TACAN, or two-way radio failure; or unless otherwise authorized by ATC in the case of a transponder failure occurring at any time, no person may operate an aircraft within a Group II terminal control area unless that aircraft is equipped with —

(i) An operable VOR or TACAN receiver (except in the case of helicopters);

(ii) An operable two-way radio capable of communicating with ATC on the appropriate frequencies for that terminal control area; and

(iii) The applicable equipment specified in 91.24, except that automatic pressure reporting equipment is not required for any operation within the terminal control area, and a transponder is not required for IFR flights operating to or from an airport outside of but in close proximity to the terminal control area, when the commonly used transition, ap-

proach, or departure procedures to such airport require flight within the terminal control area.

(c) *Group III terminal control areas.* No person may operate an aircraft within a Group III terminal control area designated in Part 71 unless the applicable provisions of 91.24(b) are complied with, except that such compliance is not required if two-way radio communications are maintained, within the TCA, between the aircraft and the ATC facility, and the pilot provides position, altitude, and proposed flight path prior to entry.

91.91 TEMPORARY FLIGHT RESTRICTIONS

(a) Whenever the Administrator determines it to be necessary in order to prevent an unsafe congestion of sight-seeing aircraft above an incident or event which may generate a high degree of public interest, or to provide a safe environment for the operation of disaster relief aircraft, a Notice to Airmen will be issued designating an area within which temporary flight restrictions apply.

(b) When a Notice to Airmen has been issued under this section, no person may operate an aircraft within the designated area unless —

(1) That aircraft is participating in disaster relief activities and is being operated under the direction of the agency responsible for relief activities;

(2) That aircraft is being operated to or from an airport within the area and is operated so as not to hamper or endanger relief activities;

(3) That operation is specifically authorized under an IFR ATC clearance;

(4) VFR flight around or above the area is impracticable due to weather; terrain, or other considerations, prior notice is given to the Air Traffic Service facility specified in the Notice to Airmen, and en route operation through the area is conducted so as not to hamper or endanger relief activities; or

(5) That aircraft is carrying properly accredited news representatives, or persons on official business concerning the incident or event which generated the issuance of the Notice to Airmen; the operation is conducted in accordance with 91.79; the operation is conducted above the altitudes being used by relief aircraft unless otherwise authorized by the

agency responsible for relief activities; and further, in connection with this type of operation, prior to entering the area the operator has filed with the Air Traffic Service facility specified in the Notice to Airmen a flight plan that includes the following information:
  (i) Aircraft identification, type and color,
  (ii) Radio communications frequencies to be used,
  (iii) Proposed times of entry and exit of the designated area,
  (iv) Name of news media or purpose of flight,
  (v) Any other information deemed necessary by ATC.

91.93 FLIGHT TEST AREAS

No person may flight test an aircraft except over open water, or sparsely populated areas, having light air traffic.

91.95 RESTRICTED AND PROHIBITED AREAS

(a) No person may operate an aircraft within a restricted area (designated in Part 73 contrary to the restrictions imposed, or within a prohibited area, unless he has the permission of the using or controlling agency, as appropriate.

(b) Each person conducting, within a restricted area, an aircraft operation (approved by the using agency) that creates the same hazards as the operations for which the restricted area was designated, may deviate from the rules of this subpart that are not compatible with his operation of the aircraft.

91.97 POSITIVE CONTROL AREAS AND ROUTE SEGMENTS

(a) Except as provided in paragraph (b) of this section, no person may operate an aircraft within a positive control area, or positive control route segment designated in Part 71 of this chapter, unless that aircraft is —
  (1) Operated under IFR at a specific flight level assigned by ATC;
  (2) Equipped with instruments and equipment required for IFR operations;
  (3) Flown by a pilot rated for instrument flight; and
  (4) Equipped, when in a positive control area, with —
    (i) The applicable equipment specified in 91.24; and

(ii) A radio providing direct pilot/controller communication on the frequency specified by ATC for the area concerned.

(b) ATC may authorize deviations from the requirements of paragraph (a) of this section. In the case of an inoperative transponder, ATC may immediately approve an operation within a positive control area allowing flight to continue, if desired, to the airport of ultimate destination, including any intermediate stops, or to proceed to a place where suitable repairs can be made, or both. A request for authorization to deviate from a requirement of paragraph (a) of this section, other than for operation with an inoperative transponder as outlined above, must be submitted at least 4 days before the proposed operation, in writing, to the ATC center having jurisdiction over the positive control area concerned. ATC may authorize a deviation on a continuing basis or for an individual flight, as appropriate.

91.101 OPERATIONS TO, OR OVER, CUBA

No person may operate a civil aircraft from the United States to Cuba unless —

(a) Departure is from an international airport of entry designated in 6.13 of the Air Commerce Regulations of the Bureau of Customs (19 CFR 6.13); and

(b) In the case of departure from any of the 48 contiguous States or the District of Columbia, the pilot in command of the aircraft has filed —
  (1) A DVFR or IFR flight plan as prescribed in 99.11 or 99.13 of this chapter; and
  (2) A written statement, within one hour before departure, with the office of Immigration and Naturalization Service at the airport of departure, containing—
    (i) All information in the flight plan;
    (ii) The name of each occupant of the aircraft;
    (iii) The number of occupants of the aircraft; and
    (iv) A description of the cargo, if any.

This section does not apply to the operation of aircraft by a scheduled air carrier over routes authorized in operations specifications issued by the Administrator.

FEDERAL AVIATION REGULATIONS

91.102 FLIGHT LIMITATION IN THE PROXIMITY OF SPACE FLIGHT RECOVERY OPERATIONS

No person may operate any aircraft of United States registry, or pilot any aircraft under the authority of an airman certificate issued by the Federal Aviation Administration within areas designated in a Notice to Airmen (NOTAM) for space flight recovery operations except when authorized by ATC, or operated under the control of the Department of Defense Manager for Manned Space Flight Support Operations.

91.104 FLIGHT RESTRICTIONS IN THE PROXIMITY OF THE PRESIDENTIAL AND OTHER PARTIES

No person may operate an aircraft over or in the vicinity of any area to be visited or traveled by the President, the Vice President, or other public figures contrary to the restrictions established by the Administrator and published in a Notice to Airmen (NOTAM).

VISUAL FLIGHT RULES

91.105 BASIC VFR WEATHER MINIMUMS

(a) Except as provided in 91.107, no person may operate an aircraft under VFR when the flight visibility is less, or at a distance from clouds that is less, than that prescribed for the corresponding altitude in the following table:

Altitude	Flight visibility	Distance from clouds
1,200 feet or less above the surface (regardless of MSL altitude)— Within controlled airspace	3 statute miles	500 feet below. 1,000 feet above. 2,000 feet horizontal.
Outside controlled airspace	1 statute mile except as provided in 91.105(b).	Clear of clouds.
More than 1,200 feet above the surface but less than 10,000 feet MSL Within controlled airspace	3 statute miles	500 feet below. 1,000 feet above. 2,000 feet horizontal.
Outside controlled airspace	1 statute mile	500 feet below. 1,000 feet above. 2,000 feet horizontal.
More than 1,200 feet above the surface and at or above 10,000 feet MSL	5 statute miles	1,000 feet below. 1,000 feet above. 1 mile horizontal.

(b) When the visibility is less than one mile, a helicopter may be operated outside con-

trolled airspace at 1,200 feet or less above the surface if operated at a speed that allows the pilot adequate opportunity to see any air traffic or other obstructions in time to avoid a collision.

(c) Except as provided in 91.107, no person may operate an aircraft, under VFR, within a control zone beneath the ceiling when the ceiling is less than 1,000 feet.

(d) Except as provided in 91.107, no person may take off or land an aircraft, or enter the traffic pattern of an airport, under VFR, within a control zone—
(1) Unless ground visibility at that airport is at least 3 statute miles; or
(2) If ground visibility is not reported at that airport, unless flight visibility during landing or takeoff, or while operating in the traffic pattern, is at least 3 statute miles.

(e) For the purposes of this section, an aircraft operating at the base altitude of a transition area or control area is considered to be within the airspace directly below that area.

91.107 SPECIAL VFR WEATHER MINIMUMS

(a) Except as provided in 93.113, when a person has received an appropriate ATC clearance, the special weather minimums of this section instead of those contained in 91.105 apply to the operation of an aircraft by that person in a control zone under VFR.

(b) No person may operate an aircraft in a control zone under VFR except clear of clouds.

(c) No person may operate an aircraft (other than a helicopter) in a control zone under VFR unless flight visibility is at least one statute mile.

(d) No person may take off or land an aircraft (other than a helicopter) at any airport in a control zone under VFR—
(1) Unless ground visibility at that airport is at least 1 statute mile; or
(2) If ground visibility is not reported at that airport, unless flight visibility during landing or takeoff is at least 1 statute mile.

(e) No person may operate an aircraft (other than a helicopter) in a control zone under the special weather minimums of this section, between sunset and sunrise (or in Alaska, when the sun is more than 6 degrees below the horizon) unless:

FEDERAL AVIATION REGULATIONS

(1) That person meets the applicable requirements for instrument flight under Part 61 of this chapter; and

(2) The aircraft is equipped as required in 91.33(d).

91.109 VFR CRUISING ALTITUDE OR FLIGHT LEVEL

Except while holding in a holding pattern of 2 minutes or less, or while turning, each person operating an aircraft under VFR in level cruising flight more than 3,000 feet above the surface shall maintain the appropriate altitude or flight level prescribed below, unless otherwise authorized by ATC.

(a) When operating below 18,000 feet MSL and —

(1) On a magnetic course of zero degrees through 179 degrees, any odd thousand foot MSL altitude plus 500 feet (such as 3,500, 5,500, or 7,500); or

(2) On a magnetic course of 180 degrees through 359 degrees, any even thousand foot MSL altitude plus 500 feet (such as 4,500, 6,500 or 8,500).

(b) When operating above 18,000 feet MSL to flight level 290 (inclusive), and —

(1) On a magnetic course of zero degrees through 179 degrees, any odd flight level plus 500 feet (such as 195, 215 or 235); or

(2) On a magnetic course of 180 degrees through 359 degrees, any even flight level plus 500 feet (such as 185, 205, or 235).

(c) When operating above flight level 290 and—

(1) On a magnetic course of zero degrees through 179 degrees, any flight level, at 4,000-foot intervals, beginning at and including flight level 300 (such as flight level 300, 340, or 380); or

(2) On a magnetic course of 180 degrees through 359 degrees, any flight level at 4,000 foot intervals, beginning at and including flight level 320 (such as flight level 320, 360, or 400).

INSTRUMENT FLIGHT RULES

91.115 ATC CLEARANCE AND FLIGHT PLAN REQUIRED

No person may operate an aircraft in controlled airspace under IFR unless —

(a) He has filed an IFR flight plan; and

(b) He has received an appropriate ATC clearance.

91.116 TAKEOFF AND LANDING UNDER IFR: GENERAL

(a) *Instrument approaches to civil airports.* Unless otherwise authorized by the Administrator (including ATC), each person operating an aircraft shall, when an instrument letdown to an airport is necessary, use a standard instrument approach procedure prescribed for that airport in Part 97 of this chapter.

(b) *Landing minimums.* Unless otherwise authorized by the Administrator, no person operating an aircraft (except a military aircraft of the United States) may land that aircraft using a standard instrument approach procedure prescribed in Part 97 of this chapter unless the visibility is at or above the landing minimum prescribed in that part for the procedure used. If the landing minimum in a standard instrument approach procedure prescribed in Part 97 of this chapter is stated in terms of ceiling and visibility, the visibility minimum applies. However, the ceiling minimum shall be added to the field elevation and that value observed as the MDA or DH, as appropriate to the procedure being executed.

(c) *Civil airport takeoff minimums.* Unless otherwise authorized by the Administrator, no person operating an aircraft under Part 121, 123, 129 or 135 of this chapter may takeoff from a civil airport under IFR unless weather conditions are at or above the weather minimums for IFR takeoff prescribed for that airport in Part 97 of this chapter. If takeoff minimums are not prescribed in Part 97 of this chapter, for a particular airport, the following minimums apply to take-offs under IFR for aircraft operating under those parts:

(1) Aircraft having two engines or less: 1 statute mile visibility.

(2) Aircraft having more than two engines: One-half statute mile visibility

(d) *Military airports.* Unless otherwise prescribed by the Administrator, each person operating a civil aircraft under IFR into, or out of, a military airport shall comply with the instrument approach procedures and the takeoff and landing minimums prescribed by the military authority having jurisdiction on that airport.

(e) Comparable values of RVR and ground visibility.

(1) If RVR minimums for takeoff or landing are prescribed in an instrument approach procedure, but RVR is not

reported for the runway of intended operation, the RVR minimum shall be converted to ground visibility in accordance with the table in subparagraph (2) of this paragraph and observed as the applicable visibility minimum for takeoff or landing on that runway.

(2)

RVR	Visibility (Statute miles)
1600 feet	1/4 mile
2400 feet	1/2 mile
3200 feet	5/8 mile
4000 feet	3/4 mile
4500 feet	7/8 mile
5000 feet	1 mile
6000 feet	1-1/4 mile

(f) *Operation on unpublished routes and use of radar in instrument approach procedures.* When radar is approved at certain locations for ATC purposes, it may be used not only for surveillance and precision radar approaches, as applicable, but also may be used in conjunction with instrument approach procedures predicated on other types of radio navigational aids. Radar vectors may be authorized to provide course guidance through the segments of an approach procedure to the final approach fix or position. When operating on an unpublished route or while being radar vectored, the pilot, when an approach clearance is received, shall, in addition to complying with 91.119, maintain his last assigned altitude (1) unless a different altitude is assigned by ATC, or (2) until the aircraft is established on a segment of a published route or instrument approach procedure. After the aircraft is so established, published altitudes apply to descent within each succeeding route or approach segment unless a different altitude is assigned by ATC. Upon reaching the final approach fix or position, the pilot may either complete his instrument approach in accordance with the procedure approved for the facility, or may continue a surveillance or precision radar approach to a landing.

(g) *Use of low or medium frequency simultaneous radio ranges for ADF procedures.* Low frequency or medium frequency simultaneous radio ranges may be used as an ADF instrument approach aid if an ADF procedure for the airport concerned is prescribed by the Administrator, or if an approach is conducted using the same

courses and altitudes for the ADF approach as those specified in the approved range procedure.

(h) *Limitations on procedure turns.* In the case of a radar initial approach to a final approach fix or position, or a timed approach from a holding fix, or where the procedure specifies "NOPT" or "FINAL," no pilot may make a procedure turn unless, when he receives his final approach clearance, he so advises ATC.

91.117 LIMITATIONS ON USE OF INSTRUMENT APPROACH PROCEDURES (OTHER THAN CATEGORY II)

(a) *General.* Unless otherwise authorized by the Administrator, each person operating an aircraft using an instrument approach procedure prescribed in Part 97 of this chapter shall comply with the requirements of this section. This section does not apply to the use of Category II approach procedures.

(b) *Descent below MDA or DH.* No person may operate an aircraft below the prescribed minimum descent altitude or continue an approach below the decision height unless—

(1) The aircraft is in a position from which a normal approach to the runway of intended landing can be made; and

(2) The approach threshold of that runway, or approach lights or other markings identifiable with the approach end of that runway, are clearly visible to the pilot.

If, upon arrival at the missed approach point or decision height, or at any time thereafter, any of the above requirements are not met, the pilot shall immediately execute the appropriate missed approach procedure.

(c) *Inoperative or unusable components and visual aids.* The basic ground components of an ILS are the localizer, glide slope, outer marker, and middle marker. The approach lights are visual aids normally associated with the ILS. In addition, if an ILS approach procedure in Part 97 of this chapter prescribes a visibility minimum of 1,800 feet or 2,000 feet RVR, high-intensity runway lights, touchdown zone lights, centerline lighting and marking and RVR are aids associated with the ILS for those minimums. Compass locator or precision radar may be substituted for the outer or middle marker. Surveillance radar may be substituted for the outer marker. Except as provided in subparagraph (c)(5) of this paragraph or unless otherwise specified by the Administrator, if a ground component, visual aid, or RVR is inoperative, or unusable or not utilized, the straight-in minimums prescribed in any approach procedure in Part 97 of this chapter are raised in accordance with the following tables. If the related airborne equipment for a ground component is inoperative or not utilized, the increased minimums applicable to the related ground component shall be used. If more than one component or aid is inoperative, or unusable, or not utilized, each minimum is raised to the highest minimum required by any one of the components or aids which is inoperative, or unusable, or not utilized.

(1) *ILS and PAR.*

Component or aid	Increase decision height	Increase visibility (statute miles)	Approach category
LOC[1]	ILS approach not authorized.	---	All
GS	As specified in the procedure.	---	All
OM,[1] MM[1]	50 feet	None	ABC
MM,[1] MM[1]	50 feet	¼	D
ALS	50 feet	¼	All
SSALSR	50 feet	¼	ABC
MALSR	50 feet	¼	ABC

[1]Not applicable to PAR.

(2) *ILS with visibility minimum of 1,800 or 2,000 feet RVR*

Component or aid	Increase decision height	Increase visibility (statute miles)	Approach category
LOC	ILS approach not authorized.	---	All
GS	As specified in the procedure.	---	All
OM, MM	50 feet	To ½ mile	ABC
OM, MM	50 feet	To ¾ mile	D
ALS	50 feet	To ¾ mile	All
HIRL, TDZL, RCLS.	None	To ½ mile	All

(2) *Continued*

Component or aid	Increase decision height	Increase visibility (statute miles)	Approach category
RCLM	As specified in the procedure.	---	All
RVR	None	To ½ mile	All

(3)   *VOR, LOC, LDA, and ASR*

Component or aid	Increase MDA	Increase visibility (statute miles)	Approach category
ALS, SSALSR, MALSR	None	½ mile	ABC
SSALS, MALS, HIRL, and REIL	None	¼ mile	ABC

(4)   *NDB(ADF) and LFR*

Component or aid	Increase MDA	Increase visibility (statute miles)	Approach category
ALS, SSALSR, MALSR	None	¼ mile	ABC

(5) The inoperative component tables in subparagraphs (1) through (4) of this paragraph do not apply to helicopter procedures. Helicopter procedure minimums are specified on each procedure for inoperative components.

91.119 MINIMUM ALTITUDES FOR IFR OPERATIONS

(a) Except when necessary for takeoff or landing, or unless otherwise authorized by the Administrator, no person may operate an aircraft under IFR below —
(1) The applicable minimum altitudes prescribed in Parts 95 (New) and 97 (New) of this chapter; or
(2) If no applicable minimum altitude is prescribed in those parts —
(i) In the case of operations over an area designated as a mountainous

area in Part 95 an altitude of 2,000 feet above the highest obstacle within a horizontal distance of five statute miles from the course to be flown; or

(ii) In any other case, an altitude of 1,000 feet above the highest obstacle within a horizontal distance of five statute miles from the course to be flown.

However, if both a MEA and a MOCA are prescribed for a particular route or route segment, a person may operate an aircraft below the MEA down to, but not below, the MOCA, when within 25 statute miles of the VOR concerned (based on the pilot's reasonable estimate of that distance).

(b) *Climb.* Climb to a higher minimum IFR altitude shall begin immediately after passing the point beyond which that minimum altitude applies, except that, when ground obstructions intervene, the point beyond which the higher minimum altitude applies shall be crossed at or above the applicable MCA.

91.121 IFR CRUISING ALTITUDE OR FLIGHT LEVEL

(a) *In controlled airspace.* Each person operating an aircraft under IFR in level cruising flight in controlled airspace shall maintain the altitude or flight level assigned that aircraft by ATC. However, if the ATC clearance assigns "VFR conditions ontop," he shall maintain an altitude or flight level as prescribed by 91.109.

(b) *In uncontrolled airspace.* Except while holding in a holding pattern of two minutes or less, or while turning, each person operating an aircraft under IFR in level cruising flight, in uncontrolled airspace, shall maintain an appropriate altitude as follows:

(1) When operating below 18,000 feet MSL and—
(i) On a magnetic course of zero degrees through 179 degrees, any odd thousand foot MSL altitude (such as 3,000, 5,000, or 7,000); or
(ii) On a magnetic course of 180 degrees through 359 degrees, any even thousand foot MSL altitude (such as 2,000, 4,000, or 6,000).

(2) When operating at or above 18,000 feet MSL but below flight level 290, and—

(i) On a magnetic course of zero degrees through 179 degrees, any odd flight level (such as 190, 210, or 230); or
(ii) On a magnetic course of 180 degrees through 359 degrees, any even flight level (such as 180, 200, or 220).

(3) When operating at flight level 290 and above, and—
(i) On a magnetic course of zero degrees through 179 degrees, any flight level, at 4,000 foot intervals, beginning at and including flight level 290 (such as flight level 290, 330, or 370); or
(ii) On a magnetic course of 180 degrees through 359 degrees, any flight level, at 4,000 foot intervals, beginning at and including flight level 310 (such as flight level 310, 350, or 390).

91.123 COURSE TO BE FLOWN

Unless otherwise authorized by ATC, no person may operate an aircraft within controlled airspace, under IFR, except as follows:
(a) On a Federal airway, along the centerline of that airway.
(b) On any other route, along the direct course between the navigational aids or fixes defining that route.

However, this section does not prohibit maneuvering the aircraft to pass well clear of other air traffic or the maneuvering of the aircraft, in VFR conditions, to clear the intended flight path both before and during climb or descent.

91.125 IFR, RADIO COMMUNICATIONS

The pilot in command of each aircraft operated under IFR in controlled airspace shall have a continuous watch maintained on the appropriate frequency and shall report by radio as soon as possible—
(a) The time and altitude of passing each designated reporting point, or the reporting points specified by ATC, except that while the aircraft is under radar control, only the passing of those reporting points specifically requested by ATC need be reported;
(b) Any unforecast weather conditions encountered; and
(c) Any other information relating to the safety of flight.

91.127 IFR OPERATIONS; TWO-WAY RADIO COMMUNICATIONS FAILURE

(a) *General.* Unless otherwise authorized by ATC, each pilot who has two-way radio communications failure when operating under IFR shall comply with the rules of this section.

(b) *VFR conditions.* If the failure occurs in VFR conditions, or if VFR conditions are encountered after the failure, each pilot shall continue the flight under VFR and land as soon as practicable.

(c) *IFR conditions.* If the failure occurs in IFR conditions, or if paragraph (b) of this section cannot be complied with, each pilot shall continue the flight according to the following:

    (1) *Route.*

        (i) By the route assigned in the last ATC clearance received;

        (ii) If being radar vectored, by the direct route from the point of radio failure to the fix, route, or airway specified in the vector clearance;

        (iii) In the absence of an assigned route, by the route that ATC has advised may be expected in a further clearance; or

        (iv) In the absence of an assigned route or a route that ATC has advised may be expected in a further clearance, by the route filed in the flight plan.

    (2) *Altitude.* At the highest of the following altitudes or flight levels for the route segment being flown:

        (i) The altitude or flight level assigned in the last ATC clearance received;

        (ii) The minimum altitude (converted, if appropriate, to minimum flight level as prescribed in 91.81 (c)) for IFR operations; or

        (iii) The altitude or flight level ATC has advised may be expected in a further clearance.

    (3) (Revoked).

    (4) *Leave holding fix.* If holding instructions have been received, leave the holding fix at the expect-further-clearance time received, or, if an expected approach clearance time has been received, leave the holding fix in order to arrive over the fix from which the approach begins as close as pos-

sible to the expected approach clearance time.

    (5) *Descent for approach.* Begin descent from the en route altitude or flight level upon reaching the fix from which the approach begins, but not before—

        (i) The expect-approach-clearance time (if received); or

        (ii) If no expect-approach-clearance time has been received, at the estimated time of arrival, shown on the flight plan, as amended with ATC.

91.129 OPERATION UNDER IFR IN CONTROLLED AIRSPACE; MALFUNCTION REPORTS

(a) The pilot in command of each aircraft operated in controlled airspace under IFR, shall report immediately to ATC any of the following malfunctions of equipment occurring in flight:

    (1) Loss of VOR, TACAN, ADF, or low frequency navigation receiver capability.

    (2) Complete or partial loss of ILS receiver capability.

    (3) Impairment of air/ground communications capability.

(b) In each report required by paragraph (a) of this section, the pilot in command shall include the—

    (1) Aircraft identification;

    (2) Equipment affected;

    (3) Degree to which the capability of the pilot to operate under IFR in the ATC system is impaired; and

    (4) Nature and extent of assistance he desires from ATC.

SUBPART C—MAINTENANCE, PREVENTIVE MAINTENANCE, AND ALTERATIONS

91.161 APPLICABILITY

(a) This subpart prescribes rules governing the maintenance, preventive maintenance, and alteration of U.S. registered civil aircraft operating within or without the United States.

(b) Sections 91.165, 91.169, 91.170, 91.171, 91.173, and 91.174 of this subpart do not apply to an aircraft maintained in accordance with a continuous airworthiness maintenance program as provided in Part 121, 127, or 135 of this chapter.

91.163 GENERAL

(a) The owner or operator of an aircraft is primarily responsible for maintaining that aircraft in an airworthy condition, including compliance with Part 39 of this chapter.

(b) No person may perform maintenance, preventive maintenance, or alterations on an aircraft other than as prescribed in this subpart and other applicable regulations, including Part 43.

(c) No person may operate a rotorcraft for which a Rotorcraft Maintenance Manual containing an "Airworthiness Limitations" section has been issued unless the replacement times, inspection intervals, and related procedures specified in that section of the manual are complied with.

91.165 MAINTENANCE REQUIRED

Each owner or operator of an aircraft shall have that aircraft inspected as prescribed in Subpart D or 91.169 of this Part, as appropriate, and 91.170 of this Part and shall, between required inspections, have defects repaired as prescribed in Part 43 of this chapter. In addition, he shall insure that maintenance personnel make appropriate entries in the aircraft and maintenance records indicating the aircraft has been released to service.

91.167 CARRYING PERSONS OTHER THAN CREWMEMBERS AFTER REPAIRS OR ALTERATIONS

(a) No person may carry any person (other than crewmembers) in an aircraft that has been repaired or altered in a manner that may have appreciably changed its flight characteristics, or substantially affected its operation in flight, until it has been approved for return to service in accordance with Part 43 and an appropriately rated pilot, with at least a private pilot's certificate, flies the aircraft, makes an operational check of the repaired or altered part, and logs the flight in the aircraft's records.

(b) Paragraph (a) of this section does not require that the aircraft be flown if ground tests or inspections, or both, show conclusively that the repair or alteration has not appreciably changed the flight characteristics, or substantially affected the flight operation of the aircraft.

91.169 INSPECTIONS

(a) Except as provided in paragraph (c) of this section, no person may operate an aircraft,

unless, within the preceding 12 calendar months, it has had—

(1) An annual inspection in accordance with Part 43 of this chapter and has been approved for return to service by a person authorized by 43.7 of this chapter; or

(2) An inspection for the issue of an airworthiness certificate.

No inspection performed under paragraph (b) of this section may be substituted for any inspection required by this paragraph unless it is performed by a person authorized to perform annual inspections, and is entered as an "annual" inspection in the required maintenance records.

(b) Except as provided in paragraph (c) of this section, no person may operate an aircraft carrying any person (other than a crewmember) for hire, and no person may give flight instruction for hire in an aircraft which that person provides, unless within the preceding 100 hours of time in service it has received an annual or 100-hour inspection and been approved for return to service in accordance with Part 43 of this chapter, or received an inspection for the issuance of an airworthiness certificate in accordance with Part 21 of this chapter. The 100-hour limitation may be exceeded by not more than 10 hours if necessary to reach a place at which the inspection can be done. The excess time, however, is included in computing the next 100 hours of time in service.

(c) Paragraphs (a) and (b) of this section do not apply to—

(1) Any aircraft for which its registered owner or operator complies with the progressive inspection requirements of 91.171 and Part 43 of this chapter;

(2) An aircraft that carries a special flight permit or a current experimental or provisional certificate;

(3) Any airplane operated by an air travel club that is inspected in accordance with Part 123 of this chapter and the operator's manual and operations specifications; or

(4) An aircraft inspected in accordance with an approved aircraft inspection program under Part 135 of this chapter and so identified by registration number in the operations specifications of the certificate holder having the approved inspection program.

(5) Any large airplane, or a turbojet or turbopropeller-powered multiengine airplane, that is inspected in accordance with an inspection program authorized under Subpart D of this Part.

91.170 ALTIMETER SYSTEM TESTS AND INSPECTIONS

(a) No person may operate an airplane in controlled airspace under IFR unless, within the preceding 24 calendar months, each static pressure system and each altimeter instrument has been tested and inspected and found to comply with Appendix E of Part 43. The static pressure system and altimeter instrument tests and inspections may be conducted by—

(1) The manufacturer of the airplane on which the tests and inspections are to be performed;

(2) A certificated repair station properly equipped to perform these functions and holding—

    (i) An instrument rating, Class I;

    (ii) A limited instrument rating appropriate to the make and model altimeter to be tested;

    (iii) A limited rating appropriate to the test to be performed;

    (iv) An airframe rating appropriate to the airplane to be tested; or

    (v) A limited rating for a manufacturer issued for the altimeter in accordance with 145.101 (b) (4) of this chapter; or

(3) A certificated mechanic with an airframe rating (static pressure system tests and inspections only).

(b) (Revoked)

(c) No person may operate an airplane in controlled airspace under IFR at an altitude above the maximum altitude to which an altimeter of that airplane has been tested.

91.171 PROGRESSIVE INSPECTION

(a) Each registered owner or operator of an aircraft desiring to use the progressive inspection must submit a written request to the Flight Standards District Office having jurisdiction over the area in which the applicant is located, and shall provide—

(1) A certificated mechanic holding an inspection authorization, a certificated airframe repair station, or the manufacturer of the aircraft, to supervise or conduct the progressive inspection;

(2) A current inspection procedures manual available and readily understandable to pilot and maintenance personnel containing, in detail—

    (i) An explanation of the progressive inspection, including the continuity of inspection responsibility, the making of reports, and the keeping of records and technical reference material;

    (ii) An inspection schedule, specifying the intervals in hours or days when routine and detailed inspections will be performed and including instructions for exceeding an inspection interval by not more than 10 hours while en route and for changing an inspection interval because of service experience;

    (iii) Sample routine and detailed inspection forms and instructions for their use; and

    (iv) Sample reports and records, and instructions for their use;

(3) Enough housing and equipment for necessary disassembly and proper inspection of the aircraft; and

(4) Appropriate current technical information for the aircraft.

(b) The frequency and detail of the progressive inspection shall provide for the complete inspection of the aircraft within each 12 calendar months and be consistent with the manufacturer's recommendations, field service experience, and the kind of operation in which the aircraft is engaged. The progressive inspection schedule must insure that the aircraft at all times will be airworthy and will conform to all applicable FAA aircraft specifications, type certificate data sheets, airworthiness directives, and other approved data.

(c) If the progressive inspection is discontinued, the owner or operator shall immediately notify the local General Aviation District Office, in writing, of the discontinuance. After the discontinuance, the first annual inspection under 91.169(a) is due within 12 calendar months after the last complete inspection of the aircraft under the progressive inspection. The 100-hour inspection under 91.169(b) is due within 100 hours after that complete inspection. A complete inspection of the aircraft, for the purpose of determining when the annual and 100-hour inspections are due, will require a detailed inspection of the aircraft and all its components in accordance with the progressive inspection. A routine inspection of the aircraft and a detailed inspection of several components is not considered to be a complete inspection.

91.173 MAINTENANCE RECORDS

(a) Except for work performed in accordance with 91.170 and 91.177, each registered owner or operator shall keep the following records for the periods specified in paragraph (b) of this section;

  (1) Records of the maintenance and alteration, and records of the 100-hour, annual, progressive, and other required or approved inspections as appropriate, for each aircraft (including the airframe) and each engine, propeller, rotor, and appliance of an aircraft. The records must include —

    (i) A description (or reference to data acceptable to the Administrator) of the work performed;

    (ii) The date of completion of the work performed; and

    (iii) The signature and certificate number of the person approving the aircraft for return to service.

  (2) Records containing the following information:

    (i) The total time in service of the airframe.

    (ii) The current status of life-limited parts of each airframe, engine, propeller, rotor, and appliance.

    (iii) The time since last overhaul of all items installed on the aircraft which are required to be overhauled on a specified time basis.

    (iv) The identification of the current inspection status of the aircraft, including the times since the last inspections required by the inspection program under which the aircraft and its appliances are maintained.

    (v) The current status of applicable airworthiness directives (AD) including, for each, the method of compliance, the AD number, and revision date. If the AD involves recurring action, the time and date when the next action is required.

    (vi) A list of current major alterations to each airframe, engine, propeller, rotor, and appliance.

(b) The owner or operator shall retain the following records for the periods prescribed:

  (1) The records specified in paragraph (a)(1) of this section shall be retained until the work is repeated or superseded by other work or for one year after the work is performed.

  (2) The records specified in paragraph (a)(2) of this section shall be retained and transferred with the aircraft at the time the aircraft is sold.

  (3) A list of defects furnished to a registered owner or operator under 43.9 of this chapter, shall be retained until the defects are repaired and the aircraft is approved for return to service.

(c) The owner or operator shall make all maintenance records required to be kept by this section available for inspection by the Administrator or any authorized representative of the National Transportation Safety Board (NTSB).

91.177 ATC TRANSPONDER TESTS AND INSPECTIONS

(a) After Janaury 1, 1976, no person may use an ATC transponder that is specified in 91.24(a), 121.345(c), 127.123(b), or 135.143(c) of this chapter, unless, within the preceding 24 calendar months, that ATC transponder has been tested and inspected and found to comply with Appendix F of Part 43* of this chapter.

(b) The tests and inspections specified in paragraph (a) of this section may be conducted by —

  (1) A certificated repair station properly equipped to perform those functions and holding —

    (i) A radio rating, class III;

    (ii) A limited radio rating appropriate to the make and model transponder to be tested;

    (iii) A limited rating appropriate to the test to be performed; or

    (iv) A limited rating for a manufacturer issued for the transponder in accordance with 145.101(b)(4) of this chapter; or

  (2) A certificate holder authorized to perform maintenance in accordance with 121.379 or 127.140 of this chapter; or

  (3) The manufacturer of the aircraft on which the transponder to be tested is installed, if the transponder was installed by that manufacturer.

SECTION C—FAR PART 135

TABLE OF CONTENTS

SUBPART A — GENERAL

135.1 APPLICABILITY

(a) Except as provided in paragraph (b) of this section, this part prescribes rules governing—

    (1) Air taxi operations conducted under the exemption authority of Part 298 of this title;

    (2) The transportation of mail by aircraft conducted under a postal service contract awarded under section 5402c of Title 39, United States Code;

    (3) The carrying in air commerce by any person, other than as an air carrier, of persons or property for compensation or hire (commercial operations) in aircraft having a maximum passenger seating configuration, excluding any pilot seat, of 30 seats or less and a maximum payload capacity of 7,500 pounds or less; and

    (4) Each person who is on board an aircraft being operated under this part.

(b) This part does not apply to—

    (1) Student instruction;

    (2) Nonstop sightseeing flights that begin and end at the same airport, and are conducted within a 25 statute mile radius of that airport;

    (3) Ferry or training flights;

    (4) Aerial work operations, including—

        (i) Crop dusting, seeding, spraying, and bird chasing;

        (ii) Banner towing;

        (iii) Aerial photography or survey;

        (iv) Fire fighting;

        (v) Helicopter operations in construction or repair work (but not including transportation to and from the site of operations); and

        (vi) Powerline or pipeline patrol;

    (5) Sightseeing flights conducted in hot air balloons;

    (6) Nonstop flights conducted within a 25 statute mile radius of the airport of takeoff carrying persons for the purpose of intentional parachute jumps;

    (7) Helicopter flights conducted within a 25 statute mile radius of the airport of takeoff, if—

        (i) Not more than two passengers are carried in the helicopter in addition to the required flight crew;

        (ii) Each flight is made under VFR during the day;

        (iii) The helicopter used is certificated in the standard category and complies with the 100-hour inspection requirements of Part 91 of this chapter;

        (iv) The operator notifies the FAA Flight Standards District Office responsible for the geographic area concerned at least 72 hours before each flight and furnishes any essential information that the office requests;

        (v) The number of flights does not exceed a total of six in any calendar year;

        (vi) Each flight has been approved by the Administrator; and

        (vii) Cargo is not carried in or on the helicopter;

    (8) Operations conducted under Part 133 or 375 of this title;

    (9) Emergency mail service conducted under section 405(h) of the Federal Aviation Act of 1958; or

    (10) Carriage of a candidate in a Federal election, an agent of the candidate, or person traveling on behalf of the candidate, if—

        (i) The principal business of the person operating the aircraft is not that of an air carrier or commercial operator; and

        (ii) The payment for the carriage is required, and does not exceed the amount required to be paid, by regulations of the Federal Election Commission (11 CFR Chapter 1).

The terms "candidate" and "election" have the same meaning as that set forth in the regulations of the Federal Election Commission.

135.3 RULES APPLICABLE TO OPERATIONS SUBJECT TO THIS PART

Each person operating an aircraft in operations under this part shall—

(a) While operating inside the United States, comply with the applicable rules of this chapter; and

(b) While operating outside the United States, comply with Annex 2, Rules of the Air, to the Convention on International Civil Aviation or the regulations of any foreign country, whichever applies, and with any rules of Parts 61 and 91 of this chapter and this part that are more restrictive than that Annex or those regulations and that can be complied with without violating that Annex or those regulations. Annex 2 is incorporated by reference in 91.1(c) of this chapter.

135.5 CERTIFICATE AND OPERATIONS SPECIFICATIONS REQUIRED

No person may operate an aircraft under this part without, or in violation of, an air taxi/commercial operator (ATCO) operating certificate and appropriate operations specifications issued under this part, or, for operations with large aircraft having a maximum passenger seating configuration, excluding any pilot seat, of more than 30 seats, or a maximum payload capacity of more than 7,500 pounds, without, or in violation of, appropriate operations specifications issued under Part 121 of this chapter.

135.10 COMPLIANCE DATES FOR CERTAIN RULES

(a) A certificate holder or pilot is allowed until June 1, 1979, to comply with the following sections:

(1) A third bank and pitch indicator (artificial horizon) (135.149(c)).

(2) Shoulder harness at flight crewmember stations (135.171(a)).

(3) Airline transport pilot certificate (135.243(a)).

(b) A certificate holder is allowed until December 1, 1979, to comply with the following sections:

(1) Cockpit voice recorder (135.151).

(2) Ground proximity warning system or other approved system (135.153).

(3) Airborne thunderstorm detection equipment (135.173).

(c) A certificate holder or pilot is allowed until December 1, 1980, to comply with the instrument rating requirement of 135.243(b)(3).

(d) A certificate holder or pilot may obtain an extension of the compliance date in paragraph (a) or (b) of this section, but not beyond December 1, 1980, from the Director, Flight Standards Service, if before the compliance date in paragraph (a) or (b) of this section —

(1) The certificate holder or pilot shows that due to circumstances beyond its control they cannot comply by that date; and

(2) The certificate holder or pilot has submitted before that date a schedule for compliance, acceptable to the Director indicating that compliance will be achieved at the earliest practicable date.

135.19 EMERGENCY OPERATIONS

(a) In an emergency involving the safety of persons or property, the certificate holder may deviate from the rules of this part relating to aircraft and equipment and weather minimums to the extent required to meet that emergency.

(b) In an emergency involving the safety of persons or property, the pilot in command may deviate from the rules of this part to the extent required to meet that emergency.

(c) Each person who, under the authority of this section, deviates from a rule of this part shall, within 10 days, excluding Saturdays, Sundays, and Federal holidays, after the deviation, send to the FAA Flight Standards District Office charged with the overall inspection of the certificate holder a complete report of the aircraft operation involved, including a description of the deviation and reasons for it.

135.21 MANUAL REQUIREMENTS

(a) Each certificate holder, other than one who is the only pilot used in the certificate holder's operations, shall prepare and keep current a manual setting forth the certificate holder's procedures and policies acceptable to the Administrator. This manual must be used by the certificate holder's flight, ground, and maintenance personnel in conducting its operations. However, the Administrator may authorize a deviation from this paragraph if the Administrator finds that, because of the limited size of the operation, all or part of the manual is not necessary for guidance of flight, ground, or maintenance personnel.

(b) Each certificate holder shall maintain at least one copy of the manual at its principal operations base.

(c) The manual must not be contrary to any applicable Federal regulations, foreign regulation applicable to the certificate holder's operations in foreign countries, or the certificate holder's operating certificate or operations specifications.

(d) A copy of the manual, or appropriate portions of the manual (and changes and additions) shall be made available to maintenance and ground operations personnel by the certificate holder and furnished to —

(1) Its flight crewmembers; and

(2) Representatives of the Administrator assigned to the certificate holder.

(e) Each employee of the certificate holder to whom a manual or appropriate portions of it are furnished under paragraph (d)(1) of this section shall keep it up to date with the changes and additions furnished to them.

(f) Except as provided in paragraph (g) of this section, each certificate holder shall carry appropriate parts of the manual on each aircraft when away from the principal operations base. The appropriate parts must be available for use by ground or flight personnel.

(g) If a certificate holder conducts aircraft inspections or maintenance at specified stations where it keeps the approved inspection program manual, it is not required to carry the manual aboard the aircraft en route to those stations.

135.25 AIRCRAFT REQUIREMENTS

(a) No certificate holder may operate an aircraft under this part unless that aircraft—

(1) Is registered as a civil aircraft of the United States and carries an appropriate and current airworthiness certificate issued under this chapter; and

(2) Is in an airworthy condition and meets the applicable airworthiness requirements of this chapter, including those relating to identification and equipment.

(b) Each certificate holder must have the exclusive use of at least one aircraft that meets the requirements for at least one kind of operation authorized in the certificate holder's operations specifications. In addition, for each kind of operation for which the certificate holder does not have the exclusive use of an aircraft, the certificate holder must have available for use under a written agreement (including arrangements for performing required maintenance) at least one aircraft that meets the requirements for that kind of operation. However, this paragraph does not prohibit the operator from using or authorizing the use of the aircraft for other than air taxi or commercial operations and does not require the certificate holder to have exclusive use of all aircraft that the certificate holder uses.

(c) For the purposes of paragraph (b) of this section, a person has exclusive use of an aircraft if that person has the sole possession, control, and use of it for flight, as owner, or has a written agreement (including arrangements for performing required maintenance), in effect when the aircraft is operated, giving the person that possession, control, and use for at least 6 consecutive months.

SUBPART B — FLIGHT OPERATIONS
135.61 GENERAL

This subpart prescribes rules, in addition to those in Part 91 of this chapter, that apply to operations under this part.

135.93 AUTOPILOT; MINIMUM ALTITUDES FOR USE

(a) Except as provided in paragraphs (b), (c), and (d) of this section, no person may use an autopilot at an altitude above the terrain which is less than 500 feet or less than twice the maximum altitude loss specified in the approved Aircraft Flight Manual or equivalent for malfunction of the autopilot, whichever is higher.

(b) When using an instrument approach facility other than ILS, no person may use an autopilot at an altitude above the terrain that is less than 50 feet below the approved minimum descent altitude for that procedure, or less than twice the maximum loss specified in the approved Airplane Flight Manual or equivalent for a malfunction of the autopilot under approach conditions, whichever is higher.

(c) For ILS approaches, when reported weather conditions are less than the basic weather conditions in 91.105 of this chapter, no person may use an autopilot with an approach coupler at an altitude above the terrain that is less than 50 feet above the terain, or the maximum altitude loss specified in the approved Airplane Flight Manual or equivalent for the malfunction of the autopilot with approach coupler, whichever is higher.

(d) Without regard to paragraphs (a), (b), or (c) of this section, the Administrator may issue operations specifications to allow the use, to touchdown, of an approved flight control guidance system with automatic capability, if—

    (1) The system does not contain any altitude loss (above zero) specified in the approved Aircraft Flight Manual or equivalent for malfunction of the autopilot with approach coupler; and

    (2) The Administrator finds that the use of the system to touchdown will not otherwise adversely affect the safety standards of this section.

(e) This section does not apply to operations conducted in rotorcraft.

135.99 COMPOSITION OF FLIGHT CREW

(a) No certificate holder may operate an aircraft with less than the minimum flight crew specified in the aircraft operating limitations or the Aircraft Flight Manual for that aircraft and required by this part for the kind of operation being conducted.

(b) No certificate holder may operate an aircraft without a second in command if that aircraft has a passenger seating configuration, excluding any pilot seat, of ten seats or more.

135.101 SECOND IN COMMAND REQUIRED IN IFR CONDITIONS

Except as provided in 135.103 and 135.105, no person may operate an aircraft carrying passengers in IFR conditions, unless there is a second in command in the aircraft.

135.103 EXCEPTION TO SECOND IN COMMAND REQUIREMENT; IFR OPERATIONS

The pilot in command of an aircraft carrying passengers may conduct IFR operations without a second in command under the following conditions:

(a) A takeoff may be conducted under IFR conditions if the weather reports or forecasts, or any combination of them, indicate that the weather along the planned route of flight allows flight under VFR within 15 minutes flying time, at normal cruise speed, from the takeoff airport.

(b) En route IFR may be conducted if unforecast weather conditions below the VFR minimums of this chapter are encountered on a flight that was planned to be conducted under VFR.

(c) An IFR approach may be conducted if, upon arrival at the destination airport, unforecast weather conditions do not allow an approach to be completed under VFR.

(d) When IFR operations are conducted under this section:

    (1) The aircraft must be properly equipped for IFR operations under this part.

    (2) The pilot must be authorized to conduct IFR operations under this part.

    (3) The flight must be conducted in accordance with an ATC IFR clearance.

IFR operations without a second in command may not be conducted under this section in an aircraft requiring a second in command under 135.99.

135.105 EXCEPTION TO SECOND IN COMMAND REQUIREMENT; APPROVAL FOR USE OF AUTOPILOT SYSTEM

(a) Except as provided in 135.99 and 135.111, unless two pilots are required by this chapter for operations under VFR, a person may operate an aircraft without a second in command if it is equipped with an operative approved autopilot system and the use of that system is authorized by appropriate operations specifications.

(b) The certificate holder may apply for an amendment of its operations specifications to authorize the use of an autopilot system in place of a second in command.

(c) The Administrator issues an amendment to the operations specifications authorizing the use of an autopilot system, in place of a second in command, if—

(1) The autopilot is capable of operating the aircraft controls to maintain flight and maneuver it about the three axes; and

(2) The certificate holder shows, to the satisfaction of the Administrator, that operations using the autopilot system can be conducted safely and in compliance with this part.

The amendment contains any conditions or limitations on the use of the autopilot system that the Administrator determines are needed in the interest of safety.

SUBPART C — AIRCRAFT AND EQUIPMENT

135.141 APPLICABILITY

This subpart prescribes aircraft and equipment requirements for operations under this part. The requirements of this subpart are in addition to the aircraft and equipment requirements of Part 91 of this chapter. However, this part does not require the duplication of any equipment required by this chapter.

135.143 GENERAL REQUIREMENTS

(a) No person may operate an aircraft under this part unless that aircraft and its equipment meet the applicable regulations of this chapter.

(b) Except as provided in 135.179, no person may operate an aircraft under this part unless the required instruments and equipment in it have been approved and are in an operable condition.

(c) ATC transponder equipment must meet the performance and environmental requirements of any Class of Technical Standard Order (TSO) C74b, or Class 1A or Class 1B of TSO-74c, as appropriate, except that the Administrator may approve the use of TSO-C74 or TSO-C74a equipment if the applicant submits data showing that the equipment meets the minimum performance standards of Class 1A or Class 1B of TSO-C74c, and the environmental conditions of the TSO under which it was manufactured.

135.149 EQUIPMENT REQUIREMENTS; GENERAL

No person may operate an aircraft unless it is equipped with—

(a) A sensitive altimeter that is adjustable for barometric pressure;

(b) Heating or deicing equipment for each carburetor or, for a pressure carburetor or, an alternate air source;

(c) For turbojet airplanes, in addition to two gyroscopic bank-and-pitch indicators (artificial horizons) for use at the pilot stations, a third indicator that —

(1) Is powered from a source independent of the aircraft's electrical generating system;

(2) Continues reliable operations for at least 30 minutes after total failure of the aircraft's electrical generating system;

(3) Operates independently of any other attitude indicating system;

(4) Is operative without selection after total failure of the aircraft's electrical generating system;

(5) Is located on the instrument panel in a position that will make it plainly visibile to, and usable by, any pilot at the pilot's station; and

(6) Is appropriately lighted during all phases of operation;

(d) For aircraft having a passenger seating configuration, excluding any pilot seat, of more than 19, a public address system and a crewmember interphone system, approved under 21.305 of this chapter, which meet 121.318 and 121.319, respectively, of this chapter; and

(e) For turbine powered aircraft, any other equipment as the Administrator may require.

SUBPART D — VFR/IFR OPERATING LIMITATIONS AND WEATHER REQUIREMENTS

135.201 APPLICABILITY

This subpart prescribes the operating limitations for VFR/IFR flight operations and associated weather requirements for operations under this part.

135.203 VFR; MINIMUM ALTITUDES

Except when necessary for takeoff and landing, no person may operate under VFR—

(a) An airplane—
  (1) During the day, below 500 feet above the surface or less than 500 feet horizontally from any obstacle; or
  (2) At night, at an altitude less than 1,000 feet above the highest obstacle within a horizontal distance of 5 miles from the course intended to be flown or, in designated mountainous terrain, less than 2,000 feet above the highest obstacle within a horizontal distance of 5 miles from the course intended to be flown; or
(b) A helicopter over a congested area at an altitude less than 300 feet above the surface.

135.205   VFR; VISIBILITY REQUIREMENTS

(a) No person may operate an airplane under VFR in uncontrolled airspace when the ceiling is less than 1,000 feet unless flight visibility is at least 2 miles.
(b) No person may operate a helicopter under VFR in uncontrolled airspace at an altitude of 1,200 feet or less above the surface or in control zones unless the visibility is at least—
  (1) During the day — ½ mile; or
  (2) At night — 1 mile.

135.209   VFR; FUEL SUPPLY

(a) No person may begin a flight operation in an airplane under VFR unless, considering wind and forecast weather conditions, it has enough fuel to fly to the first point of intended landing and, assuming normal cruising fuel consumption—
  (1) During the day, to fly after that for at least 30 minutes; or
  (2) At night, to fly after that for at least 45 minutes.
(b) No person may begin a flight operation in a helicopter under VFR unless, considering wind and forecast weather conditions, it has enough fuel to fly to the first point of intended landing and, assuming normal cruising fuel consumption, to fly after that for at least 20 minutes.

135.211   VFR: OVER-THE-TOP CARRYING PASSENGERS; OPERATING LIMITATIONS

Subject to any additional limitations in 135.181, no person may operate an aircraft under VFR over-the-top carrying passengers, unless—
(a) Weather reports or forecasts, or any combination of them, indicate that the weather at the intended point of termination of over-the-top flight—
  (1) Allows descent to beneath the ceiling under VFR and is forecast to remain so until at least 1 hour after the estimated time of arrival at that point: or
  (2) Allows an IFR approach and landing with flight clear of the clouds until reaching the prescribed initial approach altitude over the final approach facility, unless the approach is made with the use of radar under 91.116 (f) of this chapter; or
(b) It is operated under conditions allowing—
  (1) For multiengine aircraft, descent or continuation of the flight under VFR if its critical engine fails; or
  (2) For single-engine aircraft, descent under VFR if its engine fails.

135.213   WEATHER REPORTS AND FORECASTS

(a) Whenever a person operating an aircraft under this part is required to use a weather report or forecast, that person shall use that of the U.S. National Weather Service, a source approved by the U.S. National Weather Service, or a source approved by the Administrator. However, for operations under VFR, the pilot in command may, if such a report is not available, use weather information based on that pilot's own observations or on those of other persons competent to supply appropriate observations.
(b) For the purposes of paragraph (a) of this section, weather observations made and furnished to pilots to conduct IFR operations at an airport must be taken at the airport where those IFR operations are conducted, unless the Administrator issues operations specifications allowing the use of weather observations taken at a location not at the airport where the IFR operations are conducted. The

Administrator issues such operations specifications when, after investigation by the U.S. National Weather Service and the FAA Flight Standards District Office charged with the overall inspection of the certificate holder, it is found that the standards of safety for that operation would allow the deviation from this paragraph for a particular operation for which an ATCO operating certificate has been issued.

135.215 IFR; OPERATING LIMITATIONS

(a) Except as provided in paragraphs (b), (c) and (d) of this section, no person may operate an aircraft under IFR outside of controlled airspace or at any airport that does not have an approved standard instrument approach procedure.

(b) The Administrator may issue operations specifications to the certificate holder to allow it to operate under IFR over routes outside controlled airspace if—
   (1) The certificate holder shows the Administrator that the flight crew is able to navigate, without visual reference to the ground, over an intended track without deviating more than 5 degrees or 5 miles, whichever is less, from that track; and
   (2) The Administrator determines that the proposed operations can be conducted safely.

(c) A person may operate an aircraft under IFR outside of controlled airspace if the certificate holder has been approved for the operations and that operation is necessary to—
   (1) Conduct an instrument approach to an airport for which there is in use a current approved standard or special instrument approach procedure; or
   (2) Climb into controlled airspace during an approved missed approach procedure; or
   (3) Make an IFR departure from an airport having an approved instrument approach procedure.

(d) The Administrator may issue operations specifications to the certificate holder to allow it to depart at an airport that does not have an approved standard instrument approach procedure when the Administrator determines that it is necessary to make an IFR departure

from that airport and that the proposed operations can be conducted safely. The approval to operate at that airport does not include an approval to make an IFR approach to that airport.

135.217 IFR; TAKEOFF LIMITATIONS

No person may take off an aircraft under IFR from an airport where weather conditions are at or above take off minimums but are below authorized IFR landing minimums unless there is an alternate airport within 1 hour's flying time (at normal cruising speed, in still air) of the airport of departure.

135.219 IFR; DESTINATION AIRPORT WEATHER MINIMUMS

No person may take off an aircraft under IFR or begin an IFR or over-the-top operation unless the latest weather reports or forecasts, or any combination of them, indicate that weather conditions at the estimated time of arrival at the next airport of intended landing will be at or above authorized IFR landing minimums.

135.221 IFR; ALTERNATE AIRPORT WEATHER MINIMUMS

No person may designate an alternate airport unless the weather reports or forecasts, or any combination of them, indicate that the weather conditions will be at or above authorized alternate airport landing minimums for that airport at the estimated time of arrival.

135.223 IFR; ALTERNATE AIRPORT REQUIREMENTS

(a) Except as provided in paragraph (b) of this section, no person may operate an aircraft in IFR conditions unless it carries enough fuel (considering weather reports or forecasts or any combination of them) to—
   (1) Complete the flight to the first airport of intended landing:
   (2) Fly from that airport to the alternate airport; and
   (3) Fly after that for 45 minutes at normal cruising speed.

(b) Paragraph (a)(2) of this section does not apply if Part 97 of this chapter prescribes a standard instrument approach procedure for the first airport of intended landing and, for at least one hour before and after the estimated time of arrival, the appropriate weather reports or forecasts, or any combination of them, indicate that—

(1) The ceiling will be at least 1,500 feet above the lowest circling approach MDA; or

(2) If a circling instrument approach is not authorized for the airport, the ceiling will be at least 1,500 feet above the lowest published minimum or 2,000 feet above the airport elevation, whichever is higher; and

(3) Visibility for that airport is forecast to be at least three miles, or two miles more than the lowest applicable visibility minimums, whichever is the greater, for the instrument approach procedure to be used at the destination airport.

135.225 IFR; TAKEOFF, APPROACH AND LANDING MINIMUMS

(a) No pilot may begin an instrument approach procedure to an airport unless—

(1) That airport has a weather reporting facility operated by the U.S. National Weather Service, a source approved by U.S. National Weather Service, or a source approved by the Administrator; and

(2) The latest weather report issued by that weather reporting facility indicates that weather conditions are at or above the authorized IFR landing minimums for that airport.

(b) No pilot may begin the final approach segment of an instrument approach procedure to an airport unless the latest weather report by the facility described in paragraph (a)(1) of this section indicates that weather conditions are at or above the authorized IFR landing minimums for that procedure.

(c) If a pilot has begun the final approach segment of an instrument approach to an airport under paragraph (b) of this section and a later weather report indicating below minimum conditions is received after the aircraft is—

(1) On an ILS final approach and has passed the final approach fix; or

(2) On an ASR or PAR final approach and has been turned over to the final approach controller; or

(3) On a final approach using a VOR, NDB, or comparable approach procedure; and the aircraft—

(i) Has passed the appropriate facility or final approach fix; or

(ii) Where a final approach fix is not specified, has completed the procedure turn and is established inbound toward the airport on the final approach course within the distance prescribed in the procedure; the approach may be continued and a landing made if the pilot finds, upon reaching the authorized MDA or DH, that actual weather conditions are at least equal to the minimums prescribed for the procedure.

(d) The MDA or DH and visibility landing minimums prescribed in Part 97 of this chapter or in the operator's operations specifications are increased by 100 feet and ½ mile respectively, but not to exceed the ceiling and visibility minimums for that airport when used as an alternate airport, for each pilot in command of a turbine-powered airplane who has not served at least 100 hours as pilot in command in that type of airplane.

(e) Each pilot making an IFR takeoff or approach and landing at a military or foreign airport shall comply with applicable instrument approach procedures and weather minimums prescribed by the authority having jurisdiction over that airport. In addition, no pilot may, at that airport—

(1) Take off under IFR when the visibility is less than 1 mile; or

(2) Make an instrument approach when the visibility is less than ½ mile.

(f) If takeoff minimums are specified in Part 97 of this chapter for the takeoff airport, no pilot may take off an aircraft under IFR when the weather conditions reported by the facility described in paragraph (a)(1) of this section are less than the takeoff minimums specified for the takeoff airport in Part 97 or in the certificate holder's operations specifications.

(g) Except as provided in paragraph (h) of this section, if takeoff minimums are not prescribed in Part 97 of this chapter for the takeoff airport, no pilot may take off an aircraft under IFR when the weather conditions reported by the facility described in paragraph (a)(1) of this section are less than that prescribed in Part 91 of this chapter or in the certificate holder's operations specifications.

(h) At airports where straight-in instrument approach procedures are authorized, a pilot may take off an aircraft under IFR when the weather conditions reported by the facility described in paragraph (a)(1) of this section are equal to or better than the lowest straight-in landing minimums, unless otherwise restricted, if—

(1) The wind direction and velocity at the time of takeoff are such that a straight-in instrument approach can be made to the runway served by the instrument approach;

(2) The associated ground facilities upon which the landing minimums are predicated and the related airborne equipment are in normal operation; and

(3) The certificate holder has been approved for such operations.

135.227 ICING CONDITIONS; OPERATING LIMITATIONS

(a) No pilot may take off an aircraft that has—

(1) Frost, snow, or ice adhering to any rotor blade, propeller, windshield, or powerplant installation, or to an airspeed, altimeter, rate of climb, or flight attitude instrument system;

(2) Snow or ice adhering to the wings or stabilizing or control surfaces; or

(3) Any frost adhering to the wings, or stabilizing or control surfaces, unless that frost has been polished to make it smooth.

(b) Except for an airplane that has ice protection provisions that meet 34 of Appendix A, or those for transport category airplane type certification, no pilot may fly—

(1) Under IFR into known or forecast light or moderate icing conditions; or

(2) Under VFR into known light or moderate icing conditions; unless the aircraft has functioning deicing or anti-icing equipment protecting each rotor blade, propeller, windshield, wing, stabilizing or control surface, and each airspeed, altimeter, rate of

climb or flight attitude instrument system.

(c) Except for an airplane that has ice protection provisions that meet 34 of Appendix A, or those for transport category airplane type certification, no pilot may fly an aircraft into known or forecast severe icing conditions.

(d) If current weather reports and briefing information relied upon by the pilot in command indicate that the forecast icing condition that would otherwise prohibit the flight will not be encountered during the flight because of changed weather conditions since the forecast, the restrictions in paragraphs (b) and (c) of this section based on forecast conditions do not apply.

135.229 AIRPORT REQUIREMENTS

(a) No certificate holder may use any airport unless it is adequate for the proposed operation, considering such items as size, surface, obstructions and lighting.

(b) No pilot of an aircraft carrying passengers at night may take off from, or land on, an airport unless —

(1) That pilot has determined the wind direction from an illuminated wind direction indicator or local ground communications or, in the case of takeoff, that pilot's personal observations; and

(2) The limits of the area to be used for landing or takeoff are clearly shown—

(i) For airplanes, by boundary or runway marker lights;

(ii) For helicopters, by boundary or runway marker lights or reflective material.

(c) For the purpose of paragraph (b) of this section, if the area to be used for takeoff or landing is marked by flare pots or lanterns, their use must be approved by the Administrator.

SUBPART E — FLIGHT CREWMEMBER REQUIREMENTS

135.241 APPLICABILITY

This subpart prescribes the flight crewmember requirements for operations under this part.

135.243 PILOT IN COMMAND QUALIFICATIONS

(a) No certificate holder may use a person, nor may any person serve, as pilot in command in passenger-carrying operations of a turbojet airplane, of an airplane having a passenger seating configuration, excluding any pilot seat, of 10 seats or more, or a multiengine airplane being operated by the "Commuter Air Carrier" (as defined in Part 298 of this title), unless that person holds an airline transport pilot certificate with appropriate category and class ratings and, if required, an appropriate type rating for that airplane.

(b) Except as provided in paragraph (a) of this section, no certificate holder may use a person, nor may any person serve, as pilot in command of an aircraft under VFR unless that person—

(1) Holds at least a commercial pilot certificate with appropriate category and class ratings and, if required, an appropriate type rating for that aircraft; and

(2) Has had at least 500 hours of flight time as a pilot, including at least 100 hours of cross-country flight time, at least 25 hours of which were at night; and

(3) For an airplane, holds an instrument rating or an airline transport pilot certificate with an airplane category rating; or

(4) For helicopter operations conducted VFR over-the-top, holds a helicopter instrument rating, or an airline transport pilot certificate with a category and class rating for that aircraft, not limited to VFR.

(c) Except as provided in paragraph (a) of this section, no certificate holder may use a person, nor may any person serve, as pilot in command of an aircraft under IFR unless that person—

(1) Holds at least a commercial pilot certificate with appropriate category and class ratings and, if required, an appropriate type rating for that aircraft; and

(2) Has had at least 1,200 hours of flight time as a pilot, including 500 hours of cross-country flight time, 100 hours of night flight time, and 75 hours of actual or simulated instrument time at least 50 hours of which were in actual flight; and

(3) For an airplane, holds an instrument rating or an airline transport pilot certificate with an airplane category rating; or

(4) For a helicopter, holds a helicopter instrument rating, or an airline transport pilot certificate with a category and class rating for that aircraft, not limited to VFR.

135.245 SECOND IN COMMAND QUALIFICATIONS

(a) Except as provided in paragraph (b), no certificate holder may use any person, nor may any person serve, as second in command of an aircraft unless that person holds at least a commercial pilot certificate with appropriate category and class ratings and an instrument rating. For flight under IFR, that person must meet the recent instrument experience requirements of Part 61 of this chapter.

(b) A second in command of a helicopter operated under VFR, other than over-the-top, must have at least a commercial pilot certificate with an appropriate aircraft category and class rating.

135.247 PILOT QUALIFICATIONS: RECENT EXPERIENCE

(a) No certificate holder may use any person, nor may any person serve, as pilot in command of an aircraft carrying passengers unless, within the preceding 90 days, that person has—

(1) Made three takeoffs and three landings as the sole manipulator of the flight controls in an aircraft of the same category and class and, if a type rating is required, of the same type in which that person is to serve; or

(2) For operation during the period beginning 1 hour after sunset and ending 1 hour before sunrise (as published in the Air Almanac), made three takeoffs and three landings during that period as the sole manipulator of the flight controls in an aircraft of the same category and class and, if a type rating is required, of the same type in which that person is to serve.

A person who complies with paragraph (a)(2) of this paragraph need not comply with paragraph (a)(1) of this paragraph.

(b) For the purpose of paragraph (a) of this section, if the aircraft is a tailwheel airplane, each takeoff must be made in a tailwheel airplane and each landing must be made to a full stop in a tailwheel airplane.

SUBPART H — TRAINING

135.341 PILOT AND FLIGHT ATTENDANT CREWMEMBER TRAINING PROGRAMS

(a) Each certificate holder, other than one who is the only pilot used in the certificate holder's operation, shall establish and maintain an approved pilot training program, and each certificate holder who uses a flight attendant crewmember shall establish and maintain an approved flight attendant training program, that is appropriate to the operations to which each pilot and flight attendant is to be assigned, and will ensure that they are adequately trained to meet the applicable knowledge and practical testing requirements of 135.293 through 135.301. However, the Administrator may authorize a deviation from this section if the Administrator finds that, because of the limited size and scope of the operation, safety will allow a deviation from these requirements.

(b) Each certificate holder required to have a training program by paragraph (a) of this section shall include in that program ground and flight training curriculums for —
  (1) Initial training;
  (2) Transition training;
  (3) Upgrade training;
  (4) Differences training; and
  (5) Recurrent training.

(c) Each certificate holder required to have a training program by paragraph (a) of this section shall provide current and appropriate study materials for use by each required pilot and flight attendant.

(d) The certificate holder shall furnish copies of the pilot and flight attendant crewmember training program, and all changes and additions, to the assigned representative of the Administrator. If the certificate holder uses training facilities of other persons, a copy of those training programs or appropriate portions used for those facilities shall also be furnished. Curricula that follow FAA published curricula may be cited by reference in the copy of the training program furnished to the representative of the Administrator and need not be furnished with the program.

FAR PARTS 133 AND 137

FAR Part 133 governs the commercial use of rotorcraft for carrying external loads. Since it is primarily of interest to a limited segment of the aviation industry, it is not included in this manual.

This part of the FARs specifies who must obtain a rotorcraft external-load operator certificate, establishes limitations on its use, and provides procedures under which it can be amended, suspended, revoked, or voluntarily surrendered. In addition, it establishes the requirement for exclusive use of at least one rotorcraft, and specifies certain knowledge and skill requirements which must be demonstrated by the crew.

To provide for the safety of the crew and the general public, Part 133 also specifies operating rules and related requirements, such as approved rotorcraft-load combinations. In addition, it requires load stability checks and places certain restrictions on operating activities.

Part 137 prescribes the rules governing operation of agricultural aircraft. It also provides for the issuance of operator certificates for those operations.

Agricultural aircraft operators utilize aircraft to apply agricultural chemicals to crops in farmers' fields. Due to the low flying and the types of chemical poisons used, these operations also require special knowledge and training. The applicant may be required to demonstrate safe handling techniques and display knowledge of the toxic effects of the agricultural chemicals normally used. In addition, he may be asked to demonstrate skill in operating the agricultural aircraft.

SECTION D—NTSB REGULATION PART 830

TABLE OF CONTENTS

SUBPART A—GENERAL

830.1 APPLICABILITY

This part contains rules pertaining to:

(a) Providing notice of and reporting, aircraft accidents and incidents and certain other occurrences in the operation of aircraft when they involve civil aircraft of the United States wherever they occur, or foreign civil aircraft when such events occur in the United States, its territories or possessions.

(b) Preservation of aircraft wreckage, mail, cargo, and records involving all civil aircraft in the United States its territories or possessions.

830.2 DEFINITIONS

As used in this part the following words or phrases are defined as follows:

AIRCRAFT ACCIDENT means an occurrence associated with the operation of an aircraft which takes place between the time any person boards the aircraft with the intention of flight until such time as all such persons have disembarked, and in which any person suffers death or serious injury as a result of being in or upon the aircraft or by direct contact with the aircraft or anything attached thereto, or in which the aircraft receives substantial damage.

FATAL INJURY means any injury which results in death within 7 days of the accident.

OPERATOR means any person who causes or authorizes the operation of an aircraft, such as the owner, lessee, or bailee of an aircraft.

SERIOUS INJURY means any injury which:
(1) Requires hospitalization for more than 48 hours, commencing within 7 days from the date the injury was received;
(2) Results in a fracture of any bone (except simple fractures of fingers, toes, or nose);
(3) Involves lacerations which cause severe hemorrhages, nerve, muscle, or tendon damage;
(4) Involves injury to any internal organ; or
(5) Involves second or third degree burns; or burns affecting more than 5 percent of the body surface.

SUBSTANTIAL DAMAGE:
(1) Except as provided in subparagraph (2) of this paragraph, substantial damage means damage or structural failure which adversely affects the structural strength, performance, or flight characteristics of the aircraft, and which would normally require major repair or replacement of the affected component.
(2) Engine failure, damage limited to an engine, bent fairings or cowling, dented

skin, small punctured holes in the skin or fabric, ground damage to rotor or propeller blades, damage to landing gear, wheels, tires, flaps, engine accessories, brakes, or wingtips are not considered "substantial damage" for the purpose of this part.

SUBPART B—INITIAL NOTIFICATION OF AIRCRAFT ACCIDENTS, INCIDENTS, AND OVERDUE AIRCRAFT

830.5 IMMEDIATE NOTIFICATION

The operator of an aircraft shall immediately, and by the most expeditious means available, notify the nearest National Transportation Safety Board (Board), Bureau of Aviation Safety field office when:

(a) An aircraft accident or any of the following listed incidents occur:
   (1) Flight control system malfunction or failure;
   (2) Inability of any required flightcrew member to perform his normal flight duties as a result of injury or illness;
   (3) Turbine engine rotor failures excluding compressor blades and turbine buckets;
   (4) In-flight fire; or
   (5) Aircraft collide in flight.

(b) An aircraft is overdue and is believed to have been involved in an accident.

830.6 INFORMATION TO BE GIVEN IN NOTIFICATION

The notification required in 830.5 shall contain the following information, if available:

(a) Type, nationality, and registration marks of the aircraft;
(b) Name of owner, and operator of the aircraft;
(c) Name of the pilot in command;
(d) Date and time of the accident;
(e) Last point of departure and point of intended landing of the aircraft;
(f) Position of the aircraft with reference to some easily defined geographical point;
(g) Number of persons aboard, number killed, and number seriously injured;
(h) Nature of the accident including weather and the extent of damage to the aircraft so far as is known; and
(i) A description of any explosives, radioactive materials, or other dangerous articles carried.

SUBPART C—PRESERVATION, ACCESS TO AND RELEASE OF AIRCRAFT WRECKAGE, MAIL, CARGO, AND RECORDS

830.10 PRESERVATION OF AIRCRAFT WRECKAGE, MAIL, CARGO, AND RECORDS

(a) The operator of an aircraft is responsible for preserving to the extent possible any aircraft wreckage, cargo, and mail aboard the aircraft, and all records, including tapes of flight recorders and voice recorders, pertaining to the operation and maintenance of the aircraft and to the airmen involved in an accident or incident for which notification must be given until the Board takes custody thereof or a release is granted pursuant to 831.17.

(b) Prior to the time the Board or its authorized representative takes custody of aircraft wreckage, mail, or cargo, such wreckage, mail and cargo may not be disturbed or moved except to the extent necessary:
   (1) To remove persons injured or trapped;
   (2) To protect the wreckage from further damage; or
   (3) To protect the public from injury.

(c) Where it is necessary to disturb or move aircraft wreckage, mail, or cargo, sketches, descriptive notes, and photographs shall be made, if possible, of the accident locale including original position and condition of the wreckage and any significant impact marks.

(d) The operator of an aircraft involved in an accident or incident as defined in this Part shall retain all records and reports, including all internal documents and memoranda dealing with the accident or incident, until authorized by the Board to the contrary.

SUBPART D—REPORTING OF AIRCRAFT ACCIDENTS, INCIDENTS, AND OVERDUE AIRCRAFT

830.15 REPORTS AND STATEMENTS TO BE FILED

(a) *Reports.* The operator of an aircraft shall file a report as provided in paragraph (c) of this section on Board Form 6120.1 or Board Form 6120.2 within 10 days after an accident, or after 7 days if an overdue aircraft is still missing. A report on an incident for which notification is required by 830.5(a) shall be filed only as requested by an authorized representative of the Board.

(b) *Crewmember statement.* Each crewmember, if physically able at the time the report is submitted, shall attach thereto a statement setting forth the facts, conditions, and circumstances relating to the accident or incident as they appear to him to the best of his knowledge and belief. If the crewmember is incapacitated, he shall submit the statement as soon as he is physically able.

(c) *Where to file the reports.* The operator of an aircraft shall file with the field office of the Board nearest the accident or incident any report required by this section.

NOTE:
National Transportation Safety Board Forms 6120.1 and 6120.2 are not included in this coverage because of their extensive length. These forms are available at the nearest National Transportation Safety Board, Bureau of Aviation Safety Field Office.

HMR 175

HMR 175* governs the carriage of dangerous articles and magnetized materials onboard any civil aircraft in the United States, as well as any civil aircraft of U.S. registry anywhere in air commerce. This regulation does not specifically identify each item classified as dangerous. Instead, it references other Department of Transportation regulations governing their shipment.

Dangerous articles regulated by HMR 175 fall into the following general classes.

1. *Explosives*
2. *Flammable liquids and solids, including paint removers, liquid flavoring extracts, rubber cement, paints and varnishes, alcohol, matches, and charcoal*
3. *Oxidizing materials, such as nitrates, that readily yield oxygen to stimulate combustion*
4. *Corrosive liquids, including battery acid, some cleaning compounds and rust removing or prevention compounds*
5. *Compressed gases, including most household sprays*
6. *Posions, such as pesticides, roach powder and motor-fuel antiknock compound*
7. *Etiological agents, including medical and diagnostic supplies such as serums, specimens, and vaccines*
8. *Radioactive materials*

These general classes cover thousands of items, including many common household products. The types of items listed either require special handling, must be packaged in

a specific manner, can be carried only in limited quantities, or are totally prohibited from transport by air.

Items commonly carried by the uninformed pilot include aerosol spray cans and other pressurized containers, such as filled scuba tanks, which can explode at high altitudes in an unpressurized aircraft. Medicinal and toilet articles in this category, however, are exempt from the regulation when carried by a crew member or passenger, provided they do not exceed specified small quantities. Even the carriage of survival items, such as fire extinguishers, oxygen tanks, matches, lighter fluid, signal flares, and small arms ammunition are regulated, unless they are carried in small quantities or are specially packaged.

Final responsibility for compliance with these rules is placed on the pilot in command. Since severe penalties are imposed for noncompliance, each pilot should familiarize himself with the general requirements of HMR 175. He must make certain that no dangerous materials are carried in his aircraft unless properly packed and loaded. Included in his responsibility are requirements for visual inspection of the product for container damage or leakage. Compatibility with other products, persons, or living animals, as well as the potential for contamination of food, are listed among pilot responsibilities. If a pilot is in doubt as to what he may carry in the aircraft, he should contact the local General Aviation District Office for guidance.

* *HMR 175 not published herein*

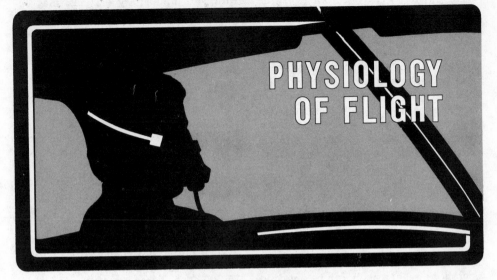

chapter 6

PHYSIOLOGY
OF FLIGHT

INTRODUCTION

With the development of lightweight construction materials and more powerful aircraft engines, general aviation aircraft are being designed for progressively higher flight into the upper atmosphere. While flights at the higher altitudes have increased the efficiency of aircraft operations, man's basic physiological and psychological processes have not been changed. Pressurized cabins or supplemental oxygen must be used to allow man to fly at high altitudes.

SECTION A—OXYGEN REQUIREMENTS

HYPOXIA

Hypoxia occurs when an insufficient quantity of oxygen is available for use by the cells of the body. In aviation, this condition generally is caused by breathing the less dense air at high altitudes. Other frequently encountered causes are illnesses which reduce the quantity of red blood cells and poisons which displace the oxygen in the red blood cells. These factors may combine to vary the pilot's altitude tolerance from day to day. Since the density of the air decreases with altitude, less oxygen is available for respiration. Consequently, some degree of physiological impairment begins to occur in most healthy persons at approximately 10,000 feet.

The most hazardous single characteristic of hypoxia is its insidious onset. In fact,

hypoxia can produce a sense of well-being called euphoria, which obscures a person's ability and desire to be critical of himself. Since he is unable to recognize his hypoxic condition, the individual believes that things are getting progressively better as he nears total mental and physical impairment.

The onset of hypoxia does not affect all individuals in the same manner. One or more of the following common symptoms may occur.

1. Impaired judgment
2. Increased breathing rate
3. Lightheaded or dizzy sensations
4. Tingling or warm sensations
5. Perspiration
6. Reduced visual acuity
7. Sleepiness

8. Cyanosis (blue coloring of the skin, fingernails, and lips)
9. Changes in behavior

Many pilots mistakenly believe that it is possible to learn their own early symptoms of hypoxia and take corrective action after these symptoms are noted. This theory is extremely dangerous because one of the earliest symptoms of hypoxia is impaired judgment. Therefore, even if an early symptom is noted, it may be disregarded or the corrective action initiated may be in error. Another important consideration is that the symptoms most commonly experienced by an individual may change from time to time.

If hypoxia is caused by high altitude operations, relief usually can be obtained by descending to a lower altitude or by using supplemental oxygen. If 100 percent oxygen is used, partial recovery normally occurs within 15 seconds.

However, momentary dizziness may occur during recovery. Although partial recovery is usually quite rapid, a person recovering from severe hypoxia may suffer measurable deficiency in mental and physical performance for several hours.

To guard against hypoxia, FAR Part 91.32 specifies the pilot and required flight crew must use supplemental oxygen for that portion of any flight above a cabin pressure altitude of 12,500 feet which exceeds 30 minutes. The pilot and crew must use oxygen continuously for flight above a cabin pressure altitude of 14,000 feet. In addition, supplemental oxygen must be available to all passengers when flying at cabin altitudes above 15,000 feet. These requirements are depicted in figure 6-1. Oxygen use requirements for FAR Part 135 operations are more stringent than those listed in FAR Part 91.

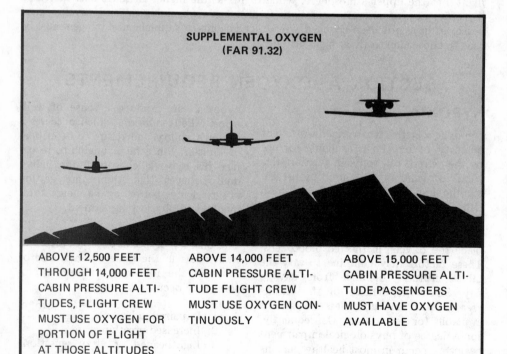

SUPPLEMENTAL OXYGEN
(FAR 91.32)

| ABOVE 12,500 FEET THROUGH 14,000 FEET CABIN PRESSURE ALTITUDES, FLIGHT CREW MUST USE OXYGEN FOR PORTION OF FLIGHT AT THOSE ALTITUDES BEYOND 30 MINUTES | ABOVE 14,000 FEET CABIN PRESSURE ALTITUDE FLIGHT CREW MUST USE OXYGEN CONTINUOUSLY | ABOVE 15,000 FEET CABIN PRESSURE ALTITUDE PASSENGERS MUST HAVE OXYGEN AVAILABLE |

Fig. 6-1. Supplemental Oxygen Requirements

HYPERVENTILATION

Normally, the respiratory center of the brain reacts to the amount of carbon dioxide produced by the body. When a person is in a physically relaxed state, the respiratory center senses the amount of carbon dioxide in the bloodstream and stabilizes the breathing rate at about 12 to 16 breaths per minute. Physical activity causes the body cells to use more oxygen resulting in increased production of carbon dioxide. The respiratory center senses the additional carbon dioxide in the bloodstream and increases the rate and depth of breathing to remove the excess. An excessive increase in breathing rate and depth is termed hyperventilation.

Within the context of flying, hyperventilation usually occurs as a result of emotional tension, anxiety, or apprehension. The resulting washout of carbon dioxide may produce the following symptoms, which are sometimes mistaken for hypoxia.

1. Sensation of being very warm
2. Nausea
3. Tingling of the fingers and toes
4. Muscle spasms
5. Unconsciousness

An individual may assume that he has hypoxia when, in fact, he is hyperventilating. This is particularly true of individuals who have been briefed inadequately or improperly on the use of oxygen equipment. If symptoms occur that cannot definitely be identified as either hypoxia or hyperventilation, it is recommended that three or four deep breaths of 100 percent oxygen be taken. If the condition experienced is hypoxia, the symptoms should diminish markedly. On the other hand, if the symptoms persist, the individual should make a conscious effort to slow his breathing rate or hold his breath for 30 to 45 seconds, then resume breathing at a normal rate. Rebreathing of the expelled air, which contains a concentration of carbon dioxide, will expedite the recovery from hyperventilation. This can be accomplished by breathing into a paper bag. A rebreather type of oxygen mask also can be used, provided it is not being supplied with oxygen. Since hyperventilation is caused primarily by anxiety and tension, the individual must make a conscious and deliberate effort to relax and slow his breathing rate.

EFFECTS OF PRESSURE CHANGE

The volume of a gas varies inversely with the applied pressure. That is, as pressure decreases, the volume of the gas increases and as pressure increases, the volume decreases. For example, the volume of a given quantity of gas at sea level doubles at 18,000 feet. At 25,000 feet, this same amount of gas occupies three times as much space as it did at sea level.

When gases are trapped in body cavities, such as the middle ear, sinuses, or intestinal tract, this change in volume can result in a painful condition called *dysbarism*. This condition can be caused by either an altitude change in an unpressurized airplane or decompression of a pressurized airplane.

MIDDLE EAR

As illustrated in figure 6-2, the middle ear is an air-filled cavity which is vented to the atmosphere through the eustachian tube. This tube opens into the

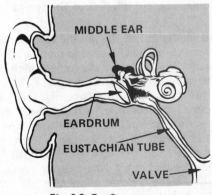

MIDDLE EAR

EARDRUM

EUSTACHIAN TUBE

VALVE

Fig. 6-2. Ear Structure

back of the throat and is constructed something like a check valve, allowing air to flow out of the ear more easily than back into the ear.

During ascent, the air pressure within the middle ear expands as the atmospheric pressure decreases. This causes the eardrum to bulge outward until the excess pressure in the middle ear is relieved as the eustachian tube is forced open. Therefore, ascent is generally noneventful, except for slight clicking and popping sensations which are caused by the eardrum flexing as the pressure changes.

During descent, the situation is reversed. As the atmospheric pressure increases, it presses against the area of lower pressure within the middle ear and causes the eardrum to bulge inward. As the aircraft descends, the individual usually is aware of the low pressure area in the middle ear through a sense of eardrum tension, a partial loss of hearing, and a vague discomfort which can turn into actual pain if the valve blocks the air movement.

An individual who attempts to fly with a cold or sinus condition is most susceptible to an ear blockage. However, when a person is healthy, chewing, yawning, or swallowing will cause the small muscles around the eustachian tube valve to contract, holding the tube open. These actions usually are followed by pressure equalization between the middle and outer ear, giving relief of the symptoms.

If reinflation of the middle ear does not occur, additional measures may be necessary. One of the most efficient methods is called the Valsalva technique. To use this technique, the nostrils are held closed to form an airtight seal, then pressure is built up in the nose slowly and gently. In severe cases, it may be necessary to increase altitude until the middle and outer ear pressures equalize, then make a slower descent while using the Valsalva technique periodically.

SINUS CAVITIES

The sinuses also are air-filled cavities which vent into the nose, as shown in figure 6-3. Occasionally, sinus blockages may occur due to altitude changes. In this situation, the techniques used to relieve pressure on the middle ear can be used to clear the sinuses.

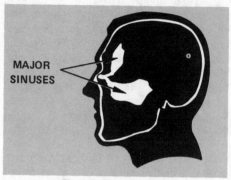

MAJOR
SINUSES

Fig. 6-3. Sinus Cavities

INTESTINAL TRACT

At sea level, the intestinal tract normally contains about a quart of gas consisting of swallowed air and some gas given off by the food digestion process. During a climb to altitude, these gases expand and can cause discomfort. This discomfort is aggravated by foods that increase sensitivity to intestinal gas expansion. Onions, cabbage, raw apples, radishes, beans, cucumbers, and melons are examples of foods that may cause excessive amounts of gas. A good diet and regular eating habits are considered to be important factors in avoiding abdominal stress.

DECOMPRESSION

During normal physiological processes, a considerable volume of gas, primarily nitrogen, is dissolved in the blood and intracellular fluids. If the pressure outside the body is reduced suddenly, these gases tend to come out of solution and form bubbles which can cause pain. Although this reaction occurs to a small degree during a climb to a higher altitude in an unpressurized airplane, the effects are more significant when an airplane at a high altitude loses pressurization.

Nitrogen bubbles can cause pain in various parts of the body. Pain experienced primarily in the joints is referred to as the *bends*, while bubble formation in the respiratory system can cause a burning discomfort called the *chokes*. Although these symptoms rarely occur below 20,000 feet, they can be experienced at much lower altitudes by a person who has recently been scuba diving. The excess nitrogen absorbed into the diver's body under the increased pressure of the water is released as bubbles at low altitudes. A general guideline for avoiding the bends or chokes after scuba diving is that flight above a cabin pressure altitude of 12,000 feet should be avoided within 12 hours after a dive to 12 feet or more. Specific information can be obtained in diving manuals.

While the symptoms due to the expansion of trapped gas develop almost immediately following loss of pressurization, the problems that result from bubble formation normally do not occur for a considerable period of time. For example, if aircraft pressurization is lost at altitudes of 35,000 to 40,000 feet, approximately 20 minutes is required for the average person to develop severe or incapacitating symptoms. The onset of these symptoms also is affected by the speed and severity of the decompression.

SLOW DECOMPRESSION

Slow decompression normally is indicated on the cabin-pressure altimeter and rate-of-pressure-change instrument. In this case, the pilot usually has adequate time to take corrective action or begin a descent to lower altitudes where pressurization is not required.

RAPID DECOMPRESSION

Rapid decompression usually results from a breakdown of the pressurized section of the aircraft, such as a ruptured fuselage or a failed windshield or window. It normally is indicated by an initial explosive noise, followed by a rapid rush of cabin air toward the opening which caused the decompression. There also is a noticeable decrease in cabin temperature and a marked fogging effect due to the rapid reduction in cabin pressure and temperature.

A number of experiments indicate that healthy individuals may experience a rapid decompression from a cabin altitude of 8,000 to 35,000 feet in less than one-tenth of a second without physical damage. However, several physiological changes occur as the body adjusts to the reduced pressure. These changes include a noticeable feeling of abdominal fullness, and momentary pain in the ears and sinuses.

The greatest hazard of a rapid decompression is not physical damage, but the possible subsequent hypoxia. To avoid hypoxia, oxygen must be administered immediately and an emergency descent initiated to a lower altitude where pressurization is not required.

FATIGUE

Simply defined, fatigue is weariness from bodily labor or mental exertion. Excessive fatigue can lead to a decline in efficiency and performance. Since efficiency is impaired, a pilot in an emergency situation may fail to respond either rapidly or appropriately.

Physical fatigue can be caused by several factors. It can result from unusual physical exercise, excessive loss of sleep, illness, or advancing age. The following list contains some of the symptoms of physical fatigue.

1. Decreased strength
2. Decreased muscular coordination
3. Slower reaction time
4. Increased time for the eyes to respond to light
5. Increased time for the eyes to focus when alternating between nearby and distant objects

Mental fatigue can be the result of physical fatigue, but also can exist within an individual who is otherwise in a physically rested state. Mental fatigue can be caused by repeated sleep inadequacies, time-pressure stresses, frequent, unanticipated interruption of work schedules, and sudden changes in schedules involving shortened overnight stops, frequent emergencies, and interrupted family life.

CIRCADIAN RHYTHMS

The body undergoes several periodic, rhythmic cycles called circadian rhythms which are repeated at intervals of approximately 24 hours. Since these cycles are not directly related to the incidence of daylight and darkness, a traveler who crosses several time zones arrives at his destination out-of-step with the local day-to-day activities. Even without daylight and darkness, his body still tends to maintain a normal sleep cycle. If he is deprived of sleep during this cycle, regardless of the time of day in the new time zone, he is likely to perform below

normal. Blood pressure and the activities of the liver, kidneys, and other organs and glands are similarly out of phase when a rapid change of time zones takes place.

When an individual travels through several time zones rapidly, the internal "biological clock" begins to adjust body functions. However, the time required for adjustment varies with individuals and may require several days. As the individual adapts to the new timetable, his biological functions return to normal.

Certain actions may be taken to aid in adjusting to a new time zone. First, the traveler should be adequately rested prior to departure. Then, after arriving at the destination, he should get a good night's sleep or a nap. Second, excessive alcohol and heavy eating should be avoided. Last, any essential work should be scheduled after the first full rest period, preferably on the following day.

SECTION B—VERTIGO AND VISION

SENSORY ILLUSIONS

The human body depends on several information sources to determine its position in space. The most pronounced of these sources are visual sense, vestibular sense, and kinesthetic sense. When one or more of these sources are rendered inoperative or provide information in conflict with the other senses, spatial disorientation results. This mental conflict, often called *vertigo*, can cause sensory confusion, disorientation, dizziness, or nausea.

VISUAL SENSE

Vision is the most important of the senses used to maintain balance. Physiologists have found that if the brain is confronted with conflicting signals from various sensory inputs, interpretation of the individual's orientation in space is made primarily by visual means. Since flight in actual instrument conditions, marginal VFR conditions, or at night may cause the outside visual references to become unreliable, the visual system must be trained to correctly interpret information obtained from the flight instruments.

VESTIBULAR SENSE

The organs that control the vestibular sense are the semicircular canals and the static organ. As shown in figure 6-4, these structures are located in the inner ear, very close to the sensory hearing center.

SEMICIRCULAR CANALS

There are three fluid-filled semicircular canals located near each ear. One of the canals lies in the horizontal plane, while the other two are in vertical planes. Inside the canals, in the area near their junction, are numerous tiny hair cells. These hair cells project from the lining of the canals into the fluid. When a canal is moved, inertia causes the fluid to resist movement, thus applying pressure to the

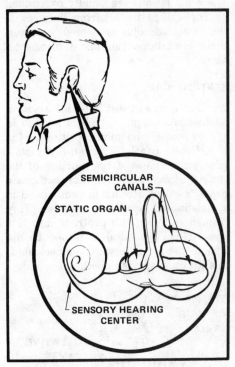

Fig. 6-4. Vestibular Sense Mechanism

hair cells. The nervous system translates this pressure into a sense of movement. For example, when the head is tipped forward or backward, the bone structure of the head rotates around the fluid and stimulates the hair cells in the vertically oriented canal. The stimulus is interpreted as forward or backward motion. The canal in the horizontal plane is stimulated in a similar manner by turning motions, and the remaining canal is stimulated by the motions involved in rolling the head to the left or to the right.

Although the semicircular canals are useful in sensing movement, they have certain limitations. One of the most significant of these is an inability to detect a rate of rotation of less than three degrees per second. Also, if a uniform rate of movement continues for an extended period of time the fluid in the canals will "catch up" and stabilize, so that there is no turning sensation. These limitations are usually overridden by correcting stimulus from the eyes. If the visual stimulus is denied, however, these limitations can cause disorientation.

STATIC ORGAN

Another source of vestibular information is the static organ, which is located in approximately the same position as the semicircular canals. Figure 6-5 depicts a microscopic view of one portion of the static organ. Tiny calcium carbonate deposits called otoliths are embedded in a gelatinous layer of material. Tiny filaments of hair cells protrude into this layer. When the head is tipped to the left, to the right, forward, or backward, this structure also is tipped.

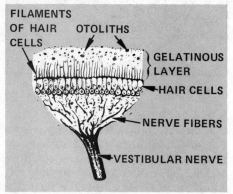

Fig. 6-5. Static Organ

The tiny otoliths cause the gelatinous layer to be deflected by the pull of gravity (or G forces). Since the otoliths respond to these forces, they cause the hair filaments to generate a nervous impulse which is interpreted as linear acceleration. In this manner, the static organ senses acceleration, deceleration, and sideways motion.

KINESTHETIC SENSE

Kinesthetic sense sometimes is referred to as "the seat of the pants" sense. The muscles and skeletal structure of the body report their state of contraction and pressure to the brain for interpreta-

tion. In turn, the brain translates these sensations into position information. However, confusion results when the brain is unable to interpret whether the pressure and tension reported are the result of gravity or the result of load factors induced by coordinated flight maneuvers.

FAA aeromedical personnel have investigated vertigo with the aid of vertigo simulators like the one shown in figure 6-6. Test subjects in the simulator are instructed to tilt their heads sideways approximately 30° from the vertical while the simulator begins a slow rotation in the horizontal plane.

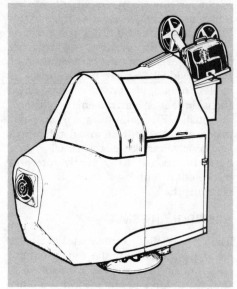

Fig. 6-6. Vertigo Simulator

When rotational motion has apparently ceased, the pilot is instructed to move his head upright. Almost immediately he grabs for the control wheel, because he feels his airplane has gone into a steep diving or climbing turn.

The tests also showed that leaning the head forward produces apparent rolls to the right and returning the head to a normal position produces a sensation of a left roll. The doctors pointed out that such movements as leaning forward to retrieve a pencil or to change the fuel selector can cause similar reactions under actual instrument conditions.

MOTION ILLUSIONS

Spatial disorientation is a common phenomenon experienced by non-instrument qualified pilots who attempt to fly in adverse weather conditions. The disorientation typically begins with an unintentional turn which is undetected because the rate of change is not sufficient to stimulate the semicircular canals. Then, the bank increases and the airplane begins a descending spiral. As the pilot becomes aware of increased engine speed and loss of altitude, he pulls back on the wheel in an attempt to recover from an apparent wings-level dive. This action only tightens the spiral. If uncorrected, this situation can cause the structural limits of the airplane to be exceeded.

Even experienced pilots can lapse into a similar situation because of distraction and may find the recovery produces strong erroneous sensations. For example, in a recovery from a level turn, the pilot may feel he has entered a descent. In a prolonged turn, the pilot may feel he is flying straight and level because the fluid in the semicircular canals has stabilized and registers no rate of change. If this occurs, the roll-out from the turn may induce a strong sensation of entering a turn in the opposite direction. In a skidding, flat turn, the pilot may feel that he is banking in the opposite direction because of G forces pulling on the otoliths.

VISUAL ILLUSIONS

Vision itself may contribute to certain illusions such as the autokinetic phenomenon. This occurs when a pilot stares at a single light against a totally dark background and the light suddenly appears to move. This phenomenon is especially prevalent during turbulent conditions and can give the impression that the airplane has entered a side slip.

Another area of confusion can occur during flight above a sloping cloud layer. Because the pilot is using the tilted layer as the horizon, he may actually be in a bank while thinking the aircraft is in level flight. During night flight in or near clouds, a rotating beacon can induce a sensation of turning. Another nighttime visual illusion that can cause disorientation is the sensation of a false horizon caused by the apparent intermingling of ground lights with stars, as illustrated in figure 6-7. This is especially true where a definite visual horizon is not readily apparent.

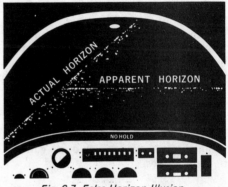

Fig. 6-7. False Horizon Illusion

FLICKER VERTIGO

A light which flickers at a constant rate between approximately 240 and 1,200 times per minute can cause unpleasant and sometimes dangerous physiological reactions. Although the degree of impairment varies between individuals, susceptibility appears to be increased if one is fatigued or in a mild state of hypoxia. This phenomenon is most likely to occur during landing or ground operations when the slowly turning propeller causes the rays of a setting or rising sun to become interrupted flashes of light. A change in r.p.m. usually eliminates flicker vertigo.

VERTIGO PREVENTION

To overcome the effects of vertigo, the pilot must trust the aircraft instruments, not his physical senses. The following paragraphs contain several suggestions for avoiding or minimizing the effects of vertigo.

The pilot should be aware of the limitations of the balance mechanism and the false sensations which may occur. If possible, he should experience the various vertigo sensations under the guidance of a flight instructor or in a vertigo trainer. This experience will help him recognize the effects of vertigo.

During flight in instrument conditions, *sudden head movements should be avoided*, particularly when the aircraft is changing attitude. Vertigo induced by sudden head movements is referred to as "coriolis illusion." This type of vertigo may occur in conjunction with sudden head movements anytime that instrument reference is temporarily lost. Examples include map reading, changing a radio channel, searching for an approach chart, fuel managing, computing a navigational problem, or performing other in-flight duties.

If vertigo is encountered and the instruments indicate the airplane is in straight-and-level flight, this attitude should be held for a few minutes to allow the effects of vertigo to pass. The airplane should be trimmed properly, especially in straight-and-level flight. If vertigo is experienced and the airplane varies from this configuration, it can be returned to level flight, then the controls released until disorientation subsides. If a critical attitude is encountered, aircraft attitude should be determined by reference to the instruments, then corrective control pressures should be applied smoothly.

During an instrument approach, the instruments should be cross-checked, even after visual contact with the runway is established. Then, if disorientation is experienced, the instrument indications can be used to maintain the desired attitude.

Aeromedical researchers have determined that an increase in mental effort makes an individual more susceptible to vertigo. This simply means that since instrument flight is less demanding on a highly skilled, proficient instrument pilot, he is less susceptible to vertigo than a pilot who is not as proficient.

VISION

The ease with which an object can be seen depends on many factors, such as illumination, contrast, perspective, viewing time, and atmospheric clarity. To a certain extent, a deficiency in one of these areas may be compensated for by an increase in another. For example, an airplane can be made more visible by increasing its contrast through the use of appropriate paint schemes and external lighting. The method of looking at an object also influences its clarity. To see an object clearly under normal illumination, the individual should look directly at the object. At night, he should focus his eyes approximately 4° to 12° off the center of the object.

LIGHT SENSITIVITY

The light-sensitive area at the back of the eye is called the retina. As illustrated in figure 6-8, this photosensitive layer is made up of two perceptual elements called *cones* and *rods*. Cones are more numerous in the central area of the retina and provide the sharpest vision when the illumination is greater than that provided by a full moon. Below this level of brightness, the cones become relatively unusable and the rods are utilized.

DARK ADAPTATION

While the rods provide the maximum amount of night vision, they require a period of time to adjust to darkened conditions. The principle of dark adaption can be illustrated by going into a darkened movie theater during the day. At first, little can be seen. Then, after a few minutes, the eyes become capable of

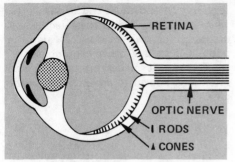

Fig. 6-8. Photosensitive Eye Structures

making out dim forms and large outlines. Eventually, smaller details can be seen in the darkened environment.

The rate and degree of dark adaption can vary considerably. In the theater, it is fairly rapid due to the illumination from the movie screen. However, after a night departure from a brightly lit airport into a moonless sky, more time is required for adaptation.

Approximately 30 minutes normally is required for complete dark adaptation to occur. Since exposure to a bright light significantly extends time required for dark adaption, the pilot should avoid looking directly at bright lights during the 30 minutes before a planned flight. If the pilot must face a bright light, such as an airplane landing light, just prior to takeoff, he should shield one eye so that it is not required to readapt. In addition, if variable intensity runway lights are too bright, the pilot should ask the tower controller to reduce the intensity.

Exposure to bright sunlight has a cumulative and adverse effect on dark adaption. If an afternoon is spent in very bright sunlight, the eyes' sensitivity to low levels of light can be decreased significantly for as much as five hours. However, the time required to adapt can be reduced greatly if adequate sunglasses are worn.

When flying in the vicinity of thunderstorms, lightning flashes can affect dark adaption and cause temporary "blindness." To minimize this effect, the pilot should increase the intensity of the cabin lighting. Although outside vision will be diminished, the ability to read the flight instruments will be retained.

In addition to exposure to bright light, several factors affect night vision. For example, any condition which reduces the supply of oxygen decreases night vision and causes an increase in the time required for dark adaption. While flying at 12,000 feet without supplemental oxygen, an individual's night vision is only about one-half of that normally experienced at sea level.

Smoking also has a detrimental effect on night vision. Three cigarettes smoked at night can reduce visual sensitivity as much as an altitude increase of 8,000 feet.

An adequate supply of vitamin A also is necessary for good night vision. The role vitamin C plays in night vision is not completely understood. However, it appears that a diet deficient in vitamin C may result in impaired night vision.

SCANNING TECHNIQUE

Proper scanning technique is the basis of collision avoidance. It involves a systematic sweep of the entire visual field by use of both eye and head movements. However, this technique is most effective when the sky is scanned by sectors, rather than by a continuous sweeping motion because the eye perceives poorly if an image is moving across the retina. The sharpest image is formed if each sector of the sky is brought into focus on or near the center of the retina before moving on to the next sector.

Scanning efficiency can be increased further through use of clearing turns to expose the airspace hidden by the aircraft structure. Additional airspace can be exposed during climbout from an airport if the airplane is accelerated to the normal climb speed when a safe altitude is reached. The higher airspeed results in a lower pitch attitude and increased forward visibility.

To supplement visual scanning, the pilot should utilize such aids as airport advisory service and radar traffic advisiores, when available. Use of these facilities is desirable for two reasons. It aids the pilot in detecting otherwise unobserved traffic, and it makes his position and intentions known to other aircraft in the area.

chapter 7

INTRODUCTION

Current technology has greatly increased the operational capabilities of general aviation aircraft. Airplanes are capable of flying higher and often are equipped to fly through icing conditions. To utilize the airplane's altitude and weather capabilities, the advanced pilot must understand the use of oxygen systems, pressurization, and de-icing and anti-icing equipment.

SECTION A—OXYGEN SYSTEMS

Supplemental oxygen is available to the general aviation pilot through three basic types of oxygen delivery systems. The most common type is the *continuous flow* system. It may be installed as optional equipment in nearly all modern production aircraft and is also available in smaller, portable units. The second type of oxygen system is the *diluter-demand* system, which increases the utility of the basic continuous flow system by conserving oxygen at lower altitudes and increasing the oxygen flow at higher altitudes. The third type is the *pressure-demand* oxygen system, normally found on high-performance turboprops and jet aircraft.

2. Regulator
3. Distribution system
4. Continuous flow masks

A supply of high-pressure oxygen is maintained in a storage cylinder of the type shown in figure 7-1. A regulator valve (item 2), usually incorporating an ON/OFF valve (item 3) which is controllable from the cabin, reduces the high-pressure oxygen to a lower, usable pressure. The distribution system (item 4) routes the low-pressure oxygen to convenient outlets throughout the cabin (item 5). The pilot and passengers may then plug their individual masks into outlets when supplemental oxygen is desired.

CONTINUOUS FLOW OXYGEN SYSTEM

Continuous flow oxygen delivery systems normally consist of four main components
1. High-pressure storage cylinder

OXYGEN STORAGE CYLINDER

The oxygen supply is contained in one or more high-pressure cylinders. These cylinders are subject to strict regulation by the Department of Transportation and are stamped with a material quality

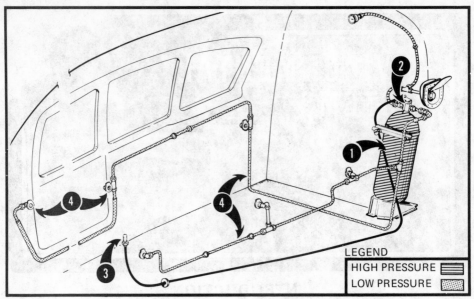

LEGEND
HIGH PRESSURE
LOW PRESSURE

Fig. 7-1. Continuous Flow Oxygen System

code, serial number, pressure rating, and test dates. The capacity of the oxygen storage cylinders found in light, general aviation aircraft varies from approximately 11 cubic feet to over 100 cubic feet.

Most oxygen storage systems have an external filler valve located in a convenient place to permit filling the storage cylinder without removal from the aircraft. Some filler valves are automatically self-closing, while others require that the cylinder ON/OFF valve be positioned manually when the cylinders are being filled. It is important that the specific operating procedures found in the aircraft's flight manual be followed carefully when the cylinder is being filled or when preparations are made for a flight in which the use of oxygen is anticipated.

OXYGEN REGULATORS

Several types of manual and automatic regulators are used to control the flow of oxygen through the distribution system. Manual regulators incorporate a pilot-operated flow control valve, while automatic regulators utilize the atmo-

spheric and cylinder pressure differential to maintain the proper flow rate.

DISTRIBUTION SYSTEM

Oxygen is routed from the regulator to the oxygen outlets, as shown in figure 7-2. These outlets contain spring-loaded shutoff valves which close automatically when the mask is disconnected. Plugging the mask into the outlets opens the spring-loaded shutoff valve, allowing the low-pressure oxygen to flow to the mask, as shown on the right side of figure 7-2.

The amount of oxygen flowing into the mask is dependent upon two factors — the *oxygen pressure* supplied to the outlet and the *size of the restricted opening* in each outlet or plug-in. Since the oxygen pressure reaching the outlet is constant, the mask's plug-in fitting and the outlet work together to control the oxygen flow into the face mask by means of an *oxygen flow restrictor*.

FLOW RESTRICTORS

The flow restrictor in the oxygen mask plug-in connector may be provided with a dense fiberglass packing or a small,

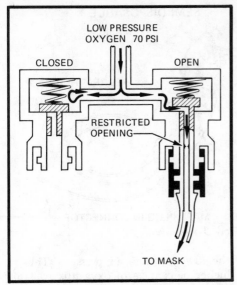

Fig. 7-2. Oxygen Outlets

orifice can be used to increase the flow rate.

Since the amount of oxygen required varies with altitude and physical activity of the user, flow restrictors come in various sizes. Pilots normally require more oxygen than passengers; therefore, the plug-in for the pilot's mask usually has a *larger* calibrated orifice or a *lower* density fiberglass packing. The pilot's mask plug-in usually has a *red band* to denote its greater flow rate. This distinguishes it from the other oxygen masks which are marked with *gold bands*. Flow rate is usually measured in liters per hour (LPH).

OXYGEN MASKS

The continuous flow oxygen mask assembly, as shown in figure 7-4, consists of a plug-in connector, flow indicator, rebreather bag, and mask. When the connector is plugged into the outlet, oxygen flows through the plug-in connector, past the flow indicator, into the rebreather bag, and then to the face mask. The flow indicator is a simple check valve; the red indicator is deflected toward the mask when oxygen is flowing, as shown in figure 7-5.

calibrated orifice. As shown in figure 7-3, the flow rate is determined by either the *density* of the fiberglass packing or the *size* of the calibrated orifice. The rate of oxygen flow may be reduced either by increasing the density of the fiberglass packing or reducing the size of the calibrated orifice. Conversely, a less dense fiberglass packing or a larger calibrated

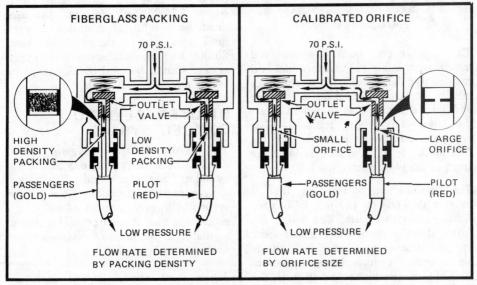

Fig. 7-3. Flow Rate Restrictors

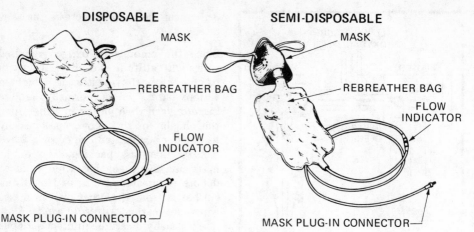

Fig. 7-4. Continuous Flow Oxygen Masks

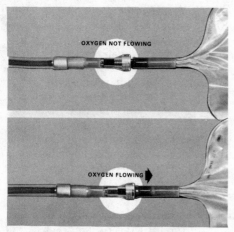

Fig. 7-5. Oxygen Flow Indicator

The mask covers both the nose and mouth, providing a comfortable and reasonably tight seal. When the user inhales, oxygen is drawn out of the bag and into the lungs, as shown in figure 7-6, item 1. As the rebreather bag collapses, outside air is drawn into the face mask through the small holes in the front of the plastic mask (item 2).

The amount of outside air that is inhaled depends on the rate of oxygen flowing into the mask. The higher the flow rate, the more the bag and mask are pressurized, resulting in less outside air entering the mask during inhalation. In addition, the higher the altitude, the more the rebreather bag expands due to

the lower outside air pressure. Thus, a higher percentage of oxygen is available as the outside air pressure diminishes.

The rebreather bag becomes repressurized both by the incoming oxygen from the distribution system and the initial exhalation from the lungs. The remaining volume of exhaled air is forced out the vent holes into the outside air, as shown in figure 7-6, item 3.

The continuous flow rebreather-type oxygen mask can provide an adequate oxygen supply *up to 25,000 feet.* Above 17,000 feet, however, the user must be careful to maintain a tight mask seal. For continued flight above 25,000 feet, the diluter-demand oxygen system should be used by all occupants of the aircraft.

DILUTER–DEMAND OXYGEN SYSTEM

The diluter-demand oxygen system utilizes the same type of oxygen supply cylinder, regulator, and distribution system as the continuous flow oxygen system. However, instead of utilizing a rebreather bag, it incorporates a second regulator in the mask or hose assembly, as shown in figure 7-7.

When used above 32,000 feet, the diluter-demand regulator should be set

Oxygen flow rate increases as outside pressure decreases.	Rebreather bag collapses as air is inhaled. After bag collapses, air enters small holes in bag or mask.	Air partially expelled through small holes in mask. Rebreather bag filled by fresh oxygen and exhaled air

Fig. 7-6. Oxygen Rebreather Bags

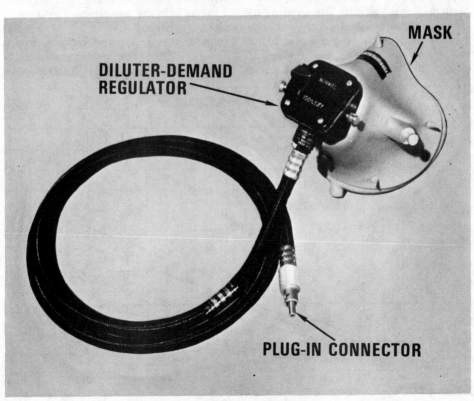

Fig. 7-7. Diluter-Demand Regulator

for 100 percent oxygen. The use of pure oxygen enables the diluter-demand mask to be used safely *up to an altitude of 35,000 feet.*

PRESSURE-DEMAND OXYGEN SYSTEM

Flight above 35,000 feet requires a special oxygen system that delivers pressurized oxygen to the user's lungs. The pressure-demand system generally is found in jet and high-performance turboprop aircraft. A pressure-demand system differs from the continuous flow and diluter-demand systems because oxygen is supplied under a positive pressure. Thus, the individual must forcibly exhale against the pressure of the incoming oxygen.

OXYGEN SUPPLY DURATION

Determining how long an aircraft's oxygen supply will last is an important preflight consideration. The duration of an oxygen supply depends on the *amount of oxygen available* and the *total consumption rate.* The amount of oxygen available is measured in terms

of oxygen pressure within the storage cylinder. The total consumption rate is determined by adding the consumption rate of each user. The total rate is measured in terms of the amount of pressure (pounds per square inch) consumed per hour. Oxygen consumption and system duration data is provided in the aircraft flight manual in the form of tables or graphs.

One method of presenting the oxygen duration data is the oxygen consumption graph shown in figure 7-8. Presentation of the information in graph form eliminates the need for mathematical computation, enabling the pilot to read the system duration directly. The pilot needs to know only the *pressure in the oxygen cylinder* and the *number of passengers using the system.*

If, for example, a pilot is planning a trip carrying three passengers and the oxygen cylinder pressure is 1,800 p.s.i., the following method should be used to determine the oxygen supply duration. The pilot locates the intersection of the diagonal line on the graph

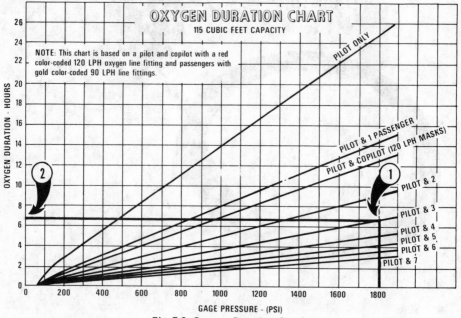

Fig. 7-8. Oxygen Duration Graph

representing the pilot and three passengers and the vertical line representing 1,800 p.s.i. (item 1). Then, by proceeding horizontally, he can determine the oxygen duration of 6.9 hours (item 2).

The graph method of presenting oxygen duration data has a slight disadvantage because it is accurate only if the pilot uses the red plug-in connector and all the passengers use gold plug-in connectors. Other methods of presenting oxygen duration may be encountered, but the ready use of sample calculations or tables makes the computation of oxygen duration relatively simple.

SECTION B—CABIN PRESSURIZATION

Technological advances have developed rapidly in the past 10 years. Turbocharging and high altitude flight capability for general aviation aircraft have presented new problems as well as new vistas. Now the pilot and his passengers enjoy the comfort and convenience of their ground environment without the discomfort and restrictions of wearing an oxygen mask and being "tethered" to an oxygen outlet.

Pressurization eliminates the need for wearing oxygen masks at altitude. In addition, pressurization adds to general passenger comfort at higher altitudes.

OPERATION

Although individual systems may differ, the basic principle of operation is the same. The system pressurizes the cabin area to some value above the outside air pressure and then maintains that pressure through a wide range of altitudes.

There are two basic systems which are representative of those used by most general aviation manufacturers. Figure 7-9 illustrates a typical pressurization system.

The *standard* system automatically begins presurizing the cabin as the aircraft climbs through 8,000 feet. (This altitude may vary with different manufacturers.) As the climb is continued, the cabin pressure altitude remains at 8,000 feet until the airplane reaches 20,000 feet. If the aircraft continues to climb above this altitude, the cabin pressure will slowly decrease; however, a cabin pressure regulator maintains a pressure *differential* of 4.2 p.s.i. up to the aircraft's service ceiling.

Some pressurization systems, however, permit the cabin pressure to be adjusted slowly as the airplane climbs or descends. For example, an aircraft may take off at sea level and climb at a rate of 1,500 feet per minute, but the "cabin rate of climb" may be set for a comfortable 250 f.p.m. rate of change. At flight altitudes up to approximately 9,000 feet, the cabin pressure altitude can remain *at sea level.* Above 9,000 feet the system permits the pressure altitude to slowly increase, so that the 4.2 p.s.i. *differential* will not be exceeded.

During the operation of this system, ram air is taken from a scoop on the side of the engine nacelle and delivered to the engine turbochargers. (See Fig. 7-9, item 1.) Compressed air from the compressor side of the turbochargers is delivered to the cabin through ducting and cabin outlets. Since the compression of air in the turbocharger generates considerable heat, a heat exchanger (item 15) is provided which cools the air during warm weather operations before it actually enters the cabin. The heat exchanger is exposed to the outside air by a scoop underneath the fuselage. After the hot, compressed air is cooled in the heat exchanger, it is delivered directly to the cabin via the system outlets (items 16 and 17).

During cold weather operations, a mixer valve (item 4) directly routes hot, compressed air from the turbocharger to the blower (item 2) of the ventilation system rather than the heat exchanger. From the ventilation blower, air is routed through the cabin heat and defroster outlets (items 16 and 17). A gasoline heater also is provided for supplemental cabin heating or for use during periods when the aircraft is not pressurized. During operations at moderate outside temperatures, the mixture valve has a capability of modulating hot, compressed air from the turbocharger by sending part of the air through the heat exchanger and part through the heater ventilation system.

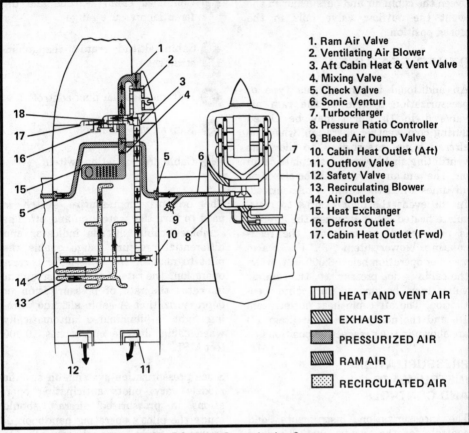

1. Ram Air Valve
2. Ventilating Air Blower
3. Aft Cabin Heat & Vent Valve
4. Mixing Valve
5. Check Valve
6. Sonic Venturi
7. Turbocharger
8. Pressure Ratio Controller
9. Bleed Air Dump Valve
10. Cabin Heat Outlet (Aft)
11. Outflow Valve
12. Safety Valve
13. Recirculating Blower
14. Air Outlet
15. Heat Exchanger
16. Defrost Outlet
17. Cabin Heat Outlet (Fwd)

▥ HEAT AND VENT AIR
▧ EXHAUST
▨ PRESSURIZED AIR
▨ RAM AIR
▨ RECIRCULATED AIR

Fig. 7-9. Cabin Pressurization System

SAFETY FEATURES

Since turbocharged air is supplied from both engines, check valves (item 5) are provided to prevent reverse airflow and decompression in the event one engine or turbocharger should fail. Other safety devices include a pressure ratio controller (item 8), which stabilizes compressor discharge pressure so that variations in turbocharger output will not cause the cabin pressure to vary. A bleed air dump valve (item 9), which is manually controlled by the pilot, is provided for unpressurized operations or for elimination of noxious fumes which may enter the turbocharger compressor. By opening these valves, the pilot can prevent the cabin from being pressurized or the fumes from entering the cabin.

The function of the sonic venturi (item 6) is to prevent the noise of the turbocharger from being transferred to the cabin through the ducting and cabin outlets.

Within the cabin, two additional safety devices are included — the outflow valve (item 11) and the safety valve (item 12). Both valves generally are located in the rear of the cabin on the aft pressure bulkhead. The outflow valve functions automatically and allows "used" cabin air to be exhausted at a controlled rate so the desired cabin altitude is maintained. The safety valve, controlled from the instrument panel, is used for normal decompression and also prevents the cabin altitude from exceeding the 4.2 p.s.i. differential between the cabin air and outside air in the event the outflow valve fails in the closed position.

OTHER FEATURES

An additional feature of this type of pressurization system is the ram air valve (item 1), which may be closed during cold weather operation, when the aircraft is not pressurized, to allow the ventilating air blower to recirculate cabin air. The ram air valve should be closed at all times when the cabin is pressurized. In the event the pilot desires to recirculate heated cabin air when the aircraft is pressurized, he may use the recirculating blower (item 13). For warm weather operation below 8,000 feet, when the cabin is not pressurized, the ram air valve may be opened for cabin ventilation. The aft cabin heat outlet (item 10) and the normal air outlet (item 14) are shown in their respective positions.

PRESSURIZATION INSTRUMENTS AND CONTROLS

The pressurization instruments and controls for the system just described are as follows. (See Fig. 7-10).

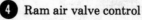

1 Combined cabin altitude and differential pressure gauge

2 Cabin altitude rate-of-change instrument

3 Left and right air duct control

4 Ram air valve control

5 Cabin pressurization switch

The pressurize/depressurize switch is used to turn the system on and off. The combined cabin altitude indicator and differential pressure gauge enable the pilot to monitor the system for correct operation. The rate-of-change instrument indicates the rate of pressurization or depressurization. A cabin altitude warning light is illuminated automatically when cabin altitude approaches 10,000 feet MSL.

Since pressurization systems on specific models vary, pilots anticipating operations in pressurized aircraft should study the pilot's operating handbook or approved flight manual carefully to insure correct operation of the system.

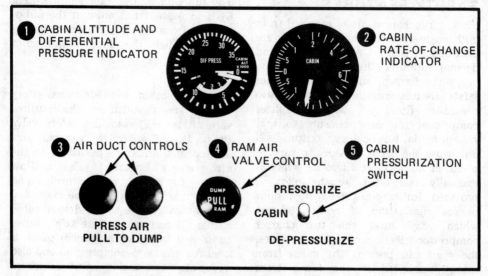

Fig. 7-10. Pressurization Instruments and Controls

SECTION C
STRUCTURAL ICE CONTROL SYSTEMS

The increased need for utilization of modern-day aircraft during all weather conditions has led to the development of de-icing and anti-icing equipment. De-icing means *removal*, whereas anti-icing denotes *ice prevention*.

ICE CONTROL EQUIPMENT AND SYSTEMS

There are several types of icing equipment employed in modern aircraft and each type may have two or more variations. Some of the systems available are as follows.

1. Propeller (alcohol or electrical)
2. Wing and tail surfaces (pneumatic boots or hot air)
3. Windshield, pitot tube, and fuel vent heaters (electrical)

Also available for use in conjunction with these systems are such items as shielded antennas (to insure adequate reception and transmission) and wing ice lights (to illuminate areas of possible ice accumulation). The following discussion of de-icing and anti-icing systems, installations, and general operations pertains to systems which are typical of most light/medium aircraft used in general aviation.

ELECTRICAL PROPELLER ANTI-ICE

The electrical propeller anti-ice system employs heating elements to reduce the adhesion between the ice and propeller. To activate the system, the pilot simply turns an electrical switch to the ON position. With the system in operation in icing conditions, the heating elements soften the layer of ice adhering to the propeller blades. Centrifugal force and airflow over the propeller cause the ice to be thrown from the blades.

HEATING ELEMENTS

The heating elements consist of heater wires enclosed in rubber pads. To pro-

vide additional strength, the rubber pads incorporate fabric plys similar to those of automobile and aircraft tires. The dull, porous side of the rubber pad is cemented to the leading edge of the propeller blades. The area covered extends from the blade root part way up the leading edge. The outer portion of the heating pad has a very smooth, glossy surface. This type of surface reduces ice adherence. A propeller with heating pads installed is shown in figure 7-11.

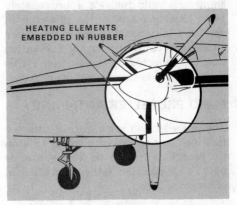

HEATING ELEMENTS EMBEDDED IN RUBBER

Fig. 7-11. Electric Propeller Heat Elements

The heating pad contains two elements—an inboard heater (near the propeller hub) and an outboard heater. These heating elements are used individually and cycled to reduce the amount of electrical current required at any one time.

TIMER

Many light twin-engine aircraft utilize a timer to cycle the electrical current between the right and left propeller heating elements every minute, creating a two minute cycle. In a given one minute period, the outboard heaters of the right propeller operate for 30 seconds, followed by a 30-second operation of the inboard heaters. During the next minute, the left propeller heating elements operate. In this manner electrical energy is conserved.

SLIP RINGS AND BRUSHES

A slip ring and brush assembly is utilized to provide electrical energy to the heating elements of the rotating propeller. Electricity is transferred by a set of brushes which make contact with the slip ring as the propeller rotates.

AMMETER

The ammeter in this system provides a means of checking heater operation. In a three-bladed propeller system, the ammeter should indicate approximately 14 to 18 amperes when the system is in use. In addition, the timer cycles every 30 seconds, causing a current fluctuation which is reflected by the ammeter. This fluctuation indicates correct operation.

FLUID PROPELLER ANTI-ICING

The propellers on some aircraft utilize a fluid (usually isopropyl alcohol) to keep the propellers free of ice. This system is based on prevention, rather than removal of propeller icing.

As shown in figure 7-12 alcohol is piped to the propeller slinger ring assembly which, in turn, directs the fluid to the leading edge of the propeller. As the alcohol flows over the propeller's leading edge, ice formation is prevented. Although this system was at one time popular, it is giving way to electrically heated propeller systems.

WING DE-ICING AND ANTI-ICING EQUIPMENT

Wing de-icing and anti-icing equipment on modern aircraft falls within two categories — pneumatic boots and "hot wings." Pneumatic boots break ice from the wing by expanding and the hot wing prevents ice formation by channeling hot air through the wing's leading edge. The pneumatic system is found primarily on

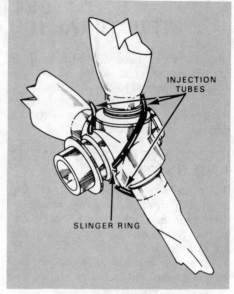

Fig. 7-12. Propeller Alcohol

light and medium weight aircraft, while the hot wing system normally is used on jet aircraft.

PNEUMATIC DE-ICE SYSTEM

A typical pneumatic wing de-ice system is shown in figure 7-13. This system consists of the following components:

1. Inflation boots
2. Timer
3. Pneumatic regulators
4. Engine-driven pressure and vacuum sources

Inflation Boots

The inflation boots are fabric reinforced rubber sheets containing inflation tubes. The inflation boots are cemented to the leading edges of the wings, horizontal stabilizer, and vertical stabilizer. When the de-ice switch is turned on, all of the boots may operate simultaneously or alternately.

During normal operation, the boots are held in the deflated position by slight vacuum pressure. When the system is energized, approximately 18 p.s.i. of positive pressure is applied to the inflation tubes. This pressure inflates the

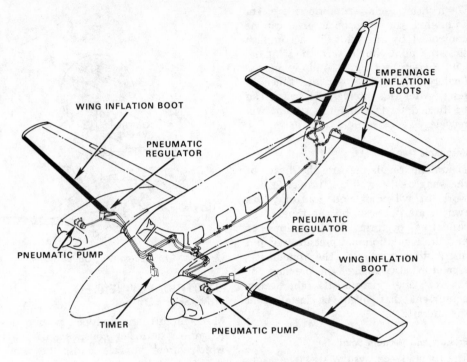

Fig. 7-13. Pneumatic Wing De-Ice System

boots as shown in figure 7-14 separating the ice from the leading edge. The airflow over the airfoil carries the ice away.

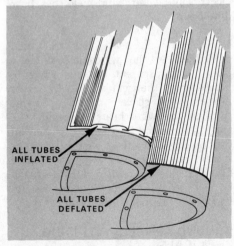

Fig. 7-14. Pneumatic De-Ice Boots

The de-ice boots should not be operated until one-fourth to one-half inch of ice has accumulated on the air-

foil's leading edge. If the boots are operated with less ice accumulation, they will tend to mold the ice to the new shape rather than breaking it from the airfoil's surface. If this occurs, ice will accumulate on the contour formed by the inflated boot and further operation of the de-ice system will have no effect.

Timer

When the de-ice switch is activated, the timer energizes the pneumatic pressure control valves for a few seconds. During this interval, pressure is applied to the inflation tubes, resulting in expansion of the boots. Then, the timer automatically de-energizes the control valves, permitting the pressurized air to be exhausted overboard. The cycle is completed when a vacuum is reapplied to the boots, holding them in the deflated position. If the control switch is left in the ON position in some aircraft, the timer will provide an automatic cycling operation every three minutes.

When heavy icing conditions are encountered, the inflation interval can be controlled by the pilot. To accomplish this, the pilot should turn the wing de-icing switch to OFF and allow approximately 15 seconds for the timer to reset. After this interval, the switch can be turned to ON and the system will recycle.

Pneumatic Regulators

Pneumatic regulators are the heart of the wing de-ice system. Through a network of solenoids and control valves (which are operated by the timer), the regulators perform the functions of pressure regulation and pressure/vacuum distribution control. The pneumatic regulators also control the pressure for the airplane instruments and other equipment that might be installed in the aircraft.

Pressure and Vacuum Source

The wing de-ice system uses the same pressure/vacuum source that powers the gyro instruments. These systems utilize a pneumatic pump located on each engine. In case of a single pump failure, the remaining pump will supply adequate pressure and vacuum to operate the gyro flight instruments and wing de-ice systems.

HEATED WING ANTI-ICE SYSTEM

The heated wing anti-ice system is normally found on turbojet or turboprop aircraft. This is because the jet engine has a ready source of hot air that can be used to heat the wing. In this system, hot air is bled from one of the later stages of the compressor section of the engine and channeled to the aircraft wings.

The leading edge is enclosed and becomes a heated chamber. As the hot air from the engines flows through this chamber, it warms the leading edge to a temperature above freezing, thus preventing ice formation. A typical hot wing is illustrated in figure 7-15.

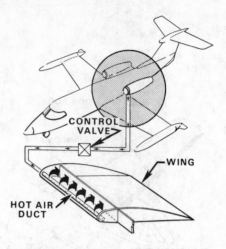

Fig. 7-15. Heated-Wing De-Ice System

ELECTRICALLY-HEATED WINDSHIELD

Most aircraft are equipped with a defogger or defroster consisting of vents which direct hot air across the windshield on the inside of the cabin. Although this system is adequate for some operations, flight in icing conditions may cause ice to adhere to the windshield, severely restricting visibility. It is for this reason that the electrically-heated windshield has been developed.

In this system, heat wires are either embedded in the windshield or in a piece of transparent material which is bonded to the windshield. In either system, electrical current flowing through the wires heats the windshield and prevents ice formation. To prevent overheating of the windshield, the system should be operated only during flight. If the windshield does overheat, it may become "milky" in appearance and greatly reduce visibility.

GROUND APPLIED ANTI-ICING CHEMICALS

Certain anti-icing chemicals are now available for general aviation use. These chemicals provide a very smooth, slick surface to which ice will not adhere readily. They are most effective when used in conjunction with de-icing systems. For example, wing de-ice boots coated with an anti-icing chemical are much more effective than those which are uncoated. On aircraft without de-icing equipment, the anti-icing chemicals are most effective if applied to rubber abrasion boots.

Although these chemicals will not prevent ice formation, they will greatly decrease the tendency of the ice to adhere to the treated surfaces. Ice may form on the leading edge of a wing or propeller that has been treated with chemicals, but since it does not firmly adhere to the surface, it can be more easily removed by centrifugal force and the impact of the airflow.

OPERATION OF ICING EQUIPMENT

Prior to operations in known icing conditions or conditions conducive to structural icing the pilot should make certain preparations. Since each piece of icing equipment falls within one of two categories (prevention or removal) there will be slightly different techniques in usage of the systems. The prevention (anti-ice) equipment should be turned on prior to entering the icing conditions or at the first indication of icing. It is necessary to do this because most anti-icing equipment must "heat up" to normal operating temperatures before it is effective. For example, the electrically heated windshield, heated pitot, and heated fuel vent systems will not operate efficiently until they attain normal operating temperatures.

Equipment should be checked in flight before entering possible icing conditions. This test should be made *in addition to* ground checks performed prior to takeoff. The pilot should cycle the wing de-ice boots and visually check for correct operation. During this time, the electric propeller anti-icer can be turned on and the ammeter observed for proper indications.

chapter 8

OPERATING PROCEDURES AND FLIGHT INFORMATION

INTRODUCTION

The national airspace system has expanded steadily to keep pace with the rapidly developing aviation community. The advanced pilot must become familiar with several areas of knowledge, including collision avoidance, airspace divisions, chart interpretation, navigation aids, communication facilities, radio frequency allocation, radar service, and airport lighting and runway markings. In addition, an understanding of the sources of flight information is necessary to plan and conduct safe flight operations in an environment which is becoming increasingly more complex.

SECTION A—AIRSPACE AND AIRPORTS

COLLISION AVOIDANCE

In today's VFR flight environment, the responsibility for collision avoidance rests entirely with the pilot. Although several systems have been designed as safety aids, nothing can replace pilot vigilance. The pilot should continually practice collision avoidance procedures and strive to develop them into positive habits. The VFR pilot should concentrate his attention *outside* the airplane. Visual scanning involves a systematic sweep of the entire visual field through use of both eye and head movements.

Airport operations require close attention on the part of the pilot to minimize collision potential. The pilot should make a point of checking that both the approach and departure paths are clear prior to takeoff. This procedure should be followed at both controlled and uncontrolled airports, because it is the pilot's responsibility to be aware of all traffic in the area. During climbout, the airplane should be accelerated to the cruise climb speed as soon as a safe altitude is reached. The higher speed will result in a lower pitch attitude and increased forward visibility. Turns of more than 90° should be avoided while in the traffic pattern. If a 360° turn is required for proper spacing, it should be executed as four 90° turns. This procedure allows better observation of other traffic.

The pilot should utilize such aids as airport advisory service and radar traffic information service, when available. Not only does participation aid the pilot in detecting otherwise unobserved traffic, but it also makes his position and intentions known.

Night scanning requires a slightly different technique than that used for daylight operations. As discussed in Chapter 6, a blind spot exists in the area of direct visual concentration at night. As a result, a known object is seen best when the pilot directs his vision slightly to the side of the object. The pilot should use short pauses during night scanning to aid detection of unknown objects.

During all operations, the pilot must maintain an awareness of the blind spots inherent in the design of the airplane. Clearing turns should be employed to expose the airspace which has been hidden by the nose and wings of the airplane. During a climb and prior to flight maneuvers, the pilot should perform two 90° turns. Before beginning a turn, the pilot must pay special attention to clearing the airspace which will become blocked by the wing.

VFR AND IFR CRUISING ALTITUDES/FLIGHT LEVELS

As an additional aid to collision avoidance, cruising altitudes have been established for VFR and IFR traffic. The VFR altitudes apply in both uncontrolled and controlled airspace, while the IFR altitudes apply only in uncontrolled airspace. ATC assigns IFR cruising altitudes for use in controlled airspace.

In the conterminous United States, a VFR pilot flying below 18,000 feet MSL and above 3,000 feet AGL on an easterly magnetic *course* (360° through 179°) should maintain an odd thousand plus 500-foot cruising altitude, such as 3,500 or 5,500 feet MSL. On a westerly magnetic *course* (180° through 359°), he should maintain an even thousand plus 500-foot altitude, such as 4,500 or 6,500.

Pilots of IFR aircraft operating below 18,000 feet MSL in uncontrolled airspace on easterly magnetic *courses* should maintain odd thousand foot MSL altitudes, such as 3,000 or 5,000. If a westerly magnetic *course* is flown, the cruising altitude should be an even thousand foot MSL altitude, such as 4,000 or 6,000. Above 18,000 feet MSL, the altitude is called a flight level (FL) and the altimeter is set to 29.92. From 18,000 feet MSL to FL 290, odd-numbered flight levels, such as 190 or 210, are used on easterly courses and even-numbered flight levels, such as 180 or 200, are used on westerly courses. IFR cruising altitudes/flight levels, clearances for VFR over-the-top, and lowest usable flight levels are covered in detail in Chapter 10.

All pilots operating below 18,000 feet MSL are expected to keep their altimeters adjusted to the current setting, as reported by a station within 100 nautical miles of the aircraft. In areas where stations are more than 100 nautical miles from the aircraft, the altimeter setting of the closest appropriate station may be used. FAR 91.81 should be consulted for additional rules which apply in unusual situations.

Collision avoidance also is one of the primary reasons for the designation of various airspace segments. Therefore, it is important for pilots to understand other operating rules and procedures which apply to flights conducted within each segment of the national airspace system.

UNCONTROLLED AIRSPACE

Uncontrolled airspace is that area which has not been designated as the positive control area, a control area, transition area, the continental control area, control zone, or a terminal control area. The amount of uncontrolled airspace is quickly decreasing because of the expanding need to exercise control over aircraft operating within the airspace of

VFR IN UNCONTROLLED AIRSPACE

ALTITUDE	FLIGHT VISIBILITY	DISTANCE FROM CLOUDS
1,200 feet or less above the surface (regardless of MSL altitude)	1 statute mile	Clear of clouds
More than 1,200 feet above the surface, but less than 10,000 feet MSL	1 statute mile	500 feet below 1,000 feet above 2,000 feet horizontal
More than 1,200 feet above the surface and at or above 10,000 feet MSL	5 statute miles	1,000 feet below 1,000 feet above 1 mile horizontal

the United States. Although ATC does not have the responsibility or authority to exercise control over aircraft in uncontrolled airspace, several regulations apply to flight operations conducted in this important airspace segment.

VFR weather minimums in uncontrolled airspace are shown in the table. Normally, all uncontrolled airspace terminates at the base of the continental control area, which begins at 14,500 feet MSL. An exception to this rule occurs when 14,500 feet MSL is less than 1,500 feet AGL. In this situation, uncontrolled airspace continues up to 1,500 feet above the surface, as shown in figure 8-1.

CONTROLLED AIRSPACE

Controlled airspace consists of those areas designated as the positive control area, control areas, transition areas, the continental control area, control zones, and terminal control areas within which some or all aircraft may be subject to air traffic control. These areas are depicted in figure 8-1, and VFR flight is permitted in all of the control areas except positive control where each aircraft must be on an IFR flight plan with an ATC clearance. Basic VFR flight visibilities and cloud clearance minimums are increased in controlled airspace, as shown in the table.

After July 1, 1975, all airplanes conducting flights in controlled airspace within the contiguous United States must meet special equipment requirements. At altitudes above 12,500 feet MSL (excluding 2,500 feet AGL and below), the aircraft must be equipped with a 4096-code transponder and automatic pressure altitude reporting equipment. Exceptions to this rule are described in FAR 91.24.

VFR IN CONTROLLED AIRSPACE

ALTITUDE	FLIGHT VISIBILITY	DISTANCE FROM CLOUDS
1,200 feet or less above the surface (regardless of MSL altitude)	3 statute miles	500 feet below 1,000 feet above 2,000 feet horizontal
More than 1,200 feet above the surface, but less than 10,000 feet MSL	3 statute miles	500 feet below 1,000 feet above 2,000 feet horizontal
More than 1,200 feet above the surface and at or above 10,000 feet MSL	5 statute miles	1,000 feet below 1,000 feet above 1 mile horizontal

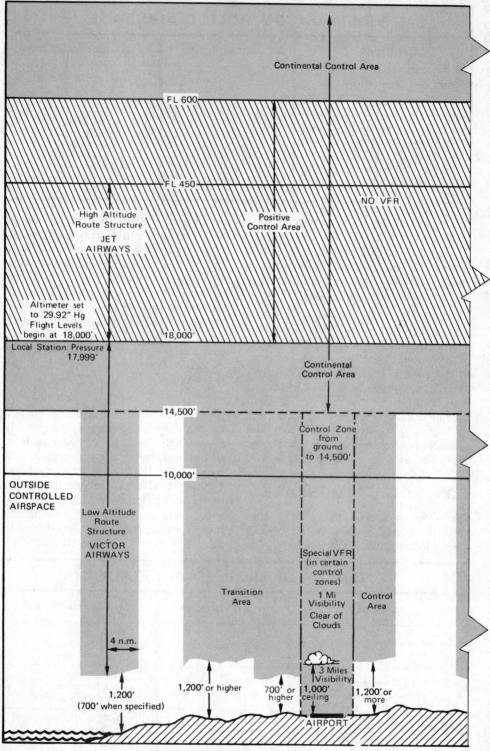

Fig. 8-1. Airspace Utilization Plan

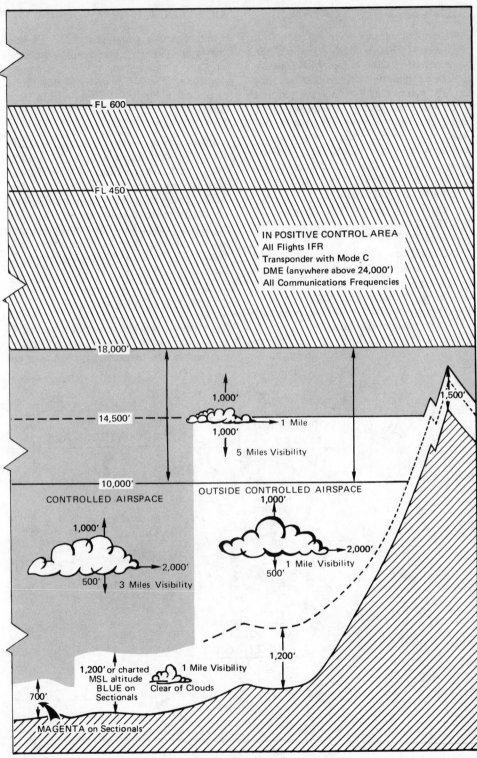

FL 600

FL 450

IN POSITIVE CONTROL AREA
All Flights IFR
Transponder with Mode C
DME (anywhere above 24,000')
All Communications Frequencies

18,000'

1,000'

14,500' — — — — 1 Mile

1,000'

5 Miles Visibility

1,500'

10,000'

CONTROLLED AIRSPACE

OUTSIDE CONTROLLED AIRSPACE

1,000'

1,000'

2,000'

1 Mile Visibility

500'   3 Miles Visibility

2,000'

500'

1,200'

1,200' or charted   1 Mile Visibility
MSL altitude
BLUE on   Clear of Clouds
Sectionals

700'

MAGENTA on Sectionals

Fig. 8-1. (Cont.)

POSITIVE CONTROL AREA

The positive control area extends from 18,000 feet MSL to flight level (FL) 600 (approximately 60,000 feet MSL), within the conterminous United States, and aircraft within this airspace are required to be operated under instrument flight rules. Positive control airspace is not shown on sectional charts; however, it is depicted on instrument high altitude enroute charts. For operations within positive control areas, aircraft must meet the following specifications.

1. Operated under IFR at specified flight levels assigned by air traffic control

2. Equipped with instruments and equipment required for IFR operations and flown by a pilot rated for instrument flight

3. Equipped with an altitude reporting radar beacon transponder

4. Radio equipped to provide direct pilot-to-controller communications

CONTROL AREAS

Control areas consist of VOR Federal airways (Victor airways), additional control areas, and control area extensions. The VFR weather minimums depicted in figure 8-1 apply within these areas.

Control areas normally begin at 1,200 feet AGL and continue up to 14,500 feet MSL, with the exception of VOR Federal airways which terminate at 18,000 feet MSL. These areas are shown on sectional charts by blue-tinted boundary lines, as depicted in figure 8-2. If the control area begins at an altitude other than 1,200 feet AGL, its base is given as an MSL altitude.

TRANSITION AREAS

Transition areas are designated to enable IFR flights to remain in controlled airspace while transitioning between en-

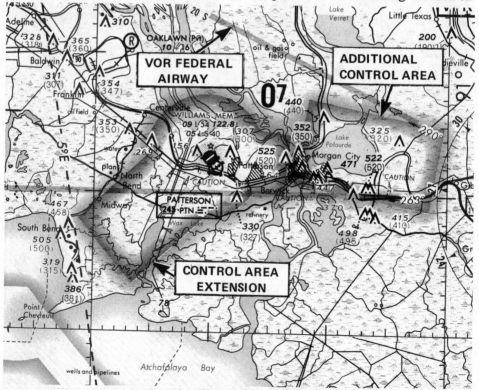

Fig. 8-2. Control Areas and Sectional Charts

route and terminal areas. The base of this airspace is at 700 feet AGL when it is used in conjunction with an airport and 1,200 feet when used in conjunction with an airway. All transition areas terminate at the base of the overlying airspace. VFR flight visibility and cloud clearance minimums are the same as those for controlled airspace below 10,000 feet MSL. On sectional charts, transition areas are shown in magenta. The outer limits of the area are indicated by the darker, more definite edge, as shown in figure 8-3.

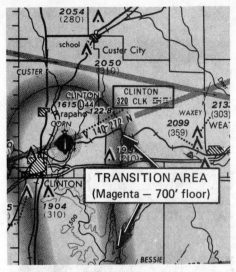

Fig. 8-3. Transition Area

CONTINENTAL CONTROL AREA

The continental control area consists of the airspace over the 48 states, District of Columbia, and that area of Alaska east of 160° west longitude. This airspace begins at 14,500 feet MSL, but does not include the airspace below 1,500 feet AGL or restricted and prohibited areas. The VFR weather minimums for controlled airspace above 10,000 feet MSL apply within the continental control area. Because this area includes most of the United States, it is not shown on navigation charts.

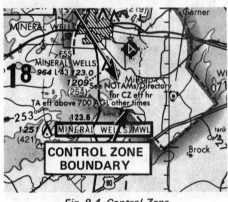

Fig. 8-4. Control Zone

CONTROL ZONES

Controlled airspace which extends upward from the surface and terminates at the base of the continental control area is called a *control zone*. Control zones that do not underlie the continental control area have no upper limit. A control zone may include one or more airports and is normally a circular area with a radius of five statute miles and any extensions necessary to include instrument departure and arrival paths.

Control zones are designated on sectional charts by broken blue lines. If a control zone is effective only during certain hours of the day, this fact also is noted on the chart, as shown in figure 8-4. Pilots often erroneously assume that a control zone exists only where there is a control tower; however, this is not the

case. Many control zones are designated at airports without control towers.

Unless the visibility is at least three miles and the ceiling is at least 1,000 feet, VFR operations (traffic pattern entry, takeoffs, landings) are *not* permitted within a control zone *without* a special VFR clearance from ATC. With this special clearance, daytime VFR operations are permitted within a control zone if the visibility is at least one mile and the aircraft can remain clear of clouds. Special VFR is not permitted between sunset and sunrise unless the pilot is instrument rated and the aircraft is instrument equipped.

Some major terminals have such high traffic density that special VFR clearances are incompatible with maximum safety and separation of special VFR aircraft from IFR operations. Therefore, there are a number of terminals where special VFR clearances are not issued. The control zones for these airports are outlined with a series of the letter "T," as shown in figure 8-5.

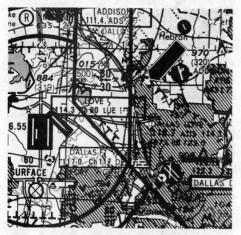

Fig. 8-5. Control Zone without Special VFR

AIRPORT TRAFFIC AREAS

An *airport traffic area* is defined as the airspace within five statute miles of an airport center at which a control tower is in operation. This airspace extends from the ground up to, but not including, 3,000 feet above the ground. The boundaries are not depicted on aeronautical charts; however, the existence of an airport traffic area is indicated by the letters "CT" (control tower) and the control tower frequency listed in the airport data, as shown in figure 8-6.

The FARs state that a pilot operating to, from, or on an airport serviced by a control tower must establish and maintain radio communications with the tower while in the airport traffic area. In addition, operation, other than for takeoffs and landings, in an airport traffic area also requires ATC authorization.

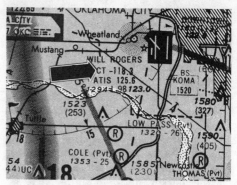

Fig. 8-6. Indicator of an Airport Traffic Area

AIRPORT ADVISORY AREAS

The area within five statute miles of an airport where a control tower is *not* operating, but where a flight service station is located, is called an *airport advisory area*. As illustrated in figure 8-7, an airport advisory area is indicated on sectional charts by the letters "FSS" above the other airport data. At such locations, flight service stations provide advisory service to arriving and departing aircraft. Recommended traffic advisory practices are outlined in the *Airman's Information Manual*.

TERMINAL CONTROL AREAS

Terminal control areas have been established to separate all arriving and departing traffic, both VFR and IFR, at large airports. A TCA may be designated as Group I, Group II, or Group III. Each terminal control area is designed to facilitate traffic separation at a particular terminal and, therefore, is different from other terminal control areas. Within the expanding controlled airspace of the

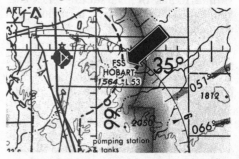

Fig. 8-7. Indicator of Airport Advisory Area

terminal control area, all aircraft are subject to operating rules and pilot and equipment requirements, as specified by FAR 91.24 and 91.90.

Pilot participation is mandatory and an ATC clearance must be received before entering a Group I TCA. To take off or land at the primary airport in a Group I TCA, the pilot also must possess at least a private pilot certificate. The airplane must be equipped with a VOR or TACAN receiver, two-way radio, a transponder with 4096-code capability, and automatic pressure altitude reporting equipment.

Within Group II TCAs, there are no minimum pilot certification requirements. The aircraft must be equipped as in a Group I TCA except that automatic pressure altitude reporting equipment is not required. In addition, a transponder is not required for those IFR flights operating to or from an airport outside of but in close proximity to the TCA when

the commonly used approach, departure, or transition procedures require flight within the TCA. Also, no person may operate an aircraft within a Group II terminal control area unless he has received an appropriate authorization from ATC prior to operation of that aircraft in that area. Finally, two-way radio communications must be maintained with ATC.

The requirements for the Group III TCA are the least restrictive of the three groups. There are no minimum pilot certification requirements. A transponder is not required if the pilot is capable of maintaining two-way communications with ATC while in the TCA boundaries and provides altitude, position, and proposed route of flight information to ATC prior to entering the TCA.

Each terminal control area includes at least one primary airport. These control areas are depicted on sectional charts by a dark blue border. (See Fig. 8-8.)

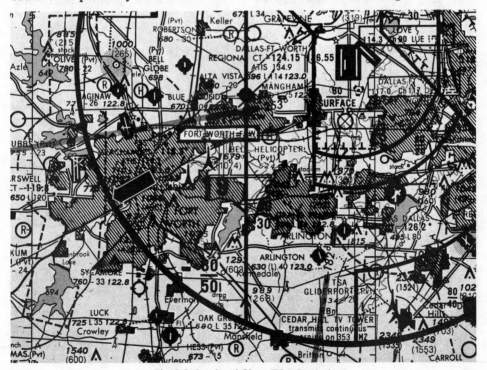

Fig. 8-8. Sectional Chart TCA Depiction

A plan view of the Los Angeles Terminal Control Area is shown in figure 8-9. The controlled airspace is divided into ceilings and floors. For instance, the ceiling for the entire terminal control area is 7,000 feet and the lowest floor is at the surface. A pilot wishing to operate through this area without meeting the necessary pilot and equipment requirements, could do so only if he flew above 7,000 feet or through the VFR corridor. VFR terminal area charts should be used for navigation through TCAs.

DEPARTURE AND ARRIVAL

The VFR pilot departing an airport within a TCA is normally instructed to advise the ground control or clearance delivery service of his intended route of flight and altitude. Pilots of aircraft arriving at airports located within a TCA should contact approach control on the appropriate frequency prior to entry and state their position in relationship to geographic or navaid fixes shown on the appropriate chart.

SPECIAL USE AIRSPACE

Occasionally, operations conducted within the airspace or on the surface are such that they can be hazardous to other aircraft operations. These areas are shown on sectional charts according to the following types.

1. Prohibited area
2. Restricted area
3. Warning area
4. Alert area
5. Military operations area (MOA)

Except for an MOA, the number of a special use airspace area is preceded by a letter designating its type. For example, "P" indicates prohibited; "R,"

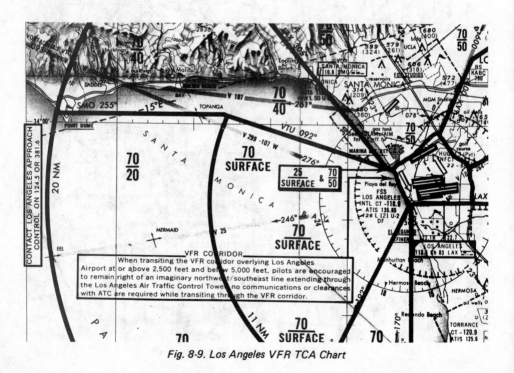

Fig. 8-9. Los Angeles VFR TCA Chart

PROHIBITED, RESTRICTED, WARNING, AND ALERT AREAS
ON DALLAS-FT WORTH SECTIONAL CHART

NO.	NAME	ALTITUDE	TIME	APPROPRIATE AUTHORITY
R-5601A	Fort Sill, Okla.	To 23,000	Continuous	C. G. Fort Sill, Okla.
R-5601B	Fort Sill, Okla.	To 23,000	Continuous	† FAA, Fort Worth ARTC Center or area FSS, C. G. Fort Sill, Oklahoma
A-631	Fort Wolters, Texas	To 3000	0700-0100	C. O. U. S. Army Primary Helicopter School/Center, Fort Wolters, Texas

P - Prohibited   R - Restricted   W - Warning   A - Alert   † - Controlling Agency

Unless otherwise noted: Altitudes are MSL and in feet; time is local.

No person shall operate an aircraft within a Prohibited Area, or within a Restricted Area between the designated altitudes during the time of designation unless prior permission has been issued by the appropriate authority as listed above. The appropriate authority is defined as either the controlling agency (†) or the using agency.

Flight within Alert Areas is not restricted, but pilots are advised to exercise extreme caution.

Fig. 8-10. Sectional Chart Listing

restricted; "W," warning; and "A," alert.

A list of prohibited, restricted, warning, and alert areas appearing on each sectional chart is found on the back of the chart panel, as shown in figure 8-10. The last entry at the right indicates the appropriate authority to contact if transition through a restricted or warning area is desired.

PROHIBITED AREAS

Prohibited areas are portions of the airspace within which the flight of aircraft is not permitted. Such areas are generally established for reasons of national security or national welfare. An example of a prohibited area is the area surrounding the Rocky Mountain Arsenal near Stapleton International Airport, Denver, Colorado. (See Fig. 8-11.)

RESTRICTED AREAS

Restricted areas include the airspace within which the flight of aircraft, while not wholly prohibited, is subject to certain limitations. These areas denote the existence of unusual, often invisible, hazards to aircraft, such as artillery firing, aerial gunnery, or the flight of guided missiles. Penetration of restricted areas without authorization from the controlling agency may be extremely hazardous. An example of a restricted

Fig. 8-11. Prohibited Area

area as it appears on a sectional chart is shown in figure 8-12.

WARNING AREAS

A *warning area* is that airspace which may contain hazards to nonparticipating aircraft in international airspace; therefore, warning areas are established beyond the three-mile limit. Although the activities conducted within warning areas may be as hazardous as those in restricted areas, warning areas cannot be legally designated as restricted because they are over international waters.

Fig. 8-12. Restricted Area

ALERT AREAS

Alert areas contain airspace which is depicted on sectional charts to inform transient or cross-country pilots of areas that may contain a high volume of pilot training or an unusual type of aerial activity. The example shown in figure 8-13 shows an alert area where a high volume of helicopter and airplane pilot training activity is occurring. Flight within alert areas is not restricted, but pilots are urged to exercise extreme caution. Pilots of aircraft participating in the alert area, as well as pilots transiting the area, are fully responsible for collision avoidance.

MILITARY OPERATIONS AREAS

Military operations areas, or MOAs, consist of airspace of defined vertical and lateral limits established to separate certain military training activities from IFR traffic. Nonparticipating IFR traffic may be cleared through an active MOA, if ATC can provide separation. Otherwise, ATC will reroute or restrict nonparticipating IFR traffic.

Pilots operating under VFR should exercise extra caution within an active MOA. Information regarding MOA activity is available from any FSS within 200 nautical miles of the area. Established MOAs are depicted on sectional, VFR terminal, and low altitude enroute charts. Depictions identify the MOA and provide a brief summary of boundaries and operational hours, as shown in figure 8-14.

MILITARY TRAINING ROUTES

Normally, military training routes (MTRs) are established below 10,000 feet MSL for operations at speeds in excess of 250 knots. However, route segments may exist at higher altitudes for route continuity, particularly in mountainous areas. MTRs involve both IFR and VFR operations. The IFR routes (IRs) may be conducted in IFR or VFR conditions, while VFR routes (VRs) are conducted under VFR conditions only. Those with segments above 1,500 feet AGL are shown on low altitude enroute charts. MTR information is available from FSSs within 200 miles.

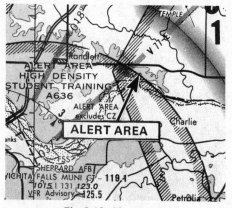

Fig. 8-13. Alert Area

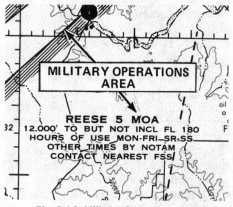

Fig. 8-14. Military Operations Area

Detailed information on MTRs is also available to the general public in Department of Defense Flight Information Publications (FLIP). The AP/1B Chart is a FLIP containing both charted and narrative descriptions of all MTRs. This chart is used by flight service stations and at many airports for pilot briefings. It can be obtained from any Government Printing Office.

NAVIGATIONAL AIDS AND FREQUENCIES

Various types of navigational aids are in use today. Each system has been designed to provide a high degree of accuracy and dependability, and each greatly simplifies cross-country navigation. This section provides information on the identification of the navigational facilities and frequencies on sectional charts. The use of each system is explained in Chapter 4.

VOR/VORTAC

The VOR and VORTAC are the most widely used navigational systems. These facilities provide azimuth information on the VHF radio band and, therefore, are virtually free of interference. The facilities operate within the 108.00 MHz to 117.95 MHz frequency band. This frequency range provides 200 navigation channels when 50 kHz spacing is utilized.

The VOR station provides only course guidance information. The VORTAC combines the VOR course information with the military TACAN distance information, thus providing the pilot with DME data. Figure 8-15 shows the sectional chart depiction of a VOR station and figure 8-16 shows the VORTAC symbol. In addition to the difference between the actual station symbols, the frequency box for the VORTAC contains the TACAN UHF channel. All VOR and VORTAC information and symbols are depicted in

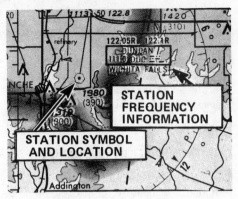

Fig. 8-15. VOR Depiction on Sectional Charts

blue. A few VOR/DME facilities also are utilized, and they provide course guidance and distance information similar to a VORTAC. However, these facilities do not provide the TACAN azimuth information necessary for military utilization.

NONDIRECTIONAL BEACONS

Nondirectional beacons are also a valuable navigational aid, which serve mainly as a backup system during VFR operations. The NDB transmits within the low frequency range from 200 kHz to 415 kHz. The facility is depicted on a sectional chart as a magenta-colored circle comprised of dots, as shown in figure 8-17.

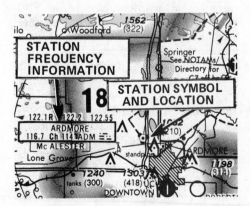

Fig. 8-16. VORTAC Depiction on Sectional Charts

Commercial broadcast stations which are reliable for VFR navigation also are shown on the sectional charts. Figure 8-18 shows the chart depiction, including the station call sign. If the station operates other than 24 hours a day, the general time of operation is indicated.

AIRPORTS

COMMUNICATION FACILITIES

There are many communication facilities provided for use by pilots. Some are primarily for VFR use, while others are for IFR use. Regardless of a facility's primary function, service normally is available to any pilot on request. To efficiently operate in the national airspace system, the pilot must be familiar with each of these facilities and the services provided.

FLIGHT SERVICE STATIONS

Flight service stations provide the largest variety of services in the airspace system. These services are important to both the VFR and IFR pilot. The following discussion provides a review of each of the FSS's services.

WEATHER BRIEFING

Flight service stations generally are the most widely used weather briefing facilities. The National Weather Service (NWS) collects, analyzes, and distributes current weather information to the FSS system for use in preflight weather briefings. The pilot can obtain this information through a personal visit to the FSS, by telephone, or via the aircraft radio.

In addition to ground briefings, FSSs provide in-flight information service on selected VOR and NDB frequencies. *Unscheduled* broadcasts are made when significant weather conditions or other critical aeronautical data warrant wide dissemination. These broadcasts report data within 150 miles of the station.

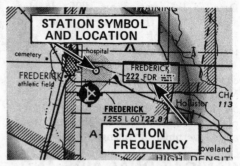

Fig. 8-17. NDB Depiction on Sectional Charts

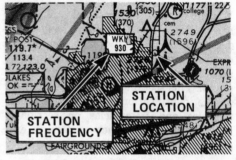

Fig. 8-18. Commercial Broadcast Station

Transcribed weather broadcasts, or TWEBs, are transmitted continuously and normally cover stations within 400 miles of the broadcast station. Flight service stations also broadcast special reports at unscheduled times to distribute notices to airmen, pilot reports, and significant weather changes.

An additional weather reporting service is available from selected flight service stations. This service is called *enroute flight advisory service* and is designed to provide current weather information for the enroute pilot. The service is *not* intended to be used for preflight weather briefings or for filing and closing flight plans.

The service is obtained by calling the controlling FSS on the standard enroute flight advisory service frequency of 122.00 MHz. On the initial callup, the pilot should use the words *"Flight Watch"*; for example, *"Oakland Flight Watch, Beech Sierra 2536W."* The tri-

Fig. 8-19. Chart Symbol for Enroute Flight Advisory Service

angular corners of the VORTAC facility box, shown in figure 8-19, item 1, indicate the availability of this service and a remote communications facility for enroute flight advisory service is depicted by item 2.

FLIGHT PLAN PROCESSING

Flight plan processing is another service provided by the FSS. Once the pilot has received a preflight weather briefing, either a VFR or IFR flight plan can be filed with the flight service station. In the case of a VFR flight plan, it is processed entirely by the FSS. IFR flight plans are transmitted from the FSS to the nearest air route traffic control center for processing. Whenever possible, flight plan filing should be done in person or by telephone to relieve radio congestion.

FSS will also monitor the progress of VFR flights. This is done by enroute position reports to the nearest FSS. This procedure is highly recommended because it aids in search and rescue efforts in the event of a lost aircraft.

SEARCH AND RESCUE

Flight service stations are responsible for initiating search and rescue anytime a pilot has not reported or closed his VFR flight plan within 30 minutes of the estimated time of arrival indicated in the flight plan. This time limit is reduced to 15 minutes for jet aircraft.

Lost or disoriented pilots also can receive aid by contacting the FSS. Select

stations can provide VHF/UHF direction finding assistance. If the contacted FSS cannot provide this service, it will relay the necessary information to another facility, which can provide the needed assistance.

AIRPORT ADVISORY SERVICE

Flight service stations provide airport advisory information at airports without control towers or when the tower is not operating. The advisory provides information about the wind speed and direction, favored runway, altimeter setting, and known traffic. This is only an advisory service, and air traffic control is not exercised.

The following table lists the frequency that should be used to contact an operating FSS for airport advisories or to broadcast the pilot's intentions if the FSS is not operating.

AIRPORT FACILITY	FREQUENCY
Full-time FSS when tower is closed	Local tower frequency
Part-time FSS when closed (no tower)	123.60 MHz
Full-time or part-time FSS when operating (no tower)	123.60 MHz

ARTCC COMMUNICATIONS RELAY

Flight service stations also relay communications between air route traffic control centers and aircraft, when difficulties with direct communication are experienced between the pilot and the ARTCC facility. The FSS also will relay IFR clearances to pilots operating from uncontrolled airports.

RADIO FREQUENCIES AND CHART SYMBOLS

Several VHF frequencies have been allocated to the flight service station system. Each station does not have all frequencies, but the pilot can determine which frequencies are available by the sectional chart facility box used to identify the appropriate station.

Figure 8-20 shows the various chart symbols used to identify flight service stations. An information box with a heavy-lined border (items 1 and 2) indicates a flight service station. The standard simplex frequency of 122.20 MHz and the emergency frequency of 121.50 MHz are available at all stations and, therefore, are not shown above the box. If any other frequencies are available, they are listed above the information box. If a "T" appears after a frequency, it indicates the FSS can only transmit on that frequency. An "R" indicates the FSS can only receive on that frequency.

If the flight service station does not require the use of a nearby navaid for communications, only the name of the FSS is shown in the heavy-lined box (item 1). If the FSS uses a nearby navaid, it is depicted differently (item 2). In this example, Abilene FSS could be contacted by transmitting on 122.10 MHz and receiving on 113.70 MHz (VORTAC frequency), or by using either 122.60 MHz or 123.60 MHz, which are both simplex frequencies. The darkened square on this box and the Paris VOR indicates TWEB facilities.

An information box with a thin-lined border and a bracket under the box (item 3) indicates a navigation facility which has remote communications capability and is linked to the controlling area FSS. In this example, the Dallas FSS is contacted by transmitting on 122.10 MHz and receiving on 113.60 MHz (Paris VOR). Communications through a remote facility depend on altitude and terrain in relation to that facility and not in relation to the controlling FSS.

A navigation aid which *does not* have FSS communications capability is shown by a thin-lined box. Only the navigation frequency and TACAN channel of the navaid are shown within the box (item 4).

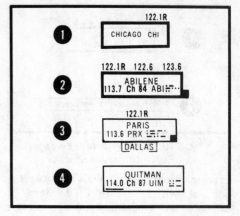

Fig. 8-20. FSS Frequency Boxes

Since FSS communications frequencies are not available, they do not appear above the box and the bracket for a controlling area FSS does not appear below the box. A line beneath a frequency means that voice communications are not available on that frequency.

UNICOM

Many airports which do not have tower or flight service station facilities are assigned a simplex VHF frequency, which can be used for air/ground communications. This frequency can be used by a pilot to obtain an airport advisory of wind direction and velocity, favored runway, and known traffic. Additionally, requests for transportation, aircraft service, and relay of personal messages can be transmitted on this frequency.

When an airport has an FSS or tower, a different UNICOM frequency is assigned. All of the previously mentioned services, except airport advisories, are provided on this frequency.

UNICOM frequencies are shown on sectional charts following the length of the runway in the airport data notation. Availability of this service, along with the frequency, is listed in the *Airport/ Facility Directory* under the airport communications data.

The Federal Communication Commission (FCC) has designated certain frequencies for UNICOM aeronautical advisory stations. These include:

Frequency Use

122.700	Uncontrolled fields
122.725	Private airports (not open to public)
122.750	Private airports (not open to public) and air-to-air communications
122.800	Uncontrolled airports
122.950	Airports with a control tower
122.975	High altitude
123.000	Uncontrolled airports
123.050	Heliports
123.075	Heliports

GROUND CONTROL

The frequency most commonly used for ground control is 121.90 MHz, with 121.70, 121.80, and 121.60 MHz used where there is a possibility of interference from another ground control station nearby. Knowing that specific frequencies are assigned for controlling the movements of aircraft on the ground, the pilot must determine which frequency is used at any particular airport. These frequencies can be found in the *Airport/Facility Directory*.

Ground control communications can be very useful in providing the pilot with valuable information at any airport with these capabilities. The following are examples of ground control services.

1. Precise taxi instructions to the runway of intended takeoff
2. Information concerning any hazards which might exist between the pilot and the point on the airport to which he intends to proceed
3. After landing at an unfamiliar airport, directions and information about tiedown, ramp service, or maintenance
4. The ATC clearance prior to an IFR departure, unless a separate *clearance delivery* frequency is available.

CLEARANCE DELIVERY

In order to relieve congestion on the ground control frequencies at large airports, a discrete clearance delivery frequency is provided. Some clearance delivery facilities allow a pilot to receive an IFR clearance 10 minutes prior to taxi. Additionally, this service, if available, is used by the VFR pilot to receive an ATC clearance when departing a TCA and to receive a departure control frequency and transponder code when departing an airport within a terminal radar service area.

CONTROL TOWER

Towers are responsible for the control of all airborne traffic which is landing, taking off, and operating within their airport traffic area. After takeoff, the pilot is required to remain in communication with the tower until at least five miles away or 3,000 feet above the field elevation. If leaving the pattern in any way other than along the standard route, the pilot should obtain permission from the tower before beginning the first turn after takeoff. When arriving at a controlled airport, it is necessary to contact the tower when at least five miles out.

Tower frequencies can be found on the sectional chart in the airport data notation next to the airport, as shown in figure 8-21. They also can be found in the control tower frequency listing on the back of the chart panel and in the *Airport/Facility Directory*.

APPROACH AND DEPARTURE CONTROL

Air traffic control for arrivals and departures is exercised by approach and departure control. Since these facilities coordinate closely with the control tower and the air route traffic control center (ARTCC) in handling air traffic, they act as go-betweens for the pilot when he transitions from the terminal to enroute operations, or vice versa.

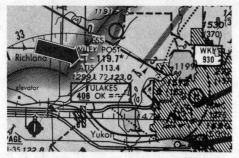

Fig. 8-21. Control Tower Frequency

Approach and departure control have the primary responsibility of sequencing and separating IFR aircraft. In addition, separation is provided between IFR traffic and known VFR traffic.

The individual frequencies utilized for approach and departure control are between 118.00 MHz and 135.95 MHz. The frequencies are found in the *Airport/ Facility Directory* and on the various IFR charts. The availability of radar service can be determined from the same sources.

Radar service is also provided to VFR aircraft and is designated Stage I, II, or III service. Stage I service provides traffic information and limited radar vectoring if the controller's workload permits.

Stage II service is provided to adjust the flow of VFR and IFR traffic. If the controller's workload permits, radar traffic advisory and sequencing are provided. When Stage II service is provided, pilots of VFR aircraft should contact approach control when approximately 25 miles from the airport. Approach control then provides standard separation between IFR aircraft, but separation is not provided between VFR, or VFR and IFR aircraft. The terminal locations offering Stage II services and the appropriate frequencies are listed in the *Airport/Facility Directory*.

Stage III service is available at certain terminal locations. This service provides standard traffic separation between both VFR and IFR traffic operating in the terminal radar service area (TRSA).

Additionally, radar vectoring and sequencing are provided for operations to and from the primary airport.

This service, like Stage I and II service, is not mandatory, but pilot participation is urged. These radar services *do not* relieve the pilot of the responsibility to see and avoid other traffic when operating in VFR weather conditions.

The AIM provides a description of TRSA operational procedures for both pilots and air traffic controllers. In addition, the Graphic Notices and Supplemental Data publication contains charts of each terminal radar service area in the United States.

The terminal radar service area should not be confused with terminal control areas (TCAs), which are located at *very large* airports with high density traffic. In TCAs, participation is mandatory, and all aircraft are subject to definite operating rules and specific pilot certification and aircraft equipment are required. In addition, an ATC clearance normally must be received by all pilots before flight operations are conducted within the TCA. Specific rules are listed in FAR 91.24 and 91.90.

ATIS

Automatic terminal information service (ATIS) is provided at busy terminal airports. The information transmitted by this service is broadcast continuously and includes such information as runways and instrument approaches in use, tower frequencies, and surface winds. These broadcasts are updated whenever conditions change, and each new broadcast is labeled with a phonetic letter, such as alpha or bravo. On initial callup to the tower, approach control, or ground control, the pilot should indicate which ATIS information he has received by repeating the phonetic designation. ATIS may be assigned a certain VHF tower frequency or broadcast over the voice feature of a navaid near the airport. The correct frequencies may be found on the sectional chart, IFR enroute chart, IFR approach chart, or in the *Airport/ Facility Directory*. Figure 8-22 shows the entry for Stapleton International Airport in Denver, Colorado.

The Denver ATIS information is presented on two separate frequencies. Arrival information is provided on 125.60 MHz and departure information is given on 124.45 MHz. Because of radio equipment limitations, some aircraft may not be able to receive the information presented on a given ATIS frequency. In this case, the pilot should inform the controller that he has *not* received the ATIS information.

The following is a sample broadcast of an ATIS recording for arriving aircraft.

"Stapleton Airport, arrival information Charlie, the 1500 Greenwich weather, 800 scattered, ceiling measured 4,000 overcast, visibility 20, wind 180 at four, temperature 38, altimeter 30.32, ILS approach runway 26L in use, landing runway 26L and 26R, frequency 118.3, departure runway 26R and 26L, frequency 119.5. Notice to airmen, runway 35 closed until 1600 Zulu. Airman advisory, fog bank east of the airport, visibility three miles. Stapleton VFR arrivals contact approach control, north 120.5 south 127.05. All others transiting the TCA use 119.3 for TCA clearance. VFR departures, contact clearance delivery, 127.6. Inform controller on initial contact that you have received information Charlie."

As indicated in the last sentence of the recording, the pilot should notify the controller on his initial contact that he has received the ATIS information. As

an example, *"Denver Approach, Cessna 6721X, 20 miles north squawking 1200, landing Stapleton, information Charlie."* This initial contact should be as brief as possible; any additional information required will be requested by the radar controller. When weather conditions are below a 5,000-foot ceiling or the visibility is less than five miles, the time of the observation will be included at the beginning of the ATIS broadcast.

AIR ROUTE TRAFFIC CONTROL CENTERS

ARTCCs are the central authority for issuing IFR clearances. There are more than 20 centers established in the United States, with associated radar and communication facilities. Each of these centers is further divided into sectors to provide adequate communication and radar surveillance for enroute IFR aircraft.

The IFR flight plan filed by the pilot is processed by the ARTCC in which the flight originates. Due to the time involved in checking the route of flight for other air traffic, weather hazards, and issuing the appropriate clearance, the pilot should file his flight plan at least 30 minutes before the intended departure time.

ARTCCs also provide services to VFR pilots. If the controller's workload permits, he will provide traffic advisories and, in some cases, course guidance (radar vectoring) if the pilot so requests. Because of ARTCC's extensive radar coverage, the facility can be of great assistance to lost and disoriented pilots. A pilot should never hesitate to request assistance.

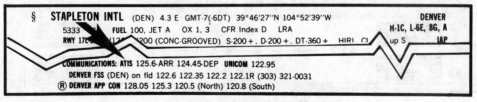

Fig. 8-22. ATIS Frequencies

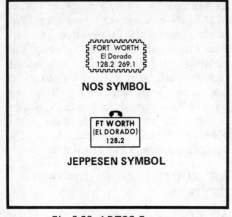

Fig. 8-23. ARTCC Frequency Identification

Center frequencies are found on both Jeppesen and NOS enroute charts, as shown in figure 8-23. Jeppesen charts show center frequencies in boxes along specific IFR routes. NOS charts follow the same format. The frequencies for these centers range from 118.00 through 135.95 MHz.

AIRPORT MARKINGS

Airport markings vary from airport to airport. These markings are determined by the type of runway, its direction, and the types of operations that are permitted.

BASIC RUNWAY

The basic runway, is used for operations under visual flight rules. Its markings include the runway number and centerline. Runways are numbered to the nearest $10°$ in relation to magnetic north, with the last digit omitted. For example, a runway with a magnetic heading of $084°$ is marked with the numeral 8. The opposite end of the runway is marked with the reciprocal of that heading (26 in this case). Three parallel runways are designated by the same number with the addition of an "L," "C," and "R" to indicate the left, center, and right runways, respectively, as shown in figure 8-24. The centerline marking consists of a white, dashed line.

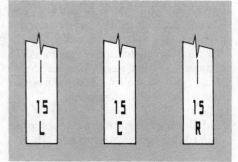

Fig. 8-24. Parallel Basic Runways

NONPRECISION INSTRUMENT RUNWAY

A nonprecision instrument runway incorporates basic runway markings and threshold markings, as shown in figure 8-25. A nonvisual, nonprecision navigation aid (VOR, NDB) serves this type of runway.

PRECISION INSTRUMENT RUNWAY

Precision instrument runways are served by nonvisual precision approach aids, such as the instrument landing system (ILS) or precision approach radar (PAR). Both provide glide slope information. In addition to the nonprecision instrument runway markings, precision runways incorporate touchdown zone markings, fixed distance markings, and side stripes, as shown in figure 8-26.

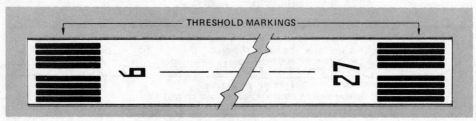

Fig. 8-25. Nonprecision Instrument Runway

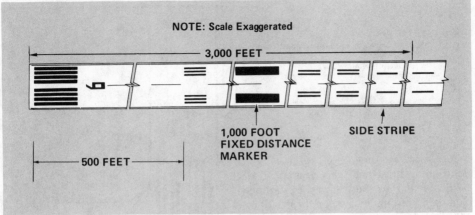

NOTE: Scale Exaggerated

3,000 FEET

1,000 FOOT FIXED DISTANCE MARKER

SIDE STRIPE

500 FEET

Fig. 8-26. Precision Instrument Runway

Special Purpose Areas

Closed or overrun/stopway areas are designated as special purpose areas. These terms refer to any surface or area which appears usable, but which, due to the nature of its structure, is unusable. Several special purpose areas are shown in figure 8-27. The stopway is an area which may be used to decelerate an aircraft in case of an aborted takeoff. This area will support the aircraft, but, due to its structural nature, it is not designed for continuous operational use.

In addition to normal runway markings, short takeoff and landing (STOL) runways have the letters "STOL" painted on the approach end of the runway and a touchdown aim point designated, as shown in figure 8-28. These runways, as the name implies, are to be used for aircraft designed for short takeoffs and landings.

Taxiway centerlines are marked with a continuous yellow line. Taxiway edges are marked with two continuous lines six

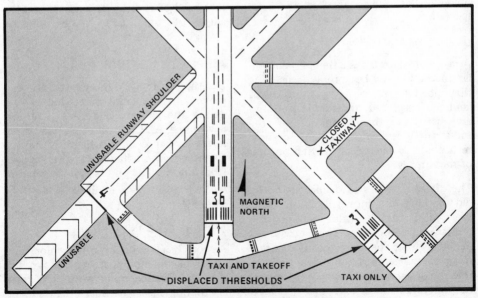

UNUSABLE RUNWAY SHOULDER

UNUSABLE

CLOSED X-TAXIWAY

MAGNETIC NORTH

36

31

TAXI AND TAKEOFF

DISPLACED THRESHOLDS

TAXI ONLY

Fig. 8-27. Special Airport Markings

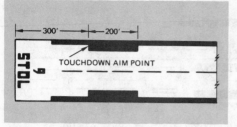

Fig. 8-28. STOL Runways

inches apart. Holding lines consist of two continuous lines and two dashed lines, perpendicular to the taxiway centerline. Standard holding lines will appear 100 to 200 feet from the runway edge. Holding lines for runways authorized for Category II operations will be at least 200 feet from the runway edge, as shown in figure 8-29.

NOTE:

A Category II approach is a precision approach that requires specific equipment and authorization and allows descents below normal ILS minimums.

The Category II holding line need not be observed when Category II approaches are not in operation. A standard holding line will accompany the Category II holding line, unless the two are collocated.

Displaced Thresholds

A *threshold marking* is a line perpendicular to the runway centerline designating that portion of a runway usable for landing. Displaced threshold markings are used at the beginning of the full-strength runway pavement to show restrictions to the use of the first portion of the runway.

The different types of displaced threshold markings are shown in figure 8-27. The pilot should land beyond the displaced threshold marking, because it denotes either the presence of *obstructions* in the aircraft approach path or that the designated area *may not support* the aircraft's weight. If the displaced threshold area is marked by arrows

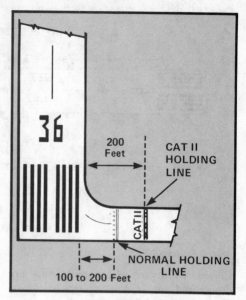

Fig. 8-29. Holding Lines

leading to the full-strength runway, as on runway 36 in figure 8-27, the pilot may use the area for taxiing or takeoff only. Should the area be marked with chevrons, as on runway 4, the area may only be used for blastpad, overrun, or stopway purposes, and may *not* be used for taxiing, takeoff, or landing. The perpendicular lines on the displaced threshold of runway 31 indicate that the edges of the taxiway are not full strength.

AIRPORT LIGHTING

Lighting and marking systems are employed to help the pilot locate and define the runway and general airport environment. The following discussion refers to figure 8-30, which illustrates a complete airport lighting system, as seen from the air. The pilot should familiarize himself with each type of lighting and its meaning.

AIRPORT BEACONS

Airport beacons incorporate color combinations which indicate various types of airports. For example, white and green alternating flashes denote a lighted land airport; while white and yellow flashes

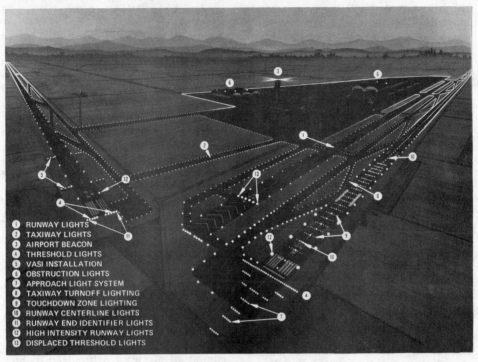

Fig. 8-30. Airport Lighting

1. RUNWAY LIGHTS
2. TAXIWAY LIGHTS
3. AIRPORT BEACON
4. THRESHOLD LIGHTS
5. VASI INSTALLATION
6. OBSTRUCTION LIGHTS
7. APPROACH LIGHT SYSTEM
8. TAXIWAY TURNOFF LIGHTING
9. TOUCHDOWN ZONE LIGHTING
10. RUNWAY CENTERLINE LIGHTS
11. RUNWAY END IDENTIFIER LIGHTS
12. HIGH INTENSITY RUNWAY LIGHTS
13. DISPLACED THRESHOLD LIGHTS

inform the pilot that the beacon serves a lighted water airport. Military airport beacons flash *alternating* white and green, but are differentiated from civilian airport beacons by two quick white flashes between the green flashes.

Operation of the airport rotating beacon during daylight hours indicates that the airport is below VFR landing minimums; therefore, the ground visibility in the airport control zone is less than three miles and/or the ceiling is less than 1,000 feet. This means a special VFR or IFR clearance is required for landings and takeoffs at airports in a control zone. During the hours of darkness, instrument conditions are indicated by flashing lights outlining the tetrahedron or wind tee.

OBSTRUCTION LIGHTS

In the event an obstruction is present which may be hazardous to flight operations in the terminal area, a steady red light is found on the obstruction. A

flashing red light indicates the marking of an enroute obstruction.

TAXIWAY LIGHTS

Taxiway lights are blue to distinguish them from the runway lights. These lights outline the taxi areas and, at some airports, their intensity or brightness can be adjusted.

THRESHOLD LIGHTS

Threshold lights mark the beginning of the landing surface at both ends of the runway. For each end of the runway, they consist of four or more green lights, two located on each side of the runway centerline. When used in conjunction with an approach lighting system, additional threshold lights may be added to the basic configurations.

RUNWAY LIGHTING

Taxiway Turnoff Lights

Taxiway turnoff lights are similar to runway centerline lights. They generally are flush-mounted and spaced at 50-foot intervals. They define the curved path of an aircraft from a point near the runway centerline to the center of the intersecting taxiway. Taxiway centerline lights further define the taxiway.

Runway Edge Light Systems

The airport runway edge lights are white, and are used to outline the runway during periods of darkness or restricted visibility. These light systems are classified according to their brightness. The different classifications are high intensity runway lights (HIRL), medium intensity runway lights (MIRL), and low intensity runway lights (LIRL). The HIRL and MIRL systems have variable intensity controls, while the LIRL system normally has only one intensity setting.

When the HIRL system is installed on an instrument runway, the last 2,000 feet of runway (viewed from the takeoff direction) is equipped with bidirectional lights. This provides the pilot with *yellow edge lights*, rather than white, to identify the last 2,000 feet of available runway. The intensity of the HIRL and MIRL systems may be adjusted from the control tower.

Touchdown Zone Lighting

Touchdown zone (TDZ) lighting is provided to aid the pilot in locating the touchdown zone during reduced visibility situations. TDZ lighting consists of a series of white lights flush-mounted in the runway, beginning 75 to 125 feet from the landing threshold and extending 3,000 feet down the runway.

Runway Centerline Lights

Runway centerline lights (CL) are white lights flush-mounted in the runway. These lights are used primarily during takeoff and landing to aid the pilot in remaining in the center of the runway. The centerline lights are spaced at intervals of 50 feet, beginning 75 feet from the landing threshold and extend-

ing to within 75 feet of the opposite end of the runway.

The portion of the runway with between 3,000 feet and 1,000 feet remaining is equipped with alternate bidirectional red and white lights. However, all of the lights in the final 1,000 feet of runway are bidirectional and are seen as *red* from the takeoff direction. Therefore, when landing or departing, the centerline lights appear as all white for the first part of the runway, then change to alternate red and white lights when 3,000 feet of runway remains, and finally show all red in the last 1,000 feet of remaining runway.

Runway End Identifier Lights

Runway end identifier lights (REIL) are installed at larger terminals to provide positive identification of the approach end of the runway. This system is comprised of two synchronized flashing white lights, one on each side of the approach end of the runway. REIL is especially beneficial when used on runways that have many lights in the general airport vicinity.

Displaced Threshold Lighting

Due to the reduced visibility encountered in night or IFR operations, displaced threshold markings are extremely difficult to see. For this reason, displaced lighting systems are used.

Standard displaced threshold lighting employs a combination of green, blue, red, and white lights to denote the permitted and restricted operations. No landings are permitted short of the *green* displaced threshold lights. Additionally, the *absence* of runway edge lights in this area indicates that no operations are authorized short of the displaced threshold. When *blue* runway edge lights are used in the area short of the displaced threshold lights, the area may be used only for taxi purposes.

The area short of the displaced threshold lights can be used for takeoff purposes when the runway edge lights appear in one of the following combinations.

1. Red runway edge lights located with visible displaced threshold lights, as viewed from the displaced threshold end of the runway
2. White runway edge lights located with no visible threshold lights, as viewed from the runway end opposite the displaced threshold.

APPROACH LIGHT SYSTEMS

The instrument approach light system (ALS) aids the pilot in transitioning from instrument reference to visual flight during the approach to landing. The ALS makes the runway environment more apparent in low visibility conditions. Although there are many lighting systems in operation, only the more common ones will be illustrated in this section.

The most common approach light system in the United States is the U. S. Standard ALSF-1 lighting system, shown in figure 8-31. This system is comprised of 30 light bars spaced 100 feet apart and arranged about the extended runway centerline. A distance marker light bar is located at 1,000 feet from the threshold. At this point, sequence flashing lights (if installed) begin and extend outward into the approach zone 2,000 feet, along with the rest of the standard lighting system.

Sequenced Flashing Lights

Condenser-discharge sequenced flashing light (SFL) systems are installed in conjunction with the U.S. Standard ALSF-1 and ALSF-2 systems at some large airports. The SFL system consists of a series of brilliant blue-white bursts of light flashing in sequence along the approach lights. From the pilot's viewpoint, the system gives the impression of a ball of light traveling at high speed toward the approach end of the runway.

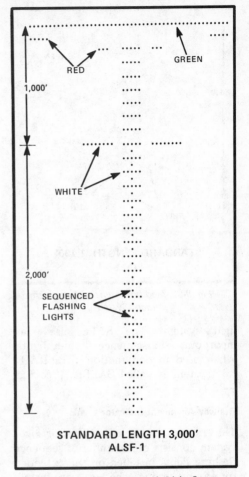

STANDARD LENGTH 3,000'
ALSF-1

Fig. 8-31. ALSF-1 Approach Light System

Medium Intensity Approach Lights

The *medium intensity approach lighting system* (MALS) consists of seven light bars spaced 200 feet apart along the extended runway centerline, as shown in figure 8-32. The entire system extends into the approach zone approximately 1,400 feet. When used in conjunction with runway alignment indicator lights (RAIL), the system is abbreviated MALSR. A description of RAIL will follow in this discussion.

Short Approach Lights

The *U.S. short approach light system* (SALS) consists of the inner 1,500 feet of the U.S. Standard ALSF-1 approach

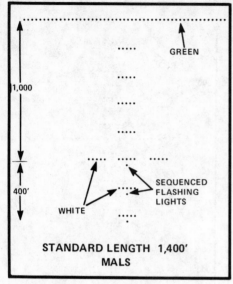

Fig. 8-32. Medium Intensity Approach Light System

light system. The SALS also may incorporate the sequence flashing lights. When used in conjunction with RAIL, this system is called SALSR. (See Fig. 8-33.)

Runway Alignment Indicator Lights

The *runway alignment indicator light* system consists of a number of sequence flashing lights installed on the extended runway centerline. The lights are install-

ed at approximately 200-foot intervals and provide directional guidance to the runway. Figure 8-34 shows a RAIL installation used in conjunction with a medium intensity approach light system.

VASI Installations

The most common visual approach slope indicator (VASI) is the two-bar type. When using this system, the pilot should attempt to fly an approach which will result in the upwind bars indicating red, and the downwind bars showing white. When the approach is too low, both bars will appear red; when the approach is too high, both bars will appear white. The different VASI indicators are shown in figure 8-35.

Some airports serving long-bodied aircraft are equipped with three-bar VASI systems, providing two visual glide paths to the same runway. The first glide path (when approaching the runway) is the same as that provided by a standard two-bar VASI installation. However, the second glide path, which must be used by pilots of long-bodied aircraft, is about one-half of a degree higher than the first.

The upwind bar in a three-bar VASI installation is located approximately 700 feet upwind of the middle bar. The *upwind glide path* also can be used by

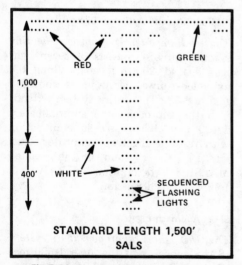

Fig. 8-33. Short Approach Light System

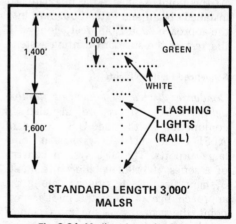

Fig. 8-34. Medium Intensity System with Rail

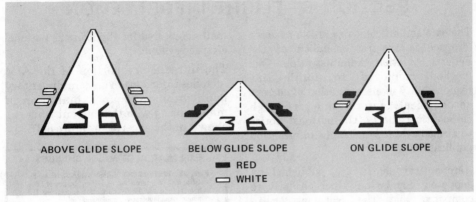

ABOVE GLIDE SLOPE   BELOW GLIDE SLOPE   ON GLIDE SLOPE

■ RED
☐ WHITE

Fig. 8-35. Two-Bar VASI

pilots of small aircraft to avoid the possibility of *wake turbulence* generated on the lower glide path.

A new type of tri-color VASI system also is being used at several airports. This system consists of a single light unit, projecting a three-color visual approach slope. The below-glide-path indication is a red light, the above-glide-path indication is amber, and the on-glide-path indication is a green light. These systems generally have a daytime useful range of approximately one-half to one mile. Night useful range, depending upon visibility conditions, varies from one to five miles.

PILOT-CONTROLLED LIGHTING

Pilot-controlled lighting (PCL) is designed primarily to conserve energy and is found at airports without a tower or an FSS. Airports with part-time towers may also have this equipment for use when the tower is closed. PCL facilities are listed in the *Airport/Facility Directory* and on aeronautical charts near the airport data. The chart symbol for PCL is an "L" enclosed in a circle.

Control of the lights is possible within 15 miles of the airport. Only one lighting system per runway may be operated by the pilot control system. Where a single runway is equipped with both approach lights and runway edge lights, priority for pilot control will be given to approach lights. If no approach lights are installed, priority will be given to runway edge lights, in preference to other lighting such as REIL or VASI.

FAA approved systems provide for three types of radio controls — a three-step system, a two-step system that selects medium or high intensity, and a single-step system for ON and OFF control only. Each activation or change of intensity starts a preset time of 15 minutes (normally long enough to complete an approach, landing, and the necessary taxiing).

Instrument approach charts include sufficient data to identify the PCL equipment, the lighting system, and the control frequency. For example, a three-step system for a MALSR on runway 25 that is controlled by 122.8 MHz would be noted on the instrument approach chart as "three-step MALSR Rwy 25 — 122.8."

Suggested usage is published in the AIM and in the introductory section of approach chart booklets. The procedure requires keying the aircraft microphone a specified number of times within a given time to activate the lights or select the desired intensity. For instance, with a standard three-step system, keying the microphone five times within five seconds activates the lighting and selects a medium intensity.

SECTION B—FLIGHT INFORMATION

The safe and efficient use of the nation's airspace is the responsibility of the Federal Aviation Administration. One method employed to fulfill this responsibility is dissemination of current aeronautical information through aeronautical charts, the national notice to airmen system, and flight information publications.

Aeronautical charts are published by Jeppesen Sanderson, Inc., a private company, and the National Ocean Survey, a government agency. To the extent possible, they reflect the most current information available at the time of printing.

The notice to airmen (NOTAM) system is used to disseminate information of a "time-critical nature." This information is required for flight planning, but is not known sufficiently in advance to permit publication elsewhere.

THE AIM

The *Airman's Information Manual* (Basic Flight Information and ATC Procedures) is shown in figure 8-36. The manual is generally referred to as the AIM. It contains fundamental infor-

Fig. 8-36. AIM Basic Flight Information and ATC Procedures

mation required for flight in the national airspace system.

The introductory portion of the AIM includes information on complimentary publications and an explanation of major changes to the current issue, as shown in the excerpt in figure 8-37.

EXPLANATION OF MAJOR CHANGES

Para. 12 INSTRUMENT LANDING SYSTEM—Revised to include information regarding the use of DME and to include additional information concerning ILS minimums and inoperative components.

Para. 47 RADIO CONTROL OF AIRPORT LIGHTING—Revised in its entirety for clarification and to provide additional information.

Para. 132 MILITARY TRAINING ROUTES—Revised to encourage the VFR pilot to solicit current MTR route information from the FSS.

Para. 155. AIRPORT ADVISORY PRACTICES—Revised in its entirety for clarification.

Para. 156 AERONAUTICAL ADVISORY STATIONS (UNICOM)—Revised for clarification.

Para. 172 HAZARDOUS AREA REPORTING SERVICE, LAKE/ISLAND, MOUNTAIN AND SWAMP REPORTING SERVICE GRAPHIC—Revised to include the Southern Appalachian Mountain Reporting Service.

Para. 227. LOW—LEVEL WIND SHEAR ALERT SYSTEM—Added to provide an operational description of the system.

Para. 230 INTERSECTION TAKEOFFS—Revised to provide in-depth description of wake turbulence procedures for intersection departures.

Para. 552 AIR TRAFFIC WAKE TURBULENCE SEPARATIONS—Revised to provide in-depth description of wake turbulence procedures for aircraft departing behind heavy aircraft.

Fig. 8-37. AIM, Summary of Major Changes Excerpt

The main subjects covered in the AIM include:
— Navigation Aids
— Airport, Air Navigation Lighting and Marking Aids
— Airspace — Air Traffic Control
— Emergency Procedures
— Safety of Flight
— Medical Facts for Pilots
— Aeronautical Charts and Related Publications
— Pilot/Controller Glossary

Navigation Aids — This section contains a detailed description of all the navaids used in the national airspace system. The discussion also addresses the components, limitations, and operational use of each.

Airport, Air Navigation Lighting and Marking Aids — The AIM coverage of these subjects includes comprehensive illustrations of the most commonly used airport marking aids. For example, basic runway markings, hold lines, threshold markings, and touchdown zone markers are shown.

Airspace — This part contains pertinent information for both VFR and IFR pilots. It covers the VFR visibility and distance criteria for controlled and uncontrolled airspace, as well as the required altitudes and flight levels to be used in VFR and IFR operations.

Special use and other airspace areas are also defined. These include prohibited, restricted, warning, alert, and military operations areas. Other special airspace subjects, such as airport traffic/advisory areas, military training routes, and general airspace segments and dimensions also are described.

Air Traffic Control — This is one of the most important AIM segments for all pilots, but especially commercial and instrument pilots. It covers services available to pilots, radio communications phraseology, and airport operations for controlled and uncontrolled airports.

In addition, this section also lists practical steps for preflight planning and provides an insight into ATC clearance/separation practices during flight. National security and interception procedures are described at the end of this part.

Emergency Procedures — Portions dealing with emergency procedures involve topics such as common accident cause factors, the national search and rescue plan, and the rules pertaining to the aviation safety reporting program. The procedures and signals for aircraft in emergency situations also are described.

Safety of Flight — Included in this section is a discussion of weather information sources, altimetry, wake turbulence, and bird hazards. Important topics like the "do's and don'ts" of thunderstorm flying, clear air turbulence, wind shear, and vortex avoidance procedures also are included.

Medical Facts for Pilots — This section reviews various aspects of fatigue, hypoxia, oxygen requirements, drugs/alcohol, carbon monoxide, and orientation as they relate to flight. Other subjects of interest include vision, middle ear discomfort, and vertigo.

Aeronautical Charts and Related Publications — The coverage in this section lists the types of charts available and their appropriate uses. The discussion contains a detailed description of each chart series, miscellaneous auxiliary charts, and related publications.

Pilot/Controller Glossary — This glossary, located in the back of the manual, is designed to promote a common understanding of terms used in air traffic control. Because of the international nature of flying, terms used by the International Civil Aviation Organization (ICAO) are included when they differ from FAA definitions. These ICAO terms are *italicized* in the glossary, as shown in figure 8-38.

AIRMAN'S INFORMATION MANUAL/ AIM— A publication containing Basic Flight Information and ATC Procedures designed primarily as a pilot's instructional manual for use in the National Airspace System of the United States.

ICAO — AERONAUTICAL INFORMATION PUBLICATION—A publication issued by or with the authority of a state and containing aeronautical information of a lasting character essential to air navigation.

AIRMET/AIRMAN'S METEOROLOGICAL INFORMATION—Inflight weather advisories which cover moderate icing, moderate turbulence, sustained winds of 30 knots or more within 2,000 feet of the surface and the initial onset of phenomena producing extensive areas of visibilities below 3 miles or ceilings less than 1,000 feet.

Fig. 8-38. Glossary of Aeronautical Terms

AIRPORT/FACILITY DIRECTORY

The *Airport/Facility Directory* is published by NOS in seven booklets — one for each of seven regional areas in the United States. Effective dates and the area of coverage for each are shown on the cover. (See Fig. 8-39.) Contents include a tabulation of all data on record with the FAA for public use civil airports, associated terminal control facilities, air route traffic control centers, and radio aids to navigation. Each booklet also contains additional data such as special notices, operational procedures, and preferred routes relevant to the coverage area.

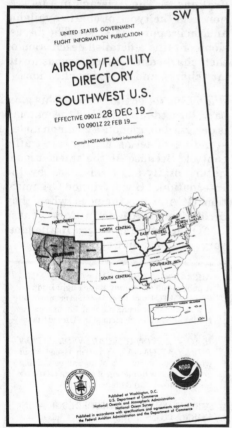

Fig. 8-39. Airport/Facility Directory

Listings are alphabetical by state and cities within states. A cross reference system is used for the names of facilities. Airports are listed by associated city name and cross-referenced by airport name. Facilities associated with an airport, but with different names, are listed individually in the alphabetical tabulation under their own names, as well as under the associated airport name.

LEGEND

A comprehensive legend example is printed in the first few pages of each regional directory. The format, although similar to that used in many aeronautical publications, contains several unique abbreviations and symbols. Pilots should become familiar with the directory legend. A sample legend is shown in figure 8-40.

In addition to airport information, each directory lists all national airspace system radio navigation aids within the area. An example of a listing from the southwest directory is illustrated in figure 8-41. Radio facilities with a name different than an associated airport are listed separately under their own name and included in the airport data.

SPECIAL NOTICES

Most of each regional directory is devoted to the airport/facility listing; however, other important information is included. Each directory has a special notices section. This section lists "hard to find" significant information. For example, civil use of military fields, newly certified airports, and continuous power facilities are explained, and special procedures are identified. Special notices also contains a complete listing of useful telephone numbers. These include FSS, combined station/tower, national weather service, and fast file flight plan telephone numbers. All listings are alphabetical by state. An excerpt of this listing is shown in figure 8-42.

VOR RECEIVER CHECKPOINTS

VOR receiver checkpoint procedures were covered in Chapter 4 and are also discussed in the AIM. The information

CITY NAME
§   **AIRPORT NAME**   (ORL)   2.6 E   GMT –5(–4DT)   28°32′43″N 81°20′10″W   **JACKSONVILLE**
      113   B   S4   FUEL 100, JET A   OX 1, 2, 3   TPA—1000(800)   AOE   CFR   Index A   Not insp.   **H-4G, L-19C**
                                                                                            IAP

(18) ► **RWY 07-25:** H6000X150 (ASPH)   S-90, D-160, DT-300   HIRL
       RWY 07: ALSF1. Trees.   **RWY 25:** REIL. Rgt tfc.
       RWY 13-31: H4620X100 (ASPH)   HIRL
       RWY 13: VASI—GA 3.3° TCH 89′. Pole.   **RWY 31:** VASI—GA 3.1° TCH 36′. Tree. Rgt tfc.
(19) ► **AIRPORT REMARKS:** Attended 1200-0300Z‡. LLWSAS. Acft 100,000 lbs or over ctc Director of Aviation for
       approval (305) 894-9831. Fee for all airline charters, travel clubs and certain revenue producing acft.
(20) ► **COMMUNICATIONS:** ATIS 127.25   **UNICOM** 123.0
       NAME FSS (ORL) on fld   123.65 122.65 122.2 122.1R 112.2T   (305) 894-0861
      ℝ **NAME APP CON** 124.8 (337°-179°)   120.15 (180°-336°)
       TOWER 118.7   **GND CON** 121.7   **CLNC DEL** 125.55   **PRE TAXI CLNC** 125.5
      ℝ **DEP CON** 124.8 (337°-179°)   120.15 (180°-336°)
       STAGE I SVC ctc ORLANDO APP CON
(21) ► **RADIO AIDS TO NAVIGATION:** VHF/DF ctc PHOENIX FSS
       NAME (H) VORTAC 112.2   ORL   Chan 59   28°32′33″N 81°20′07″W   at fld.   1110/8E
            VOR unusable 050-060° beyond 5000′
       HERNY NDB (LOM) 221   OR   28°30′24″N 81°26′03″W   067° 5.4 NM to fld.
       ILS 109.9 I-ORL Rwy 07. LOM HERNY NDB
       ASR/PAR
(22) ► **COMM/NAVAID REMARKS:** Emerg frequency 121.5 not available at tower.

(1) City/Airport Name	(12) Fuel
(2) NOTAM Service	(13) Oxygen
(3) Location Identifier	(14) Traffic Pattern Altitude
(4) Airport Location	(15) Airport of Entry and Landing Rights Airports
(5) Time Conversion	(16) Certificated Airport (FAR 139) and
(6) Geographic Position of Airport	(17) FAA Inspection
(7) Charts	(18) Runway Data
(8) Instrument Approach Procedures	(19) Airport Remarks
(9) Elevation	(20) Communications
(10) Rotating Beacon	(21) Radio Aids to Navigation
(11) Servicing	(22) Comm/Navaid Remarks

Fig. 8-40. Airport/Facility Directory Legend Excerpt

in the *Airport/Facility Directory* on VOR checkpoints lists each regional facility, the identifier, type of checkpoint, distance/azimuth, and a description, if necessary. Again, the listing is alphabetical by state. A typical listing of VOR receiver checkpoints is depicted in figure 8-43. VOT facilities are listed in the same section below the VOR checkpoints.

COCHISE   32°02′00″N 109°45′27″W   **PHOENIX**
   (H) BVORTAC 115.8 Chan 105   317° 14.8 NM to Cochise County Arpt   **H-2G, L-4F**
     VORTAC unusable 005°-015° beyond 35 NM below 10,000′
                   015°-030° beyond 25 NM below 10,000′
                   030°-040° beyond 35 NM below 10,000′
                   190°-220° beyond 30 NM below 9000′
                   220°-240° beyond 25 NM below 9500′
   COCHISE LRCO 122.1R 115.8T (TUCSON FSS)

Fig. 8-41. Radio Navigation Aid Listing

FSS-CS/T AND NATIONAL WEATHER
SERVICE TELEPHONE NUMBERS

Flight Service Stations (FSS) and Combined Station/Tower (CS/T) provide information on airport conditions, radio aids and other facilities, and process flight plans. CS/T personnel are not certified pilot weather briefers; however, they provide factual data from weather reports and forecasts. Airport Advisory Service is provided at the pilot's request on 123.6 by FSSs located at airports where there are no control towers in operation. (See Airman's Information Manual, Basic Flight Information and ATC Procedures.)

"Numerous additional telephone numbers are listed under COMMUNICATIONS in the Airport/Facility Directory tabulation. If you wish to call an FSS, but do not have access to a directory listing telephone numbers, call the toll-free information number 800-555-1212. Many FAA Flight Service Station numbers may be obtained through this service."

The telephone area code number is shown in parentheses. Each number given is the preferred telephone number to obtain flight weather information. Automatic answering devices are sometimes used on listed lines to give general local weather information during peak workloads. To avoid getting the recorded general weather announcement, use the selected telephone number listed.

FAST FILE FLIGHT PLAN SYSTEM

Some Flight Service Stations have inaugurated this system for pilots who desire to file IFR/VFR flight plans. Pilots may call the discrete telephone numbers listed and file flight plans in accordance with prerecorded taped instructions. IFR flight plans will be extracted from the recorder and subsequently entered in the appropriate ARTCC computer. VFR flight plans will be transcribed; and both IFR/VFR flight plans will be filed in the FSS. This equipment is designed to automatically disconnect after 8 seconds of no transmission, so pilots are instructed to speak at a normal speech rate without lengthy pauses between flight plan elements. Pilots are urged to file flight plans into this system at least 30 minutes in advance of proposed departure. The system may be used to close and cancel flight plans.

Preflight weather briefing services remain available through regular telephone numbers.

★ Indicates Pilot's Automatic Telephone Weather Answering Service (PATWAS) or telephone connected to the Transcribed Weather Broadcast (TWEB) providing transcribed aviation weather information.

◆ Indicates a restricted number, used for aviation weather information.

■ Call FSS for "one call" FSS—Weather Service (WS) Briefing Service

\# Automatic Aviation Weather Service (AAWS)

§§ Indicates Fast File telephone number for pre-recorded and transcribed flight plan filing only.

Location and Identifier		Area Code	Telephone
IDAHO			
Boise BOI (Air Terminal)	FSS	(208)	343-2525 ■
	FSS	(208)	345-6163/4 ★
Burley BYI (Burley)	FSS	(208)	678-8361/2
Idaho Falls IDA (Fanning Field)	FSS	(208)	522-9024
Lewiston	WS	(208)	743-3841
			(1130-0330Z‡)
Pocatello	WS	(208)	232-0143 ◆
			(1200-0400Z‡)

Fig. 8-42. FSS-CS/T and National Weather Service Telephone Numbers Excerpt

VOR RECEIVER CHECK POINTS
VOR/VORTAC

The list of VOR airborne and ground check points are included in this section. Use of these check points is explained in Airman's Information Manual, Basic Flight Information and ATC Procedures.

NOTE: Under column headed "Type Check Pt. Gnd. AB/ALT", G stands for ground, A/ stands for airborne followed by a number (2300) indicating the altitude above mean sea level at which the check should be conducted. Facilities are listed in alphabetical order, in the state where the check points are located.

Facility Name (Arpt Name)	Freq/Ident	Type Check Pt. Gnd. AB/ALT	Azimuth from Fac. Mag	Dist. from Fac. N.M.	Check Point Description
CONNECTICUT					
Carmel (Danbury Muni)	116.6/CMK	A/1500	050	6.7	Over apch end of Rwy 08.
Hartford (Hartford-Brainard)	114.9/HFD	G	337	7.8	On parking ramp S of terminal bldg.
Hartford (Rentschler)	114.9/HFD	G	347	8.0	On taxi strip E side S of service hangar ramp.

Fig. 8-43. VOR Receiver Checkpoint Excerpt

PREFERRED IFR ROUTES

Certain preferred routes have been designated by the FAA. The objective is to facilitate the flow of air traffic into and out of major terminal areas. The directory lists established preferred IFR routes for each region. Pilots who plan to transit a busy air terminal area during a flight should consult the preferred route section of the directory before filing an IFR flight plan. These routes pertain to both high and low altitude airspace, as shown in figure 8-44.

AERONAUTICAL CHART BULLETIN

The last section of the *Airport/Facility Directory* lists changes to aeronautical charts within the region. Generally, only changes to controlled and special use airspace which could pose a hazard to flight or impose a restriction are published in this section. Major changes to airport or radio navigation facilities are also included. When the affected aeronautical chart is republished, changes are included and the chart

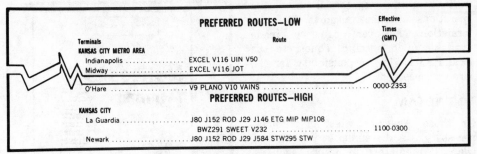

Terminals	Route	Effective Times (GMT)
PREFERRED ROUTES—LOW		
KANSAS CITY METRO AREA		
Indianapolis	EXCEL V116 UIN V50	
Midway	EXCEL V116 JOT	
O'Hare	V9 PLANO V10 VAINS	0000-2353
PREFERRED ROUTES—HIGH		
KANSAS CITY		
La Guardia	J80 J152 ROD J29 J146 ETG MIP MIP108	
	BWZ291 SWEET V232	1100-0300
Newark	J80 J152 ROD J29 J584 STW295 STW	

Fig. 8-44. Preferred Route Excerpt

bulletins are removed from the directory. A chart bulletin excerpt is illustrated in figure 8-45.

NOTICES TO AIRMEN

Time-critical aeronautical information that was not known at the time of publication of aeronautical charts or other documents receives immediate dissemination via the national notice to airmen service, a telecommunications system. Two general types of NOTAMs exist — the NOTAM-D and the NOTAM-L. In certain circumstances, a third category — the Flight Data Center (FDC) NOTAM — may be issued. An FDC NOTAM contains regulatory information.

NOTAM information is regularly passed to pilots by telephone or radio. The FAA also produces a separate publication, called *Notices to Airmen*, to provide further dissemination.

NOTAM-D

Information designated for NOTAM-D dissemination is the type that could affect a pilot's decision to make a flight. Events such as airport closure, interruptions in service of navigational aids, ILS, or radar service are appropriate NOTAM-D material. NOTAM-D information is provided for all navigation facilities, all IFR airports (with approved instrument approach procedures), and for VFR airports annotated by the NOTAM symbol (§) in the *Airport/Facility Directory*.

NOTAM-L

NOTAM-L information is that which is of an advisory, or nice to know, nature. It includes such information as taxiway closings, men and equipment near or crossing runways, and information on airports not annotated with the NOTAM symbol (§) in the *Airport/Facility Directory*. NOTAM-L information is maintained on file only at those local air

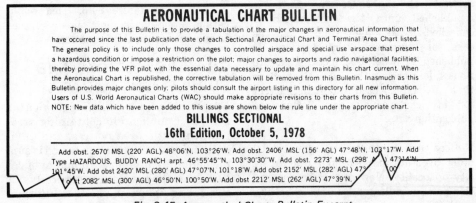

AERONAUTICAL CHART BULLETIN

The purpose of this Bulletin is to provide a tabulation of the major changes in aeronautical information that have occurred since the last publication date of each Sectional Aeronautical Chart and Terminal Area Chart listed. The general policy is to include only those changes to controlled airspace and special use airspace that present a hazardous condition or impose a restriction on the pilot; major changes to airports and radio navigational facilities, thereby providing the VFR pilot with the essential data necessary to update and maintain his chart current. When the Aeronautical Chart is republished, the corrective tabulation will be removed from this Bulletin. Inasmuch as this Bulletin provides major changes only; pilots should consult the airport listing in this directory for all new information. Users of U.S. World Aeronautical Charts (WAC) should make appropriate revisions to their charts from this Bulletin. NOTE: New data which have been added to this issue are shown below the rule line under the appropriate chart.

BILLINGS SECTIONAL
16th Edition, October 5, 1978

Add obst. 2670' MSL (220' AGL) 48°06'N, 103°26'W. Add obst. 2406' MSL (156' AGL) 47°48'N, 103°17'W. Add Type HAZARDOUS, BUDDY RANCH arpt. 46°55'45''N, 103°30'30''W. Add obst. 2273' MSL (298' ___ ___ 47°14'N, 101°45'W. Add obst 2420' MSL (280' AGL) 47°07'N, 101°18'W. Add obst 2152' MSL (282' AGL) 47° ___ ___ ___ __ ___t 2082' MSL (300' AGL) 46°50'N, 100°50'W. Add obst 2212' MSL (262' AGL) 47°39'N, ___

Fig. 8-45. Aeronautical Chart Bulletin Excerpt

traffic facilities concerned with the operations at these airports. This information, however, can be made available upon specific request to the local FSS having responsibility for the airport concerned.

FDC NOTAM

On those occasions when it becomes necessary to disseminate information which is regulatory in nature, such as amendments to aeronautical charts, instrument approach procedures, or to effect restrictions to flight, the National FDC in Washington, D.C., will issue the NOTAM containing the regulatory information as an FDC NOTAM. FDC NOTAMs are distributed through the National Communications Center in Kansas City for transmission to all air traffic facilities with telecommunications access. Current FDC NOTAMs are published in their entirety in the *Notices to Airmen* publication and also as part of the instrument approach procedure charts.

NOTICES TO AIRMEN (CLASS II)

The *Notices to Airmen* publication contains three basic parts, or subdivisions. The first part consists of notices which meet the NOTAM-D criteria and are expected to remain in effect for an extended period. These NOTAMs are included to reduce teletype circuit congestion. NOTAM-L and other special notices may be included in the interest of flight safety. Data is republished until the information is cancelled, is no longer valid or, in the case of permanent information, is published in other documents that are revised less frequently. All notices in the first part are expected to remain in effect for at least seven days after the publication date.

Notices are arranged in alphabetical order by state and within the state by city or locality. New or revised data, in this part, is indicated by bold italicizing of the airport name. It is important to

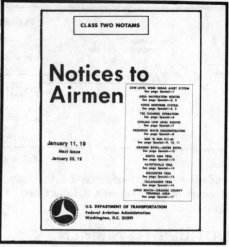

Fig. 8-46. Notices to Airmen

note that, unless stated otherwise, all times are local.

The second part contains all FDC NOTAMs current through specific FDC NOTAM number and date. This is listed in the FDC legend, which is shown in figure 8-47.

The third part contains special notices that, either because they are too long or because they concern a wide or unspecified geographic area, are not suitable for inclusion in the general notices. Contents of the special notices vary widely. The main criteria for inclusion of these special notices is enhancement of flight safety. Each biweekly publication of the *Notices to Airmen* (Class II) publication lists the special notices on the cover, as illustrated in figure 8-46. This publication is one of the most timely sources of new aeronautical information.

GRAPHIC NOTICES AND SUPPLEMENTAL DATA

Graphic Notices and Supplemental Data is a publication containing aeronautical data, area notices, and navigational route information which is supplemental to other operational publications and charts. Data is generally not subject to frequent change. Information that appears in this publication;

F.A.A. NATIONAL FLIGHT DATA CENTER
FDC NOTAMS

THE LISTING BELOW INCLUDES, IN PART, CHANGES IN FLIGHT DATA, PARTICULARLY OF A REGULATORY NATURE, WHICH AFFECT STANDARD INSTRUMENT APPROACH PROCEDURES, AERONAUTICAL CHARTS AND SELECTED FLIGHT RESTRICTIONS, PRIOR TO THEIR NORMAL PUBLICATION CYCLE. THEREFORE, THEY SHOULD BE REVIEWED DURING PRE-FLIGHT PLANNING. THIS LISTING INCLUDES ALL FDC NOTAMS CURRENT THRU FDC NOTAM NUMBER SHOWN BELOW.

LEGEND

FDC ------- NATIONAL FLIGHT DATA CENTER
6/103 ----- ACCOUNTABILITY NUMBER ASSIGNED TO THE MESSAGE ORIGINATOR BY FDC
FI/T ------ FLIGHT INFORMATION/TEMPORARY
FI/P ------ FLIGHT INFORMATION/PERMANENT
--------- NEW NOTAM

THE FOLLOWING LISTING CONTAINS FDC NOTAMS
THRU FDC 8/1876 DEC 28, 19—

EAST CENTRAL
ILLINOIS

FDC 8/446 FI/T (MVN) MT VERNON-OUTLAND MT VERNON IL. ILS RWY 23 AMDT 2 STRAIGHT-IN DECISION HEIGHT 721 FEET VISIBILITY 3/4 MILE HEIGHT ABOVE TOUCHDOWN 250 FEET ALL CATEGORIES. STRAIGHT-IN LOCALIZER VISIBILITY 3/4 MILE CATEGORY A B AND C. VOR RWY 23 AMDT 7 STRAIGHT-IN VISIBILITY 3/4 MILE CATEOGRY A AND B.

#FDC 8/1810 FI/T (FWA) FORT WAYNE MUNI (BAER FIELD) FORT WAYNE IN. ILS RWY 31 AMDT 19 ILS SI RWY 31 RVR 5000 FT ALL CATS. LOC SI RWY 31 RVR 5000 FT CAT A B AND C. RADAR-1 AMDT 12 SI RWY 31 RVR 5000 FT CAT A B AND C.

MICHIGAN

FDC 8/650 FI/T (MKG) MUSKEGON COUNTY MUSKEGON MI. ILS RWY 32 AMDT 9 STRAIGHT IN RWY 32 DECISION HEIGHT 877 FEET HEIGHT ABOVE TOUCHDOWN 250 FEET VISIBILITY RVR 4000 FEET ALL CATEGORIES, STRAIGHT IN LOCALIZER RWY 32 VISIBILITY RVR 4000 FEET ALL CATEGORIES. RADAR-1 AMDT 3 RWY 32 VISIBILITY RVR 4000 FEET CATEGORIES A B AND C. TAKEOFF MINIMUMS RWY 32 RVR 4000 FEET AUTHORIZED FOR FAR 135 OPERATORS.

Fig. 8-47. Notices to Airmen Excerpts

however, may be revised by inclusion in *Notices to Airmen (Class II)* which is published more frequently.

Graphic Notices and Supplemental Data is a quarterly publication available through subscription from the Superintendent of Documents. The effective dates of each issue are printed on the cover, as shown in figure 8-48.

The major sections include Area Advisories, Area Navigation (RNAV) Routes, North Atlantic Routes (NAR), Terminal Area Graphics, and Terminal Radar Service Area Graphics.

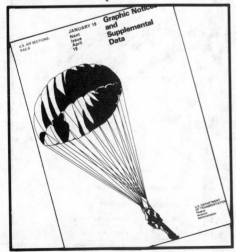

Fig. 8-48. Graphic Notices and Supplemental Data

AREA ADVISORIES

This section is limited to information that does not concern a specific airport or navaid and, at the same time, does not meet the criteria for inclusion into other more permanent publications such as the *Airport/Facility Directory*. The advisories are grouped under state headings and, where appropriate, under city or geographical locations.

RNAV AND NORTH ATLANTIC ROUTES

The next section contains a listing of *area navigation*, or RNAV, routes. Guidelines for use of these routes within the national airspace system specify the use of approved navigation systems such as Doppler radar, inertial or courseline computers. A description of the route numbering system is also provided.

North American Routes for North Atlantic Traffic are described and listed in the next section. These routes, which generally pertain to air carrier operations, are referred to by the acronym NAR.

TERMINAL AREA GRAPHIC NOTICES

The majority of *Graphic Notices and Supplemental Data* is devoted to terminal area graphic notices and terminal radar service areas (TRSA). Both of these sections are preceded by a map and an index of the respective graphic depictions. Listings are alphabetical by city.

Terminal area graphic notices are published for areas of concentrated IFR traffic. Normally, these areas have at least one busy air terminal with a complex air traffic flow involving a mixture of commercial, general aviation, and military aircraft. The graphics are intended to assist VFR pilots planning flights in the areas, and in many cases

recommended VFR routes or corridors are shown. The information presented is advisory only. Pilots flying within these areas are encouraged to use the graphic information and any other radar or advisory service. A typical terminal area graphic notice is shown in figure 8-49.

TERMINAL RADAR SERVICE AREAS

As discussed earlier, the radar service programs available to VFR pilots include Stage I (advisory), Stage II (advisory and sequencing), and Stage III (sequencing and separation). Where Stage III service is implemented, the

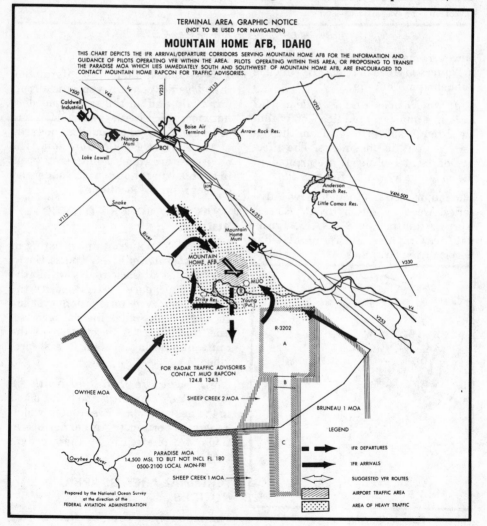

Fig. 8-49. Terminal Area Graphic Notice

area is called a terminal radar service area, or a TRSA. All TRSAs in the United States are depicted in *Graphic Notices and Supplemental Data*. A typical illustration, as shown in figure 8-50, contains frequencies, checkpoints, and airspace boundaries.

In addition, this section also contains a description of the services provided and pilot/controller procedures. Both the service and the procedures are predicated on what is essentially an IFR environment. IFR pilots operate according to normal IFR; VFR pilots are expected to contact the controlling agency whenever they depart, arrive, or transit a TRSA. VFR participation is not mandatory; however, it is encouraged.

Normally, TRSA service consists of vectoring, sequencing, and separation of both VFR and IFR traffic landing at the primary airport. Separation service and advisories on unknown aircraft also are provided to all participating aircraft on a controller workload basis. *Participating traffic* is defined as an aircraft in radar and radio contact with approach or departure control.

The terminal radar service areas should not be confused with terminal control

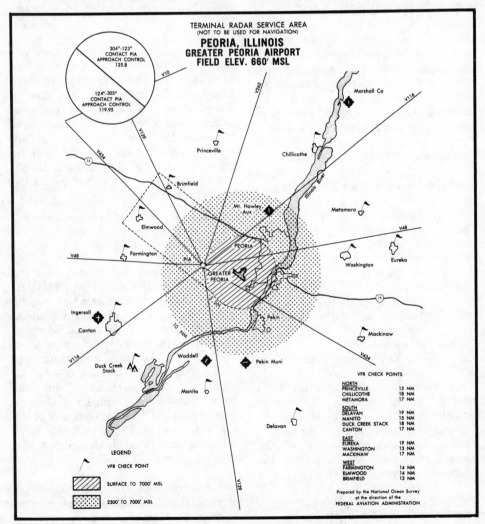

Fig. 8-50. Terminal Radar Service Area

areas (TCAs), which are located at very large airports with high density traffic. In the TCAs, *all* aircraft are subject to definite operating rules, specific pilot certification, and equipment requirements. Also, both VFR and IFR pilots normally must operate in accordance with an ATC clearance within the terminal control area. Areas having a TCA are depicted on aeronautical charts. Basic information is found on the world aeronautical charts and sectional charts while specific TCA information is shown on a VFR terminal area chart.

ADVISORY CIRCULARS

Advisory circulars are issued by the FAA to provide aviation information of a nonregulatory nature. Although the contents of most advisory circulars are not binding on the public, they contain information and accepted procedures necessary for good operating practices.

Each of the subjects covered is identified by a general subject number, followed by the number for the specific subject matter, as shown in the following list.

00	General
10	Procedural
20	Aircraft
60	Airmen
70	Airspace
90	Air Traffic Control and General Operations
140	Schools and Other Certified Agencies
150	Airports
170	Air Navigational Facilities

When the volume of circulars in a general series warrants a further breakdown, the general number is followed by a slash and a specific subject number. For example, some of the Airports series (150) are issued under the following numbers.

150/4000	Resource Management
150/5000	Airport Planning
150/5200	Airport Safety — General
150/5210	Airport Safety Operations (Recommended Training, Standards, Manning)
150/5220	Airport Safety Equipment and Facilities
150/5230	Airport Ground Safety System

Each circular has a subject number followed by a dash and a sequential number identifying the individual circular (150/4000-1). Changes to circulars have the notation 'CHG 1," "CHG 2," etc. after the identification number on pages that have changed. The date on a revised page reflects the effective date of change.

The subjects covered by advisory circulars and the availability of each are contained in the Advisory Circular Checklist. Generally, this checklist is issued three times each year and contains a listing of all current circulars, those circulars which have been canceled, and any additions since the last checklist was printed. This checklist can be obtained free of charge by writing to the following address.

U.S. Department of Transportation
Publications Section, M 443.1
Washington, D.C. 20590

Figure 8-51 shows an excerpt from the Advisory Circular Checklist. This excerpt contains one circular which may be obtained free of charge and one which must be purchased. It should be noted that after the narrative description of AC 61-64A, the price and source are listed. This advisory circular costs $1.30 and can be purchased from the Superintendent of Documents, Government Printing Office (GPO) or any of the GPO bookstores. The appropriate GPO addresses are listed in the front of the Advisory Circular Checklist.

The description of AC 61-65 does not list a price, therefore, this advisory circular is free. To request a free advisory circular or to be placed on the FAA's

> 61—64A Flight Test Guide—Instrument Pilot Helicopter (5/25/—).
>
> Assist the applicant and the instructor in preparing for the flight test for the Instrument Pilot Helicopter Rating. Contains information and guidance concerning the pilot operations, procedures, and maneuvers relevant to the flight test. ($1.30 Supt. Docs.) SN 050-007-00404-4.
>
> 61—65 Part 61 (Revised) Certification: Pilot and Flight Instructors (9/5/—).
>
> Informs pilots and flight instructors of the changes in Part 61, revised January 23, 1973, their effects, and the standards and procedures which will be used in implementing them.

Fig. 8-51. Advisory Circular Checklist Excerpt

mailing list for future circulars, a request should be sent to the previously listed address for the Department of Transportation. When requesting future circulars, the subject matter desired must be identified by the subject numbers and titles, as shown in the Advisory Circular Checklist. For example, use 00 General, 10 Procedural, or 20 Aircraft.

JEPPESEN J-AID

The *Jeppesen Airport and Information Directory (J-AID)* is a comprehensive collection of current airport and aeronautical information. This looseleaf reference book, shown in figure 8-52, is the same size as the Jeppesen approach chart binders, and contains information applicable to both VFR and IFR pilots.

Fig. 8-52. J-AID

The *J-AID* includes the material covered in the Airman's Information Manual and other aeronautical publications, plus information on many other aeronautical knowledge areas. For this reason, FAR Part 135.81 authorizes it as a substitute for the above publications during air taxi and commercial operations. Because it contains more information and is frequently revised, many airlines and commercial operators prefer its use.

There are two basic revision cycles employed with the *Jeppesen J-AID*. First, revisions to information concerning air traffic control are distributed approximately 10 times a year. Second, airport diagrams and related information are revised and disseminated every four months.

J-AID SECTIONS

The *J-AID* is divided into seven basic sections — introduction, radio facilities, airport directory, meteorology, tables and codes, air traffic control, and regulations. All material relating to a specific subject is included in the section.

INTRODUCTION

The introduction section contains a table of contents, a revision record, and any recently issued Jeppesen briefing bulletins. The briefing bulletins deal primarily with new material or subjects that must be specifically brought to the attention of the pilot.

RADIO FACILITIES

Information contained in the radio facilities section pertains to frequency allocation, characteristics of navigation facilities, location of radar units, direction finding procedures, and the location of direction finding stations. In addition, it lists locations and frequencies for commercial broadcast stations and provides information concerning VOR receiver checkpoints and test signals. Unlike the *Airport/*

Facility Directory, all published VOR receiver tests are listed in this one section. Information also is presented concerning the locations and frequencies of navigation aids within that region.

AIRPORT DIRECTORY

The airport directory section for the United States is divided into three geographic regions — east, central, and west. The airports within each region are listed alphabetically by state, then by locations within the states (and by airport names, if they differ). The airport listings of each state are preceded by a map of the state showing all of the locations under which airports are indexed. The state maps can be used with sectional and enroute charts for selection of the airport nearest the destination.

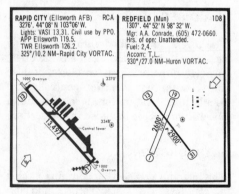

Fig. 8-53. J-AID Airport Diagrams

An airport diagram and tabular airport information are provided for each airport, as shown in figure 8-53. The tabular information includes the airport name, elevation, geographic coordinates, manager's name and telephone number, hours of operation, service facilities available, runway information, communications facilities, and the distance and direction from a local navaid.

METEOROLOGY

The meteorology section contains general information concerning the weather services available and the meanings of weather station models, symbols, and codes used on various weather charts and forecasts. In addition, it lists all continuous automatic transcribed weather broadcast (TWEB) stations and National Weather Service and flight service station telephone numbers.

TABLES AND CODES

A comprehensive collection of conversion tables and data on commonly used codes is included in the tables and codes portion of the *J-AID*. For example, there are tables for converting temperatures from Celsius to Fahrenheit and making various metric conversions. The phonetic alphabet, Morse code, wind component table, and sunrise, sunset, and twilight tables also are provided.

AIR TRAFFIC CONTROL

The air traffic control section consists of the basic information contained in AIM, Basic Flight Information and ATC Procedures. This includes data pertaining to airspace, services available to pilots, radiotelephone phraseology and technique, clearances, emergency procedures, and departure, enroute, and arrival procedures. It also provides data concerning wake turbulence avoidance, bird hazards, safety of flight, and good operating practices.

REGULATIONS

The last section of the *J-AID* provides a current set of Federal Aviation Regulations reprinted from Parts 1, 61, 91, 121, 135, 141, HMR 175, and NTSB 830. The regulations are updated for changes on a timely basis. The regulations also may be purchased separately from the *J-AID* with update service.

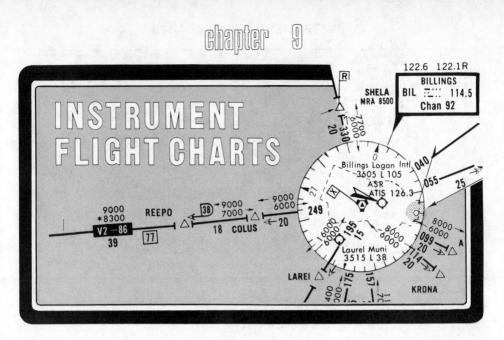

chapter 9

INSTRUMENT FLIGHT CHARTS

INTRODUCTION

A study of IFR navigation charts will enable the pilot to transition quickly from VFR to IFR navigation. During IFR operations, the pilot becomes more dependent upon navigation charts for all aspects of cross-country flying. In this chapter, the information presented on enroute, area, SID, STAR, profile descent, and approach charts will be studied closely to show the extensive information available.

There are two major sources of charts for the IFR pilot — Jeppesen Sanderson, Inc. and the National Ocean Survey (NOS). Both contain instrument navigation data compiled from information supplied by the Federal Aviation Administration and both are printed in two colors. The main differences between Jeppesen and NOS charts involve format and symbology. Sections A and B of this chapter cover NOS charts, and Section C is included to introduce Jeppesen charts.

SECTION A—ENROUTE AND AREA CHARTS

Sectional and WAC charts are commonly used for VFR cross-country flights because of their highly detailed nature. Pertinent terrain features and ground object information are displayed on these charts. A pilot flying an IFR cross country, however, must use an enroute or area chart. These charts display vast amounts of data regarding the route of flight, radio facilities used for enroute navigation, identification of instrument fixes, airport information, communications available, altitudes that guarantee proper reception of navigation signals, and terrain clearance.

The low altitude enroute and area charts are for use up to, but not including, 18,000 feet MSL. Since general aviation instrument pilots operate almost exclusively within this airspace, the emphasis is placed on the low altitude charts. The high altitude enroute charts are designed for use at and above 18,000 feet. They have basically the same symbology as lower altitude charts and

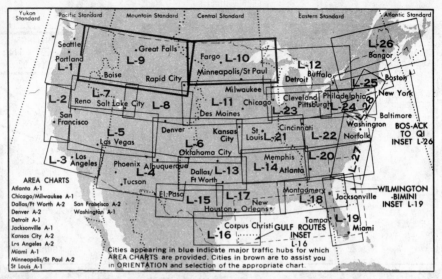

Fig. 9-1. NOS Enroute Chart Index

allow the pilot to easily transition from one chart to the other.

The charts for a particular flight can be selected from an index on the front panel of any chart. (See Fig. 9-1.) The charts are printed front and back, with areas one and two printed on one chart, three and four on the next, etc.

ENROUTE AND AREA CHART SYMBOLS

Symbols used on NOS charts are explained in the legend which is on the front panel of each chart. Pilots should maintain a working knowledge of the symbology and periodically review the legend in order to stay abreast of changes that update and improve chart format. Throughout this portion of the text, common NOS chart symbols are described and illustrated.

NAVIGATION FACILITY SYMBOLS

The VOR symbol is depicted as a compass rose oriented to magnetic north. (See Fig. 9-2.) The center of the compass rose is a hexagon which shows where the station is located.

The symbol for a TACAN facility resembles a triangle with the points cut off. (See Fig. 9-3.) TACAN stations are normally, but not always, collocated with VOR facilities.

When a VOR and a TACAN are collocated, the facility is called a VORTAC. The symbol for this type of navigation aid is shown in figure 9-4.

NAVIGATION FACILITY BOX

Information in the facility box provides the pilot with the name of the facility, the frequency on which it transmits, and the three-letter and Morse code identifiers. The illustrated information facility box in figure 9-5 is a VORTAC. It lists the identifiers, the VOR frequency, and the TACAN channel. Civil radios utilize the VOR frequency for azimuth and DME; military radio equipment is designed to operate on the TACAN channel (in this case, 117).

On the NOS charts, all available communications frequencies, except 121.50 and 122.20 MHz, are listed above the facility box. A heavy-lined box indicates a flight service station. An "R" or "T" following the frequency denotes "receive only" or "transmit only" capability.

FIG.	DESCRIPTION	SYMBOL
9-2.	VOR Facility	
9-3.	TACAN Facility	△
9-4.	VORTAC Facility	
9-5.	Facility Box	122.6 122.35 122.1R DENVER DEN ⟷ 117.0 Chan 117
9-6.	Victor Airway VOR Radial	039
9-7.	Victor Airways	V-448 V-448 S

VICTOR AIRWAYS

The designated routes between VOR stations are marked as Victor airways. These airways are formed by the VOR facilities and are designated as radials outbound from the VORs. This radial is the angle measured from *magnetic north* clockwise to the airway. In figure 9-6, the outbound radial is 039°.

Victor airways are marked with a number that indicates their general direction. (See Fig. 9-7.) Even-numbered airways usually are oriented in an east-west direction while odd-numbered airways are oriented in a north-south direction. In the example, V-448 is an east-west airway.

There are two classifications of airways on enroute charts. One is the primary airway and the other is an alternate. Alternate airways are used to provide a means of routing aircraft around areas of heavy traffic. They are marked by the addition of a letter suffix that denotes the general position of the alternate in relation to the primary airway. In the example, V-448S is south of V-448.

Airways normally extend four nautical miles each side of centerline and provide the pilot a total airway width of eight nautical miles. (See Fig. 9-8.) This holds true until a point 51 nautical miles from the navaid is reached. When the airway extends beyond 51 miles from the nearest navaid, it includes the airspace between lines diverging at angles of 4.5° from the centerline of each airway and extending until they intersect the diverging lines from the other navigational aid.

MILEAGE NUMBERS

All mileage numbers on enroute charts are expressed in nautical miles. The mileage number *enclosed* within an outlined box indicates mileage between VORs or between a VOR and a compulsory reporting point. (See Fig. 9-9.) A mileage number that is *not enclosed* in an outline box indicates the mileage between intersections, navigation aids, or mileage breakdown points.

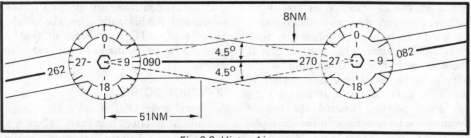

Fig. 9-8. Victor Airways

FIG.	DESCRIPTION	SYMBOL
9-9.	Mileage Numbers	[102] **V-448** 20
9-10.	Mileage Breakdown	⟋ ×
9-11.	Intersection	YUBIC
9-12.	Intersection — VOR Radial	RIDDY △ —214

MILEAGE BREAKDOWN

The mileage breakdown is shown on enroute charts by a small "x" on the airway. (See Fig. 9-10.) Generally, this symbol indicates the airway course change at a place where an intersection name is not provided. This small "x" must not be confused with the "x" enclosed in a flag on NOS charts. The flag-enclosed "x" on NOS charts signifies a minimum crossing altitude, which will be explained later.

INTERSECTIONS

Intersections are checkpoints on the airways which provide air traffic control definite positions to use in checking the progress of an aircraft. (See Fig. 9-11.) They are often located at points where the airway turns and the pilot needs a positive means to establish position. For ease of identification, intersections generally are named after cities and towns that are in close proximity.

The actual location of an intersection is based on the intersection of two VOR radials; however, other navaids also may be used, such as a localizer or nondirectional beacon. (See Fig. 9-12.) If there is any doubt concerning which navaid forms the intersection, an arrow is placed next to the intersection with the stem pointing toward the navaid forming the intersection. In the example, the Riddy Intersection is established by

the 214° radial of the Berkshire VOR and the airway radial.

An intersection that is defined by DME is depicted by an open arrow. (See Fig. 9-13.) These arrows are located near and point to the intersection. The mileage from the navaid to the first intersection is found along the airway and is the standard mileage number.

When not otherwise obvious, mileage between points is encircled by a letter "D" with an indicating arrow. This represents cumulative distance to the fix identified by the arrow. (See Fig. 9-14.)

FIG.	DESCRIPTION	SYMBOL
9-13.	Intersection — DME	△
9-14.	DME Mileage	[23]

Intersections are designated as either compulsory or noncompulsory reporting points. Compulsory reporting points require position reports; noncompulsory reporting points require reports only upon request from air traffic control.

Compulsory reporting points are identified by a *solid triangle*. A pilot passing over a compulsory reporting point must furnish ATC with a position report. However, a position report need not be made if ATC advises that radar contact is established. The pilot must resume normal position reporting if ATC advises *radar contact lost or radar service terminated*.

Noncompulsory reporting points are identified by an *open triangle*. These reporting points can become compulsory if the ATC controller so specifies in the clearance. Additionally, as the flight progresses, ATC may request that a position report be made at any specified point.

CONTROL ZONES

A control zone depicted on a chart may actually be in effect less than 24 hours a day. The control zones that have specific hours of operation are noted on the chart in the vicinity of that control zone. (See Fig. 9-15.)

When special VFR is not authorized within a specific control zone, it is shown with a series of the letter "T" surrounding the control zone. (See Fig. 9-16.)

FIG.	DESCRIPTION	SYMBOL
9-15.	*Control Zone Effective Times*	CONTROL ZONE EFFECTIVE 1500-0700Z‡
9-16.	*Control Zone — No Special VFR*	
9-17.	*Nondirectional Radio Beacon*	
9-18.	*NDB Facility Box*	LOM JEEP IA :– 383
9-19.	*Fan Marker*	

NONDIRECTIONAL RADIO BEACONS

The nondirectional radio beacon (NDB) is a low frequency navaid which may be used for instrument approaches. (See Fig. 9-17.) When the NDB is used as a navaid collocated with a marker beacon in the instrument landing system, it is called a *compass locator*. When it is combined with an outer marker, it is called an LOM, or outer compass locator. In combination with a middle marker, it is called an LMM, or middle compass locator. Combined facilities are clearly identified on instrument charts.

The name, frequency, and identification code of an NDB are provided in an adjacent facility grouping. (See Fig. 9-18.) On NOS charts, an underlined frequency indicates that no voice communications are available on that frequency.

FAN MARKERS

A fan marker, shown in figure 9-19, is a beacon that broadcasts a continuous

signal on 75 MHz. Originally, fan markers were used as distance markers with the low frequency airway system. This airway system has now been phased out; however, there are still a few fan markers in use on the Victor airways.

The outer marker (OM) and the middle marker (MM) beacons use the same symbols; however, they are smaller than fan marker symbols. They also broadcast on 75 MHz and are used as fixes during instrument approaches.

INSTRUMENT LANDING SYSTEMS

An instrument landing system (ILS) is depicted on enroute charts by a localizer symbol. (See Fig. 9-20.) A miniature symbol is utilized if the localizer is not used to form an enroute fix or airway. A localizer that is used as an enroute fix for an airway or an enroute portion of the airway is depicted with a large localizer symbol feathered on the right side. On NOS charts, a frequency is provided only for those ILS systems used to form an enroute fix or airway.

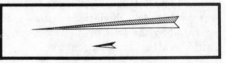

Fig. 9-20. ILS

COMMERCIAL BROADCAST STATIONS

Selected commercial broadcast stations are also included on enroute charts. (See Fig. 9-21.) These stations can be used as navigation aids by aircraft equipped with ADF receivers. Since commercial broadcast stations do not transmit a continuous identification, they are often difficult to identify.

HOLDING PATTERNS

A holding pattern symbol printed at a navaid depicts the preferred holding pattern to be used at that point. If the clearance limit is to an intersection with a holding pattern symbol shown, ATC expects the pilot to enter the pattern depicted unless instructed differently. (See Fig. 9-22.)

FIG.	DESCRIPTION	SYMBOL
9-21.	Commercial Broadcast Station	⊙
9-22.	Holding Pattern	

MINIMUM ENROUTE ALTITUDE

The minimum enroute altitude (MEA) is usually the lowest altitude a pilot can fly during a cross-country flight. The hemispheric rule for IFR flight specified in the FARs applies to flight in *uncontrolled* airspace. IFR altitudes for flight in controlled airspace are specified by ATC. Most pilots file IFR altitudes above the MEA which agree with the hemispheric rule. ATC usually assigns even-thousand foot altitudes for westbound flights below 18,000 feet MSL (4,000, 6,000, 8,000, etc.) and odd-thousand foot altitudes for eastbound flights (3,000, 5,000, 7,000, etc.). However, altitude deviations may be requested by the pilot or ATC because of traffic, weather, or other reasons.

The obstruction clearance altitude guaranteed by the MEA is 1,000 feet above the highest obstacle within five statute miles of the airway centerline in non-mountainous terrain. In mountainous terrain, the MEA provides an obstacle clearance criteria of 2,000 feet above the highest obstacle within five statute miles of centerline. MEA obstruction clearance is illustrated in figure 9-23.

In addition to obstruction clearance, the minimum enroute altitude also guarantees reception of a navigation signal at any point along the airway. The pilot flying at or above the minimum enroute altitude can be assured that proper terrain clearance and usable navigational signals are available.

On NOS charts the MEA is shown above the airway centerline. It is often the first of the two altitudes listed or, if only one is shown, it is the MEA. (See Fig. 9-24.)

MINIMUM OBSTRUCTION CLEARANCE ALTITUDE

The minimum obstruction clearance altitude (MOCA) is identified by an asterisk, as shown in figure 9-25. MOCA guarantees the same terrain clearance as does the MEA. The major difference between the two altitudes is that MOCA assures a reliable navigation signal only within 22 nautical miles of the VOR facility; conversely, the MEA guarantees reliable navigation signals throughout the segment, as shown in figure 9-26.

FIG.	DESCRIPTION	SYMBOL
9-24.	Minimum Enroute Altitude	4000 △
9-25.	Minimum Obstruction Clearance Altitude	4000 *3600

When an aircraft is flying more than 22 nautical miles from the VOR station at the MOCA, adequate terrain clearance is

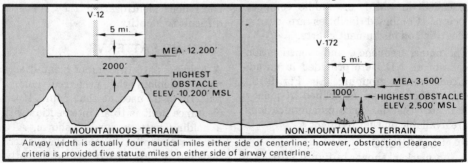

Fig. 9-23. Minimum Enroute Altitude

Airway width is actually four nautical miles either side of centerline; however, obstruction clearance criteria is provided five statute miles on either side of airway centerline.

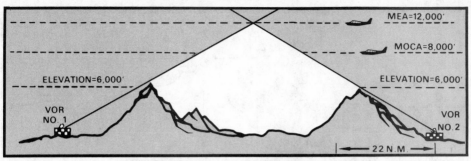

Fig. 9-26. Minimum Obstruction Clearance Altitude

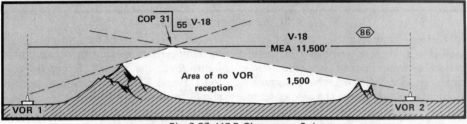

Fig. 9-27. VOR Changeover Point

assured. However, the altitude is not sufficient to receive line-of-sight transmissions from the VOR facility and to navigate on the airway. MOCA may be used during an emergency. It may also be used if the pilot is within 22 miles of the VOR and has either an approach clearance or cruise clearance.

CHANGEOVER POINT

Normally, the pilot on an IFR cross-country flight will change frequencies midway between the navigation aids. However, if a pilot is flying outbound from VOR 1, as shown in figure 9-27, the navigation signals cannot be received beyond a certain point so a changeover point (COP) is indicated.

These changeover points, shown as nautical miles to or from the navigation aids, indicate at which point the pilot should change frequencies to ensure a usable navigation signal throughout the entire course. (See Fig. 9-28.) If the pilot does not change from one VOR station to another at the proper changeover point, a weak signal or erratic indications on the VOR may result.

CHANGE IN MEA

On enroute charts, a bar crossing the airway at an intersection indicates a change in MEA. (See Fig. 9-29.) On the NOS charts it may also indicate a change in MOCA or maximum authorized altitude (MAA). A pilot should compare MEAs and MOCAs along the route or look for a maximum authorized altitude to determine the basis for change.

MINIMUM CROSSING ALTITUDE

The minimum crossing altitude (MCA) is an obstruction clearance requirement for crossing certain fixes. The MCA is determined by the MOCA of the route segment being flown and the locations of obstacles along the route. Because the mountain in figure 9-30 is situated very close to the Zambi Intersection, it is apparent that the pilot must climb soon enough to *cross* Zambi Intersection at or above the MCA (7,800 feet) when flying eastbound.

FIG.	DESCRIPTION	SYMBOL
9-28.	VOR Changeover Point	44 / 57
9-29.	MEA Change	⊢ △ ⊢

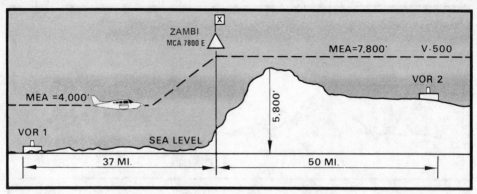

Fig. 9-30. Minimum Crossing Altitude

In certain circumstances, the MCA is used to guarantee reception of navigation signals instead of obstruction clearance. An MCA may be designated at an intersection where the airway turns and has a large change in MEA between the route segments. The pilot flying onto the route segment with the higher MEA will have to cross the intersection at an altitude high enough to ensure a usable navigation signal.

The MCA is shown on enroute charts by an information grouping that provides the intersection or VOR name, the Victor airway number, the change in altitude required, and the direction of flight for which the change must be made. As shown in figure 9-31, a flag containing an "x" originating from the intersection or VOR indicates a minimum crossing altitude. In this case, the MCA is indicated adjacent to the flag.

MINIMUM RECEPTION ALTITUDE

The minimum reception altitude (MRA) is the lowest altitude which will ensure

adequate reception of navigation signals forming an intersection or other fix. In figure 9-32, the aircraft flying between VOR 1 and VOR 2 can receive a good signal from these VORs at the MEA of 3,000 feet; however, since VOR 3 is located behind the mountains, the aircraft must be at a higher altitude in order to receive VOR 3 and make a positive identification of the fix. The MRA ensures reception of navigation signals, not terrain clearance. The MRA is used *only* if it is above the MEA.

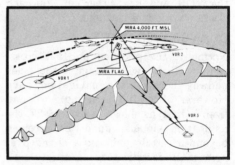

Fig. 9-32. Minimum Reception Altitude

NOS charts show an MRA by an "R" enclosed in a flag. The altitude is included in the associated information grouping. (See Fig. 9-33.)

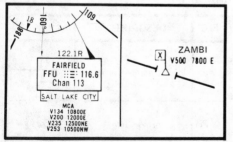

Fig. 9-31. MCA Information

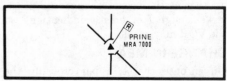

Fig. 9-33. Minimum Reception Altitude

The MRA is of importance when a position report is required over an intersection with a published MRA. When the reporting point is noncompulsory, the pilot need only be concerned with the MRA when using the reporting point as a means of establishing position.

MAXIMUM AUTHORIZED ALTITUDE

The maximum authorized altitude (MAA) is based on the transmitting distance of VOR stations which are on the same frequency. Since there are only 160 frequencies for VOR transmitters, there is a necessity for duplication of frequencies. The MAA is established when the distance between two VOR stations on the same frequency is such that both signals can be received at the same time and, therefore, give the pilot an unreliable navigation signal. This is illustrated in figure 9-34.

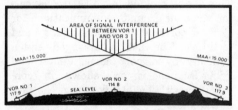

Fig. 9-34. Maximum Authorized Altitude

The MAA is shown along the airways on the charts with the letters MAA followed by the altitude. Unless the MAA is shown on the chart, VOR stations transmitting on the same frequency are located far enough apart to ensure against a reception problem.

AIR ROUTE TRAFFIC CONTROL CENTER REMOTE SITES

The air route traffic control center (ARTCC) remote radio site information box informs the pilot that Seattle Center can be contacted through a remote antenna located near the city of Redmond. (See Fig. 9-35.) Each air route traffic control center has certain frequencies for communication between

air traffic control personnel and IFR pilots operating in the general vicinity of the center. Additionally, certain remote station sites have been set up throughout the various sectors of each center. These remote sites provide adequate communication throughout the area served by the center.

The information for center communications is printed in a remote site box. It contains the associated VHF and UHF discrete frequencies used for that sector of the center.

The division line between air route traffic control centers is designated by an irregular line. (See Fig. 9-36.) The name of the controlling center is printed on its respective side.

FIG.	DESCRIPTION	SYMBOL
9-35.	ARTCC Remote Site	SEATTLE (REDMOND) 120.9 307.1
9-36.	ARTCC Boundary	SEATTLE HARROLL

SPECIAL USE AIRSPACE

Due to hazards or special activities, special use airspace is designated and identified as either restricted, prohibited, warning, alert, or military operations areas. (See Fig. 9-37.) All areas are defined by a blue border except an MOA which is outlined in brown.

The charts show the following information in or near the special use airspace.

1. Area boundary
2. Altitudes affected
3. Operating times when operation is other than continuous
4. Weather conditions if used only during IFR or VFR
5. Name of the controlling agency if air/ground communications are available

DESCRIPTION	SYMBOL
Restricted Area	R-2712 TO UNL HARROLL CENTER/FSS
Prohibited Area	P-2712 TO UNL HARROLL CENTER/FSS
Warning Area	W-2712 TO UNL HARROLL CENTER/FSS
Military Operations Area	KING MOA 12000 AND ABOVE 1300-0200Z MON.- FRI.
Military Training Route (IR/VR)	—— IR 276 ——→ ←—— VR 284 ——

Fig. 9-37. Special Use Airspace

FIG.	DESCRIPTION	SYMBOL
9-38.	Isogonic Line	
9-39.	Time Zone Boundaries	Eastern Std / Central Std. +5 = GMT / +6 = GMT

MILITARY TRAINING ROUTES

Military training routes, or MTRs, are classified as either visual (VR) or instrument (IR). VR indicates VFR flight only, and IR means the route may be used in VFR or IFR conditions. These routes extend from the surface to above 18,000 feet MSL, but they are usually concentrated below 10,000 feet. MTR segments are now depicted on enroute charts (See Fig. 9-37.)

Information concerning military training flights on MTRs is available from the nearest FSS within 200 miles. It is a good practice to check activity with flight service before transiting MTRs.

ISOGONIC LINES

Magnetic variation in an area is shown on the *edge* of the charts. There is a small line originating at the periphery of the chart with the variation in degrees printed at the border of the chart. (See Fig. 9-38.)

TIME ZONE BOUNDARIES

Boundaries between time zones are shown on NOS charts as a dotted line. The time zone and the conversion data are indicated next to the dotted line. (See Fig. 9-39.)

COMMUNICATIONS FREQUENCIES

Part of the frequencies available for air/ground communications are listed on the front panel of the enroute charts. This listing includes all ATC frequencies for voice air/ground communications for civil airports with terminal air/ground facilities. The list is arranged alphabetically by airport name. Center and FSS frequencies are shown in conjunction with facility boxes on the face of the chart.

As an ATC controller "hands off" the instrument flight to the next controller, the pilot is advised of the frequency to use. However, it will aid the pilot to know what frequency to expect and what additional frequencies may be required. The enroute charts are updated frequently, so the current chart should have the correct frequency.

AERODROME SYMBOLS

Aerodrome symbols are divided into two basic categories — those aerodromes with a published instrument approach procedure and those without such a procedure. Airports with an instrument approach procedure are printed in blue; airports without an instrument approach procedure are printed in brown.

SECTION B — SID, STAR, AND APPROACH CHARTS

Standard instrument departures (SIDs), standard terminal arrival routes (STARs), and profile descent procedures are used where complex air traffic conditions exist. Normally, these procedures are implemented to enhance safety and expedite the flow of arriving or departing traffic. However, fuel conservation and noise abatement are other considerations. Possession of the appropriate chart, or at least a textual description, allows the pilot to file, accept, or fly a given procedure.

SID SYMBOLOGY

Figure 9-40 illustrates the format used most frequently on SID charts published by NOS. Typical information elements are described by the numbered callouts.

❶ NOS indexes its charts according to the airport name in a separate book which contains only SIDs.

❷ This item refers to the actual name of the departure. In this case, the SID is the Manta One Departure. Usually, SIDs are named in reference to a specific landmark, town, intersection, navaid, or prominent area. In addition, if the SID contains transitions, the three-letter grouping (HTO or ACK) identifies the fix from which the transitions begin.

❸ Each chart gives a textual description of the departure, including any transition routes that may be used when flying the SID. The specific SID procedure depends on what runway is used for takeoff; thus, the textual description is arranged by runways.

❹ The chart depicts the primary departure route with a heavy dark arrow, and the transition route with a thin-lined arrow. The names of the transition routes are not always identified outside the narrative on NOS charts.

Transition routes provide a departure route from the final SID fix to the enroute course. They are referred to by means of a code when filing a flight plan. For example, a pilot using the Manta One Departure and the Hampton Transition would use the following code when filing the flight plan: MANTA 1.HTO. This code is comprised of acronyms and identifiers for the SID and terminating facility.

❺ Appropriate navaid frequency information is provided to satisfy SID requirements.

❻ This item refers to the magnetic course needed to track to the turning point between Casvi and Manta Intersections. Also included is the distance, in nautical miles. The turning point at Manta Intersection is identified by the 122° radial of Robinsville VORTAC and the 059° radial of Sea Isle VORTAC. The indicated DME mileage may also be used.

❼ Airways are depicted when appropriate. In this case, the Victor airway, V-139, and the overlying Jet airway, J-121, are shown.

❽ The frequencies used for departure are published by NOS on the SID charts.

❾ A mandatory altitude is indicated by a line above and below the specified figure. Minimum altitudes have a line below the altitude and maximum altitudes have a line above the altitude.

❿ An airport diagram is included in the lower right corner of the chart.

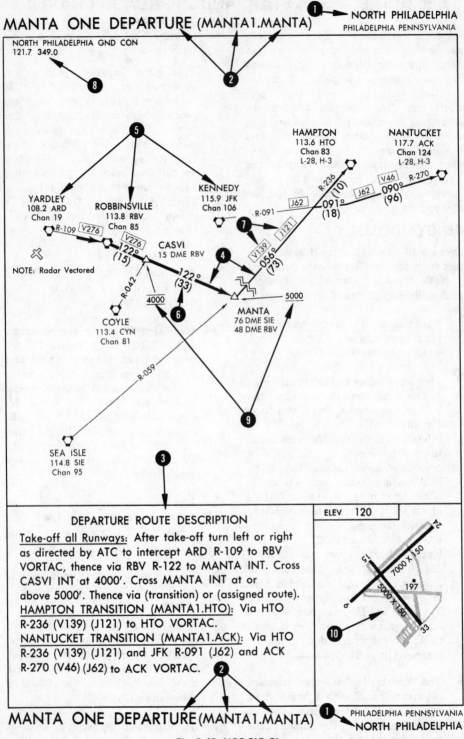

MANTA ONE DEPARTURE (MANTA1.MANTA)

DEPARTURE ROUTE DESCRIPTION

<u>Take-off all Runways:</u> After take-off turn left or right as directed by ATC to intercept ARD R-109 to RBV VORTAC, thence via RBV R-122 to MANTA INT. Cross CASVI INT at 4000'. Cross MANTA INT at or above 5000'. Thence via (transition) or (assigned route).

<u>HAMPTON TRANSITION (MANTA1.HTO):</u> Via HTO R-236 (V139) (J121) to HTO VORTAC.

<u>NANTUCKET TRANSITION (MANTA1.ACK):</u> Via HTO R-236 (V139) (J121) and JFK R-091 (J62) and ACK R-270 (V46) (J62) to ACK VORTAC.

MANTA ONE DEPARTURE (MANTA1.MANTA)

Fig. 9-40. NOS SID Chart

The diagram shows elevation data, shape, and dimensions. Control tower position and elevation is indicated in this example by the dark square.

Occasionally, SIDs have a climb restriction. When this is the case, aircraft performance must comply with the SID climb requirements or the SID cannot be used. Speed restrictions, if applicable, are described in the textual portion of the SID chart.

STAR SYMBOLOGY

In most respects, STAR charts are the same as SIDs in terms of method of routing and symbology. Figure 9-41 illustrates an NOS STAR chart.

❶ Minimum enroute altitudes and mileages may be indicated on STAR routes. The pilot should be cautioned that these MEAs are not to be used unless cleared by ATC. MEAs are occasionally found on SID charts as well as on STAR charts. The same limitations apply to both.

❷ Mileage breaks are indicated on the NOS STAR charts, but are not shown on the NOS SID charts.

❸ The transition routing is listed in a manner similar to that found on SID charts. For example, if a pilot files for the Maxon Transition to Houston Intercontinental Airport, this request should be noted on the flight plan. The following entry should be made after the enroute segment: MAXON.DAS2

❹ The STAR terminates at Innis Intersection. After departing this intersection on a heading of 260°, the pilot can expect radar vectors to the final approach course.

PROFILE DESCENTS

Profile descents are instrument procedures similar to STARs to facilitate the transition from the IFR enroute portion of the flight to an arrival segment. These procedures are designed to reduce low-altitude flying time of high performance aircraft, including turbojet and any turboprop aircraft weighing over 12,500 pounds.

Basically, the profile descent is an uninterrupted descent from cruising altitude to interception of a minimum altitude specified for the initial or intermediate segment of an instrument approach, based on descending at approximately 300 feet per nautical mile from cruise altitude. When crossing altitudes and speed restrictions are listed, ATC expects the pilot to descend to the crossing altitude first and then reduce speed. All pilots receiving a profile descent clearance are expected to advise ATC if they do not have a profile descent on board or cannot comply with procedures.

The profile descent clearance does not constitute a clearance to fly the complete instrument approach procedure. The last "maintain altitude" specified in the procedure, or the last altitude assigned by ATC, is the clearance limit. Pilots should review runway profile descent charts before flights into airports with charted procedures.

APPROACH CHARTS

Approach charts provide the pilot with detailed information regarding prescribed instrument procedures, appropriate radio frequencies, airport data, local terrain, and other items pertinent to the approach being shown. A legend in the front of each book shows the symbols and abbreviations used, along with a brief explanation of each.

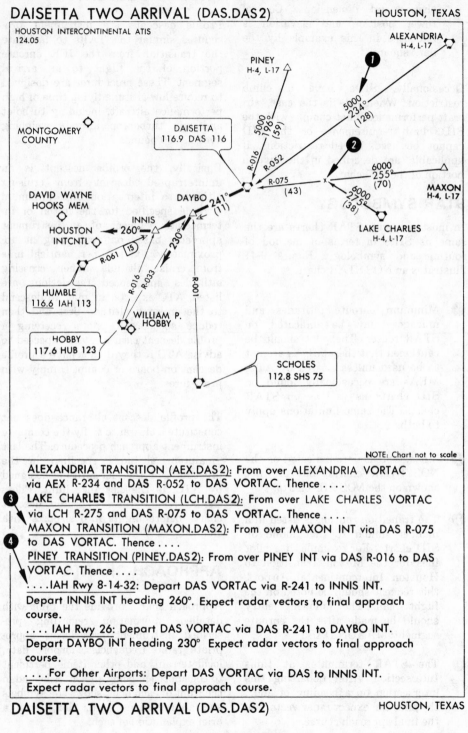

DAISETTA TWO ARRIVAL (DAS.DAS 2)   HOUSTON, TEXAS

ALEXANDRIA TRANSITION (AEX.DAS 2): From over ALEXANDRIA VORTAC via AEX R-234 and DAS R-052 to DAS VORTAC. Thence . . . .

LAKE CHARLES TRANSITION (LCH.DAS 2): From over LAKE CHARLES VORTAC via LCH R-275 and DAS R-075 to DAS VORTAC. Thence . . . .

MAXON TRANSITION (MAXON.DAS 2): From over MAXON INT via DAS R-075 to DAS VORTAC. Thence . . . .

PINEY TRANSITION (PINEY.DAS 2): From over PINEY INT via DAS R-016 to DAS VORTAC. Thence . . . .

. . . .**IAH Rwy 8-14-32:** Depart DAS VORTAC via R-241 to INNIS INT. Depart INNIS INT heading 260°. Expect radar vectors to final approach course.

. . . . **IAH Rwy 26:** Depart DAS VORTAC via DAS R-241 to DAYBO INT. Depart DAYBO INT heading 230° Expect radar vectors to final approach course.

. . . .**For Other Airports:** Depart DAS VORTAC via DAS to INNIS INT. Expect radar vectors to final approach course.

DAISETTA TWO ARRIVAL (DAS.DAS2)   HOUSTON, TEXAS

Fig. 9-41. NOS STAR Chart

There is a total of 15 volumes, or booklets, covering the continental United States. The area of coverage and effective dates for each are clearly indicated on the cover, as shown in figure 9-42.

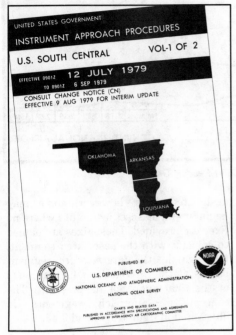

Fig. 9-42. NOS Approach Charts

FORMAT

The NOS approach chart consists of a heading group, communications group, approach plan view, approach profile view, landing minimums, notes and cautions, and an airport plan view. These are all contained on a single page.

HEADING AND BORDER DATA

This information is split on the NOS chart; some of the information appears at the top of the page and some appears at the bottom. The callout numbers which follow refer to the chart excerpt shown in figure 9-43.

❶   Geographic Name

❷   Name of Airport

❸   The code number which appears on the NOS charts refers to the FAA airport designation only. All of the charts for a given airport will have the same number.

❹   Name of Procedure

❺   Approach Control Frequency —
At some airports, different frequencies are assigned to different sectors. In this case, only two frequencies are given. The first is the VHF frequency and the second figure shown is a UHF frequency which is primarily used by the military.

❻   Tower Frequency —
The first frequency is the primary VHF tower frequency — 118.7 MHz. The second frequency listed in this example, 258.7 MHz, is a common tower frequency normally used for communications with military aircraft.

❼   Ground Control Frequencies

❽   Clearance Delivery Frequency

❾   Radar Services Available —
When ASR appears, it indicates that both radar vectoring and ASR instrument approaches are available.

❿   Automatic Terminal Information Service —
The automatic terminal information service (ATIS) is a transcribed advisory which presents traffic information and existing weather and field conditions. The information is transmitted continuously and updated as necessary by the tower or approach control.

⓫   Latitude and Longitude —
This is the precise geographic latitude and longitude of the air-

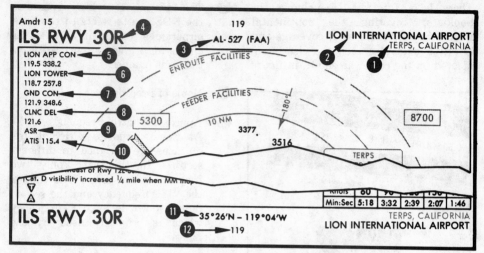

Fig. 9-43. Approach Chart Heading Group

port. The information is used primarily by pilots flying aircraft with inertial or light weight navigation equipment.

12 Page Number

APPROACH SEGMENTS

An instrument approach procedure may be divided into as many as four separate segments — *initial, intermediate, final,* and *missed approach.* Approach segments usually begin and end at designated fixes; however, some may begin or end at specified points where no fixes are provided. These fixes are named to coincide with the associated segment; for example, the *intermediate* segment begins at the *intermediate* fix and ends at the final approach fix or point. The concept of approach segments is illustrated in figures 9-44 and 9-45.

FEEDER ROUTES

Feeder (terminal) routes are given in the approach plan view to provide for

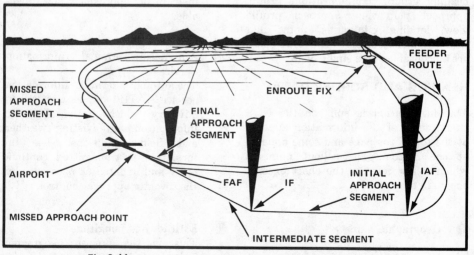

Fig. 9-44. Approach Segment Designation — No Procedure Turn

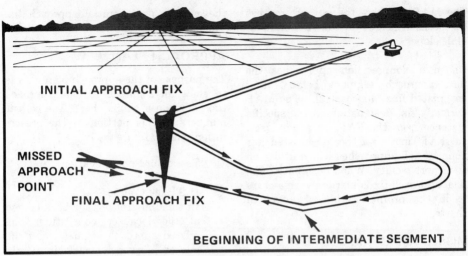

Fig. 9-45. Approach Segment Designation — With Procedure Turn

navigation from the enroute structure to initial approach fixes. They terminate with a prominent arrowhead. Altitude, course, and distance are shown from each enroute fix to its respective initial approach fix.

INITIAL APPROACH SEGMENT

The *initial approach segment* may be made along an arc, radial, course, heading, radar vector, or a combination of any of these. Procedure turns, holding pattern descents, and high altitude jet penetrations are initial approach segments.

More than one initial approach may be established for a given approach procedure, depending on the direction from which the aircraft is approaching the airport. Minimum altitudes may be prescribed for the initial approach segment and shown on the approach chart; however, the altitudes assigned by ATC for a given approach must be followed.

Sometimes the initial approach fix is collocated with the final approach fix. This is the case with the NDB approach shown in figure 9-45. The initial approach segment begins when the aircraft passes the nondirectional beacon outbound; it continues through the proce-

dure turn and terminates as the aircraft intercepts the approach course inbound.

INTERMEDIATE SEGMENT

The *intermediate segment* begins at an intermediate fix (IF) and ends at the final approach fix (FAF). It may consist of a radial, course, or arc. Its function is to connect the initial approach segment with the final approach segment. The intermediate segment course must not vary from the final approach course by more than 30°. The intermediate segment, shown in figure 9-45, begins at the completion of the procedure turn and ends at the final approach fix. The intermediate segment is not utilized for on-airport facilities when a final approach fix is not designated.

It is desirable to cross the final approach fix completely ready for the landing. Therefore, such items as adjustments in course and speed and the completion of the prelanding checklist must be accomplished during the intermediate approach segment.

FINAL APPROACH SEGMENT

The final approach segment of a precision approach extends from the point of glide slope interception to the runway or missed approach point (MAP).

The MAP is where the aircraft reaches the decision height on the ILS or radar glide slope.

On most nonprecision approaches the final approach segment begins at a designated final approach fix. The MAP normally is designated at a specific distance from the FAF. In some cases, an FAF may not be designated for nonprecision approaches which utilize an on-airport facility. When designated, the final approach fix is marked with a *cross* ✚ in the profile section of approach charts.

MISSED APPROACH SEGMENT

The *missed approach segment* begins at the missed approach point and ends at the enroute fix or initial approach fix. This segment is illustrated in figure 9-44.

APPROACH PLAN VIEW

The purpose of the approach plan view is to show all segments of the approach procedure on a single chart. The callout numbers in this portion of the presentation refer to figure 9-46.

❶ Terrain or Spot Elevation

❷ ILS Back Course —
In this illustration, the back course of the localizer consititutes the missed approach segment, and the missed approach track is nearly straight ahead. If the missed approach procedure provides for

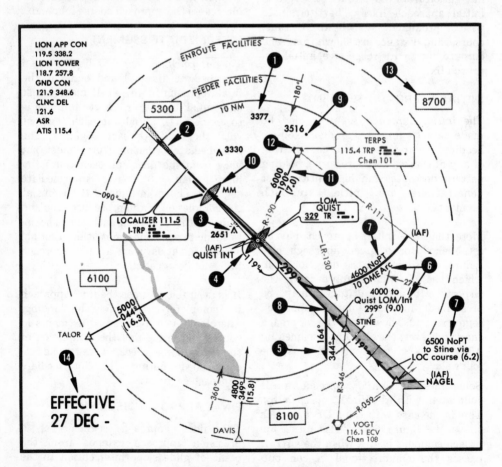

Fig. 9-46. NOS Approach Plan View

divergence from the back course ILS, the missed approach track will be shown by a dashed arrow curving in the direction specified by the procedure. NOS shows *all* missed approach tracks by a series of dashes in the direction in which the missed approach is to be made.

❸ Man-made Obstruction

❹ Outer Marker and Outer Compass Locator —
This may be the initial approach fix as well as the final approach fix.

NOTE:

It is the final approach fix only when the aircraft is aligned within 30° of the final approach course.

---

❺ Procedure Turn —
When the procedure turn is depicted with a barb, as in this example, the pilot may reverse course in any way desired as long as the procedure is executed on the same side of the approach course indicated by the barb. Should the course reversal be diagrammed as a racetrack or teardrop pattern, the indicated procedure is mandatory. The procedure turn constitutes an initial approach segment terminating at the point where the aircraft intercepts the approach course inbound, as previously shown in figure 9-45. The intermediate segment begins at this point and terminates at the final approach fix.

❻ Feeder Routes to Final Approach Course —
These routes provide for transition from the enroute phase to the approach phase.

❼ NoPT —
This indicates no procedure turn is

to be executed unless permission is issued by ATC.

❽ Beginning of Intermediate Segment —
Interception of the approach course inbound constitutes the beginning of the intermediate segment when the procedure turn is used.

❾ Highest Obstacle Charted —
The highest obstacle is identified by a larger dot in the obstruction symbol and by printing the elevation in heavier type than that used for other obstructions.

❿ Middle Marker —
The middle marker is placed approximately 3,500 feet from the runway threshold and is depicted with a fan-shaped symbol on the plan view. The middle marker is located near the missed approach point on Category I ILS approaches. It should be understood that the missed approach point on ILS approaches is determined by the decision height and not the middle marker.

⓫ Feeder (Terminal) Route to Outer Marker Initial Approach Fix —
A procedure turn is required upon arrival at the outer marker.

⓬ VORTAC —
On this approach, the VORTAC is the beginning of the feeder route. The facility provides for navigation from the enroute structure to the initial approach fix.

⓭ Minimum Sector Altitude —
In an emergency situation within 25 nautical miles of the Quist outer compass locator, the lowest altitude a pilot should fly between the 180° and 270° bearing to the Quist LOM is 8,700 feet MSL. Arrows on the distance circle identify sectors.

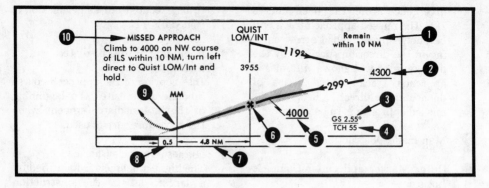

Fig. 9-47. Approach Profile Views

14 Effective Date —
When the effective date is different than the effective date of the book, it is indicated on the chart.

APPROACH PROFILE VIEW

The approach profile view shows the segments of the approach with particular emphasis on altitudes at various points along the approaches. The numbered callouts in the following text correspond with those in figure 9-47.

1 Distance —
This is the distance within which the procedure turn must be completed.

2 Procedure Turn Altitude —
A line under the altitude indicates a minimum altitude and a line above the altitude indicates a maximum altitude. Mandatory altitudes are indicated by lines above and below.

3 Glide Slope Angle —
The projected path of the glide slope above the horizontal is normally 3°. Thus, the illustrated angle is relatively shallow.

4 Threshold Crossing Height —
This is the height of the glide slope at the point where it crosses the runway threshold.

5 Glide Slope Interception Altitude—
This altitude will be different than the FAF crossing altitude when the glide slope is intercepted before reaching the FAF.

6 Final Approach Fix —
When flying on the glide slope shown in the example, the pilot will cross the FAF at 3,955 feet MSL. The FAF is identified by a cross.

7 Distance —
This is the distance between the outer marker and middle marker.

8 Middle Marker —
The distance shown is the distance of the middle marker from the runway threshold.

9 Missed Approach Point for Category I ILS

10 Narrative of Missed Approach Procedure

TAKEOFF MINIMUMS

Statistics show that aircraft malfunctions are more likely to occur at the beginning of a flight than at any other time. For this reason, the FAA has established rules which provide takeoff minimums for aircraft operated under FAR Parts 121, 123, 129, and 135. These rules provide for return to the departure airport or flight to another nearby airport should difficulties occur immediately after takeoff. These rules do not specifically apply to aircraft operating under FAR Part 91; however, commonsense and good judgment both suggest that all pilots should comply with these minimums.

The standard takeoff minimum for aircraft with two engines or less is one statute mile visibility. For aircraft with more than two engines, the minimum is one-half statute mile visibility.

If other than standard minimums are established at an airport, the symbol ▼ will appear in the information box at the bottom of the chart. This indicates the pilot must consult the tabulations of IFR takeoff minimums which accompany the NOS approach chart.

LANDING MINIMUMS

Minimums have been established for each approach procedure by the FAA. These minimums vary from airport to airport because of the existence of obstacles within the approach or missed approach path, lighting aids, and the number of radio approach aids operating at any given time.

Unless the pilot has *visual contact* with the *runway environment* upon arriving at the missed approach point (MAP), a missed approach is *mandatory*. The runway environment may be defined as the runway itself, any lighting associated with the runway, or the approach path. Minimums are shown on the front side of each approach chart, as in figure 9-48. These minimums apply only to the approach pictured.

AIRCRAFT CATEGORIES

Different approach minimums are provided for different aircraft categories. Aircraft categories are based on aircraft approach speed and maximum certificated landing weight. Aircraft approach speed is established as 130

percent of the stall speed in the landing configuration at the maximum landing weight and is expressed as 1.3 times V_{SO}. Category A is the lowest category. If it is necessary to maneuver at speed in excess of a speed range for a given category, the minimums for the next higher category should be used. The aircraft categories are defined in the following table and listed across the top of the minimums box on NOS charts. (See Fig. 9-48, item 1.)

AIRCRAFT CATEGORY	SPEED
A	Less than 91 knots
B	91 knots or more but less than 121 knots
C	121 knots or more but less than 141 knots
D	141 knots or more but less than 166 knots
E	166 knots or more

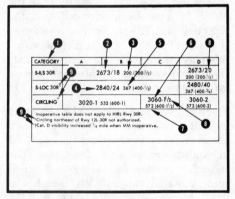

Fig. 9-48. Minimums Presentation

DESCENT LIMITS

Descent limits are minimum altitudes to which an aircraft may descend during an instrument approach while the pilot is referring solely to instrument references. For *precision approaches*, this altitude is called the *decision height* (DH) and is shown in the minimums presentation as an MSL altitude in bold type. (See Fig. 9-48, item 2.) The height above touchdown (HAT) is shown to the right of the visibility (item 3). At the DH on a precision approach, a pilot must *decide* whether to continue the approach to a landing by reference to *external visual cues* or to execute the missed approach procedure.

For nonprecision approaches, the descent limit is the *minimum descent altitude* (MDA). It is shown in bold type (item 4) as an MSL altitude. It is also shown for straight-in approaches as a height above touchdown (HAT) to the right of the visibility (item 5). Circling approaches are nonprecision approaches by definition. As such, the minimum altitudes are MDAs (item 6) which are expressed as a height above the airport (item 7).

VISIBILITY REQUIREMENTS

When the missed approach point (MAP) has been reached, the pilot must either proceed visually or execute a missed approach procedure. For this reason, visibility criteria have been established which *indicate* whether it will be possible for the pilot to proceed visually from the MAP. It must be understood that the reported visibility is only a *prediction* that the pilot will have sufficient visual reference to continue the approach since there is no way to guarantee this from a ground observation.

There are two methods used to measure visibility. One method utilizes a human observer. This measurement is reported in statute miles and fractions. The second is a more precise method called runway visual range (RVR) which utilizes electronic equipment to measure the opacity of the air along a runway. The RVR measurement is reported in hundreds of feet of horizontal visibility along the runway indicated. There is a possibility that both RVR and visibility may be reported at the same time. The visibility requirements for executing an approach are shown in figure 9-48, item 8.

INOPERATIVE COMPONENTS AND VISUAL AIDS

The listed minimums are for a normal approach with all of the ILS components and visual aids installed and operating. This condition allows the lowest possible minimums. Higher minimums apply when the required components or visual aids are inoperative. When using NOS charts, the pilot should check the notes (Fig. 9-48, item 9) or refer to the inoperative components or visual aids.

GROUNDSPEED/TIME/RATE-OF-DESCENT TABLES

Approach charts provide tables which show the time required to fly from the final approach fix (FAF) to the missed approach point (MAP) at various groundspeeds. For ILS approaches, this data is used when the electronic glide slope is not available. If this occurs, the approach becomes a nonprecision procedure, different minimums apply, and the pilot must determine the missed approach point by timing from the FAF.

The pilot must apply the headwind component to the approach airspeed to arrive at the approach groundspeed. By applying the approach groundspeed to the final approach distance, the pilot can determine the final approach time. A simple method of doing this is by using the timing table on the approach chart. For example, in the table in figure 9-49, time from the final approach fix to the missed approach point at a groundspeed of 90 knots is 3 minutes, 32 seconds. At a groundspeed of 120 knots, the time is 2 minutes, 39 seconds. If the groundspeed is determined to be 110 knots, the pilot must interpolate between the two time figures. At 110 knots, the time from the final approach fix to missed approach point will be approximately 2 minutes, 57 seconds.

FAF to MAP 5.3 NM				
Knots	60	90	120	150	180
Min:Sec	5:18	3:32	2:39	2:07	1:46

Fig. 9-49. Groundspeed/Time

In addition to timing tables, instrument approach books also contain a rate-of-descent table. The table is in the front of the book following the legend pages. It provides a rate of descent for various angles of descent and groundspeeds.

When the approach radio facility is located at the airport, no timing figure is provided within the table for non-precision approaches. This is because the missed approach point is designated by passing the station, rather than by timing the approach.

AIRPORT DIAGRAMS AND FACILITIES

The airport diagram is located on the face of each chart in the lower right-hand corner. The following items refer to figure 9-50.

❶ Airport Elevation

❷ Obstructions and Physical Features

❸ Runway Number to Nearest 10° Magnetic

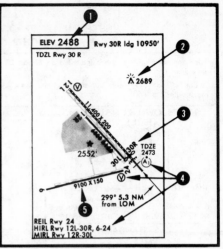

Fig. 9-50. Airport Diagrams and Facilities

❹ Approach Light Configuration

❺ Runway Length and Width

The symbols and explanations which appear on airport diagrams are shown in figure 9-51. Additionally, lighting symbols used on NOS charts are shown in figure 9-52.

JEPPESEN	NOS	DESCRIPTION
▭	▦	Unpaved runway
▬	▨	Pierced steel planking (PSP) or metal surface
= = ⊐	⦙⦙⦙⦙⦙	Runway under construction
✖	▭	Closed runway
▬⊐	■	Stopway or overrun
= = = ⊐	NO SYMBOL	Seaplane operating area
▬┣	▨	Displaced landing threshold
⌐┼┼┼─	NO SYMBOL	Approach lights extending to displaced landing threshold
▲ ⩕	Ⓗ	Helicopter landing pad
Control Tower 812′ (58′)	■	Control tower (NOS - When tower and rotating beacon are collocated, beacon symbol will be used with TWR indicated.)
⊛	☆	Rotating beacon
NO SYMBOL	0.8% UP	Total runway gradient (Shown when runway gradient exceeds 0.3%)

Fig. 9-51. Airport Diagram Symbols

LEGEND
INSTRUMENT APPROACH PROCEDURES (CHARTS)
APPROACH LIGHTING SYSTEMS – UNITED STATES

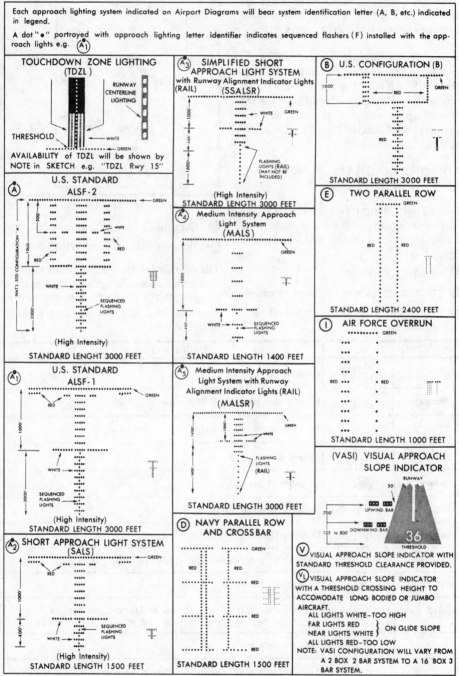

Each approach lighting system indicated on Airport Diagrams will bear system identification letter (A, B, etc.) indicated in legend.

A dot "•" portrayed with approach lighting letter identifier indicates sequenced flashers (F) installed with the approach lights e.g. (A₁)

8 MAR. 19

PUBLISHED BY NOS, NOAA, TO IACC SPECIFICATIONS

Fig. 9-52. NOS Approach Lighting Legend

SECTION C — JEPPESEN INSTRUMENT FLIGHT CHARTS

Currently, only knowledge of NOS charts is required for FAA written examinations. However, since Jeppesen charts contain additional data, and because most airlines, air taxi services, and commercial operators use Jeppesen charts, familiarity with both types is desirable. The remainder of this chapter contains a brief description of the Jeppesen charts. The discussion is oriented toward the format and symbology differences in the two products.

AVIGATION AND AREA CHARTS

Jeppesen enroute charts are usually called *avigation charts*. The term avigation (pertaining to navigation of airplanes), however, may be considered synonymous with enroute. An index of avigation charts (Fig. 9-53, item 1) and area charts (item 2) is printed on the cover panel of each chart. The distinctive symbols that are used on all Jeppesen charts are explained fully in the introductory section of the approach chart binder and briefly in this section.

NAVIGATION FACILITY SYMBOLS

The VOR symbol is a compass rose with a dot over the station location. An arrow, extending through magnetic north, is useful for plotting magnetic courses. (See Fig. 9-54.)

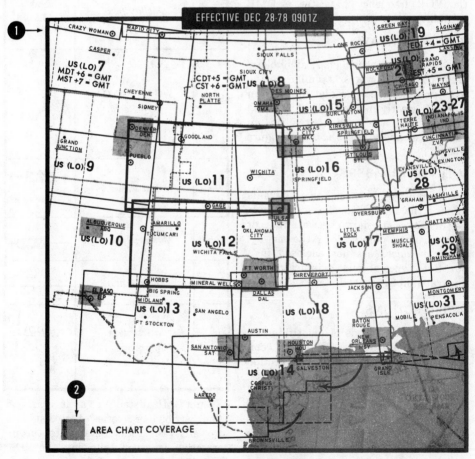

Fig. 9-53. Enroute and Area Charts

A TACAN facility (see Fig. 9-55) is symbolized by a circle with a serrated edge. When the TACAN facility is collocated with a VOR, a VORTAC facility is indicated. (See Fig. 9-56.)

NAVIGATION FACILITY BOX

All available communications frequencies, except 121.50 MHz, are listed above the facility box. The numbers above the box are the last two numbers of each frequency on which air/ground communications may be conducted (2.1 = 122.1 MHz). A "G" or "T" following the frequency denotes "guard" (receive) or "transmit" only capability. The shadowbox or heavy line on the illustrated box indicates that this facility is used as an airway or route component. (See Fig. 9-57.) The small "D" preceding the VOR frequency indicates a DME capability.

VICTOR AIRWAYS

The Jeppesen avigation chart symbology used to depict airways is similar to the NOS presentation. A radial forming an airway is clearly marked. (See Fig. 9-58.) Primary and alternate routes on an airway are annotated, as shown in figure 9-59.

MILEAGE NUMBERS

Total mileage between two navaids forming the airway is enclosed in a box. Leg distances are shown between fixes or mileage break points along the airway. These distances are not enclosed in a box. Both types of mileage indicators are illustrated in figure 9-60.

INTERSECTIONS

Two common methods of identifying an intersection are by a VOR radial combined with DME, and by the intersection of two VOR radials. On Jeppesen charts, intersections of VOR radials and DME arcs are indicated by the letter "D" and an arrow, as illustrated in figure 9-61. Riddy Intersection (see Fig. 9-62), on the other hand, is formed by the BRK 034° radial and a Victor airway.

FIG.	DESCRIPTION	SYMBOL
9-54.	VOR Facility	
9-55.	TACAN Facility	
9-56.	VORTAC Facility	
9-57.	Facility Box	2.1G-2.2-2.35-2.6 DENVER ᴰ116.3 DEN
9-58.	Victor Airways — VOR Radial	039°
9-59.	Victor Airways	V-448 - -V-448S- -
9-60.	Mileage Number	(102) 20 V-448
9-61.	Intersection	YUBIC D
9-62.	Intersection — VOR Radial	RIDDY BRK 034° 116.6

When a DME distance to an intersection is not obvious, or a series of leg distances are listed, the total distance to the intersection is given following the "D." This is shown in figure 9-63.

CONTROL ZONES

A control zone which is in effect less than 24 hours is shown by the symbol illustrated in figure 9-64. For example, the Floral Control Zone is only in effect between 0700 and 2300 hours local time.

The heavy dashed lines outlining a control zone indicate that special VFR is not authorized at any time, regardless of pilot qualifications, aircraft equipment, or time of day. An IFR clearance is required to enter this type of control zone whenever weather conditions are less than VFR. (See Fig. 9-65.)

MINIMUM ALTITUDES

A minimum enroute altitude (MEA) is always shown along each segment of an airway. When two minimum altitudes are depicted (see Fig. 9-66), the first is the MEA and the second is a minimum obstruction clearance altitude (MOCA). Figure 9-67 shows a MOCA of 3,600 feet. The "T" in conjunction with a MOCA indicates the obstruction is terrain.

If a change in altitude is required to comply with obstruction clearance criteria, it is indicated either by an MEA or MOCA change at a navaid or at an intersection. The symbol is a line perpendicular to the airway. Normally, an IFR pilot begins the climb to a higher MEA or MOCA at an intermediate navaid or intersection. In some cases, however, a minimum crossing altitude (MCA) is specified at the fix because of obstructions. This requires a climb prior to the fix to ensure crossing at or above the MCA. Examples of an MCA are shown in figures 9-68 and 9-69.

Some intersections also have a minimum reception altitude (MRA). The MRA is the lowest altitude at which an intersection can be identified. Figure 9-70 illustrates the avigation chart symbol for an MRA.

FIG.	DESCRIPTION	SYMBOL
9-63.	DME Mileage	
9-64.	Control Zone — Effective Time	
9-65.	Control Zone — No Special VFR	
9-66.	Minimum Enroute Altitude	
9-67.	Minimum Obstruction Clearance Altitude	
9-68.	Minimum Crossing Altitude	

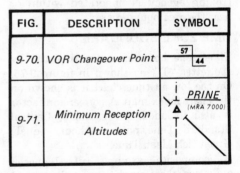

MINIMUM CROSSING ALTITUDE			
❶ Berkshire VOR	V-112-182	4700	E
	V-520	4700	E
	V-448	9400	NE
	V-448S	4500	NE

Fig. 9-69. Minimum Crossing Altitudes

FIG.	DESCRIPTION	SYMBOL
9-70.	VOR Changeover Point	
9-71.	Minimum Reception Altitudes	

VOR CHANGEOVER POINTS

The Jeppesen depiction of a VOR changeover point, other than at the midpoint of the leg, is almost identical to the NOS depiction. Figure 9-71 shows a changeover point that is 55 nautical miles from the VOR on the left and 44 nautical miles from the VOR on the right.

AIR ROUTE TRAFFIC CONTROL CENTERS

Centers are established primarily to provide air traffic control service to IFR flights within controlled airspace, principally during enroute operations. An ARTCC is divided into sectors. Each sector is operated by one or a team of controllers and has its own sector discrete frequency. As a flight progresses from one sector to another, the pilot is requested to change to the appropriate sector frequency.

Normally, ARTCCs are capable of maintaining direct communications with IFR traffic. In some areas remote center air/ground (RCAG) sites provide additional frequencies to augment communication. Remote site frequencies and the name of the site are shown on avigation charts. (See Fig. 9-72.) ARTCC boundaries are also indicated by a dotted line and the names of the adjoining centers, as illustrated in figure 9-73.

SPECIAL USE AIRSPACE

Special use airspace is outlined as shown in figure 9-74. Information such as identification, altitudes, and the controlling agency is annotated within or near the area boundaries.

TIME ZONE BOUNDARIES

Time zone boundaries are depicted by the letter "T," as shown in figure 9-75. On the low altitude chart it is shown on the chart index map. A conversion factor is also included; for example, Central Standard Time plus six hours equals Greenwich Mean Time.

A composite example of Jeppesen avigation chart symbology is illustrated in figure 9-76. Typical symbols are explained by numbered callouts.

1 ARTCC (center) boundary.

2 Englewood VOR has minimum crossing altitude (MCA) of 6300 feet for aircraft westbound on V-270.

3 VORTAC shown by compass rose and scalloped circle. Solid triangle in center indicates compulsory reporting point (except if in radar contact).

FIG.	DESCRIPTION	SYMBOL
9-72.	ARTCC Remote Site	SEATTLE (ZINC) 120.9
9-73.	ARTCC Boundary	SEATTLE HARROLL

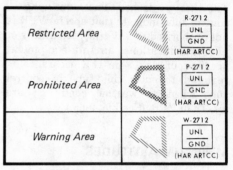

Restricted Area	R-2712 / UNL / GND (HAR ARTCC)
Prohibited Area	P-2712 / UNL / GND (HAR ARTCC)
Warning Area	W-2712 / UNL / GND (HAR ARTCC)

Fig. 9-74. Special Use Airspace

CENTRAL STANDARD TIME +6 = GMT   EASTERN STANDARD TIME +5 = GMT

Fig. 9-75. Time Zone Boundary

4 Airport advisory service (AAS) shown with frequency and letters AAS.

5 City and state name printed using all capital letters indicates published instrument approach procedure.

6 ARTCC communications with New York Center on 128.65 and 126.85 MHz.

7 Intersection of latitude/longitude coordinates every 30'.

8 High altitude jet routes are depicted for transitioning between high and low altitude structures.

9 Automatic transcribed weather broadcast (TWEB) available at Castle VORTAC on 111.2 MHz.

10 Holding pattern with direction indicated by arrows.

11 Allen intersection has minimum crossing altitude (MCA) of 4300 feet for aircraft southeast bound on V-36.

12 Nondirectional Radio Beacon (NDB) forming enroute intersection.

13 Mileage in box (79) indicates total mileage between navaids.

14 Airway leg segment mileage.

15 Armstead Airport does not have published instrument approach, indicated by name in upper and lower case letters.

INSTRUMENT FLIGHT CHARTS

16 R-3515 is restricted from 0900 to 0300 local time (LT) from the ground up to 18000 feet.

17 Navigation frequency changeover point (COP) is 19 nautical miles from Castle VORTAC and 69 nautical miles from the next VORTAC.

18 Duane is 19 DME from Inverness VORTAC. Shown as D̄ and uses airway leg segment mileage for DME distance.

19 Minimum reception altitude (MRA) at Duane is 4500 feet.

20 DME distance is shown as D63 when intersection is not first fix away from VORTAC.

21 Minimum enroute altitude (MEA).

22 Minimum obstruction clearance altitude (MOCA) shown as **3500T**.

23 Maximum authorized altitude (MAA).

24 VOR identifier, frequency, and radial from distant navaid.

25 Enroute flight advisory service (EFAS) available by calling Inverness Flight Watch on 122.0 MHz. Shown as **INV WX-2.0**.

26 Communications available with Inverness FSS by calling on 122.1 MHz and receiving on 114.4 MHz or transmitting and receiving on 122.2 and 122.65 MHz. Since all FSS frequencies are in the 122.0 to 123.65 MHz range, the numbers "12" are omitted, i.e., 2.2 represents 122.2 MHz.

27 Shadow box indicates Inverness VORTAC is an airway navaid. DME at Inverness indicated by letter "D" left of frequency.

28 Trout intersection is compulsory reporting point (except if in radar contact).

29 Special VFR not authorized is symbolized with ········

30 Localizer symbol, frequency, identifier, Morse code and inbound courses are shown when localizer forms an intersection. Localizer symbol only shown when localizer does not provide enroute function.

31 Non-directional radio beacon (NDB) off of an airway.

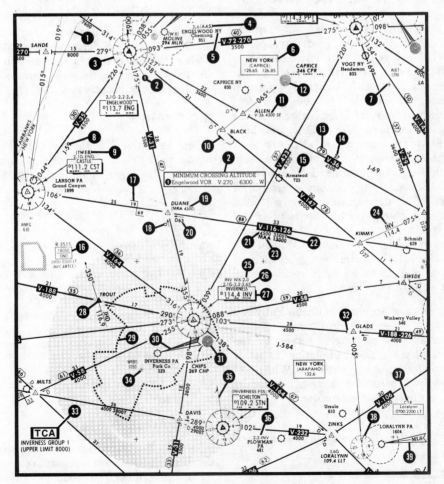

Fig. 9-76. Jeppesen Avigation Chart Symbols

(32) Bar at end of airway centerline indicates MEA change at intersection.

(33) Inverness Group I Terminal Control Area (TCA). Lateral limits shown with waffle patterned shaded area. Associated note shows city, group I or II and upper TCA limit.

(34) Commercial broadcast station WRBO on 1050 kHz.

(35) Magnetic north tick on all navaids for plotting magnetic courses with Jeppesen PV-2 plotter.

(36) Remote communication location for Inverness FSS on 122.3 MHz located at Plowman Airport.

(37) Control zone information shown by ICAO abbreviation "CTR" and effective hours in local time.

(38) Loralynn is terminal (T) class VOR indicated by smaller compass rose.

(39) Microwave Landing System (MLS) shown as

JEPPESEN AIRWAY MANUAL

The *Jeppesen Airway Manual* contains all of the information needed to operate within a given airport environment in IFR conditions. SID, STAR, profile descent, and all published approach charts are included in one loose leaf binder. Additional information, such as detailed airport data, TCA, and high density area charts are also provided. Although coverage is world wide, subscriptions can be tailored to individual requirements. For example, geographical code "T" indicates southwestern United States coverage only. Currency of information is maintained by frequent revisions. Thus, the Airway Manual is a single-source publication, in condensed form, that meets all FAA requirements for aeronautical charts.

Charts are arranged alphabetically by state. The geographical name used is generally the major city served by the civil airport. The installation name is used for military airports. When applicable, charts for a specific airport appear in the following order.

(1) Area chart

(2) TCA depiction (or orientation only)

(3) STARs

(4) Profile descents

(5) SIDs

(6) Taxiway and parking facility diagram

(7) Approach charts (airport chart)

The approach charts are generally arranged with the approach containing the lowest minimums first, followed by the next lowest, etc. The taxiway/parking diagram is provided only for the major air terminals. Airport charts for other airports are printed on the back of the first approach chart.

In addition to charts, an airway manual contains a revision record, table of contents, and an introductory section. The introduction includes a chart glossary, an explanation of abbreviations, and detailed legend descriptions for all Jeppesen charts.

Since most of these Jeppesen charts are similar to the NOS depictions described earlier, the discussion in this section is limited to a few distinctive features of the Jeppesen publications

SID CHARTS

A representative SID chart is illustrated in figure 9-77. The numbered callouts identify the significant parts of this chart.

(1) Index according to the nearest major city

(2) ATC name of the departure

(3) Textural description of the departure and transition routes

(4) Departure routes depicted with solid black arrows, transition routes shown by dashed arrows and the transition route name

(5) Appropriate navaid frequency information

(6) Magnetic course and distance in nautical miles to the turning point, Manta Intersection, formed by the RBY $122°$ radial and the Sea Isle (SIE) $059°$ radial

(7) Airway route, V-139, and the overlying jet route, J-121

APPROACH CHARTS

Approach charts provide the pilot with detailed information regarding prescribed instrument procedures, airport data, local terrain, and other items

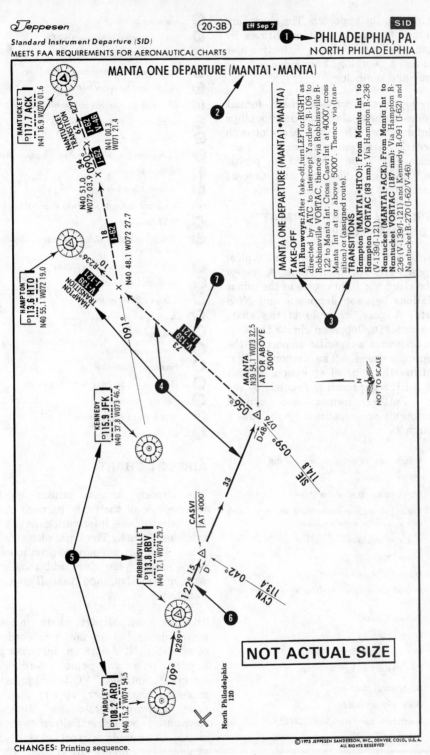

Fig. 9-77. Jeppesen SID Chart

pertinent to the approach. The charts are designed for use in IFR conditions by instrument rated pilots. Effective use requires a working knowledge of the format and symbology.

The Jeppesen approach chart format includes distinct elements or groupings of information. The main parts of each approach chart are the heading, communications data, plan view, profile view, landing minimums, and descent information.

APPROACH CHART FORMAT AND SYMBOLOGY

Figure 9-78, part 1, shows a typical Jeppesen ILS approach chart. A review of the chart highlights some of the minor variations between Jeppesen and NOS charts. A good example is the chart index code. On Jeppesen charts the first digit indicates a specific airport in the geographic area. The second digit identifies the type of approach. In this case, an ILS approach is denoted by the "-1." Further format and symbol descriptions are explained by callouts 1 through 25.

1. Frequencies for arrival in order of use
2. Effective date
3. Minimum sector altitudes (MSA)
4. Charts indexed alphabetically by city name within state (or airline manual)
5. Approach procedure identification
6. Airport elevation
7. Primary approach facility
8. Highest obstruction in plan view shown with arrow
9. Terminal route
10. Water bodies
11. Morse code for forming facilities
12. Plan view drawn to scale
13. Nonprecision profile
14. Glide slope altitudes
15. Touchdown zone elevation (TDZE)
16. Missed approach procedure
17. Straight-in landing minimums

18. Localizer minimums
19. Height above touchdown (HAT)
20. Circle-to-land minimums
21. Not all military minimums shown
22. Height above airport (HAA)
23. Complete component-out minimums
24. Descent rate in feet per minute
25. Changes from previous chart
26. Coordinates for airport reference point (ARP)
27. Airport variation
28. Airport identifier
29. Frequencies for departure in order of use
30. VOT frequency
31. Notes (including noise abatement procedures) for airport
32. Airport reference point (ARP)
33. Latitude/longitude grid
34. Taxiway designators
35. Airport diagram scale
36. Runway lighting
37. Runway grooving
38. Runway restrictions
39. Distance beyond displaced threshold
40. Takeoff minimums
41. IFR departure procedures
42. Alternate minimums

AIRPORT CHART

The airport chart is printed on the reverse side of the first approach chart. It also displays information in an established format. The basic elements include heading, departure communications, airport plan view, additional runway information, and takeoff/alternate minimums.

The Jeppesen airport chart includes useful data that is not published on comparable NOS charts; for example, airport reference point coordinates, airport identifier, VOR frequencies, notes on the airport, airport diagram scale, runway restrictions, threshold elevation, and takeoff/alternate minimums. A sample airport chart, with explanatory callouts 26 though 42, is shown in figure 9-78, part 2.

INSTRUMENT FLIGHT CHARTS

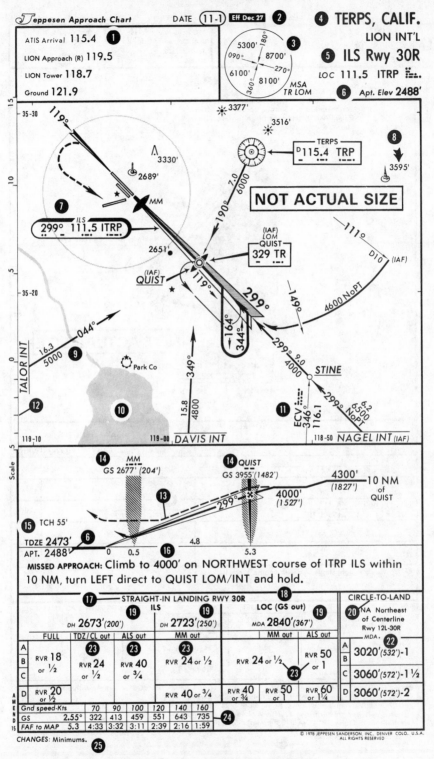

Jeppesen Approach Chart DATE (11-1) **Eff Dec 27** ②

④ **TERPS, CALIF.**
LION INT'L
⑤ **ILS Rwy 30R**
LOC 111.5 ITRP

① ATIS Arrival 115.4
LION Approach (R) 119.5
LION Tower 118.7
Ground 121.9

③ 5300' 180°
090° 8700'
6100' 270°
8100' 360°
MSA TR LOM

⑥ Apt. Elev **2488'**

NOT ACTUAL SIZE

D 115.4 TRP **TERPS**

⑦ ILS 299° 111.5 ITRP

(IAF) LOM QUIST **329 TR**

(IAF) QUIST

MISSED APPROACH: Climb to 4000' on NORTHWEST course of ITRP ILS within 10 NM, turn LEFT direct to QUIST LOM/INT and hold.

⑭ MM GS 2677' (204')
⑭ QUIST GS 3955'(1482')
4300' (1827') 10 NM of QUIST
4000' (1527')
⑬ 299°
⑮ TCH 55'
TDZE 2473'
⑥ APT. 2488'
0   0.5   ⑯   4.8   5.3

⑰ STRAIGHT-IN LANDING RWY 30R				⑱ LOC (GS out)		CIRCLE-TO-LAND
⑲ ILS DH 2673'(200')		DH 2723'(250') ⑲		MDA 2840'(367') ⑲		⑳ NA Northeast of Centerline Rwy 12L-30R
FULL	TDZ/CL out ㉓	ALS out ㉓	MM out ㉓	MM out	ALS out	MDA. ㉒
A	RVR 18 or ½	RVR 24 or ½	RVR 40 or ¾	RVR 24 or ½	RVR 24 or ½	RVR 50 or 1 ㉓	A 3020'(532')-1
B						B
C						C 3060'(572')-1½
D	RVR 20 or ½			RVR 40 or ¾	RVR 40 or ¾	RVR 50 or 1 / RVR 60 or 1¼	D 3060'(572')-2

Gnd speed-Kts		70	90	100	120	140	160	
GS	2.55°	322	413	459	551	643	735	㉔
FAF to MAP	5.3	4:33	3:32	3:11	2:39	2:16	1:59	

CHANGES: Minimums. ㉕

© 1978 JEPPESEN SANDERSON INC. DENVER COLO. U.S.A. ALL RIGHTS RESERVED

Fig. 9-78. Part 1 — Jeppesen Approach Chart

INSTRUMENT FLIGHT CHARTS

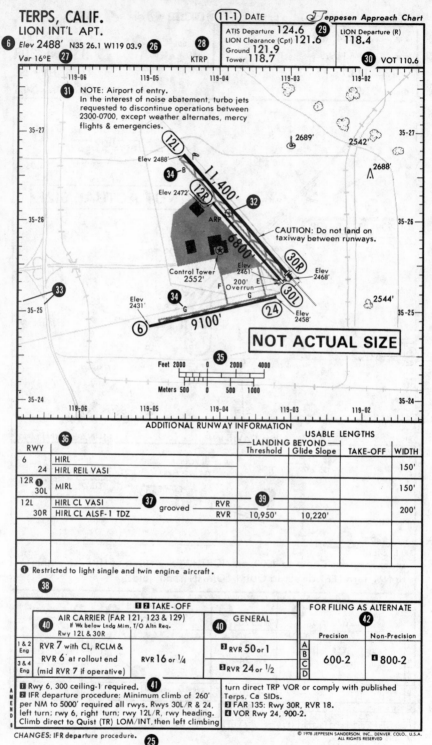

TERPS, CALIF.
LION INT'L APT.

(11-1) DATE

Jeppesen Approach Chart

6 Elev 2488' N35 26.1 W119 03.9 **26**

28 KTRP

Var 16°E **27**

ATIS Departure 124.6 **29**
LION Clearance (Cpt) 121.6
Ground 121.9
Tower 118.7

LION Departure (R) 118.4

30 VOT 110.6

31 NOTE: Airport of entry.
In the interest of noise abatement, turbo jets requested to discontinue operations between 2300-0700, except weather alternates, mercy flights & emergencies.

12L
Elev 2488'
34 B
12R
Elev 2472'
ARP
11,400'
2689'
2542'
2688'
32
6800'
CAUTION: Do not land on taxiway between runways.
30R
Elev 2468'
Control Tower 2552'
Elev 2461'
200' Overrun
E
F
30L
Elev 2458'
2544'
33
Elev 2431'
34 G
6
9100'
24

NOT ACTUAL SIZE

Feet 2000   0   2000   4000   **35**
Meters 500   0   500   1000

ADDITIONAL RUNWAY INFORMATION

RWY **36**			USABLE LENGTHS			
			LANDING BEYOND		TAKE-OFF	WIDTH
			Threshold	Glide Slope		
6	HIRL					
24	HIRL REIL VASI					150'
12R ❶	MIRL					
30L						150'
12L	HIRL CL VASI	**37** grooved	RVR	**39**		
30R	HIRL CL ALSF-1 TDZ		RVR	10,950'	10,220'	200'

❶ Restricted to light single and twin engine aircraft.
38

1 2 TAKE-OFF			FOR FILING AS ALTERNATE		
40 AIR CARRIER (FAR 121, 123 & 129) If Wx below Lndg Mim, T/O Altn Req. Rwy 12L & 30R		GENERAL **40**	**42**	Precision	Non-Precision
1 & 2 Eng	RVR 7 with CL, RCLM & RVR 6 at rollout end (mid RVR 7 if operative)	RVR 16 or 1/4	**3** RVR 50 or 1	A B C D	600-2
3 & 4 Eng			**3** RVR 24 or 1/2			800-2 **4**

41
❶ Rwy 6, 300 ceiling-1 required.
❷ IFR departure procedure: Minimum climb of 260' per NM to 5000' required all rwys. Rwys 30L/R & 24, left turn; rwy 6, right turn; rwy 12L/R, rwy heading. Climb direct to Quist (TR) LOM/INT, then left climbing

turn direct TRP VOR or comply with published Terps, Ca SIDs.
3 FAR 135: Rwy 30R, RVR 18.
4 VOR Rwy 24, 900-2.

CHANGES: IFR departure procedure. **25**

© 1978 JEPPESEN SANDERSON, INC., DENVER COLO., U.S.A.
ALL RIGHTS RESERVED

AMEND 8

Fig. 9-78. Part 2 — Jeppesen Airport Chart

chapter 10

INSTRUMENT PROCEDURES

INTRODUCTION

Traffic separation, a responsibility of both the pilot and controller, is one advantage of flying under IFR. Air traffic control can provide traffic separation between all IFR flights in controlled airspace, as well as between IFR flights and known VFR flights in certain situations. Efficient traffic control depends on all pilots and controllers adhering to the same procedures. It is necessary for the instrument pilot to become acquainted with these air traffic control procedures. In addition, frequent reference and study of the *Airman's Information Manual* will enable the IFR pilot to keep up to date on the latest recommended procedures.

SECTION A—AIR TRAFFIC CONTROL

IFR DEPARTURES

Takeoff and transition to the enroute phase can be accomplished smoothly and efficiently when the pilot is familiar with departure procedures. This keeps radio communications to a minimum and allows the pilot to concentrate on the transition to instrument references. The navigation workload varies with the procedure used. It may be as simple as holding an assigned heading while monitoring navigation aids or adhering to a detailed standard instrument departure (SID) procedure. At some airports, the pilot may perform the departure procedure without SIDs or radar assistance.

TAKEOFF MINIMUMS

IFR takeoff minimums are specified by FAR 91.116(c). Essentially, these minimums prevent IFR departures from an airport when weather conditions are below the lowest landing minimum at that airport or at a nearby airport. If these restrictions are adhered to, the pilot can return to the departure airport or one nearby (takeoff alternate) if serious mechanical difficulties should develop during a departure.

Although these requirements do not specifically apply to private aircraft operations as conducted under Part 91, good judgment dictates compliance. The prudence of an IFR departure in a light aircraft when weather conditions are known to be below landing minimums is, to say the least, questionable.

FAR Part 97 prescribes standard instrument approach procedures for instrument letdowns to airports in the United States. It also prescribes the weather minimums that apply to *takeoffs*, as well as landings under IFR. Takeoff minimums apply to the following specific types of operations.

FAR Part 121 . . . Air carrier (domestic, flag, and supplemental) and commercial operators of large aircraft
FAR Part 123 . . . Air travel clubs using large airplanes
FAR Part 129 . . . Foreign air carriers
FAR Part 135 . . . Air taxi and commercial operators

If takeoff minimums for a particular airport are *not* prescribed in Part 97, the following *standard minimums apply* — one mile visibility for single-engine and twin-engine aircraft and one-half statute mile visibility for aircraft with *more than* two engines.

Provisions also are made for *reduction* of takeoff minimums based on the designation of a takeoff alternate. In addition, the availability of centerline lights or other aids may reduce takeoff minimums; however, these reductions do not apply to operations under FAR Part 91.

In other cases, greater than standard takeoff minimums may be specified because of terrain clearance or other obstructions. Ceilings, as well as visibilities, are specified where a minimum ceiling is required in order to avoid obstructions during departures. Where necessary, detailed departure procedures, including items such as routes and minimum altitudes, are provided.

VISIBILITY AND RVR

Normally, minimums are expressed in terms of prevailing visibility, runway visibility value (RVV), or runway visual range (RVR). Prevailing visibility is the greatest distance an observer can see throughout half of the horizon, RVV is a transmissometer derived visibility for a particular runway. Both prevailing visibility and RVV are reported in statute miles or fractions of miles. When available, RVV is used in lieu of prevailing visibility. RVR, also an instrumentally measured value, represents the distance a pilot can expect to see down the runway from the approach end. RVR, when available, is used instead of RVV or prevailing visibility in determining minimums for a particular runway; RVR is always reported in hundreds of feet.

If an RVR minimum is specified for takeoff, but the RVR equipment is out of service, RVR minimums are converted to the appropriate visibility in statute miles, as shown in figure 10-1.

RVR (Feet)	VISIBILITY (Statute Miles)
1,600	1/4
2,400	1/2
3,200	5/8
4,000	3/4
4,500	7/8
5,000	1
6,000	1-1/4

Fig. 10-1. RVR and Statute Miles

TAKEOFF MINIMUMS

Takeoff minimums are not stated on NOS approach charts; however, the symbol ▼ in the information box at the bottom of the chart indicates that special minimums and/or procedures have been established for that airport.

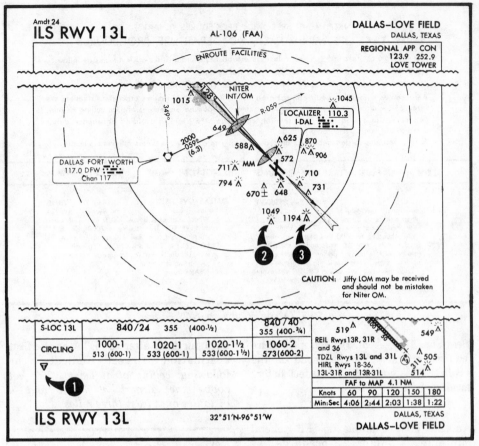

Fig. 10-2. IFR Takeoff Minimums (NOS Format)

(See Fig. 10-2, item 1). Generally, the procedures are necessary because of obstructions in the departure paths (items 2 and 3) which are especially hazardous in low visibility conditions. Special takeoff minimums are published only at airports with instrument approach procedures. When applicable, the pilot must consult the separate listing in the front of each regional approach chart book. The listing is entitled " ▼ IFR Takeoff Minimums and Departure Procedures," as shown in figure 10-3.

Takeoff minimums apply only to FAR Part 135 operations. Takeoff minimums for Parts 121, 123, and 129 are not shown in the NOS tabulation. ATC expects pilots of air carriers and FAR Part 135 operators to comply with estab-

lished takeoff minimums. However, in accordance with rigid visibility criteria, controllers will deny takeoff clearance to air carrier and other commercial aircraft carrying passengers or cargo for hire if the visibility is too low. These visibility criteria are published in the AIM under "Instrument Departures."

As a practical consideration, pilots operating under Part 91 should also consult takeoff minimum listings. For example, if a general aviation pilot plans a low visibility takeoff from runway 13L, Dallas-Love Field, disregard for the special takeoff procedure could be critical. As shown in figure 10-2, obstacles exist near the departure path, and a procedure is specified for runway 13L when the weather is below 800-1.

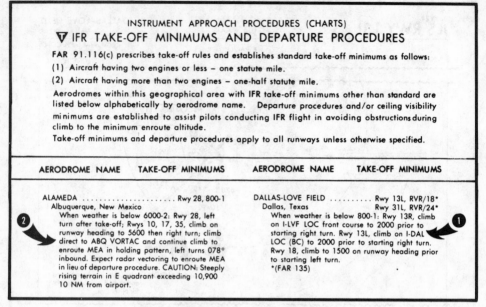

INSTRUMENT APPROACH PROCEDURES (CHARTS)
▽ IFR TAKE-OFF MINIMUMS AND DEPARTURE PROCEDURES

FAR 91.116(c) prescribes take-off rules and establishes standard take-off minimums as follows:

(1) Aircraft having two engines or less – one statute mile.

(2) Aircraft having more than two engines – one-half statute mile.

Aerodromes within this geographical area with IFR take-off minimums other than standard are listed below alphabetically by aerodrome name. Departure procedures and/or ceiling visibility minimums are established to assist pilots conducting IFR flight in avoiding obstructions during climb to the minimum enroute altitude.

Take-off minimums and departure procedures apply to all runways unless otherwise specified.

AERODROME NAME	TAKE-OFF MINIMUMS	AERODROME NAME	TAKE-OFF MINIMUMS

ALAMEDA .... Rwy 28, 800-1
Albuquerque, New Mexico
When weather is below 6000-2: Rwy 28, left turn after take-off; Rwys 10, 17, 35, climb on runway heading to 5600 then right turn; climb direct to ABQ VORTAC and continue climb to enroute MEA in holding pattern, left turns 078° inbound. Expect radar vectoring to enroute MEA in lieu of departure procedure. CAUTION: Steeply rising terrain in E quadrant exceeding 10,900 10 NM from airport.

DALLAS-LOVE FIELD .... Rwy 13L, RVR/18*
Dallas, Texas   Rwy 31L, RVR/24*
When weather is below 800-1: Rwy 13R, climb on I-LVF LOC front course to 2000 prior to starting right turn. Rwy 13L, climb on I-DAL LOC (BC) to 2000 prior to starting right turn. Rwy 18, climb to 1500 on runway heading prior to starting left turn.
*(FAR 135)

Fig. 10-3. Takeoff Minimums (NOS Format)

(See Fig. 10-3, item 1). The procedure requires a climb straight ahead on the localizer back course to 2,000 feet before turning right.

Another good example of IFR takeoff minimums and/or procedures is illustrated in figure 10-3, item 2. In this case, the steeply rising terrain in the east quadrant dictates a special procedure. All of these procedures are based on realistic obstacle clearance criteria. They are published specifically to advise and protect commercial air carriers during IFR conditions, but are recommended for all IFR operations.

ALTERNATE LANDING AIRPORT REQUIREMENTS

FAR 91.83 specifies rigid rules for selection of a landing alternate for an IFR destination airport. These rules are based on weather forecasts at the first airport of intended landing, as well as the alternate airport, when required. An alternate airport is *not required* if weather forecasts from one hour before until one hour after the ETA at the first destination airport indicate the following: *ceiling of at least 2,000 feet above the airport elevation and a visibility of at least three miles.*

NOTE:
Forecast ceiling altitudes are given in 100-foot increments for the first 2,000 feet AGL, 500-foot increments from 2,000 to 5,000 feet AGL, and 1,000-foot increments above 5,000 feet AGL.

QUALIFYING AN ALTERNATE AIRPORT

For an airport with a published instrument approach procedure to qualify as an alternate airport, the weather forecast at the ETA at that airport must not be less than 600 feet and two statute miles visibility for a precision approach or 800 feet and two statute miles for a nonprecision approach. However, once the pilot receives clearance to the alternate, the published instrument approach minimums apply.

NOS charts do not show standard alternate minimums (600 or 800 feet and two statute miles visibility). However, if the symbol ▲ appears in the information box, the airport has nonstandard minimums and the pilot must then consult a separate NOS tabulation of " ▲ IFR Alternate Minimums." This tabulation is contained in the front of the appropriate approach chart book. An excerpt is shown in figure 10-4.

Airports without a published instrument approach procedure also may be used as an alternate airport. However, forecast weather conditions at the estimated arrival time must allow a descent, approach, and landing from the MEA in VFR conditions.

RADAR DEPARTURE

Radar departures are performed with the aid of radar-equipped approach control facilities. The approach and departure controllers normally operate in close proximity to each other for the obvious reason of traffic coordination.

At some airports without ASR equipment, ARTCC may provide approach and departure radar service. In such cases, center facilities must be adequate for direct pilot-controller communications and good radar coverage at low altitudes must be available.

CLEARANCE

When an IFR departure is to be vectored immediately following takeoff, the pilot will be advised prior to departure of the initial heading to be flown. Initial IFR clearances usually contain this information, as well as the departure control frequencies and transponder codes (if

---

INSTRUMENT APPROACH PROCEDURES (CHARTS)
SOUTHWEST UNITED STATES
△ IFR ALTERNATE MINIMUMS
(Not applicable to USAF/USN)

Standard alternate minimums for nonprecision approaches are 800-2 (NDB, VOR, LOC, TACAN, LDA, VORTAC, VOR/DME or ASR); for precision approaches 600-2 (ILS or PAR). Aerodromes within this geographical area that require alternate minimums other than standard or alternate minimums with restrictions are listed below. NA- means IFR minimums are not authorized for alternate use due to unmonitored facility or absence of weather reporting service. U. S. Army pilots refer to Army Reg. 95-1 for additional application. Civil pilots see FAR 91.83. USAF/USN pilots refer to appropriate regulations.

AERODROME NAME ALTERNATE MINIMUMS	AERODROME NAME ALTERNATE MINIMUMS
ADDISON . . . . .VOR-A 　Dallas, Texas　　　　　　　　　　VOR Rwy 15 　　　　　　　　　　　　　　　　VOR Rwy 33 　NA when control zone not effective.	ENID WOODRING MUNI . . . . VOR Rwy 17 　Enid, Oklahoma　　　　　　　　VOR Rwy 35 　　NA when control zone not effective, 　　except for operators with approved weather 　　reporting service.
ALICE INTNL . . . . .VOR-1, 1000-2 　Alice, Texas	FAYETTEVILLE MUNI-DRAKE FIELD . . . . .VOR-1 　Fayetteville, Arkansas 　　Category A, 1000-2; Category B, 1100-2; 　　Category C, 1200-2
ARANSAS COUNTY . . . .NDB (ADF) Rwy 14　NA 　Rockport, Texas　　　　　　VOR/DME-1　NA	

Fig. 10-4. NOS Alternate Minimums

appropriate). For example, the departure instructions contained in one ATC clearance may specify, "*. . . maintain runway heading for departure vectors. Departure control frequency will be 124.0. Squawk 0100 just before departure.*" A typical radar departure is depicted in figure 10-5.

PROCEDURE

When executing a radar departure, the pilot will be instructed by the tower to contact departure control. After establishing radar contact, the controller usually provides a brief explanation as to what the radar vector will achieve. An example of this would be a clearance to "*. . . turn left heading 320⁰, intercept V-81, on course.*" Other instructions are included, such as altitude or climb restrictions to assist in moving the flight quickly and safely out of the terminal area. This information is vital in the event of a two-way communications failure after takeoff.

Radar departure control will vector a flight to either a navigation aid or an appropriate enroute position. At that point, the pilot usually is advised to intercept and proceed on course.

The pilot should carefully monitor his position in relation to navigation aids during radar control and may not rely completely on controller guidance. Continuous orientation to the route specified in the clearance should be maintained, and the time over compulsory checkpoints should be recorded. This is advisable since radar service may suddenly be terminated for a variety of reasons, such as controller workload, transponder failure, or emergency handling of another flight.

When flying a radar-controlled departure, the pilot is still responsible for the safe conduct of the flight. Therefore, pilots should be prepared before takeoff to conduct their own navigation during

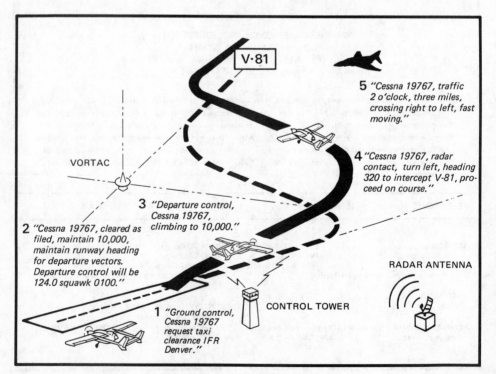

Fig. 10-5. Typical Radar Departure

the departure and to comply with their ATC clearance. This means that VOR receivers should be operationally checked and properly tuned *before departure.*

NONRADAR DEPARTURE

In the absence of radar facilities, IFR separation is based on reserving a specific airspace block for one aircraft at a given time. A clearance may contain specific departure instructions: " . . . *turn right after takeoff, climb on course,*" or, as shown in figure 10-6, *". . . after takeoff, track eastbound on the 08 localizer course to Arlee Intersection; turn right heading 110° to intercept V-220."*

Specific departure procedures also may be prescribed in the takeoff minimums for the airport concerned; however, take-off minimums and departure procedures are not specified for airports which do not have published instrument approach procedures.

UNCONTROLLED FIELDS

In many cases, specific departure instructions are not given in the clearance. In such cases, the pilot is expected to proceed on course via the most direct route. An example is a departure from an uncontrolled field not served by a terminal approach/departure control facility or flight service station. *When IFR conditions prevail* at the airport, the

clearance usually is received by telephone. Normally, a clearance void time also will be specified; for example " . . . *clearance void if not airborne by 1000Z."* When VFR conditions prevail, pilots normally receive the IFR clearance via radio after takeoff, as depicted in figure 10-7.

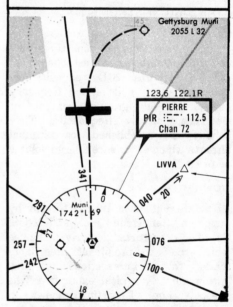

"Minneapolis Center, Cherokee 6141N 25 DME north of Pierre climbing to 6,000 requesting clearance to Rapid City."

"Cherokee 6141N maintain VFR, stand-by for clearance."

Fig. 10-7. Departure in VFR Conditions

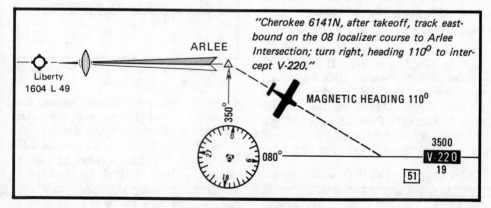

"Cherokee 6141N, after takeoff, track eastbound on the 08 localizer course to Arlee Intersection; turn right, heading 110° to intercept V-220."

Fig. 10-6. Radio Navigation Departure

At airports which have flight service stations only, the clearance is relayed from ARTCC to the FSS. The pilot then receives the clearance via radio just prior to departure. If the airport has a published instrument approach procedure, the pilot should check the remarks section of the approach chart to determine if special departure procedures are required. If instrument approach procedures have not been established (hence no departure procedures), pilots are expected to take whatever action is necessary to accomplish a safe departure.

STANDARD INSTRUMENT DEPARTURES

Standard instrument departures are coded departure routes established at selected airports. SIDs expedite departure routing and reduce frequency congestion on ground control or clearance delivery frequencies. They usually are established for terminal airports which experience a large volume of air traffic.

SID CHARTS

SIDs are published in chart form by Jeppesen Sanderson Inc. and NOS. Specific departures are given names which refer to prominent area landmarks, towns, intersections, or navigation aids. A typical example is the Prescott Four Departure, shown in figure 10-8. A narrative summary of the SID is presented in addition to the plan view of the procedure and routing.

PROCEDURES

The departure procedure for runways 8L and 8R (Fig. 10-8, item 1) requires a climb to the Rio Salado NDB, a left turn to intercept the 310° radial of the Phoenix VORTAC to Navjo (item 2), and then direct to the Prescott VORTAC via the 153° radial. A minimum altitude of 10,000 feet MSL is specified at Navjo.

Before accepting this SID, a pilot should check to see if the aircraft's climb rate is sufficient to meet the 10,000-foot altitude restriction. The net altitude gain

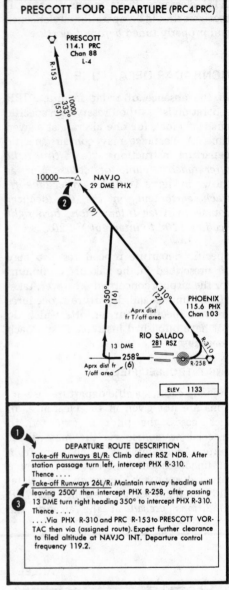

Fig. 10-8. Standard Instrument Departure (NOS Format)

is 8,867 feet (10,000 feet minus the elevation of 1,133 feet) and the total distance to Navjo is approximately 36 miles (27 plus 9). Thus, a climb of 246 feet per mile (8,867 divided by 36) is required. Many SID charts include a notation indicating the minimum climb per nautical mile required to achieve a given altitude.

To use the example chart, however, a rate of climb in feet per minute is a more useful figure. Assume the estimated groundspeed is 120 knots. Then, the time to Navjo is 18 minutes, and a rate of climb of 493 feet per minute (8,867 feet divided by 18 minutes) is the minimum required to meet the altitude restriction.

Departures from runways 26L and 26R (item 3) must maintain runway heading until leaving 2,500 feet, intercept the Phoenix 258° radial and, after passing the 13 nautical mile DME fix, turn right to a heading of 350° to intercept the Phoenix 310° radial. The remainder of the SID is the same.

ISSUANCE OF SIDs

Pilots of aircraft operating from locations where SID procedures are effective may expect an ATC clearance containing a SID. Pilots who do not wish to use a SID should file, "NO SID" in the remarks section of their flight plan. Before a pilot accepts a SID in an IFR clearance, he must have at least the narrative form of the procedure in his personal possession. In addition, he must be sure the performance capability of the aircraft will allow compliance with the procedure. For example, in the discussion of the SID departure for Phoenix, Sky Harbor Airport, an amended clearance should be requested if the aircraft is unable to climb at 493 feet per minute. Once accepted, the SID procedure becomes mandatory unless ATC approves a deviation.

ENROUTE OPERATIONS

The enroute segment of an IFR flight offers a detailed, challenging environment for the instrument pilot. The occurrence of IFR weather conditions is most prevalent below 18,000 feet MSL; ironically, most general aviation aircraft operations are conducted within this altitude range. Today, light aircraft are regularly conducting IFR flights in weather conditions which only transport aircraft attempted a few years ago.

Communications and navigation facilities in the national airspace system have improved dramatically, resulting in safer and more reliable flight operations. Although delays and subsequent holding procedures may be encountered, their occurrence is becoming less frequent.

ENROUTE RADAR PROCEDURES

Air route traffic control centers receive the majority of IFR traffic from radar equipped departure control facilities. A radar handoff is a quick and simple procedure. For example, departure control will instruct the pilot to " . . . contact Fort Worth Center now on 127.15." The pilot's initial callup to center simply states the center call sign, aircraft identification, and altitude or flight level assigned. For example, "Fort Worth Center, Cheyenne 131PT, 7,000." When climbing, the pilot should so state; for example, " . . . 6,000 climbing to 7,000." To verify position and establish radar contact, the center controller usually will instruct the pilot to "IDENT" on the assigned transponder code.

Subsequent handoffs are made between center sectors or between centers on discrete frequencies as the flight progresses. It is not uncommon for an IFR flight to be in continuous radar contact from takeoff to touchdown.

Occasionally, short IFR flights are shuttled between two terminal radar facilities rather than handed off to ARTCC. Essentially, the flight is transferred from departure control at one airport to approach control at another. This procedure depends on such factors as distance between terminals and radar coverage over the route of flight.

In addition, departures from uncontrolled fields may contact center for radar identification immediately following takeoff. Instrument flights are often conducted between smaller airports under the exclusive control of ARTCC.

INSTRUMENT PROCEDURES

Although radar negates the need for standard position reporting, certain reports are compulsory, regardless of the availability of radar service. These reports are summarized in figure 10-9. Additional reports are required whenever any of the following equipment *malfunctions* occur.

1. Loss of VOR, TACAN, or ADF receiver capability
2. Complete or partial loss of ILS receiver capability
3. Impairment of air/ground communications capability

The pilot should advise the controller of the degree to which the flight's operational capabilities are limited. He should also specify the type and extent of assistance that will be required from ATC.

NONRADAR PROCEDURES

Before the installation of radar facilities, aircraft separation was based on dif-

ferent altitude assignments, different routes, and time/distance intervals between flights. Although less effective in terms of handling large volumes of air traffic, this system is still used on some low altitude routes.

Since radar and transponder signals operate on the line-of-sight principle, signal blockage and low altitude dead spots may create areas where radar coverage is not adequate for safe separation. Also, airborne transponder failure or severe weather conditions may degrade radar reception, preventing positive aircraft identification.

POSITION REPORTS

In order to maintain separation in the nonradar environment, ATC must be provided with frequent position and altitude reports. In addition, estimated times of arrival over succeeding navigation aids or fixes must be accurately calculated and reported to ATC by the pilot. Therefore, navigation logs should

SITUATION	SAMPLE TRANSMISSION
Vacating one assigned altitude for another	*"Bellanca 1776R, leaving 7,000 climbing to 10,000."*
Missed approach	*"Bellanca 1776R, missed approach, request clearance to Omaha."*
VFR on top change in altitude	*"Bellanca 1776R, VFR on top, climbing to 10,500."*
Unanticipated hazardous weather or conditions	*"Bellanca 1776R, experiencing moderate turbulence at 10,000."*
TAS variation of plus or minus five percent, or 10 knots, whichever is greater.	*"Bellanca 1776R, advises TAS decrease to 150 knots."*

Fig. 10-9. Compulsory IFR Reports—Radar/Nonradar

INSTRUMENT PROCEDURES

be updated continuously. This is equally important for operations conducted in radar contact, since radar service may be terminated.

Federal Aviation Regulations require pilots to maintain a "listening watch" on appropriate frequencies during all IFR operations. In addition, the pilot must furnish position reports to ATC without request when crossing compulsory reporting points. An example of the standard position report format used for nonradar operations is shown in figure 10-10, along with certain additional reports which are required.

On initial callups, the pilot should specify the facility call sign, aircraft identification, and location. The pilot should then wait for a reply *before* giving the report.

CENTER COMMUNICATIONS

In most instances, the distribution of remote center air/ground (RCAG) sites is adequate for direct pilot/controller communications. Each sector controller or team has its own discrete frequency. These frequencies are shown on IFR enroute charts. However, flight plan filing and requests for weather or similar data should be made through the nearest FSS. In cases where direct pilot/controller *communication is lost* and cannot be reestablished, the pilot should furnish the IFR position reports to the closest FSS. The FSS attendant then provides a communications relay between the pilot and the ARTCC controller.

VFR CONDITIONS ON TOP

When IFR operations are conducted in VFR weather conditions *on top* of a

STANDARD POSITION REPORT

Identification	*"Comanche 8852P,*
Position	*Shreveport,*
Time	*15,*
Altitude/Flight Level	*11,000,*
IFR or VFR for report to FSS only	*IFR,*
ETA over the next reporting fix	*Quitman 40,*
Succeeding reporting points	*Scurry next."*
Pertinent remarks	*(Infrequently Used)*

ADDITIONAL REPORTS

Time and altitude reaching a clearance limit	*"Comanche 8852P, Monte Intersection at 05, 10,000 holding, requesting further clearance."*
Revised estimate in excess of three minutes	*"Comanche 8852P, revising Scurry estimate to 55."*

Fig. 10-10. Compulsory Reports—Nonradar

cloud layer, a pilot may request clearance for *"VFR conditions on top"* in lieu of an assigned altitude. If ATC authorizes a VFR conditions-on-top clearance, the following procedures apply.

1. The flight must maintain an appropriate east/west VFR cruising altitude.
2. The pilot must adhere to the VFR cloud clearance requirements for that flight altitude.
3. Normal IFR reporting procedures remain in effect.
4. VFR altitude changes may be made at the pilot's discretion, but they must be reported immediately to ATC.
5. Separation is not provided by ATC, although information pertaining to IFR traffic is provided.
6. ATC must be notified if the flight is unable to maintain VFR conditions on top.
7. An amended clearance with an altitude assignment must be obtained *before* entering instrument conditions.

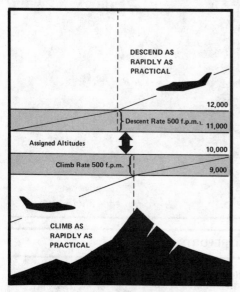

Fig. 10-11. Climb and Descent Rates

IFR CLIMBS AND DESCENTS

When ATC requires an IFR flight to climb or descend, the pilot is expected to initiate the maneuver immediately upon receipt of the clearance. Large climbs or descents are to be made as rapidly as practical. However, climb and descent rates of 500 feet per minute are expected for small altitude changes (1,000 feet or less) or for the last 1,000 feet of larger altitude changes, as shown in figure 10-11.

Occasionally, it may be necessary for a flight to level off at an *intermediary altitude* because of aircraft speed restrictions at that altitude, turbulence, or ATC requests. When this occurs, the pilot is expected to inform ATC of the altitude at leveloff, since the handling of other aircraft within that airspace may be affected.

CRUISING ALTITUDES AND ALTIMETER SETTINGS

The hemispheric rule for IFR flight specified in FAR 91.121 applies to flight in uncontrolled airspace. IFR altitudes for flight in controlled airspace are specified by ATC. Since most pilots file IFR altitudes which agree with the hemispheric rule, ATC usually assigns even thousand foot altitudes for westbound flights below 18,000 feet MSL (4,000, 6,000, 8,000, etc.) and odd thousand foot altitudes for eastbound flights (3,000, 5,000, 7,000, etc.). However, altitude deviations may be requested by either the pilot or ATC because of traffic, weather, or other reasons.

Pilots of IFR aircraft operating below 18,000 feet MSL are expected to keep their altimeters adjusted to the current setting, as reported by a station within 100 nautical miles of the aircraft. In areas where stations are more than 100 nautical miles from the aircraft, the closest appropriate station's altimeter setting may be used.

At or above 18,000 feet MSL, the pilot should set the altimeter to 29.92. This requirement results in some problems when actual altimeter settings along the route of flight are lower than 29.92; for example, an aircraft flying at FL 180 using an altimeter setting of 29.92 (assuming standard temperature) will be at the same true altitude as an aircraft in the low altitude sector indicating 17,000 feet MSL and using an altimeter setting of 28.92. Consequently, FAR 91.81 specifies the *lowest usable flight levels* for given altimeter setting ranges, as shown in figure 10-12. As local altimeter settings *fall below 29.92*, a pilot in the high altitude sector must cruise at progressively higher indicated altitudes to ensure adequate separation from other aircraft operating in the low altitude structure.

APPROACHES

Instrument approach procedures are designed to ensure a safe descent from the enroute environment to a point where a safe landing can be made. A pilot adhering to the altitudes, flight paths, and weather minimums depicted on the instrument approach procedure chart is assured of obstruction clearance and runway or airport alignment.

Several instrument approach procedures, using various navigation or approach aids, may be authorized for an airport. ATC may advise that a particular approach procedure is being used, primarily to expedite traffic. If a pilot is issued a clearance that specifies a particular approach procedure, he is expected to notify ATC immediately if he desires a different one. In this event it may be necessary for ATC to withhold clearance for the different approach until such time as traffic conditions permit.

TRANSITION

The transition from the enroute phase to the approach phase may be accomplished using radar vectors, feeder routes, STARs, or a combination of these procedures. Radar has the primary advantage of increasing the volume of traffic that can be handled safely in a given time frame. Since standard termi-

AT OR ABOVE 18,000 FT. MSL	
Current Altimeter Setting	Lowest Usable Flight Level
29.92 (or higher)	180
29.91 thru 29.42	185
29.41 thru 28.92	190
28.91 thru 28.42	195
28.41 thru 27.92	200
27.91 thru 27.42	205
27.41 thru 26.92	210

Fig. 10-12. Lowest Usable Flight Levels

nal arrival routes usually are designated for busier airports, STARs often terminate with radar vectors to the final approach course. Feeder routes are most often used at those terminals which do not possess a radar capability.

RADAR APPROACH CONTROL

ARTCCs normally provide radar handoffs to radar-equipped approach control facilities. This handoff usually is accomplished before the flight reaches the clearance limit. Radar approach control then provides separation and radar vectors to the final approach course.

The radar controller usually will issue a clearance for an approach after the final vector to intercept the approach course is given. An example of such a clearance is *"Bonanza, 9014V, three miles from outer marker, turn left heading 010°, cleared for the ILS runway 36 approach. Contact tower on 118.3 outer marker inbound."*

The purpose of the final vector is to achieve interception of the final approach course. Upon interception, the pilot is expected to establish the aircraft on the final approach course and execute the remaining part of the approach procedure using radio navigation. After passing the final approach fix (FAF), the pilot is expected to complete the approach or execute a missed approach procedure, if necessary. Radar service is automatically terminated when the pilot completes the landing, or when the tower controller has the aircraft in sight.

FEEDER ROUTES

Feeder routes, also called terminal routes, provide an alternate method for transitioning to the approach phase. At airports without radar capability, feeder routes are used exclusively between enroute and approach facilities. These routes are designated in terminal approach procedures when the approach does not begin with an enroute facility. The feeder route allows the pilot to navigate from the last enroute fix to the point at which a particular approach begins.

Feeder routes are shown on the plan view of instrument approach charts. They are depicted as prominent arrows connecting enroute fixes with the first point of the approach. It should be noted that several feeder routes may be provided for a particular approach. In addition, each feeder route indicates the magnetic course, distance, and minimum altitude between the applicable fixes.

STANDARD TERMINAL ARRIVAL ROUTES

STARs are coded IFR arrival routes which are established for specific airports. STARs are used in the arrival phase, just as SIDs are used in the departure phase. Both are used to simplify clearances.

Normally, STARs terminate at a fix near the airport concerned, then a radar vector or feeder route is used for transition to the approach phase. In some cases, STARs may be designed to intercept an approach course, as shown in figure 10-13.

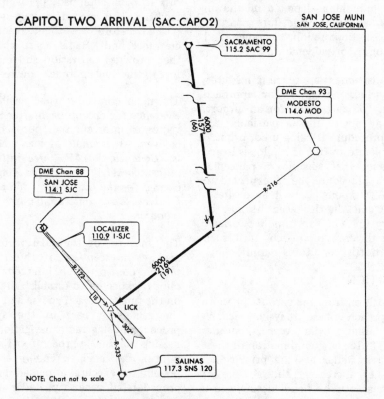

Fig. 10-13. Transition via STAR

ATC may issue a STAR to a particular aircraft whenever it is deemed appropriate. Pilots who do not wish to use STARs should file "NO STAR" in the remarks section of the flight plan. The less desirable method of verbally advising ATC also may be used.

Regular STAR procedures are produced in chart form by both Jeppesen Sanderson Inc. and NOS. When a pilot accepts a STAR in an IFR clearance, he must have the approved STAR procedure in his personal possession.

GENERAL APPROACH PROCEDURES

Instrument approach procedures provide for safe descent in IFR conditions to a specific airport or runway at that airport. Each approach must conform with criteria prescribed by the *United States Standards for Terminal Instrument Procedures (TERPs)*. Before a procedure is published in chart form, it is thoroughly checked and flight tested by the FAA. The procedure is periodically reviewed and, if changes are made, a revised approach procedure chart is published.

TYPES OF APPROACHES

All instrument approaches are divided into two broad categories — *precision approach procedures* and *nonprecision approach procedures*. Both approaches provide course guidance (azimuth) to an airport or to a specific runway. The precision approach provides vertical guidance (glide slope) as well as course guidance to the runway.

PRECISION APPROACHES

Precision approaches are designed so the final approach course is always aligned with a specific runway. During final, the pilot can tell his position in relation to the approach course and the glide path. Normally, precision approach descents continue to 200 feet above the runway. At this point, called the decision height (DH), the pilot must decide whether to continue the approach or to execute a missed approach.

The instrument landing system (ILS) is an example of a precision approach where the pilot relies exclusively on navigation indications within the aircraft. Precision approach radar (PAR), another type of precision approach, utilizes only radio communications from the radar controller to provide course correction and descent instructions. Figure 10-14 illustrates course guidance and vertical guidance used during precision approaches.

NONPRECISION APPROACHES

Nonprecision approaches require segmented descents at various points in the procedure. Since glide slope information is not provided, the pilot cannot tell the exact rate or angle of descent required at a given time. This is also true of the final segment and, for this reason, higher minimums are required for nonprecision approaches. The lowest altitude to which an aircraft may descend during a nonprecision approach is termed the minimum descent altitude (MDA).

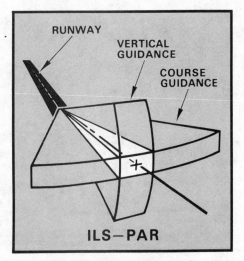

Fig. 10-14. Precision Approach

Examples of nonprecision approaches include VOR, VORTAC (VOR/DME), NDB (ADF), and ASR procedures. ILS approaches also are categorized as nonprecision approaches when the glide slope is not used; in this case, they are simply referred to as *localizer* approaches. Figure 10-15 depicts a simplified nonprecision approach procedure.

STRAIGHT-IN LANDINGS AND CIRCLING APPROACHES

A straight-in landing to a runway can be made when the final instrument approach course is aligned within plus or minus 30° of that runway. Straight-in landings require a minimum of maneuvering to align the aircraft with the

Fig. 10-15. Nonprecision Approach

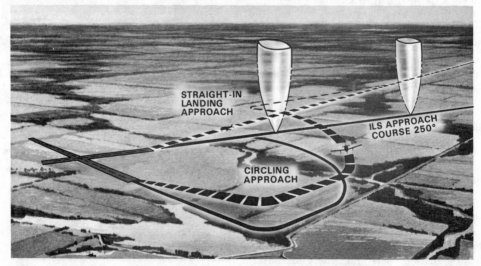

Fig. 10-16. Straight-in and Circling Procedures

INSTRUMENT PROCEDURES

runway. If the final approach course is not properly aligned or if it is desirable to land on a different runway, a circling approach may be used. Figure 10-16 depicts straight-in and circling procedures.

Straight-in landings and straight-in approaches should not be confused. The controller terminology " . . . *cleared for straight-in approach . . .* " means that the published procedure turn should not be utilized. For example, the pilot could be " . . . *cleared for straight-in ILS runway 25 approach, circle to land runway 34.* "

Most approach procedures provide for both straight-in and circling maneuvers. Others may be limited to circling only. For example, an approach from a VOR facility not closely aligned with any of the runways on the airport would authorize only circling maneuvers.

Straight-in landing procedures are named to identify the type of navaid which provides final course guidance. They also are numbered to identify the runway which is aligned with the final approach course. For example, ILS RWY 11 means that an instrument landing system is aligned with runway 11. VOR RWY 7 means a VHF omnirange provides course alignment with runway 7. However, the approach procedure also provides for an optional circling procedure when landing on another runway.

Procedures which are exclusively circling also have distinctive names. For example, VOR-A means that a VHF omnirange provides final course guidance to the airport. The letter "A" means that it is the *first nonprecision circling approach* established for the airport. Successive approaches are numbered VOR-B, VOR-C, etc.

APPROACH MINIMUMS

During the final approach, the minimum altitude to which a specific airplane may descend before the runway or runway environment is seen may be limited by several factors. In addition to the types of approaches (precision/nonprecision) and the type of maneuver (straight-in or circling), these include the following.

1. Category of aircraft
2. Associated visual aids
3. Inoperative components

Category of Aircraft

Minimum descent altitudes and decision heights are specified for different categories of aircraft. These categories are determined by approach speed. The approach speed is based on 1.3 times the stall speed in the landing configuration at the maximum landing weight. Aircraft approach categories are shown in the following table.

APPROACH CATEGORY	SPEED (KNOTS)
A	Less than 91 knots
B	91 knots or more but less than 121 knots
C	121 knots or more but less than 141 knots
D	141 knots or more but less than 166 knots
E	166 knots or more

An aircraft category also may vary with the type of approach used because of a different landing configuration. For example, a circling approach usually requires a higher speed and a different approach configuration than a straight-in landing. Therefore, a circling approach may place a particular aircraft in a higher approach category.

All approach charts show aircraft categories in the minimums section. Category E concerns military aircraft only and is not shown on civil approach charts. The single-engine and light twin-engine aircraft used in general aviation fall almost exclusively into category A.

Associated Visual Aids

Approach lighting systems make the runway environment more apparent in low visibilities; therefore, credit to reduce minimum landing visibility is required with some lighting systems. The amount of reduction follows rigid requirements specified in TERPs. Other factors, such as runway markings, the approach course, and obstacles, also are considered when determining the amount of reduction authorized.

Landing minimums published on instrument approach charts are based on full operation of all components and visual aids associated with the approach procedure being used. Higher minimums are required when one or more of the components or visual aids are inoperative or otherwise unavailable.

Inoperative Components

According to FAR 91.117(c), a higher visibility and MDA or DH may be required with inoperative components or visual aids. To determine the increase in the required minimums, pilots must consult a special chart entitled "Inoperative Components or Visual Aids Table." This table, depicted in figure 10-17, is found in the front of each NOS approach chart book. For ILS approaches, the inoperative component table adjustments apply to both ground and airborne equipment outages.

The minimums section of Jeppesen charts shows the increase in visibilities and MDA or DH resulting from various inoperative components and visual aids. Because they utilize more components and visual aids, ILS approaches are the most detailed. In some cases, more than one component or visual aid may be inoperative, requiring the pilot to select the highest of the two appropriate minimums.

ABBREVIATED APPROACH PROCEDURES

Contact and visual approaches abbreviate instrument approach procedures. They also permit the pilot to shift to visual references when the destination airport is VFR or near VFR. Both of these procedures relieve the pilot of the requirement to fly the complete instrument procedure.

CONTACT APPROACHES

ATC issues clearances for contact approaches upon *pilot request* when the reported ground visibility at the destination is one statute mile or greater and the airport has a standard or special instrument approach procedure. ATC cannot initiate a contact approach.

When operating under a clearance for a contact approach, the pilot must be able to remain clear of clouds and maintain one mile visibility to the airport (special VFR minimums). Contact approaches place the responsibility for obstruction clearance on the pilot, but ATC provides separation from other IFR or special VFR traffic. Separation from normal VFR traffic is not provided.

Contact approaches have certain advantages for the instrument pilot. For example, they require less time than the published instrument procedure, allow the pilot to retain his IFR clearance, and provide separation from IFR and special VFR traffic. On the other hand, obstruction clearance and VFR traffic avoidance become the pilot's responsibility. In addition, weather conditions can deteriorate below the required one-mile visibility. In this case, the pilot is expected to advise ATC immediately and proceed according to the instructions received. In cases where weather conditions are marginal, these instructions may be issued by ATC with the initial approach clearance. An example of such a clearance is, "*Bellanca 1776R, cleared for contact approach at or below 2,000, direct to the airport; if not possible, maintain 2,000 direct to the Taylor VOR and advise."*

Contact approaches are issued only for airports with published approach procedures (public or private). They should

---

Instrument Approach Procedures (Charts)
INOPERATIVE COMPONENTS OR VISUAL AIDS TABLE
Civil Pilots see FAR 91.117(c)

Landing minimums published on instrument approach procedure charts are based upon full operation of all components and visual aids associated with the particular instrument approach chart being used. Higher minimums are required with inoperative components or visual aids as indicated below. If more than one component is inoperative, each minimum is raised to the highest minimum required by any single component that is inoperative. ILS glide slope inoperative minimums are published on instrument approach charts as localizer minimums. This table may be amended by notes on the approach chart. Such notes apply only to the particular approach category(ies) as stated. See legend page for description of components indicated below.

(1) ILS, MLS, and PAR

Inoperative Component or Aid	Approach Category	Increase DH	Increase Visibility
MM*	ABC	50 feet	None
MM*	D	50 feet	¼ mile
ALSF 1 & 2, MALSR, & SSALR	ABCD	None	¼ mile

*Not applicable to PAR

(2) ILS with visibility minimum of 1,800 or 2,000 RVR.

MM	ABC	50 feet	To 2400 RVR
MM	D	50 feet	To 4000 RVR
ALSF 1 & 2, MALSR, & SSALR	ABCD	None	To 4000 RVR
TDZL, RCLS	ABCD	None	To 2400 RVR
RVR	ABCD	None	To ½ mile

(3) VOR, VOR/DME, VORTAC, VOR (TAC), VOR/DME (TAC), LOC, LOC/DME, LDA, LDA/DME, SDF, SDF/DME, RNAV, and ASR

Inoperative Visual Aid	Approach Category	Increase MDA	Increase Visibility
ALSF 1 & 2, MALSR, & SSALR	ABCD	None	½ mile
SSALS, MALS & ODALS	ABC	None	¼ mile

(4) NDB

ALSF 1 & 2, MALSR, & SSALR	C	None	½ mile
	ABD	None	¼ mile
MALS, SSALS, ODALS	ABC	None	¼ mile

Fig. 10-17. NOS Inoperative Components

not be used to proceed VFR to another airport which is not listed as the destination airport on the IFR flight plan.

VISUAL APPROACHES

A visual approach also authorizes an IFR pilot to expedite an approach when in flight to and landing at the airport can be accomplished under VFR. A visual approach clearance is initiated by the controller when the pilot reports the airport or the preceding aircraft in sight. A safe landing interval and wake turbulence separation are the pilot's responsibility during a visual approach. Authorization to fly a visual approach does not relieve the pilot of the responsibility to cancel the IFR flight plan.

When visual approaches are in progress at an airport with an operating control tower, the controller may alert the pilot by advising the following; *"Expect vector to the airport traffic pattern."* An example of a visual approach clearance is: *"Bonanza 9014V is cleared for a visual approach to follow the Lear at two o'clock four miles. Contact the tower 118.1 crossing the interstate."*

At airports with parallel runways separated by less than 2,500 feet, the succeeding aircraft must report sighting the preceding aircraft before ATC may authorize a visual approach. When the parallel runways are separated by 2,500 feet or more, or converging runways are in use, ATC may authorize a visual approach after advising all aircraft that other aircraft are conducting approaches to the other runway.

At airports without an operating control tower and no weather reporting facility, ATC may authorize a visual approach only if the pilot reports that descent and flight to the destination airport can be made under VFR.

ADVANCE APPROACH INFORMATION

When IFR conditions prevail at certain airports, ATC will provide arriving pilots with advance approach information. This service is provided for airports with approach control facilities where more than one published approach procedure is available.

The service is suspended when visibility is three miles or greater, and the ceiling is at or above the highest initial approach altitude. In addition, the service is not provided at locations where ATIS is available and has been received by the pilot.

Advance approach information, when issued, is not an ATC clearance or commitment, as fluctuating weather, shifting winds, or a blocked runway may require the use of a different approach. In most cases, however, the service allows the pilot to be better prepared for the approach he will likely receive.

DESCENT FOR APPROACH
FAR PART 91.116(f)

When an approach clearance is received, each pilot, operating under IFR on an unpublished route or being radar vectored, is required to maintain his last assigned altitude (1) unless a different altitude is assigned by ATC, or (2) until the aircraft is established on a segment of a published route or instrument approach procedure. However, if a pilot desires an altitude change after an approach clearance is received, he may request an appropriate clearance from ATC until the aircraft is established on a published route or instrument approach procedure. At that time the pilot may, on his own initiative, descend to the published minimum altitude for the route segment or approach procedure segment, as appropriate, unless cleared for another altitude by ATC. In this connection, it should be emphasized that an ATC clearance does not relieve the pilot of his direct responsibility for, and his final authority as to, the operation of his aircraft. This responsibility is clearly set forth in 91.3(a).

SECTION B—HOLDING PATTERNS

HOLDING PROCEDURES

Holding patterns are used to delay aircraft for various reasons. ARTCCs may assign holding patterns to regulate the flow of traffic and maintain separation. Approach control facilities often use a holding "stack" to sequence aircraft for the active instrument approach. In other cases, an aircraft may climb in a holding pattern to the MEA when enroute obstruction clearance so dictates. Holding patterns are used automatically by pilots in some cases, such as when they reach a clearance limit or during missed approach procedures. In addition, pilots may request holding patterns to wait for weather improvement.

STANDARD HOLDING PATTERN

A standard holding pattern is a racetrack-shaped maneuver. The turns are performed to the *right* at a standard rate of three degrees per second, provided the angle of bank does not exceed 30°. If a flight director system is used, the bank limit is 25°. A nonstandard holding pattern utilizes the same procedure, but employs *left turns*.

The length of the holding pattern legs varies with the groundspeed of the aircraft. In a no-wind condition, each leg is flown for 1 minute (1-1/2 minutes above 14,000 feet MSL). Figure 10-18 depicts an aircraft flying a standard holding pattern using standard-rate turns in a no-wind condition. In the example shown, the aircraft groundspeed is 120 knots, resulting in leg lengths of two nautical miles.

OUTBOUND AND INBOUND TIMING

After entry into a holding pattern, the initial outbound leg should be flown for 1 or 1-1/2 minutes, whichever is appropriate. The timing for subsequent outbound legs should be adjusted to achieve *proper inbound timing* (1 minute or 1-1/2 minutes). This procedure is required because of the effect of wind which may cause significant differences between the inbound and outbound leg groundspeed.

If the inbound leg of a holding pattern requires 45 seconds instead of one minute, the outbound leg should be lengthened. The normal procedure is to lengthen the outbound leg by the same amount that the wind has shortened the inbound leg (in this case, 15 seconds). Although this procedure results in slightly unequal time for the two legs, it will suffice

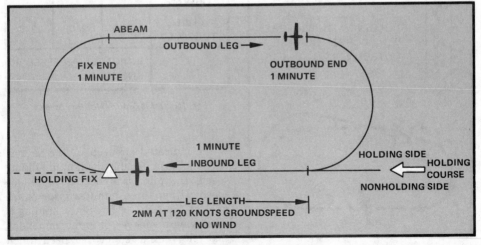

Fig. 10-18. Standard Holding Pattern

unless winds are extremely high in relation to the true airspeed of the aircraft. Pilots should continue to check the inbound timing and make outbound adjustments as necessary.

CROSSWIND CORRECTION

Crosswind conditions produce the necessity for pronounced heading corrections. During inbound tracking, the pilot can determine the wind correction angle (WCA) necessary to maintain course

from the navigation indicators. However, as shown in figure 10-19, item 1, if the same amount of wind correction is applied during the outbound leg, the aircraft will overshoot the course following the turn to the inbound leg. Item 2 shows the result of *doubling* the WCA when flying the outbound leg. Failure to apply this technique may result in penetration of the airspace on the nonholding side. In addition, it may be difficult to become established on the inbound course before reaching the fix, resulting in more pattern irregularity and possibly contributing to disorientation.

MAXIMUM HOLDING SPEED

Obviously, as the aircraft's speed increases, the holding pattern is lengthened. In order to reduce the amount of airspace that must be protected by ATC, maximum holding speeds have been designated for specific altitude ranges. These speeds and effective altitudes are shown in the table in figure 10-20.

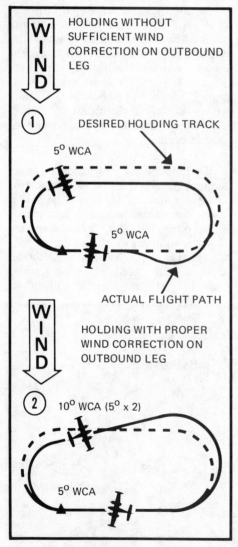

Fig. 10-19. Holding in a Crosswind

	MSL ALTITUDES		
AIRCRAFT	6,000 AND BELOW	6,001 TO 14,000	ABOVE 14,000
PROPELLER-DRIVEN	175	175	175
CIVIL TURBOJET	200	210	230
	INDICATED AIRSPEED IN KNOTS		

Fig. 10-20. Maximum Holding Speeds

If the indicated airspeed of the aircraft exceeds the applicable maximum holding speed, the pilot is expected to reduce speed within three minutes *prior to his ETA* at the holding fix. Since holding is a delaying maneuver, it is recommended that pilots use a reduced airspeed which will result in greater endurance.

HOLDING PATTERNS AND FIXES

Holding patterns may utilize VORs, VORTACs, NDBs, localizers, or combinations of navaids. Figure 10-21 depicts two variations of holding patterns which may be assigned by ATC. One procedure utilizes two VORs, and the other employs an ILS localizer course with a compass locator at the outer marker.

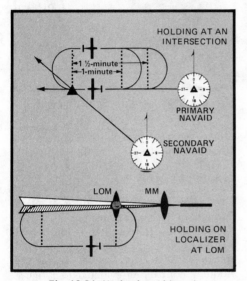

Fig. 10-21. Navigation Aids and
Holding Patterns

Figure 10-22, item 1, depicts a DME hold at the 20 DME fix on the 090° radial of a VORTAC utilizing 10 nautical mile legs. Controllers may assign any DME fix and utilize a wide range of leg lengths.

The holding pattern in item 2 shows the application of RNAV to the same DME hold. The pilot has simply "offset" the VORTAC to the DME fix location. In this case, the turn from the outbound leg begins at the 10 DME point, rather than the 30 DME point, which would normally be used.

HOLDING PATTERN ENTRIES

Standard holding pattern entry procedures are designed to reduce maneuvering and conserve airspace during the

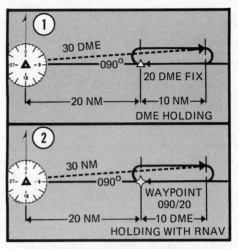

Fig. 10-22. Holding with DME and
Area Navigation

initial phase of the holding procedure. Three types of entry procedures are used.

1. Direct
2. Teardrop
3. Parallel

As shown in figure 10-23, the direct entry applies to the sectors 70° left through 110° right of the holding course, as viewed from the holding fix. The teardrop sector covers 70° of azimuth, and the parallel sector includes 110°. Aircraft magnetic *heading* upon arrival at the fix determines the type of

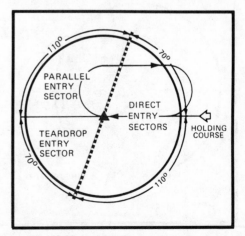

Fig. 10-23. Holding Pattern Entry Sectors

entry to use. Plus or minus five degrees in heading is considered within good operating limits for determining the correct entry. Therefore, flights approaching a fix on sector boundaries may use either of two procedures in most cases.

DIRECT ENTRY

The direct entry procedure is the simplest pattern entry. It is also the one most often encountered because it can be applied throughout 180° of azimuth in relation to the holding fix. When using a direct entry to a standard pattern, the pilot simply crosses the fix, turns right to the outbound heading, and flys the pattern. Direct entry procedures are depicted in figure 10-24. Notice in the two examples that the aircraft may not be perfectly established on the holding course until the second circuit of the holding pattern.

TEARDROP ENTRY

The teardrop entry is the next simplest procedure. After crossing the fix, the pilot should turn to an outbound heading which diverges approximately 30° toward the holding side of the course, as shown in figure 10-25. After holding the heading for 1 minute (or 1-1/2 minutes, if appropriate), the aircraft should be

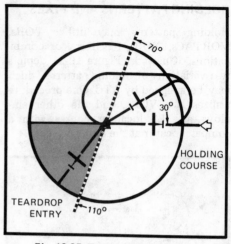

Fig. 10-25. Teardrop Entry Sector

turned to intercept the holding course inbound and return to the fix.

PARALLEL ENTRY

The parallel entry procedure is used throughout 110° of azimuth and involves paralleling the holding course outbound on the nonholding side. After one minute, a turn is made to intercept the inbound course. As evidenced in figure 10-26, it may be difficult to actually intercept the holding course before recrossing the fix.

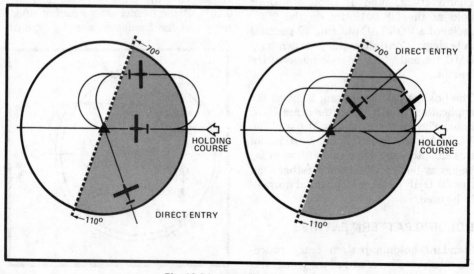

Fig. 10-24. Direct Entry Sector

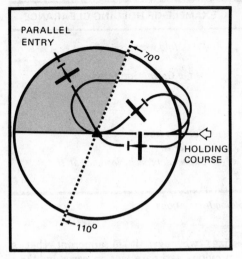

Fig. 10-26. Parallel Entry Sector

VISUALIZING ENTRY PROCEDURES

Pilots have improvised various methods for visualization of entry procedures prior to arrival over the fix. They include drawing holding patterns on aeronautical charts, using the wind side of a flight computer, employing the aircraft heading indicator, referring to a holding pattern inscription on a plotter, or using specially designed pattern entry computers. The value of any of these methods is directly proportional to how well they actually help the pilot *mentally visualize* the holding pattern and the appropriate entry procedure.

An alternate method which does not require separate "paraphernalia" may be the most advantageous. In many cases, holding patterns may be assigned suddenly, leaving little time for a busy pilot to determine the proper procedure with the use of separate tools or devices.

One of the alternate methods requires the pilot to visualize his arrival at the fix. If the holding course is behind the aircraft upon arrival at the fix, a *direct entry* is appropriate. When the holding course is *ahead* and to the *right* of the aircraft, a *teardrop entry* may be used. A *parallel entry* is appropriate if the holding course is ahead and to the *left* of the aircraft as it crosses the fix.

This method of visualization and the various methods of entry may also be applied to nonstandard holding patterns. The direct entry sector is still behind the aircraft; however, holding courses ahead and to the right of the aircraft require a parallel entry. Conversely, holding courses ahead and to the left of the aircraft require a teardrop entry.

HOLDING PATTERNS ON AERONAUTICAL CHARTS

Frequently used holding patterns are depicted on both Jeppesen and NOS charts. Figure 10-27 is an excerpt from an NOS enroute chart showing holding

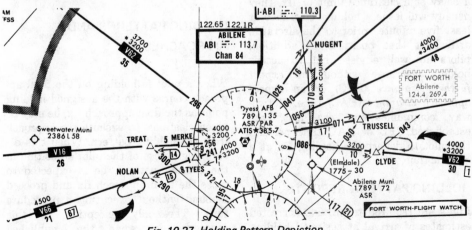

Fig. 10-27. Holding Pattern Depiction

ELEMENTS OF HOLDING CLEARANCE	EXAMPLE OF HOLDING CLEARANCE
1. The direction to hold from the holding fix	*". . . Hold west*
2. Holding fix	*of the Greenwood Intersection*
3. The specified radial, course, magnetic bearing, airway number, or jet route	*on V-8,*
4. The outbound leg length in minutes or nautical miles when DME is used	*five-mile legs,*
5. Nonstandard pattern if used	*left turns.*
6. Expect further clearance or expect approach clearance time	*Expect approach clearance at 15."*

Fig. 10-28. ATC Holding Instructions

patterns in the vicinity of the Abilene VORTAC. These holding patterns are located at Nolan, Trussell, and Clyde Intersections. All three depictions indicate standard (right hand) patterns.

ATC HOLDING INSTRUCTIONS

If the holding pattern assigned by ATC is depicted on the appropriate aeronautical chart, the pilot is expected to hold according to the procedure depicted, unless advised otherwise by ATC. An ATC clearance assigning a holding pattern which is not depicted on the appropriate chart will contain the information shown in figure 10-28.

Pilots are to hold at the last assigned altitude unless a new altitude is specifically given. When controllers anticipate a delay at a clearance limit or fix, they usually will issue a holding clearance at least five minutes prior to the aircraft's arrival at that position. In addition, pilots are well advised not to accept holding clearance without an *expect further clearance* (EFC) or an *expect approach clearance* (EAC) time. If two-way communications are lost, the established EFC or EAC time permits the pilot to depart the holding fix at a specific time.

HOLDING PATTERN REPORTS

Pilots are required to provide corrected estimates of arrival at assigned holding fixes whenever it is apparent that a previous estimate was in error by *three minutes or more.* Similarly, pilots are expected to report *entering* and *departing* the holding pattern. However, revised estimates and entry/exit reports are *not* required when in radar contact. *Changes in altitude* while holding must be reported *at all times.* After departing a holding pattern, a pilot is expected to maintain normal speeds consistent with the subsequent route. In a terminal area, appropriate speed restrictions apply. If proceeding enroute, the pilot is expected to resume the true airspeed shown on the flight plan or provide a corrected estimate when the variation is *plus or minus five percent, or 10 knots,* whichever is greater.

HOLDING PATTERNS AND
APPROACHES

When a pilot is holding on the final approach course with the assigned holding point as the final approach fix, he may be given clearance to execute the approach from the holding pattern. When this occurs, regardless of the pilot's position in the holding pattern, he is expected to cross the final approach fix and proceed inbound without executing a procedure turn. The only exception to this procedure is when the published approach procedure states that final approach from a holding pattern is not authorized. In this case, the pilot must comply with the printed procedure. As a result, he will turn outbound and execute the procedure turn or other course reversals indicated in the published approach procedure.

SECTION C—IFR CLEARANCE SHORTHAND

ATC PLANNING

Air traffic control planning for an IFR flight begins in the air route traffic control center (ARTCC). Here, the IFR flight plan is received, processed, and compared with other flight plans. An IFR clearance is prepared and distributed to the controllers in each sector through which the flight will pass. Then, it is forwarded to the pilot via the appropriate ATC facility or flight service station. Although each step in this process is executed rapidly, sometimes with the aid of an immense computer system, the entire process requires approximately 30 minutes for an average flight. It is necessary, therefore, for the pilot to allow at least 30 minutes between filing an IFR flight plan with ATC and requesting the IFR clearance.

IFR clearances also can be requested while enroute. The recommended procedure for such requests is to first file an IFR flight plan with the nearest flight service station. The pilot must then wait, in VFR conditions, for instructions as to what facility and frequency to use in receiving the clearance. In some situations, a clearance may be requested and received directly from the controller. These requests are called "pop-ups" and generally are discouraged by ATC.

Unless authorized by the responsible controller, pilots requesting an IFR clearance are required by FAR 91.115 to file an IFR flight plan containing the information established in FAR 91.83. Parts of the flight plan are used by the controller and pilot as a basis for a plan of action in the event of lost communications while flying IFR.

ATC CLEARANCE

Aircraft flying in *controlled* airspace under IFR must file an IFR flight plan.

Additonally, an ATC clearance must be obtained. A pilot flying *outside* of controlled airspace is *not* required to obtain an ATC clearance; however, the pilot should remember that other aircraft may be operating in the same area, and IFR traffic separation is not provided.

Compliance with an ATC clearance is *required* by regulations after the clearance is accepted. The pilot in command may not deviate from that clearance, unless an amended clearance is obtained, or an emergency so dictates. If a pilot is *unable* to comply with a clearance, he should refuse to accept it and request a substitute. In addition, if a pilot is *uncertain of the meaning of an ATC clearance*, he is *required* by regulation (91.75) *to immediately request clarification from ATC.*

The pilot may cancel an IFR clearance anytime the aircraft is operating in VFR weather below 18,000 feet MSL. It should be remembered at this point, that the flight must be conducted *strictly* in VFR conditions *from that point on*, and should IFR weather again be encountered, the pilot must *file* a new flight plan and *obtain* an IFR clearance or *adjust course* to remain VFR.

If several clearances are obtained while enroute, the last clearance received has *precedence* over all *related* items in any preceding clearances. If deviation from a clearance is required by an emergency, and ATC has given priority to the aircraft, the pilot in command *may* be requested to submit a written report within 48 hours to the chief of that ATC facility.

CLEARANCE READBACK

There is no requirement that an ATC clearance be read back as an unsolicited or spontaneous action. Controllers may request that a clearance be read back when the complexity of the clearance or any other factors indicate a need.

The pilot should read back the clearance if he feels the need for confirmation. Even though it is not specifically stated, it is generally expected that the pilot read back the enroute clearance when received from clearance delivery, ground control, or a flight service station.

"ATC CLEARS"

The term "ATC clears" is used only when a facility *other* than air traffic control is used to transmit an IFR clearance. For example, when receiving a clearance from the flight service station, the enroute clearance will be preceded with the term "ATC clears."

A pilot may lose communications with an air route traffic control center in remote areas even though he is navigating at, or above, the MEA. In this case, the pilot may still be able to communicate with a flight service station, and they will relay all clearances and requests from air traffic control to the pilot.

ENROUTE CLEARANCES

It is easier to copy IFR clearances if the general format of each clearance is known prior to the clearance being issued by air traffic control. Generally, the controllers will use the following order when issuing enroute clearances:

   Aircraft identification
   Clearance limit
   Departure procedure
   Route of flight
   Altitude data in the order flown
   Holding instructions
   Any special information
   Frequency and transponder code information

Some of the information listed, such as the departure procedure and holding in-

structions, may not be issued with an enroute clearance.

When requesting clearances from air traffic control or a flight service station, certain terminologies are accepted and should be utilized by pilots. The following discussions are samples of clearance requests.

CLEARANCE DELIVERY

This example illustrates the recommended phraseology to be used when requesting an IFR enroute clearance from clearance delivery.

"Denver Clearance, Skyflyer 1234X, request IFR clearance to Omaha."

GROUND CONTROL

The following terminology should be used when requesting an IFR clearance from ground control when no clearance delivery is available:

"Midway Ground, Skyflyer 1234X, at Butler, taxi, IFR, Rockford, with Lima."

The tower will reply:

"Skyflyer 1234X, taxi to runway 30, clearance on request."

In the previous example, ATIS was available. If ATIS is not available, the clearance can be used as is, except the term "with Lima" is not applicable.

When copying an enroute clearance, the pilot should *not* be taxiing. If he is advised while taxiing that his clearance is ready, he should ask that his clearance be held until he is ready to copy it.

"VFR-CONDITIONS-ON-TOP" CLEARANCE

When requesting an IFR clearance to VFR conditions on top at a tower controlled field, it may not be necessary to file an IFR flight plan with the flight service station. The initial request for a VFR-on-top clearance can be made with clearance delivery or ground control. When IFR conditions exist at an airport where an ATC facility is *not* available, a request for clearance *to* VFR conditions on top should be made with a filed flight plan.

The following clearance is an example of the proper communications to be used when requesting an IFR clearance to VFR conditions on top when ground control, but not clearance delivery, is avialable.

"Great Falls Ground, Skyflyer 1234X, at Holman Aviation, request IFR clearance to VFR conditions on top, southbound."

Note, in the previous clearance, that the direction of flight was included in the initial request to enable ground control to issue a clearance in the direction appropriate to the planned flight.

When issuing IFR clearances to "VFR conditions on top," ATC will include a clearance limit, route of flight, and an altitude. The clearance limit will usually be a fix in the terminal area in the direction of flight requested by the pilot. This type of clearance should not be confused with an IFR flight plan to the destination with an altitude request of "VFR conditions on top" instead of a specific altitude request. The following terminology is an example of a VFR-conditions-on-top clearance.

"Skyflyer 1234X, cleared to the Naperville VOR, radar vectors, maintain VFR conditions on top, if not VFR on top at 4,000 feet, maintain 4,000 feet and advise."

TOWER-TO-TOWER CLEARANCE

When flying IFR between two airports, there is a possibility that the pilot will not come under the jursidiction of the air route traffic control center if the two airports are in close proximity to each other and their respective approach control areas of responsibility overlap. In this case, the pilot can request a tower-to-tower clearance without filing an IFR flight plan. The following request is an example of the recommended procedure when calling ground control.

"Peterson Ground, Skyflyer 1234X, request IFR tower-to-tower clearance to Denver."

THROUGH CLEARANCES

When making an intermediate stop at an airport enroute to the eventual destination, a single "through" IFR flight plan can be issued at the departure airport. When filing this type IFR flight plan, a pilot can expect to receive a through clearance prior to arriving at the intermediate stop. In the through clearance, air traffic control will issue the approach clearance, followed by the through clearance, which includes a clearance to the destination airport. The following example illustrates a through clearance that might be issued in the Denver area.

"Skyflyer 1234X, cleared for Greeley VOR approach, cleared through Greeley airport to the Denver airport via the 211° radial of Gill, Victor 81, maintain 8,000 feet. Contact Denver Center 124.1 passing through 6,000 feet."

PREFERRED ROUTES

To simplify copying IFR clearances, it is very important that the pilot file preferred routes, when available. When filing preferred routes, the pilot's clearance from air traffic control will usually be similar to the following:

"Skyflyer 1234X, cleared as filed, maintain . . "

If a preferred route is not used, it may be necessary to clear a pilot via a route other than the one filed. In this case, it is usually necessary for the IFR clearance to contain detailed and complex routing assignments. Therefore, the pilot should *file preferred routes!*

When departing from an airport where radar is available, the term *"cleared as filed"* usually will be followed by the altitude assignment, similar to the following:

"Skyflyer 1234X, cleared as filed, maintain 8,000. Maintain runway heading for departure vectors, Departure Control will be 124.8 . Squawk 1013."

When radar is not available at the departure airport, the clearance will usually include one or two of the first enroute fixes after the phrase *"cleared as filed."* The following clearance is an example of an enroute clearance from a nonradar airport.

"Skyflyer 1234X, cleared as filed via Lamar. Maintain 10,000. Contact Denver Center 126.6 passing through 6,000."

When air traffic control must restrict the altitude until the aircraft departs the terminal area, the clearance may be issued as follows:

". . . maintain 6,000 feet, expect 11,000 feet 10 miles east . . ."

At some airports, rather than giving the altitude restriction in the enroute clearance, the altitude restriction will be included with the takeoff clearance when it is issued to the tower. In addition, this clearance may include a geographical restriction in a local area, as shown in the following:

"Skyflyer 1234X, cleared for takeoff, turn left heading 270°, maintain 2,000 feet. After departure, remain south of the 073° radial of Naperville."

FLIGHT SERVICE STATION

When departing an airport without a control tower, but where a flight service station is available to relay clearances from air traffic control, the following communications procedures should be used.

"Akron Radio, Skyflyer 1234X on the ramp, request advisories for taxi, IFR, Salt Lake City."

When departing IFR from an airport where no radio communications are available, it is necessary to call the flight service station after filing the flight plan and request the IFR clearance over the telephone.

AIR ROUTE TRAFFIC CONTROL CENTER

After flying in VFR conditions from a departure airport, the pilot may find the weather along his route of flight dictates the need for an IFR clearance. In this case, it is best to call the flight service station and file an IFR flight plan while enroute. *After* the IFR flight plan is filed, the flight service station may advise the pilot to contact the ARTCC on an assigned frequency to receive the clearance directly from the air route traffic control center. In some cases, the FSS will give the clearance followed by the appropriate center frequency. Since the IFR clearance in this case, begins at an enroute facility rather than the departure airport, the first fix on the clearance is usually over that enroute facility. The following example is the recommended procedure when requesting an IFR clearance direct from center.

"Ft. Worth Center, Skyflyer 1234X, request IFR clearance from over Ardmore to Dallas."

All of the clearance requests just discussed are based on the assumption that an IFR flight plan had been filed prior to the clearance request. There are times when an IFR clearance can be requested even though a flight plan has not been filed with the flight service station. The IFR clearances that are requested while enroute are called "pop up" clearances and are generally discouraged by air traffic control.

DETOUR CLEARANCES

While enroute, it may be necessary to detour around thunderstorms. According to the regulations, pilots are not authorized to deviate from stated clearances unless an amended clearance is received from air traffic control. Assuming that a large thunderstorm is straight ahead and visible to the pilot, his request should be similar to the following:

"Denver Center, Skyflyer 1234X, a large cumulus buildup is at our 12 o'clock position, request deviation to the south."

If the pilot is in an area where thunderstorms have been reported, he can make the following request when in radar contact:

"Denver Center, Skyflyer 1234X, request vectors around the thunderstorm area."

AMENDED CLEARANCES

For various reasons, sometimes the pilot may wish to change his destination airport while enroute. When the pilot requests a deviation from the flight plan and wants an amended clearance, the following sample communications should be used:

"Chicago Center, Skyflyer 1234X, request change of the destination airport from Peoria to Springfield, Illinois."

After the above clearance request is made, the pilot should be ready to copy his new clearance which will include the normal IFR enroute clearance information.

CRUISE CLEARANCE

When operating in accordance with a cruise clearance, the pilot may climb *to and descend from* the assigned altitude *at his discretion.* However, once the pilot has reported leaving an altitude in a descent, he may not return to that altitude without further ATC clearance. Furthermore, a cruise clearance is approval for the pilot to proceed to and make an approach at the destination airport. This procedure also permits the pilot to descend and land in accordance with applicable FARs governing VFR flight operations.

For example, consider the following clearance:

"ATC clears Skyflyer 1234X to the Sipple Ranch Airport, direct, cruise 3,000."

In such a clearance, the term "cruise" means that the pilot is cleared to the destination airport and also to climb to 3,000 feet and descend to the MEA or MOCA at his discretion, without further clearance. Additionally, it is clearance to execute the appropriate approved instrument approach. However, if an approved approach is not available, the pilot may not descend below the MEA or MOCA, unless he is in VFR weather conditions.

APPROACH CONTROL

When requesting a clearance for an approach to an airport, the clearance will be issued to the pilot either as an actual IFR clearance or a clearance to practice an approach in VFR conditions, depending on the terminology used by the pilot when making the approach clearance request. If the pilot is making a request to do a practice ILS approach in VFR conditions, the following sample terminology should be used:

"Denver Approach, Skyflyer 1234X, request a practice ILS approach to Denver."

If the weather conditions at Denver require an IFR clearance to land, the terminology should be similar to the following example:

"Denver Approach, Skyflyer 1234X, over the Kiowa VOR, request IFR clearance, Denver."

In the previous clearance, note that the location of the aircraft was given. This gives the controller an immediate indication of the aircraft's position to help him locate the aircraft on the radar screen and plan a "slot" for the new IFR arrival. The technique of identifying the aircraft's position on initial callup when requesting an IFR clearance is also recommended when making an IFR clearance request while enroute.

HOLDING CLEARANCES

If a delay is anticipated in the terminal area, the center or approach control will issue a holding clearance at least five minutes before the aircraft is estimated to reach the clearance limit. The holding pattern clearance given by air traffic control will be issued using the following format:

1. Aircraft number
2. Direction of the hold from the fix
3. Holding fix
4. Radial, course, bearing, or airway on which the aircraft is to hold
5. Outbound leg length in miles if DME or RNAV is to be used
6. Direction of holding pattern turns if left turns are to be made
7. Expect further clearance or expect approach clearance time

For example:

"Skyflyer 1234X, hold north of the Jay VOR on the 350° radial, left turns, 8,000 feet, expect further clearance at one five."

APPROACH CLEARANCES

If only one instrument approach procedure exists at an airport, or if air traffic control wishes to authorize the pilot to execute an instrument approach of his choice, the controller will issue the following clearance:

"Skyflyer 1234X, cleared for the approach."

If more than one approach is available at an airport, and air traffic control wants the pilot to execute a specific approach such as the ILS runway 26 left approach, he may issue the clearance in this manner:

"Skyflyer 1234X, cleared for the ILS runway 26 left approach."

When approach control is providing radar vectors for a straight-in approach, the controller will state the distance from the final approach fix, issue a new heading to intercept the final approach course, and give the approach clearance. As an example, the controller might give the following clearance:

"Skyflyer 1234X, three miles from outer marker, turn right heading 240°, cleared for straight-in ILS runway 26 left approach. Contact Denver tower 118.3 outer marker inbound."

Note in the previous clearance that the controller issues the distance from the final approach fix to confirm to the pilot that he is in the intermediate segment, allowing him to descend to the final approach fix crossing altitude.

CLEARANCE SHORTHAND

To operate efficiently in an IFR environment, the pilot must be able to copy and thoroughly understand IFR clearances. Copying IFR clearances becomes easy with practice. Although numerous changes have been made since the acceptance of the first shorthand used by early instrument pilots, many of the original symbols have been retained. The shorthand symbols in this chapter are considered by the Federal Aviation Administration and experienced instrument pilots to be the best. However, the most important consideration is not what symbol the pilot uses, but the fact that the symbols represent meaningful information after a period of time. The following symbols and contractions represent words and phrases frequently used in clearances.

WORDS AND   SHORTHAND
PHRASES

ABOVE .... ABV
ABOVE ("Above Six Thousand") . . .60
ADVISE .... ADV
AFTER (Passing) .... < or AFT
AIRPORT .... A
(ALTERNATE INSTRUCTIONS) . . ( )
ALTITUDE 6,000—17,000 60-170
AND .... &
APPROACH .... APP
  FINAL .... F
  VOR .... VOR or ⊙
NONDIRECTIONAL BEACON
  (ADF) .... ADF
SURVEILLANCE RADAR ...... ASR
LOCALIZER BACK COURSE ... LBC
INSTRUMENT LANDING
  SYSTEM .... ILS
LOCALIZER ONLY .... LCO
PRECISION (Approach) RADAR . PAR
APPROACH CONTROL .... APC
AT (Usually Omitted) .... @
(ATC) ADVISES .... C ADV
(ATC) CLEARS or CLEARED C
(ATC) REQUESTS .... C R
BEARING .... BR
BEFORE (Reaching, Passing) ..... >
BELOW .... BLO
BELOW ("Below Six Thousand") . . .60
CENTER .... CTR
CLEARED AS FILED .... CAF
CLIMB (TO) .... ↑
CONTACT .... CT
COURSE .... CRS
CROSS (Crossing) X
CRUISE ....→

DEPART (Departure) .... DEP
DESCENT (TO) .... ↓
DIRECT .... DR
DME FIX (15 DME Mile Fix) ..... ⑮
EACH .... ea
EXPECT .... EX
EXPECT APPROACH CLEARANCE
  (Time) .... EAC
EXPECT   FURTHER   CLEARANCE
  (Time or Location) .... EFC
FLIGHT LEVEL .... FL
FLIGHT PLANNED ROUTE .... FPR
FOR FURTHER CLEARANCE .. FFC
HEADING .... HDG
HOLD (Direction) (Hold West) ... H-W
HOLDING PATTERN .... ⊂⊃
IF NOT POSSIBLE .... or
ILS LOCALIZER L
INBOUND .... IB
INTERSECTION .... △
INTERCEPT .... △
MAINTAIN (or Magnetic) ...... M
MAINTAIN VFR ON TOP ...... VFR
MIDDLE MARKER .... MM
  LOW FREQUENCY BEACON
  LOCATED AT MM .... LMM
OUTBOUND .... OB
OUTER MARKER .... OM
  LOW FREQUENCY BEACON
  LOCATED AT OM .... LOM
OVER (Ident. Over the Line) .... OKC
PROCEDURE TURN .... PT
RADAR VECTOR .... RV
RADIAL (092 Radial) 092R
REPORT .... Rp
  REPORT LEAVING .... RL
  REPORT ON COURSE .... RC
  REPORT OVER .... RO
  REPORT PASSING .... RP
  REPORT REACHING .... RR
  REPORT STARTING PROCEDURE
  TURN .... RSPT
REVERSE COURSE .... RC
RUNWAY .... RW
SQUAWK .... SQ
STANDBY .... STBY
TAKEOFF .... T-O
TOWER .... Z
TRACK .... TR
TURN LEFT, OR TURN LEFT
  AFTER TAKEOFF .... ↰ or LT
TURN RIGHT, OR TURN RIGHT
  AFTER TAKEOFF .... ↱ or RT

UNTIL . . . . til
UNTIL ADVISED (By) . . . . .ADV
UNTIL FURTHER ADVISED . . FADV
VICTOR (Airway Number). V294
VOR . . . . $\odot$
VORTAC . . . . $\textcircled{T}$

SAMPLE CLEARANCES

The following examples are presented to illustrate how the shorthand symbols are used to copy an ATC clearance. Proficiency in copying clearances can be attained only by practice. This can be done quite easily by listening to a recording of practice clearances offered by Jeppesen Sanderson, Inc. 8025 East 40th Avenue, Denver, Colorado, 80207. This recording gives clearances, slowly at first, to permit the beginner to keep up. Then, the clearances are sped up to normal clearance copying speed as the student becomes more proficient. The final five clearances are faster than normal to challenge the accomplished copier.

ATC clears Skyflyer one two three four Xray to the Laconia Municipal Airport via Victor one forty-one Concord Vortac, Victor one forty-one East Gunstock intersection. Turn left after takeoff, climb to and maintain eighteen hundred to Great Point intersection. Cross Nantucket Vortac at or below eighteen hundred. After passing Great Point intersection, climb to and maintain seven thousand. Cross Hyannis Vortac at seven thousand. Squawk one zero zero zero just before departure. Otis departure control frequency will be 118.2.

C 34X LCI A VI41 CON $\textcircled{T}$ VI41E
GUN△. ↟↑ M 18 GRT PT△. X ACK $\textcircled{T}$
@ 18. < GRT PT△ ↑ M 70. X HYA $\textcircled{T}$
@ 70. SQ 1000 > DEP. OTIS DEP 118.2.

ATC clears Skyflyer one two three four Xray to the St. Louis VORTAC via Victor niner. Maintain four thousand. Expect one zero thousand thirty DME miles after passing Memphis VORTAC. Maintain runway heading for radar vectors to Memphis VORTAC. Departure control one two six point seven.

C 34X STL $\textcircled{T}$ V9. M 40. EX 100 $\boxed{30}$
< MEM $\textcircled{T}$. M RW HDG RV MEM $\textcircled{T}$.
DEP 126.7.

Skyflyer one two three four Xray is cleared to hold south of St. Louis VORTAC on the one six five radial. Maintian five thousand feet until further advised. Expect further clearance at zero five.

34X C H-S STL $\textcircled{T}$ 165R. M 50 FADV.
EFC 05.

Skyflyer one two three four Xray is cleared to the Phoenix airport via Jet nineteen. Maintain five thousand. Maintain runway heading. Expect flight level two zero zero thirty miles southwest of the Wichita VORTAC. Tower one one niner point five. Departure control one two four point five. Squawk one zero zero zero.

34X C PHX A J19. M 50. M RW HDG.
EX FL 200 30 SW ICT $\textcircled{T}$. Z 119.5.
DEP 124.5. SQ 1000.

Skyflyer one two three four Xray cleared to the Dallas VORTAC via radar vectors. Climb and maintain VFR conditions on top. If not on top at five thousand, maintain five thousand and advise. Maintain runway heading for radar vectors. In the event of radio communications failure before reaching VFR conditions on top, execute a localizer back course approach to Wichita Municipal within two zero minutes after departure.

34X C DAL $\textcircled{T}$ RV. ↑ M VFR. NOT VFR
50 (M 50 & ADV). M RW HDG RV. RAD
COM FAIL > VFR LBC APP ICT A
>20 < DEP.

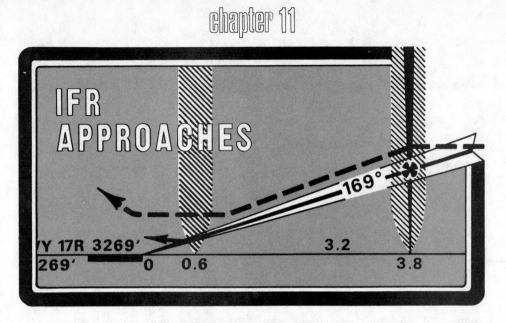

chapter 11

IFR APPROACHES

INTRODUCTION

Various procedures for instrument approaches have been established for use in the national airspace system. The approach procedures discussed in this chapter include ILS, VOR, VORTAC (VOR/DME), NDB (ADF), LDA, SDF, ASR, and PAR. The types of approaches available at a particular airport depend on airport/approach facilities and navigation aids.

Each procedure has several unique features which apply only to that particular approach. However, there are also many factors common to all instrument approach procedures. For example, approach segments, weather minimums, descent limits, missed approach procedures, and aircraft categories are specified in all approach procedures.

The execution of instrument approaches necessitates a high level of instrument proficiency. Aircraft control, navigation, chart interpretation, ATC procedures, and radio communication all are involved in instrument approaches. The function of instrument flight training is to teach smooth, accurate coordination of these operations and procedures.

SECTION A—ILS APPROACHES

The instrument landing system (ILS) has several advantages over nonprecision approach procedures as it provides highly accurate course, glide slope, and distance guidance to a given runway. Therefore, ILS approaches allow safer descents to lower minimums than most other procedures. Since civil PAR installations are very rare, ILS has become the principal precision approach in the national airspace system. An ILS approach normally provides for descents to 200 feet above the runway in visibilities as low as one-half statute mile.

ILS COMPONENTS AND VISUAL AIDS

The *basic ground components* of an ILS are the *localizer, glide slope, outer marker, and middle marker.* These items are depicted for a typical ILS installation in

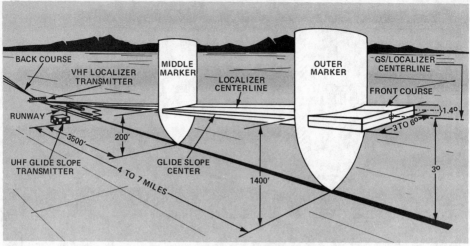

Fig. 11-1. Instrument Landing System

figure 11-1. Specific installations may vary somewhat from the format shown in terms of glide slope elevation, localizer width, or marker utilization and placement. In addition, an ILS will normally have several associated visual aids, such as runway lighting systems and RVR equipment.

LOCALIZER

The localizer transmitter is placed at the far end of the runway, opposite the approach end (front course), and emits a navigational array which provides course guidance to the *runway centerline*. This transmitter also radiates a back course signal in the direction opposite the front course. The angular width of the localizer is between three and six degrees, as necessary to provide a linear width of approximately 700 feet at the runway approach threshold.

Course information is accurate within a specific altitude block out to a range of at least 18 nautical miles from the antenna. The localizer minimum reception altitude at 18 nautical miles is 1,000 feet above the highest terrain along the approach course. The maximum reception altitude is 4,500 feet above the elevation of the antenna throughout the approach course.

The operational service volume of a localizer extends through an angular area 35° either side of the course, out to a range of 10 nautical miles. From 10 to 18 nautical miles, this area is reduced to 10° either side, as shown in figure 11-2.

Originally, localizers utilized only *20-odd-tenth frequencies* in the VHF frequency band from 108.10 MHz through 111.90 MHz (108.10, 108.30, 108.50. etc.). However, with the use of 50 kHz

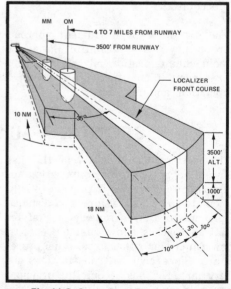

Fig. 11-2. Operational Service Volume

spacing 40 ILS channels are available (108.10, 108.15, 108.30, 108.35 MHz through 111.95 MHz). Many of the newer 200-channel navigation receivers incorporate 40-channel ILS capability.

Localizer audio identification consists of a three-letter Morse code identifier preceded by the letter "I." Since the Morse code for the letter "I" is two dots, localizers have a distinctive identification feature. For example, Dallas-Love Field, Dallas, Texas, has two separate ILS approaches. One localizer identifier is "IDAL" and the other is "ILVF."

Another distinctive feature of the ILS is greater tracking sensitivity of the course deviation indicator. Full-scale CDI movement represents a 20° radial span with VOR signals; however, when using localizer signals, the span is 5° (2.5° each side of the course).

The advantage of greater receiver sensitivity is that a localizer course can be tracked with a theoretical accuracy four times that of a VOR radial. However, since CDI movement is more rapid during localizer tracking, the pilot must make smaller course corrections than with VOR tracking. These corrections

also must be made more quickly. Since the localizer's signal represents only one magnetic course to the runway, the omnibearing selector of a navigation indicator does not affect course tracking. Regardless of what bearing is selected, the standard CDI senses off-course position with respect only to the localizer course. However, pilots often set the published front course of the ILS in the navigation indicator to serve as an orientation aid during tracking and heading corrections. In addition, pilots using flight director systems must set the horizontal situation indicator (HSI) to the approach course.

When tracking the front course of an ILS toward the runway, CDI sensing is normal; that is, right heading corrections are applied to right deflections of the CDI. Reverse CDI sensing occurs whenever the aircraft travels on the reciprocal heading of the localizer front course. The CDI sensing on the localizer is depicted in **figure 11-3.** *Normal sensing* occurs inbound on the front course and outbound on the back course. *Reverse sensing* occurs inbound on the back course and outbound on the front course. However, some currently manufactured navigation receivers provide a "reverse" or "back

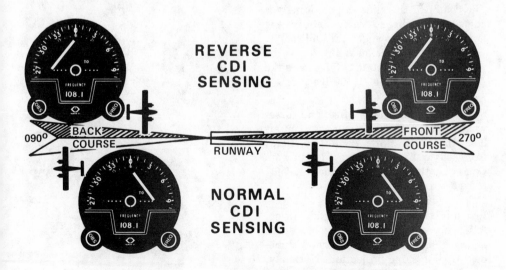

Fig. 11-3. Course Deviations on the Localizer

course" feature. This reverse sensing mode enables the pilot to select correct sensing regardless of the direction of travel on the localizer front or back course.

GLIDE SLOPE

The UHF glide slope transmitter usually is placed 750 to 1,250 feet down the runway from the approach end and is offset 400 to 600 feet from the runway centerline. Normally, glide slope signals are directed only to the front course. Glide slope information can be provided for the back course if an additional transmitter is installed near the appropriate end of the runway. These installations are increasing in number and when they occur, they are indicated by the bold notation, "BACK COURSE WITH GLIDE SLOPE" on Jeppesen charts or "BACK COURSE/GLIDE SLOPE" on NOS charts.

The glide slope transmitter operates on a UHF frequency which is paired to the associated VHF localizer frequency. When the pilot tunes the VHF localizer frequency on most general aviation navigation receivers, he also channels the appropriate UHF glide slope frequency.

The center of the glide slope normally is adjusted to three degrees above the horizontal. At this angle, the glide slope, which is 1.4° in thickness, intercepts the middle marker at about 200 feet and the outer marker at about 1,400 feet.

Since the transmitter is offset and somewhat elevated from the runway centerline, the glide slope centerline flares from 18 to 27 feet above the runway. Consequently, glide slope guidance is not provided to the point of touchdown.

In addition to the normal glide slope, false slopes and reverse sensing can occur at high angles *above* the normal three-degree glide slope projection. Normally, the existence of false glide slopes is not a problem, provided the pilot intercepts

the glide slope at or near the altitude prescribed on the approach chart. The pilot should disregard the glide slope indications until he is approaching the prescribed intercept altitude.

The localizer and glide slope information which is presented on the navigation indicator is shown in figure 11-4. A position only slightly off the glide slope or localizer centerline will produce large needle deflections on the navigation indicator. When navigating the ILS, the pilot must respond immediately to needle movement with heading, pitch, and/or power changes.

ILS MARKER BEACONS

ILS marker beacons provide the pilot with distance information with respect to the runway during the approach. All ILS marker beacons emit coded 75 MHz signals and project an elliptical array upward from the antenna site. At 1,000 feet above the antenna, the array is 2,400 feet in thickness and 4,200 feet in width. At 1,000 feet AGL, an aircraft flying through the array at 120 knots would receive the signal for about 15 seconds.

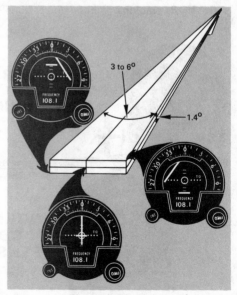

*Fig. 11-4. Localizer and
Glide Slope Indications*

Ordinarily, there are two marker beacons associated with an ILS—the outer marker (OM) and middle marker (MM). The placement of the outer marker varies from four to seven miles from the runway, depending on the installation. Normally, it is placed below the point where an aircraft executing the ILS approach procedure would intercept the glide slope. The outer marker (OM) is identified by a continuous series of dashes at the rate of two per second, or 120 per minute.

The middle marker (MM) is usually placed 3,500 feet from the landing threshold with its signal array intercepting the glide slope at approximately 200 feet above the touchdown zone. The identification feature of the MM is alternate dots and dashes keyed at the rate of 190 characters per minute.

At some locations where Category II ILS operations have been certified, an inner marker (IM) is employed. The inner marker is placed below the point where an aircraft on a CAT II approach reaches the appropriate decision height. This point is between the middle marker and the landing threshold. The IM is identified with dots keyed at the rate of six per second, or 360 per minute.

Occasionally, marker beacons may be utilized on the ILS back course as the final approach fix. Back course markers (BCM) are keyed with two dots at a rate between 144 and 190 characters per minute.

MARKER BEACON RECEIVER

Marker beacon receivers utilize three separate lights corresponding to the three ILS marker beacons, as shown in figure 11-5. The white light labeled A is also actuated by airway fan markers. This marker receiver is incorporated in the audio control console for the entire radio installation. Other models of marker receivers may be placed remotely.

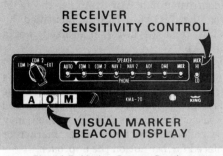

Fig. 11-5. Marker Beacon Receiver

The colors and labels for the marker beacon receiver lights are shown in the Marker Beacon Table. These lights flash as the aircraft passes through the signal array of the respective marker beacons. In addition to the lights, the audio identification of each marker beacon is presented over the speaker during station passage. Usually, a control is provided for high or low receiver sensitivity; the normal selection is the *low* position.

MARKER BEACON TABLE		
MARKER RECEIVER	COLOR	LABEL
OUTER	BLUE	O
MIDDLE	AMBER	M
INNER	WHITE	A

COMPASS LOCATORS

Many ILS systems utilize an NDB (compass locator) which normally is collocated with the outer marker. The combined facility is called an outer marker compass locator (LOM).

Compass locators normally utilize a power output of less than 25 watts, resulting in a reception range of at least 15 miles. The frequency range for compass locators is 200 to 415 kHz, the same as for standard NDBs.

At a few locations, compass locators are installed at the middle marker (LMM). Compass locators transmit a two-letter Morse code identifier taken from the ILS identifier group. For example, the LOM for the "IDAL" ILS is identified by "DA" and the LMM, if utilized, would be "AL."

At other locations, high powered NDBs (400 watts) may be utilized. These facilities usually carry transcribed weather broadcasts (TWEBs). They may be collocated with the outer marker or placed farther out on the approach.

When a compass locator is collocated with a marker beacon, the locator may be substituted for the beacon in the event of beacon failure. This means the pilot may still use the lowest approach minimum for the category of aircraft being operated. However, if the marker beacon *receiver* fails, the approach minimums will increase unless a compass locator also is collocated with the middle marker.

A compass locator used in conjunction with the ILS provides a means of transitioning to the approach course and better orientation during the approach procedure. ADF equipment also may function as a valuable backup system in the event of VHF/UHF navigation failure during an ILS approach.

ILS WITH DME

Occasionally, DME transmitters are collocated with the ILS glide slope transmitter. This type of installation provides the pilot with direct runway distance information.

ILS VISUAL AIDS

Approach lighting systems are visual aids which normally are associated with the ILS. In addition, whenever the minimum landing visibility for an ILS approach is specified as 1,800 or 2,000 feet runway visual range (RVR), other visual aids are included. They are high intensity runway lights, touchdown zone lights, centerline lights and markings, and RVR. These visual aids are described in Chapters 8 and 10.

When any basic ILS ground component or required visual aid is *inoperative, unusable, or not utilized*, the standard straight-in landing minimums prescribed for the approach are raised according to FAR 91.117. The Jeppesen charts show the increase in minimums directly on the chart. NOS users are provided with a tabulation derived from FAR 91.117 entitled, "Inoperative Components and Visual Aids Table." The pilot must then compute the higher minimums based on the applicable equipment failure.

ILS CATEGORIES

The basic ILS approach is termed Category I; it requires only that the pilot be instrument rated and that the aircraft be equipped with marker beacon, localizer, and glide slope receivers. Normally, minimum visibility is one-half statute mile, or RVR 2400, but it may be reduced to RVR 1800 when centerline and touchdown zone lights are provided. Decision height (DH) is 200 feet above the touchdown zone elevation.

Category II ILS minimums require special certification for operators, pilots, aircraft, and air/ground equipment. Normally, only air carrier operators possess the training facilities and equipment necessary for CAT II certification. "Interim" CAT II minimums authorize a DH of 150 feet and an RVR of 1600. After a period of consistent successful operations with interim minimums, the operator may be authorized "full" CAT II minimums as low as a DH of 100 feet and an RVR of 1200.

To accommodate future technological progress, Category III has been established. Category III miniumums include IIIa (DH — 0 feet, RVR — 700), IIIb (DH — 0 feet, RVR — 150), and IIIc (DH — 0 feet, RVR — 0). Due to the cost and complexity of equipment, it is likely that only the largest operators will qualify for CAT III ILS minimums.

FLYING THE ILS APPROACH

ILS approach training introduces elevation guidance by radio navigation. A pilot tracking a VOR radial interprets CDI deflections as *horizontal* movement of the aircraft away from the selected course. When the aircraft is on course, the CDI is centered regardless of altitude. On the other hand, the glide slope indicator senses the *vertical* movement of the aircraft in relation to an inclined plane projected from the glide slope transmitter. The pilot flying an ILS actually tracks a line formed by the intersection of the glide slope and localizer courses, as shown in figure 11-6.

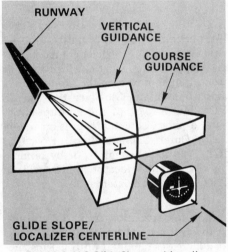

Fig. 11-6. ILS Glide Slope and Localizer

Prior to ILS glide slope interception, the pilot's primary concern is to stabilize airspeed and altitude, and arrive at a magnetic heading which will maintain the aircraft on the localizer centerline. Constant airspeed is not only desirable, but essential for smooth, accurate descents to MDA or DH. For example, the times to the MAP shown on approach charts are predicated on the basis of constant groundspeeds during the ILS approach. By maintaining a constant indicated approach speed, variation in groundspeed may be minimized and many pitch and power corrections elim-

inated. However, continuous small corrections are required on the ILS final approach course, because the wind usually varies in direction and/or velocity as the aircraft descends.

Pitch and power adjustments and configuration changes normally are required at glide slope interception to initiate the descent. In fixed-gear aircraft, a power reduction usually is required at glide slope interception. The amount of reduction depends on whether the flap configuration also is changed. In retractable gear aircraft, when the landing gear is lowered as the glide slope is approached, a pitch and power change may not be required. However, when such adjustments are required, retrimming the aircraft often is necessary.

Since the aircraft usually is below the glide slope during the intermediate approach segment, the glide slope indicator will display a full-up needle deflection, as shown in figure 11-7, item 1. The pilot should observe the initial downward movement of the indicator (item 2) and lead the descent to intercept the glide slope centerline accordingly.

After the descent rate stabilizes, power should be used, as necessary, to maintain a constant approach speed. Pitch changes normally are used to maintain the glide slope. However, if the glide slope indicator approaches full scale deflection, the pilot should respond immediately with pitch and power adjustments to reintercept the glide slope. As proficiency increases, tracking should be accurate enough to preclude any full-scale deflection of the glide slope indicator during the final approach segment. As the aircraft approaches MDA or DH, the pilot should be prepared to lead the leveloff by smoothly increasing back pressure on the elevator (stabilator) and increasing power to stop the descent without a reduction of airspeed.

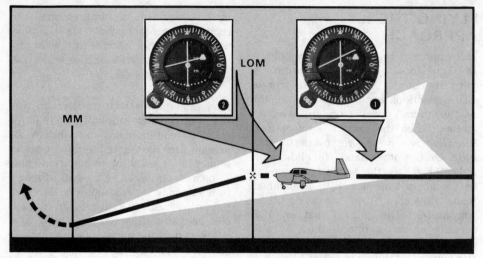

Fig. 11-7. Anticipating Glide Slope Interception

During actual IFR weather conditions, it usually is apparent to the pilot when the approach can be continued visually. However, prior to DH or MDA, the pilot should continue the instrument cross-check with only brief glances outside until he is sure that positive visual contact with the runway environment is established. It is not unusual for a pilot on an ILS approach to establish visual contact at 500 to 600 feet AGL and then lose outside visual references as the descent continues to minimums. For example, a very low fog layer which does not preclude visual contact from above can easily result in complete loss of visual cues on a horizontal plane within the layer. For this reason, descents below the glide slope should be avoided during the final landing maneuver.

ILS PROCEDURES WITH RADAR

Most instrument landing systems are installed at terminal airports with radar equipped approach facilities. A typical example is the ILS runway 1R approach for the Wichita Mid-Continent Airport, Wichita, Kansas, shown in figure 11-8. In addition to radar service, this approach provides for several other methods of transitioning to the final approach course. For example, a flight making an ILS approach to runway 1R from Makes Intersection (item 1) must proceed straight-in on the localizer course, unless ATC approves a deviation. The same is true of an approach on the 15-mile DME arcs (items 2 and 3). Since the Wichita VORTAC is part of the enroute structure, a pilot also could transition to the Piche Outer Compass Locator via the ICT 172° radial (item 4), or by homing on the compass locator, which will be discussed in detail later.

During the transition from the enroute to the approach phase, the pilot's workload increases rapidly. Controller instructions must be acknowledged and complied with, the aircraft speed and configuration usually must be adjusted, and the navigation equipment must be set up for the approach. Additional items include performing the prelanding checklist, reviewing the approach procedure chart, and concentrating on the applicable DH and missed approach procedure.

When radar vectors to the ILS approach course are to be utilized, the pilot will be advised verbally by the controller or through ATIS. The following is an example of a typical vector clearance.

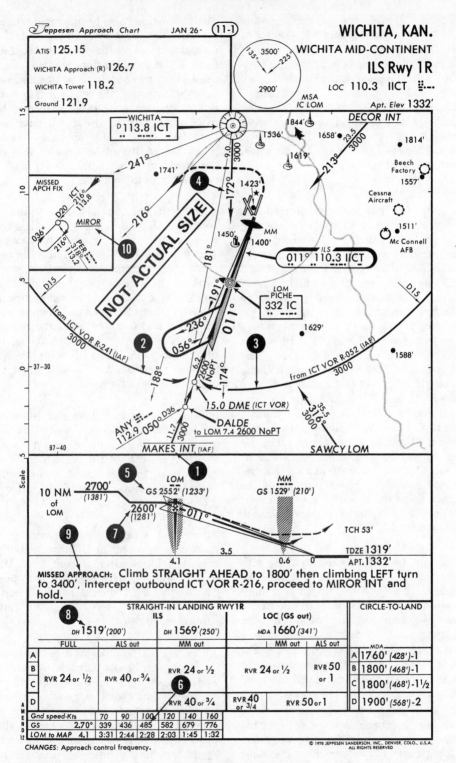

Fig. 11-8. ILS Approach

"Mooney 9161K, descend and maintain 3,000, turn right heading 340° vector to the ILS runway 1R approach course." As the flight approaches course interception, a final vector and approach clearance will be issued. For example, *"Mooney 9161K, position 1-1/2 miles south of the outer marker; turn right heading 360° to intercept the localizer; cleared for the ILS runway 1R approach; contact the tower 118.2 at the outer marker."*

Immediately upon localizer interception, the pilot should concentrate on selecting a magnetic heading which will maintain the localizer centerline. If this can be accomplished prior to the final approach fix, the entire approach will be easier. However, the final heading must be adjusted throughout the approach because of variations in wind or changes in approach speed. Figure 11-8 illustrates that the altitude of the glide slope at the LOM is 2,552 feet MSL (item 5). If the aircraft is at 2,600 feet and approaching the LOM at 100 knots groundspeed, transition to the glide slope can be accomplished by making pitch and power adjustments and/or lowering the gear to establish a 485 f.p.m. descent (item 6). The time of marker passage should be noted and a report should be furnished to the tower. *"Wichita Tower, Mooney 9161K, outer marker inbound, ILS runway 1R."*

It should be remembered that the altitude prescribed for the intermediate segment, 2,600 feet (item 7), is a minimum altitude. It is not unusual for a flight to arrive at the LOM on final approach at a higher altitude. If this occurs, the pilot should expedite descent in the early part of the approach to ensure glide slope interception well before reaching the middle marker.

The final approach segment requires the pilot to concentrate intently on maintaining correct localizer and glide slope position. He must continue to make small adjustments to heading and rate of descent. The category A DH with all ILS components operating is 1,519 feet (item 8). If the glide slope is maintained, the DH on this approach will be reached at approximately the same location as the middle marker. Although DH may be reached at or near the middle marker, the MAP for an ILS approach is the point where the glide slope intercepts the decision height. This point is not necessarily at the marker.

At DH, the pilot must decide to either continue the approach to landing or execute the missed approach procedure. The determination to continue the approach to landing is based on two factors. One, the *aircraft must be in a position from which a normal approach to the runway of intended landing can be made;* and two, *the approach threshold of the runway, approach lights, or other markings identifiable with the approach end of that runway must be clearly visible to the pilot.*

In addition, these requirements must be met throughout the final descent to the runway. If these conditions are not met at DH, or cannot be maintained to touchdown, the pilot must immediately execute the appropriate missed approach procedure.

Although the runway environment may be readily apparent at DH, the visibility may deteriorate after descent from DH to the runway. Because of this possibility the pilot should never descend below the glide slope during the final landing maneuver.

All instrument approach procedures provide for a missed approach maneuver. Figure 11-8, item 9, shows the missed approach for the ILS runway 1R at Wichita Mid-Continent Airport. Unless otherwise directed by the controller, this procedure provides a climbing left turn to 3,400 feet MSL to intercept the Wichita 216° radial and proceed outbound 20 miles to Miror Intersection (item 10). The flight should then enter a holding pattern southwest of the intersection, utilizing right turns. After the missed approach is declared in the procedure, the flight most likely would be handed back to Wichita Approach Control. Based on the pilot's intentions, additional clearance would be provided for another approach or diversion to the alternate.

NONRADAR ILS PROCEDURES

The advantages of the instrument landing system have resulted in widespread utilization of ILS approaches. This system is available not only at large, radar-equipped terminal locations, but also at smaller, nonradar terminals as well.

ADVANCE APPROACH INFORMATION

The aircraft, shown in figure 11-9, is enroute to Pueblo, Colorado, from Denver, via V-19. Denver Center advises, *"Comanche 8852P, expect handoff to Pueblo Approach Control at Hanko Intersection, ILS runway 25R approaches in progress . . . "*

Although approach control service is provided at this controlled airport, radar transitions to the final approach course are not available. Consequently, the pilot must transition from the enroute phase to the approach phase using radio navigation. ADF homing, VOR navigation, DME arcs, or a combination of these procedures are available, as depicted on the NOS approach chart in figure 11-10.

APPROACH CHART REVIEW

The ILS runway 25R approach chart depicts a 10-mile DME arc beginning at the 333° radial of the Pueblo VORTAC. In this case, the aircraft will be inbound on the 351° radial (V-19). When this procedure is used, the intersection of the 351° radial from Pueblo and the 10-mile DME arc is the beginning of the initial approach segment.

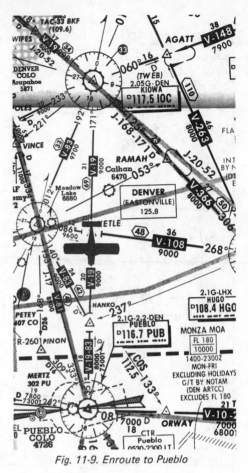

Fig. 11-9. Enroute to Pueblo

For this approach, the minimum altitude for navigation on the DME arc is 7,000 feet MSL. The notation "NoPT" means that a procedure turn is *not required or expected* by the controller. A specific pilot request for a procedure turn could be approved but it would only complicate the approach.

The procedure requires a right turn to intercept the localizer after crossing the Pueblo 068° radial. Glide slope interception will occur before reaching the Aruba LOM at an altitude of 6,500 feet MSL. The DH with all ILS components operative is 4,906 feet MSL (250 feet AGL). A note in the remarks section indicates the approach is not authorized when the control zone is not in effect.

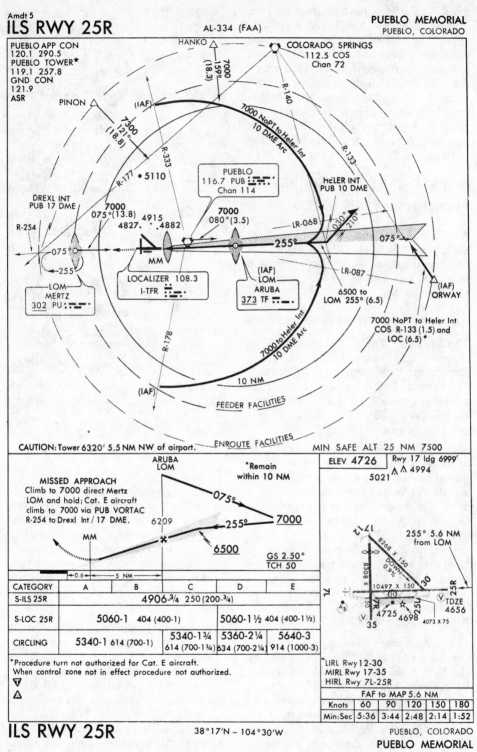

Amdt 5
ILS RWY 25R

AL-334 (FAA)

PUEBLO MEMORIAL
PUEBLO, COLORADO

PUEBLO APP CON
120.1 290.5
PUEBLO TOWER*
119.1 257.8
GND CON
121.9
ASR

Fig. 11-10. Pueblo ILS Runway 25R

ILS RWY 25R

38°17'N – 104°30'W

PUEBLO, COLORADO
PUEBLO MEMORIAL

CATEGORY	A	B	C	D	E
S-ILS 25R	4906-¾ 250(200-¾)				
S-LOC 25R	5060-1 404 (400-1)			5060-1½ 404 (400-1½)	
CIRCLING	5340-1 614 (700-1)		5340-1¾ 614 (700-1¾)	5360-2¼ 634 (700-2¼)	5640-3 914 (1000-3)

*Procedure turn not authorized for Cat. E aircraft.
When control zone not in effect procedure not authorized.

MISSED APPROACH
Climb to 7000 direct Mertz
LOM and hold; Cat. E aircraft
climb to 7000 via PUB VORTAC
R-254 to Drexl Int / 17 DME.

ARUBA LOM

*Remain within 10 NM

075°

255° **7000**

6500

GS 2.50°
TCH 50

MM
6209

0.6 ← → 5 NM

CAUTION: Tower 6320' 5.5 NM NW of airport.

MIN SAFE ALT 25 NM 7500

ELEV 4726	Rwy 17 ldg 6999'

5021 ∧ ∧ 4994

255° 5.6 NM
from LOM

TDZE 4656
4725 4698
4073 X 75

*LIRL Rwy 12-30
MIRL Rwy 17-35
HIRL Rwy 7L-25R

FAF to MAP 5.6 NM					
Knots	60	90	120	150	180
Min:Sec	5:36	3:44	2:48	2:14	1:52

The missed approach procedure requires a climb to 7,000 feet direct to the Mertz LOM. A standard holding pattern west of the LOM is prescribed. Depending on the wind, either a parallel or teardrop entry is appropriate.

High intensity runway lights and VASI are available for runway 25R. (See Fig. 11-10.) The approach path is free from obstructions; however, a caution note lists a tower which is 6,320 feet MSL northwest of the airport. Runway 25R is 10,497 feet long and 150 feet wide.

SETTING UP THE APPROACH

After Denver Center's handoff to Pueblo Approach Control, the following clearance is received. *"Comanche 8852P, Pueblo weather 300 overcast, three-fourths of a mile in light snow showers, wind 280° at 15, altimeter 29.97; cleared ILS approach 25R via the 10 DME arc, report intercepting the localizer."*

The pilot should reset the altimeter and tune the communications and navigation equipment for the approach. The ADF should be set to 373 kHz (LOM) and the VOR/LOC receiver to 108.30 MHz (localizer). The number two communications radio should be set to the tower frequency of 119.10 MHz while the other VOR receiver and the DME receiver remain tuned to the Pueblo VORTAC. All navaid frequencies should be verified by listening to the identification feature, and the marker beacon receiver should be turned on and checked for proper operation.

TRANSITION VIA DME ARC

The initial turn to intercept the DME arc should be started before the aircraft actually crosses the 10-mile DME point. By using the DME distance indicator, the pilot can select exact *leadpoints*. Although the amount of lead varies with the speed of the aircraft, a lead factor of .5 nautical miles is satisfactory for groundspeeds below 150 knots. As the aircraft reaches the 10.5 DME leadpoint on V-19, the pilot should turn to a heading of 081°, which forms a 90° angle to the 351° radial. The bearing selector should then be reset to 360° and a very slow turn initiated to a heading of 090° (tangential heading). As the aircraft crosses the 360° radial, the pilot should set the bearing selector ahead another 10° and turn to a 90° intercept heading for that radial. The same procedure should be repeated as the aircraft progresses around the 10-mile DME arc. This technique is illustrated in figure 11-11. By using the 90° index marker on the heading indicator, the need for continuous mental calculations is eliminated.

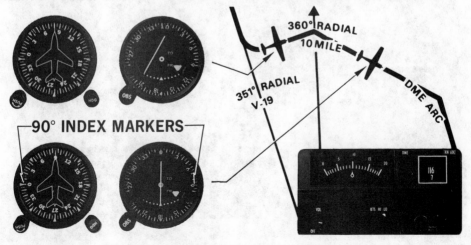

Fig. 11-11. Flying the DME Arc

While navigating the DME arc, some heading variation is necessary to compensate for off-course positions resulting from wind drift and over-shooting or undershooting the initial turn to intercept the arc. In addition to repeated changes in heading and omni-bearing selection, final adjustments to other navigational equipment must be made and the prelanding checklist completed.

After crossing the 068° lead radial, the pilot should turn to intercept the localizer course and establish an approach speed of 90 knots. Course interception is apparent from the movement of the CDI to the center position and the indication of a zero degree relative bearing as the aircraft rolls out on a heading of 255°. After course interception, the pilot should apply wind correction to keep the localizer needle centered and report to the controller, *"Pueblo Approach Control, Comanche 8852P, localizer inbound."* A typical

controller reply would be, *"Comanche 8852P, roger; contact tower on 119.1 at the outer marker."*

FINAL APPROACH FIX INBOUND

At a normal approach speed of 90 knots, the time to MAP should be approximately 3 minutes, 44 seconds. At this speed, the descent rate required on the glide slope is about 400 f.p.m. However, because of the headwind component, a slower descent rate of approximately 300 f.p.m. is more appropriate. At glide slope interception, the gear should be lowered while pitch and power are adjusted, as necessary, to maintain an indicated approach speed of 90 knots and a descent rate of about 300 f.p.m. (See Fig. 11-12.) As the ADF bearing indicator switches to 180° and the blue marker beacon flashes, the pilot should report to the tower, *"Pueblo Tower, Comanche 8852P, Aruba inbound."* Pueblo Tower will advise, *"Comanche 8852P, roger, winds 280° at 12, gusting to 20; report runway in sight."*

Fig. 11-12. Glide Slope Interception

DECISION HEIGHT

During the descent to DH (4,906 feet MSL), the pilot's primary concern is maintaining the localizer and glide slope centerline. Variations in wind will require constant, small adjustments to descent rate and heading. The pilot should respond immediately to movement of the glide slope indicator with appropriate pitch changes and not allow needle deflections to approach full scale. The landing runway threshold or VASI lights must be clearly visible to the pilot at DH or a missed approach must be executed.

Even if the criteria for descent below DH are met, the pilot should be careful not to descend below the glide slope during the final landing maneuver. A descent below the glide slope would place the aircraft in a precarious position in the event of sudden loss of visual references.

ADF TRANSITION

Transitions from enroute to approach also may be accomplished using ADF navigation, provided an NDB is utilized on an ILS approach. For example, if DME equipment had not been available for the previous approach, the following procedure would have been appropriate.

Prior to Hanko Intersection, the following clearance is received from Denver Center, "*Comanche 8852P, radar service terminated; contact Pueblo Approach Control 120.1 passing Hanko; expect ILS runway 25R approach; Pueblo altimeter 29.97.*

A review of the Jeppesen approach chart excerpt in figure 11-13 reveals a feeder route from Hanko Intersection to the Aruba LOM. This route provides a transition from Hanko to the approach course using ADF navigation. Descent to 7,000 feet MSL is authorized. The procedure turn altitude is also 7,000 feet MSL and the glide slope interception altitude is 6,500 feet MSL.

FLYING THE APPROACH

Prior to reaching Hanko, the ADF should be tuned to 373 kHz (Aruba LOM), the code identified, and the ADF bearing indicator checked for proper operation. At Hanko Intersection, the pilot should make the following report, "*Pueblo Approach Control, Comanche 8852P, Hanko 41, 11,000, Pueblo 49, request current Pueblo weather.*" The controller will reply, "*Comanche 8852P, Pueblo weather 300 overcast, visibility three-fourths of a mile in light snow showers, wind 280° at 14, altimeter 29.97. Cleared for ILS runway 25R approach; report Aruba outbound.*"

The pilot should immediately turn left until the ADF bearing indicator points directly ahead of the nose of the aircraft, then start descent to 7,000 feet MSL. Normal procedure requires a report leaving 11,000 feet and a check of the ADF bearing indicator for any apparent wind drift while stabilizing the descent. It may be necessary to apply wind correction while transitioning to the LOM.

APPROACH COURSE OUTBOUND

Since the aircraft will be approaching the localizer course outbound, reverse CDI sensing will be apparent. The pilot should watch for movement of the localizer needle and ADF bearing indicator. As the localizer needle moves from full left deflection, the ADF bearing indicator will begin to move away from the nose position and the blue marker beacon light will begin to flash. At this point, the aircraft should be turned to an outbound heading of 075° (localizer course outbound). Then, the pilot should report, "*Pueblo Approach Control, Comanche 8852P, Aruba outbound.*" Pueblo Approach Control will instruct, "*Comanche 8852P, report Aruba inbound to the tower on 119.1.*" The instrument indications during the turn will be as shown in figure 11-14.

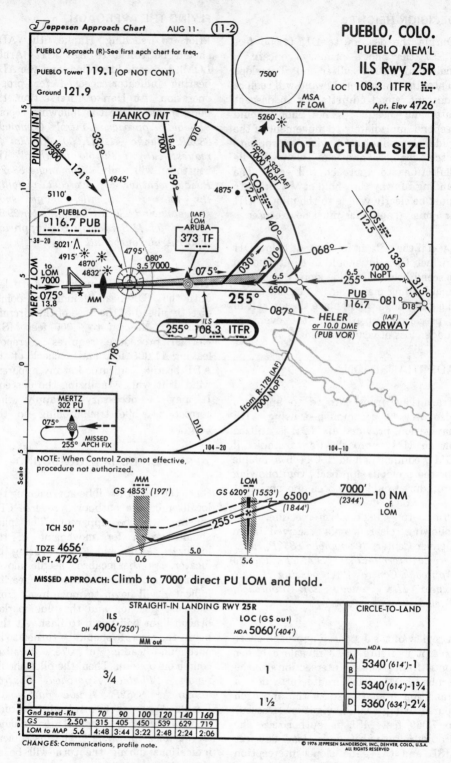

Fig. 11-13. ADF Transition

PROCEDURE TURN

After tracking 1-1/2 minutes outbound because of the west-northwest winds, the aircraft is turned to 030° (procedure turn outbound) for approximately one minute. During this segment, the pre-landing checklist is completed. Following the turn to 210° (procedure turn inbound), the bearing selector may be set to 255° to provide better orientation on the approach. Course interception is apparent from the CDI information, as well as a 45° relative bearing on the ADF indicator. After course interception, the pilot applies wind correction in order to keep the localizer needle centered and completes the approach to DH as previously described. However, when the glide slope is inoperative, the pilot descends to the localizer MDA (5,060 feet MSL) as shown in the approach chart minima section.

Fig. 11-14. Localizer Course Outbound

SECTION B—VOR AND RADAR APPROACHES

VOR and VORTAC (VOR/DME) approaches are widely used in the national airspace system. These approaches provide for final descents as low as 250 feet above the airport or runway. However, the MDAs for most VOR approach procedures range from 500 to 1,000 feet AGL.

APPROACH CLEARANCE

The pilot receives the approach clearance from an approach facility at locations where this service is provided. At locations which do not have approach control, the clearance is issued directly from an ARTCC, if air/ground communications permit, or indirectly through flight service stations.

A typical VOR approach clearance from a radar equipped approach control facility may be issued as follows: *"Mooney 9161K, now three and one-half miles north of the VOR; turn right heading 180°, cleared for the VOR runway 20 approach; contact the tower 118.3 over the VOR inbound."* In this case, a radar vector is provided in lieu of the initial approach segment, and the published procedure turn or other initial approach segment will not be utilized.

At a nonradar equipped approach facility, the following clearance may be issued. *"Mooney 9161K, cleared for VOR approach, report the VOR inbound to the tower on 118.3."* In this case, if more than one VOR approach is available, the pilot may have his choice of procedures. When the controller desires a specific procedure he will so specify; for example, *"Mooney 9161K, cleared for VOR runway 36 approach, circle to land runway 14."*

At nontower airports without approach control service, the ARTCC may issue a "cruise" clearance. An example of such a clearance is *"Mooney 9161K, cleared to the Winnsboro Airport, cruise 5,000."*

The word "cruise" is used in lieu of "maintain" and authorizes the pilot to climb to or descend from his assigned altitude (within the limits of the MEA or MOCA) without further clearance from ATC. However, once the pilot starts a descent and reports leaving an altitude in the block, he may not return to that altitude without additional ATC clearance. If the pilot has been issued a cruise clearance, he may proceed to the destination airport, execute any published approach procedure available, and land if visibility minimums are met. Normally, cruise clearances are used for relatively short flights in uncongested areas.

VOR APPROACH PROCEDURE

Nonprecision approaches are of two general types—those that utilize a navaid located beyond the airport boundaries and those with the navaid located on the airport. The approach chart profiles in figure 11-15 illustrate the basic differences in these two types of approaches.

The VOR approach procedure for Winnsboro, Texas (NOS format), as shown in figure 11-16, utilizes the Quitman VORTAC which is located 5.7 nautical miles southwest of the airport. The navigation facility for this approach (Quitman VORTAC) is also part of the enroute structure. Consequently, feeder routes, which normally provide a means of transitioning from the enroute structure, are not required. In addition, the

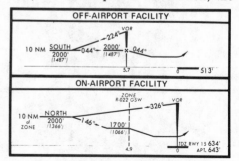

Fig. 11-15. VOR Approach Profiles

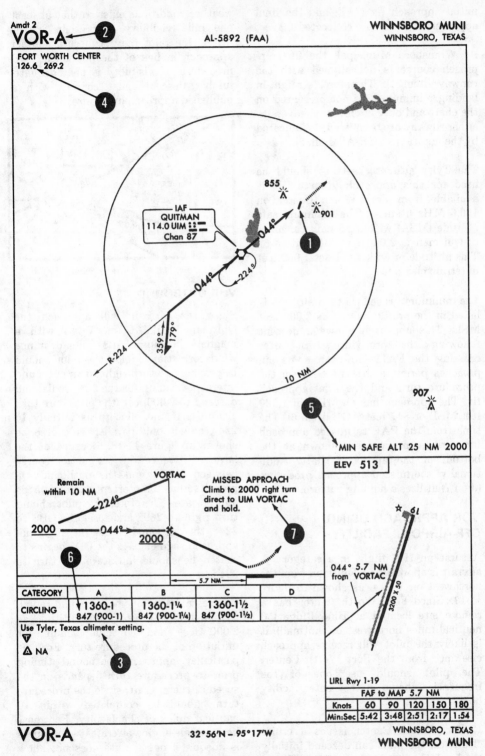

Amdt 2
VOR-A ← ②

AL-5892 (FAA)

WINNSBORO MUNI
WINNSBORO, TEXAS

FORT WORTH CENTER
126.6 269.2

④

855

901

IAF
QUITMAN
114.0 UIM
Chan 87

044°

①

044°

224°

359°

179°

R-224

10 NM

907

⑤

MIN SAFE ALT 25 NM 2000

ELEV 513

Remain within 10 NM	VORTAC	MISSED APPROACH

224°

2000   044°   2000

Climb to 2000 right turn
direct to UIM VORTAC
and hold.

⑦

⑥

5.7 NM

044° 5.7 NM
from VORTAC

3200 X 50

CATEGORY	A	B	C	D
CIRCLING	1360-1 847 (900-1)	1360-1¼ 847 (900-1¼)	1360-1½ 847 (900-1½)	

Use Tyler, Texas altimeter setting.
▽
⚠ NA

③

LIRL Rwy 1-19

FAF to MAP 5.7 NM					
Knots	60	90	120	150	180
Min:Sec	5:42	3:48	2:51	2:17	1:54

VOR-A

32°56'N – 95°17'W

WINNSBORO, TEXAS
WINNSBORO MUNI

Fig. 11-16. Circling VOR Approach

initial approach fix (IAF) and the final approach fix (FAF) are collocated.

At Winnsboro Municipal, the final approach course is not aligned with the runway (item 1). Therefore, straight-in landing minimums are not presented on the chart and only circling maneuvers to either runway are permitted, as indicated by the notation "VOR-A" (item 2).

The Tyler altimeter setting should be used for this approach (item 3). It is available from Fort Worth Center on 126.6 MHz (item 4). The minimum safe altitude (MSA) within 25 nautical miles of Quitman is 2,000 feet MSL (item 5). This altitude provides at least 1,000 feet of terrain clearance.

The minimum procedure turn altitude is listed in the profile section as 2,000 feet MSL. This approach allows a descent following the procedure turn after crossing the FAF. However, some approaches permit a descent between the procedure turn and the final approach fix. The approach has an MDA of 1,360 feet MSL or 847 feet AGL (item 6). The time from the FAF to missed approach for various airspeeds is shown at the bottom of the approach chart. Additionally, the missed approach procedure (item 7) utilizes a holding pattern.

VOR APPROACH USING OFF-AIRPORT FACILITY

Assume an IFR flight in a category A aircraft is approaching Quitman from the northwest on V-114, as shown in figure 11-17. Since Fort Worth Center has a remote site located at Blue Ridge (56 nautical miles northwest of Quitman), it is likely the pilot will receive approach clearance from the Fort Worth Center. The pilot should use one of the frequencies shown in the center facility box.

If Fort Worth Center issues a cruise clearance, the pilot can descend initially to the MEA (2,300 feet MSL). Should

weather conditions exist so that at least one mile visibility is present at the MEA, the pilot may request a contact approach in lieu of the published VOR procedure. If visibility is not adequate, further descent must comply with a published approach procedure.

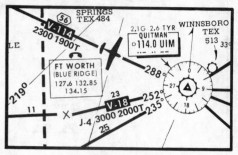

Fig. 11-17. Enroute Segment

VOR OUTBOUND

Since the aircraft will approach the Quitman VORTAC on V-114 with a magnetic heading of 108° (plus or minus wind correction angle), the pilot should be prepared to turn right to an outbound intercept heading for the 224° radial and descend to 2,000 feet (the procedure turn altitude). If the pilot turns initially to 224°, he will only parallel the course, as shown in figure 11-18. Because of the large difference in magnetic course between V-114 and the outbound approach radial, an intercept angle of 45° is appropriate. Therefore, the pilot should turn right to 269° and reset the OBS to 224°, the outbound course for the initial approach segment. As the CDI begins to center, he should initiate a left turn to 224°.

Once established on the outbound radial, the pilot should verify the altitude as 2,000 feet and continue timing for initiation of the procedure turn. For this particular approach, outbound timing prior to procedure turn depends on the speed of the aircraft, since the procedure turn should be completed within 10 nautical miles of the facility. For most light, single-engine aircraft, two minutes is adequate; one minute does not allow enough time for tracking inbound and

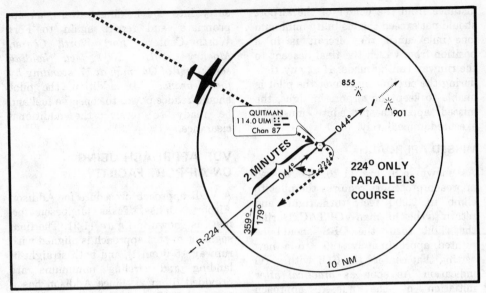

Fig. 11-18. Outbound Intercept

three minutes may extend the procedure turn close to or beyond the 10 nautical mile limit. Outbound timing also should be adjusted, for the effects of known wind conditions.

PROCEDURE TURN

The outbound portion of the procedure turn requires the pilot to turn left to a magnetic heading of 179° and maintain that heading for one minute, as shown in figure 11-18. The course selector should be adjusted to the inbound approach course (044°) and, at the end of one minute, a standard-rate turn should be made to an inbound procedure turn heading of 359°. During the procedure turn (initial segment), the airspeed and configuration *may be* set up for final approach. Immediately following inbound course interception, the pilot should determine the heading required to maintain course. The heading indicator should be checked against the magnetic compass and reset, if necessary.

VOR INBOUND

Upon reaching the VOR inbound, the pilot must note the time of station

passage, begin a descent, and report the FAF inbound to Fort Worth Center. Assuming an approach groundspeed of 90 knots, the time from FAF to MAP will be 3 minutes, 48 seconds, as shown in figure 11-19. The descent to the category A MDA (1,360 feet MSL) should be accomplished well before this time has elapsed. As the aircraft approaches the time limit, the pilot should attempt to establish visual contact with the airport. If the airport has not been located at the end of 3 minutes, 48 seconds, the missed approach procedure must be executed.

FAF to MAP 5.7 NM					
Knots	60	90	120	150	180
Min: Sec	5:42	3:48	2:51	2:17	1:54

Fig. 11-19. Approach Timing

If the airport and runway environment are clearly visible before reaching the MAP and, in the pilot's judgment, a safe approach and landing can be made, he may initiate a circling maneuver to the favored runway. However, descent must not be made below the MDA (1,360 feet MSL), and it is recommended that the distance from the center of the airport should not exceed the visibility minimum (one mile) until the aircraft is in a position from which the final descent to the runway can be made. If at any time during the circling maneuver the pilot is unable to keep the airport in sight, the missed approach procedure must be executed immediately.

MISSED APPROACH

As shown in figure 11-20, the missed approach procedure requires the pilot to climb to 2,000 feet, turn right, and return to the Quitman VORTAC. During the right turn, the OBS should be rotated approximately 180° to a new setting that centers the CDI with a TO indication. As soon as *practical* after initiation of the missed approach procedure, the pilot should make a report to Fort Worth Center similar to the following, *"Forth Worth Center, Mooney 9161K, missed approach at 14, request clearance for another approach (or clearance to the alternate)."*

If the aircraft reaches Quitman before additional clearance is received, the pilot should execute a teardrop or parallel

entry into the holding pattern, as appropriate, and report again to Fort Worth Center. *"Fort Worth Center, Mooney 9161K, 2000 feet, holding southwest of Quitman at 17, standing by for clearance."* In addition, the pilot should reduce power to conserve fuel and be ready to receive the additional clearance.

VOR APPROACH USING ON-AIRPORT FACILITY

A VOR approach procedure for Addison Airport, Dallas, Texas (Jeppesen format), is shown in figure 11-21. The final segment of this approach is aligned with runway 15 (item 1), and both straight-in landing and circling minimums are provided (item 2). Since Addison has a terminal VOR facility (item 3) which is not part of the enroute structure, feeder routes are provided for transition from the Blue Ridge and Dallas-Fort Worth VORTACs.

Addison Airport is served by Regional Approach Control (item 4). This facility will issue the approach clearance after it receives the flight from Fort Worth ARTCC. Additionally, radar vectoring will be available and the pilot can utilize this service in lieu of the feeder routes shown.

The minimum altitude for the procedure turn shown in the profile section is 2,100 feet MSL, while the minimum altitude for crossing Zonee Intersection (item 5) is 1,700 feet MSL. The pilot may descend initially to a minimum of 2,100 feet for the procedure turn and then down to 1,700 feet after completion of the procedure turn.

Zonee Intersection is identified by the 326° radial of the Addison VOR and the 026° radial of the Dallas-Fort Worth VORTAC. The final descent to the MDA for a category A aircraft can be made to 1,040 feet MSL for a straight-in landing on runway 15, or to 1,100 feet MSL for a circling approach. The visibility required

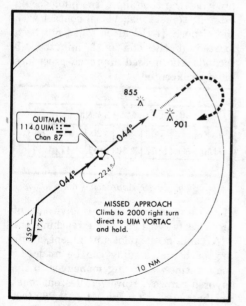

Fig. 11-20. Missed Approach Procedure

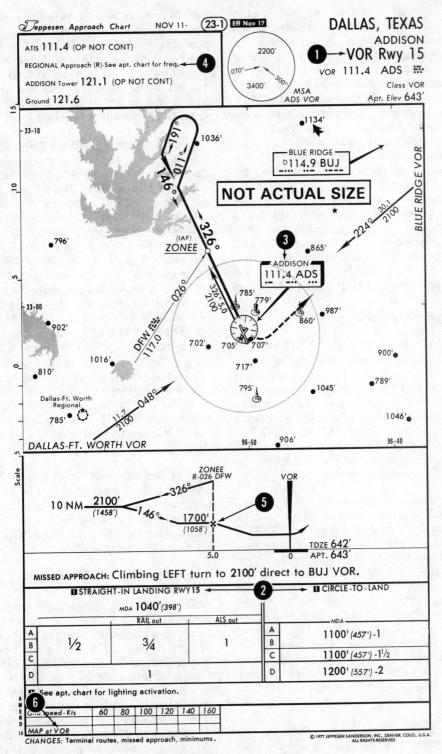

Fig. 11-21. Straight-In VOR Approach

is one-half mile and one mile respectively. Since the *VOR is the MAP* in this procedure, timing from Zonee Intersection is not required or shown on the chart (item 6). If the runway environment for runway 15 (or the airport when circling) is not visible at the MAP, the pilot must execute the missed approach procedure. Furthermore, in a situation where visual contact with the runway (or the airport when circling) is lost during the final descent from the MDA to the runway, the missed approach procedure also applies. Should the missed approach be required, a climbing left turn to 2,100 feet on a direct route to the Blue Ridge VORTAC is prescribed unless otherwise directed by the controller. Further clearance will be provided by Regional Approach Control.

VOR/DME APPROACHES

When the notation "VORTAC" or "VOR/DME" appears on an approach procedure, the use of DME equipment is mandatory for execution of the approach. Although many procedures utilize *supplemental* DME fixes, the absence of the notation "VORTAC" or "DME" in the chart heading means that the use of DME equipment is not mandatory for execution of the approach.

An approach procedure (NOS format) which requires DME navigation equipment is shown in figure 11-22. This approach provides for a procedure turn and two 14-mile DME arcs for transition to the final approach course. If the procedure turn is employed, the pilot should utilize the 142° radial of the Gregg County VORTAC to arrive at the eight-mile DME fix (item 1). As shown by the profile view, a descent should then be made to 2,000 feet (the procedure turn altitude) and the final descent initiated crossing the eight-mile DME fix inbound.

The limits of the DME arcs are marked by the 059° radial (item 2) and the 172° radial (item 3). In many cases these

radials coincide with airways and a pilot approaching on any airway within this span can intercept the 14 DME arc and proceed with the approach. However, a procedure turn is not authorized (or needed) when the DME arcs are used. The procedure for flying a DME arc is described in Section A of this chapter.

After the flight is handed off from Ft. Worth Center to Longview Approach Control, the pilot will be provided with an approach clearance. The following is an example of an approach clearance utilizing a DME arc, *"Grumman 121GA, cleared for VOR/DME runway 35 approach to the Gregg County Airport via the 14-DME arc. Contact Gregg Tower 119.2 crossing the eight-mile DME fix inbound."* A cross designates the FAF in the profile section at the point where the final descent begins (item 4). The MAP on VOR/DME (VORTAC) approaches is based on DME distance rather than time. The missed approach procedure requires a climbing left turn to 2,000 feet, via the Gregg County 172° radial, to a holding pattern south of Pipes Intersection (item 5). This requires either a teardrop or parallel holding pattern entry.

If a missed approach is executed, the pilot normally is instructed by the tower to contact approach control. If additional clearance is not received before reaching the intersection, the pilot should report entering the holding pattern.

RADAR APPROACHES

ASR and PAR approaches have a distinct advantage over other approach procedures because the only VHF equipment required is a two-way communications radio. Consequently, radar approaches often are used by distressed aircraft that have experienced loss of navigation capability or some type of inflight emergency. When available, radar approaches are provided upon pilot request or they may be suggested by the controller.

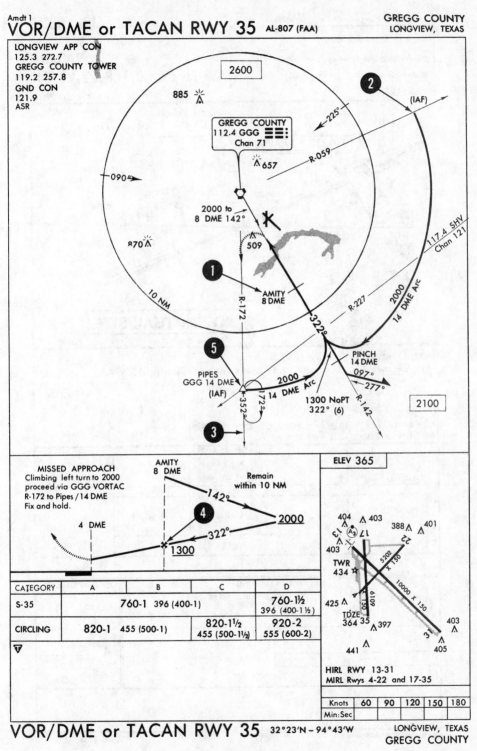

Amdt 1
VOR/DME or TACAN RWY 35 AL-807 (FAA)

GREGG COUNTY
LONGVIEW, TEXAS

LONGVIEW APP CON
125.3 272.7
GREGG COUNTY TOWER
119.2 257.8
GND CON
121.9
ASR

2600

885

GREGG COUNTY
112.4 GGG
Chan 71

657

090°

225°

R-059

(IAF)

2

2000 to
8 DME 142°

509

117.4 SHV
Chan 121

870

R-172

1

AMITY
8 DME

R-227

2000

14 DME Arc

322°

10 NM

5

PINCH
14 DME

097°

PIPES
GGG 14 DME
(IAF)

352°

172°

2000

14 DME Arc

277°

1300 NoPT
322° (6)

R-142

2100

3

MISSED APPROACH
Climbing left turn to 2000
proceed via GGG VORTAC
R-172 to Pipes/14 DME
Fix and hold.

AMITY
8 DME

Remain
within 10 NM

142°

4

2000

4 DME

322°

1300

ELEV 365

404   403
388   101
403
TWR
434
5202 X 150

10000 X 150

425
TDZE
364 35   397
403
441   405

HIRL RWY 13-31
MIRL Rwys 4-22 and 17-35

CATEGORY	A	B	C	D
S-35	760-1 396 (400-1)			760-1½ 396 (400-1½)
CIRCLING	820-1 455 (500-1)		820-1½ 455 (500-1½)	920-2 555 (600-2)

Knots	60	90	120	150	180
Min:Sec					

VOR/DME or TACAN RWY 35 32°23'N – 94°43'W

LONGVIEW, TEXAS
GREGG COUNTY

Fig. 11-22. VORTAC Approach

11-25

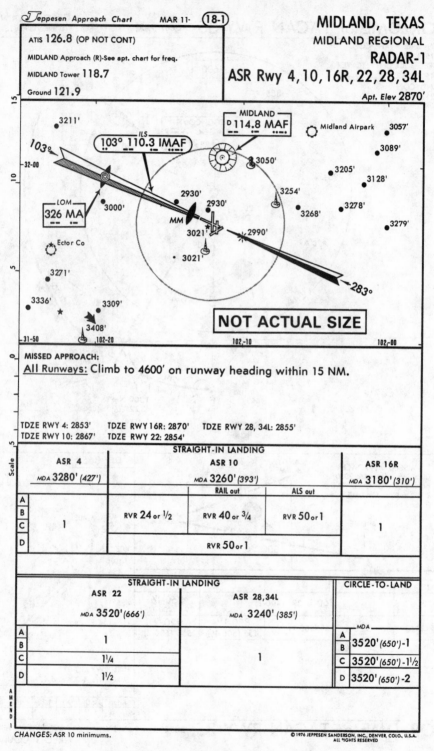

ATIS **126.8** (OP NOT CONT)

MIDLAND Approach (R)-See apt. chart for freq.

MIDLAND Tower **118.7**

Ground **121.9**

MIDLAND, TEXAS
MIDLAND REGIONAL
RADAR-1
ASR Rwy 4,10,16R,22,28,34L
Apt. Elev **2870'**

NOT ACTUAL SIZE

MISSED APPROACH:
All Runways: Climb to 4600' on runway heading within 15 NM.

TDZE RWY 4: 2853'	TDZE RWY 16R: 2870'	TDZE RWY 28, 34L: 2855'
TDZE RWY 10: 2867'	TDZE RWY 22: 2854'	

	STRAIGHT-IN LANDING			ASR 16R
ASR 4 MDA **3280'** *(427')*	ASR 10 MDA **3260'** *(393')*			MDA **3180'** *(310')*
		RAIL out	ALS out	
A				
B		RVR **40** or ¾	RVR **50** or 1	
C	1	RVR **24** or ½		1
D		RVR **50** or 1		

	STRAIGHT-IN LANDING		CIRCLE-TO-LAND
	ASR 22 MDA **3520'** *(666')*	ASR 28,34L MDA **3240'** *(385')*	MDA
A			A 3520' *(650')*-1
B	1		B
C	1¼	1	C 3520' *(650')*-1½
D	1½		D 3520' *(650')*-2

AMEND 1

CHANGES: ASR 10 minimums.

© 1976 JEPPESEN SANDERSON, INC., DENVER, COLO., U.S.A.
ALL RIGHTS RESERVED

Fig. 11-23. Airport Surveillance Radar Approach

ASR APPROACHES

Most radar approaches are conducted using airport surveillance radar facilities. ASR approach minimums vary slightly, depending on the local terrain at each terminal radar location. Generally, they provide for MDAs between 300 and 800 feet AGL with visibilities ranging from one-half to two statute miles. ASR procedures may provide for circling as well as straight-in landing minimums.

A typical ASR approach is the ASR procedure for Midland Regional Airport, Midland, Texas (Jeppesen format), shown in figure 11-23. Prominent navaid locations are shown in the approach plan view to facilitate orientation. This procedure shows the landing minimums for six of the runways at Midland. The straight-in landing minimums vary slightly between the runways; however, circling minimums and missed approach procedures are identical for all of the runways.

NOS provides radar minimums alphabetically by airport on separate pages in the approach chart binders. An excerpt of the Midland Regional ASR minimums is shown in figure 11-24. The NOS format does not show the published missed approach procedure. The controller will provide these instructions, as well as lost communications procedures, verbally during the initial portion of the approach.

Acceptance of a radar approach by a pilot does not waive the prescribed landing visibility minimums for the airport as they apply to a particular aircraft operator. The pilot is responsible for determining if the approach *and landing* are authorized under existing weather minimums. Controller instructions are mandatory from the initial radar contact to the MAP. However, if the pilot establishes visual contact with the airport or runway prior to reaching minimums, or if he wishes to discontinue the approach, he should advise the controller.

CIVIL RADAR INSTRUMENT APPROACH MINIMUMS

LUBBOCK INTL TX   Amdt. 4, FEB 23, 1978   ELEV **3281**

RWY	CAT	DH/ MDA-VIS	HAT/ HAA	CEIL-VIS	CAT	DH/ MDA-VIS	HAT/ HAA	CEIL-VIS
35L	ABCDE	3560—1	306	(300—1)				
17R	ABC	3620/24	339	(400—½)	DE	3620/50	339	(400—1)
26	ABCDE	3660—1	408	(400—1)				
CIRCLING	A	3700—1	419	(500—1)	B	3740—1	459	(500—1)
	C	3740—1½	459	(500—1½)	D	3840—2	559	(600—2)
	E	3980—2	699	(700—2)				

▽

MIDLAND REGIONAL AIR TERMINAL TX   Amdt. 1, FEB 12, 1976   ELEV **2870**

RWY	CAT	DH/ MDA-VIS	HAT/ HAA	CEIL-VIS	CAT	DH/ MDA-VIS	HAT/ HAA	CEIL-VIS
16R	ABCDE	3180—1	310	(400—1)				
34L	ABCDE	3240—1	385	(400—1)				
10	ABC	3260/24	393	(400—½)	DE	3260/50	393	(400—1)
28	ABCDE	3240—1	385	(400—1)				
4	ABCDE	3280—1	427	(500—1)				
22	AB	3520—1	666	(700—1)	C	3520—1¼	666	(700—1¼)
	DE	3520—1½	666	(700—1½)				
CIRCLING	AB	3520—1	650	(700—1)	C	3520—1½	650	(700—1½)
	D	3520—2	650	(700—2)	E	3560—2	690	(700—2)

▽ △

Fig. 11-24. NOS Radar Approach Minimums

Should radio communication be lost for a time interval specified by the controller (not more than one minute) on vector to final approach or for 15 seconds while on final approach, the *lost communication procedure* should be initiated.

The *missed approach procedure* should be executed under the following conditions: when visual contact with the runway (or airport, if circling) is not established before reaching the MAP or not maintained after descent from the MDA and when the landing is not accomplished.

CONTROLLER COMMUNICATIONS

The following controller communications are typical of an ASR approach in IFR conditions. *"Bonanza 9014V, how do you hear me?"*

(Pilot acknowledges.)

"Bonanza 9014V, squawk (appropriate code) and IDENT."

"Bonanza 9014V, radar contact; your position 10 miles east northeast of the airport. Turn right heading 260°, vector to the final approach course, descend and maintain 5,500."

(Pilot acknowledges.)

"14V, this will be a surveillance approach to runway 22. If no transmissions are received for one minute in the pattern or for 15 seconds on final approach, attempt contact on 119.15. If unable, proceed with ILS runway 10 approach."

(Pilot acknowledges.)

"14V, perform landing check."

(Pilot acknowledges.)

"14V, turn left heading 220° final approach course. Descend and maintain 5,000. Your missed approach procedure is climb on runway heading to 4,600 feet within 15 nautical miles."

(Pilot acknowledges and requests that the controller provide recommended altitudes on final approach.)

"14V, recommended altitude will be furnished each mile on final approach, except the last mile. Prepare to descend in two miles; published minimum descent altitude 3,520 feet."

(Pilot acknowledges.)

"14V, do not acknowledge further transmissions. Turn right heading 225°, eight miles from runway, slightly left of course."

"14V, turn left heading 220°, seven miles from runway, on course. Descend to your minimum descent altitude."

"14V, heading 220°, six miles from runway, on course, altitude should be 4,700."

"14V, turn right heading 222° five and one-half miles from runway on course, your altitude should be 4,400."

(Controller instructions continue for the next three miles at less than 15 second intervals.)

"14V, two miles from runway on course, altitude should be 3,700 report approach lights in sight. Cleared to land runway 22, wind 250° at 5."

"14V, one and one-half miles from runway on course."

"14V, one mile from runway, on course, take over visually; if approach lights not in sight, execute missed approach. Acknowledge."

(Pilot acknowledges.)

NO-GYRO APPROACHES

No-gyro approaches may be requested by pilots under radar control who have experienced failure of the gyroscopic heading indicator. During a no-gyro approach, the controller instructs the pilot to *"start turn"* followed by *"stop turn"* at the appropriate time. Using this technique, the controller can provide guidance to the airport or runway in IFR conditions, similar to a normal ASR approach. Pilots are instructed by the controller to use standard-rate turns until final approach, and one-half standard-rate turns thereafter.

PAR APPROACHES

Precision approach radar installations are being phased out at civilian airports. A few have been retained at joint civil/military or affiliated airports. Although PAR is still widely used by the military, their facilities may not be used in IFR conditions by civilian pilots without prior permission, except in an emergency.

During a PAR approach, the controller can provide exact course and glide path guidance to the decision height. In addition, the pilot will be told when to anticipate glide path interception at the beginning of the approach. Deviations from the course or glide path are relayed promptly by the controller. For example, *"Cessna 6721X, turn left heading 147°, two miles from runway, well right of course, slightly below glide path."*

Range from touchdown is provided at least once each mile. After reaching DH, the controller continues to advise the pilot of any deviation from the runway centerline, until the aircraft crosses the runway threshold for landing. Radar service is terminated automatically upon completion of the approach. Should radio communications be lost for five seconds while on final approach, the pilot should execute the missed approach procedure.

Figure 11-25 shows one of the few remaining civil PAR approaches (Jeppesen format), located at Duluth International Airport, Duluth, Minnesota. This PAR approach may be used for runway 9 and ASR approaches also may be conducted to runways 3, 9, 21, and 27.

RADAR MONITORING OF INSTRUMENT APPROACHES

Radar monitoring of instrument approaches is another function of precision approach radar. This service is performed on request during IFR weather conditions at civil or military airports *which have PAR equipment.* Monitoring is available only for those approaches where the final segment coincides with the final PAR course. Prior to starting the procedure, the pilot is informed of the frequency that will be used for the advisories.

The pilot is advised when he is passing the final approach fix inbound. Additional advisories are issued with respect to azimuth only for nonprecision approaches, while azimuth and elevation advisories are provided for ILS approaches. For example, *"Cessna 6721X, radar observes your position slightly below glide slope and well right of the localizer course for runway 9."* If, after repeated advisories, an aircraft exceeds the PAR safety limit, or if a radical deviation is observed, the pilot will be advised to execute the appropriate missed approach procedure.

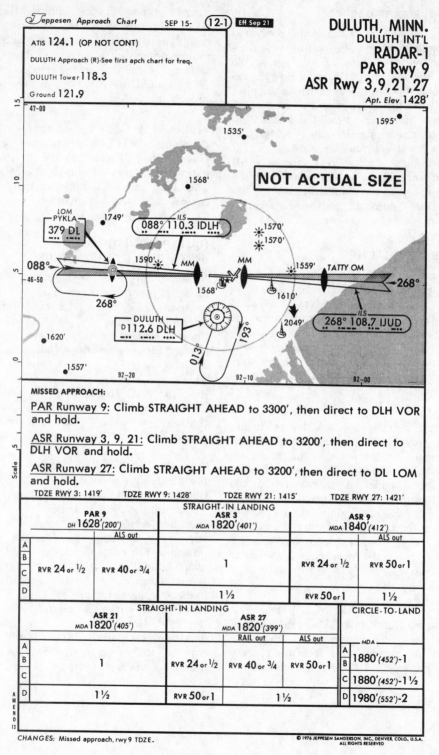

DULUTH, MINN.
DULUTH INT'L
RADAR-1
PAR Rwy 9
ASR Rwy 3,9,21,27
Apt. Elev 1428'

ATIS **124.1** (OP NOT CONT)

DULUTH Approach (R)-See first apch chart for freq.

DULUTH Tower **118.3**

Ground **121.9**

NOT ACTUAL SIZE

LOM PYKLA
379 DL

ILS
088° 110.3 IDLH

088°

268°

268°

268° 108.7 IJUD

DULUTH
D **112.6 DLH**

TATTY OM

268°

193°

013°

MISSED APPROACH:

PAR Runway 9: Climb STRAIGHT AHEAD to 3300', then direct to DLH VOR and hold.

ASR Runway 3, 9, 21: Climb STRAIGHT AHEAD to 3200', then direct to DLH VOR and hold.

ASR Runway 27: Climb STRAIGHT AHEAD to 3200', then direct to DL LOM and hold.

TDZE RWY 3: 1419'   TDZE RWY 9: 1428'   TDZE RWY 21: 1415'   TDZE RWY 27: 1421'

	STRAIGHT-IN LANDING					
	PAR 9 DH **1628'**(200')		**ASR 3** MDA **1820'**(401')		**ASR 9** MDA **1840'**(412')	
		ALS out				ALS out
A B C	RVR **24** or 1/2	RVR **40** or 3/4	1		RVR **24** or 1/2	RVR **50** or 1
D			1 1/2		RVR **50** or 1	1 1/2

	STRAIGHT-IN LANDING				CIRCLE-TO-LAND	
	ASR 21 MDA **1820'**(405')		**ASR 27** MDA **1820'**(399')			
				RAIL out	ALS out	MDA
A B C	1		RVR **24** or 1/2	RVR **40** or 3/4	RVR **50** or 1	A B **1880'**(452')-1
						C **1880'**(452')-1 1/2
D	1 1/2		RVR **50** or 1	1 1/2		D **1980'**(552')-2

CHANGES: Missed approach, rwy 9 TDZE.   © 1976 JEPPESEN SANDERSON, INC., DENVER, COLO., U.S.A.
ALL RIGHTS RESERVED

Fig. 11-25. PAR Approach

SECTION C — NDB, LDA, AND SDF APPROACHES

In actual practice, ILS, VOR, and VORTAC (VOR/DME) approaches are the most frequently used instrument procedures. At terminal locations, NDB (ADF) and radar approaches often are referred to as "back up" procedures, because they provide an alternative if VHF navigation failure occurs.

NDB procedures often are used in terminal areas when the instrument landing system is shut down for maintenance. NDBs also are encountered at small airports which are relatively remote from VHF navigation aids. At many of these locations, NDBs provide the only means of executing an instrument approach.

NDB, like VOR or VORTAC approaches, may utilize either on-airport or off-airport facilities. In addition, they may provide for straight-in landings and/or circling maneuvers. The navigation facilities used may be low powered ILS compass locators or high powered NDBs.

Many terminal airports with ILS systems utilize an NDB approach which coincides with the ILS approach course. The NDB straight-in landing minimums are higher, however, because NDB approaches are in the nonprecision approach category.

NDB APPROACH CHARTS

Except for Category II ILS procedures, Jeppesen approach charts often show NDB and ILS approaches combined on one chart. This format is utilized when the approach segments for both approaches coincide. The Jeppesen format provides for a rapid transition to an NDB approach should VHF navigation failure occur during an ILS approach. Figure 11-26 shows an example of such a procedure for the ILS/NDB runway 22 approach at Eau Claire, Wisconsin.

Although radar vectoring is not provided, this approach procedure provides several terminal routes for transition from the enroute to the approach phase. A transition may be made from the Eau Claire VORTAC to the Maggs LOM, along the Eau Claire (EAU) 054° radial (item 1). Since the VORTAC is part of the enroute structure, a clearance may be issued to transition to the final approach course by the 11 nautical mile DME arc (item 2). Final descent using the NDB procedure begins at the LOM, as indicated by the dashed line in the profile section (item 3). However, the ILS procedure indicates that the descent following glide slope interception should be initiated just *before* reaching the LOM.

The NDB straight-in landing minimums for category A aircraft (item 4) are an MDA of 1,400 feet and three-fourths of a statute mile visibility. If the approach lighting system (ALS) is inoperative, the visibility minimum increases to one statute mile, but the MDA remains the same. The circling minimums (item 5) are the same for both the NDB and ILS procedures. The missed approach procedure (item 6) also can be applied to either approach. When flying the NDB procedure, the time to the MAP at 100 knots (item 7) is 3 minutes, 36 seconds.

NOS publishes each NDB approach procedure separately and utilizes the title "NDB" in the chart heading. An example of an NDB approach chart using the NOS format is shown in figure 11-28 for Dawson Community Airport, Glendive, Montana.

NDB APPROACH PROCEDURES

Although the accuracy of an NDB approach depends upon the pilot's skill using ADF navigation, the approach has some advantages over VOR procedures. For example, changes in bearing selection are not required and position orien-

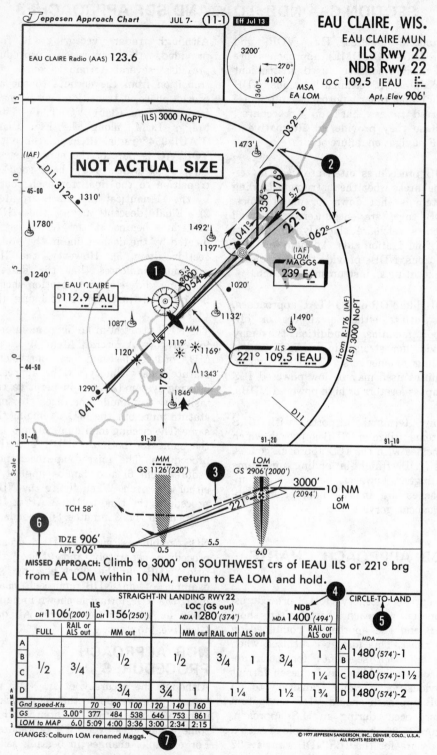

Jeppesen Approach Chart   JUL 7- (11-1) Eff Jul 13

EAU CLAIRE, WIS.
EAU CLAIRE MUN
ILS Rwy 22
NDB Rwy 22
LOC 109.5 IEAU
Apt. Elev 906'

EAU CLAIRE Radio (AAS) 123.6

3200'
270°
360°
4100'
MSA
EA LOM

NOT ACTUAL SIZE

(ILS) 3000 NoPT

(IAF)
D11 312°

032°
1473'

356° 176°
221°
041°
062°
5.7

(IAF)
LOM
MAGGS
239 EA

EAU CLAIRE
D112.9 EAU

5.3
3000
054°

1020'

from R-176 (IAF)
(ILS) 3000 NoPT

MM
1132'
1490'

1087'
1119'
1169'
ILS
221° 109.5 IEAU

1120'
176°
1343'
1846'

1290'
041°

D11

MISSED APPROACH: Climb to 3000' on SOUTHWEST crs of IEAU ILS or 221° brg from EA LOM within 10 NM, return to EA LOM and hold.

MM
GS 1126'(220')

LOM
GS 2906'(2000')

3000'
(2094')

10 NM
of
LOM

221°

TCH 58'

TDZE 906'
APT. 906'
0   0.5   5.5   6.0

	STRAIGHT-IN LANDING RWY 22								CIRCLE-TO-LAND		
	ILS DH 1106'(200')	DH 1156'(250')	**LOC (GS out)** MDA 1280'(374')				**NDB** MDA 1400'(494')					
	FULL	RAIL or ALS out	MM out		MM out	RAIL out	ALS out		RAIL or ALS out			MDA
A	1/2	3/4	1/2	1/2		3/4	1	3/4	1	A B	1480'(574')-1	
B												
C									1 1/4	C	1480'(574')-1 1/2	
D			3/4	3/4	1	1 1/4		1 1/2	1 3/4	D	1480'(574')-2	
Gnd speed-Kts		70	90	100	120	140	160					
GS	3.00°	377	484	538	646	753	861					
LOM to MAP	6.0	5:09	4:00	3:36	3:00	2:34	2:15					

CHANGES: Colburn LOM renamed Maggs.

© 1977 JEPPESEN SANDERSON, INC., DENVER, COLO., U.S.A.
ALL RIGHTS RESERVED

Fig. 11-26. Combined NDB and ILS Approach Chart

tation is somewhat easier throughout the approach because of the ADF bearing indicator.

The flight shown in figure 11-27 is enroute from Miles City, Montana, to Dawson Community Airport, Glendive, Montana, via V-465E. On this route structure, radar coverage and direct center communications often are unreliable below 10,000 feet MSL. In addition, the Miles City altimeter setting must be used for the approach to the Dawson Airport. For this reason Salt Lake Center may issue a cruise clearance for a light aircraft inbound to Glendive. For example, the following clearance may be issued over Miles City. *"Bellanca 1776R, cleared to Dawson Community*

Airport via V-465E Marro, direct Glendive, cruise 7,000, Miles City altimeter 29.87, report procedure turn inbound to Glendive Radio on 122.2."

APPROACH CHART REVIEW

In this case, the only published approach at Glendive is the NDB runway 12 (NOS format), as shown in figure 11-28. This procedure provides a transition via the feeder route from Marro Intersection to the Glendive NDB. The minimum altitude for this segment is 5,000 feet MSL and, after departing the airway, the entire procedure must be flown using ADF navigation. A procedure turn is mandatory and the minimum procedure turn altitude specified is 4,000 feet MSL.

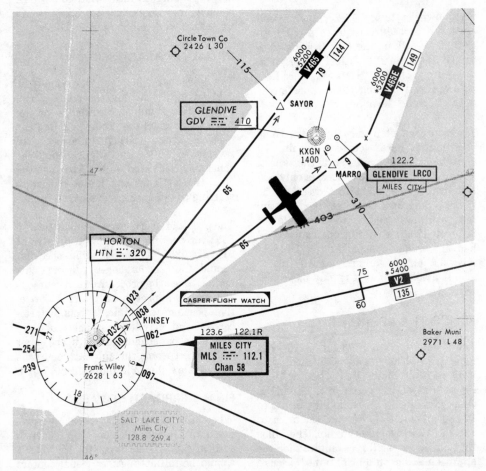

Fig. 11-27. Enroute to Glendive

The consecutive course changes after V-465E are 310° (feeder route and initial segment), 265°, 085° (initial segment), and 130° (final segment). Since the Glendive NDB is an on-airport facility, an intermediate approach segment is not required. A cross does not appear in the profile section because an FAF is not designated and the time to MAP is not specified on the chart. This procedure allows the pilot to track directly to the MAP. When flying this approach, the task of determining the missed approach point is eliminated since the MAP is the NDB. The MDA for category A aircraft is 3,580 feet MSL for both straight-in landings and circling approaches, and the visibility minimum is one and one-fourth miles.

As shown in figure 11-28, the missed approach procedure requires a climb to 4,000 feet MSL on the 130° bearing from the NDB within 10 nautical miles. Then, a return to the NDB is specified, followed by a holding pattern northwest of the NDB on the approach course.

The approach plan view indicates three obstructions are located within 10 nautical miles of the airport; the tallest, a spot elevation of 2,950 feet, is only 630 feet below the 3,580-foot MDA. The airport diagram indicates medium intensity runway lights are available for runway 12/30. In addition, runway 12 has an available length of 5,704 feet. Another unlighted turf runway (2/20) also is available, but it is only 3,074 feet in length.

FLYING THE APPROACH

The Glendive NDB frequency (410 kHz) must be selected and identified. The VOR receiver should be set to the Miles City VORTAC frequency of 112.10 MHz. One communications radio may be set to 122.80 MHz (UNICOM) and the other to 122.20 MHz (Glendive Radio). The Miles City altimeter setting is required for the approach and should be obtained prior to reaching Marro Intersection.

TRANSITION

As the flight approaches Marro Intersection on V-465E, the pilot may notice that a magnetic heading of 045° is required to maintain the airway centerline. By applying the ADF formula [magnetic bearing (310°) − magnetic heading (45°) = relative bearing], the pilot will conclude that the aircraft is over the intersection when the relative bearing is 265°. At that point, the aircraft should be turned left to a 30° intercept heading of 280° and the descent to 5,000 feet MSL initiated. When the ADF indicator shows 030°, the course has been intercepted and the aircraft should be turned to a heading of 310°. This procedure is illustrated in figure 11-29. Depending on local wind conditions, it may be necessary to apply wind correction while inbound to the NDB.

INITIAL APPROACH SEGMENT

The descent to 4,000 feet MSL should be delayed until reaching the NDB. Then, the aircraft should be slowed to an approach speed of 90 knots. At station passage, the bearing indicator will reverse to 180°. The flight should be continued outbound on the 310° bearing from the NDB for two minutes prior to starting the procedure turn.

The procedure turn requires a left turn to 265° for one minute followed by a right turn to 085°. The prelanding checklist should be accomplished during this period. Since the procedure turn course is 45° to the approach course, a 45° relative bearing will indicate course interception and completion of the procedure turn. The panel indications at the point where the turn to the approach course is initiated are shown in figure 11-30.

FINAL APPROACH SEGMENT

When inbound, a report should be provided to Glendive Radio, as requested, and a prompt descent to the MDA should be initiated. After visual contact is established, the windsock/tetrahedron

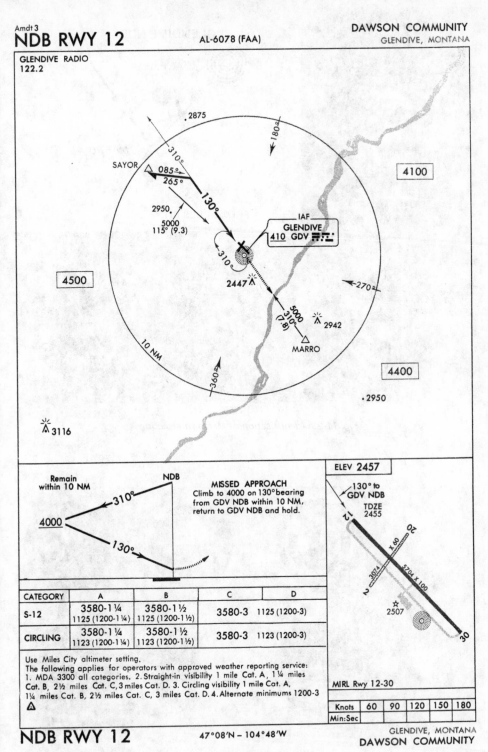

Amdt 3
NDB RWY 12
AL-6078 (FAA)

DAWSON COMMUNITY
GLENDIVE, MONTANA

GLENDIVE RADIO
122.2

. 2875

SAYOR

085°
265°
130°
310°

2950.
5000
115° (9.3)

4100

IAF
GLENDIVE
410 GDV

4500

310°

2447

10 NM

5000
(7.8)
310°

2942

MARRO

270°

-360°

4400

.2950

A 3116

Remain within 10 NM

NDB

310°

4000

130°

MISSED APPROACH
Climb to 4000 on 130° bearing
from GDV NDB within 10 NM,
return to GDV NDB and hold.

ELEV 2457

130° to
GDV NDB

TDZE
2455

12

20

5704 X 100

2

30

2507

CATEGORY	A	B	C	D
S-12	3580-1¼ 1125 (1200-1¼)	3580-1½ 1125 (1200-1½)	3580-3 1125 (1200-3)	
CIRCLING	3580-1¼ 1123 (1200-1¼)	3580-1½ 1123 (1200-1½)	3580-3 1123 (1200-3)	

Use Miles City altimeter setting.
The following applies for operators with approved weather reporting service:
1. MDA 3300 all categories. 2. Straight-in visibility 1 mile Cat. A, 1¼ miles
Cat. B, 2½ miles Cat. C, 3 miles Cat. D. 3. Circling visibility 1 mile Cat. A,
1¼ miles Cat. B, 2½ miles Cat. C, 3 miles Cat. D. 4. Alternate minimums 1200-3
△

MIRL Rwy 12-30

Knots	60	90	120	150	180
Min:Sec					

NDB RWY 12

47°08'N – 104°48'W

GLENDIVE, MONTANA
DAWSON COMMUNITY

Fig. 11-28. NDB Approach

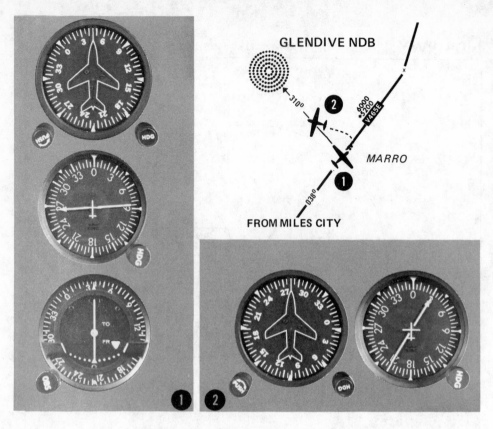

Fig. 11-29. Identification of Marro Intersection

Fig. 11-30. Instruments at Course Interception

should be observed to confirm whether a straight-in landing for runway 12 or a circling approach to runway 30 should be initiated.

MISSED APPROACH

If the runway threshold for 12 cannot be identified clearly prior to the MAP (station passage) on a straight-in landing approach, the missed approach procedure should be executed. The pilot should make an immediate climb on the extended approach course to 4,000 feet, then return to the NDB and enter the holding pattern depicted on the approach chart. Additional clearance should then be requested through Glendive Radio.

LDA AND SDF APPROACHES

The *localizer-type directional aid* (LDA) and the *simplified directional facility* (SDF) are very similar to a standard localizer. Each of these systems operates within a frequency range of 108.10 MHz to 111.95 MHz and provides course guidance to a specific runway.

The approach techniques and procedures to be used with both the LDA and SDF approaches are essentially identical to those employed while executing a standard localizer approach. Since both facilities transmit the same type of signal as a standard localizer, the pilot simply tunes his navigation radio to the appropriate frequency and monitors the navigation indicator. The course selector setting has no effect on the CDI indications.

The primary differences between the localizer, LDA, and SDF facilities are the placement of the transmitting antenna, course width, and course alignment. Some of these differences are shown in figure 11-31. Due to these differences, most LDA and SDF approaches do not have usable back courses.

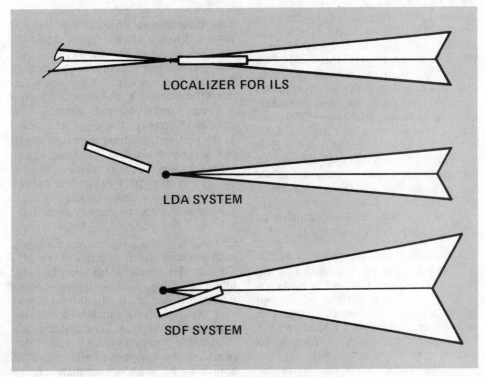

LOCALIZER FOR ILS

LDA SYSTEM

SDF SYSTEM

Fig. 11-31. Guidance System Comparison

LOCALIZER-TYPE DIRECTION AID

The LDA facility employs the same utility and accuracy of a localizer, but is not part of a complete ILS system. However, the facility itself is identified much the same as a standard localizer. For example, the LDA facility is identified by a three-letter code prefixed by the letter "I," as shown in figure 11-32, item 1. In addition, the LDA course width is adjusted between three and six degrees, as is the standard localizer.

The transmitting antenna for the LDA normally is located off the airport or at the approach end of the corresponding runway. Figure 11-31 illustrates an example of a transmitting antenna located at the approach end of a runway with the antenna array aimed at an angle to the runway centerline.

The antenna location causes an apparent difference in course sensitivity between the LDA and the ILS localizer. Most ILS localizers with an angular width between three and six degrees provide an approach course width of approximately 700 feet at the runway threshold. This means that when an aircraft one mile from touchdown is displaced horizontally 350 feet from the runway centerline, it will display half-scale CDI deflection. If the antenna in a similar LDA system is located at the approach end of the runway, the horizontal distance of the course width is much smaller on final approach. At one mile from touchdown, a 350-foot lateral course error will cause a full scale CDI deflection compared to the half-scale deflection for the ILS.

The LDA approach may employ lead-in (LDIN) lights for visual guidance to the runway. Generally, the lead-in lights are used for the visual portion of the approach after passing the missed approach point. Item 2 of figure 11-32 shows the lead-in lights for the LDA runway 18 approach to Washington National Airport. The lead-in lights can be in the form of a single light or three to five lights in short sequence. Additionally, a series of single or multiple array lights can be employed to guide the pilot in a straight or curved path to the approach end of the runway.

SIMPLIFIED DIRECTIONAL FACILITY

The SDF approach facility normally is identified by a three-letter code. However, unlike the LDA and localizer facilities, the three-letter identifier is not prefixed with the letter "I."

The antenna array for an SDF approach can be placed in various locations and provides an approach course which is seldom aligned with an extended runway centerline. The SDF example in figure 11-31 shows the antenna array located next to the runway with the approach course crossing the runway threshold. The antenna array also can be located near the approach or departure end of the runway.

The transmitting antenna for the approach illustrated in figure 11-33 is installed north of the runway and provides an approach course which almost parallels the runway. In this case, an aircraft maintaining the course centerline will fly parallel to and alongside the runway. Normally, the angle of convergence between the final approach course and a runway heading is not more than three degrees. This provides good accuracy to the runway and does not require excessive maneuvering to align the aircraft with the runway centerline.

The SDF antenna array transmits a signal with a course width of either 6° or 12°. This angular course width provides maximum usability and optimum course quality. However, it should be noted that this provides a much wider course than the localizer or LDA systems. Although the greater angular course width provides less precision with an SDF approach, it provides adequate course guidance for a safe approach.

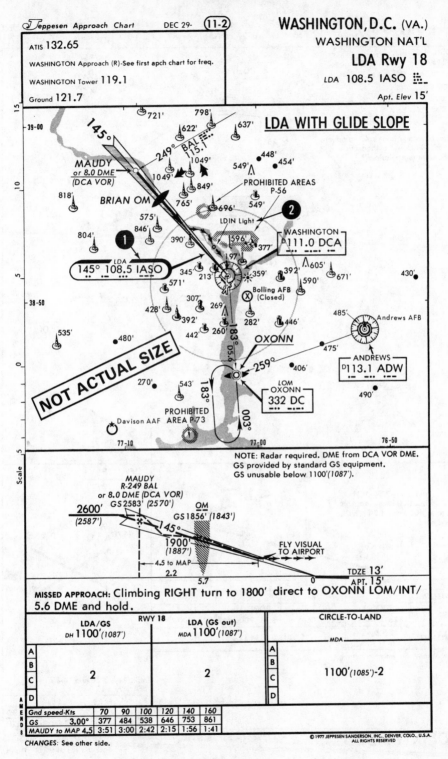

Jeppesen Approach Chart   DEC 29- (11-2)

ATIS **132.65**

WASHINGTON Approach (R)-See first apch chart for freq.

WASHINGTON Tower **119.1**

Ground **121.7**

WASHINGTON, D.C. (VA.)
WASHINGTON NAT'L
LDA Rwy 18

LDA **108.5 IASO**

Apt. Elev 15'

LDA WITH GLIDE SLOPE

145°

249°

BAL 115.1

MAUDY or 8.0 DME (DCA VOR)

BRIAN OM

1 LDA **145° 108.5 IASO**

PROHIBITED AREAS P-56

LDIN Light

2 WASHINGTON **111.0 DCA**

Bolling AFB (Closed)

183° D5.6

OXONN

259°

ANDREWS **113.1 ADW**

Andrews AFB

LOM OXONN **332 DC**

183°

003°

PROHIBITED AREA P-73

Davison AAF

NOT ACTUAL SIZE

NOTE: Radar required. DME from DCA VOR DME.
GS provided by standard GS equipment.
GS unusable below 1100'(1087').

MAUDY
R-249 BAL
or 8.0 DME (DCA VOR)
GS 2583' (2570')

2600'
(2587')

145°

OM
GS 1856' (1843')

1900'
(1887')

FLY VISUAL TO AIRPORT

4.5 to MAP
2.2
5.7

0

TDZE 13'
APT. 15'

MISSED APPROACH: Climbing **RIGHT** turn to 1800' direct to OXONN LOM/INT/ 5.6 DME and hold.

	LDA/GS DH 1100'(1087')	RWY 18	LDA (GS out) MDA 1100'(1087')		CIRCLE-TO-LAND
					MDA
A				A	
B	2		2	B	1100'(1085')-2
C				C	
D				D	

Gnd speed-Kts	70	90	100	120	140	160
GS 3.00°	377	484	538	646	753	861
MAUDY to MAP 4.5	3:51	3:00	2:42	2:15	1:56	1:41

CHANGES: See other side.

© 1977 JEPPESEN SANDERSON, INC., DENVER, COLO., U.S.A.
ALL RIGHTS RESERVED

Fig. 11-32. LDA Approach

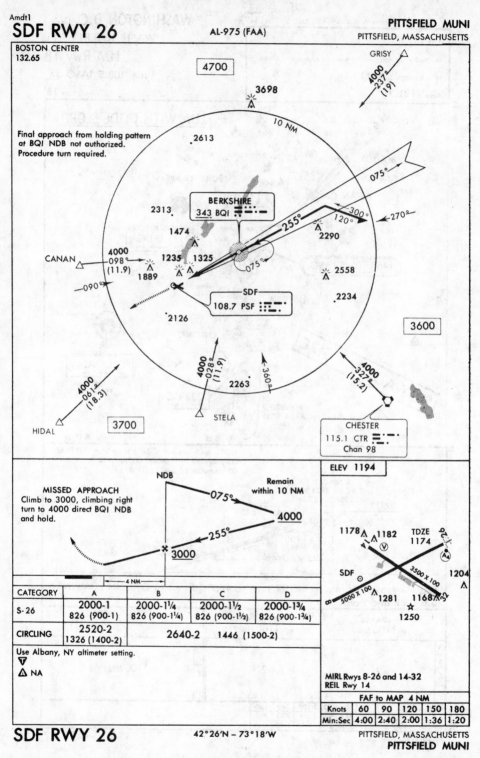

Amdt 1
SDF RWY 26
AL-975 (FAA)

PITTSFIELD MUNI
PITTSFIELD, MASSACHUSETTS

BOSTON CENTER
132.65

GRISY

4700

3698

Final approach from holding pattern
at BQI NDB not authorized.
Procedure turn required.

10 NM

.2613

075°

4000
237°
(19)

075°

BERKSHIRE
343 BQI

2313.

255°

300°

270°

120°

2290

1474

CANAN
4000
098°
(11.9)

1235 1325

1889

-090°

075°

2558

2234

SDF
108.7 PSF

3600

.2126

4000
028°
(11.9)

.2263

360°

4000
06
(18.3)

HIDAL

3700

STELA

4000
32
(15.2)

CHESTER
115.1 CTR
Chan 98

ELEV 1194

MISSED APPROACH
Climb to 3000, climbing right
turn to 4000 direct BQI NDB
and hold.

NDB

075°

Remain
within 10 NM

4000

255°

3000

4 NM

1178   1182
TDZE
1174

SDF

3500 X 100

1204

5000 X 100   1281

1168

1250

CATEGORY	A	B	C	D
S-26	2000-1 826 (900-1)	2000-1¼ 826 (900-1¼)	2000-1½ 826 (900-1½)	2000-1¾ 826 (900-1¾)
CIRCLING	2520-2 1326 (1400-2)	2640-2 1446 (1500-2)		

Use Albany, NY altimeter setting.

▽

⚠ NA

MIRL Rwys 8-26 and 14-32
REIL Rwy 14

FAF to MAP 4 NM					
Knots	60	90	120	150	180
Min:Sec	4:00	2:40	2:00	1:36	1:20

SDF RWY 26

42°26'N – 73°18'W

PITTSFIELD, MASSACHUSETTS
PITTSFIELD MUNI

Fig. 11-33. SDF Approach

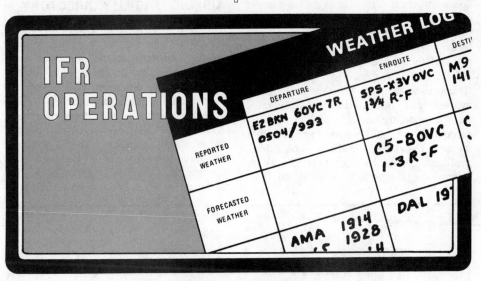

chapter 12

IFR OPERATIONS

WEATHER LOG

INTRODUCTION

This chapter takes the pilot through IFR flight planning, followed by a simulated IFR flight, and concludes with a discussion of emergency procedures. With this information, the pilot will be able to place in perspective various areas of training and knowledge gained throughout the instrument course.

SECTION A — IFR PLANNING

Adequate instrument flight planning is a prerequisite for a successful IFR flight. In addition, Federal Aviation Regulations impose certain preflight planning requirements. FAR 91.5 states that the pilot in command must familiarize himself with all available information concerning that flight. For an IFR flight, this information must include the weather reports and forecasts, fuel requirements, and landing/takeoff distance requirements. Additionally, the pilot must allow for any known traffic delays and have a plan of action in case the planned flight cannot be completed.

THE FLIGHT

This section takes the pilot through the preflight planning process required for a flight from Childress Municipal Airport (34°26'N, 100°18'W) to Meacham Field at Fort Worth, Texas (32°49'N, 97°22'W). The flight is scheduled to depart Childress at 1600Z. The aircraft,

Skyflyer 1234X, is equipped with dual nav/coms, glide slope, ADF, transponder and DME. Section B describes how this flight might actually be conducted.

FLIGHT PUBLICATIONS

A pilot preparing for an IFR flight should consult specific publications to ensure the flight can be completed safely and in accordance with current information. These publications include the *Airman's Information Manual* (AIM), the *Airport/Facility Directory*, the NOTAM publication, and *Graphic Notices and Supplemental Data.*

AIRMAN'S INFORMATION MANUAL

The *Airman's Information Manual Basic Flight Information and ATC Procedures* is generally referred to as the AIM. This manual is designed to provide airmen with the fundamental knowledge required to fly within the national airspace system. It contains a comprehensive description of established facilities and procedures. Items of interest to pilots, concerning health, medical factors, factors affecting flight safety, a pilot/controller glossary of terms used in the air traffic control system, and information on accident/hazard reporting, are also addressed. The discussion of ATC procedures, radio usage, clearance, traffic separation, preflight, departure, enroute, and arrival operations is especially relevant to IFR pilots.

AIRPORT/FACILITY DIRECTORY

The *Airport/Facility Directory* is a complimentary publication that contains specific information on airports, communications, navigational aids, instrument landing systems, VOR receiver checkpoints, preferred routes, FSS/Weather Service telephone numbers, ARTCC frequencies, part-time control zones, and various other pertinent special notices essential to air navigation. Regional directories are updated every eight weeks. Effective

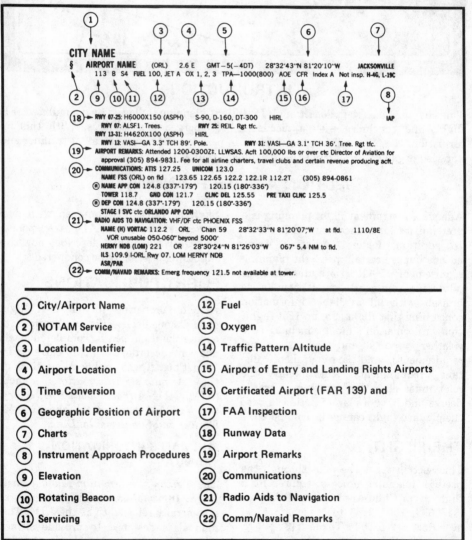

① City/Airport Name	⑫ Fuel
② NOTAM Service	⑬ Oxygen
③ Location Identifier	⑭ Traffic Pattern Altitude
④ Airport Location	⑮ Airport of Entry and Landing Rights Airports
⑤ Time Conversion	⑯ Certificated Airport (FAR 139) and
⑥ Geographic Position of Airport	⑰ FAA Inspection
⑦ Charts	⑱ Runway Data
⑧ Instrument Approach Procedures	⑲ Airport Remarks
⑨ Elevation	⑳ Communications
⑩ Rotating Beacon	㉑ Radio Aids to Navigation
⑪ Servicing	㉒ Comm/Navaid Remarks

Fig. 12-1. Airport/Facility Directory Legend Excerpt

dates and areas of coverage are indicated on the cover page. A legend sample is included in each publication, as illustrated in figure 12-1.

An excerpt of directory data for the departure and destination airport is shown in figure 12-2. Both airports have instrument approach procedures (item 1). Meacham Field is a controlled airport (item 2) with radar services for arriving (item 3) and departing (item 4) aircraft.

Fig. 12-2. Airport/Facility Directory Excerpt

NOTICES TO AIRMEN (CLASS II)

The *Notices to Airmen* publication is one of the most timely sources of new information. The example listing in figure 12-3 shows no significant general NOTAMs for the planned route of flight.

TEXAS

CANADIAN, HEMPHILL COUNTY ARPT: TPA 1000 ft. Right tfc rwys 4, 22 and 17. (1/79-2)
COLEMAN MUNI ARPT: Rotating bcn and UNICOM OTS. (1/78)
DALLAS, ADDISON ARPT; Unlgtd 75 ft AGL tower 2 NM NE. (10/78)
DALLAS-FT WORTH REGIONAL ARPT: Rwys 35R and 35L now SSALR. Rwy 17R now ALSF2. (1/79-2)
LAREDO INTL ARPT: Pilot controlled lighting OTS. (11/78)
MIDLAND AIRPARK: Thr rwy 16 dsplcd 350 ft. (1/79-2). Rwy 7–25 now 5810 by 75 ft. (2/79-2)
MIDLAND REGIONAL ARPT: Rwy lights rwy 4–22 OTS. (11/78)
MULESHOE, EDWARD WARREN FIELD: Rwy lights OTS. UNICOM OTS. (1/79-2)
NAVASOTA MUNI ARPT: Rotating beacon OTS. (3/76-9)
OLNEY MUNI ARPT: Thr rwy 17 no longer dsplcd 430 ft. (2/79-2)

Fig. 12-3. Notices to Airmen Excerpt

GRAPHIC NOTICES AND SUPPLEMENTAL DATA

Graphic Notices and Supplemental Data lists area advisories, Area Navigation (RNAV) Routes, North Atlantic Routes, Terminal Area Graphics, Terminal Radar Service Area (TRSA) graphics, civil flight test areas, and other data not subject to frequent change, as required. This quarterly publication, although primarily intended for VFR planning, also contains useful information for the IFR pilot.

ROUTE OF FLIGHT

One of the most important flight planning tasks is route selection. It involves research of route alternatives, evaluation of weather, aircraft performance, economy, personal limitations and, finally, a decision. As discussed in Chapter 9, instrument charts depict the basic route information and the flight publications provide additional guidance.

Preferred IFR routes are established between many busy terminal areas. These preferred routes are published in the *Airport/Facility Directory*. As shown in figure 12-4, a preferred route is not available between Childress, Texas, and the Dallas-Fort Worth metro area.

PREFERRED ROUTES—LOW

Terminals	Route	Effective Times (GMT)
DALLAS/FORT WORTH AREA		
Atlanta	V18 UIM V54 TXK V278 BHM V18N	
	MAYES V325 DALAS ATL	0000-2359
Houston	ENNIS LOA322 LOA V477W TNV	0000-2359
Memphis	V18 UIM V16 RAMSY	1200-1400
		1800-0000
Midway	DFW017 MLC202 MLC V63 UIN V116 JOT	0000-2359
New Orleans	V18 UIM V114 VEILS	0000-2359
O'Hare	DFW017 MLC202 MLC V63 UIN V116	
	PIA V262 BDF V10 VAINS	0000-2359
San Antonio	V358 ACT V17 WINKS	0000-2359

Fig. 12-4. Preferred Routes

There is a standard terminal arrival route (STAR), as shown in figure 12-5, that can be used. The Boids Four Arrival with the Wichita Falls transition

BOIDS FOUR ARRIVAL (BPR.BOIDS4)
DALLAS-FORT WORTH, TEXAS

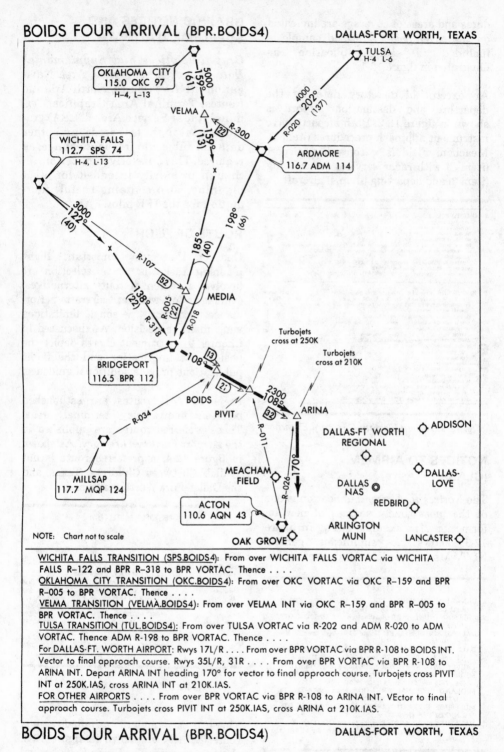

BOIDS FOUR ARRIVAL (BPR.BOIDS4)
DALLAS-FORT WORTH, TEXAS

WICHITA FALLS TRANSITION (SPS.BOIDS4): From over WICHITA FALLS VORTAC via WICHITA FALLS R–122 and BPR R–318 to BPR VORTAC. Thence . . . .

OKLAHOMA CITY TRANSITION (OKC.BOIDS4): From over OKC VORTAC via OKC R–159 and BPR R–005 to BPR VORTAC. Thence . . . .

VELMA TRANSITION (VELMA.BOIDS4): From over VELMA INT via OKC R–159 and BPR R–005 to BPR VORTAC. Thence . . . .

TULSA TRANSITION (TUL.BOIDS4): From over TULSA VORTAC via R–202 and ADM R–020 to ADM VORTAC. Thence ADM R–198 to BPR VORTAC. Thence . . . .

For DALLAS-FT. WORTH AIRPORT: Rwys 17L/R . . . . From over BPR VORTAC via BPR R–108 to BOIDS INT. Vector to final approach course. Rwys 35L/R, 31R . . . . From over BPR VORTAC via BPR R–108 to ARINA INT. Depart ARINA INT heading 170° for vector to final approach course. Turbojets cross PIVIT INT at 250K.IAS, cross ARINA INT at 210K.IAS.

FOR OTHER AIRPORTS . . . . From over BPR VORTAC via BPR R–108 to ARINA INT. VEctor to final approach course. Turbojets cross PIVIT INT at 250K.IAS, cross ARINA at 210K.IAS.

BOIDS FOUR ARRIVAL (BPR.BOIDS4)
DALLAS-FORT WORTH, TEXAS

Fig. 12-5. Standard Terminal Arrival Route (STAR)

provides a route of flight from the Wichita Falls VORTAC to the Dallas metro area. Since a STAR is essentially a preferred route, it not only provides a route of flight, but also simplifies clearance delivery instructions. The route chosen for this flight utilizes V-114 and the Boids Four STAR. The route filed on the flight plan is CDS-V-114-SPS.BOIDS 4.

VOR RECEIVER CHECKPOINT

The pilot preparing for this flight has two means of accomplishing a VOR check, if required. First, as shown in figure 12-6, Childress Municipal Airport has a ground VOR checkpoint at the intersection of the ramp and the center taxi strip. Second, since the airplane to be flown on this trip has dual VORs, the pilot can compare VOR indications when both radios are tuned to the same facility. The maximum permissible error when performing any ground VOR check or dual VOR check is four degrees.

SPECIAL OPERATIONS

Graphic Notices and Supplemental Data and *Notices to Airmen* provide data on special flight activities. Military training routes are depicted on enroute charts. Pilots can also request ATC advisories concerning any unusual civil or military flight operations.

WEATHER INFORMATION

Another important aspect of instrument flight planning is devising a plan of action based on expected weather conditions. *Will weather conditions alter the route of flight? Is an instrument approach available or necessary? Is an alternate airport required and, if so, which airport can be used?* These are the main questions that should be resolved while studying weather reports and forecasts.

To obtain the total weather picture, a logical sequence must be used for gathering information. The weather charts can provide a view of the general weather pattern, and the weather reports and forecasts can supply specific information. This check of the weather gives the pilot the maximum amount of information with the least expenditure of effort and time.

WEATHER DEPICTION CHARTS

The weather depiction chart, illustrated in figure 12-7, indicates the information gathered at 1300Z (item 1). Throughout the area of central Texas where the flight will be conducted, the ceilings are below 1,000 feet and/or general visibilities below three miles. This is indicated by the solid line enclosing the area of IFR conditions (item 2). A typical station within this area (item 3) is reporting three miles visibility in rain and fog, with an overcast ceiling of 700 feet.

Facility Name (Arpt Name)	Freq/Ident	Type Check Pt. Gnd. AB/ALT	Azimuth from Fac. Mag	Dist. from Fac. N.M.	Check Point Description
		TEXAS			
Abilene	113.7/ABI	A/2800	047	10.1	Over silos in center of Ft Phantom Lake.
Addison (Addison)	111.4/ADS	G	162	0.55	At intersection of center and parallel twys.
Alice (Alice International)	114.5/ALI	G	270	0.5	On twy N of hangar.
Amarillo (Amarillo International)	117.2/AMA	G	207	4.5	On east runup pad rwy 21
Austin (Robert Mueller Muni)	114.6/AUS	G	011	0.3	On runup area on twy to rwy 16L.
	114.6/AUS	G	117	0.7	On runup area of twy to rwy 30L
	114.6/AUS	G	315	0.4	On runup area on twy to rwy 12R.
Beaumont (Jefferson County)	114.5/BPT	G	310	1 0	On runup area for rwy 11.
Big Spring	114.3/BGS	A, 3500	106	10	Over water tank in Coahoma.
Brownsville (Brownsville Intl)	116.3/BRO	G	247	3.2	On NE corner of parking ramp.
Brownwood (Brownwood Muni)	108.6/BWD	A/2600	169	6.2	Over rotating bcn.
Childress (Childress Muni)	117.6/CDS	G	353	3.7	At intersection of edge of ramp at center twy.

Fig. 12-6. VOR Receiver Checkpoints

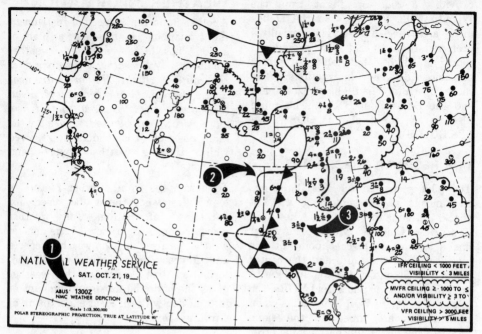

Fig. 12-7. Weather Depiction Chart

LOW-LEVEL PROGNOSTIC CHARTS

The low-level prognostic chart, illustrated in figure 12-8, indicates that at 1800Z (item 1), the area of the flight should be experiencing marginal VFR conditions. This is depicted on the chart by an enclosed area with scalloped lines (item 2). In addition, moderate turbulence is expected below 20,000 feet in parts of Kansas, Missouri, Nebraska, and Iowa (item 3).

The surface prognosis shown in the lower panel depicts the expected location of a cold front at 1800Z (item 4). A warm front (item 5) extends from the cold front easterly through the Gulf of Mexico and into the Atlantic Ocean. The area north of Texas (item 6) should have continuous rain over more than one half of the area.

The radar summary chart, illustrated in figure 12-9, shows an area of echoes in southern and eastern Texas (item 1). In the area of flight, there are echo returns covering three-tenths to four-tenths of the area with rain decreasing in intensity (item 2) and echo tops at 40,000 feet (item 3). The movement of the cells is to the southeast at 20 knots (item 4).

SURFACE ANALYSIS CHARTS

The pilot can determine the exact location of fronts and general wind flow from the barometric pressure by referring to the surface analysis chart. Specific information is also printed on the chart in the general location of each reporting station.

CHART INFORMATION SUMMARY

By checking the weather charts, the pilot has determined that the area in which the flight will be conducted is primarily affected by a cold front with resulting precipitation, low ceilings and low visibility. The precipitation will be in the form of light rain and the area should not be affected by severe weather.

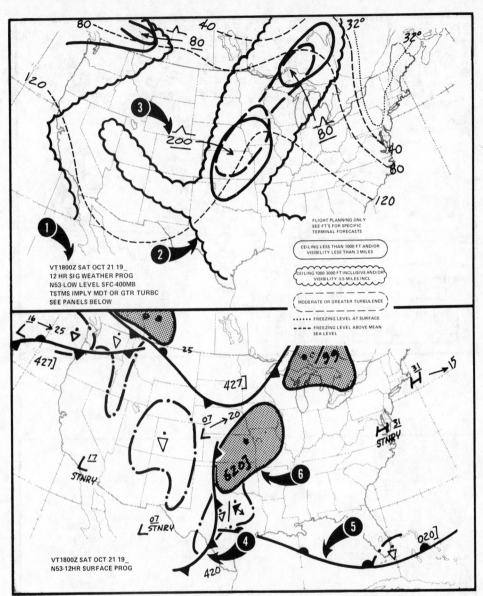

Fig. 12-8. Low-Level Prognostic Chart Excerpt

Now that the pilot has a general weather picture, he will check the reports and forecasts to obtain specific information.

AREA FORECAST

As shown in figure 12-10, the area forecast that includes the route of flight concerns New Mexico, Oklahoma, Texas and the coastal waters area (item 1). The weather synopsis mentions a weak cold front extending from western Kansas to near Del Rio, Texas, and a warm front extending eastward from this cold front to southwestern Louisiana (item 2).

The next portion of the area forecast includes the clouds and weather over the

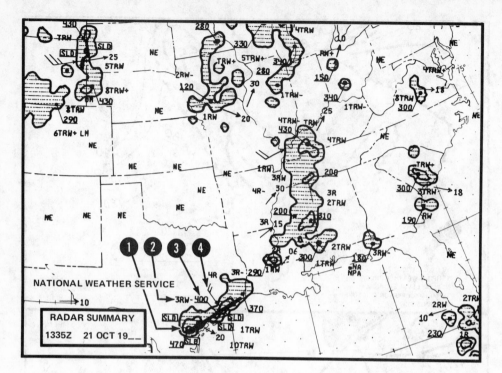

Fig. 12-9. Radar Summary Chart

```
DFW FA 211240
13Z SAT-07Z SUN.
OTLK 07Z-19Z SUN.

NM OK TX AND CSTL WTRS

HGTS ASL UNLESS NOTED

SYNS...WK CDFNT 13Z WRN KS SWD NR AMARILLO-DEL RIO LN WL MOV INTO
WRN AR SWD NR TEXARKANA-BEAUMONT LN ARND 07Z. AT 13Z WRM FRN NR
LAREDO-PALACIOS LN WL MOV NWD DURG AFTN EXTDG EWD FM CDFNT NR LUFKIN-
SWRN LA LN BY 07Z.

SIGCLD AND WX...
OVR OK AND TX.
GENLY E OF GAGE-HOBBS-MARFA LN AND N OF EAGLE PASS-BEAUMONT LN. CIGS
FQTLY LWRG BLO 1 THSD FT VSBYS BLO 3RF. TOPS LYRD ABV 150.
SOME IPVMT THRU THE WRN AND SRN SXNS BCMG CIGS 10-18 BKN VRBL OVC 3-
6RW-F S OF DEL RIO-LUFKIN LN AND W OF ENID-MIDLAND-MARFA LN ARND 2100Z
BUT LWRG AGN BY 02Z. NMRS SHRWS AND SCTD TSTMS CIGS BLO 1 THSD FT VSBYS
BLO 3 RWF THRU SWRN OK AND MOST SXNS OF TX EXCP THE NERN PTN. TSTM
TOPS NEAR 350. TSTMS AND SHWRS WL SPRD EWD AND NEWD INTO ERN OK ERN
TX DURG AFTN AND ERY NGT. TSTMS GENLY EMBOD IN MULTI LYRD CLDS. OTLK
...E OF CDFNT MVFR. W OF CDFNT MVFR BCMG VFR BY 12Z.

ICG...MDT MXD ICG ABV FRZLVL IN TSTMS. FRZLVL 75-85 THRU NM SLPG TO
120-130 OVR OK AND WRN TX AND TO 140-150 THRU SRN AND SERN TX.
```

Fig. 12-10. Area Forecast

```
FT22


FT211040

GAG 211111 C8 OVC 2315 OCNL C5 OVC 5RW-F. 15Z C15 OVC 2315. 23Z
 C25 BKN. 05Z VFR..

PNC 211111 5 SCT C15 OVC 4L-F 1512 SCT V BKN. 05Z MVFR LF..

TUL 211111 C18 OVC OCNL C5 BKN 12 OVC 5RW-F. 05Z MVFR RW..

FYV 211111 C18 BKN 50 OVC 7 BKN V OVC OCNL C6 OVC 2RWF. 05Z IFR RW...

AMA 211111 C2X 2F OCNL C1X 1/2F. 16Z 10 SCT C60 BKN. 18Z 25 SCT.
 05Z VFR..

OKC 211111 5 SCT C15 OVC 4F OCNL C5 BKN 10 OVC 4RW-F. 18Z C15 OVC
 6F CHC TRW-. 05Z VFR..

MLC 211111 C18 OVC OCNL C10 OVC 5R-F. 05Z IFR RF..

SPS 211111 C2 OVC 1/2R-F. 14Z C5 OVC 1R-F VRBL C8 OVC 3R-F. 05Z MVFR
 RF..

ADM 211111 C15 OVC 6L-F OCNL C8 OVC 3RW-F. 05Z MVFR RW..

ABI 211111 C1X 1R-F VRBL C3 OVC 2R--F. 16Z C6 OVC 2R-F OCNL C8 OVC
 4R-F SLT CHC TRW- TIL 05Z. 05Z MVFR TRW..

DFW 211111 C8 OVC 2R-F VRBL C10 OVC 3R-F CHC TRW- AFT 23Z. 05Z
 IFR RF..

DAL 211111 C8 OVC 2R-F VRBL C10 OVC 3R-F CHC TRW- AFT 23Z. 05Z
 IFR RF..

TYR 211111 C8 OVC 4R-F VRBL C5 OVC 2R-F. 05Z IFR RF..
```

Fig. 12-11. Terminal Forecast

area. The expected ceilings, visibilities, precipitation, and thunderstorm activities also are detailed.

TERMINAL FORECAST

On the terminal forecast, illustrated in figure 12-11, both Dallas-Fort Worth Regional (DFW) and Dallas Love (DAL) are forecast to have ceilings of 800 overcast and visibilities of two miles in light rain and fog. Conditions are expected to be variable to 1,000 overcast, three miles visibility in light rain and fog, with a chance of thunderstorms and light rain showers after 2300Z.

Since the forecast ceiling within one hour of the ETA is considerably less than 2,000 feet above the airport elevation, the pilot must choose an alternate airport. A suitable alternate airport should be at a feasible distance from the destination, provide an instrument approach, and be situated in an area where forecast weather is above alternate IFR landing minimums. According to the enroute chart, Mineral Wells (located approximately 33 nautical miles west of Meacham Field) has an instrument approach. The alternate minimums for Mineral Wells (MWL) indicate the airport will qualify as an alternate as long as the forecast ceiling at the ETA is 800 feet or above and the visibility is two miles or greater. Since Mineral Wells is close to Dallas, the terminal forecasts for the Dallas-Fort Worth area are used to determine the forecast ceiling and visibility for the alternate. Since Mineral Wells meets all of the required criteria, it is selected as the alternate.

```
SA29 211505
ABI SP 211502 M12 BKN 80 OVC 15R- 122/62/59/1717/992/RWU SW
MAF SP 211504 M11 OVC 21/2F 117/56/55/2604/994
AMA E50 BKN 200 BKN 7 108/56/47/2604/989/VSBY LWR W
CDS E2 BKN 6 OVC 7R- 134/53/51/0504/993/
GAG 30 SCT E100 OVC 20+ 118/54/51/2315/989/BINOVC W
HBR SP 211501 E4 BKN 16 OVC 3R-F 133/54/54/1007/993
SPS -XM3 VOVC 13/4R-F 127/59/59/1309/992/R15RVV3V7 CIG 2V5
MWL M9 OVC 4R-F 130/65/64/1412/993


TEXAS 211507
DAL M14 OVC 5F 145/69/66/1812/997
FTW SP 211503 M8 OVC 3F 137/68/66/1412/995
DFW SP 211502 M8 OVC 2F 137/68/66/1410/995
TYR SP 211505 M6 OVC 2F 69/67/1612/RE10
```

Fig. 12-12. Surface Aviation Weather Reports

SURFACE AVIATION WEATHER REPORT

The pilot should also check the surface aviation weather report, sometimes called an hourly report, to determine the actual weather at the destination and alternate. The report in figure 12-12 shows that a special weather report has been issued stating that the Fort Worth (FTW) weather (item 1) is "measured ceiling 800 feet overcast, three miles visibility and fog." Mineral Wells (MWL), the alternate (item 2), has "measured ceiling 900 feet overcast, four miles visibility, light rain and fog."

The pilot is not limited to checking the weather only at the destination and alternate airports. By observing the weather reports for the area surrounding the destination, weather trends can be

```
VALID 211800Z FOR USE 1500-2100Z.   TEMPS NEG ABV 24000


FT  3000  6000  9000  12000  18000  24000  30000  34000  39000


ABI       1924+12 2132+07 2240+02 2254-10 2257-21 226134 236543 246854
AMA       1914    2121+05 2231-02 2251-15 2261-23 227335 227944 237452
DAL 1721  1932+13 2035+09 2037/04 2244-09 2249-20 225535 235644 245654
OKC 1918  1928+11 2136+07 2136+02 2252-11 2260-21 217135 227044 236854
```

Fig. 12-13. Winds Aloft Forecast

detected. For example, Dallas (DAL) (item 3) has a 1,400-foot ceiling (Dallas is just east of Fort Worth) and Abilene (ABI) (item 4) has a 1,200-foot broken ceiling. Thus, the cold front and area of lowest ceiling and poorest visibility is presently passing through the Fort Worth area. As long as the cold front continues to move, conditions at the destination airport should be improving by the arrival time.

WINDS AND TEMPERATURES ALOFT FORECAST

The next item the pilot should check is the winds and temperatures aloft forecast. Since the flight originates a short distance southeast of Amarillo, passes between Oklahoma City and Abilene, and terminates near Dallas-Fort Worth, wind data for these four reporting stations should be used. (See Fig. 12-13.)

The general direction of the winds aloft is approximately the same for each of the stations; however, the velocity varies (using 6,000-foot level) from 14 knots at Amarillo (AMA) to 32 knots at Dallas (DAL). Abilene (ABI) and Oklahoma City (OKC), the stations along the route of flight, are calling for 24- and 28-knot winds. Therefore, the wind direction should remain constant and the wind velocity should increase along the route of flight. A comparison of the surface winds and winds aloft indicates the *average enroute winds* encountered during the flight will be 190° at 25 knots.

WEATHER LOG

To aid the pilot in compiling weather data, a weather log is useful, as shown in figure 12-14. A similar weather log should be completed for every flight.

NAVIGATION LOG

The complete navigation log for this flight is illustrated in figure 12-15. The following paragraphs discuss each section in detail.

CLEARANCE SECTION

The clearance section of the navigation log is an excellent place to write information that may be needed quickly. For example, based on the forecast wind and approaches available, the most logical approach to expect at Meacham Field is the ILS RWY 16L. This type of information should be noted in the navigation log (item 1).

An examination of the approach chart and route of flight indicates the pilot should expect to intercept the ILS localizer on a radar vector approximately 10 nautical miles north of Meacham Field (item 2). Since the navigation log will be on a clipboard for ready reference during the flight, part of the clearance section (item 3) can be used for copying clearances.

ENROUTE SECTION

RADIO NAVIGATION

In the navigation portion of the log, the pilot notes the checkpoints and fixes to be used, the VOR frequencies, identifiers, and course and/or route of flight. Since a significant portion of the route is the Boids Four STAR, the fixes will include STAR intersections and a course change. When tracking outbound from the Wichita Falls VORTAC, the pilot will use the 122° radial until intercepting the 318° radial from the Bridgeport VORTAC (item 4). At this point, the pilot will track inbound to the Bridgeport VORTAC on the 318° radial. The next fix to be identified is the Bridgeport VORTAC (item 5).

WEATHER LOG

	DEPARTURE	ENROUTE	DESTINATION	ALTERNATE
REPORTED WEATHER	E 2BKN 60VC 7R 0504/993	SPS′-XM3V OVC 1¾ R-F	M 8 OVC 3F 1412/995	M 9 OVC 4R -F 1412/993
FORECAST WEATHER		C 5-8 OVC 1-3R-F	C8 OVC 2R-F VRBL C10 OVC 3R-F	C 8 OVC 2R-F VRBL C10 OVC 3R-F
WINDS ALOFT	AMA 1914 DAL 1932 OKC 1928 ABI 1924 AVERAGE 190°@ 25K			
ICING & TURBULENCE	ICG ABV 12,000 MDT TO SVR TURBC NR TSTMS			
CLOUD TOPS	ABV 15,000			
SIGMETS & AIRMETS				
PILOT & RADAR REPORTS	R-TOPS ABV 40,000			

Fig. 12-14. Weather Log

ALTITUDE, WIND, AND HEADING

The altitude chosen for the first segment of flight is 5,000 feet. A power setting of 70 percent at this altitude will provide a TAS of 107 knots. The altitude to be flown from the Wichita Falls VORTAC will be assigned by ATC while the pilot is navigating according to Boids Four Arrival.

The pilot will then calculate wind correction angle and groundspeed. Although the wind correction angle is quite important in dead reckoning navigation, it is used primarily for planning purposes during an IFR flight since the actual aircraft heading is determined by the VOR indications. However, the computation of the magnetic heading will provide the pilot with a starting place and, therefore, eliminate much of the trial and error.

FUEL CONSUMPTION

At the power setting used for this trip (70 percent), the aircraft will burn 7.9 gallons of fuel per hour. The expected time enroute for each leg of the flight is computed (item 6). Next, the pilot should calculate and add the amount of fuel required for takeoff, cruise, approach, flight to the alternate, and the required reserve (item 7) to arrive at the total fuel required for the trip. (item 8). Since Skyflyer 1234X holds 50 gallons of fuel, more than an adequate supply is available for the trip.

CLEARANCES

EXPECT ILS 16L

EXPECT VECTOR ILS 10 N.M. NORTH OF MEACHAM

FIXES	ROUTE	MC	MH	GS	DIST	ETE	ETA	ATA
						TIME OFF		
CHILDRESS VORTAC 117.6	D→		1	KTS.	3	:03		
WICHITA FALLS VORTAC 112.7	V114	095°	109°	102	87	:51		
BPR 318°R 116.5	SPS 122°R	122°	135°	99	40	:24		
BRIDGEPORT VORTAC 116.5	BPR 318°R	138°	149°	93	22	:14		
FORT WORTH LOM 365.	BPR 128°R	128°	140°	96	29	:18		
MEACHAM	ATIS 120.7	APP 120.5	TWR 118.3	FSS 122.6				
CHILDRESS	FSS 123.6							
DESTINATION					181	1:50		
MINERAL WELLS (ALT.) MQP 117.7	V18	253°	241°	90	33	:22		
TRIP TOTALS					214	2:12		

FUEL		
TAXI/TO	1.0	
CLIMB	1.2	
CRUISE	14.2	
APPROACH	.8	
ALTERNATE	2.9	
RESERVE	6.0	
TOTAL	26.1	

TC → ± VAR = MC → ± DEV = CC
↓
± WCA   ± WCA
↓
TH → ± VAR = MH → ± DEV = CH

BLOCK IN

BLOCK OUT

LOG TIME

TIME FLIGHT PLAN EXPIRES

POSITION REPORT

Acft. Ident.	Position	Time	Alt.	IFR/VFR	Est. Next Fix	Name Next Fix

Fig. 12-15. Navigation Log

AIRPORT INFORMATION

The various communications frequencies to be used at each airport can be listed on the navigation log (item 9). The communication frequency listed for Childress, which is an uncontrolled airport, is 123.60 MHz for the airport advisory service. While using this frequency, the flight service station will provide the pilot with his IFR clearance, information regarding his departure, and the correct frequencies to be used to contact air traffic control.

The *time off* (item 10) should be logged upon receipt of takeoff clearance or taxiing onto the runway for takeoff (such as would be done at Childress).

Additionally, the ETAs and ATAs for the trip can be entered as the flight progresses.

SUMMARY

It can be seen that IFR flight planning is basically an extension of VFR flight planning. The information required for an IFR cross-country flight is much the same as that for a VFR flight with the major difference being that the pilot must put the major emphasis on different areas of planning and perform more detailed checks. By incorporating the proper flight planning techniques, the pilot is assured of safe, efficient flight.

SECTION B — IFR FLIGHT

After the preflight planning is complete and the IFR flight plan is filed, the pilot is ready for the operational portion of the IFR flight. During the preflight check, the aircraft documents were checked to confirm the aircraft had the required weight and balance papers, registration and airworthiness certificates, and radio station license. In addition, the aircraft and engine logs were checked to confirm that the aircraft had the necessary inspections.

LAST MINUTE PREPARATIONS

Prior to starting the engine, the pilot should organize the clipboard and navigation charts for easy reference during the flight and review the approach chart for Childress Municipal Airport. This is a good practice because an aircraft problem shortly after takeoff could necessitate a return to Childress Airport. After these preparations are completed, the pilot is ready to start the engine and taxi to the runway.

VOR ACCURACY CHECK

The pilot first taxies to the intersection of the center taxiway and the parking ramp. At this location (as noted in the *Airport/Facility Directory*), the required VOR accuracy test is performed. Whenever possible, this check should be performed to ensure VOR accuracy, even if the VOR receivers have been checked within the preceding 30 days.

Next, the pilot calls Childress Flight Service Station and requests a relay of the clearance: *"Childress Radio, this is Skyflyer 1234X, IFR to Meacham Field, Ft. Worth, request clearance."* The flight service station replies, *"ATC clears Skyflyer 1234X, as filed, via Childress,*

Wichita Falls. Maintain 5,000. Advise when reaching Childress, squawk code 0325." The pilot may acknowledge receipt of the clearance by a readback.

ENROUTE

TAKEOFF

Since the surface winds at Childress are 050° at four knots, the pilot decides to depart from runway four. In addition to being aligned with the surface winds, a takeoff on this runway provides the pilot with an opportunity to climb to the enroute altitude of 5,000 feet before reaching the Childress VORTAC.

The number one VOR frequency selector is set to the Childress VORTAC and the course selector adjusted to the approximate course required for the flight to the navaid before the aircraft reaches the active runway. The pilot then calls the flight service station, *"Childress Radio, Skyflyer 1234X, taxiing onto 04 for takeoff, IFR Meacham."* The flight service station replies, *"34X, no reported traffic in the area, winds 050° at 04. altimeter 29.93."* The pilot sets the altimeter to 29.93 and it correctly indicates the field elevation of 1,952 feet MSL.

CLIMBOUT

The pilot smoothly applies takeoff power, makes a time check, and begins the roll. After liftoff, the aircraft is stabilized at the best rate-of-climb speed and the runway heading maintained until the flight reaches approximately 1,000 feet AGL, at which time the turn to the VORTAC is begun.

HANDOFF

The pilot maintains approximately 500 f.p.m. rate of climb and reaches the enroute altitude of 5,000 feet just prior to arrival at the Childress VORTAC. At station passage, the pilot turns left to intercept V-114, records the time, and contacts the flight service station, *". . . Skyflyer 1234X, Childress VORTAC, level at 5,000."* The flight service station replies, *"Skyflyer 34X, contact Ft. Worth Center 135.6."* The pilot writes the frequency in the clearance section of the navigation log and acknowledges receipt of the transmission. Next, Ft. Worth Center is contacted. *"Ft. Worth Center, Skyflyer 1234X, Childress VORTAC, 5,000."* Ft. Worth Center replies, *"Skyflyer 1234X, squawk code 0325, and IDENT."* After turning the transponder to code 0325 and depressing the IDENT feature, Ft. Worth Center calls, *"Skyflyer 34X, radar contact. Maintain 5,000."* The pilot now proceeds on course.

ROUTE CHANGE

Prior to reaching Vernon Intersection, ATC advises, *"Skyflyer, radar shows a buildup developing along and north of V-114, approximately 14 miles ahead of you. Turn right heading 135°, proceed to Elect Intersection, V-102 to Wichita Falls VORTAC."* After acknowledging the transmission and turning to the new heading, the pilot ensures the number one VOR is tuned to the Wichita Falls VORTAC and the course selector is set to 072°. The number two VOR is tuned to the Hobart VORTAC (111.80 MHz) with the course selector set at 171°. Thus, when the DME reads 25 nautical miles on the 252° radial of Wichita Falls VORTAC, or when both VOR needles center, the flight will be at Elect Intersection.

BOIDS FOUR ARRIVAL

Over the Wichita Falls VORTAC, the pilot sets the navigation indicator to the 122° radial and turns onto the initial route segment of the Boids Four Arrival, as shown in figure 12-16. Proceeding outbound on the 122° radial of Wichita Falls VORTAC, the pilot sets the

number two VOR receiver to the Bridgeport VORTAC and turns the course selector to 138° (the reciprocal of the 318° radial). When the 318° radial of Bridgeport is intercepted, the pilot turns inbound and heads toward the Bridgeport VORTAC.

A SHORT DELAY

Ft. Worth Center contacts the pilot prior to reaching the Bridgeport VORTAC and instructs, *"Hold northwest of the Bridgeport VORTAC on 318° radial. Expect further clearance at 35."*

As the DME for the number two VOR reaches 5, the pilot begins to slow to holding speed. Although propeller driven aircraft can enter a holding pattern at any airspeed up to 175 knots, it is preferable to use economy cruise while in the holding pattern. This will provide for easier control, a smaller holding pattern, and less fuel consumption. As the number two VOR flag changes to FROM, the pilot notes the time is 28 minutes past the hour. This means a seven minute holding pattern will be required. Seven minutes equals one normal holding pattern (four minutes) and one pattern with the outbound and inbound legs approximately 30 seconds shorter in a no-wind condition. However, after flying the first pattern, the second pattern should be adjusted for the effect of wind to ensure arrival over Bridgeport VORTAC at the "expect further clearance" time.

While flying outbound in the second holding pattern, Ft. Worth Center calls, *"Proceed direct to the Boids Intersection. Maintain 5,000. Contact Regional Approach on 120.5."* The pilot acknowledges, turns inbound, and proceeds to the Bridgeport VORTAC.

FINAL APPROACH COURSE

Crossing the Bridgeport VORTAC, the pilot calls Regional Approach, *"Regional*

BOIDS FOUR ARRIVAL (BPR.BOIDS4) DALLAS-FORT WORTH, TEXAS

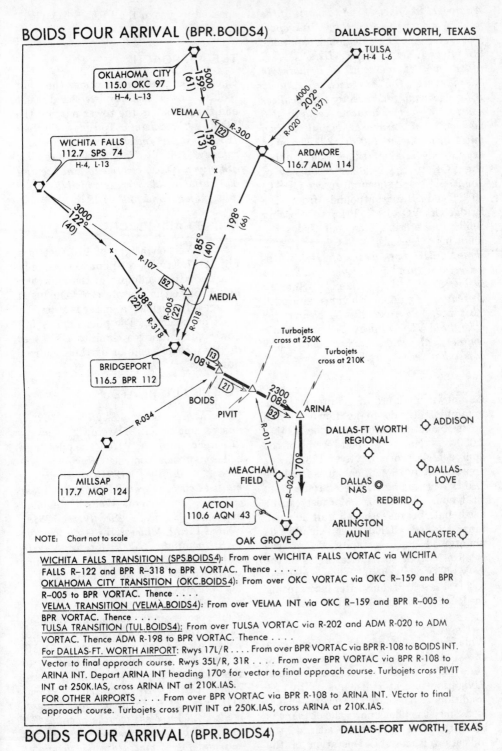

NOTE: Chart not to scale

WICHITA FALLS TRANSITION (SPS.BOIDS4): From over WICHITA FALLS VORTAC via WICHITA
FALLS R–122 and BPR R–318 to BPR VORTAC. Thence . . . .
OKLAHOMA CITY TRANSITION (OKC.BOIDS4): From over OKC VORTAC via OKC R–159 and BPR
R–005 to BPR VORTAC. Thence . . . .
VELMA TRANSITION (VELMA.BOIDS4): From over VELMA INT via OKC R–159 and BPR R–005 to
BPR VORTAC. Thence . . . .
TULSA TRANSITION (TUL.BOIDS4): From over TULSA VORTAC via R-202 and ADM R-020 to ADM
VORTAC. Thence ADM R-198 to BPR VORTAC. Thence . . . .
For DALLAS-FT. WORTH AIRPORT: Rwys 17L/R . . . . From over BPR VORTAC via BPR R-108 to BOIDS INT.
Vector to final approach course. Rwys 35L/R, 31R . . . . From over BPR VORTAC via BPR R-108 to
ARINA INT. Depart ARINA INT heading 170° for vector to final approach course. Turbojets cross PIVIT
INT at 250K.IAS, cross ARINA INT at 210K.IAS.
FOR OTHER AIRPORTS . . . . From over BPR VORTAC via BPR R-108 to ARINA INT. VEctor to final
approach course. Turbojets cross PIVIT INT at 250K.IAS, cross ARINA at 210K.IAS.

BOIDS FOUR ARRIVAL (BPR.BOIDS4) DALLAS-FORT WORTH, TEXAS

Fig. 12-16. Boids Four Arrival

Approach, Skyflyer 1234X, departing the holding pattern at the Bridgeport VORTAC, 5,000." Regional answers, *"Skyflyer 1234X, roger, IDENT . . . radar contact, descend and maintain 3,000, expect ILS approach to runway 16L, Meacham, radar vectors to localizer course. Meacham weather: ceiling 300 variable 400 overcast, visibility two miles in fog, wind 140 at 12."* The pilot acknowledges, then tunes the number one VOR to the localizer frequency of 109.90 MHz and the number two OBS to 108° and flies outbound from the Bridgeport VORTAC. Prior to crossing Boids Intersection, Regional issues the following clearance, *"Skyflyer 1234X, three miles northwest of Boids Intersection, turn right heading 125° to intercept the localizer."* Shortly thereafter, Regional provides approach clearance, *"Skyflyer 1234X, cleared for straight-in ILS runway 16L approach, contact Meacham tower on 118.3 crossing outer marker."*

As shown in figure 12-17 (item 1), the minimum altitude to be flown from a point 10 nautical miles out to the LOM is 2,000 feet. However, upon receipt of the approach clearance, Skyflyer 1234X was approximately 18 nautical miles from the LOM. When using the feeder route from Bridgeport VORTAC, 2,500 feet can be used; but, because the aircraft is on a radar vector, 3,000 feet should be maintained until established on the localizer within 10 nautical miles of the LOM. The pilot should begin a descent to 2,000 feet MSL only after intercepting the localizer within 10 nautical miles.

While flying inbound, the pilot makes a check of the navigation indicator. The glide slope needle in the number one navigation indicator displays a "fly-up" condition as the aircraft reaches 2,000 feet. Since the pilot knows the airplane is below the glide slope at this altitude, the indication is correct. Operation of the marker beacon receiver should also be checked by use of the PRESS TO TEST function.

THE APPROACH

Upon glide slope interception, the pilot reduces power to establish the descent and then contacts the tower passing the LOM, *"Meacham Tower, Skyflyer 1234X, outer marker inbound, ILS runway 16L."* The tower replies, *"Skyflyer 1234X, cleared to land, ceiling 300 variable 400 overcast, visibility two miles in fog, wind 140° at 12."*

MISSED APPROACH

At the decision height of 910 feet (see Fig. 12-17, item 2), the pilot receives only an intermittent glimpse of the approach lights. Since the runway environment is not clearly visible, a missed approach must be executed. The pilot applies full power and initiates a climb to 2,500 feet on the south course of the localizer (item 3).

TO THE ALTERNATE

"Meacham Tower, Skyflyer 1234X, missed approach." The tower answers *"Contact approach 120.5."* The pilot then calls approach control, *"Regional Approach, Skyflyer 1234X, executing missed approach from Meacham, request clearance to Mineral Wells."* Regional approach replies, *"Skyflyer 1234X, cleared to the Mineral Wells airport via V-18, maintain 3,000, intercept V-18 westbound."* At this point, the pilot starts a right turn to intercept V-18 to the Millsap VORTAC.

While proceeding westbound, the pilot studies the approach chart for Mineral Wells Airport, shown in figure 12-18. Approach control calls with the type of approach to expect and the Mineral Wells weather. *"Skyflyer 1234X, expect VOR runway 31 approach at Mineral Wells. Mineral Wells weather: ceiling 800 overcast, four miles visibility, very light rain and fog, temperature 65, dewpoint 64, wind 140 at 12, altimeter 29.93."*

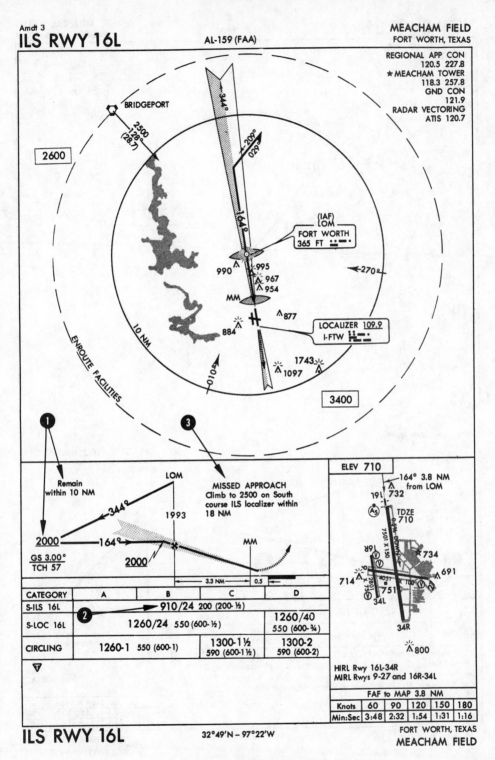

Fig. 12-17. Meacham Approach

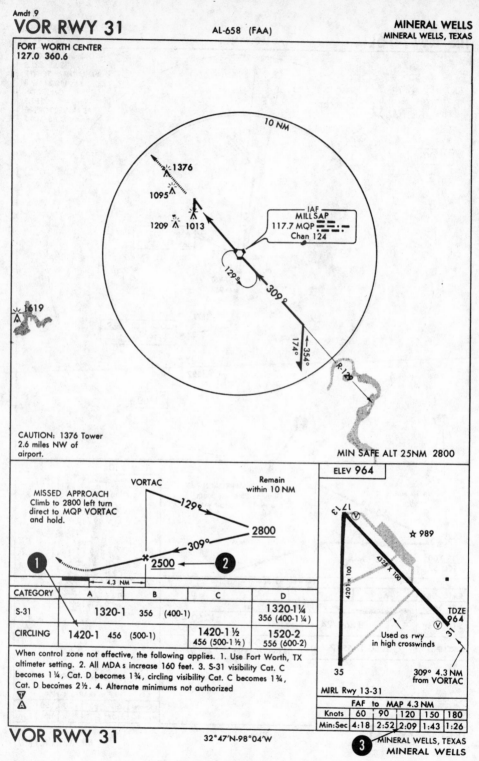

Amdt 9
VOR RWY 31

AL-658 (FAA)

MINERAL WELLS
MINERAL WELLS, TEXAS

FORT WORTH CENTER
127.0 360.6

10 NM

1376

1095

1209 1013

IAF
MILLSAP
117.7 MQP
Chan 124

129°

309°

174° 354°

R-129

1619

CAUTION: 1376 Tower
2.6 miles NW of
airport.

MIN SAFE ALT 25NM 2800

ELEV 964

MISSED APPROACH
Climb to 2800 left turn
direct to MQP VORTAC
and hold.

VORTAC

Remain
within 10 NM

129°

2800

309°

2500

4.3 NM

1713

☆ 989

420' x 100

4325 x 100

35

TDZE
964

31

Used as rwy
in high crosswinds

309° 4.3 NM
from VORTAC

MIRL Rwy 13-31

CATEGORY	A	B	C	D
S-31	1320-1	356 (400-1)		1320-1¼ 356 (400-1¼)
CIRCLING	1420-1	456 (500-1)	1420-1½ 456 (500-1½)	1520-2 556 (600-2)

When control zone not effective, the following applies. 1. Use Fort Worth, TX
altimeter setting. 2. All MDA s increase 160 feet. 3. S-31 visibility Cat. C
becomes 1¼, Cat. D becomes 1¾, circling visibility Cat. C becomes 1¾,
Cat. D becomes 2½. 4. Alternate minimums not authorized

FAF to MAP 4.3 NM					
Knots	60	90	120	150	180
Min:Sec	4:18	2:52	2:09	1:43	1:26

VOR RWY 31

32°47'N-98°04'W

MINERAL WELLS, TEXAS
MINERAL WELLS

Fig. 12-18. Mineral Wells Approach

Just prior to reaching the Millsap VORTAC, approach control issues an approach clearance, *"Skyflyer 1234X, cleared for Mineral Wells VOR runway 31 approach, circle to land runway 13, change to the Mineral Wells advisory frequency approved at the VOR inbound."* The pilot crosses the Millsap VORTAC, starts turning outbound, and begins timing for the procedure turn. The final check of the approach chart indicates the circling MDA is 1,420 feet (item 1). With an 800-foot ceiling, this provides a good margin. Upon interception of the course inbound (intermediate approach segment) the pilot begins the descent to 2,500 feet MSL (item 2). The time is noted crossing the VOR and the descent initiated. Then, the pilot calls Mineral Wells radio on 123.60. *"Mineral Wells Radio, Skyflyer 1234X, VOR inbound."*

Since the estimated groundspeed is approximately 100 knots during the final approach, it will take two minutes and 38 seconds (item 3) to fly to the missed approach point. At 1,700 feet MSL, the pilot breaks out of the clouds, observes the approach lights about two miles ahead, and starts to maneuver the aircraft to enter a left downwind for runway 13. The airport must remain visible throughout the landing maneuver and the descent not made below 1,420 feet until the aircraft is in a position for the final descent to the runway.

Taxiing to the ramp after landing, the pilot calls Mineral Wells Radio to close the IFR flight plan. At an uncontrolled airport, the pilot must initiate the action to close the flight plan. If the landing was made at Meacham, the tower would have closed the flight plan automatically.

SECTION C—IFR EMERGENCY PROCEDURES

Whether or not a given situation constitutes an emergency may be determined by either the pilot or ATC controller. In an emergency, pilots are authorized to deviate from any rule in FAR Part 91, Subparts A and B, to the extent necessary to meet the emergency. The pilot may, however, be requested to defend his actions in a written report to the chief of the ATC facility concerned.

The determination that an emergency situation exists or is developing may not always be evident from either the pilot's or controller's viewpoint. Such factors as the experience of the pilot or controller, aircraft and equipment capabilities, or unexpected weather conditions may alter the decision to declare an emergency.

A complete loss of communications and navigation capability in *IFR conditions* is considered an emergency. However, should only one of these systems become inoperative, the flight may be expected to continue safely, provided ATC has been alerted. Situations associated with weather, such as inadvertent entry into a thunderstorm, hail, severe turbulence, or icing, clearly point to a probable emergency. Fuel starvation or inability to maintain the MEA are undeniable emergencies. If, after considering the particular circumstances of his flight, the pilot *feels* a potentially dangerous or unsafe situation exists, he should declare an emergency.

In any case, the pilot should remember the four "C's."

1. *Confess* the predicament as soon as it becomes apparent. The longer the delay the more grave the situation becomes.

2. *Communicate* as much of the distress message as possible during the initial transmission. ATC needs complete information to provide adequate service.

3. *Climb*, if possible, for better radio, radar, and direction finding (DF) reception. Remember that these systems transmit and receive on an approximate line-of-sight basis. However, when operating on an IFR clearance in IFR conditions, an unauthorized climb could reduce separation, thus creating another dangerous situation.

4. *Comply* with the advice and instructions received. Help from ATC is of no value unless it is followed.

DECLARING AN EMERGENCY

To declare an emergency when operating with an IFR clearance, the pilot should contact ATC on the currently assigned frequency. If no response is received, the emergency frequency of 121.50 MHz should be used. Pilots should be aware that the ARTCC emergency frequency reception range may not extend to the limits of radar coverage. Thus, if no response is received on the assigned frequency or 121.50 MHz, the emergency should be declared to the nearest FSS or ATC control tower on the appropriate frequency.

When not under ATC control, the pilot should transmit the emergency message on the FSS or ATC frequency being monitored. If a particular frequency is not being monitored by the pilot, he should use 121.50 MHz. In either case, the information summarized in figure 12-19 should be transmitted.

At the end of the transmission, the microphone should be "keyed" for two 10-second dashes, with or without voice, followed by the aircraft identification and the word "over." This procedure may enable a ground station to obtain a DF fix.

Distress or Uncertainty or alert	"MAYDAY, MAYDAY, MAYDAY, or "PAN, PAN, PAN,
Aircraft identification (repeated three times)	N6174P N6174P N6174P
Type of aircraft	Piper Comanche,
Position or estimated position (specify)	30 DME west of Salina, V-4S,
True or magnetic heading (specify)	heading 260° magnetic,
True airspeed or estimated true airspeed (specify)	estimated 120 knots true airspeed,
Altitude	6,000 feet, descending,
Fuel remaining in hours and minutes	two hours, three zero minutes fuel remaining,
Nature of distress	experiencing severe clear icing,
Pilot's intentions (ditch, emergency landing, etc.)	will attempt landing at Russell Airport,
Assistance desired (fix, steer, bearing, escort, etc.)	request vector to initial approach fix."

Fig. 12-19. Emergency Communications

In addition, the pilot of an aircraft equipped with a transponder may declare the emergency by squawking code 7700. The double hashmarks associated with code 7700 will normally be observed by radar controllers if *the aircraft is within radar range.*

SPECIAL EMERGENCY (AIR PIRACY)

A special emergency is a condition of air piracy, or other hostile act by a person, or persons, aboard an aircraft, which threatens the safety of the aircraft or its passengers. Although these incidents rarely involve the average pilot in command, all pilots should be aware of the recommended ATC procedures.

Normal distress or urgency procedures should be employed, if possible. When circumstances do not permit prescribed distress or urgency procedures, a message consisting of as much of the following information as practical should be transmitted on the air-ground frequency in use at the time.

1. Name of the station addressed
2. Identification of the aircraft and present position
3. Nature of the special emergency condition and the pilot's intentions

If unable to provide the above information, the pilot should use the code words and/or transponder setting as follows:

Spoken words — *Transponder Seven Five Zero Zero* (meaning "I am being hijacked/forced to a new destination.")

Transponder setting — Mode 3/A, Code 7500 (See Fig. 12-20).

COMMUNICATIONS FAILURE

Two-way radio communications failure procedures for IFR flights are outlined in Federal Aviation Regulation 91.127 and are reiterated in the *Airman's Information Manual.* Unless otherwise

Fig. 12-20. Transponder Setting

authorized by ATC, pilots operating under IFR are expected to comply with this regulation. The procedure varies with the type of weather conditions in which the flight is operating at the time of the failure.

ALERTING ATC

To alert ATC of a radio communications failure, transponder equipped aircraft should squawk code 7700 for one minute, then squawk code 7600 for a period of 15 minutes, or the remainder of the flight, whichever occurs first. The sequence may be repeated, as necessary. This procedure is especially valuable in the approach phase. However, some radar facilities are not equipped to display code 7600 automatically and will interrogate 7600 only when the aircraft is under direct radar control at the time of the radio failure. During the enroute phase, the absence of communications with the pilot will be interpreted as a communications failure.

In addition, pilots are urged to listen for ATC instructions on any operational radio receiver. Controllers have the capability to transmit on most navigation aids such as VORs, VORTACs, NDBs, or localizers.

IN VFR CONDITIONS

The primary objective of FAR 91.127 is to preclude extended IFR operations in the air traffic control system for aircraft experiencing communication failure. If a two-way radio communication failure occurs in VFR conditions or if VFR conditions are encountered at any time after the failure, the pilot should continue the flight under VFR and land as soon as practicable. The terminology "land as soon as practicable" should not be construed to mean "land as soon as possible." For example, the pilot is not expected to land at an unauthorized or unsuitable airport or to land minutes short of his destination.

IN IFR CONDITIONS

If IFR conditions prevail at the time of two-way communication failure, the pilot must comply with detailed procedures to ensure aircraft separation. These procedures establish the *route* and *altitude* to be used for extended operations when two-way communications are not possible.

ROUTE

The flight should be continued under IFR by one of the following routes, in the order shown.

1. The route assigned by the last accepted ATC clearance

2. A direct course to the fix, route, or airway *specified in a radar vector clearance*

3. By the route ATC has advised may be expected in a further clearance

4. The route specified in the flight plan if items 1, 2, and 3 have not been specified by ATC

ALTITUDE

The altitude flown should be at the *highest* of the following altitudes for the particular *route segment* being flown.

1. The MEA

2. The last altitude assigned by ATC

3. The altitude ATC has advised may be expected in a further clearance

If it becomes necessary for the pilot to climb to an MEA which is higher than the last assigned altitude or the altitude expected in a further clearance, the *higher* altitude (MEA) should be flown, but *only* over the route segment to which the MEA applies, as shown in figure 12-21. If the succeeding route segment has a lower MEA, descent should be made to the applicable altitude—either the last assigned altitude or the altitude expected in a further clearance.

HOLDING

If the two-way communication failure occurs during a holding pattern, the pilot is expected to continue to hold *until* the "expect further clearance" time. Then the flight should proceed via the route and altitude, as previously specified in this section.

If an "expect approach clearance" time has been specified, the pilot should depart the holding fix so as to arrive over the initial approach fix at the specified time. However, if an "expect approach clearance" time has not been provided and the flight arrives at the destination before the ETA, the pilot should hold at the initial approach fix until the ETA.

DESCENT FOR APPROACH

The descent for the approach begins from the enroute altitude when over the approach fix. The descent may not begin before the "expect approach clearance" time (if received). If the "expect approach clearance" time has not been received, the descent is begun at the ETA, as shown on the flight plan with any amendments by ATC included.

If more than one fix is available for starting the approach, the pilot may choose whichever fix he deems appropriate. ATC will provide separation for the flight, regardless of the initial approach fix used.

It is impossible to construct procedures for every situation; as a result, pilots who are confronted by a situation not covered in the regulations are expected to exercise good judgment in whatever action is taken. For example, only general procedures are specified for a flight which experiences communications failure before reaching the first destination airport, and continues to the alternate because of poor weather conditions.

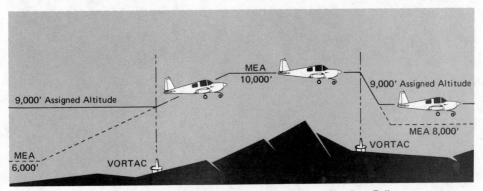

Fig. 12-21. Altitude Selection for Two-Way Communications Failure

APPENDIX I
FLIGHT MANEUVERS

COMMERCIAL FLIGHT MANEUVERS
ATTITUDE INSTRUMENT FLYING

COMMERCIAL FLIGHT MANEUVERS

INTRODUCTION

The appendix presents the performance criteria for the precision flight maneuvers which are required for the commercial pilot applicant. The training and certification concepts in FAR Part 61 require the pilot to receive instruction and demonstrate competency in all pilot operations listed in the pertinent sections of this regulation. The procedures and maneuvers used to test the pilot's competency are outlined in the Commercial Pilot Flight Test Guide. It should be noted that the examiner may specify only the initial portions of some maneuvers, depending on aircraft performance and/or flight conditions.

STEEP POWER TURNS AND CHANDELLES

STEEP POWER TURNS

Steep power turns are excellent maneuvers to help a pilot develop a fine control touch and analysis of control functions. Through them, the pilot will learn to accurately maneuver the aircraft near its performance limits.

Steep power turns aid in the development of proper coordination and accuracy in turning, since the pilot must recognize the control pressures needed for entry, execution, and recovery. In addition, it is the type of maneuver that helps pilots develop judgment and the ability to plan ahead.

Fig. A-1. Instrument Indications in Steep Turns

DESCRIPTION

The steep power turn is a turn with a bank of *at least* 50° maintained through at least two complete turns. Care must be exercised during turns in excess of 50° of bank that the normal flight limitations are not unintentionally exceeded. The instrument indications in figure A-1 display a turn to the left with 50° of bank. This maneuver usually consists of turns in one direction immediately followed with another series of turns in the opposite direction.

During the early phases of training in this maneuver, the pilot may briefly fly straight and level between the two turns. This allows stabilization and preparation for the next turn; however, as proficiency is developed, a roll from one turn directly into the other will be expected.

PROCEDURE

As is the case with all training maneuvers, the pilot must be aware of other traffic within the area. Therefore, before beginning the maneuver, clearing turns should be made to ensure that the practice area is free of conflicting traffic. As the maneuver is performed, it is the pilot's responsibility to remain vigilant and avoid other traffic in the area.

The pilot should prepare for this maneuver by stabilizing the aircraft altitude, airspeed, and heading. Beginning the maneuver from a stabilized condition will allow the pilot to do a much better job of precision flying. Section lines or prominent land features should be used to establish heading and aid in orientation.

TURN ENTRY

The entry should be smooth and precise. Generally, the best entry results from a smooth roll-in that requires 25° of heading change. This rule is based on using one-half of the desired bank as the

degree of heading change used for roll-in (50° ÷ 2 = 25°).

During the entry, the pilot should smoothly apply sufficient power to help maintain level flight in the steep turn. The additional power provides lift to balance the increased load factor created by centrifugal force. As shown in figure A-2, an aircraft in a 60° bank must develop sufficient lift to support two times the aircraft's weight (two Gs).

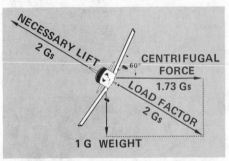

Fig. A-2. Load Factor in Steep Turns

As the desired bank is reached, the pilot should briefly check the attitude indicator to confirm the degree of bank, and the altimeter and vertical velocity indicators to confirm pitch. Reference to the aircraft instruments must be used *only* as a cross-check to confirm the indications gained from outside visual references.

PITCH TRIM

Some instructors encourage the use of trim to help maintain the correct pitch attitude. The use of trim will simplify the pilot's task during the turn; however, forward elevator control pressure on recovery must be anticipated and trim *readjusted* as needed. Use of trim is a matter of personal preference and should be determined individually.

VISUAL REFERENCE

Throughout the maneuver, the altitude is maintained by the pitch attitude of the aircraft. The pilot must adjust the control pressures, as needed, to maintain the pitch angle that results in level flight. The easiest way to do this is to pick a spot on the windshield directly in front of the pilot's eyes that is aligned with the horizon, as shown in figure A-3. This spot provides the pitch reference in the same manner as does the miniature aircraft in the attitude indicator, as shown in figure A-4.

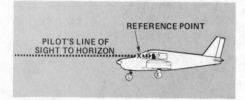

Fig. A-3. Picking a Reference Point

Fig. A-4. Attitude Indicator

If the pilot uses a spot on the windshield rather than the cowling of the aircraft for pitch indication, he will find that the indication is identical in both left and right turns. Figure A-5 illustrates the visual reference the pilot has in straight and turning flight. As the aircraft rolls into a bank, the reference spot moves to a point above the horizon because of the increased angle of attack.

If the pilot were to use the cowling of the aircraft for the pitch angle reference, he would have a different indication for left and right turns. This happens because the pilot is sitting to the left side of the aircraft and not along the centerline.

IMPORTANCE OF BANK

Maintenance of bank angle in the steep power turn is of utmost importance, since effects of the bank change are cumulative. When the bank changes, pitch requirements change and, therefore, the airspeed and altitude also change.

It can be seen that if the bank is decreased, the elevator control pressure needed to maintain level flight at the greater bank causes the nose to rise with a resulting increase in altitude. At this point, a frustrated pilot would be *chasing his instruments* trying to adjust bank angle, altitude, and airspeed. The correct recovery procedure is to adjust the pitch attitude, roll the aircraft to 50° of bank, and let the aircraft return to normal airspeed for the steep turn.

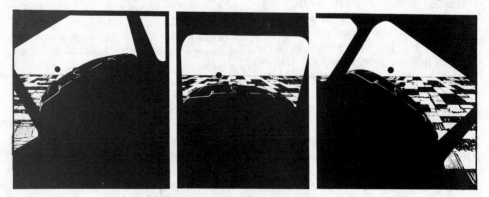

Fig. A-5. Pitch Indications with Spot Method

ALTITUDE CORRECTIONS

Altitude corrections in steep turns deserve special consideration. If altitude is being lost because of a nose-low attitude, simply pulling back on the control wheel *is not* a satisfactory correction. An aircraft in a *constant altitude*, 60° bank has a load factor of two Gs. While *climbing* or *stopping a rate of descent* in a 60° bank, it is possible to exert a force greater than two Gs upon the aircraft. The pilot trying to stop a descent by pulling back on the control wheel simply tightens the turn and may cause an accelerated stall or damage to the aircraft. Figure A-6 shows the result of using elevator control to recover altitude in a steep turn.

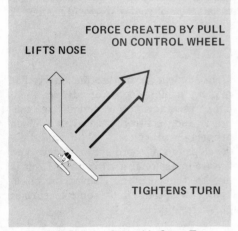

Fig. A-6. Elevator Control in Steep Turns

The proper correction is to *reduce the angle of bank* causing the nose to rise. When the pitch angle of the aircraft has returned to level, the pilot should return to the desired angle of bank and apply slightly more back pressure as the bank is increased.

RECOVERY

Recovery should be smooth and precise, utilizing the approximate rate of roll used for entry. As the pilot decreases the bank, enough back pressure must be released to maintain altitude. If the control pressure is released in proper proportion to the rate of roll, the spot on the windshield will seem to move downward to the horizon and the aircraft *altitude* will remain constant throughout the recovery.

The recovery should be planned so the wings roll level as the aircraft reaches the original heading. The pilot should practice steep turns which incorporate a roll-out to a level flight attitude for several seconds before entering the second steep turn. As the pilot becomes proficient in making smooth roll-outs and recovering with proper heading and altitude, he should begin to roll from one turn directly into the other.

During the roll from one turn to the turn in the opposite direction, the ailerons should be deflected at approximately a constant rate. As the roll is begun, the back pressure should be gradually reduced until the aircraft is in wings-level flight. As the aircraft passes through wings-level flight, the pilot must begin to increase aft control pressure gradually to adjust the pitch angle and maintain altitude. The pitch angle will be changed slightly throughout the roll from one turn to the other.

EVALUATION

This maneuver is evaluated on the basis of planning, coordination, smoothness, prompt stabilization of turns, and orientation. The pilot is expected to plan the entries and recoveries for a smooth, prompt roll-in and roll-out. The bank should be maintained within five degrees. During the flight test, the applicant may be asked to execute steep turns in either direction using a bank of at least 50°, but not greater than 60°. By proper anticipation of control pressures, the pilot is able to perform a smooth maneuver without a loss or gain in altitude. The FAA evaluation criteria include maintenance of altitude within 100 feet of the entry altitude. Throughout the maneuver, the pilot must maintain vigilance for other air traffic.

COMMON ERRORS

IMPROPER PITCH CHANGE

The most common fault of the pilot performing these maneuvers is the improper amount of pitch change during entry or recovery. Many pilots over-anticipate the pitch requirements and make excessive changes when rolling into or out of the turn. The pilot must recognize that the pitch change required for the turn is very small. The pitch change should not be confused with the control pressures which change significantly upon entry or recovery from the turn.

The pilot who makes no pitch change on entry or recovery displays a lack of planning since only the degree of bank and not the control pressure requirements are considered. During the entry and recovery, the pilot will find that each of the three controls must be used to achieve the desired result.

ROUGH CONTROL HANDLING

Rough control handling may be due to lack of planning and loss of orientation. It is normally due to this lack of planning and orientation that the pilot suddenly discovers a large control movement must be made to attain the desired result. To avoid this, the pilot must anticipate the control pressures needed and apply them smoothly.

EARLY RECOVERY

Another common error is initiation of recovery too early in the maneuver. Since the rate of turn in a steep power turn is quite rapid, the pilot may misjudge the amount of lead required for roll-out. A smooth, gentle roll-out should be initiated at a heading approximately 25° (one-half the degree of bank) before the desired recovery heading.

LOSS OF ORIENTATION

Loss of orientation is caused by either forgetting the heading from which the maneuver was entered, or by spatial disorientation. The pilot performing a seemingly perfect maneuver may be dismayed to find the wrong recovery heading was selected. Before entering the maneuver, the pilot should take definite note of the aircraft heading. The easiest way to do this is to align the aircraft with a section line or some other prominent landmark outside the aircraft. Then, each time the aircraft nose approaches this landmark, the aircraft will have completed 360° of turn and the roll-out can be planned accordingly.

Spatial disorientation may occur during initial training because of the effect of the rapid turn rate on the inner ear. However, after adequate exposure, pilots usually develop some degree of immunity to this type of spatial disorientation.

CHANDELLES

The chandelle is another maneuver that requires a high degree of advance planning, accuracy, coordination, smoothness, and control sensitivity. When properly practiced, the chandelle develops good coordination habits and finesse in use of aircraft controls. This is due to the constant changes in pitch, bank, airspeed, and control surface pressures.

DESCRIPTION

A chandelle may be described as a maximum performance climbing turn of 180°. Throughout the maneuver, the aircraft speed is smoothly adjusted from entry speed to a few knots above the stall speed by controlling the pitch attitude. As airspeed is reduced, full power is smoothly applied and a 180° climbing turn is executed. Figure A-7 illustrates a chandelle.

PROCEDURE

Although the prevailing winds have little or no effect on the chandelle, the pilot

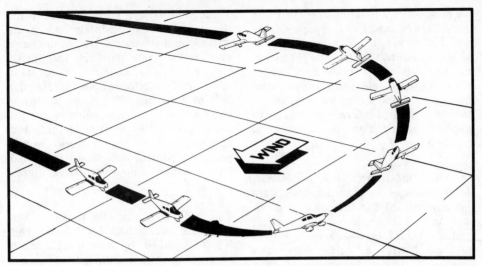

Fig. A-7. Chandelle

will find it best to begin this maneuver crosswind. By turning into the wind, the smallest amount of wind drift results; therefore, the pilot will find it easier to remain in the practice area. As with all training maneuvers, the pilot should make the necessary clearing turns and check the training area for other traffic.

ENTRY

The chandelle should be entered from level flight at cruising speed. If the cruising speed of the aircraft is higher than maneuvering speed, the aircraft should be slowed to maneuvering speed, or the recommended entry speed, whichever is less. The sequence of events and the relationship between pitch angle and bank angle is illustrated in figure A-8.

When the chandelle is properly performed, the increase in load factor on the aircraft is extremely small. The load factor encountered in this maneuver should not exceed approximately 1-1/2

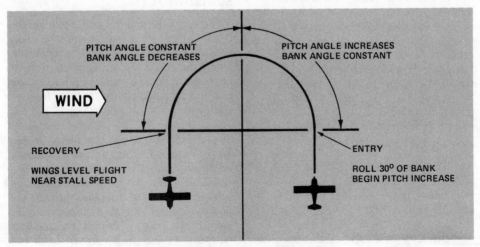

Fig. A-8. Plan View of Chandelle

Gs; however, by entering the maneuver at or below maneuvering speed, the load factor should not exceed that for which the aircraft is stressed. Maneuvering speed is the maximum speed at which the pilot may use abrupt control movement. Good operating practice in turbulent air is to slow the aircraft to maneuvering speed to reduce stress on the aircraft.

As with most precision maneuvers, visual references outside the aircraft are the primary aid for the pilot in maintaining orientation and precision control. Therefore, the aircraft should be aligned with a section line or a prominent landmark to begin the maneuver. (See Fig. A-9, position 1.) While on the desired heading, the pilot should begin a coordinated roll to the desired bank, as shown by the aircraft in position 2. Although 20° to 30° of bank may be used in this maneuver, 30° is recommended, since it provides the pilot with a smoother, easier maneuver.

FIRST 90° OF TURN

After the bank is established, the pilot applies back pressure to the elevator control to begin the climbing turn. As the climbing turn is initiated, the pilot should apply full power gradually in an attempt to maintain cruise r.p.m. as long as possible. If the pilot applies power in this manner he will not exceed the maximum r.p.m. for the engine. Throughout the first 90° of turn, the bank of 30° must be maintained. Also, the pitch attitude should be increased at a *constant rate* throughout the first 90° of turn.

SECOND 90° OF TURN

At the completion of the first 90° of turn, the aircraft should still be in a 30° bank and have the highest pitch attitude which will be utilized during the maneuver. The aircraft in position 3 of figure A-9 illustrates an aircraft after 90° of turn.

Throughout the second 90° of turn, the pilot should maintain the pitch attitude and slowly roll out of the bank at *a constant rate* until the 180° point is reached. To maintain a constant pitch attitude throughout the second 90° of turn the pilot needs to slowly increase back pressure. As the aircraft loses speed, the elevators become less effective and, therefore, more elevator pressure (control deflection) is needed to maintain the established pitch attitude.

The roll-out should be timed so the wings are level at the 180° point. This is accomplished by *reducing the bank at a constant rate* after the 90° point. As the speed of the aircraft decreases and the power is increased, the left-turning tendency, caused by P-factor and the propeller slipstream, is more prevalent. During the second 90° of turn the rudder pressure needed will be noticeably different in right and left turns.

RECOVERY

Recovery is completed by gradually lowering the nose to level flight attitude and allowing the aircraft to accelerate while maintaining a constant altitude. Figure A-9, position 4, illustrates an aircraft at the 180° point.

EVALUATION

The chandelle will be evaluated on the basis of planning, airspeed control, coordination, smoothness, and orientation. Since the coordination elements learned in this maneuver are required when performing lazy eights, a high level of proficiency should be attained.

The chandelle must be completed within 10° of desired heading and at an airspeed not more than five knots above stalling speed. The amount of altitude gained in this maneuver is not the measure of quality. The pilot should obtain from his aircraft the best climb performance consistent with the proper use of bank and existing conditions of flight.

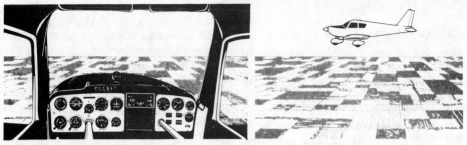

1. At or below maneuvering speed select a reference, such as a road, and line up with it.

2. Bank the airplane 30° with coordinated controls and apply steady back pressure.

3. The roll out is started at the 90° position and the pitch attitude is maintained.

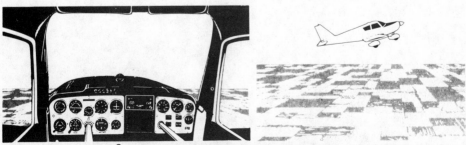

4. At the 180° position, the wings are level and the airspeed just above a stall.

Fig. A-9. Executing the Chandelle

COMMON ERRORS

LACK OF COORDINATION

The most common problem experienced by the pilot is lack of coordination. Coordination generally is good until the airspeed starts to decrease and left-turning tendency becomes a factor. Generally, insufficient right rudder is the major coordination problem. Necessary control pressures vary greatly throughout the maneuver as the angle of attack changes and, therefore, the left-turning tendency changes.

IMPROPER BANK

The pilot should roll into the desired amount of bank at the beginning of the maneuver and maintain it until 90° of turn, at which point a constant rate roll-out is started. The pilot should not be so engrossed with other facets of the maneuver that he neglects proper bank control.

Some pilots have a tendency to roll into an initial bank that is too steep, resulting in a loss of performance. The pilot will find that with too steep a bank, the aircraft will turn more rapidly and arrive at the recovery point before the airspeed is slowed to the desired speed, or the pilot may find that he is rolling all the bank out in the last 10° to 15° of turn. Also, during the turn with an excessive angle of bank, lift that would otherwise result in altitude gain will be used to offset the increased bank.

As the airplane is placed in a climbing attitude during the first 90° of turn, it will appear to the pilot that the bank is increasing; therefore, the pilot will have a tendency to shallow the bank. The attitude indicator may be checked occasionally to confirm the angle of bank. It should be emphasized that the roll-out from the 90° point to the 180° point should be at a constant rate and the aircraft should arrive at the recovery point in wings-level flight.

PITCH ANGLE

The pitch angle should increase at a constant rate from the entry to the 90° point of the turn. At this time, the pitch angle stabilizes and remains constant throughout the second 90° of turn. With proper planning, the pilot will initiate a pitch angle that causes the aircraft to arrive at the 180° point of turn at a speed slightly above stall speed. With a little practice and the use of outside visual references, the pilot will be able to select a pitch angle that provides the desired results.

If the pitch angle is too great, the possibility of stalling the aircraft before reaching the recovery point exists. With too small a pitch angle, the pilot finds that he arrives at the recovery point with an airspeed greater than five knots above stalling speed. The pilot should remember that since full power is used throughout the last portion of this maneuver, the airspeed is controlled by the pitch angle of the aircraft. Because of this, the maintenance of the proper pitch angle is of utmost importance.

STEEP SPIRALS AND MAXIMUM PERFORMANCE TAKEOFFS AND LANDINGS

STEEP SPIRALS

Steep spirals are valuable for teaching coordination, planning, precise speed control, and orientation. Although steep spirals are practiced primarily as a coordination exercise, they also have practical aspects, such as descending to a landing approach from an altitude higher than the normal traffic pattern. If the pilot experiences a power failure at high altitudes, this maneuver provides an excellent procedure for an approach to an emergency landing. Figure A-10 illustrates an aircraft performing a steep spiral to a point of intended landing.

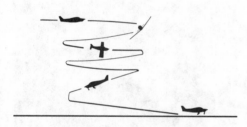

Fig. A-10. Profile of Steep Spiral

The practice of this maneuver improves the pilot's orientation under difficult circumstances. In addition, this maneuver develops the pilot's ability to maintain precise speed control, which is essential in all flight maneuvers.

DESCRIPTION

The steep spiral is nothing more than a steep bank held through a series of gliding turns. During the spiral, a uniform radius is maintained about a reference point on the ground. An intersection of roads or fields provides the pilot with an excellent reference point. To compensate for wind drift, the angle of bank should vary, as necessary;

however, the pilot should use at least 50° of bank at the steepest point in each turn.

PROCEDURE

Before attempting this maneuver, it is recommended that the pilot have sufficient altitude to make at least three steep spirals (1080° of turn) and *recover more than 1,500 feet above the ground.* The amount of altitude required will vary with different types of aircraft.

Since the aircraft will be descending throughout this maneuver, it is important that the pilot clear the area below as well as around the aircraft. The safest and most positive way to accomplish this is to perform clearing turns and observe the affected airspace as the entry position is approached.

ENTRY

Although this maneuver can be entered from any position relative to the wind, it is advisable to enter it downwind, approximately one-quarter of a mile from the point around which the maneuver will be flown. If the entry is downwind, the steepest angle of bank will occur at the beginning of the maneuver. This allows the pilot to readily adjust the radius of turn as needed to circle the reference point. Entering the maneuver one-quarter of a mile from the selected point generally positions the aircraft so a bank of at least 50° can be used at the steepest point of each turn.

During the approach to the entry point, a prominent landmark downwind of the ground reference should be chosen to aid in orientation during both the maneuver and the roll-out. Through the use of outside reference points for both pitch attitude and orientation, a smooth accurate maneuver and recovery can be

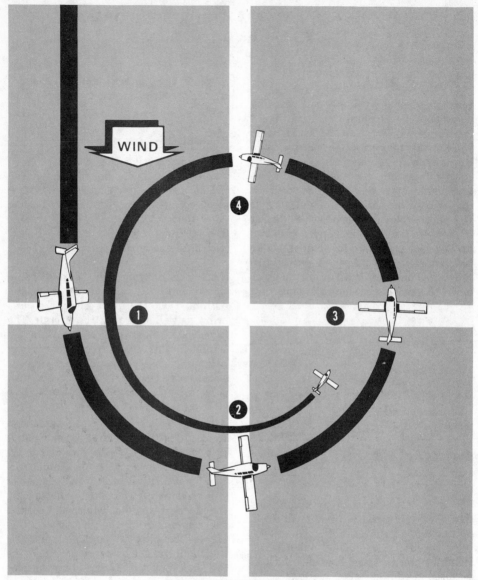

Fig. A-11. Wind Drift Correction

performed. Upon arrival at the entry point, carburetor heat is applied (if required), throttle closed, and a steep spiral begun by rolling into the desired angle of bank. (See Fig. A-11, position 1.)

AIRSPEED

The speed recommended for this maneuver by the Federal Aviation Administration is 150 percent of the stall speed of the aircraft. This speed provides the pilot with a safe margin above stall speed and a solid, responsive feel of the controls throughout the maneuver.

Since power is reduced to idle, airspeed is controlled solely by the pitch attitude of the aircraft. As the pilot rolls into the bank, he must lower the nose of the aircraft to maintain the correct airspeed. The pilot should establish a pitch attitude that provides the speed desired and then maintain that pitch attitude through outside visual references. The airspeed indicator should be checked only to confirm the pitch attitude.

WIND DRIFT

Since the pilot must maintain a constant radius about the selected point, proper wind drift correction is essential. The proper radius can be maintained by varying the wind drift correction angle and the angle of bank as in the turns about a point and S-turns. On the downwind side of the turn, the bank is the steepest since the groundspeed is the greatest. On the upwind side of the turn, the bank is the shallowest. In figure A-11, the aircraft at position 1 is downwind and, consequently, has the steepest bank. From position 1 to position 3, the bank angle of the aircraft gradually descreases from the steepest to the shallowest point as it turns upwind. From position 3 to position 1, the bank gradually increases until it is once again at the steepest point at position 1.

Since this maneuver is entered from a relatively high altitude, the point is more difficult to see and, therefore, to hold at the beginning of the maneuver. As the aircraft descends, the pilot finds that the constant radius around the reference is easier to maintain. The normal pitch attitude in a steep spiral to the right is illustrated in figure A-12.

LOAD FACTOR

An aircraft in a *constant altitude* turn with 60° of bank experiences a load factor of two Gs. Since the steep spiral is not a constant altitude maneuver, there is less than two Gs of load factor exerted upon the aircraft. However, it is possible for the load factor to increase signifi-

Fig. A-12. Pitch Attitude in Steep Spiral

cantly as the result of the pilot's control usage. If the pilot lets the airspeed increase above normal and then slows the aircraft by raising the nose, the load factor exerted upon the aircraft will increase. Raising the nose of the aircraft tends to tighten the turn instead of providing corrective action; therefore, the load factor can greatly increase with little airspeed adjustment.

The increase in stall speed which accompanies the increased load factor can cause an accelerated stall. As shown in figure A-13, an aircraft with a two-G load factor has a stall speed 41 percent greater than normal. With a three-G load factor, the stall speed is increased by 73 percent. In terms of airspeed, this means that an aircraft with a normal *indicated* stall speed of 53 knots will stall at 75 knots with a two-G load factor and at 92 knots with a three-G load factor.

LOAD FACTOR	INCREASE IN NORMAL STALL SPEED
1.0	0%
1.5	22%
2.0	41%
2.5	58%
3.0	73%
3.5	87%
4.0	100%

Fig. A-13. Load Factors

As the maneuver progresses, the pilot must not become lax in his search for other aircraft. A constant vigilance for other aircraft in the area must be exercised at all times.

LANDING APPROACH

If the pilot has sufficient altitude and experiences a power failure, he can use a steep spiral to position the aircraft for an actual landing approach. The pilot finds that it is easier and safer to lose altitude over the point of intended landing than to execute S-turns or other maneuvers that are performed away from the landing area. In the event of a power failure, the pilot should fly his aircraft directly to a point over his intended landing field and then begin the steep spiral.

The spiral approach also provides the pilot with an opportunity to inspect his intended landing field before he actually commits himself to final approach. Once the aircraft is on final approach, it is too late for a pilot to change his mind because of obstacles and try to reach another field.

The pilot should plan the spiral approach so he will recover approximately 1,500 feet above ground level heading *upwind*. At this point, a 360° overhead approach is entered. A spiral approach to a landing pattern is illustrated in figure A-14. The final approach direction is chosen by the pilot during the steep spiral (if he does not know the surface wind direction), since he has the opportunity to gauge wind direction and make estimations of his final approach path.

RECOVERY

Normal recovery from a steep spiral should be made at 1,500 feet above ground level. It is recommended this maneuver not be flown lower than 1,000 feet AGL.

The recovery should be made without a change in airspeed when the straight

glide is resumed. As the pilot rolls out of the bank to his original entry heading, he should adjust the pitch attitude of the aircraft to maintain the airspeed. The pilot will discover that adequate practice is the solution to rolling out with the proper pitch control and coordination.

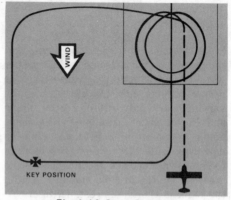

Fig. A-14. Steep Spiral to Landing Approach

EVALUATION

Evaluation criteria are based on competency in entering, maintaining, and recovering from steep spirals using smooth, coordinated control. Loss of orientation, descent below a safe altitude, or excessive variation of pitch attitude is disqualifying. The performance of this maneuver with proper drift correction, airspeed control, and coordination indicates that the pilot has learned the elements necessary for the performance of subsequent precision maneuvers.

During the flight test, the pilot is expected to control his airspeed within 10 knots of that desired and his bank between 50° and 55° at the steepest point. A uniform radius around the reference point should be maintained and recovery should be made at the specified point or at a safe altitude.

COMMON ERRORS

AIRSPEED CONTROL

Probably the most common difficulty encountered during steep spirals is proper maintenance of airspeed. Generally, the pilot concentrates too heavily on wind drift control and the bank of the aircraft and finds himself constantly raising or lowering the nose of the aircraft. As the nose of the aircraft is raised or lowered, the airspeed will change appreciably. Through the use of a reference spot on the windshield (as used with previous maneuvers), the pilot can maintain a more uniform pitch attitude and, therefore, control the airspeed.

ORIENTATION

Since the pilot is flying the aircraft in a steep bank with three consecutive turns, there is a tendency to become disoriented. If possible, the pilot should pick a prominent landmark in the direction of the original heading and then count the number of times he passes it. The pilot greatly improves his orientation by maintaining visual reference to objects outside the aircraft.

Another way to maintain orientation is to use shallower banks and maintain a larger radius of turn during the early periods of training in this maneuver. Once the pilot becomes adjusted to spirals of a more gentle nature, he can progress to the normal steep spirals.

POOR COORDINATION

The changing angle of bank required when the maneuver is performed with a wind may contribute to poor coordination. Since the bank angle varies (with wind) from approximately 50° to that of a shallow bank, the pilot must vary rudder pressure to maintain coordination. The sense of coordination developed in previous maneuvers will be of great value to the pilot during gliding spirals.

SHORT-FIELD TAKEOFFS

DESCRIPTION

During short-field practice sessions, it usually is assumed that, in addition to a short runway, there is an obstruction on each end of the runway that must be cleared. The obstruction is considered to be approximately 50 feet in height. (See Fig. A-15.)

Fig. A-15. Typical Short Field

The pretakeoff checklist is the same for a short-field takeoff as for normal takeoff procedures, except that the manufacturer's recommended flap setting is used to achieve the best angle of climb. The recommended flap setting will vary with different types of aircraft.

PROCEDURE

The short-field takeoff may be initiated by holding the brakes, applying full power, and then releasing the brakes. This procedure enables the pilot to see that the engine is functioning properly before takeoff from a field where power availability is especially critical. However, this procedure is not mandatory and, in some situations, the technique of holding the brakes may not be necessary. A takeoff immediately after a high-speed taxi turn is not recommended because it does not permit stabilization of fuel level in the tanks.

Directional control is maintained with rudder pressure. The aircraft should be allowed to roll on the full weight of its wheels in an attitude that results in minimum drag, as shown in figure A-16, positions 1 and 2.

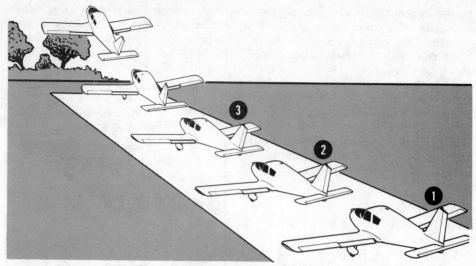

Fig. A-16. Short-Field Takeoff Technique

The initial takeoff roll involves *little* or *no use of the elevator control* beyond permitting it to assume a neutral position. When the aircraft accelerates to a speed slightly slower than best angle-of-climb (position 3), back pressure is applied to the control wheel to rotate the aircraft to the takeoff attitude. After breaking ground, the aircraft is accelerated to the best angle-of-climb speed and that speed is maintained until the obstacle is cleared. Caution should be taken to avoid raising the nose too soon. *A premature, nose-high attitude will produce more drag and cause a longer takeoff roll.*

The wing flaps, if used, are retracted after the obstacle is cleared and the *best rate-of-climb* speed has been attained. Flap retraction completes the short-field takeoff procedure and normal climbout and level off procedures are resumed.

EVALUATION

The short-field takeoff is executed with prompt, smooth application of power and a steady climb at best angle-of-climb airspeed. Evaluation is based on planning, smoothness, accuracy, and directional control. The criteria for acceptable performance indicate that the liftoff and climb are to be performed within five knots of best angle-of-climb speed.

Performance which is comparable to that presented in the airplane's performance data should be obtained. Improper flap or propeller setting, or premature retraction of the landing gear is disqualifying.

COMMON ERRORS

PREMATURE TAKEOFF AND CLIMB

An essential aspect of the short-field takeoff is the acceleration to the proper airspeed prior to liftoff. If the aircraft is allowed to lift off at a speed considerably lower than best angle-of-climb speed, valuable altitude is sacrificed while accelerating to the proper speed. If the climb is initiated prematurely, the angle of climb will be considerably less, defeating the purpose of the takeoff.

FAILURE TO MAINTAIN PROPER ATTITUDE DURING THE INITIAL CLIMB

Failure to maintain the proper attitude during the initial climb results in an airspeed which is either too fast or too slow. The pilot should learn what attitude produces the best angle-of-climb airspeed and assume this attitude with

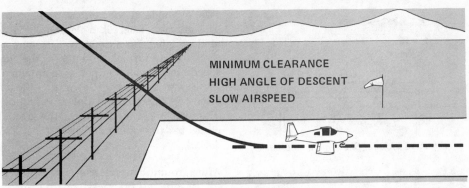

Fig. A-17. Short-Field Landing

minor adjustments for density, altitude, etc.

SHORT-FIELD LANDINGS
DESCRIPTION

A successful short-field landing over an obstacle begins with *good* planning. In order to achieve a landing roll that is as short as possible, it is desirable to touch down at minimum airspeed as close to the obstacle as possible. This means clearing the obstacle by a minimum amount at a *high angle-of-descent and slow airspeed*. (See Fig. A-17.)

PROCEDURE

The early part of the approach on the downwind leg and through the turn to base leg is very similar to a normal approach. Many pilots prefer to extend the first third of the flaps during the latter portion of the downwind leg, the second third on base, and full flaps on final approach, while progressively reducing the airspeed. This enables the pilot to make the transition to the short-field approach speed in smooth, easy steps. During the transition, the trim tab should be used to relieve excessive control pressures.

After the flaps are extended to the full down position and the aircraft is trimmed on final approach, the aircraft will be in a configuration very similar to that practiced at minimum controllable airspeed — high drag and slow speed; however, the pitch attitude will be slightly nose down. Therefore, it is par-

ticularly important for the pilot to remember the lessons learned at minimum controllable airspeed with regard to the interrelationship of power and elevator when making changes in airspeed and altitude.

In the slow flight configuration, back pressure on the control wheel will raise the nose, slow the airspeed, and *increase the rate of descent*. Altitude and angle of glide are controlled by power. Power is added to *decrease* the rate of descent and angle of glide. To *steepen* the glide angle, power is reduced, and attitude and airspeed control are maintained with the elevator. On a short-field approach, minimal power may be carried throughout the final approach up to the time of roundout, or flare.

If the approach to the runway resembles the illustration in figure A-18, the wires will be cleared. If the appearance changes to that shown in figure A-19, power should be added to slow the rate of descent as the aircraft is *too low*. If it changes to that depicted in figure A-20, power should be *decreased* because the aircraft is *too high*.

The typical reaction is to pull back on the yoke when the approach is low. However, that will only slow the speed more and increase the rate of descent. When the aircraft is low and slow, the nose position should be adjusted downward, although it may appear to the pilot that he is pushing himself into the

Fig. A-18. Correct Short-Field Approach

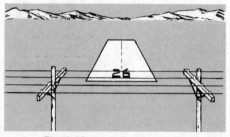

Fig. A-19. Approach Too Low

Fig. A-20. Approach Too High

obstacle or will land short of the field. The nose should be lowered and a substantial amount of power added to decrease the rate of descent and extend the flight path. The pilot must anticipate these responses and conditions, and learn to make the proper attitude and power adjustments.

The pilot should plan to cross the obstacle at a speed that is equal to approximately 1.3 times the power-off stalling speed with fully extended flaps. For example, in an aircraft which stalls at 55 knots with full flaps, the speed should be approximately 72 knots when crossing the obstacle.

After passing over the obstacle, there should be no attempt to change the

rate or angle of descent until flareout. The altitude where the flareout is initiated will be approximately the same as that for a normal landing. If the airspeed has been properly maintained, there will be very little or no "float" after the flareout and power reduction. The airplane should contact the ground close to the stalling speed. (See Fig. A-21.)

After ground contact, the nose is lowered as soon as practical and the brakes are applied. There will be less chance of skidding the tires if the flaps are retracted before applying the brakes. Braking is most effective when back pressure is applied to the control wheel, putting most of the aircraft weight on the main wheels. The properly executed short-field landing will result in an *extremely* short landing roll. When landings are being made on actual short fields, preflight planning should be exercised to insure that the aircraft can take off from the *short field* into which it has been flown.

EVALUATION

Performance is evaluated on the basis of planning, coordination, smoothness, and accuracy. The angle of descent and airspeed must be controlled on final approach so that floating is minimized during the flare. After touchdown, the airplane should be brought to a stop within the shortest possible distance, consistent with safety. Improper or incomplete prelanding procedures, touching down with an excessive side load on the landing gear, or poor directional control is disqualifying.

COMMON ERRORS

EXCESSIVE NOSE-DOWN ATTITUDE AFTER CLEARING THE OBSTACLE

The stabilized approach should always be used, and at no time should the pilot clear an obstacle, immediately reduce power, and dive to the runway. This creates a very hazardous situation. The proper procedure is to reduce power when the obstacle has been cleared, then resume a normal glide to a landing.

EXCESSIVE SPEED DURING LANDING

The recommended approach and landing procedure is to use a stabilized approach at 1.3 times the power-off stalling speed. If an airspeed higher than that prescribed is utilized, the landing distance is increased and the aircraft deceleration on the ground becomes difficult and, at times, hazardous.

In a short-field landing, the airplane should land firmly at nearly the power-off stalling speed. Then wing flaps should be retracted and braking should be used as necessary. Heavy braking should not be used when the wing flaps are extended, as the weight being applied to the landing gear is small, and the chance of locking the wheels and sliding the tires becomes great. Therefore, the best procedure is to maintain back pressure on the control yoke and retract the flaps prior to applying the brakes.

IMPROPER FLARE ALTITUDE

Additional attention should be given to the flare following the short-field approach. In the full-flap, power-off configuration, the airspeed will dissipate rapidly when the attitude reaches level flight. The pilot should guard against initiating his landing flare at an exces-

sive altitude. If this is done, power should be added and a go-around initiated, or the airplane should be eased down gently to the runway by the use of power.

SOFT-FIELD TAKEOFF

DESCRIPTION

The soft-field takeoff technique is used whenever the takeoff surface is covered with snow, mud, high grass, loose rocks, or the overall terrain is rough. Therefore, the objective of the soft-field takeoff is to transfer the weight of the aircraft from the *wheels to the wings* as rapidly as possible and lift the aircraft clear of the retarding effects of the surface condition.

PROCEDURE

The soft-field takeoff technique begins with the completion of the pretakeoff checklist and as in the short-field procedures, the flaps are set according to the manufacturer's recommendations. After completing the checklist, the aircraft should be slowly taxied toward the takeoff position without stopping, to prevent the aircraft from "bogging down." At the same time, full back pressure should be maintained to place minimum weight on the nosewheel. This turning takeoff procedure should not be used with low fuel quantities in the tanks.

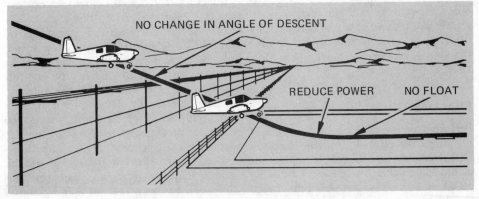

Fig. A-21. Ideal Short-Field Approach and Landing

Fig. A-22. Soft-Field Takeoff

At no time during taxi operations on a soft runway surface should the aircraft be allowed to stop; rather, alignment with the center of the takeoff area should be performed while taxiing and the throttle should be smoothly advanced to takeoff power. As the speed increases, some of the elevator back pressure must be relaxed; however, sufficient pressure should be maintained to lift the nose gear clear of the surface as soon as possible. When this is accomplished, the aircraft will no longer benefit from the effects of nosewheel steering and prompt positive rudder control pressure is necessary in order to maintain directional control (as in flight at minimum controllable airspeed).

The nose position is considerably higher than in a normal takeoff and may require the pilot to sight along the edge of the cowling in order to have adequate forward vision. The high angle of attack and *ground effect* will result in a liftoff speed that is actually *lower* than the power-off stall speed. (See Fig. A-22.)

EVALUATION

Performance is evaluated on the basis of planning, directional control, smoothness, and accuracy. Liftoff should occur at not higher than the power-off stalling speed and the best rate-of-climb speed should be maintained. Improper flap or propeller setting or premature retraction of the landing gear is disqualifying.

COMMON ERRORS

POOR DIRECTIONAL CONTROL ON THE RUNWAY

Full-up elevator travel will produce lift as soon as possible, reducing the load on the nosewheel. As the aircraft gains flying speed, the pilot reduces the amount of elevator travel to prevent initiation of a premature takeoff. Directional control also should be monitored. Nosewheel steering is less effective as the result of the decreased load; therefore, increased rudder travel will be used to maintain directional control.

IMPROPER ELEVATOR MANAGEMENT AND FAILURE TO REDUCE PITCH ATTITUDE AFTER LIFTOFF

The soft-field takeoff technique produces a liftoff speed below that normally sufficient to sustain flight. After liftoff, the aircraft attitude must be reduced to gain additional flying speed; however, this reduction should never be made to a point where the aircraft again makes contact with the runway. The reduction in elevator back pressure to reduce pitch attitude must be smooth and precise to allow the aircraft to accelerate to best angle-of-climb airspeed. Once this speed is achieved, the flaps may be retracted, the speed increased to best rate of climb, and a normal climb initiated.

SOFT-FIELD LANDINGS

DESCRIPTION

The soft-field landing also assumes that the runway surface is covered with snow, mud, high grass, loose rocks, or that the overall terrain is quite rough. The objective of this type of landing is to support the weight of the aircraft with the wings as long as possible during the landing roll and delay the weight transfer to the wheels during the roll-out until the aircraft attains the slowest possible speed.

PROCEDURE

The airspeed used for the *short-field landing* is appropriate for the soft-field landing, and a normal full-flap landing approach is recommended. There is no reason for a steep approach path *unless*, obstacles are present in the final approach course.

A small amount of power should be maintained throughout the flareout to assist in decreasing the rate of descent while permitting the speed of the aircraft to be reduced to the lowest possible value. Use of power also permits the aircraft to contact the ground as softly and smoothly as possible. The use of full flaps is recommended because it is necessary to contact the ground at the minimum safe speed. (See Fig. A-23.

On soft surfaces, deceleration is rather rapid after touchdown, so braking usually is not required. Braking at this time may even cause a nose-over tendency. In order to prevent nose gear or propeller damage, it is desirable to hold the nosewheel off the ground as long as possible by progressively increasing the elevator back pressure as the aircraft is decelerated during the landing roll-out. This procedure is illustrated in figure A-24.

EVALUATION

Performance is evaluated on the basis of planning, smoothness, and accuracy. Final approach airspeed should be maintained within plus or minus five knots of that prescribed. During flap retraction (if appropriate), extreme caution should be exercised to maintain positive control. Improper or incomplete prelanding procedures, touching down with an excessive side load on the landing gear, or poor directional control is disqualifying.

COMMON ERRORS

IMPROPER PITCH CONTROL DURING LANDING FLARE AND TOUCHDOWN

The soft-field landing is a normal, full flap approach with a specialty landing flare and touchdown. The actual soft-field landing is accomplished in a relatively nose-high attitude using power to gently ease the airplane to the runway. The transition from the descent to the flare may be described in the following manner. Step 1 is the normal descent. Step 2 is a level flight attitude, accomplished with a small amount of power. Step 3 is the transition from level flight to a shallow climb attitude, again using a small amount of power. Step 4 is maintenance of a nose-high attitude after touchdown.

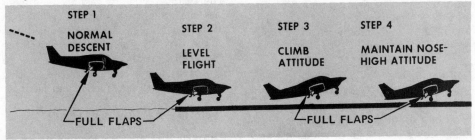

STEP 1 — NORMAL DESCENT

STEP 2 — LEVEL FLIGHT

STEP 3 — CLIMB ATTITUDE

STEP 4 — MAINTAIN NOSE-HIGH ATTITUDE

FULL FLAPS   FULL FLAPS

Fig. A-23. Soft-Field Landing

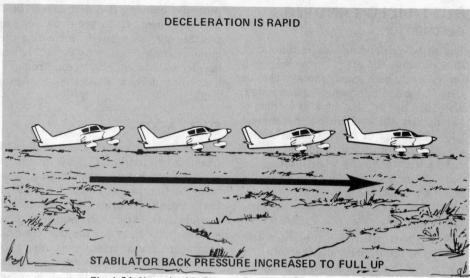

DECELERATION IS RAPID

STABILATOR BACK PRESSURE INCREASED TO FULL UP

Fig. A-24. Nosewheel is Clear of Surface for as Long as Possible

If the flare is initiated too high above the ground, the airspeed dissipates rapidly and a hard landing occurs. Also, if the power is reduced during the flare, the nosewheel will come in contact with the landing surface prematurely, defeating the purpose of the landing.

COMBINING TECHNIQUES FOR TAKEOFFS AND LANDINGS

Throughout the discussion, one specialized takeoff or landing technique has been dealt with at a time for the sake of simplicity and ease of description. However, it is possible to have situations where it is necessary or desirable to use a combination of two or more techniques. For example, the pilot could encounter a situation involving a *soft field* that has *obstacles* at the end of the runway and a *crosswind component*. A combination of soft-field, short-field, and crosswind techniques would be required.

All possible situations cannot be covered in one manual. There will be times when the techniques learned must be modified to fit existing conditions. The flight instructor will provide guidance for additional techniques that the stu-

dent may be required to use. As the pilot gains experience, he will develop proficiency in *combining* the various techniques to fit the existing flight conditions.

For example, modification of landing technique is required when the winds are high, gusty, and variable. In this situation, the final approach airspeed is higher and the touchdown attitude is less nose high. Also, the touchdown should be at a higher airspeed to provide positive and prompt control responses throughout the flareout. Similarly, in high, gusty winds, takeoff airspeeds should be higher and the nosewheel held on the ground longer to enhance directional control.

The various types of takeoffs and landings are taught so that the pilot may utilize the full performance capabilities of the aircraft. When he has achieved the mastery of his aircraft, he will be able to approach a wide variety of existing conditions with confidence and security.

ACCURACY LANDINGS

Through the accuracy landing, the pilot learns the technique of landing his aircraft when, where, and how he chooses. As the pilot develops the ability to make accuracy landings, he will find that techniques learned in this maneuver will be carried over to his everyday flying.

The accuracy landing, sometimes called a spot or precision landing, also may be used in case of an emergency requiring a landing other than at an airport. Should the situation *arise*, the pilot who is proficient in this maneuver will be prepared to make a safe, smooth, accurate landing under emergency conditions.

DESCRIPTION

The approach to an accuracy landing normally is begun at pattern altitude. The approach to a landing should contain a 180° change in direction with the recommended minimum power setting and a touchdown in a normal landing attitude beyond and within 200 feet of a line or predetermined mark. A typical approach to an accuracy landing is illustrated in figure A-25.

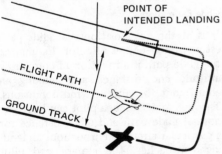

APPROXIMATELY 2500 FT.

POINT OF INTENDED LANDING

FLIGHT PATH

GROUND TRACK

Fig. A-25. Accuracy Landing

A pilot can lengthen or shorten turns, extend flaps, S-turn, or slip to maneuver the aircraft to the desired touchdown point. Additionally, any combination of these can be used as long as they are within the operating limitations of the aircraft. Many aircraft manufacturers restrict the use of slips with flaps extended.

APPROACH AND LANDING

The consistent performance of accurate landings is the result of proper planning. The pilot must plan the approach so there are as few variables as possible. If the pilot always enters the maneuver from the same altitude, airspeed, and distance from the runway, the glide path will be more uniform and easier to estimate. With these factors constant, the glide path must be altered only to compensate for wind effects.

DOWNWIND LEG

The prelanding checklist should be completed early on the downwind leg. Then, while approaching the spot opposite the intended landing point (the 180° point), the pilot should check for other traffic in the pattern.

The downwind leg should be flown at normal traffic pattern altitude and at a distance of approximately 2,500 feet (one-half mile) from the runway in use. The aircraft's ground track should parallel the runway with no tendency to drift toward or away from the runway. Any deviation from a parallel downwind leg will cause the traffic pattern to have an abnormal shape which greatly influences the length of the pattern and, therefore, the glide path.

At the 180° point, the pilot should reduce power to initiate the descent. If a power-off approach is being used, the throttle should be completely closed at this point. For a power approach, the power should be reduced initially, and then held constant until the start of the flare. Both power-on and power-off approaches are made with a constant power setting.

After the power has been set, a normal approach speed should be established promptly. This is accomplished by attempting to hold a level pitch attitude with increased elevator back pressure until the speed decreases to the desired range. Then, the pitch attitude of the aircraft is lowered to hold the approach speed while continuing downwind to the position where the turn to base leg normally is made.

Flaps

Flaps may be used as needed to steepen the landing approach. The recommended procedure is to extend the flaps in increments throughout the approach as required. Once flaps have been extended, they should not be retracted before the landing touchdown unless the pilot must initiate a go-around.

BASE LEG

The principal indication of when to begin the turn to base leg will come from sighting the aircraft's position relative to the runway. The point of intended landing in a no-wind situation should appear to be approximately 45° behind the wing.

During the turn to base leg, the pilot should use between 20° and 30° of bank. The exact amount of bank used for the turn will depend on wind conditions. To maintain consistency, the same degree of bank should be used for all turns throughout the accuracy landing. Turns with a greater degree of bank than 30° should be avoided within the traffic pattern due to the increased altitude loss.

Key Position

Once the aircraft turns onto base leg, it will be at the key position. The key position is the point from which the pilot can tell whether he is able to glide safely to the field.

It is at the key position that the pilot must determine if he needs to conserve or lose altitude. The key position and the change in traffic pattern needed to conserve or lose altitude is shown in figure A-26.

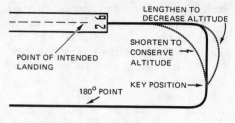

Fig. A-26. Key Position

The pilot should make altitude judgments by a method that has been successfully used by many others. This is the spot method by which the pilot observes his intended point of landing. If the point of intended landing *appears* to be moving down in relation to the aircraft, as shown in figure A-27, it indicates that the pilot's glide path is high and that he will have to lengthen his base and final legs to lose this additional altitude. If the point of intended landing *appears* to be moving up, the pilot will need to shorten his base and final approach legs by turning toward the runway from this point. As shown in figure A-28, the pilot may vary the position of the base leg in order to hold the reference point in a constant relationship to the aircraft.

Glide Estimation

It is at the key position that glide path estimation becomes a factor. Estimating the glide path is a function of comparing altitude and distance and making an adjustment for surface wind conditions. Through experience, a pilot can learn the normal glide path and glide distance for a particular aircraft. Throughout all landing approaches, the experienced pilot will be able to accurately establish a uniform rate of descent and, therefore, be able to make accurate glide path estimations by comparing the angle of descent with the surface winds.

If the pilot slows the aircraft, a more shallow glide path will result. If the aircraft is slowed further, the glide path will steepen considerably. As the aircraft is slowed below the speed which gives

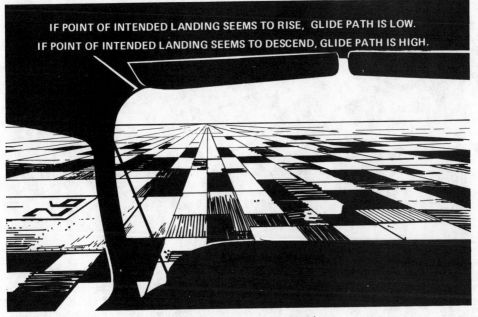

IF POINT OF INTENDED LANDING SEEMS TO RISE, GLIDE PATH IS LOW.

IF POINT OF INTENDED LANDING SEEMS TO DESCEND, GLIDE PATH IS HIGH.

Fig. A-27. Glide Path Determination

the greatest glide distance, the lift-drag ratio causes the aircraft to descend in a steeper glide.

FINAL APPROACH

Before turning to the final approach leg, the pilot should look in all directions for other traffic. If the area is clear, the turn to final can be made.

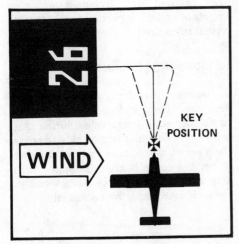

KEY POSITION

WIND

Fig. A-28. Adjusting Base Leg

The pilot must plan the turn to final approach so that the aircraft rolls out on an extension of the runway centerline. The final approach should require *no* sharp angling toward the runway (aircraft too low), nor should it require violent S-turns (aircraft too high). A straight-line approach at the desired airspeed should be maintained through "final" until the beginning of the landing flare.

Figure A-29 shows that the steeper uniform angle of descent approach provided by use of full flaps is much more accurate than a landing approach without flaps. Because of the steep glide, a 50-foot error in altitude will not cause as large a lateral error in touchdown as a more shallow glide angle.

Slips

Throughout the landing approach, the pilot may use a slip as necessary to lose altitude. The pilot may vary the amount of slip to lose altitude, but the aircraft must be in a normal landing attitude for the actual touchdown.

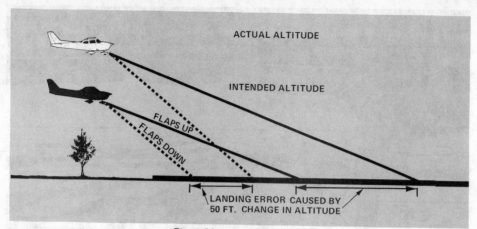

Fig. A-29. Approach Accuracy

EVALUATION

The maneuver will be evaluated on the correctness of procedures, airspeed control, coordination, smoothness, and accuracy of the touchdown. The two most important facets of this maneuver are airspeed control and ability to estimate the glide path. The pilot who can maintain accurate control of the airspeed will be able to make an accurate glide path estimation.

The aircraft must touch down in a normal landing attitude slightly above a stall speed, and beyond but within 200 feet of the anticipated point. Violent maneuvering while making this approach or excessive drift while landing is disqualifying.

COMMON ERRORS

FIXED OBJECT AS KEY POSITION

Many pilots have a tendency to use a fixed object on the ground as the key position. When landing at a different field or making an emergency landing, this fixed object will not be present and the pilot may be unable to accurately determine the key position. Therefore, the key position should be considered a point in the air a certain distance and angle from the point of intended landing.

AIRSPEED CONTROL

Optimum glide distance can be achieved only with a specified airspeed. Thus, airspeed control is a critical element of accuracy landings. However, a pilot flying this type of approach usually finds it necessary to concentrate on visual cues outside of the aircraft with minimum time available for monitoring the airspeed indicator. This dilemma can be resolved by an occasional glance at the airspeed and by maintaining a constant pitch attitude using outside visual references.

UNCOORDINATED TURNS

The sense of coordination that the pilot developed when performing steep power turns will be of great value during this maneuver. The pilot will be able to sense the aircraft movements and tell whether or not the controls are coordinated with only an occasional check of the ball in the turn coordinator for confirmation.

LAZY EIGHTS

The lazy eight is a training maneuver that combines dives, climbs, turns, and various combinations of each. Through this maneuver, the pilot continues to develop his coordination, speed sense, and feel of the aircraft.

During lazy eights, control pressures are constantly changing, necessitating careful advance planning of control usage to perform the maneuver well. Because of this constant control pressure change, the lazy eight cannot be done mechanically or automatically. The flight path of an aircraft performing a lazy eight is illustrated in figure A-30.

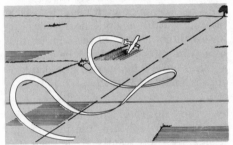

Fig. A-30. Flight Path of Lazy Eight

DESCRIPTION

The lazy eight is essentially two 180° turns in opposite directions, one following the other, with each turn having a climb and a dive. It is called a lazy eight because the longitudinal axis of the aircraft appears to outline a figure eight in a horizontal plane.

To execute a smooth, precision maneuver, all turns within the lazy eight must not exceed a bank of 30°. If the pilot uses a steeper bank, the maneuver becomes hurried and looses the smoothness that is desired.

A plan view of the lazy eight is shown in figure A-31. This illustration shows that the highest pitch attitude in the climb comes after 45° of turn, and that the lowest pitch attitude in a dive comes after 135° of turn. During the first 90° the bank angle is increasing at a constant rate until it reaches 30°. Throughout the second 90° of turn, the bank angle is decreasing constantly until wings-level flight is reached after 180° of turn.

EFFECTS OF WIND

The turns of a lazy eight should be made into the wind; if this is not done, the loops of the lazy eight will not appear to be of equal size. If the maneuver is executed crosswind, the wind will make the loops of the lazy eight cross the horizon at different points and the longitudinal axis of the aircraft will draw an unsymmetrical eight about the horizon. Making turns into the wind also will tend to keep the aircraft within the training area.

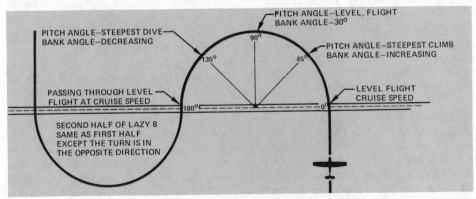

PITCH ANGLE—LEVEL, FLIGHT
BANK ANGLE—30°

PITCH ANGLE—STEEPEST DIVE
BANK ANGLE—DECREASING

90°

PITCH ANGLE—STEEPEST CLIMB
BANK ANGLE—INCREASING

135°   45°

PASSING THROUGH LEVEL
FLIGHT AT CRUISE SPEED

LEVEL FLIGHT
CRUISE SPEED

180°   0°

SECOND HALF OF LAZY 8
SAME AS FIRST HALF
EXCEPT THE TURN IS IN
THE OPPOSITE DIRECTION

Fig. A-31. Plan View of Lazy Eight

PROCEDURE

As is the case prior to any training maneuver, the pilot must first clear the area for other traffic. During the lazy eight, the aircraft will be changing directions and altitudes constantly, and the pilot must first clear the area and then maintain vigilance throughout the maneuver for other traffic.

The pilot should choose a reference object on the horizon as a center point for the eight that is outlined about the horizon. This reference object should be the point that the longitudinal axis of the aircraft passes through at the center of the figure eight. A section line, building, or prominent landmark on the horizon are all good reference objects. In any case, the reference object should be directly upwind of the aircraft and aligned with the wingtip at the start of the maneuver.

ENTRY

This maneuver should be entered from straight-and-level flight at cruising speed, maneuvering speed, or recommended entry speed, whichever is lowest. The power setting used for this maneuver normally will be cruise power; however, once the pilot selects a power setting, it should not be changed throughout the maneuver.

FIRST 90° OF TURN

Figure A-32 illustrates the sequence of events that occur throughout the lazy eight. The pilot begins the lazy eight by initiating a gentle climbing turn. Through the first 45° of turn, the bank angle is increasing slowly, and the pitch angle is increasing to maximum.

At the 45° point of the turn as illustrated in position one of figure A-32 the aircraft is at the highest pitch attitude and the bank is still increasing. As the aircraft passes through the 45° point of the turn the pilot begins to lower the nose gently so the aircraft will reach a level flight pitch attitude after 90° of turn. Throughout the first 90° of turn, the bank angle is increasing at a constant rate so the desired bank of 30° is reached at the 90° point of turn.

SECOND 90° OF TURN

As shown in position two of figure A-32, the aircraft is in level pitch attitude and 30° bank after 90° of turn. It should be noted that as the aircraft passes through level flight the extended longitudinal axis intersects the reference object.

After passing through the first 90° of turn, the pilot initiates a constant rate roll-out timed so the aircraft will complete the first 180° of turn in a wings level attitude. After passing the first 90° of turn, the pilot continues decreasing his pitch attitude until he reaches the lowest pitch at 135° of turn. In position three, the pitch attitude of the aircraft is at the lowest point and the bank is approximately 15° to 20°.

As the nose of the aircraft passes through 135° of turn, the pilot begins raising the nose gently to increase the pitch attitude. Through the last 45° of turn, the pitch attitude rises to level flight and the bank angle continues to decrease.

RECOVERY

Recovery should be timed so the bank angle reaches 0° and the pitch attitude reaches level flight after 180° of turn. In addition, the aircraft should recover at the entry speed and altitude.

The same procedure is used throughout the next 180° of turn in the opposite direction. As the aircraft reaches level flight after 180° of turn, the pilot immediately begins the climbing turn in the opposite direction. The airplane is not flown in straight-and-level flight, but only passes through the straight-and-level attitude at the 180° point of turn as it is rolled into the next turn.

1. At 45° of turn, the pitch angle is highest and bank (approx. 15° - 20°) is increasing.

2. At 90° of turn, the bank is at its steepest (30°), airspeed at its lowest, and the nose is passing through level flight.

3. At 135° of turn, pitch angle is lowest and bank (approx. 15° - 20°) is decreasing.

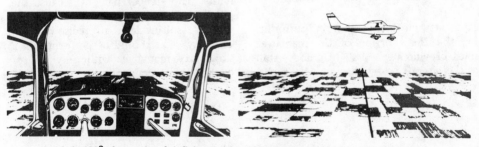

4. At 180° of turn, aircraft is flying straight and level at entry speed as next turn is begun.

Fig. A-32. Executing the Lazy Eight

EVALUATION

Performance is based on the planning, orientation, coordination, smoothness, attitude, and airspeed control demonstrated by the pilot. Since the attitude, altitude, and speed of the airplane are constantly changing, the pilot must display a high degree of skill in the proper performance of this maneuver. Repeated slipping or a persistent gain or loss in altitude at the completion of the maneuver will be disqualifying factors.

COMMON ERRORS

IMPROPER PLANNING

The pilot should plan this maneuver so the peaks of the loops both above and below the horizon come at the proper location within the maneuver. The peak of the loop above the horizon should come at approximately 90° of turn, and the lowest altitude should come as the aircraft is passing through straight-and-level flight. Additionally, the pilot must plan for the changing bank angle which is used throughout the maneuver. Therefore, proper attention to bank angle, pitch angle, and aircraft heading becomes absolutely necessary.

The pilot can simplify his orientation and planning by dividing each 180° of turn into four segments of 45° each. Preplanning the events in each 45° segment insures complete understanding and makes proper anticipation a simple matter.

UNSYMMETRICAL LOOPS

When properly performed, the peak of a loop above the horizon is approximately the same size and shape as the peak below the horizon. Through proper airspeed control, the pilot can make symmetrical loops in this maneuver.

Pitch attitude in the climbing turn during the first portion of the maneuver must provide a speed slightly above stall as the aircraft passes through level flight.

In similar fashion, the pitch angle in the diving turn must allow the aircraft to accelerate to entry speed after 180° of turn. If these two criteria are adhered to, loops will be approximately symmetrical and equal in size.

EXCESSIVE PITCH ATTITUDE

If the pilot uses too steep a pitch attitude in the climbing turn, the aircraft may stall before reaching the 90° point. The nose of the aircraft should pass through the reference point after 90° of turn at the minimum maneuver speed. This speed is normally slightly above stall speed.

Too low a pitch attitude in the second portion of the turn results in an excessive dive which causes the aircraft to exceed entry speed at the 180° point. The excessive pitch attitude with a resultant gain in airspeed causes the pilot to lose altitude in the maneuver and to enter the second half of the lazy eight at the wrong airspeed.

EXCESSIVE BANK

Since the maneuver seems easier to perform with steeper than medium banks, some pilots have a tendency to steepen the bank angle beyond normal limits. The steeper bank will cause the pilot to hurry through the maneuver with a resulting lack of precise control. The lazy eight should be performed as a slow, lazy maneuver with only 30° of bank at the steepest point.

ATTITUDE INSTRUMENT FLYING

INTRODUCTION

Attitude instrument flying is a fundamental method for controlling an aircraft by reference to instruments. It is based upon an understanding of the flight instruments and systems and the development of the skills required to interpret and translate the information presented by the instruments into precise aircraft control. This section begins with a discussion of the flight instruments used in attitude instrument flying and concludes with a description of instrument flight maneuvers.

FLIGHT INSTRUMENTS

The progress of attitude instrument flying in general aviation has paralleled the design and manufacture of accurate, reliable, low cost flight instruments. The instrumentation of modern light aircraft provides many safety features for the instrument pilot. Panel layouts are arranged logically to promote rapid scanning and built-in system redundancy prevents the failure of one instrument or component from causing complete loss of attitude reference. To further promote safety, a fundamental part of instrument training involves learning the capabilities and limitations of flight instruments and supporting systems.

PITOT-STATIC INSTRUMENTS

The pitot-static instruments, shown in figure A-33, are the airspeed indicator, altimeter, and vertical velocity indicator. All of these instruments operate on the principle of differential air pressure. Pressure sensitive mechanisms convert pressure supplied by the pitot-static system to a measurement of aircraft speed, altitude, and vertical velocity. Pitot pressure, also called ram or dynamic pressure, is directed only to the airspeed indicator, but static (ambient) pressure is directed to all three instruments, as shown in figure A-34.

Since the information supplied by these instruments is vital to instrument flight, the pilot is provided alternatives in case either the pitot head or static source becomes blocked. To assure continuous airspeed indications in IFR conditions, pitot tubes may have an electrical heating element which prevents the formation of ice. In airplanes equipped this way, the pitot heat switch in the cabin should be turned on before flying through visible moisture. In many aircraft, an alternate static source is provided in case the main static system is obstructed by ice or otherwise fails. When installed, the alternate static source usually is located inside the aircraft.

For those aircraft without an alternate static source, an emergency source of static pressure can be obtained by breaking the glass face on the vertical velocity indicator. When this is done, a lower or higher static pressure is sensed, causing slightly different altimeter and airspeed readings and a momentary climb or descent indication on the vertical velocity indicator.

AIRSPEED INDICATOR

Airspeed is measured by comparing the difference between the pitot and static pressures and, through mechanical linkages, displaying the resultant on the airspeed indicator. Three types of airspeeds need to be considered by the general aviation pilot.

Indicated airspeed (IAS) is read directly from the dial of the airspeed indicator. It equals true airspeed only at sea level on a standard day.

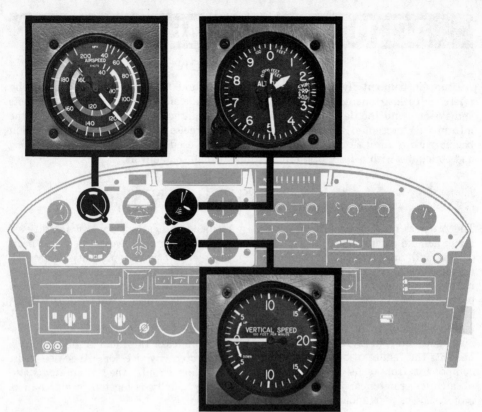

Fig. A-33. Pitot-Static Instruments

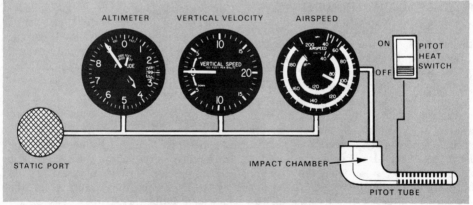

Fig. A-34. Pitot-Static Pressure Flow Diagram

Calibrated airspeed (CAS) is indicated airspeed corrected for errors introduced by the pitot-static system. An airspeed correction table is provided by the aircraft manufacturer when the difference between indicated airspeed and calibrated airspeed is significant.

True airspeed (TAS) is the actual speed of the aircraft through the air and is found by correcting calibrated airspeed for nonstandard temperature and pressure. The airspeed indicator is calibrated at standard sea level conditions. Therefore, as an aircraft climbs and temperature and pressure decrease, the airspeed indicator reads slower than the aircraft actually is flying. Therefore, indicated airspeed normally is slower than true airspeed. TAS can be determined by use of a true airspeed indicator, flight computer, or cruise performance chart in the pilots operating handbook (POH).

V-SPEEDS AND AIRSPEED COLOR MARKINGS

Colored arcs and radials on the face of the airspeed indicator define aircraft speed limits and operating ranges, as shown in figure A-35. The following is a list of commonly used V-speeds and color codings.

V_{NE} — Never exceed (red line)

V_{NO} — Maximum for normal operations (high speed end of green arc)

V_{FE} — Maximum with flaps extended (high speed end of white arc)

V_{S1} — Stall, power off, clean configuration (low speed end of green arc)

V_{SO} — Stall, power off, landing configuration (low speed end of white arc)

During gusty or turbulent atmospheric conditions, the aircraft should be flown at or below the design maneuvering speed (V_A) but with sufficient margin to avoid a stall. This important limiting speed normally is not marked on the airspeed indicator, but is listed in the airplane owner's manual or on a placard on the instrument panel near the airspeed indicator.

Two other important limiting speeds for airplanes with retractable landing gear are V_{LE}, the maximum landing gear

extended speed, and V_{LO}, the maximum landing gear operating speed. Both of these are located in the POH.

ALTIMETER

The altimeter senses the normal decrease in atmospheric pressure when an aircraft ascends, then indicates height in feet above the barometric pressure level set in the altimeter setting window. For example, if 29.82 is set in the window, the altimeter indicates the height of the airplane above a pressure level of 29.82. When using the current altimeter setting, the altimeter indicates the aircraft's height above mean sea level.

When a pilot uses the altimeter setting of a nearby station while enroute, his indicated altitude may be different from true altitude. Therefore, when terrain or obstacle clearance is a factor in selecting a cruising altitude, it should be remembered that colder-than-standard temperatures will place the aircraft lower than the altitude displayed on the altimeter. Also, when flying from a high pressure area to a lower pressure area without resetting the barometric pressure, the airplane actually descends if the pilot

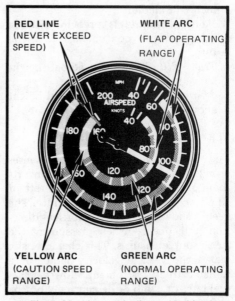

Fig. A-35. Airspeed Indicator Markings

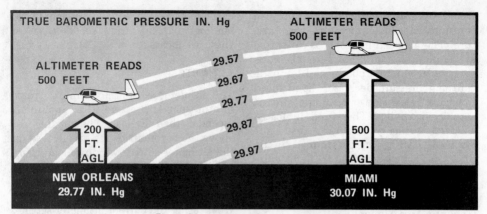

Fig. A-36. Pressure Effects on Altimeter

maintains the same indicated altitude, as shown in figure A-36. An aid to remembering this relationship is the saying, "From high to low or hot to cold, look out below."

There are five definitions of altitude that the pilot should recall from private pilot training.

1. *Indicated altitude* is read directly from the altimeter when set to the current altimeter setting.
2. *Pressure altitude* is read from the altimeter when set to the standard atmosphere sea level pressure of 29.92 inches of mercury.
3. *Density altitude* is pressure altitude corrected for nonstandard temperature.
4. *True altitude* is the actual height above mean sea level.
5. *Absolute altitude* is the actual height above the earth's surface.

VERTICAL VELOCITY INDICATOR

The vertical velocity indicator senses changes in static pressure and converts these pressure changes to indicate rate of climb or descent in feet per minute. The needle shows a change in vertical direction immediately when pressure at the static source changes. This characteristic makes the vertical velocity indicator a valuable trend instrument. However, actual rates of climb or descent may not be obtained for as long as nine seconds

because of a restriction in air flow through a calibrated leak in the instrument.

During preflight inspection or while taxiing, the vertical velocity indicator should be checked to see that the pointer is at zero. If it is not, a gentle tap on the glass cover of the instrument may cause the needle to return to the proper position. Otherwise, the ground indication can be used as the zero reference in flight.

GYROSCOPIC INSTRUMENTS

The three gyroscopic instruments used in general aviation are shown in figure A-37. They are the attitude indicator, heading indicator, and turn coordinator. These instruments employ two fundamental properties of the gyroscope—rigidity in space and precession.

ATTITUDE INDICATOR

The attitude indicator uses rigidity in space to provide a stable reference line (the horizon bar) and erection devices (precession) to keep the horizon bar orientated to the earth's surface. Every pilot is taught to maintain the attitude of an aircraft with reference to the horizon. When the natural horizon is no longer visible, the attitude indicator provides a substitute. This instrument is the only one that provides an immediate and direct picture of the airplane's pitch and bank attitude in relation to the earth's horizon. Pitch changes, in bar widths or

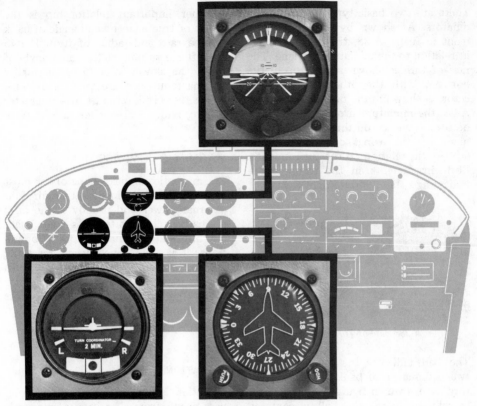

Fig. A-37. Gyroscopic Instruments

fractions of bar widths, are made with reference to the movement of the miniature airplane in relation to the horizon bar. Bank changes are made by adjusting the bank angle of the aircraft in relation to the pointer and bank indexes of the instrument.

One of the characteristics of the gyroscopic attitude indicator is acceleration/deceleration error. This is most noticeable during acceleration on the takeoff roll when the horizon bar on the attitude indicator dips slightly below the horizon, giving a false indication of a climb.

HEADING INDICATOR

The heading indicator utilizes a gyro for stability, eliminating magnetic compass-type errors, such as oscillation, northerly turning error, and acceleration error. Since the heading indicator does not have a direction-seeking capability, it should be checked and set by reference to the magnetic compass prior to take-off.

While airborne, precession causes the heading indicator to gradually drift away from the correct magnetic heading. Therefore, it should be checked and reset against the magnetic compass at least every 15 minutes, but only during straight-and-level, unaccelerated flight.

TURN COORDINATOR

The turn-and-slip indicator has been replaced by a turn coordinator on most new training airplanes. This instrument uses a miniature airplane instead of a turn needle to pictorially indicate a turn. The turn coordinator is really two separate instruments. The miniature airplane provides information about the direction and rate of turn, while the ball independently provides information about the coordination of the turn.

There are two basic types of turn coordinators. As shown by the left instrument in figure A-38, the horizon banks in relation to the miniature airplane. The rate of turn is shown at the top of the horizon. With the other type of indicator, as shown in the right side of figure A-38, the miniature airplane banks. Rate of turn is shown on this type of instrument by the wings of the miniature airplane in relation to the turn indexes. Both instruments in the example are indicating a standard-rate right turn.

Fig. A-38. Rate-of-Turn Indicators

The ball indicates the relationship between the angle of bank and the rate of turn, as shown in figure A-39. During a coordinated turn, the ball is centered because the forces acting on it are balanced (instrument 1). In an uncoordinated turn, unequal forces acting on the ball move it away from the center, indicating either a skid or a slip. In a skid (instrument 2), the rate of turn is too great for the angle of bank. Conversely, in a slip (instrument 3), the rate of turn is too small for the angle of bank. In either case, an adjustment to the angle of bank or rate of turn is required.

Another important relationship is the effect of true airspeed and angle of bank on the rate and radius of turn. If two aircraft are turning at the same angle of bank, the slower aircraft has a smaller turning radius and greater rate of turn, while the faster aircraft has a greater turning radius and smaller rate of turn.

MAGNETIC COMPASS

The magnetic compass is one of the most basic aircraft instruments. It requires no external power and usually is the only means the pilot has to cross-check heading information. During normal operations, it is used primarily to reset the heading indicator. The magnetic compass can display reliable directional guidance if its limitations and inherent errors (deviation, variation, and magnetic dip) are understood.

DEVIATION

Deviation is the deflection of the compass needle from a position of magnetic north as a result of local magnetic disturbances in the aircraft. The amount of deviation also varies with the operation of the aircraft's electrical equipment. Since these disturbances change with the passage of time, the compass must be swung (calibrated) periodically to compensate for these errors. The errors remaining after the compass has been swung are recorded on a compass correction card.

Fig. A-39. Quality-of-Turn Indicators

VARIATION

Magnetic compasses present directional information in terms of magnetic north. In order to convert directions expressed in terms of true north to magnetic north, the angular difference between true and magnetic north (variation) is applied. Easterly variation is subtracted from and westerly variation is added to the true direction to determine the magnetic direction.

MAGNETIC DIP

Magnetic dip is the tendency of the compass needle to point downward as it moves closer to one of the magnetic poles. This tendency causes errors in compass readings during turns, acceleration, and deceleration.

Northerly Turning Error

Northerly turning error is most apparent when turning to or from a heading of north or south. When making a turn from a northerly heading in the Northern Hemisphere, the compass gives a brief indication of a turn in the opposite direction. Then *lags* behind the actual heading until rollout or until approaching a heading of east or west. Very little northerly turning error is apparent on an easterly or westerly heading. When making a turn from a southerly heading, the compass gives an indication of a turn in the correct direction, but at a much faster rate. The magnetic compass heading then *leads* the actual aircraft heading.

Acceleration and Deceleration Errors

Acceleration and deceleration errors occur during airspeed changes and are most apparent on headings of east and west. When the aircraft is accelerating on either of these headings, a turn to the north is indicated. An aid for remembering this relationship between acceleration and deceleration is the acronym ANDS, or "accelerate north, decelerate south."

TURNS USING THE MAGNETIC COMPASS

A maximum of 15° of bank should be used when turning to headings utilizing the magnetic compass. When a 15° bank is used in turning north or south, the amount of roll-out lead is proportional to the latitude. For example, in turning from south to north in the area of 30° north latitude, a pilot would start a roll-out 30° prior to reaching north, plus a 5° lead to allow time for roll-out from the banking attitude. Therefore, the roll-out should be initiated at either 035° or 325° depending on the direction of the turn.

To roll out on a heading of south, it is necessary to fly past 180°, the number of degrees of latitude minus the 5° lead. For example, in making a right turn from east to south at 30° north latitude with 15° bank, the roll-out should begin on a heading of 205°.

INSTRUMENT FLIGHT MANEUVERS

Attitude instrument flying is an extension of the concept of attitude flying. That is, the establishment of a specific pitch and bank attitude accompanied by a designated power setting results in predictable aircraft performance. If pitch, bank, and power are established by reference to the flight instruments and the desired performance confirmed by instrument indications, the definition and technique of attitude instrument flight are clearly evident.

This type of flight has three basic ingredients—scan, interpretation, and aircraft control. As in visual flying, instrument flying requires that certain instruments be used more often during one maneuver than another.

Proper instrument scan is of extreme importance to the instrument pilot. Because the attitude indicator replaces the normal outside visual references, it is considered to be the principal attitude control instrument used in instrument flight. The role of the attitude indicator with respect to other flight instruments is analogous to a wheel; the hub of the wheel is the attitude indicator and the spokes extend to the other instruments. The pilot should incorporate this concept into the instrument scan, as shown in figure A-40. As shown, the instruments are not connected to each other, but to the attitude indicator. This scan method utilizes the other instruments to confirm the performance indicated by the attitude indicator.

The instrument scan table illustrates that the attitude indicator is the *control* instrument for maintaining airplane attitude, while the instruments used to determine the pitch and bank quality change for various flight maneuvers. The table also illustrates that the majority of the pilot's scan is directed to the control instrument and the pitch and bank quality instruments.

The second important ingredient in instrument flying is proper instrument interpretation. Since the attitude indicator provides the pilot with an artificial horizon which replaces the natural horizon, proper interpretation of this principal attitude control instrument is extremely important. Reference to the other instruments is essentially the same under instrument conditions as under visual conditions.

The final ingredient, aircraft control, is actually the result of scan and interpretation. After proper instrument scan and interpretation are accomplished, it is simply a matter of applying the proper control pressures to attain the desired airplane performance. Because the human body is subjected to sensations which may be unreliable when interpreting the airplane's actual attitude, it is necessary that the pilot learn to disregard these sensations. The aircraft must be controlled through proper scan and interpretation of the flight instruments.

STRAIGHT-AND-LEVEL FLIGHT

During straight-and-level, unaccelerated flight, the miniature airplane on the attitude indicator should be aligned with the artificial horizon bar. This reference is used as a basis for estimating changes in pitch or bank when performing any of the other instrument flight maneuvers. Changes in this reference are reflected immediately on other instruments. That

Fig. A-40. Scan Pattern

ATTITUDE INSTRUMENT FLYING

MANEUVER	CONTROL INSTRUMENT	PITCH QUALITY INSTRUMENT	BANK QUALITY INSTRUMENT	POWER QUALITY INSTRUMENT	ADDITIONAL QUALITY PITCH & BANK INSTRUMENTS
STRAIGHT-AND-LEVEL FLIGHT	ATTITUDE INDICATOR	ALTIMETER VERTICAL VELOCITY	HEADING INDICATOR	AIRSPEED INDICATOR	TURN COORDINATOR COORDINATED BALL
CLIMBS AND DESCENTS — CONSTANT AIRSPEED	ATTITUDE INDICATOR	AIRSPEED INDICATOR	HEADING INDICATOR	VERTICAL VELOCITY INDICATOR	TURN COORDINATOR ALTIMETER COORDINATED BALL
CLIMBS AND DESCENTS — CONSTANT RATE	ATTITUDE INDICATOR	VERTICAL VELOCITY INDICATOR	HEADING INDICATOR	AIRSPEED INDICATOR	TURN COORDINATOR HEADING INDICATOR
TURNS— CONSTANT ANGLE OF BANK	ATTITUDE INDICATOR COORDINATED BALL	ALTIMETER VERTICAL VELOCITY INDICATOR	ATTITUDE INDICATOR	AIRSPEED INDICATOR	HEADING INDICATOR TURN COORDINATOR
TURNS— CONSTANT RATE	ATTITUDE INDICATOR COORDINATED BALL	ALTIMETER VERTICAL VELOCITY INDICATOR	TURN COORDINATOR	AIRSPEED INDICATOR	HEADING INDICATOR
CLIMBING OR DESCENDING TURNS— CONSTANT AIRSPEED	ATTITUDE INDICATOR COORDINATED BALL	AIRSPEED INDICATOR	ATTITUDE INDICATOR	VERTICAL VELOCITY INDICATOR	HEADING INDICATOR ALTIMETER
CLIMBING OR DESCENDING TURNS— CONSTANT RATE	ATTITUDE INDICATOR COORDINATED BALL	VERTICAL VELOCITY INDICATOR	TURN COORDINATOR	AIRSPEED INDICATOR	HEADING INDICATOR ALTIMETER

|←————— MAJOR SCAN —————→|←——— MINOR SCAN ———→|

INSTRUMENT SCAN TABLE

is, a bank change also is apparent on the heading indicator and turn coordinator, while a pitch change is reflected on the altimeter, vertical velocity indicator, and airspeed indicator. However, attitude adjustments always are made on the attitude indicator, not the supporting instruments.

ALTITUDE CONTROL

A desired altitude is maintained by establishing a specific pitch attitude on the attitude indicator and trimming the aircraft properly. When the attitude has been established, the vertical velocity indicator, altimeter, and airspeed indi-

cator are scanned to determine if any change is occurring. If a departure from the desired altitude occurs, the first indication is reflected on the vertical velocity indicator and next on the altimeter. By evaluating the initial rate of movement of these instruments, a pilot can estimate the amount of pitch change required to restore level flight. The amount of change needed usually is small and requires only a fraction of a bar width of change on the attitude indicator.

When a deviation from the desired altitude occurs, pilot judgment and experience in a particular aircraft dictate the rate of correction. As a guide, the pitch attitude should be adjusted to produce a rate of change which is double the amount of altitude deviation and power should be used, as necessary. The aircraft illustrated in figure A-41 is descending at 300 f.p.m. and is 100 feet below the desired altitude. To correct back to altitude, a climb rate of 200 f.p.m. is selected. An initial pitch adjustment is made to stop the descent and initiate the approximate climb rate. This pitch attitude is maintained on the attitude indicator until the vertical velocity stabilizes. A further pitch adjustment may be necessary to produce the desired climb rate.

CLIMBING AT 200' PER MINUTE

When approaching a predetermined altitude, a leadpoint is selected on the altimeter for initiating a leveloff pitch attitude change. This leadpoint is estimated by using 10 percent of the vertical velocity rate. As shown in figure A-42, if the rate of correction to the desired altitude is 200 f.p.m., the leveloff should begin 20 feet before reaching the desired altitude.

HEADING CONTROL

A desired heading is maintained by establishing a zero bank attitude on the attitude indicator, with deviations being detected on the heading indicator. When

LEAD THE ALTITUDE 20 FEET

Fig. A-42. Leading the Leveloff

The aircraft is descending at 300 fpm.

The aircraft is 100 ft below the desired altitude. A climb back at 200 fpm is indicated.

With practice a close estimate of the amount of pitch change required to return to the desired altitude can be made.

Fig. A-41. Altitude Corrections

a deviation occurs, a definite angle of bank is established on the attitude indicator to produce a suitable rate of turn. When a heading variation of up to 15° occurs, an angle of bank equal to the degrees of heading deviation is used. As shown in figure A-43, if the heading change is 10°, a 10° bank produces a suitable rate of correction.

If a heading variation exceeds 15°, the degree of bank which produces a standard-rate turn is appropriate; however, the maximum angle of bank should not exceed 30°.

10° REQUIRED HEADING CHANGE

10° DESIRED ANGLE OF BANK

Fig. A-43. Heading Corrections

AIRSPEED CONTROL

To maintain airspeed, reference is made to the airspeed indicator and adjustments are made either to the pitch or the power setting. If a change in the power setting is indicated, the approximate setting is selected and the airspeed indicator is checked to determine whether further corrections to power and/or pitch are required.

To make suitable power adjustments, a knowledge of the approximate power required to establish a desired airspeed is needed. If this information is unknown or not readily available, it should be acquired by actual flight experience in various configurations before entering instrument conditions.

Pitch and power adjustments are closely related. Adjustment of one usually requires appropriate adjustment of the other. For example, a pitch adjustment during flight at the desired airspeed also requires a power adjustment to prevent a change in airspeed. To increase the airspeed while maintaining straight-and-level flight, power is advanced beyond the setting required to maintain the new desired airspeed. As the airspeed increases, the pitch attitude is adjusted downward to maintain altitude. When the airspeed approaches the desired indication, the power is reduced to an estimated setting that maintains the new airspeed. When reducing airspeed, this procedure is reversed.

LEVEL TURNS
BANK CONTROL

To enter a turn, the desired angle of bank is established by reference to the bank index on the attitude indicator. The turn coordinator is scanned to confirm control coordination and proper bank angle for the desired rate of turn.

Rate of turn varies as true airspeed changes. The approximate angle of bank required for a standard-rate turn can be calculated quickly by dividing the true airspeed in knots by a factor of 10 and adding 5° to the resultant figure. For example, the angle of bank required for a standard-rate turn at a cruise speed of 110 KTAS is 11 plus 5°, or a 16° angle of bank.

To roll out of a turn on a desired heading, a leadpoint must be estimated. As a guide, one-half of the angle of bank is used. For example, if the bank angle is 10°, a roll-out is initiated five degrees prior to the desired heading. However, as the pilot gains experience, the leadpoint may be varied to meet individual piloting techniques.

ALTITUDE CONTROL

When a turn is initiated and the bank increases, the aircraft tends to descend due to loss of vertical lift. Therefore, the pitch attitude is adjusted by reference to the attitude indicator, and the altimeter and vertical velocity indicator are scanned to confirm that pitch adjustments are adequate.

When rolling out of a turn, the back pressure or trim used to maintain altitude during the turn is reduced sufficiently to prevent the aircraft from

climbing because of the increased vertical lift available. Therefore, the pitch attitude shown on the attitude indicator is scanned in the same manner as during roll-in.

AIRSPEED CONTROL

The aircraft tends to lose airspeed in a turn because induced drag increases. The amount of power required varies with airspeed; that is, the slower the airspeed, the greater the power requirement. At slow speeds, it may be desirable to add an estimated amount of power as the turn is established, rather than waiting until an airspeed loss becomes apparent.

STEEP TURNS

Steep turns by instrument reference normally are performed using a bank angle of 45°. The roll-in is performed slowly using the attitude indicator for pitch and bank references. As the bank angle steepens, increased back pressure and power are required to maintain altitude and airspeed. After the turn is established, the aircraft should be retrimmed, as necessary. The instrument indications of a steep turn to the left are shown in figure A-44.

Fig. A-44. Performing the Steep Turn

The airspeed indicator, altimeter, and vertical velocity indicator are scanned to determine whether adjustments to the aircraft attitude or power are required. Adjustments to pitch and bank are made immediately and precisely, before the point is reached where back elevator pressure tightens the turn without raising the nose. If a steep bank occurs, the bank angle must be reduced prior to increasing the back elevator pressure.

A tendency to climb should be expected when rolling out of a steep turn and adjustments should be made to the trim, power, and back pressure. Steep turns are a confidence maneuver and are not recommended for normal instrument flight.

CLIMBS AND DESCENTS

Climbing and descending maneuvers are divided into two general categories—*constant airspeed* or *constant rate*. The constant airspeed maneuver is accomplished by maintaining a constant power indication and varying the pitch attitude as required to maintain a specific airspeed. The constant rate maneuver is accomplished by varying both power and pitch as required to maintain a constant airspeed and vertical velocity. Either type of climb or descent may be performed while maintaining a constant heading or while turning. These maneuvers should be practiced using airspeeds, configurations, and altitudes corresponding to those which will be used in actual instrument flight.

CONSTANT AIRSPEED CLIMBS AND DESCENTS
CONSTANT AIRSPEED CLIMBS

To enter a climb from straight-and-level flight at cruise airspeed, the power is increased to the climb power setting and the miniature airplane on the attitude indicator is adjusted to approximately two bar widths above the horizon. This pitch adjustment is an average and varies with the aircraft used, the desired airspeed, and rate of climb selected. A smooth, slow power application increases the pitch attitude so that only slight control pressures are needed to effect the desired pitch change. During the transition and climb, the turn coordinator and heading indicator are scanned to confirm coordinated straight flight. Since the combination of climb power, torque, and P-factor causes a left-turning tendency, right rudder pressure is required to maintain a constant heading.

With climb power constant, the pitch attitude is adjusted to establish and maintain the best rate-of-climb speed, as illustrated in figure A-45. However, when a pitch adjustment is made to correct for an airspeed deviation, the airspeed indicator does not reflect an immediate change. The vertical velocity indicator will generally show the result of the pitch change more quickly than the airspeed indicator. Therefore, the vertical velocity indicator is an excellent aid in maintaining constant airspeed.

CONSTANT AIRSPEED DESCENTS

Constant airspeed descents are performed in a similar procedural manner by using the pitch attitude of the airplane to control airspeed and engine power to control rate of descent. For example, to enter a descent from cruise without a change in airspeed, the power is reduced smoothly to the desired setting and the pitch attitude is reduced slightly so the airspeed remains constant. The degree of pitch change and power reduction will vary according to the particular airplane used for training. Once the power and pitch attitude are established, the pilot begins to cross-reference the airspeed indicator with the attitude indicator. The airspeed indicator is the main quality instrument *until the desired attitude is stabilized*. Once the airplane is stabilized at the desired speed, the attitude indicator becomes the pilot's control instrument.

When the airplane is descending at cruise airspeed, the rate of descent is controlled

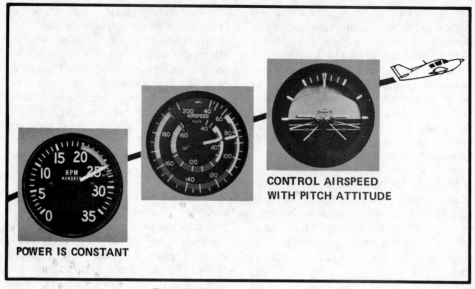

POWER IS CONSTANT

CONTROL AIRSPEED
WITH PITCH ATTITUDE

Fig. A-45. Constant Airspeed Climb

by small power adjustments. However, when a power change is made, the pilot must cross-reference the airspeed indicator and attitude indicator to assure the speed remains constant. This procedure becomes important because any change in power also requires a corresponding change in pitch attitude to maintain a constant airspeed during the descent.

CONSTANT RATE CLIMBS

Constant rate climbs are accomplished by maintaining the desired constant vertical velocity and airspeed. It should be noted that the procedural technique used for constant rate climbs is the opposite of the technique used for constant airspeed climbs.

During this maneuver, *pitch attitude control* is used to establish and maintain the *vertical velocity*, while *power* is used to *control the airspeed*. For example, if the airplane is in level flight at cruise power and airspeed, the first step in entering the maneuver is to establish the desired rate of climb. This is accomplished by increasing the control back pressure and cross-checking the vertical

velocity indicator and the attitude indicator. Power is applied simultaneously in anticipation of the airspeed decrease. Once the pitch attitude has been established to produce the desired rate of climb, the power is adjusted to maintain the desired airspeed. A cross-check of the vertical velocity indicates the need for subsequent pitch adjustments and a cross-check of the airspeed shows the need for resultant power adjustments.

It should be noted that due to the performance capabilities of most training airplanes, a constant airspeed may not be possible if a constant vertical velocity is maintained. For example, in nonturbocharged airplanes, as the altitude increases, the performance capabilities decrease. Therefore, to maintain a constant rate of climb, the control back pressure is increased, which decreases the airspeed. If the power is increased gradually to maintain the airspeed, maximum power is applied at some point and the airspeed continues to dissipate. However, in spite of this factor, it is important for the pilot to understand the principles of the maneuver so the techniques may be utilized when he transitions to higher performance airplanes.

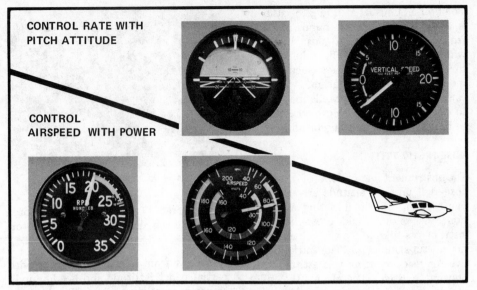

CONTROL RATE WITH
PITCH ATTITUDE

CONTROL
AIRSPEED WITH POWER

Fig. A-46. Constant Rate Descent

CONSTANT RATE DESCENTS

Whether a constant rate descent is made at cruise speed or approach speed, the control procedures are identical. As in a constant rate climb, power controls airspeed and pitch attitude controls rate. This concept is illustrated in figure A-46.

The descent is entered by simultaneously adjusting the nose of the miniature airplane just below the horizon bar on the attitude indicator and reducing power to a predetermined setting. When power is reduced, the aircraft often tends to turn right, so slight left rudder pressure may be required.

Techniques for scanning the other instruments are the same as those used in a climb. Since a constant rate is desired in addition to a constant airspeed, scan of the vertical velocity indicator is important.

LEVELOFF LEADPOINT

The leveloff leadpoint for both climbs and descents is determined using 10 percent of the vertical velocity rate when approaching the desired altitude. For example, if the climb or descent rate is

500 f.p.m., the appropriate leveloff procedure should be initiated when the airplane is 50 feet from the desired altitude. Then, the nose is positioned to a level flight attitude and the altimeter and vertical velocity are monitored to maintain level flight. The power is adjusted until the desired cruise airspeed is obtained and trim is adjusted to relieve control pressure.

CLIMBING AND DESCENDING TURNS

When climbing or descending during a turn, the procedures previously discussed are combined. Since the vertical component of lift decreases in turns, more emphasis is placed on pitch control. When performing a rate climb or descent in a turn, pitch is adjusted to maintain the desired rate and power is adjusted to maintain the desired airspeed.

UNUSUAL ATTITUDE RECOVERY

Spatial disorientation, wake turbulence, lapse of attention, or abnormal trim conditions can cause a pilot to enter an unusual flight attitude. Although such cases are rare, a pilot must know how to recover from an unusual attitude during instrument flight.

To enter an unusual attitude, the student is asked to remove his hands and feet from the controls and close his eyes, while the instructor flies the aircraft through various maneuvers calculated to induce spatial disorientation. At a critical point, the instructor tells the student to open his eyes and recover the aircraft to the original altitude and heading.

NOSE-HIGH ATTITUDE

The instrument indications of a typical nose-high unusual attitude are shown in figure A-47. Before initiating a correction, the pilot should cross-check the instruments to confirm the reliability of the attitude indicator. The initial objective for recovery from this attitude is to prevent a stall. Therefore, the pilot should simultaneously decrease pitch (reducing angle of attack), increase power, and roll the wings level.

Fig. A-47. Nose-High Attitude

NOSE-LOW ATTITUDE

The indications of a nose-low unusual attitude are a nose-low attitude, increasing airspeed, rapid loss of altitude, and a high rate of descent, as illustrated in figure A-48. The primary objective of a nose-low unusual attitude recovery is to avoid a critically high airspeed and load factor. In this case, the pilot should simultaneously reduce power, roll wings level, increase pitch attitude to stop acceleration, and gently raise the nose to the level flight attitude. If the pilot raises the nose before rolling the wings level, the increased load factor may result in

Fig. A-48. Nose-Low Attitude

an accelerated stall, a spin, or a force exceeding the aircraft design load factor.

Recovery from unusual attitudes with partial panel (attitude and heading indicators inoperative) is basically the same as that with a full panel, except that the turn coordinator is used to stop the turn. In addition, the pressure instruments (airspeed, altimeter, and vertical velocity) must be used for pitch attitude reference. Reversal of the altimeter, airspeed, and vertical velocity trends indicates passage through the level flight attitude. At this point, elevator pressure is neutralized to maintain a level pitch attitude.

STALLS

During instrument training, stalls may be practiced to demonstrate that recognition and recovery procedures under instrument conditions are exactly the same as under visual conditions. Recovery is accomplished by immediately reducing the angle of attack and positively regaining normal flight attitude by coordinated use of flight and power controls.

It is not necessary to practice full stalls, since performance of stalls is not required during an instrument rating flight test and a commercial pilot applicant is required to perform only imminent stalls. Therefore, recovery should be initiated at the first aerodynamic indication of the stall.

PARTIAL PANEL FLYING

Basic partial panel airwork is not required for commercial pilot certification. However, to increase basic instrument flying skills and aircraft control, partial panel airwork has been included.

ATTITUDE INDICATOR

Airliners, most military aircraft, and some light aircraft have attitude indicators which are powered by the aircraft electrical system. This type of indicator is equipped with an OFF flag which appears when the electrical power fails or the gyro is not operating at the proper speed. If the attitude indicator fails on an aircraft equipped this way, the pilot should check the circuit breakers to see whether power can be restored to the instrument.

Failure of a vacuum operated attitude indicator often is indicated by a vacuum pressure loss or inconsistencies with associated flight instruments. For example, if the attitude indicator shows that the aircraft is sharply nose-up, but the airspeed is not decreasing and the altitude is not increasing, it may be presumed that the attitude indicator is inaccurate. In this case, the pilot has no choice but to use other sources for aircraft attitude information.

The turn coordinator provides a reliable indication of wing position when used in conjunction with the heading indicator. It functions much like the attitude indicator with respect to bank attitude, as long as the ball is centered. However, when the aircraft is banked, but not actually turning because of cross-control pressures, the miniature airplane in the turn coordinator indicates a normal wings-level flight attitude with the ball in the inclinometer off center.

If the aircraft is equipped with a turn-and-slip indicator, it may be used for heading change information. However, the vertical needle of the turn-and-slip indicator deflects only when the aircraft actually is turning. In addition, the vertical turn needle is somewhat sensitive, so an average reading must be used in turbulent air.

The vertical velocity indicator, together with the altimeter and the airspeed indicator, gives a very accurate indication of pitch attitude. If the nose is raised and the aircraft begins to climb while the power setting is constant, the vertical velocity indicator shows a positive indication, the altimeter shows an increase in altitude, and the airspeed indicator shows a decrease.

When the attitude indicator has failed, the pilot must modify his scan pattern, omitting the failed instrument from his cross-check. Because several instruments must be used to provide the same information usually obtained from the attitude indicator, the pilot must keep his scan pattern moving continuously. Some pilots find it easier to fly partial panel by covering the inoperative attitude indicator with a piece of paper, or anything else available, to prevent the subconscious use of the false indications displayed.

When a pilot applies a flight control movement, the aircraft must overcome a small amount of inertia while becoming established on the new flight path. When the attitude indicator is inoperative, this lag becomes very noticeable, especially if large or rapid corrective control movements are applied. Therefore, the pilot should keep the aircraft trimmed properly at all times and make small, well-controlled corrections.

HEADING INDICATOR

While flying IFR, the pilot is most likely to detect a failure of the heading indicator if he experiences difficulty remaining on the intended course, as depicted by the VOR navigation indicator. When this type of deviation occurs, the pilot should check the heading indicator against the magnetic compass.

If the attitude indicator is operating, it can assist the pilot in maintaining his course. A heading also can be maintained simply by keeping the miniature airplane and the inclinometer ball of the turn coordinator centered. The pilot can use the magnetic compass for heading information, provided the aircraft is in wings-level, unaccelerated flight.

TIMED TURNS

Timed turns are made by initiating a standard-rate turn with reference to the turn coordinator. This type of turn results in a heading change at the rate of three degrees per second. If a pilot wishes to make a 30° turn, for example, he begins timing as he rolls into the turn, maintains the wingtip on the index for 10 seconds, then starts recovery to straight-and-level flight.

For increased accuracy, the turn should be started when the second hand on the aircraft clock passes one of the cardinal numbers. At the end of the predetermined number of seconds required to make the desired heading change, the pilot should begin to roll out of the turn. He should attempt to make the rate of roll constant for both rolling in and rolling out of the turn.

After the aircraft has stabilized in level flight, the pilot checks the magnetic compass to determine whether the turn was completed on the desired heading. Any necessary corrections are accomplished by using the same procedure, then rechecking the magnetic compass after it has stabilized.

IFR flight with gyro-stabilized instruments inoperative is considered a *semi-emergency situation* because the pilot may not be able to comply immediately and accurately with all ATC clearances. ATC should be notified of the situation *as soon as it occurs*. When an approach must be made without the use of the heading indicator, the pilot should use a no-gyro radar approach if the destination

airport has this capability. However, diversion to an alternate airport which has more favorable weather conditions is usually a better course of action.

BASIC VOR NAVIGATION

Several methods are used to position an aircraft on a specific VOR radial to obtain course guidance. All methods use magnetic headings which intercept the course or airway at a specific angle. The intercept angle is the number of degrees formed by the intersection of the projected aircraft heading and the desired course.

INTERCEPTING VOR RADIALS

In figure A-49 for example, an aircraft departing the airport may select a heading of 300° to intercept V-14 westbound. This procedure results in a 30° outbound intercept. At course interception, the CDI centers, and the aircraft should be turned to a heading of 270°. Depending on airport location and local terrain, a different intercept angle may be used. However, 30° is a popular angle for enroute operations. This intercept allows the pilot time to turn, upon interception of the selected radial, without "overshooting." In cases where large intercept angles are used, such as 60° or 90°, it becomes necessary to *"lead"* the turn to the selected radial. "Lead" is used in close proximity operations to a VOR and prevents overshooting. The degree of lead varies with the ground-speed of the aircraft and the distance from the navaid.

A situation in which a pilot plans to fly eastbound on V-14 after departing from the airport is depicted in figure A-50. An intercept heading of 360° could be used, resulting in a 90° inbound intercept. The turn on course (090°) requires a lead factor of approximately five degrees. However, an initial bearing selection of 085° could also be used to indicate when the inbound turn should begin. After starting the turn, the course selector should be changed to 090°. The actual

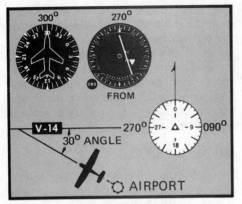

Fig. A-49. Outbound Intercept

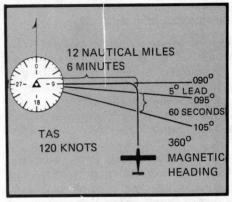

Fig. A-51. VOR Time and Distance

rollout heading will depend on the CDI deflection and rate of movement when approaching a heading of 090°. A wide range of *intercept angles* may be suitable; however, the angle of intercept obviously must not exceed 90°.

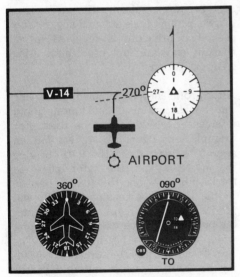

Fig. A-50. Inbound Intercept

TIME AND DISTANCE

A popular training maneuver, used to determine time and distance to a navaid, is illustrated in figure A-51. While on a near perpendicular course to a VOR radial, the time required to cross a predetermined *radial span* can be used to determine the time and distance to the navaid.

In the example shown, the pilot plans a 90° intercept for the 090° radial. The passage of a 10° change (105° to 095°), while on a heading of 360°, requires 60 seconds. Radial spans of 5°, 15°, or 20° may also be used; however, the 10° radial span facilitates division. By applying the following formula, the approximate time to the station can be determined:

$$\frac{\text{Time in seconds}}{\text{Number of degrees}} = \text{Minutes to the station}$$

or

$$\frac{60\ \text{seconds}}{10\ \text{degrees}} = 6\ \text{minutes}$$

Therefore, if the time check is completed at 1215Z, the airplane will arrive over the VOR at approximately 1221Z. At a speed of 120 knots TAS (approximately two nautical miles per minute depending upon wind), the aircraft will be 12 nautical miles east of the VOR at the completion of the time check (2NM/MIN X 6 MIN = 12 NM).

Time and distance checks are useful training maneuvers, because good position visualization and mental calculations are required while flying the aircraft. However, they have little practical application, except in an emergency, since DME equipment lessens the need for this procedure in normal operations.

REVERSE SENSING AND RECIPROCAL BEARINGS

One of the few disadvantages of VOR navigation is that of reciprocal bearing selection. For example, reverse CDI sensing will result if a pilot, intending to track *inbound* on the 270° radial of a VOR, selects 270° on the omnibearing selector rather than 090°. The FROM flag will be displayed instead of the TO flag and course corrections, using the CDI, will carry the aircraft farther and farther from the selected radial, as shown in figure A-52.

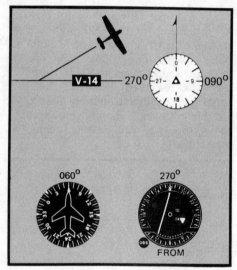

Fig. A-52. VOR Reverse Sensing

The best way to avoid reciprocal tuning and reverse sensing is to mentally verify that the *desired magnetic course*, *actual magnetic heading*, and *course selection* are in general agreement. When this is accomplished, a TO indication is always displayed approaching a VOR, and a FROM indication will occur when flying outbound from a VOR.

BASIC ADF NAVIGATION

Tracking to an ADF facility in a *no-wind condition* simply requires turning the aircraft to a heading which results in a zero degree relative bearing. The pilot then maintains a constant heading which results in a straight course to a navaid.

The same is true when tracking away from the NDB; in this instance, however, the relative bearing is 180°. ADF tracking in a *crosswind* is somewhat more involved, since unlike VOR, ADF does not provide an automatic wind correction angle. ADF orientation, tracking, and bracketing procedures are described in Chapter 4.

ADF INTERCEPTS

During initial practice of ADF intercepts, it may be beneficial to parallel the desired course before beginning the intercept. For example, in figure A-53, the pilot determines his position to be on the 195° bearing from an NDB. If the desired inbound course is the 360° bearing, a turn is made to a heading of 360° to parallel course. From this position, it is easier to visualize the intercept procedure. The selection of a 30° intercept heading results in the intersection of two parallel lines at equal angles. This geometric principle is involved in all tracking and intercept procedures using ADF navigation.

After proficiency is obtained, paralleling can be discontinued and more rapid intercept procedures can be used. For example, in figure A-54, assume an aircraft is located on the 070° bearing to an NDB and the pilot plans to track inbound on the 090° bearing to the station. A heading of 060° will produce a 30° intercept angle; therefore, the pilot will intercept the 090° bearing when the relative bearing is 30°. The aircraft should then be turned to a heading of 090° to track inbound to the station.

Assume that the pilot now plans to depart the NDB on the 180° bearing, as shown in figure A-55. As in VOR operations, various intercept angles may be used. In this case, a 30° intercept heading of 210° is chosen.

The turn on course should be started when the station's bearing from the tail

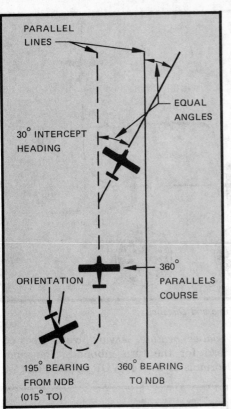

Fig. A-53 Paralleling the Course

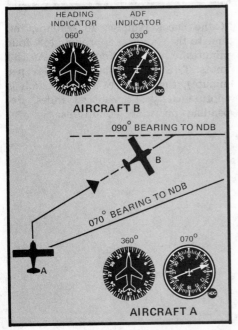

Fig. A-54. Inbound Intercept

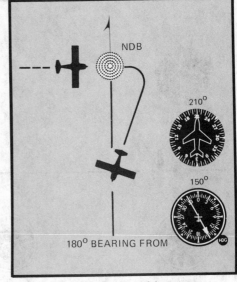

Fig. A-55. Outbound Intercept

of the aircraft approaches the intercept angle (30°). In this example, when a relative bearing of 150° is approached, the pilot should turn the aircraft to a heading of 180° and track outbound. A continuous 180° relative bearing indicates that the aircraft is maintaining course.

The pilot should be aware that *reliable ADF navigation* is dependent upon the *accuracy* of the *heading indicator*. If the heading indicator has precessed 10°, the tracking procedures and intercepts will be in error 10°. Although this will not be very significant during inbound tracking, during outbound tracking over large distances, the error is multiplied. A pilot can be miles off course and yet be completely unaware of his predicament, unless he confirms agreement between the magnetic compass and the heading indicator.

TIME AND DISTANCE

Time and distance checks are similar to those used with VOR. The ADF procedure is somewhat easier, since the consecutive course selector changes required for VOR are not needed with ADF. In

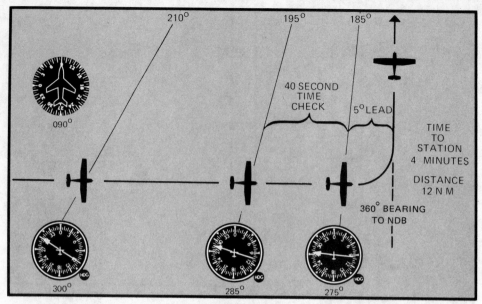

Fig. A-56. ADF Time and Distance

figure A-56, assume the pilot performs an ADF orientation and determines his location to be on the 210° bearing from an NDB. A 90° inbound intercept is planned for the 360° bearing with a time and distance check enroute.

The first step is to turn the aircraft to a heading of 90°, which gives a 90° intercept to the 360° bearing. Since a relative bearing of 270° will indicate interception of the 360° bearing, the time check should begin 15° before interception, or at a *relative bearing of 285°*. The check should be completed at 275°

relative bearing, leaving five degrees of lead for the turn inbound. The same formula as used in VOR applies, that is:

$$\frac{\text{Time in Seconds}}{\text{Number of Degrees}} = \text{Minutes to the Station}$$

If the check requires 40 seconds, the time to the station is approximately four minutes in a no-wind condition. At 180 knots TAS (three nautical miles per minute), the distance to the station is approximately 12 nautical miles, depending on wind conditions.

ALPHABETICAL INDEX

A

B

C

U

V

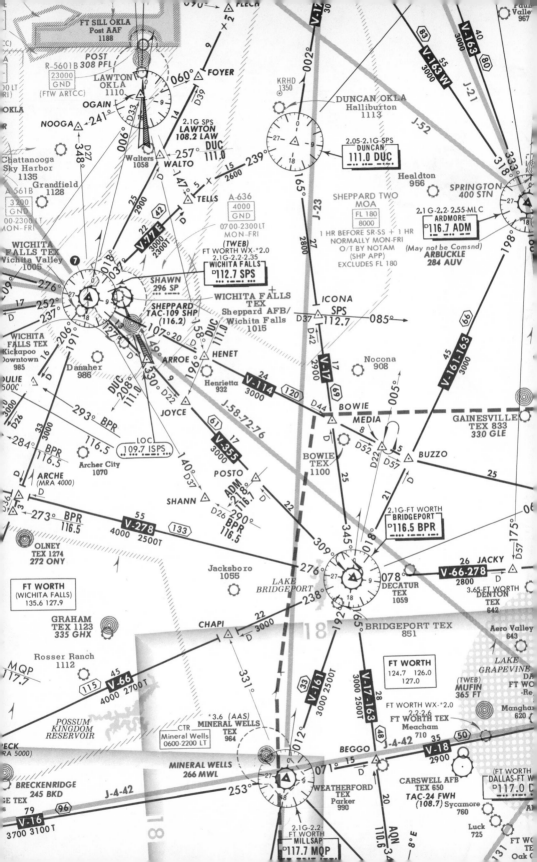

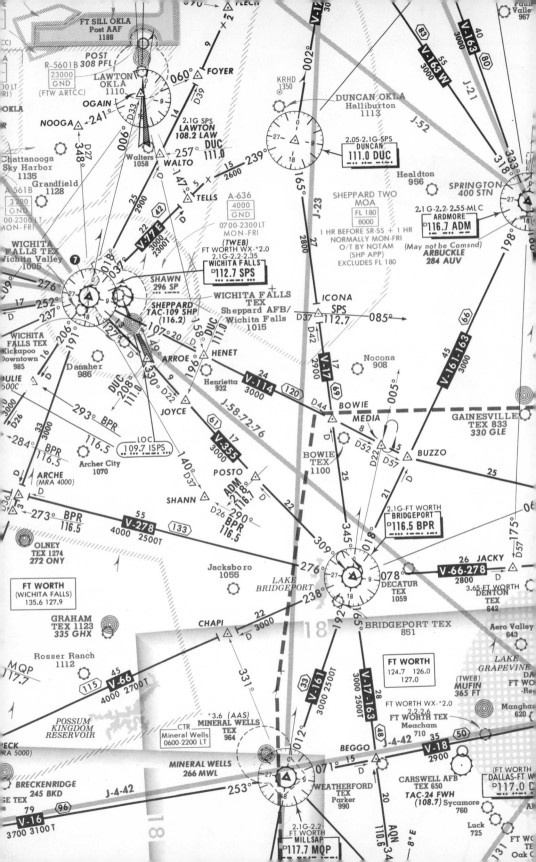